The

SUICIDE

of

CHRISTIAN THEOLOGY

The
SUICIDE
of
CHRISTIAN THEOLOGY

by
JOHN WARWICK
MONTGOMERY

Trinity Press
A Publishing Ministry of
Trinity College & Seminary
Newburgh IN 47630

The Suicide of Christian Theology
by John Warwick Montgomery

Seventh printing, 1998

Library of Congress Catalog Card Number 70-270170

ISBN 0-87123-521-8

Copyright   1970

John Warwick Montgomery
All Rights Reserved

Trinity Press
A Publishing Ministry of
Trinity College & Seminary
Newburgh IN 47630

Printed in The United States of America

À
la Faculté de Théologie Protestante
de l'Université de Strasbourg

John Warwick Montgomery is Professor of Law & Humanities at the Luton University, England, and Director of its Human Rights Centre and annual summer program at the International Institute of Human Rights, Strasbourg, France. He also serves on the Adjunct Faculty of Trinity College of the Bible and Trinity Theological Seminary, Newburgh, Indiana, and conducts seminars on "Defending the Biblical Gospel" under their auspices. He holds eight earned degrees besides the LL.B.: the A.B. with distinction in Philosophy (Cornell University; Phi Beta Kappa), B.L.S. and M.A. (University of California at Berkeley), B.D. and S.T.M. (Wittenberg University, Springfield, Ohio), M. Phil. in Law (University of Essex, England), Ph.D. (University of Chicago), and the Doctorat d'Universite from Strasbourg, France. He is author of over one hundred scholarly journal articles, and more than 40 books in English, French, Spanish, and German. He is internationally regarded, both as a theologian (his debates with the late Bishop James Pike, death-of-God advocate Thomas Altizer, and situation-ethicist Joseph Fletcher are historic), and as a lawyer (barrister-at-law of Middle Temple and Lincoln's Inn, England; member of the California, Virginia, Washington State, and District of Columbia Bars and the Bar of the Supreme Court of the United States). He is one of only six persons to have received the Diploma of the International Institute of Human Rights cum laude, and was the Institute's Director of Studies from 1979 to 1981. From 1980 to 1983 he served on the Human Rights Committee of the California Bar Association, and is presently a member of the Human Rights Task Force of the Bar of England and Wales. He is honored by inclusion in *Who's Who in America, Who's Who in American Law, The Directory of American Scholars, Contemporary Authors, Who's Who in France, Who's Who in Europe, International Scholars Directory* (editor-in-chief), *Who's Who in the World,* and the *International Who's Who.*

Preface

In Negro legend, the devil meets his victim at a cross-road. Contemporary theology—and the church life which it so directly influences—stands at just such a crossroad, and the next step is fraught with tremendous peril.

The locus of this intersection in the history of 20th century theological thought is formed by two coordinates. First, and most readily observed, is the disappearance of the charismatic personalities who have dominated the stage since the collapse of the old modernism in the second decade of the century.

Barth and Brunner, the twin incarnations of neo-orthodoxy, have left a void that extends from Basel and Zurich to the ends of the theological spectrum. The shade of Bonhoeffer now flutters weakly over a bewildering number of conflicting interpretations of his fragmentary literary remains—unable to restrain lesser men from using him to support their pre-set ideologies.

Tillich, half-expecting like Aquinas never to finish his magnum opus, did in fact complete the *Systematic Theology*, but much of the magic of that convoluted and germanic trilogy seemed to·depart with its author. Even the pontifex maximus of liberal religious causes in America, Bishop James Pike, has completed his flamboyant career—with an exit that leaves his followers as spiritually bereft as were his séances. Only Rudolf Bultmann remains, but as a superannuated oracle who looks down from the lofty heights of Marburg on the clashes of his former disciples on the broad and utterly fragmented plain of German university theology.

Natura abhorret vacuum, Rabelais tells us, following Cicero. This is certainly true of ideological vacuums and we are thus brought to the second coordinate pinpointing the critical state of today's theology: a groping reintroduction of 19th century values—confidence in man's corporate ability to achieve in the vague future what he has not been able to accomplish in past or present.

On the Protestant side, Jürgen Moltmann, in depend

A Culture of Relativism

ence on renegade Marxist Ernst Bloch, substitutes *spero ut intellegam* and *spes quaerens intellectum* for the faith principle of Augustine and Anselm, warns us that we cannot have God "in us or over us but always only before us" (*The Theology of Hope*) and draws out the revolutionary implications of such unqualifiedly futuristic thinking (*Religion, Revolution and the Future*). In the Roman Catholic sphere, the posthumous dominance of Pierre Teilhard de Chardin increases daily: the dominance of an esoteric "hyperphysics" which, by subordinating entropic drift to organic evolution (in defiance of all modern physical theory), offers a progressive, evolving future where God waits for us "up ahead" at a mystical, Christic "Omega-point."

And both Catholics and Protestants are becoming more and more enamored of the varieties of "process theology" stemming from the philosophical labors of Whitehead and Hartshorne; by eschewing all absolute categories and by interlocking God with the actions of his creatures, these positions make peace with the relativism of the contemporary mind, turn the Christ into an exemplary symbol of man's potentialities, and elevate humanistic goals to the level of divine action (cf. John B. Cobb, Jr., *A Christian Natural Theology;* Norman Pittenger, *Process Thought and Christian Faith;* and Leslie Dewart's *The Foundations of Belief,* of which the late Bishop Pike wrote: "It would appear that what we have here is a sophisticated para-Thomistic statement of panentheism").

In this tentative repristination of 19th century, idealistic, progressivistic humanism—paralleling so closely western Europe's fading memory of Dachau and America's phoenix-like new confidence in her unlimited possibilities—Protestants and Catholics are discovering a new kind of ecumenicity. We have just seen that futurism is characteristic of influential thinking in both camps. Indeed, as Father Robert Campbell's two books (*Spectrum of Protestant Beliefs, Spectrum of Catholic Attitudes*) have recently made crystal clear, the same general spread of liberal-to-conservative positions can be found in both communions, and the alignments in this regard often prove to be far more significant than the Catholic-

Protestant distinction itself!

Under these new and unique conditions, it becomes of utmost consequence what path today's theology will follow when it moves from its present crossroad. A perceptive French critic of Chardin, Louis Salleron, has given dire warning of the results when the current "process" option is pursued: "The gospel is almost absent. . . . Faith in the world is not faith in God; it is precisely its contrary. Heaven and earth will pass away. To believe in the Holy Evolution of heaven and earth is to deny the truth of Christianity." * If this analysis is correct, to follow the path away from the solidity of the once-for-all historical revelation of God in Jesus Christ to a chimerical and unknowable futurism is to give the devil full rein at the crossroad; it is to cleanse the house of one demon only to invite "seven other spirits more wicked than himself," so that indeed "the last state is worse than the first."

But what alternative is possible? To the present writer, the answer is to go back (which in theology is the only way ever to go forward): back to the general and ecumenical creeds of the church, which convey the unchanging heart of its teachings—that "God was in Christ, reconciling the world unto Himself." The Apostles', Nicene, and Athanasian symbols are as capable as ever of carrying the present theological generation to the scriptural sources and to the Christ on whom the entire biblical revelation centers.

A simplistic solution? Perhaps, but the questioner has no right to assume this without studying carefully the essays and reviews which comprise this book. To discover whether indeed the faith of the ecumenical creeds can stand today, one must first critically and courageously determine why the maverick theology of our century has failed so badly, and then analyze the historic Christian position to see whether it has a structure capable of coping with the ideological challenges of our time. This is what the present volume attempts to do. If a motto were essential to its task, it would be that remarkable biblical couplet so antithetical to all theological rela-

---

* *Contre Teilhard de Chardin* ("Collection Pour ou Contre," 2; Nancy: Berger-Levrault, 1967), pp. 48-49.

tivism: "Jesus Christ the same yesterday, and today, and for ever. Be not carried about with divers and strange doctrines" (Hebrews 13:8-9).

JOHN WARWICK MONTGOMERY

29 September 1969
St. Michael and All Angels

Acknowledgments

The articles contained in this book have appeared previously in various theological publications; bibliographical data on their original publication follows:

"The Suicide of Christian Theology and a Modest Proposal for its Resurrection": *Bulletin of the Evangelical Theological Society*, Spring, 1968; *The Springfielder*, Spring, 1968; *His*, November, 1969-February, 1970.

"Agent 666: Bishop Pike and His Treasure Hunt": *The Sunday School Times*, April 30 and May 7, 1966.

"Dialogue on the New Morality": *Christianity Today*, July 21, 1967; transcribed from "The Bible and the New Morality," a film in the series "God and Man in the Twentieth Century," produced by Educational Communication Association, Indianapolis, Indiana.

"The Gospel According to LSD": *Christianity Today*, July 8, 1966.

"Morticians of the Absolute": *The Springfielder*, Spring, 1966; *The Asbury Seminarian*, Spring, 1966; *The Meaning of the Death of God*, ed. by Bernard Murchland (Random House, 1967); *The 'Is God Dead?' Controversy* (Zondervan, 1966).

"Wagering on the Death of God" and "The Altizer-Montgomery Debate": *The Altizer-Montgomery Dialogue* (Inter-Varsity, 1967).

"The Death of God Becomes More Deadly": *Christianity Today*, December 9, 1966.

"Altizer and Rome": *Christianity Today*, November 24, 1967; *Ecumenicity, Evangelicals, and Rome* (Zondervan, 1969), (under the title: "Rome and the 'Death of God' ").

"On Taking a European Theological Doctorate": *Christianity Today*, January 15, 1965.

"Bibliographical Bigotry": *Christianity Today*, August 19, 1966.

"Why Churches Decline": *Christianity Today*, December 3, 1965.

"Barth in Chicago": *Dialog*, Fall, 1962.

"Vidler at Strasbourg": *Christianity Today*, May 26, 1967.

"Kirchentag 1967": *Christianity Today*, September 1, 1967.

"Fresh Spirit in Continental Theology": *Christianity Today*, July 5, 1968.

"France in Flame": *Christianity Today*, August 16, 1968.

"Marcuse": *Christianity Today*, April 24, 1970.

"Freedom and the Gospel": *Christianity Today*, September 30, 1966.

"Dissecting Courage": *Christianity Today*, December 6, 1968.

"Theological Expo 69": *Christianity Today*, September 26, 1969.

"Georgia Harkness": *Christianity Today*, January 5, 1962.

"Martin Marty": *Christianity Today*, August 30, 1963.

"Gustaf Wingren": *Christianity Today*, November 5, 1965.

"James A. Pike": *Christianity Today*, April 29, 1966.

"Frederick Herzog": *Bulletin of the Evangelical Theological Society*, Summer, 1968.

"E. Schillebeeckx": *Christianity Today*, March 14, 1969.

"Robert M. Grant": *Bulletin of the Evangelical Theological Society*, Summer, 1965.

"G. Ernest Wright": *Journal of the Evangelical Theological Society*, Fall, 1969.

"Is Man His Own God?": *Journal of the Evangelical Theological Society*, Spring, 1969.

"The Theologian's Craft": *Concordia Theological Monthly*, February, 1966; *Journal of the American Scientific Affiliation*, September, 1966.

"Inspiration and Infallibility: A New Departure": *Bulletin of the Evangelical Theological Society*, Spring, 1965; *Crisis in Lutheran Theology*, Volume I (Baker, 1967).

"Inductive Inerrancy": *Christianity Today*, March 3, 1967.

"The Relevance of Scripture Today": *Christianity Today*, November 10, 1967 (shortened version); *The Bible: The Living Word of Revelation*, ed. by Merrill C. Tenney (Zondervan, 1968).

"God's Country?": *Christianity Today*, January 30, 1970.

"Demos and Christos": *Christianity Today*, July 18, 1969.

"Wisdom As Gift": *Interpretation*, January, 1962.

"Eros and Agape in Pico of Mirandola": *Concordia Theological Monthly*, December, 1961.

"The Law's Third Use: Sanctification": *Christianity Today*, April 26, 1963; *Crisis in Lutheran Theology*, Volume I (Baker, 1967).

"The Fourth Gospel Yesterday and Today": *Concordia Theological Monthly*, April, 1963.

"Can We Recover the Christian Devotional Life?": *Christianity Today*, September 25, 1961.

"100 Select Devotional Books": *Christianity Today*, September 25, 1961.

"Choice Books on the Holy Spirit": *Christianity Today*, January 4, 1963.

"Remythologizing Christmas": *Christianity Today*, December 20, 1968.

"Ascension Perspective": *Cresset*, May, 1961.

"The Reformation and World Evangelism": *Christianity Today*, April 29, 1966.

"95 Theses for the 450th Anniversary of the Reformation": *Christianity Today*, October 27, 1967; printed beside Luther's Theses in a booklet, *Reformation—einst und jetzt*, in Germany by Verlag Stelten; *In Defense of Martin Luther* (Northwestern, 1970).

"Renewal and Contemporary Theology"; *United Evangelical Action*, April, 1965; *Why—In the World?* ed. by Harvey C. Warner (Word, 1965).

The opportunity to collect these essays in a single volume has afforded the author an occasion to make slight improvements in style and content, and, in certain instances, to restore material which journal editors, solicitous of space limitations, dropped from the author's original manuscript texts.

Contents

III. Reconstructing

Illustrations

PART ONE

Reacting

1.

The Suicide of Christian Theology and a Modest Proposal for Its Resurrection *

A Disquieting Parabolic Introduction

Paul Tillich's Chicago University Law School lectures have just been published posthumously under the title, *My Search for Absolutes.*[1] This work is significant not only because of the lectures themselves, which represent Tillich's last major thoughts, but also because of the striking illustrations prepared for the volume by Tillich's close friend Saul Steinberg. One of Steinberg's drawings well depicts the theme of the present essay. It pictures two men on a teeter-totter poised at the edge of a cliff. The man on the end of the board which extends over the abyss is firing a fatal shot at his companion who stands on the safe end of the board. The result of this action is, of course, the destruction not only of the one who receives the bullet but also of the one who fires it, since when the shot finds it mark and the murdered man falls, the teeter-totter will throw the killer into the chasm. In killing his supposed enemy, the aggressive gunman has in reality killed himself, for he was dependent on him for his own life.

This, in my judgment, is the sad state of contemporary theology: in firing what is thought to be a fatal shot at Christian orthodoxy, the modern theologian has only succeeded in killing himself, for he has eliminated the sole *raison d'être* for his own existence. He has, in effect, committed suicide. To understand this suicidal phenomenon, we must first take a close look at its context, both secular and religious.

* An invitational presentation at the McMaster University Teach-In, Hamilton, Ontario, Canada, November 17-19, 1967, in dialogue with the Rev. Gregory Baum, O.S.A., Dr. William G. Pollard, and Resigned Bishop James A. Pike.

Notes for this section, pages 43-46.

The Secular Dilemma

Theologians of secularity such as death-of-Goders William Hamilton and Thomas Altizer, urban theologians such as Harvey Cox and Gibson Winter, and theological pundits such as James McCord of Princeton, inform us that secular society has finally overcome its neurotic guilt feelings and is on the verge of a new era of optimism, megalopolitan accomplishment, and social progress—an era which may well give rise to a new name for God and a new conception of the working of the Spirit.[2]

Sad to say, however, a closer look at the evidence belies any such interpretation. Antonioni's film *Blow-Up* has been heralded as a clear proof that the "op" generation has confidently thrown off the troubling restrictions of Christian morality and is now delightfully reinstituting Eden by a permissive sexual code and an autonomous, self-created situation ethic. But sensitive observers of *Blow-Up* will have noted the real theme of the film: the brooding, unsatisfied quest for reality in which the photographer-hero engages—a quest which is left unsatisfied by his sexual adventures and which finally collapses in his solipsistic inability to distinguish between the real world and the world of self-created photographic artistry.[3]

Three recent French films have made this point with even more telling effect. Alain Jessua's *Jeu de Massacre,* which received the best scenario award at Cannes in 1967, presents an op cartoonist who loses his wife to the absurd and immature life-model of his cartoon character, the "killer of Neuchâtel"; as in *Blow-Up,* the blending of fiction and reality in modern life is relentlessly destroying the values and personalities of the modern man who gives himself up to the spirit of the times. In *Le Grand Dadais,* a twenty-year old, taken as the symbol of contemporary youth, listens seriously to the cacophony of slogans modern life offers for achieving happiness: secular success and hedonistic love; in religiously putting these values into practice, he makes a shamble of his life. Jean-Luc Godard's *La Chinoise,* which produced an uproar at Cannes and offended both Marxists and anti-Communists, tells of the endeavor of five French students to inject meaning into their lives through Mao's "red book": instead of facing the self-centeredness which stalks them at every point, they sublimate their real motivations by absorption in the totally secularized gospel of revolutionary Communism. They think that they are following Mao's axiom: "Il faut confronter les idées vagues avec des images claires"; but in actuality they fall into the worst kind of intellectual, moral, and personal chaos.

NB

One of the best descriptions of the current secular dilemma is provided by Greenwich Village cartoonist Jules Feiffer's fable, "George's Moon."[4] George, the lone inhabitant of the moon, represents contemporary man in his fruitless search to discover meaning in life. His grandiose intellectual attempts (à la 19th century idealism) to construct a universal philosophy border on the absurd ("If I *am* here and *I* can see space then space must, in all logic, be able to see *me*...."); his endeavor to lose himself in activistic programs leave him totally unsatisfied, for they introduce no real meaning into his existence ("What good was it to collect rocks, to count craters, to fill the craters you've counted with the rocks you've collected, to empty the craters and collect the rocks all over again?"); and his existential effort to establish universal significance by total concentration on his own existence results in the loss of his personal starting-point ("Since *he* was the only thing around, George decided to believe in himself.... Then he awoke one morning and found that he had forgotten his name").

The current preoccupation with psychedelic drugs is an extension of this existential quest. Having lost confidence in the reality and significance of the external world, many today seek to uncover, through drugs, a hidden reality within themselves. The kind of "reality" encountered has been put in serious doubt by psychedelic experts such as French specialist Roger Heim, who found that a cat who has received LSD recoils in fear from a mouse;[5] but the very use of psychedelic techniques, regardless of their results, shows how dissatisfied modern man is with his secular existence and how far he will go to inject meaning into his world.

Philosopher J. Glenn Gray, in his article, "Salvation

"George's Moon"
by Jules Feiffer

George spent his days dreaming about space.

IF SPACE IS **REALLY** THERE AND I **KNOW** IT MUST BE THERE BECAUSE I CAN SEE IT.

THEN **I** MUST BE REALLY **HERE** OR ELSE I WOULDN'T KNOW ITS **THERE** BECAUSE I COULDN'T SEE IT.

AND IF **I AM** HERE AND **I** CAN SEE SPACE THEN SPACE MUST, IN ALL LOGIC, BE ABLE TO SEE **ME**.

—WHICH PROVES THAT I **EXIST**.

SPACE AND GEORGE— GEORGE AND SPACE —

A TEAM.

It almost made him feel like crying.

He was just filling up time and he knew it. What good was it to collect rocks, to count craters, to fill the craters you've counted with the rocks you've collected, to empty the craters and collect the rocks all over again?

IT LACKS DIGNITY.

Was this a way for a man to spend a life?

George recognized he had no sense of himself. Also that he had no sense of others. How could he have any dignity without a context? He didn't know who he was or what or anything.

A MAN **HAS** TO BELIEVE IN SOMETHING.

since **he** was the only thing around, George cided to believe in himself.

HAIL GEORGE.

He made up poems to himself.

GEORGE
George
GEORGE
george
GEORGE
George
GEORGE.

e made up stories o himself.

SO GEORGE CURED THE PLAGUE, ENDED THE FAMINE, TURNED BACK THE FLOOD.

And then he awoke one morning and found that he had forgotten his name.

THAT'S WHAT I GET. SERVES ME RIGHT.

So he stopped believing in himself.

on the Campus: Why Existentialism Is Capturing the Students,"[6] has perceptively argued that today's focus on existential subjectivity paradoxically arises from the desperate search for "some authority, both private and public, that will make possible authentic individuality." However, concludes Gray, who has done depth studies in German existentialism: "I doubt that Existentialist philosophy can ultimately satisfy the search for authority." At best it merely offers to those "not yet able or ready to act" an "escape from the morass of conformity, *la dolce vita,* boredom, and ... meaningless competitiveness."

Traditionally, Christian theology has seen its prime task at this very point: it has sought to lead men to the only "authority" that can create "authentic individuality"—the God who revealed Himself in the living Word, Jesus Christ, through the written Word, Holy Scripture. What about today's theology? How effectively is it carrying out this task?

The Religious Dilemma

On October 31, the 450th Anniversary of the Reformation reminded Christendom of Martin Luther, who typifies the great theologians of former days. Luther made many mistakes, but equivocation and uncertainty were not among them. His stand at Worms ("I am bound by the Scriptures adduced, and my conscience has been

Luther Statue in the Marketplace
Eisleben, East Germany

taken captive by the Word of God; I am neither able nor willing to recant"); his opposition to all relativizing of the truth of Holy Scripture ("I make it my invariable rule," he wrote to Erasmus, "steadfastly to adhere to the sacred text in all that it teaches, and to assert that teaching. . . . Uncertainty is the most miserable thing in the world"); his great hymnody ("A Mighty Fortress Is Our God")—every aspect of his career displayed his unalterable conviction that God has spoken clearly, revealing His will to man and demanding a response of trust and faith in this clear revelation.[7] A similar description could apply, with little substantive change, to Augustine, Thomas Aquinas, Wesley, Newman, or to any other great theologian of the Christian past.

If the pre-20th century theologian could be sculpted as Luther is at Worms and at Wittenberg—standing forthrightly and preaching from God's Holy Word—the contemporary theologian might be represented ·as Marcel Duchamp's "Nude Descending a Staircase": all motion and no substance. That this is by no means an exaggeration can be seen in studies made of the image of learned representatives of the faith in today's novels and films. Worden's unpublished Boston University doctoral dissertation[8] on the American film situation from 1951 to 1960 and Horton Davies study of contemporary fiction[9] display the theological representative in an exceedingly poor light. Typical is Peter DeVries' hilarious but tragic portrayal of liberal clergyman "Holy" Mackerel, whose confusion of belief is so appalling that his idea of church architecture is to create a pulpit with "four legs of four delicately differing fruitwoods, to symbolize the four Gospels, and their failure to harmonize."[10]

This is perhaps the contemporary emancipated cleric at his worst; but the extent of present theological decline is as readily shown by the common attribution of Luther-like qualities to any modern theologian who takes a stand of any kind—even if (or particularly if?) it involves his stalwart refusal to make any positive presentation of Christian doctrine at all. Luther shook the world because he courageously endeavored to reassert the biblical Gospel; today's "Luthers" are theologians who sted-

"Nude Descending a Staircase" by Marcel Duchamp.

fastly maintain their inability to believe or proclaim historic Christian truth any longer. So parched is the desert of contemporary theology that any act of faith—even if it is a commitment to unfaith—becomes a mirage suggesting Luther himself.

How has this sad state of affairs come about? Why is contemporary theology seemingly incapable of offering any firm word to modern secular man? How is it that the secular dilemma of uncertainty is matched by an equal if not greater religious uncertainty? Perhaps the best way to understand the self-destruction of contemporary theology is by way of a modern parable. I call it "The Parable of the Engineers."

Once a corps of engineers was assigned to continue the building of a magnificent cathedral which had already been under construction many centuries and which had benefitted from the devoted labor of great engineers of many generations. Some of the new engineers, however, began to question the architectural soundness of the plans. They said that the plans had numerous errors and contradictions in them. When asked for clarification by some of their fellows, they pointed out that architectural styles were changing and that the plans erroneously presented older stylistic characteristics and contradicted current styles. In reply, a few engineers noted that this did not make the plans erroneous or contradictory in themselves, and that it was the architect's business to draw the plans and the engineers' to follow them. The majority did not agree, but they did not want to cast direct aspersions on the architect or abandon the construction. So they had recourse to a number of stratagems.

1. First, they argued that though the plans were erroneous and contradictory this was not the architect's fault and should be attributed to his draughtsmen. (Intransigent engineers claimed that the architect was always responsible for his draughtsmen, but this argument was brushed aside.) Endeavors were thus made to ignore the "draughtsmen's errors" while accepting the architect's "true ideas" as conveyed by the draughtsmen's plans. But since the only knowledge of the architect's ideas came by way of the draughtsmen's plans, this endeavor miserably failed and led to more radical suggestions. (It is perhaps worth pointing out that while these discussions went on, relatively little building was done.)

2. Then the engineers argued that the purpose of the plans had been misunderstood. They were not intended to be followed as such, but contact with them would increase the engineer's inner sensitivity to true building methods. But one engineer's inner sensitivity did not produce the same results as another's,

considerable confusion set in, and a tower collapsed.

3. A particularly brilliant engineer now suggested that every-thing in the plans was symbolic of the architect himself. How-ever, it was soon discovered that if everything was symbolic and nothing literal, no engineer could determine the real meaning of any particular element in the plans. More disputes set in, and another section of the building crumbled.

4. Now the people for whom the cathedral was being built were becoming more and more agitated and many would not enter the half completed edifice at all because of the danger of falling stones, loose mortar, and buckling floors. Some were even crying for a new staff of engineers. This made the engi-neers terribly nervous and excitable, and finally some of them, to placate the mob, began to claim that there was no archi-tect at all, that the people for whom the cathedral was being built were more important than anything else, and that every-one was in as good a position as the inaccurate draughtsmen to draw up plans. Oddly enough, this seemed to infuriate the people even more, for the latter apparently considered it self-evident that the plans, the great engineers of the past who had faithfully followed them, and the earlier work on the cathedral (the work done before the present confusion) all presupposed an architect. They began to become violent and even claimed that the engineers were destroying their cathedral and making a mockery out of the engineering profession.

5. At this point a very vocal engineer tried to convince the people that such efforts as he and the others were making were really acts of tremendous heroism and that even though the plans of the architect were impossibly naive and had been hope-lessly muddled by past draughtsmen and engineers, he himself could lead them through the maze by direct communication with dead engineers of the past, thereby proving the deathless value of engineering science. But instead of being considered a repristination of heroic, reforming engineers of early times, this engineer was regarded as an epitomal fool by virtually all of his colleagues and the great mass of the people. Only the media of communication featured him, for they quickly discovered that people followed his exploits with horror and fascination even as they did the latest scandals of famous enter-tainers.

Thus did the great cathedral eventually crumble and fall, killing not only the people who had loved it but also the engi-neers responsible for its loss. Pathetically, there were a few engineers who, right up to the moment of final destruction, still pleaded that the only hope lay in following rigorously the original plans, that the engineers must bring their stylistic ideas into conformity with the architect's, and that deviations from their notions of style did not constitute genuine errors or contradictions in the plans. But their voices were scarcely heard amid the din of engineering teams working at cross-purposes to each other, and the deafening roar of falling masonry.

And the rain descended, and the floods came, and the winds blew, and beat upon that cathedral; and it fell: and great was the fall of it.

Anatomy of a Suicide

Let us now consider each of the sad stages in the destruction of the cathedral of theology. By observing the unfortunate decisions of the theological engineers assigned to the work, we will be able to understand how the current religious dilemma has arisen. And only when the religious crisis has been diagnosed can a meaningful remedy be offered.

The Gun Is Loaded in the 18th Century, Placed against the Head in the 19th Century, First Fired in the 20th

During the 18th century, when it became painfully evident that the church was identifying with certain privileged classes and neglecting others, and revolutionary opposition was directed against unjust privilege, the church fell under the revolutionary axe. Instead of seeing that the church had violated her own principles (which firmly maintained the equality of all men before God) and should be corrected on the basis of these very principles, the intelligentsia endeavored to establish a counter-religion, naturalistic Deism.[11] Philosophical objectors to historic Christianity arose, who argued that "firm and unalterable experience" eliminates the miraculous claims of Christian revelation (David Hume), and "the accidental truths of history [such as are provided by the historical revelation of Christ] can never become the proof of the necessary truths of reason" (Lessing). Attention was thus shifted to the natural laws of the external world as proofs of God's existence, and to the moral nature of man as evidence of God's moral perfection; and biblical revelation was considered superfluous if not positively misleading. Deists such as Thomas Paine (*The Age of Reason*) went to great lengths to demonstrate alleged errors and contradictions in the scriptural text.

In the 19th century[2] man's confidence in his abilities, ethical and otherwise, expanded by leaps and bounds. Reinforced by what he believed to be the scientifically-established world-view of evolution, he built metaphysical and idealistic systems to replace Christian revelation, and pragmatically endeavored to achieve a perfect society through technology, big business, and colonial expansion. Many theologians—not appreciating that the arguments of Hume, Lessing, and Paine had been well met even in the 18th century,[13] and not listening to 19th century littérateurs such as Hawthorne, Melville, and Burckhardt who reminded Western man of his finitude and presumptive selfishness—jumped on the evolutionary, perfectionistic bandwagon. They endeavored to re-do the biblical revelation in the image of the 19th century Zeitgeist, and where it did not fit, they *made* it fit—by dismembering the Old Testament texts through (non-textually based) documentary criticism so as to demonstrate the "evolution of Jewish religion," and by throwing out the miraculous in Jesus' ministry so as to turn him into an ethical example, a kind of ideal boy scout helping little old ladies across the Sea of Galilee.

Building on this base, early 20th century theological Modernism, both Protestant and Catholic, created a totally new religion of human perfectibility and social improvement, to which they attached the terminology of traditional Christianity.[14] These theological engineers justified themselves by pointing out that "architectural styles were changing and that the plans [God's revelation in the Christ of the Bible] erroneously presented older stylistic characteristics and contradicted current styles. In reply, a few engineers noted that this did not make the plans erroneous or contradictory in themselves, and that it was the architect's business to draw the plans and the engineers' to follow them." But the vast majority of theologians were too inebriated from gulping down the heady wine of early 20th century cultural self-confidence to listen to these warnings. They preferred to take their cue from such aphorisms as that of autosuggestionist Emile Coué: "Every day in every way we are becoming better and better." Thus was the first suicidal round fired against Christian theology by its own theological proponents.

Inadequate First Aid Treatment by Dr. Barth

The First World War accomplished what orthodox theologians had not been able to do: it destroyed the evolutionary, progessivistic confidence of 19th century man and of his early 20th century Modernistic counterpart. Into the theological vacuum left by the collapse of Modernism stepped Karl Barth,[15] who reasserted the ancient Christian verities: man is a sinner desperately needing the Divine grace offered by Christ's death on the Cross and proclaimed in Holy Scripture. But Barth was equally convinced that the 19th century negative criticisms of the miraculous plan of salvation and of Scripture itself could not be rejected. His solution was a "dialectic" of Yes and No: Yes, the transcendent Gospel is valid, but No, it cannot be justified evidentially through investigation of the Resurrection of Christ or through an errorless biblical revelation. The Biblical writers, asserted Barth in his *Church Dogmatics*, "have been at fault in every word, and yet according to the same scriptural witness, being justified and sanctified by grace alone, they have still spoken the Word of God in their fallible and erring human word." [16]

This attempt to have one's theological cake and eat it too was tremendously influential as long as dismal post-World War I conditions prevailed; but as soon as secular life began to recover after the War and the subsequent Depression, the inherent instabilities of Barth's dialectic caused it to lose ground. Critics soon observed[17] that what Barth gave with one hand he removed with the other: since, in the words of our Parable [1],[18] "the only knowledge of the architect's (God's) ideas came by way of the draughtsman's plans [the biblical writers' productions]," Barth's concession that the Bible was an erroneous book and that Christ's miraculous work was untestable removed all ground for accepting its Gospel message. Dr. Barth's first aid gave the suicidal patient a temporary lease on life, but his medical technique was too self-contradictory to bring about the needed recovery.

The Bultmannian and Post-Bultmannian Discharge of More Ammunition

Rudolf Bultmann recognized full well the instabilities in Barth's theology, and insisted that if the miraculous claims of the Bible could not be evidentially sustained (as the 19th century had asserted and Barth had conceded), then the only answer was to "demythologize" the Bible. One must, said he, eliminate the mythical, miraculous thought-forms with which the scriptural writers and the early church clothed the basic Christian message. What was the fundamental Gospel? For Bultmann, caught up in Heideggerian existentialism, it was "authentic self-understanding," which can (and must) be proclaimed to modern man without offensive miraculous trappings.

Barth had endeavored to discount the negative efforts of 18th and 19th century biblical and historical criticism of the Christian faith by a dialectic affirmation of the transcendent Gospel; however, his concessions to biblical criticism put a serious question mark over all biblical teaching about the transcendent God and the Gospel. Bultmann, while rejecting Barth's inconsistency, fell into a parallel difficulty: if the Bible is a mythologically corrupted work, what makes its conception of existential self-authentication valid? Why not extend demythologizing to the Christian interpretation of *Existenz?*

Moreover, if Barth's flight to a transcendent Gospel put him in a realm of unverifiability, even more so did Bultmann's descent into existential subjectivity. In theory it seemed superficially plausible that the scriptural plans for the cathedral of theology "were not intended to be followed as such, but contact with them would increase the engineer's inner sensitivity to true building methods." But in practice, "one engineer's inner sensitivity did not produce the same results as another's, considerable confusion set in, and a tower collapsed" [2]. Just as secular existentialism was unable to "satisfy the search for authority," so Bultmann's religious existentialism, founded on the Kierkegaardian axiom that "truth is subjectivity," necessarily produced relativistic chaos on the theological scene.

This has been painfully illustrated by the diverse theological views of Bultmann's disciples, the so-called "Post-Bultmannians," in their "new quest of the historical Jesus." From Fuchs' hypostatizing of language ("the Word interprets us") to Ott's rejection of all objective history ("there are no such things as objectively verifiable facts"), one sees the inevitable theological outcome of existential commitments. The Jesus of Christian proclamation almost totally disappears in the blending of revelation with the contemporary interpreter of revelation.[19] Theology degenerates to autobiography.

Tillich Fires Another Round

If the first suicidal shot against theology in the 20th century was discharged by the Modernists (using ammunition prepared by critics of the faith in the 18th and 19th centuries), and if Bultmann and the Post-Bultmannians fired rounds two and three (after Barth's first aid proved ineffective), then the fourth discharge at the victim was set off by Paul Tillich.[20]

Tillich properly saw that existential theology confused revelational answers to the human predicament with the predicament itself, and he sought to avoid this grave difficulty by giving theology an absolutely firm base in ontology—in "Being Itself." Only Being Itself (or the "Ground of all being") is worthy of ultimate concern, he maintained, and all genuine religious statements are symbolic of ultimate Being. No biblical assertions and no historical realities (including Jesus Himself) can be regarded as absolute; at best they "participate" in Being Itself, while always pointing beyond themselves to ultimacy.

But Tillich's appeal to ontology achieved little more than Barth's appeal to transcendence or Bultmann's appeal to existential experience. As analytical philosopher Paul Edwards has shown, "Tillich's theology is indeed safe from anti-theological arguments, . . . but only at the expense of being compatible with anything whatever."[21] Tillich's concept of Being Itself is technically meaningless because it is completely formal; no religious statements about it can be taken literally, and the degree to which Christian "symbols" (even the Christ) "participate" in it remains indeterminate. As our Parable says [3]: "It was soon discovered that if everything was symbolic and nothing literal, no engineer could determine the real meaning of any particular element in the plans."

Tillich, like other major theologians of the 20th century, uncritically accepted Lessing's claim that eternal truth cannot be identified with historical revelation, and likewise bought the negative biblical criticism of the 19th century. Thus he eliminated the possibility of his making concrete and verifiable statements about God or about His relation to the world. As George Tavard well noted: "Tillich has simply not been radical enough in criticizing liberal theology. He has not seen that the historians who doubt the value of the [biblical] records have failed to establish their point. Here, Paul Tillich remains a child of his generation, a victim of the historicism of the last century." [22]

The Last Two Chambers Emptied by the Secular and Death-of-God Theologians of the Sixties

Two barrels of the six-shooter were left unfired when Tillich ceased his labors, and as the theological victim, already mortally wounded, reeled back and forth on Steinberg's teeter-totter, the "secular" and "God-is-dead" theologians of our decade took careful aim and finished him off. They have yet to realize that as a result they themselves are now in what Christian poet Charles Williams referred to as "the spectral grave and the endless falling." [23]

No one should have been surprised at the secular and theothanatological turn of contemporary theology: the way had been fully prepared. [24] Death-of-God theologian Paul van Buren, who had taken his doctorate under Barth, woke up one morning to the realization that if God were indeed the transcendent "Holy Other" that Barth said He was—unverifiable in revelational history and subject only to the acknowledgment of unsupported faith—then God was in fact dead; God-language no longer had any meaningful referent. Thomas J. J. Altizer followed out Tillich's basic "Protestant principle"—that the ultimacy of all religious assertions must be negated in order to prevent non-ultimate concerns from triumphing—and applied the principle rigorously to Being Itself, thus negating the very idea of God.[25]

And why have the "secular theologians" such as Robinson, Vidler,[26] and Pike repristinated the old liberal humanism that finds God where man's social action takes place? Simply because the intermediate states of 20th century theology—Barthian neo-orthodoxy, Bultmannian and Post-Bultmannian existentialism, and Tillichian ontology—having accepted the critical approach to revelation maintained by the old Modernism, were unable to offer any stable alternatives to humanistic liberalism. Once the reliability of God's revelation in the historical Christ of Scripture is put in question, as it was in 18th and 19th century thought, secular theology is the only consistent possibility: in rejecting God's revelation, man puts himself in God's place; now all that is required is to work out the implications of man's centrality. Naturally, God will take a back seat or be redefined in terms of man's interests; naturally, human social action will become all-important; naturally (as in the theology of death-of-God advocate William Hamilton), Jesus will be transmuted into a humanistic "place to be" and "revelation" will now be found in sexual satisfaction and the amelioration of the ills of society.[27]

Ironically, however, the secular focusing of theology has not in any sense accomplished what its proponents envisaged. Instead of church life reviving through concentration on the humanistic, indifference or out-and-out antagonism has been manifested. Church interest in England is still approaching the vanishing point in spite of the efforts of Cambridge radicals and the Bishop of Woolwich to outdo each other in a "more heretical than thou" contest; in the United States, theological seminary enrollments in non-evangelical institutions have continued their steady one-half percent decline each year.[28] Young people seeking careers and older people seeking meaningful community associations have recognized what ought to have been obvious to the theologians: if Christian faith reduces to humanistic values, then why bother with church membership or church careers? The peace corps, social work, psychiatry, and the Rotary offer more mean-

ingful opportunities for secular association and service—
and they are not debilitated by a conceptual vocabulary
which even their own leaders do not take seriously. As
for committed church members, they look at the secular
theologian as little more than a betrayer; in the words of
our Parable [4]: "They [the people who desired to worship in the cathedral] began to become violent and even
claimed that the engineers were destroying their cathedral and making a mockery out of the engineering profession." The failure of the radical theologians' efforts
to make the church "relevant" through secularism suggest that there might actually be some merit in that old
teaching, "He who would save his life shall lose it."

One of the most tragic examples in the current revival of liberal theology is that of Bishop James Pike
[5], whose theological devolution took him farther and
farther left since he entered Protestantism at the point
of an unstable Barthian theology. At the time the Bishop's
work, *What Is This Treasure*, was published in 1966, he
had already come to display utter arbitrariness in accepting and rejecting biblical materials in accord
with his personal religious preferences; in a series of
critical articles on his theology published that same year
I cited a number of examples and drew conclusions from
them:

> If we can trust no revelation of God fully, then *we
> ourselves become the only remaining standard of judg-
> ment.* This is precisely the case with the Bishop of Cali-
> fornia, and the arbitrariness of his entire theology is the
> consequence. He picks and chooses Scripture according to
> his interests. Thus, as we have seen, he accepts the first
> clause of John 14:6 while rejecting the second, and uses
> the apocryphal book of Judith to argue for a loose sexual
> morality, while rejecting the absoluteness of the Ten
> Commandments found in canonical Scripture. In "How My
> Mind Has Changed," he insists on wine for Communion
> on the ground that "Jesus never drank grape juice," yet
> in *What Is This Treasure* he approvingly cites the non-
> Christian philosopher Porphyry (third century), who said
> of Jesus' healing of the Gadarene demoniac, "probably
> fictitious, but if genuine then morally discreditable"
> (p. 69). In *A Time for Christian Candor* he rejects He-
> brews 12:5, 6 as "in direct contradiction to our Lord's teach-
> ing" (p. 136).

The more one reads the bishop, the more the convic-

tion grows that in dispensing with all "earthen vessels,"
he has inevitably ended up with the earthen vessel of his
own judgment.... Pike's adventurous theological career
has made him the sole arbiter of the divine, whose increasing vagueness as the "Ground of all being" opens
the floodgates to semantic confusion, to creedal double-
think, and to moral anarchy.[29]

With the appearance of *If This Be Heresy* (1967) and
the reports of the Ford-Pike séances, the evident de-
terioration proceeded even farther. In sublime disregard of the basic Christian affirmations concerning sin,
hell, judgment, redemption, and resurrection, the Bishop
endeavored to provide "empirical" evidence for human
survival after death by way of psychic phenomena and
psi-research. As in the 18th century, when alongside a
Voltaire stood a Cagliostro, rationalism here displayed
its other face, superstition. By "superstition" we do not
mean ESP investigations as such, for this is a legitimate field of inquiry; nor do we criticize the Bishop's laud-
able appreciation of empirical method. What is sad is
the extent to which he, like the 18th and 19th century
critics of the Bible, consistently confused empirical investigation with unrecognized metaphysical and religious commitments.

The data collected by parapsychological experts
over the years has been exceedingly impressive; only
prejudicial blindness can ignore research compilations
such as those by Sidgwick, Gurney, Myers, and Tyrrell,
or the work carried on by Professor Rhine.[30] But one
cannot stress too emphatically that *the specialists in this
area have not been able to establish human survival or
any other religious doctrine on the basis of their data.*
Thus, after setting out the best evidence the ESP field
offers, Gardner Murphy—by all odds one of the foremost
American students in this field—gives this chilling personal testimony: "Trained as a psychologist, and now in
my sixties, I do not actually anticipate finding myself in
existence after physical death." [31] And in concluding
a detailed examination of the entire parapsychological
field, Castellan quotes another French expert, Robert
Amadou, and perceptively comments on his judgment:

"Il y a un immense décalage entre la connaissance
exacte que nous possédons de ces phénomènes et les sup-

positions qu'impliquent les hypotheses. . . . Nous ignorons
trop les circonstances qui entourent l'apparition des faits
psi pour pouvoir édifier une théorie satisfaisante de
ces phénomènes, immédiatement vérifiable par l'expéri-
ence." Cette remarque se dégage d'elle-même au terme de
notre étude. Les véritables métapsychistes n'ont pu poser
aucune conclusion scientifique: toute conclusion est
manifestement empreinte de métaphysique.[32]

This is the point: Pike's own metaphysic—and, in
light of the close connection between psi phenomena and
the unconscious, doubtless his personal drive toward wish-
fulfillment as well—created the "survival" interpretation he placed on psychic data. Why not other contexts
of interpretation? In the Christian world-view, there
are other spiritual powers to be reckoned with besides
God and the members of the Church Triumphant.[33]
Wrote B. Vaughan in his Foreword to a classic work by
a noted British psychical investigator: "There is a great
deal to say against Spiritism, but not much that I know
of for it. But I shall be reminded that it has disproved
the doctrine for materialism and proved the immortality
of man. Not so; it may have only proved the immortality
of demons." [34] A sobering point, and one reinforced by
the most important German theological work published
on the subject in this century: Kurt Koch's *Seelsorge und
Okkultismus*, where the author scientifically tabulates
the "frequency-ratio" of consequences connected with
spiritualist activity on the part of practitioners (mediums,
etc.) and followers; these include psychoses, horrible
death-bed scenes, suicides, apoplexy, warping and distortion of character, compulsions and fear-delusions, indifference or positive hostility to Scripture and prayer, and
obduracy (*Verkrampfung*) against Christ and God.[35]

"Test the spirits" cautions the Christian revelation,
but for Bishop Pike and the radical theology of the Sixties, testing of theological judgments has become impossible. If a recent issue of *Newsweek*[36] is right that
"Anything Goes" in our "Permissive Society" today,
then theology has become relevant beyond the wildest
dreams of its current proponents: now "anything goes"
religiously as well. And this of course applies also to the
practical ecumenical blueprints on the horizon, such as
the Blake-Pike proposal. In a prevailing atmosphere of

doctrinal vagary, with no clear standards of theological truth or error and with the inability to condemn heresy because few know what orthodoxy is,[37] church unions based on piety, sentiment, love of organization, or the simple urge for togetherness become not only live possibilities but appalling actualities. And the result is a steady devaluation of the coinage of the Gospel.

Modest Proposal for a Resurrected Theology

By strict analogy with Jonathan Swift's *Modest Proposal*, it might be thought that we would recommend that the church eat its theologians. This suggestion does not need to be entertained, since, as we have seen in the foregoing discussion, contemporary theologians have eaten each other and nearly gobbled theology down as well. Conditions have become so bad that a radical rethinking of the whole theological enterprise has become mandatory.

The lines along which theological recovery can be made have been outlined in our Parable. While the cathedral was tottering on the brink of collapse, "there were a few engineers who, right up to the moment of final destruction, still pleaded that the only hope lay in following rigorously the original plans, that the engineers must bring their stylistic ideas into conformity with the architect's, and that deviations from their notions of style did not constitute genuine errors or contradictions in the plans." Contemporary theologians have destroyed themselves by their unnecessary and unwarranted destruction of biblical revelation, on which all sound theology is based. The only hope for a resurrected theology lies in a recovery of confidence in the historical Christ and in the Scriptures He stamped with approval as God's Word.

The Divine Christ of History

Neither rejection of the historicity of a Divine Christ, nor the fear of negative consequences if the question of His Divinity is subjected to historical investigation, can in any sense be justified—though such attitudes have characterized all mainline Protestant theological positions in the 20th century. Contemporary theology has un-critically followed the 18th century dicta that history is too uncertain to ground faith (Lessing's ditch) and that universal experience rules out the miraculous (Hume). But no one is obligated to accept Hume's circular argu-ment (the very existence of evidential claims for Christ's miracles shows that no alleged "universality of experi-ence" can eliminate miracle claims *a priori*),[38] nor can anyone legitimately depreciate history as the ground for religious faith (since history is but past experience, and our every decision, religious or non-religious, involves the weighing of experiential evidence and the commitment of faith to the implications of empirical data).[39] More-over, contemporary theology is in no way required to carve up the biblical records by 19th century documen-tary methods that are in fact rooted in discredited evolu-tionary presuppositions and subjectivistic analytical techniques; in actuality, these methods have been tried and found wanting in other fields (Greco-Roman and an-cient Near Eastern studies, for example).[40] Concern-ing the destructive use of form-criticism on the New Tes-tament documents, C. S. Lewis argued with tremendous cogency just before his death that a lifetime of work on comparative literary questions had showed him the utter fallacy of the method: "The 'assured results of modern scholarship,' as to the way in which an old book was written, are 'assured,' we may conclude, only because the men who know the facts are dead and can't blow the gaff." [41]

The historical value of the New Testament records about Christ is, when considered from the objective stand-point of textual scholarship, nothing less than stellar. Writes Sir Frederic G. Kenyon, formerly director and principal librarian of the British Museum: "The interval ... between the dates of original composition and the earliest extant evidence becomes so small as to be in fact negligible, and the last foundation for any doubt that the Scriptures have come down to us substantially as they were written has now been removed. Both the *authenticity* and the *general integrity* of the books of the New Testa-ment may be regarded as finally established." [42]

And in these attested historical documents the Divine

claims of Jesus Christ and the Resurrection by which He
validated those claims are set forth in the most lucid and
persuasive terms. J. V. Langmead Casserley perceptively
noted in his 1951 Maurice Lectures at King's College,
London, that the evidence for the Resurrection is "like
a knife pointed at the throat of the irreligious man." [43]
Attempts like Schonfield's to explain it away invariably
demand more faith than the Resurrection itself, for they
fly squarely in the face of the primary-source material.[44] The saving events of the Christian Gospel are
as factually sound today as they ever were, in spite of
theological opinions to the contrary. Well ought we to
ponder Ignatius of Antioch's words, written on his way
to martyrdom under the Emperor Trajan (*ca.* A.D. 107):
Christ "suffered all these things for our sakes, that we
might attain salvation, and He truly suffered even as also
He truly raised Himself up, not, as some faithless persons
say, that his Passion was a matter of mere semblance,
whereas it is they who are mere semblance. Things will
assuredly turn out for them in accordance with their
opinions; they will find themselves disembodied and
phantasmal." [45]

The Holy Scriptures

The historical validation of a Divine Christ leads to
the establishment of the Scriptures as Divine revelation.
When one examines, purely on historical grounds, the attitude of Jesus toward the Old Testament, one finds that
He regarded it as no less than God's revealed Word. His
attitude is one of total trust: He quotes authoritatively
from the most obscure corners of the Old Testament; He
makes no attempt to distinguish "religious" or "moral"
truth from veracity in historical or "secular" matters;
and never does He subject the Old Testament to criticism.
Far from rebuking the devil himself for quoting Scripture, Jesus out-quotes him, employing the significant assertion that man lives "by every word that proceeds out
of the mouth of God." [46]

As even radical biblical critics such as Bultmann,
H. J. Cadbury, and F. C. Grant have admitted, Jesus
considered the Old Testament to be fully revelatory and
totally reliable. But if Jesus was in fact God Incarnate

as He claimed and as His Resurrection evidences, then His evaluation of Scripture is no mere human, fallible judgment, but the exact truth. And the same veracity attaches to His promise to His Apostles that His Spirit would give them "total recall" concerning His teachings,[47] thereby guaranteeing that the New Testament documents, subsequently to be written by them and by their close associates (under Apostolic guidance), would have revelatory value also.[48]

Thus can the authority of the Christian Scriptures be established on a solidly empirical, historical footing. Problems of course still remain, such as the reconciliation of biblical and scientific data concerning the origin of man and the world, alleged contradictions in Scripture or between Scripture and extra-biblical data, and moral difficulties in the scriptural narratives. But these problems now become questions of interpretation, not of authority, for Christ Himself has settled the authority issue once and for all. His testimony to the de facto revelatory character of the whole of Scripture outweighs any and every counterargument from particular difficulties; it now becomes the task of the faithful biblical interpreter, as he confronts problem passages, to seek effective solutions consistent with the high view of the Bible's authority held by the Incarnate Lord Himself.[49]

Resurrection and Life

The keystone of a resurrected theology is, then, an unqualified acceptance of the resurrected Christ. His historical Resurrection was the focal point of early Christian witness (and the early Christians were close enough to the events to know what had and what had not happened). Only when modern theology ceases its equivocation on the issue of the reality of the Resurrection will it find its way to a Divine Christ and to a fully authoritative Scripture. John Updike, in "Seven Stanzas at Easter," speaks directly to contemporary theology in this regard: [50]

> Make no mistake: if He rose at all
> it was as His body.
> if the cells' dissolution did not reverse, the molecules
>   reknit, the amino acids rekindle,
> the Church will fall.

THE SUICIDE OF CHRISTIAN THEOLOGY

It was not as the flowers,
each soft Spring recurrent;
it was not as His Spirit in the mouths and fuddled
    eyes of the eleven apostles;
it was as His flesh: ours.

The same hinged thumbs and toes,
the same valved heart
that—pierced—died, withered, paused, and then
    regathered out of enduring Might
new strength to enclose.

Let us not mock God with metaphor,
analogy, sidestepping, transcendence;
making of the event a parable, a sign painted in the
    faded credulity of earlier ages:
let us walk through the door.

The stone is rolled back, not papier-mâché,
not stone in a story,
but the vast rock of materiality that in the slow
    grinding of time will eclipse for each of us
the wide light of day.

And if we will have an angel at the tomb,
make it a real angel,
weighty with Max Planck's quanta, vivid with hair,
    opaque in the dawn light, robed in real linen
spun on a definite loom.

Let us not seek to make it less monstrous,
for our own convenience, our own sense of beauty,
lest, awakened in one unthinkable hour, we are
    embarrassed by the miracle,
and crushed by remonstrance.

Bishop Pike was right to seek empirical grounding for faith; he was wrong in looking to ambiguous psi-experiences for that experiential base, when he could have found it where Christians from earliest days to modern times have met it: in the Resurrection of Christ. Paul stated the issue precisely: "If Christ was not raised, your faith is vain and you are still in your sins. Then those also who have died in Christ have perished. If our hope in Christ is limited to this life, we are of all men most miserable. But Christ *has* been raised from the dead—the firstfruits of those that slept."[51] The evidence that man today can live forever is available where it has been for twenty centuries: at the empty tomb. "I am the Resurrection and the Life," said Christ. "He who believes in me, though he were dead, yet shall he live. And everyone who lives and believes in me shall never die. Believest thou this?" [52]

A Parable of Hope by Way of Conclusion

This presentation began with two disquieting parables: George's Moon, reflecting the contemporary secular dilemma, and the Parable of the Engineers, mapping the decline and fall of 20th century theological solutions to the secular predicament. Sad to say, uncertainty and loss of meaning in the secular realm proved to be more than matched by vagueness and indefiniteness in theology. "Physician," the secularist could well say to today's theologian, "heal thyself!"

We have been at pains to show that healing is in fact available—in contact with the Cross, the Empty Tomb, and the Holy Scriptures. There a solid foundation exists for theology, personal faith, and spiritual renewal. In stark contrast to the parables with which this essay began, listen now to a parable told in the 7th century by an adviser of King Edwin of Northumbria to show the King the wisdom of accepting the Christian faith:

> O King, this present life of men on earth, in comparison with the time that is unknown to us, seems to me as if you were sitting at a banquet with your ealdormen and thanes in the winter time with the fire burning and the hall warmed, and outside the storms of winter rain or snow were raging; and there should come a sparrow swiftly flying through the hall, coming in by one door and flying out through another. During the time it is inside it is not touched by the storm of winter; but, that little moment of quiet having passed, it soon returns from winter back to winter again, and is lost to sight. So this mortal life seems like a short interval; what may have gone before or what may come after it, we do not know. Therefore, if this new teaching has brought any greater certainty, it seems fitting that it should be followed. [53]

The new teaching did indeed bring "greater certainty"; and, in contrast to the uncertainties of contemporary speculation, religious and secular, it continues to bring that certainty to every man who, in his swift flight through the hall of this world, gives himself to the Christ

who gave His life for the sins of us all. Unremittingly He
seeks us, offering a certainty and a peace available nowhere else. In Auden's words—and we close with
them:[54]

> From no necessity [He]
> Condescended to exist and to suffer death
> And, scorned on a scaffold, ensconced in His life
> The human household. In our anguish we struggle
> To elude Him, to lie to Him, yet His love observes
> His appalling promise; His predilection
> As we wander and weep is with us to the end.

Notes

[1] New York: Simon and Schuster, 1967.

[2] See Montgomery, "The Relevance of Scripture for Current The-
ology," *Christianity Today*, November 10, 1967; reprinted in *The Bible:
The Living Word of Revelation*, ed. by Merrill C. Tenney (Grand Rapids,
Michigan: Zondervan, 1968), and in the present volume in III. 3.

[3] Cf. the excellent critical review of the film in the French news-
magazine *L'Express*, 8-14 mai, 1967.

[4] This fable is included in Feiffer's *Passionella and Other Stories*
(New York: New American Library Signet Books, 1964).

[5] See Montgomery, "The Gospel According to LSD," *Christianity
Today*, July 8, 1966; reprinted in the present volume as essay I. 4.

[6] *Harpers*, May, 1965.

[7] Cf. Montgomery, *Crisis in Lutheran Theology* (2 vols.; Grand
Rapids, Michigan: Baker Book House, 1967), Vol. 1, especially chap.
ii.

[8] James William Worden, "The Portrayal of the Protestant Minister in American Motion Pictures, 1951-1960, and Its Implications for
the Church Today" (unpublished Ph.D. dissertation, Boston University
Graduate School, 1962).

[9] Horton Davies, *A Mirror of the Ministry in Modern Novels* (New
York: Oxford University Press, 1959).

[10] Peter DeVries, *The Mackerel Plaza* (Boston: Little, Brown, 1958),
chap. i.

[11] See Peter Gay, *The Enlightenment: An Interpretation. The Rise
of Modern Paganism* (New York: Knopf, 1966).

[12] See B. M. G. Reardon, *Religious Thought in the Nineteenth
Century* (Cambridge, England: Cambridge University Press, 1966).

[13] For example, Richard Whately, in his superlative tour de force,
Historic Doubts Relative to Napoleon Buonaparte, showed that the
same arguments Hume used to eliminate the miraculous from the life

of Christ would equally well eliminate the unique from the career of Napoleon—thus destroying all meaningful historical analysis.

[14] See J. Gresham Machen, *Christianity and Liberalism* (New York: Macmillan, 1923).

[15] See Montgomery, "Karl Barth and Contemporary Theology of History," *The Cresset*, November, 1963; reprinted in my *Where Is History Going?* (Grand Rapids, Michigan: Zondervan, 1969), chap. v.

[16] *Church Dogmatics*, I/2, 529-30.

[17] Cf. Brand Blanshard, "Irrationalism in Theology: Critical Reflections on Karl Barth," in *Faith and the Philosophers*, ed. by John Hick (New York: St. Martin's Press, 1964).

[18] Bracketed figures from 1 to 5 designate numbered sections of "The Parable of the Engineers" given above.

[19] See the essays (including one by the present writer) in *Jesus of Nazareth: Saviour and Lord*, ed. by Carl F. H. Henry (Grand Rapids, Michigan: Eerdmans, 1966).

[20] See Montgomery, "Tillich's Philosophy of History," *The Gordon Review*, Summer, 1967; reprinted in my *Where Is History Going?* (Grand Rapids, Michigan: Zondervan, 1969), chap. vi.

[21] Paul Edwards, "Professor Tillich's Confusions," *Mind*, April, 1965.

[22] George H. Tavard, *Paul Tillich and the Christian Message* (New York: Scribner, 1962), chap. v.

[23] Charles Williams, *Taliessin Through Logres* (London: Oxford University Press, 1938), pp. 31-32.

[24] I have charted this development in detail in my book, *The 'Is God Dead?' Controversy* (Grand Rapids, Michigan: Zondervan, 1966); reprinted in the present volume in I. 5 as "Morticians of the Absolute."

[25] Cf. *The Altizer-Montgomery Dialogue: A Chapter in the God Is Dead Controversy* (Chicago: Inter-Varsity Press, 1967). My position paper and the dialogue itself are reprinted in the present volume in I. 5.

[26] See Montgomery, "Vidler at Strasbourg," *Christianity Today*, May 26, 1967; reprinted in the present volume in II. A. 2.

[27] See Montgomery, " 'Death of God' Becomes More Deadly," *Christianity Today*, December 9, 1966; reprinted in the present volume in I.5.

[28] This has not been equally true of orthodox, confessional seminaries. The Trinity Evangelical Divinity School has grown from 31 students five years ago to over 500 in 1970.

[29] Montgomery, "Bishop Pike and His Treasure Hunt," *The Sunday School Times*, May 7, 1966 (the first installment of the article appeared in the April 30, 1966 issue); both articles have been reprinted in revised form in the present work (see the next chapter).

[30] E. M. Sidgwick, E. Gurney, *et al.*, *Phantasms of the Living* (New Hyde Park, New York: University Books, 1962); F. W. H. Myers, *Human Personality and Its Survival of Bodily Death* (New Hyde Park: New York: University Books, 1961); G. N. M. Tyrrell, *Science and Psychical Phenomena; Apparitions* (New Hyde Park, New York: University Books, 1961); J. B Rhine, *The Reach of the Mind* (New York: William Sloane, 1947).

[31] Gardner Murphy, *Challenge of Psychical Research* (New York: Harper, 1961), p. 273.

[32] Y. Castellan, *La Métapsychique* (2ᵉ éd.; Paris: Presses Universitaires de France, 1960), p. 119. Cf. the same author's related work, *Le Spiritisme* (2ᵉ éd.; Paris: Presses Universitaires de France, 1959).

[33] Cf. *The Angels of Light and the Powers of Darkness*, ed. by E. L. Mascall (London: Faith Press, 1954), and J. H. Jung-Stilling's old but still valuable *Theory of Pneumatology*, trans. Samuel Jackson (London: Longman, 1834).

[34] In Elliot O'Donnell, *The Menace of Spiritualism* (New York: Frederick A. Stokes, 1920). Cf. the occult and demonic experiences of fin-de-siècle littérateur J.-K. Huysmans, who said after his conversion to Christianity: "With his hooked paw, the Devil drew me toward God" (See Robert Baldick, *The Life of J.-K. Huysmans* (Oxford: Clarendon Press, 1955), chaps. v-vii).

[35] Kurt E. Koch, *Seelsorge and Okkultismus*, Geleitwort von Adolf Köberle (5. Aufl.; Berghausen b. Karlsruhe: Evangelisationsverlag, 1959), pp. 162-66. Cf. the similar conclusions arrived at in *Vrais et faux possédés* (Paris: Fayard) by Dr. Jean Lhermitte, the distinguished neurologist and member of the French Académie Nationale de Médecine.

[36] November 13, 1967.

[37] This is the real tragedy of the inept heresy-trial discussions concerning Pike in the Episcopal Church. As for Stringfellow and Towne's argument in *The Bishop Pike Affair* (New York: Harper, 1967) that opposition to the Bishop stems from ultra-right-wing forces inimical to the American spirit, one can only second a recent commentator who has called this charge "galloping paranoia."

[38] Cf. C. S. Lewis, *Miracles* (New York: Macmillan, 1947), especially chap. xiii.

[39] See *Vindications: Essays on the Historical Basis of Christianity*, ed. by Anthony Hanson (New York: Morehouse-Barlow, 1966).

[40] See Edwin Yamauchi, *Composition and Corroboration in Classical and Biblical Studies* (Philadelphia: Presbyterian and Reformed Publishing Company, 1966); U. Cassuto, *The Documentary Hypothesis*, trans. Israel Abrahams (Jerusalem: Magnes Press, The Hebrew University, 1961).

[41] C. S. Lewis, "Modern Theology and Biblical Criticism," in *Christian Reflections*, ed. by Walter Hooper (Grand Rapids, Michigan: Eerdmans, 1967), p. 161. See also the excellent recent work by Augustin Cardinal Bea, *The Study of the Synoptic Gospels: New Approaches and Outlooks* (New York: Harper, 1965).

[42] Sir Frederic G. Kenyon, *The Bible and Archaeology* (New York: Harper, 1940), pp. 288-89 (Kenyon's italics). For numerous other evidential considerations along the same line, see Montgomery, "History & Christianity," *His* (Inter-Varsity Christian Fellowship), December, 1964-March, 1965 (also available as a *His* Reprint); reprinted in my *Where Is History Going?* (Grand Rapids, Michigan: Zondervan, 1969), chaps. ii and iii.

[43] J. V. Langmead Casserley, *The Retreat from Christianity in the*

Modern World (London: Longmans, Green, 1952), p. 82.

⁴⁴ Of *The Passover Plot,* Samuel Sandmel of Hebrew Union College wrote in *Saturday Review,* December 3, 1966: "Schonfield's imaginative reconstruction is devoid of a scintilla of proof, and rests on dubious inferences from passages in the Gospels whose historical reliability he himself has antecedently rejected on page after page. In my view, the book should be dismissed as the mere curiosity it is." Worthy of careful examination is the detailed scholarly review of *The Passover Plot* by Edwin M. Yamauchi in *The Gordon Review,* Summer 1967.

⁴⁵ *To the Smyrnaeans,* ii.

⁴⁶ Mt. 4:4, quoting Deut. 8:3.

⁴⁷ John 14:26-27; 16:12-15; cf. Acts 1:21-26; I Cor. 14:37; II Pet. 3:15. See also Montgomery, *The Shape of the Past: An Introduction to Philosophical Historiography* ("History in Christian Perspective," Vol. 1; Ann Arbor, Michigan: Edwards Brothers, 1963), pp. 138-39, 171-72.

⁴⁸ Cf. F. F. Bruce, *The New Testament Documents* (5th ed.; London: Inter-Varisty Fellowship, 1960).

⁴⁹ Many useful works have been written dealing with the problem passages of the Bible. Among the best in English are two books by New Testament Greek lexicographer William F. Arndt: *Bible Difficulties* (St. Louis, Missouri: Concordia, 1951), and *Does the Bible Contradict Itself?* (St. Louis, Missouri: Concordia, 1955). Cf. also B. B. Warfield, *The Inspiration and Authority of the Bible,* ed. by Samuel G. Craig (Philadelphia: Presbyterian and Reformed Publishing Company, 1948); and Montgomery, "Inductive Inerrancy," *Christianity Today,* March 3, 1967; reprinted in the present volume in III.3.

⁵⁰ John Updike, *Verse* (New York: Copyright 1961 by John Updike. Reprinted from TELEPHONE POLES AND OTHER POEMS, by John Updike, by permission of Alfred A. Knopf, Inc.) This poem was written for a religious arts festival sponsored by the Clifton Lutheran Church, of Marblehead, Mass.

⁵¹ I Cor. 15:17-20.

⁵² John 11:25-26.

⁵³ Bede, *Ecclesiastical History, ii. 13.*

⁵⁴ W. H. Auden, *The Age of Anxiety* (New York: Random House, 1947), p. 137.

2.

Agent 666: Bishop Pike and His Treasure Hunt

Gazing quizzically at America's general reader from the pages of the February 22nd, 1966, *Look* magazine was the Rt. Rev. James A. Pike, Protestant Episcopal Bishop of California. The article described Pike's "search for a space-age God" as it followed his visit to the haunts of British radical theology: the home of his friend Bishop J. A. T. Robinson, whose best-seller, *Honest to God,* a potpourri of Bultmann, Tillich, and Bonhoeffer, has stirred up debate in Europe and America; and King's College, Cambridge, where Dr. Alec Vidler and other Anglican theologians have been delivering broadsides against Christian orthodoxy.

The state of Pike's own search for religious answers was by no means clear in *Look,* but the general tenor of his thinking is reflected in the remark, "I've jettisoned the Trinity, the Virgin Birth and the Incarnation." His promised book, *What Is This Treasure,* in trying to "recast the identity of Christ," was described as "more radical" than even his *Time for Christian Candor,* written in 1964. *What Is This Treasure* (Harper and Row, 1966) does indeed offer an opportunity to assess the mind and influence of a prominent American church leader who endeavored to redo Christian theology in the interests of contemporary man. Who was Bishop Pike, what was the nature of his "treasure hunt," and what evaluation is to be placed upon it?

I.

Pike's religious and vocational life was anything but ordinary, and most of it took place in the public eye. In *Modern Canterbury Pilgrims* (1956) he tells of his loss of faith in Roman Catholicism while a student at a Jesuit college; the "closed-minded dogmatism and the overprotectiveness against 'error'" experienced there led him

47

to agnosticism. In consequence, he says, "I sought the meaning for my life in career and in a zeal for social reform—more particularly through my eventual association, as an attorney, with the New Deal." Gradually these life aims showed their "inadequacy," and "serious personal crisis" led Pike to reconsider Christianity. "Aesthetic—and, in my case, nostalgic—appeal" gave the initial push toward Episcopalianism; later, intellectual considerations confirmed the move, and after his release from the Navy Pike was ordained a priest. His rise to prominence in the Protestant Episcopal Church was meteoric; service as Dean of the Cathedral of St. John the Divine in New York was followed by elevation to episcopal rank.

Episcopal bishops are not particularly well known outside their church, but Pike became a by-word. This was due in part to his continual involvement in public issues (his book, *A Roman Catholic in the White House*, published prior to the 1960 national election, is illustrative), and to the famous "Blake-Pike proposal" (in collaboration with Eugene Carson Blake, former stated clerk of the United Presbyterian Church in the U.S.A. and now head of the World Council of Churches), whereby Episcopal-Presbyterian ecumenical union could be effected. But the most important reason for Pike's notoriety is evident from the *Look* article: it is his far left-of-center theological position.

Pike's theological pilgrimage, since his re-entrance into organized Christianity, involved a steady movement to the left. In an illuminating essay in *Christian Century's* "How My Mind Has Changed" series (published in book form in 1961), the Bishop wrote: "I am more liberal in theology than I was ten years ago. When Norman Pittenger and I were writing *The Faith of the Church* (a semi-official Episcopal book on doctrine), he did not find reason to accept the historical virgin birth; I thought I did. Our wrestling over the matter—not only a personal wrestling but a wrestling with both theological professors and bishops of our church—resulted in the book's leaving an opening for people like Dr. Pittenger. Now I am with him." Continued Pike: "More than that, my earlier neo-orthodox orientation—valuable as it was as I was coming out of agnosticism—I now find entirely too 'vertical'. . . .

I no longer regard grace, or the work of the Holy Spirit, as limited explicitly to the Christian revelation."

The momentum of Pike's swing from neo-orthodoxy to neo-liberalism increased considerably after 1961, and was punctuated by three heresy charges (all of which, however, were dismissed by his fellow bishops). In 1963, his book *Beyond the Law: The Religious and Ethical Meaning of the Lawyer's Vocation* appeared, and in it Pike denied the possibility of obtaining "specific answers from any religiously based code of ethics" and identified himself as an ethical "existentialist" (pp. xii, 4). Nineteen sixty-four saw the publication of his volume, *A Time for Christian Candor* (dedicated to his son, who tragically committed suicide); this work depends heavily upon Bishop Robinson's *Honest to God.* In 1965, Pike brought out a "new edition, completely revised" of his *Doing the Truth: A Summary of Christian Ethics,* in which (parallel with Robinson's *Christian Morals Today)* he applied his relativistic theology to the general problems of Christian conduct. That same year saw the publication of Pike's *Teen-Agers and Sex,* a manual written for parents and others who counsel young people; in this amazing volume, the author gives parallel advice to those holding an absolute, "Code" ethic and to those (with whom he clearly identifies himself) who view sex ethics "situationally and existentially," i.e., who do not unqualifiedly condemn sexual intimacy outside marriage.

Nineteen sixty-six heralded, as noted previously, the Bishop's *Look* interview and the appearance of *What Is This Treasure.* While facing the latest heresy charge against him (for denial of the Trinity, Virgin Birth, and Incarnation), Pike told *Look* that he was thinking: "If they only knew what I had in my briefcase"; this was the manuscript of *What Is This Treasure,* and its content displays how fully Pike followed the path of the new radical theology in England.

II.

Before we peer closely into the Bishop's briefcase, let us take stock of the contemporary Anglican theology to which he attached his ideological wagon. Such an examination is vital, for Pike's above-mentioned visit to England was symbolic of his thought: it is not original, but derives from others; or, perhaps more charitably stated, its originality consists in its manner of popular presentation, not in its substantive content.

Bishop Robinson, whom *Look* photographed ecstatically conducting a confirmation service assisted by Pike, was doubtless the greatest single influence upon the Bishop of California. In the Preface to his *Time for Christian Candor,* Pike wrote: "The Bishop of Woolwich was kind enough to send me an advance copy of the English edition of his *Honest to God.* His insights, his courage, and his capacity to make plain a point of view hitherto only understood by the professionals and by that particular group of laity whom we can call theological amateurs (in the best sense of the word), inspired me to think through the full implications of the positions I had heretofore taken ... and to essay a contribution to the present work of theological reconstruction."

What is Robinson's "point of view"? This is not easy to say, for the confused and ambiguous character of *Honest to God* has troubled and irritated virtually all of its critics (the most decisive counters being Leon Morris' *Abolition of Religion* and James Packer's *Keep Yourselves from Idols).* Packer calls the book "just a plateful of mashed-up Tillich fried in Bultmann and garnished with Bonhoeffer" and notes that "it bears the mark of unfinished thinking on page after page."

In general, Robinson's position (shared by Bishop Pike) is that spaceage man can no longer accept the antiquated, mythological view of the world held by the biblical writers, and that Christians must therefore recast the faith in modern, secular terms. This recasting will involve a new view of God, Christ, and ethics. We cannot any longer regard God as a supernatural Being "up there" or "out there"; he is now best understood in Tillich's terms as the "ground" or "depth" of all being. Says Robinson: "a statement is called 'theological' not because it relates to a particular Being called 'God,' but because it asks *ultimate* questions about the meaning of existence." The only true ultimate is love, and Jesus is to be regarded as the perfect mirror of it; he is best conceived simply as "the man for others." Ethical conduct can no longer be judged by adherence to biblical commands, for the Scripture itself was conditioned by the thought forms of its day. "Nothing is prescribed except love," says the Bishop, and each man must seek it in his own particular situation ("situation ethics"). One man's moral decisions will not necessarily be those of another. As Robinson puts it in his little book, *Christian Morals Today* (a sequel to *Honest to God*): "What he [God] says will not always be the same as he said to our fathers. . . . The moral teaching of Jesus is not to be judged by its adequacy as a code. As such it is entirely inadequate." Modern man becomes "new in Christ" as he endeavors to exist for others in love as Jesus did.

In a recent interview for the *New Yorker*, Bishop Robinson informed the public: "I was able to find time to write *Honest to God* because of a slipped disc." His critics have made clear that this is by no means the only thing that slipped! The Bishop of Woolwich reduces Jesus to a humanistic ethical model, relativizes the moral commands of Christian revelation, and turns the Bible into little more than a collection of ancient Near Eastern religious opinions. But he even goes beyond these heresies (shared by the modernists of the Harry Emerson Fosdick era): he offers a Tillichian view of God which is either pantheistically meaningless or in fact atheistic. Philosophers such as Paul Edwards have pointed out that if God is simply "being itself" or "the depth of being," then there is no point in talking about him at all, since this tells us nothing more than we knew before, namely, that the universe exists! ("Professor Tillich's Confusions," *Mind*, April, 1965). Robinson's countryman, philosopher-theologian Alasdair MacIntyre, comes to an even more negative conclusion: "We can see now that Dr. Robinson's voice is not just that of an individual, that his book testifies to the existence of a whole group of theologies which have retained a theistic vocabulary but acquired an atheistic substance" (*Encounter*, September, 1963).

Robinson certainly does not stand in isolation, and the so-called "Cambridge radicals" with whom Bishop Pike studied during his sojourn in England illustrates this well.

The leading figure among these self-styled "Christian radicals" is certainly Alec Vidler, dean of King's College, who was caught deep in peripatetic conversation with Pike by *Look's* photographer. Vidler describes himself thus in his work, *20th Century Defenders of the Faith* (1965): "I am more interested in other people's thoughts than in my own. I regard my proper role as an editorial one, or as that of a midwife to theologians." Vidler's midwifery is displayed in several books he had edited in recent years. *Soundings* (1962) stresses from beginning to end the tentativeness, uncertainty, and indefiniteness of Christian truth; its title page motto displays the spirit of all the contributors: "Man hath but a shallow sound, and a short reach, and dealeth onely by probabilities and likelyhoods." In an editorial note to one of the chapters, Vidler goes so far as to apply this uncertainty to the New Testament Christ: "There is an element of contingency even in the *ipsissima verba* of Christ himself in so far as they can be accurately recovered." (Eric Mascall, professor of historical theology in the University of London, has delivered a massive body blow to *Soundings* in his book, *Up and Down in Adria,* with nautical chapter titles such as "No Bottom Yet" and "Pumping Out the Bilge," and with a motto that well captures the vapidity of the radical theology: "Where lies the land to which the ship would go? Far, far ahead, is all her seamen know.") In *Objections to Christian Belief* (1963), Vidler speaks for his contributors in saying that they all "have been living with one foot in Christian belief and the other resolutely planted in the radical unbelief of the contemporary world." In his own chapter he speaks of the "striking inconsistencies" among the New Testament writers and the "extraneous elements even in the Gospel records."

The ethical consequences of this relativistic approach are evident in the contributions of H. A. Williams, dean of Trinity College, Cambridge, to *Soundings* and to *Objections to Christian Belief:* in the former he argues that when the prostitute in the Greek film *Never on Sunday* gives herself to a neurotic sailor so that "he acquires confidence and self-respect," one sees "an act of charity which proclaims the glory of God"; in the latter book, he cites approvingly a case of an Anglican who, "drunk among the bars and brothels of Tangier," told him that "words of Jesus rang in his ears like bells of victory—the words which Jesus addressed to the churchman of His day—'Verily I say unto you, that the publicans and the harlots go into the Kingdom of God before you.' " In another book edited by Vidler, *Traditional Virtues Reassessed* (1964), Glen Cavaliero informs readers that "it is time that we broadened our conception of chastity" and asserts the Robinsonian situational ethic: "Chastity could be attributed to some non-marital relationships, in so far as genuine love and self-commitment be there." ... "Whatever rules about our sexual behaviour the Church supports, those rules are always liable to be broken by individuals who in each particular situation are forced to make their own decisions."

When midwife Vidler published his systematic overview of "20th Century Defenders of the Faith" (delivered as the Robertson Lectures at Glasgow in 1964), he completely ignored the greatest Anglican apologist of our century, orthodox believer C. S. Lewis, and discussed only neo-orthodox and liberal theologians. He identifies himself with "Christian radicalism" and admits that "it is the Roman Catholic Modernists with whom I feel most kinship"—Modernists such as Loisy (excommunicated in 1908) when he approvingly quotes: "The adaptation of the gospel to the changing condition of humanity is requisite today as always and more than ever." Vidler concludes on the bright note: "I find it encouraging that, though there have naturally been expressions of alarm, churches do not at present seem to be trying to suppress their radicals."

III.

We seem to have spent far too much time on Bishop Pike's bedfellows. Is this a subtle attempt to "guilt by association"? Decidedly not; rather, it is an effort to put Pike in context—to set a stage apart from which his frequently ambiguous statements are often virtually incomprehensible. As *New Yorker* writer Ved Mehta shrewdly observed (November 13, 1965): Pike's name is "often linked with Robinson's, though Pike sounded like an instructor in a department of which Robinson was the head."

What is the content of this instructor's instruction? To be brutally frank, it is totally unoriginal as to content; it is nothing but an American version of the British radicalism we have just described. As an American, operating in a land where conservative, biblical, evangelical Christianity is still the grass-roots religion of churchgoers, Bishop Pike did not make the consistently radical pronouncements of his British confrères, who theologize in a country where the empty pews of a state church attest to the general secularization of a once Christian nation.

Pike therefore on occasion sounds remarkably orthodox, if not downright evangelical; in "How My Mind Has Changed," we read, for example: "I stand in the tradition that requires all doctrine to be under the standard of the Bible"; I shall go on doing the best I can to affirm the fact that all baptized Christians who believe in Jesus Christ as Lord and Savior are members of the Holy Catholic Church"; "The church is only possible because of the gospel"; etc. But when we look behind the verbal facade of such emotive claims, and ask what the Bishop of California *means* by his terms, we find the British radicalism patently evident. Let us quickly survey the Bishop's views on the major doctrines of the faith, using his most recent writings.

The Bible. In the article just quoted, Pike denies the verbal reliability of Scripture: "The *ipsissima verba* of the Bible are not binding." In *A Time for Christian Candor,* the Bishop sets up a ridiculous and utterly inaccurate straw man of "fundamentalism" identifying the historic, orthodox position with bibliolatry: "Sometimes the bibliolatrist focuses upon an even lesser god, namely, a particular translation; such was the lady who said, 'If the King James Version was good enough for Saint Paul, it is good enough for me!' " Pike absurdly confuses belief in the complete soundness of the Scriptural revelation with "literalism," and we are told that "such preoccupation with the literal hides the depth meaning in a mythological narrative and dims its relevance for today" (pp. 26-27). The Bishop thus confidently stands in judgment over the biblical text. For example: "Nor in the singing or reading of the Psalms should we include verses which, due either to a faulty Hebrew text that makes adequate translation impossible or to the wrong-headedness of the ideas expressed, present views of God or man that we would not be prepared to affirm as true or good" (pp. 135-36). Other examples could be given *ad nauseum* from the Bishop's publications.

The Trinity. As *Look*'s article on Pike rightly points out, the Bishop refused to identify himself with the new "God is dead" theology of Altizer, William Hamilton, and Paul van Buren: "The Bishop is still orthodox enough to recoil at their 'Christocentric atheism.' " Yet in the Introduction to *What Is This Treasure*, significantly dedicated to Tillich and Robinson, Pike snubs as the work of a "denominational guardian" the most recent and scholarly refutation of van Buren, Eric Mascall's book, *The Secularisation of Christianity* (1965). In point of fact, Pike's doctrine of God is as vague as that of Robinson or Tillich, and this is clear from his rejection of the Trinitarian formula of the historic church. "If categories of thought involved in the classical formulation of the Trinity are no longer viable, then we need not feel troubled by them in regard to the conventional Trinitarian declaration" (*A Time for Christian Candor*, p. 129).

Pike notes, however, that we should still retain "all that heretofore has been experienced" of God, and that we need not chuck the church's trinitarian liturgy, since "we can attribute a genuine measure of truth to outdated concepts and semantics." In "How My Mind Has Changed," Pike says that in conversation with Jewish philosopher Martin Buber (who understood God in terms of an existential "I-Thou" relationship between persons), Pike realized that Buber, though in no sense a trinitarian Christian, "understands what we Christians are trying to say about the remarkable—and, for Christians, unique—revelation of God in Christ." "I am with him," said Pike, "in thinking that all the *verbiage* associated with the Trinity is quite unnecessary." Pike concludes his article with his interpretation of the Anglican theme of "broad church," "low church," "high church," and says: "Perhaps *this* trinity is a measure of the truth—at least for our times."

Jesus Christ. As we saw previously, the Bishop of California moved from an earlier acceptance of the Virgin Birth to final rejection of it; in his *Look* interview he also announced his "jettison of the Incarnation" as an outmoded doctrine, incomprehensible to modern man. Pike's book, *What Is This Treasure,* was intended to "recast the identity of Christ," and here we must look for his developed views on the subject. His position is indistinguishable from that of Robinson and the Cambridge radicals: Jesus is viewed humanistically as an ethical model, and his "divinity" is understood as his ideal "openness" to the life of love. Pike summarizes as follows, with his usual olympian judgment as to what is sound and what unsound in Scripture (p. 80): " 'I am the Way, the Truth, and the Life,' we read in the Fourth Gospel (14:6). While, as we have seen, the negative conclusion of the sentence ('No one cometh to the Father but by me') won't do, the opening clause beautifully reflects the experience of the early Christian community of the role of Jesus in their lives. To sum up, in Him they say what a man is to be; and since Jesus was Himself fully this, they saw showing through Him the fullness of God as Truth (which in good measure we can see also through Socrates and Buddha as 'free and open' man) and, certainly as important, as Love."

Sin, Salvation, the Church. Pike's move from neoorthodoxy to liberal theology was accompanied by a weakening of his view of sin. As he writes in "How My Mind Has Changed": "My experience in the ministry—and as a person—has convinced me that there is much truth and goodness in natural man." Such a view of man's natural goodness entails a correspondingly weak view of salvation. As seen in the quotation from *What Is This Treasure* given above, Pike rejected the exclusiveness of John 14:6; he expressly states in many of his later writings that belief in the historic Christ is not necessary for salvation. What, then, is the essence of salvation? It is the *imitation of Christ*—standing in openness to truth and love as He stood.

What Is This Treasure ends with an unbelievably obtuse and maudlin personal statement of faith in "God, the Ultimate Ground of all being" in which man's salvatory task is described: "We identify with Him and seek to free ourselves of barriers to full relation with the Reality Who is already there, we thus being means through whom others to whom we relate as persons, may experience meaning, accepting love and new life now and always, that more and more men may be more and more free, open, and whole, like Jesus our Lord." "This is the Treasure," says Pike. "That's all there is to it." And to a creed like this, perhaps we ourselves could apply Pike's view of the historic creeds ("How My Mind Has Changed"): "There are several phrases in the Creeds that I cannot affirm as literal prose sentences, but I can certainly sing them" (though in this case, I am reasonably sure that Beatle-like dissonance would be the only appropriate musical setting!)

As for Pike's view of the Church, its function is not (as just seen) to proclaim creedal absolutes expressing God's revealed truth (the biblical revelation is but an erroneous pointer to the "Ground of being" and creeds cannot be literally subscribed to). Rather, the Church is vital in that it offers continuity during the flux of doctrinal change, and its ancient liturgies convey the old myths in a poetic form that penetrates to the unconscious of modern man. Would it be unkind to say that for the Bishop of California the Church was the way *par excellence* for 20th century man to experience psychoanalytic guilt transference and group therapy?

The Christian life. Pike's relativistic humanism was fully manifested in his attitude to prayer and the moral life. For him, prayer is basically a "horizontal," not a "vertical" activity, as is seen from his description of prayers of petition at the end of the revised (1965) edition of *Doing the Truth:* "In prayer of *petition* we focus the direction of our action, as especially concerns ourselves." Noteworthy is the complete absence of any affirmation that God supernaturally *answers* such prayers; prayers of petition have here degenerated into volitional gymnastics. As to Christian ethical standards, we have already found Pike an admitted existentialist. In point of fact, his later works in this area (*Beyond the Law; Doing the Truth,* rev. ed.; *Teen-Agers and Sex*) are direct reflections of the situational ethics we have already met in

Bishop Robinson and the Cambridge radicals. In *Doing the Truth*, Pike uses the apocryphal story of Judith (who was willing to go to bed with an Assyrian commander in order to kill him) to argue that one cannot accept "an *absolute* limitation of intercourse to marriage" (pp. 41-42, 142), and recommends that each case be determined individually by the criteria of "responsibility," "finitude" ("quantity can interfere with quality"), and "maturity." *Teen-Agers and Sex* (1965) is an incredible manual which actually gives existentially-oriented parents guidance in counselling teen-agers in the use of contraceptives. With an unmarried college couple facing pregnancy, Pike "immediately zeroed in on this question, 'How could the two of you—seniors in college—have been so irresponsible as not to have taken precautions?' " (p. 84). A passage such as the following is representative of the moral tone of the entire work: "The social milieu has changed in most strata of modern life. It would now be an exaggeration to say that a girl is 'ruined' because of an 'illegitimate' pregnancy. There are circumstances—psychological and physical—which in some states make legal abortion possible (this is all the more reason for the point made above, that young persons should be urged to notify their parents immediately should such an unfortunate outcome occur)" (p. 87). Nowhere in this book is its reader brought face to face with the moral law revealed once for all by God in Holy Scripture.

IV.

Our survey of the Bishop's theology has brought us in full circle back to his biblical position—and it is here that the key to his Pandora's box of heresy will be found. Pike's favorite scripture verse (used as the theme both for *A Time for Christian Candor* and for *What Is This Treasure*) was II Cor. 4:7: "We have this treasure in earthen vessels, that the excellency of the power may be of God, and not of us." In spite of the fact (pointed out by a priest of Pike's own diocese in *Christianity Today*, October 8, 1965) that the "earthen vessels" in this verse refer to ministers of the gospel, Pike continued to apply the phrase, à la Tillich, to all earthly expressions of divine truth (Jesus, the Bible, the creeds, etc.). "What is this treasure?" asks Pike in his book of that title. "The brief answer, and one which ultimately is adequate, is: God. No one or nothing else is final or ultimate" (p. 85).

On the surface, this seems to be a noble and lofty protest against idolatry, but a little reflection quickly shows its true character. How do we know we *are* worshipping the true God and not an idol if all earthly expressions of His will are fallible? Perhaps what we consider to be the true "Ground of all being" is actually but wish-fulfilment or even the demonic! Obviously, if we can trust no revelation of God fully, then *we ourselves become the only remaining standard of judgment.* This was precisely the case with the Bishop of California, and the arbitrariness of his entire theology is the consequence. He picks and chooses Scripture according to his interests. Thus, as we have seen, he accepts the first clause of John 14:6 while rejecting the second, and uses the apocryphal book of Judith to argue for a loose sexual morality while rejecting the absoluteness of the Ten Commandments found in canonical Scripture. In "How My Mind Has Changed," he insists on wine for Communion on the ground that "Jesus never drank grape juice"; yet in *What Is This Treasure* he approvingly cites the non-Christian philosopher Porphyry (third century), who said of Jesus' healing of the Gadarene demoniac, "probably fictitious, but if genuine then morally discreditable" (p. 69); and in *A Time for Christian Candor* he rejects Heb. 12:5-6 as "in direct contradiction to our Lord's teaching" (p. 136).

The more one reads the Bishop, the more the conviction grows that in dispensing with all "earthen vessels," he inevitably ended up with the earthen vessel of his own judgment. This is of course not accidental but inevitable, for God must meet man *somewhere* on earth in order for man to know Him; the question is, will we accept Him on *His* terms, as He reveals Himself in the Christ of Scripture, or will we endeavor to encounter Him in our personal, sin-impregnated judgment? If the latter, we will invariably create Him in *our* image instead of being recreated in His likeness (II Cor. 5:17).

The purpose of II Cor. 4:7 is precisely the reverse of

what the Bishop thought: the Apostle exhorts men to trust in God's revealed will, not in themselves. Pike and the British radical theology he mimiced arrogate God's power to themselves by making their personal judgment the measure of all things. Thus in reading the Bishop one is actually not reading theology at all; one is reading *autobiography*—the autobiography of a sinner who endeavored to restructure God's nature, revelation, and moral law in the image of his own preferences and those of his cultural epoch.

And Pike chose the right society and time for this. James Bond is its symbol: utterly independent, bound by no external standards of truth or morality, a law unto himself. As Bond's freewheeling adventures carry him through espionage situations in which (to use the words of Orwell's apocalyptic novel *1984*) "ignorance is strength," "war is peace," and "freedom is slavery," so Pike's adventurous theological career made him the sole arbiter of the Divine, whose increasing vagueness as the "Ground of all being" opens the floodgates to semantic confusion, to creedal double-think, and to moral anarchy.

It is a sobering thought that in the great apocalyptic chapter of II Thessalonians the Antichrist is referred to in the Greek as *Anomos*, "The Lawless One," the one who regards himself beyond all standards (2:8). The very essence of Antichrist lies in his lawlessness: his conviction that he will "exalt his throne above the stars of God" (Isa. 14:12-14) and become "like the most High" in serving as a law to himself. Such presumption, however, for individual or society, has only one certain result: "Thou shalt be brought down to hell, to the sides of the pit" (v. 15). In diametric contrast to this antichristic lawlessness, our Lord always kept faith with the scriptural revelation, and through the centuries those redeemed by His blood have made it their life purpose to proclaim the biblical message faithfully in word and deed.

May our spiritual treasure hunt in the space age begin and end in "the acknowledgment of God's mystery, of Christ, in whom are hid all the treasures of wisdom and knowledge. And this I say, lest any man should beguile you with enticing words. . . . Beware lest any man spoil you through philosophy and vain deceit, after the tradition of men, after the rudiments of the world, and not after Christ. For in him dwelleth all the fulness of the Godhead bodily" (Col. 2:2-9).

3.

Dialogue on the New Morality

Panelists discussing "The Bible and the New Morality" are the director of the Pastoral Doctorate Program at Fuller Theological Seminary in Pasadena, California, a minister of the Christian Reformed Church, Dr. James Daane; Chairman of the Division of Church History and History of Christian Thought at Trinity Evangelical Divinity School in Deerfield, Illinois, a minister of the Lutheran Church-Missouri Synod, Dr. John Warwick Montgomery; and, Dr. Leon Morris, Canon of St. Paul's Cathedral, Anglican, in Melbourne, Australia, where he is also Principal of Ridley College, and an author of numerous religious books. Moderator of the panel is Dr. Carl F. H. Henry, editor of Christianity Today.

DR. HENRY: Gentlemen, shouldn't we expect morals or ethics to change just as transportation does, so that what was good enough for our grandparents or godparents need not be good for us? After all, is the old morality good just because it's old? Or is the new morality rather immorality? And shouldn't one's moral decision, after all, be one's personal decision?

DR MONTGOMERY: I'm not very happy with this analogy between transportation and morality. It makes me think of the comparison between an elephant and a tube of toothpaste; neither one can ride a bicycle. It's possible to compare any two things but the question is, is there any legitimate basis for the comparison? It looks to me as if in the New Testament the Christian morality is not a traditional morality. It's set over against traditionalism. Jesus is constantly striking against the religious leaders of his day who obscured absolute truth through tradition. For him absolute truth is the most contemporaneous thing in the world and therefore his morality is the most exciting kind of guidance for life.

DR. HENRY: That is an important point, I think, that the New Testament is not simply a traditional morality.

DR. MORRIS: I think we have to be very careful

talking about the new morality because the expression can be used in more ways than one. For some people the new morality is simply an out. They want an easy way in life, and they use it as an excuse for letting down the floodgates and doing the things that they want to do that deep down they know are wrong. But for other people the new morality is a very serious attempt to think through problems of ethics and to give to men of this day an approach which will be validly based. They think that the old traditional basing is quite in error. They would feel that traditionally the Bible stands as the standard and they just don't like that. Now the new morality poses the whole problem of where do we find our standards? Are we to regard the Bible as simply giving us some nice thoughts of men of antiquity or is it the very revelation of the living God Himself.

DR. DAANE: I suspect that we can answer the question about change in morality by saying that moral responses change with the changing of the times. But the references, the objective moral standards, the Ten Commandments, if you will, by reference to which these acts are moral or immoral, do not change.

DR. HENRY: Well, let's take a look at the new morality, or situational ethics, or existential ethics, as it is sometimes called. We know that it rejects fixed moral principles, and that it reduces everything, as it were, to love. As the Anglican Bishop John Robinson would say, in *Honest to God,* love and do as you please. After all, didn't Jesus of Nazareth say that love is the new and great commandment?

DR. MORRIS: Yes, but didn't He also say that He came not to destroy the law but to fulfill it? It's just too easy, in my judgment, to say that Jesus taught an ethic of love and then to put a full stop. He did teach love but He also had a very high place for law. You take the Sermon on the Mount. You get a kind of refrain running through that. "You have heard that it was said to them of old time . . . but I say unto you . . ." But all the time what Jesus does is to reinforce what had been said in old time. He never does away with it. For instance, He takes the commandment, "Thou shalt not commit adultery," and He doesn't say "Let us do away with that and from now on anybody who wants to, can commit adultery." Rather, He says, "Whoever looks on a woman to lust after her has committed adultery in his heart." You see, He takes the law; He says that this is a good commandment; it ought to be kept, but it ought to be taken further. I think you will find that right through the teaching of Jesus there runs this emphasis on righteousness, on justice, as well as on love. Now, I'm not suggesting that we should take love lightly, but we ought to keep these things in balance.

DR. HENRY: You think it is an oversimplification to reduce the whole of biblical morality to love?

DR. MORRIS: Oh, yes.

DR. MONTGOMERY: Yes, Jesus places a great deal of stress on the combination of love and the keeping of commandments. For example, he says, "If you love Me, keep My commandments." And there is quite a contrast between this and the vagueness of the so-called new morality or situational ethics. Canon Rhymes and Joseph Fletcher maintain much the same position—hold that one acts simply in order to bring about maximum wholeness in the other person, or to bring about the greatest benefits for a group. This just begs the question. What is maximum wholeness? What is the greatest benefit? Psychoanalysis, it seems to me, has shown in the twentieth century that people are really not aware of the degree to which selfishness strikes them in their actions. You know, the statement is made that a psychiatrist and a coal miner have a good deal in common. The psychiatrist goes down deeper, stays down longer, and comes up dirtier. He comes up with more evidence of the selfishness that operates in human life. In order to deal with the problem of selfishness, it is necessary to have external objective standards by which our selfishness can be brought into the light.

DR. HENRY: Well, are you saying that the new morality has a certain vagueness that pervades it? That love as it states it is, is quite ambiguous and lacking in content and direction?

DR. MONTGOMERY: Yes, very definitely. Love is a motive. It doesn't, in itself, define the nature of the obligations.

DR. DAANE: It seems to me you can put the matter

this way. The new morality runs into difficulty when it appeals to love and when it appeals to Jesus without any specific biblical concrete context. You spoke of wholeness a moment ago. Many of these Christocentric theologians appeal to Jesus to find out what a whole new man would do in this area of sex and they run into a dead-end street, because Jesus didn't happen to get married or to court girls. And right at this point, the attempt to separate Jesus and love from the total situation of the Bible makes the new morality run into something highly abstract and even a blank at this point.

DR. HENRY: What do you mean by a Christocentric ethic in contrast with a biblical ethic?

DR. DAANE: Well, I mean the people that appeal not specifically to the Bible, but to Jesus, and to the fact that Jesus says you have to love. Now, in the area of love you can't look to Jesus, and looking at Him alone, find out how you ought to court your girl, because He set no example at this point. That is what I mean be determining an ethic in terms of Jesus alone and exclusively, apart from the Bible.

DR. MONTGOMERY: Is there any Jesus apart from the Bible? What kind of Jesus are they talking about? This is what bothers me. It looks to me as if one either obtains one's portrait of Jesus and His ethic from the primary documents, or one develops this out of one's self. One spins a Jesus out of one's own self, as the spider spins . . .

DR. DAANE: Well, particularly in the area of sex, because no one has spun it out for you.

DR. HENRY: The term Jesus or Christ becomes rather a philosophical abstraction rather than anything really identifiable in terms of the historical Jesus.

DR. DAANE: Well, He isn't a norm, I would say, at this point. Jesus by Himself, apart from the biblical context, cannot be taken for a norm in the area of sexuality, simply because He did not get married and raise a family, and so far as we know, practice sexuality of any kind.

DR. HENRY: Now, the new morality rejects fixed moral principles and it concentrates, as you know, on immediate relationships between persons, and it finds in love alone, the only fixed content of morality. Well, how does Christian ethics, authentically Christian ethics, differ from this? What difference does it make by way of contrast if one makes a moral choice in the authentically biblical tradition?

DR. MORRIS: The point that we've already made is that Jesus insisted on justice, on righteousness, as well as on love. Dr. Montgomery pointed out that Jesus said, "If you love Me, keep My commandments." Now, you can parallel this in all sorts of ways. He kept telling people that if they would follow Him they must take up their cross day by day, and follow Him. This stands for an attitude of following in the steps of Jesus, doing the things that He would have people do. Indeed, He used the expression following Him and quite a number of others will be found right through the gospels. He kept insisting that people must do righteousness, do justice, as well as do love. And I think we get the New Testament quite wrong if we omit that particular emphasis.

DR. MONTGOMERY: Yes, and He never allowed the situation to determine the ethical involvement. He didn't maintain an attitude of ethical relativity. And this is the main difficulty, as far as I can see, with the new morality, that it allows the situation to determine the ethical principles and thereby really leaves the situation without ethical principles. For example, the difference that one encounters in various cultural situations on the matter of morality. I presume that among cannibals, it is a basic ethical principle to clean your plate. But I doubt very much that Jesus would have appreciated this kind of approach.

DR. DAANE: It seems to me that the distinction between the biblical morality and the so-called new morality at this point is that in biblical thought, love is defined for you. In precepts, in commandments, in moral imperatives. The heart of Christianity, after all, is that God so loved the world that He gave His Son. So the revelation of the essence of Christianity is the love of God, which means that we have to be told what love is. Now, in the new morality you decide what love is in the heat of the moment, maybe in the back seat of the car, in the moment of uncontrolled, or, well-nigh uncontrolled passion.

DR. MONTGOMERY: Which isn't easy.

DR. DAANE: And now the Bible comes to you, and it tells you that this is love and that is love, but it doesn't let *you* decide in any given situation, and in every given situation just what is an act of love or is not. Hence, from the biblical point of view, homosexuality is ruled out as one possible expression of love.

DR. HENRY: Let's take the given moral situation in modern times. As I recall, the Kinsey Report projects— and one always has certain doubts about the reliability of statistical sampling—but at any rate, it projects that almost half of the American college women have had sexual relationships before marriage. And the American Family Service says—I presume also on the basis of a projection from a statistical sampling—that one in five brides is now pregnant at the time of marriage. Now that brings to mind a passage that would bear on this from Bishop Robinson's *Honest to God.* In *Honest to God,* Bishop Robinson wrote, and I quote: "Nothing can of itself be labeled as wrong. Sex relations before marriage or divorce may be wrong in 99 cases, or even 100 cases, out of 100, but they are not intrinsically so," he says, "for the only intrinsic evil is lack of love." Now, I submit that if Bishop Robinson's abandonment of fixed moral principles is right, his figures are capable of a complete inversion so that premarital intercourse and divorce might be right on his presuppositions, a hundred times out of a hundred, rather than one out of a hundred. What about the consequences of an unprincipled morality?

DR. MORRIS: I think that if you have that kind of morality you are shot to pieces. Once you admit the possibility of an exception, you can no longer have a morality that is worth having, because human nature being what it is, every one of us believes that the exception applies in his own particular case; the rule is for someone else, the exception is for me, and the dikes are unleashed and the floods come in. A moment ago, Dr. Daane was talking about what might happen in the back of a car. If you've got two teen-aged kids in the back of a car, and they've got in their minds firmly the idea that there can be exceptions in this matter of sex morals . . .

DR. HENRY: Because they love each other so much.

DR. MORRIS: Exactly. They see themselves as different from other people. Nobody ever had to put up with the difficulties we have to put up with. Nobody ever loved like we love. So that there is just nothing to hold them. But where they have a firm grasp on great principles of morality, then they can say immediately, "This is wrong," and they know where they are. But it seems to me that one great weakness in the new morality is that it fails to give clear guidance to people who need clear guidance.

DR. HENRY: It is interesting that here in the District of Columbia a couple of years ago, a student at one of the local universities killed a co-ed because he loved her so much. This was his report to the police—a very interesting story.

DR. DAANE: Now on the basis of the new morality this could not be judged bad. Is that right?

DR. HENRY: Well, in his *Christian Morals Today,* a later publication, after the storm over Bishop Robinson's earlier work, the Bishop backtracks a bit, and he says that in the case of premarital sex relationships, there is a bonding element between sex and marriage which is so firm that one might almost invariably say that premarital sex is wrong. My point is, that if the Bishop is here saying that in this one situation, premarital sex, there is an objective principle which controls sex in all situations and places he has introduced the very sort of principle that he said was illicit and illegitimate to begin with. You cannot have both a principled ethic and an unprincipled ethic jumbled side by side. You must have one or the other, and I don't think you can play Bishop Robinson's tune on Gabriel's horn.

DR. MORRIS: It's difficult. In that book he is desperately trying, it would seem to me, to preserve something like the traditional code of morals. You remember that he says that every society must have its net—that some nets are finer than others, but the net has to be woven by society, and people then are kept within reasonable bounds. But what he never does, it seems to me there, is to show *why* there should be a net, and *why* a net should have its strands in such and such a place. In other words, we are back to the point that I was trying to make a little while ago: For people who have to make an agonizing decision there is no clear guidance, and they are thrown back on their own resources. They may be the exception to the general rule, and there is just no way of knowing for them what is right.

DR. MONTGOMERY: The biblical morality is frequently criticized for not taking into account exceptions, for being simplistic. But it seems to me that exactly the opposite is the case. It's the new morality that is simplistic in thinking that somehow magically, out of such situations as the teen-agers in the car, you get solutions to problems like this.

DR. MORRIS: It asks too much of people.

DR. MONTGOMERY: Right. The Christian morality fully recognizes the difficulty of moral decision and frequently a Christian finds himself in a position where it is necessary to make a decision where moral principle must be violated in favor of other moral principles, but he never vindicates himself in this situation. He decides in terms of the lesser of evils or the greater of goods, and this drives him to the Cross to ask forgiveness for the human situation in which this kind of complication and ambiguity exists.

DR. HENRY: There is a difference between the exception that is recognized as wicked and sinful, and needing repentance and forgiveness, and an exception which is tolerated as presumably moral.

DR. DAANE: The exceptional ethical situation creates even for Christian morality an exceptional amount of difficulty. But in Christianity, there are exceptions, and it seems to me it is very indicative of the new morality that the exceptions, the most far out ethical situations, best illustrate the character of the new morality. It is the son and mother who alone are left after a nuclear war, who then are left with the task of re-populating the race. It is the mother in a concentration camp, who, if she gets pregnant with another man, can return to her family. These exceptional ethical situations are most indicative and illuminating for the nature of this new morality, which makes the exception the prime thing rather than in biblical morality the reverse. And as to the question why the new morality is attractive . . .

DR. HENRY: What gives it its appeal today?

DR. DAANE: It seems to me it is attractive for two reasons. Some people find it an excuse for sexual license. But others find that they warm up to the idea that what is demanded is love, which is certainly true enough; even Christians believe this. It depends, however, upon *how* you define love. And here the new morality lets love undefined, and it seems to me that this is one of the basic weaknesses of it.

DR. MONTGOMERY: Yes, Some people think also that contemporary psychology gives reasons for moving in the direction of the new morality. And here those that do take this view are very much deceived. Psychology has come to the conclusion in recent years that there must be a structure of principle within which the individual operates. Without the structure of principle, the individual gradually comes to the conclusion that no one really cares. If one attempts to bring up a child without any structure of principle, the child will keep pressuring to see if anybody out there really loves him to the extent of providing an opportunity for him to move by principle. And this means that if the structures are left out, the child or the adult destroys himself trying to create principle from within.

DR. DAANE: Which means that nobody loves to be utterly alone in the universe.

DR. MONTGOMERY: Right. C. S. Lewis has pointed out in his preface to *Paradise Lost* that Milton's greatness came from the fact that he used his genius within a framework and that this is characteristic of great art and literature through the centuries. It is also characteristic of great morality.

DR. HENRY: Well now, the new morality is not for many people who live by it, an articulate view of ethical decision. If the Bible is taken seriously, and man is a sinner who needs to be redeemed, isn't this vagabond morality what people naturally live by? What about the Gentile world that early Christianity faced? Wasn't this— look at the first chapter of Romans.

DR. MORRIS: I think that is a very important point because there are a lot of people today who've got the idea that traditional Christianity gives a good morality for people who are half inclined to be good anyway—it doesn't work in a time like the present when there is very much license, and people are doing all sorts of things they ought not to do. But they overlook altogether, the fact that Christianity was born into a world like that. You take for instance such a man as Seneca, a great and good philosopher, and he has gone on record as saying that chastity is simply a proof of ugliness. Or again he says, innocency is not rare; it is non-existent. And this kind of statement could be paralleled again and again from the classical authors of the first century. And into that world, Christianity came with its uncompromising demand that people should put away altogether what passed for sex ethics in their day. Lecky, the historian of European morals, maintains that chastity was the one new virtue that Christianity brought into the world. Now, whether you believe the truth of that, the important thing is that Christianity came into a world where it was accepted unquestioningly, that continence was an unreasonable demand to make of any man—with the women, of course, it was different.

DR. HENRY: Gentlemen, I think we have come—if you will excuse me, Dr. Morris—to just about the end of our panel, with the time only for a closing summary statement by each of the panel members. And we will begin with Dr. Daane, if you don't mind, and then we will give Dr. Morris an opportunity, after Dr. Montgomery.

DR. DAANE: Well, I would say that the new morality is in part a concession to the times. I would say one ought to be a bit careful here, alluding to what you just said a moment ago. I notice that most of the professional advocates of the new morality are men that are well on in years. Secondly, I would say that the new morality has an appeal against an excessive amount of legalism that you found in the whole church tradition. But its great weakness is that it lets the central thing it demands, namely love, undefined, without definition, and it is up to each individual to define it as he wills. And at that point, it becomes dangerous.

DR. MONTGOMERY: Ours is a day when concern for social justice has come to the fore to an extent that can't be paralleled in many generations of the past. It seems to me that this is a time of all times when an absolute ethic is a necessity. If we are concerned about people who are disenfranchised, people who are suffering from cultural prejudice and the like, we had better have a very cleancut standard of ethics, such that such prejudicial attitudes toward these people cannot be justified under any circumstances. This the Christian faith provides. The Christian faith says that there is neither Jew nor Greek, neither bond nor free; we are all one in Jesus Christ. This kind of absolute claim stands regardless of the cultural situation.

DR. HENRY: Dr. Morris.

DR. MORRIS: Two things. It seems to me that the new moralists pay insufficient attention to the fact that God has made a revelation of himself in Scripture and this revelation carries with it great principles which stand back of moral conduct. And the other thing is that this same revelation brings before us the Spirit of God Himself which helps men be the kind of people they ought to be.

DR. HENRY: Gentlemen, thanks for taking time out of your busy lives to join us on this panel. Dr. Daane of Fuller Theological Seminary in Pasadena, California; Dr. Montgomery, of the faculty of Trinity Evangelical Divinity School in Deerfield, Illinois; Dr. Leon Morris, Principal of Ridley College in Melbourne, Australia. Thank you for sharing the hour with us.

4.

The Gospel According to LSD

Karl Marx religiously believed that religion is the opiate of the people. Now the conviction is growing in avant-garde circles that an opiate can become the religion of the people.

The drug in question is D-lysergic acid diethylamide (LSD-25), one of a group of "psychedelic" (consciousness-expanding) agents that includes peyote, mescaline, psilocin, and psilocybin. In the last two decades, interest in these drugs has greatly increased. During the winter of 1962-63, President Pusey of Harvard removed from his psychology staff Drs. Timothy Leary and Richard Alpert for unscientific and dangerous experimentation with psychedelics. "You may be making Buddhas out of everyone," the university told them, "but that's not what *we're* trying to do."

Exiled from academia, Leary and Alpert devoted their energies to their "International Federation for Internal Freedom," in which continued experimentation with the drug experience could be promoted. In December, 1965, Leary was arrested in Texas for illegally transporting and failing to pay taxes on marijuana and was given the maximum sentence (thirty years plus $40,000 in fines).

Cases of psychotic behavior as a result of LSD "trips" have been making the press of late, and Dr. Donald Louria of the New York County Medical Society reports that during 1966 seventy-five persons were admitted to Bellevue as a result of LSD reactions. The serious medical literature on LSD has continued to multiply (see the exhaustive "Annotated Bibliography" published by Sandoz Pharmaceuticals, the only legal manufacturer of the drug —which recently stopped all deliveries of LSD).

Our interest here is not in the chemical or psychological aspects of the psychedelics (for a discussion of their value in controlled psychotherapy and treatment of alcoholism, consult the October, 1965, issue of *Pastoral Psychology*). We wish to focus attention on the repeated claim that

LSD offers a prime avenue to ultimate religious reality.

In the course of Leary's Harvard experiments, sixty-nine religious professionals (about half of Christian or Jewish persuasion and the rest adherents of Eastern religions) took psychedelic drugs; over 75 per cent reported intense mystico-religious experiences, and more than half asserted that they had had the deepest spiritual experience of their life (*Psychedelic Review*, I [1964], 325). Pahnke's 1963 Harvard doctoral dissertation supports these claims by reporting a statistically significant, controlled experiment in which drugs were administered to ten theology students and professors in the setting of a Good Friday service, while ten others received only placebos; "those subjects who received psilocybin experienced phenomena which were indistinguishable from, if not identical with . . . the categories . . . of mysticism." Professor Walter Clark of Andover Newton states that his psychedelic vision was "like Moses' experience of the burning bush."

What interpretation should be placed upon such claims? Roman Catholic scholar R. C. Zaehner, in his book, *Mysticism, Sacred and Profane*, argues that the drug experience, as exemplified by Aldous Huxley in his *Doors of Perception*, is at best a blend of monistic and nature mysticism but does not reach the level of genuinely theistic, Christian mysticism. The Native American Church of the North American Indians, however, claims that Jesus gave the peyote plant to them in their time of need, and, according to Slotkin, they "see visions, which may be of Christ Himself" (cf. Huston Smith, "Do Drugs Have Religious Import?," in *LSD*, ed. Solomon [1964], pp. 152-67). In these latter cases, the drug is evidently viewed as a means of grace, not as an *opus operatum* or magical device.

Yet Zaehner makes an important point: the psychedelic experience has generally been understood in terms of monistic mysticism, particularly its Eastern forms. Alan Watts relates it to Zen. Leary and Alpert have published a manual for LSD "trips" based on the Tibetan Book of the Dead. The vast majority of selections included in Ebin's anthology, *The Drug Experience* (1961; 1965), are written from non-Christian standpoints.

Why is this so? William James suggested the answer as long ago as 1902 when he described his experience with nitrous oxide: "The keynote of it is invariably a reconciliation. It is as if the opposites of the world, whose contradictoriness and conflict make all our difficulties and troubles, were melted into unity" (*The Varieties of Religious Experience*, lectures 16 and 17).

The drug experience, though it may be integrated into a Christian context, never requires such integration, and in fact leads the unwary to believe that the reconciliation of the fallen world can be achieved simply by consciousness (or unconsciousness) expansion. Scripture, however, makes clear beyond all shadow of doubt that true reconciliation occurs solely when a man faces up to his sin and accepts the atoning work of the historic Christ in his behalf. LSD offers the deceptive possibility of bypassing the Cross while achieving harmony within and without. Like Altizer's chimerical endeavor to gain the "conjunction of opposites" through the substitution of a mystical, fully kenotic "Christ" for the historical Jesus, psychedelic mysticism tries to reconcile all things apart from the only Reconciler.

The tragedy of the LSD gospel (which is not a gospel) is nowhere more evident than in its use with dying patients. Dr. Sidney Cohen reports the last days of "Irene," terminally ill with cancer. She had "no religion, no hope," and was given LSD. Then she faced death calmly: "Once you see the pattern of the vortex, it all fits," she said (*Harper's*, September, 1965). Did she see the world aright? Was her consciousness truly expanded? French psychedelic specialist Roger Heim noted that under the influence of the drug his handwriting, in reality black, appeared red; and a cat, given the drug, recoils in fear from a mouse. Reality? No. The only religious "trip" that avoids irrational fear, sees the blackness of the world for what it is, and transmutes death into life is offered freely, without need of capsule or syringe, by Christ the Way.

5.

The Death of the "Death of God"
Morticians of the Absolute*

The subject of this essay is the new theological science of Theothanatology, wherein God's mortal illness or demise serves as the starting point for a radically secular approach to the modern world.[1]

The national publicity given to this movement in general periodicals (*Time, The New Yorker, The New York Times,* etc.)[2] may produce the false impression that here Protestantism has again spawned an unstable lunatic fringe which will disappear before one knows it —or quickly be replaced, as the Beatles edged out Elvis Presley. A closer look, however, reveals that the death-of-God movement is no flash in the theological pan. Stokes, a critical colleague of theothanatologist Altizer at Emory University, has recently and accurately mapped "the nontheistic temper of the modern mind;" the death-of-God theologies are consciously relating to this temper.[3] Carl F. H. Henry, on closely observing the present European theological climate, has noted that, after the relatively brief Barthian interlude, the cold winds of rationalism are blowing again;[4] in the death-of-God movement America is beginning to feel these winds turning icy cold as they are directed through an ideological morgue. *Christian Century*'s editor, while varying the temperature, does not minimize the impact of the new theology; on December 1, 1965, he wrote of the so-called "Christian atheism": "Debate now rages: it looks as if we shall have a long, hot winter."[5] Cold or hot (Altizer would like this conjunction of opposites!), the movement is indeed to be reckoned with. Says one of its prime spokesmen, William Hamilton: "Members of this group are in touch with each other; plans are under way for a major meeting of the group and there is

* Fred C. Rutz Foundation Lecture, Concordia Theological Seminary Springfield, Illinois, February 3, 1966.
Notes for this section, pages 109-21.

even some talk of a new journal devoted to the movement." [6]

Protestants in the Reformation tradition should especially examine this new theology with care, for it is not accidental that Hamilton regularly appeals to Luther and to motifs of Reformation theology,[7] or that a critic of the movement has shrewdly written: "Soon, I predict, Luther will become the dominant symbol of the God-is-dead theology because he left the cloister and went into the 'world'—whatever that is." [8]

Even more important, as we shall see, the God-is-dead movement takes its rise from the consistent appropriation and use of a central theme in Neo-Orthodoxy —the very Neo-Orthodoxy that many Lutheran and Reformed theologians here and abroad are naively embracing today.[9] Perhaps this lecture will aid some members of the theological community to check their tickets more carefully before they board contemporary trains of thought.

As to the author's posture, let it be plainly stated at the outset: in Merrill Tenney's words, "We are not ready to be God's pallbearers yet";[10] nor are we going to function as pseudo-sophisticated embalmers of the Infinite. Rather, I find myself at the presumed death of God in the role of a coroner. My dictionary defines a coroner as "a public officer whose principal duty is to inquire into any death which there is reason to suppose is not due to natural causes." I have become convinced that there is some foul play involved in this particular death; and we shall discover, if I am not mistaken, that the death-of-God theology represents a classic case of what mystery writers call "the wrong corpse."

The Morticians in the Case

Five names have become associated, for good or for ill, with the new "Christian atheism." They are: Gabriel Vahanian of Syracuse, a French Calvinist by origin, whose 1961 book *The Death of God* gave the new movement its name; Baptist Harvey Cox of the Harvard Divinity School, rocketed to fame by his paperback, *The Secular City* (1965), which sold over 135,000 copies in its first year; Thomas J. J. Altizer, an Episcopal layman formerly on the faculty at Emory and now Professor of English at the State University of New York at Stony Brook, whose monograph carries the title *The Gospel of Christian Atheism;* William Hamilton, formerly of Colgate Rochester and now professor of religion at New College (Sarasota, Florida), a Baptist, best known for his book *The New Essence of Christianity*—which, however, now represents an earlier, more conservative stage in his development; and Paul M. van Buren, an Episcopal priest teaching in the religion department at Temple University, who took his doctorate under Karl Barth at Basel and whose book *The Secular Meaning of the Gospel* is the most substantial production yet to arise from the death-of-God camp. All of these men are "younger theologians": Cox is 40, Vahanian and Altizer are 42, and Hamilton and van Buren are 45.

Whether these five theologians actually constitute a "school" is still a matter of debate among them. Cox, speaking in Evanston some time ago at the Seventh Annual Meeting of the American Society of Christian Ethics, denied the existence of a unified movement (but then observed important common elements among the "Christian atheists");[11] Paul van Buren has remarked: "Langdon Gilkey says we belong to a 'God is dead' movement, but I think Altizer and Bill Hamilton and I are saying different things."[12] Hamilton, on the other hand, has argued cogently for the existence of a definite ideological focus shared at least by Altizer, van Buren, and himself.[13] Of course the question of a "school" depends on one's definition of the term. The fact that the above five theologians are already linked in the common mind with the God-is-dead stir requires that we look at the position of each. Having done so, we can proceed to note the common elements in their views.

We shall take up the theothanatologists in the order already employed: Vahanian, Cox, Altizer, Hamilton, and van Buren. This order represents, roughly, a continuum from "more conservative" to "more radical," with the caesura between Cox and Altizer. Such an arrangement takes into account a basic clarification made

both by Cox and by Hamilton: Cox's distinction between
the theologians (such as himself) who use the phrase
death-of-God with quotation marks around either or both
of its nouns, and the theologians (such as van Buren)
who use the phrase with no qualifications, to signify
that God is no longer alive, even if he once existed;[14]
and Hamilton's separation of the "soft" radicals ("they
have God, but sometimes for strategic reasons they may
decide not to talk about him") from "hard" radicals
such as himself:

> The hard radicals are really not interested in problems
> of communication. It is not that the old forms are out-
> moded or that modern man must be served but that the
> message itself is problematic. The hard radicals, how-
> ever varied may be their language, share first of all a
> common loss. It is not a loss of the idols, or of the God of
> theism. It is a real loss of real transcendence. It is a loss
> of God.[15]

In terms of these typologies, Vahanian and Cox are
"soft" radicals who use quotation marks, while Altizer,
Hamilton, and van Buren, by eschewing qualifications
(though admittedly not always in the most clean-cut fashion) and by endeavoring to assert the ontological demise
of deity, warrant classification as "hard" radicals.

The five death-of-God theologians may be further
distinguished by the way of their academic specializations
and temperamental orientations. Thus Vahanian is principally concerned with the relations between literature
and theology, and writes as an urbane littérateur himself;
Cox is basically a sociologist of religion,[16] endeavoring to unite Talcott Parsons with Karl Barth(!); [17] Altizer is "mystical, spiritual, and apocalyptic . . . all élan,
wildness, excessive generalization, brimming with color-
ful, flamboyant, and emotive language"; [18] Hamilton
is the theologian's theologian, having produced (before
his conversion to death-of-God thinking) such standard
fare as the *Modern Reader's Guide to the Gospels,* and
The Christian Man in Westminster Press's Layman's
Theological Library; and van Buren—"ordered, precise,
cool" [19] is ever the modern linguistic philosopher: he
"has neither wept at God's funeral nor, like Altizer and
the dancers at a Hindu procession to the burning ghat,

leaped in corybantic exultation. He plays the role of the clinical diagnostician of linguistic maladies." [20] Let us consider in turn the peculiar ideological orientation of each of these thinkers, who, in spite of their wide divergencies, are united in focusing the attention of theology on contemporary secular man rather than on transcendental deity.

Gabriel Vahanian: Mortician-Littérateur. Though Rudolf Bultmann regards Vahanian's *Death of God* as one of the most exciting books he has read in recent years, its author is now considered hopelessly conservative by the advocates of Christian atheism.[21] Why? Because he unabashedly uses the expression "death of God" in a metaphorical-literary, not literal, way. The subtitle of his book reveals his major concern: "The Culture of Our Post-Christian Era." "God's death" is evident in the fact that ours is a post-Christian world where (1) "Christianity has sunk into religiosity," (2) "modern culture is gradually losing the marks of that Christianity which brought it into being and shaped it," and (3) "tolerance has become religious syncretism." [22] In his recent book, *Wait Without Idols*, Vahanian explicates: "This does not mean, obviously, that God himself no longer is but that, regardless of whether he is or not, his reality, as the Christian tradition has presented it, has become culturally irrelevant: God is *de trop*, as Sartre would say" [23]—and he illustrates with the opening scenes of the film *La Dolce Vita*, where a huge crucifix suspended from a helicopter hovers incongruously over indifferent sunbathers below.

What is the cause of this "demise of God"? Like Paul Tillich or Christian philosopher of history Eric Voegelin,[24] Vahanian finds the basic issue in "the leveling down of transcendental values to immanental ones," [25] i.e., the worship of the idolatrous gods of cultural religiosity. In a penetrating analysis of Samuel Beckett's 1952-1953 play *En attendant Godot (Waiting for Godot)*, where Godot represents God, Vahanian concludes: "No wonder then that life is lonesomely long, when one lives it out wandering from meaninglessness to meaninglessness, from idol to idol—and not a hope in sight. Modern man's place is the right place; only his religiousness is at the wrong place, addressing itself to the Unknown God." [26]

But Vahanian has an answer for post-Christian man: he must, as his book title says, "Wait without idols." As a Calvinist and as a follower of Barth (he translated and wrote the introduction for Barth's book *The Faith of the Church*), Vahanian believes that secular "immanentism can show that God dies as soon as he becomes a cultural accessory or a human ideal; that the finite cannot comprehend the infinite (*finitum non capax infiniti*)." [27] What then does modern man wait for? The breaking in of the Wholly Other—the transcendent God who can never be "objectified." [28]

> The Christian era has bequeathed us the "death of God," but not without teaching us a lesson. God is not necessary; that is to say, he cannot be taken for granted. He cannot be used merely as a hypothesis, whether epistemological, scientific, or existential, unless we should draw the degrading conclusion that "God is reasons." On the other hand, if we can no longer assume that God is, we may once again realize that he *must* be. God is not necessary, but he is inevitable. He is wholly other and wholly present. Faith in him, the conversion of our human reality, both culturally and existentially, is the demand he still makes upon us. [29]

Harvey Cox: Mortician-Sociologist. Bishop John A. T. Robinson, of *Honest to God* fame, recently commended Cox's *Secular City* as "a major contribution by a brilliant young theologian" and pointed up its major theme: that secularization is "the fruit of the Gospel." [30] For Cox, secularization (as opposed to secularism) is a positive phenomenon, whereby "society and culture are delivered from tutelage to religious control and closed metaphysical world-views." [31] Following Eric Voegelin and Gerhard von Rad, Cox interprets the Genesis account of Creation and the Exodus narratives of the deliverance from Egypt and the Sinai covenant as secularizing-liberating myths— myths of which the secular city becomes a modern counter-part. Urban life, with its anonymity and mobility, can free modern man from bondage to closed, idolatrous value systems, and open him to that which is truly transcendent. He quotes Amos Wilder approvingly: "If we are to have any transcendence today, even Christian, it must be in and through the secular." [32] How will the liberating transcendence manifest itself? Cox suggests art, social change, and what he calls the "I-You partnership" (a teamwork relationship). Through such means the transcendent may eventually reveal to us a new name, for the word "God" has perhaps outlived its usefulness owing to its association with old idolatries. "This may mean that we shall have to stop talking about 'God' for a while, take a moratorium on speech until the new name emerges." [33] But this should not appear strange to us, since "hiddenness stands at the very center of the doctrine of God." [34] Even "in Jesus God does not stop being hidden; rather He meets man as the unavailable 'other.' He does not 'appear' but shows man that He acts, in His hiddenness, in human history." [35] Modern urban-secular life, then, is the vehicle (the "means of grace"!) by which man in our age can be freed from bondage to lesser gods and meet the Transcendent One again.

When Cox revisted his secular city in a conference several years ago, he made his position vis-à-vis the "death of God" even more explicit.[36] No, he did not accept the literal demise of deity; as a close admirer of Karl Barth, he firmly believes in a transcendent, wholly other God.[37] Indeed, it is on this basis that his book strikes out against those styles of life that capture and immanentize deity. With Friedrich Gogarten, he is convinced that apart from transcendent reality—an extrinsic point of reference—the world cannot be a world at all. (He illustrated with Muzak: if it were to go on all the time, then music would cease to exist; an anti-environment is necessary for an environment, and the wholly other God is such an anti-environment for our world.) But as to the identification of the Absolute, Cox was no less vague than in his book. There he spoke of atheists and Christians as differing not in their factual orientation but in their "stance"; in his lecture, he employed an aesthetic model for Christian social decisions, and when asked for the criteria whereby one could know that the transcendent is indeed working in a given social change, he optimistically asserted that "the hermeneutical community, with its eyes of faith, discerns 'where the action is.' " Whereupon the questioner shrewdly retorted:

"Carl McIntire's church or yours?" Cox then readily admitted his enthusiast-anabaptist frame of reference, and
noted that Lutherans and Calvinists (mainline Reformation Protestants) had been the chief critics of his *Secular City.*

Thomas J. J. Altizer: Mortician-Mystic. In spite of
their radical terminology, Vahanian and Cox are familiar
territory to those acquainted with the twentieth-century
Protestant thought world. Beginning with Barth's radical
transcendence, they condemn the false gods of cultural
immanentism and see the collapse of these idols in our
day as the entrée to a new appreciation of the Wholly
Other. They differ from Barth chiefly in the means by
which the Transcendent One will now show himself; for
Barth, it is always through the (erring but revelatory)
Word of Scripture; for Vahanian and Cox, it is through
the pulsating secular life of our time. With Altizer, however, we move into a more distinctively radical radicalism, where God's death is passionately affirmed as a real
(though dialectical) event. Altizer's difficult world-view
is best comprehended through the influences that have
played upon him:

(1) From the great phenomenologist of religion Mircea
Eliade, Altizer came to see that modern man has lost
his sense of the sacred;[38] but Altizer "refuses to follow Eliade's tempting advice to return to some sort of
precosmic primitivism and to recover the sacred in the
way archaic religion did." [39] Altizer picks up the principle of the "coincidence of opposites" (*coincidentia oppositorum*) so vital to the thinking of Eliade (and of Carl
Gustav Jung), and endeavors to apply it with ruthless
consistency: the only way to recover the sacred is to
welcome fully the secularization of the modern world.

(2) Altizer's studies in comparative religion, particularly the Eastern religions, provided considerable grist
for his mill.[40] He came to identify the basic thrusts of
Christianity and atheistic Buddhism;[41] in his judgment
both religions seek to liberate man from all dependence
on the phenomenal world (in Buddhism, the negation of
Samsara is the only means to Nirvana), yet at the same
time there is "a mystical apprehension of the oneness

of reality" (Nirvana and Samsara are mystically identified).[42] Here, according to Altizer, is a telling parallel
with the Christian Kingdom of God, which is "in the world
but not of it."

(3) From modern Protestant theology Altizer has acquired his basic understanding of Christianity. Sören
Kierkegaard has contributed the dialectical method:
"existence in faith is antithetically related to existence in objective reality; now faith becomes subjective,
momentary, and paradoxical."[43] Rudolph Otto[44] and
Karl Barth have provided a God who is wholly transcendent—who cannot be adequately represented by any
human idea. But Barth, Bultmann, and even Tillich have
not carried through the Kierkegaardian dialectic to its
consistent end, for they insist on retaining some vestige
of affirmation; they do not see that the dialectic requires
an unqualified coincidence of opposites. If only Tillich
had applied his "Protestant principle" consistently, he
could have become the father of a new theonomous age.
Wrote Altizer not long before Tillich's death:

> The death of God (which Tillich, who refuses to be fully
> dialectical, denies) must lead to a repetition of the Resur-
> rection, to a new epiphany of the New Being. Moreover
> his own principles lead Tillich to the threshold of this
> position. If Christianity will be a bearer of the religious
> answer not so long as it breaks through its own par-
> ticularity, only to the degree in which it negates itself as
> a religion, then obviously it must negate its Western form.
> Until Christianity undergoes this negation, it cannot be
> open to the depths of the ground of being. Nor will Chris-
> tianity continue to be able to embody the New Being if
> it remains closed both to non-Western history and to the
> contemporary historical present. Potentially Tillich could
> become a new Luther if he would extend his principle of
> justification by doubt to a theological affirmation of the
> death of God.[45]

Altizer now clearly sees *himself* in this role.

(4) "If radical dialectical thinking was reborn in
Kierkegaard, it was consummated in Friedrich Nietzsche,"[46] says Altizer, who sees in Nietzsche's vision
of Eternal Recurrence the ideal myth of the coincidence
of opposites, and in his passionate proclamation of God's
death—the death of metaphysical transcendence—the
essential key to a new age. For "only when God is dead,

can Being begin in every Now"[47] Therefore, to turn
the wheel of the world we must dare with William Blake
to "name God as Satan," i.e., to "identify the transcendent Lord as the ultimate source of alienation and
repression."[48] Only then can we affirm "the God beyond the Christian God, beyond the God of the historic
Church, beyond all which Christendom has known as
God."[49]

(5) By a thoroughgoing acceptance of Albert
Schweitzer's eschatological interpretation of Jesus in
his *Quest of the Historical Jesus,* Altizer claims Jesus
as the prime symbol of his world-view. "To grasp Jesus
as an historical or an objective phenomenon is to live
in unbelief."[50] Jesus is significant because of his single-
minded attention to the coming Kingdom and his sacrifice of himself for it; he thus becomes the Christ figure—
the symbol of a total rejection of the old to achieve the
new—and this "mythical symbol of Christ" is "the substance of the Christian faith."[51] So Altizer calls on
radical Christians to "rebel against the Christian churches
and their traditions" and to "defy the moral law of the
churches, identifying it as a satanic law of repression and
heteronomous compulsion."[52] As "spiritual or apocalyptic" Christians, they must "believe only in the Jesus
of the third age of the Spirit, a Jesus who is not to be
identified with the original historical Jesus, but who rather
is known here in a new and more comprehensive and
universal form, a form actualizing the eschatological
promise of Jesus."[53] The incarnate Word is thus seen
to be fully kenotic—capable of a total new expression
in the new age ushered in when dialectically we "accept
the death of God as a final and irrevocable event":

> Neither the Bible nor church history can be accepted
> as containing more than a provisional or temporary series
> of expressions of the Christian World. . . . Not only does
> Christianity now have a new meaning, it has a new reality,
> a reality created by the epiphany of a fully kenotic Word.
> Such a reality cannot be wholly understood by a word of
> the past, not even by the word "kenosis," for the Chris-
> tian Word becomes a new reality by ceasing to be itself:
> only by negating and thus transcending its previous ex-
> pressions can the Incarnate Word be a forward-moving
> process.[54]

William Hamilton: Mortician-Theologian. Though
Altizer outbarths Barth in his employment of the transcendence principle, thus apparently leaving the "soft"
radicals far behind, his affirmation of God's death is,
after all, still a dialectic affirmation: from the ashes of
God's pyre will rise, like the Phoenix, a "God beyond
God." Now let us consider a theothanatologist who has
come to reject the dialectic as well.

In a revealing autobiographical article, Hamilton
states that he did not attain his present "hard" radical
position until 1964, after he had turned forty.[55] This
is quite true, and much of the current interpretation of
Hamilton falls wide of the mark because it is based on
his 1961 book *The New Essence of Christianity,* which
explicity disavows "the non-existence of God"[56] and
even affirms Jesus' resurrection "as an ordinary event"
(though it is insignificantly relegated to a footnote!).[57]
But even at that time, the influence of Barth,[58] Niebuhr, and John Baillie[59] on Hamilton's thought was
leading to a more radical position. Thus in the spring of
1963 Hamilton wistfully attempted to save Mozart's Don
Giovanni through the employment of Kierkegaard's dialectic of good and evil; Don Giovanni seems to typify
the limbo state of the contemporary theologian—neither
damned nor saved.[60] Then came Hamilton's first direct
attempt to "see if there is anybody out there"[61]—if
there were others who shared his growing dissatisfaction
with the state of theological life: his essay "Thursday's
Child," in which he depicted the theologian of today and
tomorrow as "a man without faith, without hope, with
only the present and therefore only love to guide them"
—"a waiting man and a praying man."[62] When interviewed in 1965 by Mehta, he said: "I am beginning to
feel that the time has come for us to put up or shut
up, for me to be an in or an out."[63]

The decision to be an "out"—a "hard" radical affirming the literal death of God—was made by Hamilton last
year. In his *Christian Century* article previously referred
to, he described the breakdown of his "good old world
of middle-of-the-road, ecumenical neo-orthodoxy,"[64] and
outlined his new position in three particulars: (1) God
is indeed dead; the Neo-Orthodox "dialectic between the

presence and absence of God" has now "collapsed."
(2) A free choice is made to follow the man Jesus in
obedience—to stand where he stands.[65] (3) A new
optimism will "say Yes to the world of rapid change, new
technologies, automation and the mass media." The last
two points are clarified somewhat in Hamilton's recent
analysis of the death-of-God movement, wherein he
stakes out his position as compared with the views of
Altizer and van Buren.[66] Christologically, Hamilton,
like Altizer, commits himself to a radically hidden,
kenotic Jesus: "Jesus may be concealed in the world,
in the neighbor, in this struggle for justice, in that struggle for beauty, clarity, order. Jesus is in the world as
masked." Moreover, "Become a Christ to your neighbor,
as Luther put it." [67]

Yet the theme of the Christian as "both a waiting man
and a praying man" still remains. How is this possible
if "the breakdown of the religious a priori means that
there is no way, ontological, cultural, or psychological,
to locate a part of the self or a part of human experience
that needs God"—if "there is no God-shaped blank within man?" "Really to travel along this road means that
we trust the world, not God, to be our need fulfiller and
problem solver, and God, if he is to be for us at all, must
come in some other role." [68] Having rejected Augustine's claim that our hearts are restless till they find
their rest in God, Hamilton draws in another Augustinian
theme: the distinction between *uti* and *frui*—between
using God and enjoying Him.

> If God is not needed, if it is to the world and not to
> God that we repair for our needs and problems, then per-
> haps we may come to see that He is to be enjoyed and
> delighted in.... Our waiting for God, our godlessness, is
> partly a search for a language and a style by which we
> might be enabled to stand before Him once again, de-
> lighting in His presence.[69]

In the meantime, modern secular man must grow up
—from an Oedipus to an Orestes, from a Hamlet to a
Prospero[70]—by moving beyond the anguished quest
for salvation from sin to a confident, optimistic, secular
stance "in the world, in the city, with both the needy
neighbor and the enemy." Thus is the orthodox relation

between God and the neighbor "inverted": "we move to our neighbor, to the city and to the world out of a sense of the loss of God." [71] Man, not God, becomes the center of focus while we wait prayerfully for the epiphany of a God of delight.

Paul van Buren: Mortician-Philosopher. Officially, Hamilton rejects a dialectic view of God's existence; yet, remarkably (or paradoxically, in spite of Hamilton's formal break with neo-Protestant paradox!), a *frui* God is hoped for at the death of a *uti* divinity. Prayer is the revealing element in Hamilton's theology: he continues to pray in spite of God's death—thus forcing the conclusion that the dialectic of divine presence-absence that he claims to have rejected has not been rejected at all in practice. Through the contemporary dark night of the soul God *is* in some sense still there, waiting as we wait, the recipient of our prayers. In Paul van Buren, however, this inconsistency is overcome through the cool and rigorous application of linguistic philosophy. Significantly, van Buren recently admitted: "I don't pray. I just reflect on these things." [72]

Like the other death-of-God theologians, van Buren began his reflecting as a Barthian. We noted earlier that he took his doctorate under Barth at Basel.[73] Subsequently, however, he came into contact with the *Philosophical Investigations* of the later Wittgenstein and the writings of the so-called linguistic analysts who have followed him.[74] In the process of subjecting his own Neo-Orthodox theology to rigorous analytic and linguistic criticism, he wrote his *Secular Meaning of the Gospel,* a book which, he says, "represented an important step in a personal struggle to overcome my own theological past" [75]—but "what I'm thinking now is a lot more radical even than what I said in my book." [76]

What is van Buren's current position? It may be represented as a five-point argument, the total importance of which can hardly be overemphasized since it forms the philosophical backbone of consistent "Christian atheism":

(1) Assertions compatible with anything and everything say nothing, and this is precisely the status of Neo-

Orthodoxy's affirmation concerning a transcendental, wholly-other God. At the beginning of *The Secular Meaning of the Gospel,* van Buren approvingly quotes the well-known parable by Antony Flew and John Wisdom, demonstrating the meaningless of such God-statements:

> Once upon a time two explorers came upon a clearing in the jungle. In the clearing were growing many flowers and many weeds. One explorer says, "Some gardener must tend this plot." The other disagrees, "There is no gardener." So they pitch their tents and set a watch. No gardener is ever seen. "But perhaps he is an invisible gardener." So they set up a barbed-wire fence. They electrify it. They patrol with bloodhounds. (For they remember how H. G. Wells' *The Invisible Man* could be both smelt and touched though he could not be seen.) But no shrieks ever suggest that some intruder has received a shock. No movements of the wire ever betray an invisible climber. The bloodhounds never give cry. Yet still the Believer is not convinced. "But there is a gardener, invisible, intangible, insensible to electric shocks, a gardener who has no scent and makes no sound, a gardener who comes secretly to look after the garden which he loves." At last the Sceptic despairs, "But what remains of your original assertion? Just how does what you call an invisible, intangible, eternally elusive gardener differ from an imaginary gardener or even from no gardener at all?" [77]

An important section of van Buren's book is devoted to showing that Bultmann's existential assertions about God do not escape this "death by a thousand qualifications," and that the same holds true of Schubert Ogden's attempts (God is "experienced non-objective reality," etc.) to stiffen existential affirmations with Whitehead's process-philosophy. God, then, is literally and unqualifiedly dead, and future divine epiphanies have no more meaning than present-day expressions of God's existence.

(2) Modern life is irrevocably pluralistic and relativistic, a market place where a multitude of "language games" are played, not a Gothic cathedral where a single comprehensive world-view is possible. The non-cognitive language game of theology has to be played relativistically in this milieu.[78]

(3) If metaphysical, transcendental God-statements are literally meaningless, what is their "cash value"? The actual worth of these affirmations of faith can be

obtained only by translating them into human terms, an operation to which the concluding portion of *The Secular Meaning of the Gospel* is devoted. As van Buren put it in his recent *New Yorker* interview: "I am trying to argue that it (Christianity) is fundamentally about man, that its language about God is one way—a dated way, among a number of ways—of saying what it is Christianity wants to say about man and human life and human history." [79]

(4) This translation of God-language to man-language must be carried out particularly in reference to the central figure of Christianity, Jesus of Nazareth.

> One of the ways in which the New Testament writers speak about Jesus is in divine and quasi-divine terms— Son of God, and what have you.... What I'm trying to do is to understand the Bible on a naturalistic or humanistic level, to find out how the references to the absolute and the supernatural are used in expressing on a human level the understanding and convictions that the New Testament writers had about their world. For by using these large cosmological terms in speaking about this particular happening, this event—the history of Jesus—they were saying the most that they could say about this man. If a man in the first century had wanted to say of a certain person that he had given him an insight into what human life was all about, he would have almost normally said, "That man is divine." [80]

Van Buren claims that his secular translation of the Gospel "stands or falls with our interpretation of the language connected with Easter." [81] What is this interpretation?

> Jesus of Nazareth was a free man in his own life, who attracted followers and created enemies according to the dynamics of personality and in a manner comparable to the effect of other liberated persons in history upon people about them. He died as a result of the threat that such a free man poses for insecure and bound men. His disciples were left no less insecure and frightened. Two days later, Peter, and then other disciples, ... experienced a discernment situation in which Jesus the free man whom they had known, themselves, and indeed the whole world, were seen in a quite new way. From that moment, the disciples began to possess something of the freedom of Jesus. His freedom began to be "contagious." [82]

(5) Admittedly, theology is here reduced to ethics, but in our secular age we are unable to find any "em-

pirical linguistic anchorage" for the transcendental. After all, "alchemy was 'reduced' to chemistry by the rigorous application of an empirical method." [83] So let us frankly embrace the secular world of which we are a part. Religious thought is "responsible to human society, not to the church. Its orientation is humanistic, not divine. Its norms must lie in the role it performs in human life. . . . Any insights into the 'human situation' which our religious past may provide us, therefore, can be helpful only insofar as we bring them into a dynamic conversation with and allow them to be influenced by our rapidly changing technological culture." [84]

And here *la ronde* is complete, for in his stress on our modern cultural situation van Buren reminds us of the "soft" radicals, Vahanian and Cox, as much as of his "hard" compatriots, Altizer and Hamilton. Is there then a death-of-God school? Even with the qualifications introduced in our discussion of each of the five theothanatologists, the answer must be Yes. For in all of these thinkers the theological center shifts away from a God whose transcendence causes him to become more and more indistinct, until finally, in van Buren, he passes into the realm of analytic meaninglessness. And for all of these morticians of the Absolute, God's vague or vacated position on the theological stage is replaced by Man—literary man (Vahanian), urban man (Cox), mystical man (Altizer), social man (Hamilton), ethical man (van Buren). Correspondingly, the Christ of these "Christian atheists" moves from divine to human status: his kenosis becomes continually more pronounced until finally the divine "hiddenness" in him is absolutized, yielding a humanistic Jesus with whom modern man can truly and optimistically stand in "I-You" partnership in a world of secular challenge and dynamic change.

Efforts at Resuscitation

As the theothanatologists have taken their positions around the divine bier, ready to convey to its final resting place, resuscitator squads of theologians and clergy have rushed to the scene in a frantic effort to show that the Subject of discussion "is not dead but sleepeth." In the nine years since the appearance of Vahanian's *Death*

of God, vocal opposition to the movement has increased
not arithmetically but geometrically. The protests have
ranged widely in scope and quality—from the revival of
the anti-Nietzsche equip ("God is dead!" signed, Nietzsche; "Nietzsche is dead!" signed, God) to Eric Mascall's
The Secularisation of Christianity, a book-length criticism
of the common theological orientation of van Buren and
J. A. T. Robinson.[85] In general, it must be said that
the attempts to counter "Christian atheism," though
occasionally helpful in pointing up weaknesses in the theothanatologists' armor, do not cut decisively to the heart
of the issue. In most instances, the reason for the critical
debility lies in the dullness of the theological swords the
critics wield. Let us observe several representative efforts to slay the God-is-dead ideology, after which we
will be in a better position to offer our own critique.

Early in this paper we cited Hamilton's colleague
Charles M. Nielsen of Colgate Rochester, who evidently
has taken all that he can bear from Hamilton and his
death-of-God confrères. Nielsen is the best example of
the anti-theothanatological critics who oppose the movement through satire and ridicule. Here is a delightful
sample:

> On the subject of freedom: there is nothing quite like
> some Protestant seminaries. Presumably a medical school
> would be upset if its students became Christian Scientists
> and wanted to practice their new beliefs instead of medi-
> cine in the operating rooms of the university hospital.
> And a law school might consider it unbecoming to admit
> hordes of Anabaptists who refused on principle to have
> anything to do with law courts. But almost nothing (in-
> cluding atheism but excluding such vital matters as smok-
> ing) seems inappropriate in some Protestant settings—
> nothing, that is, except the traditions of Christianity and
> especially of Protestantism. Traditions are regarded as
> "square," supposedly because they are not new. The mod-
> ern theologian spends his time huddled over his teletype
> machine, like a nun breathless with adoration, in the hope
> that out of the latest news flash he can be the first to
> pronounce the few remainings shreds of the Protestant
> tradition "irrelevant."
> So powerful is the thrust toward novelty that a famous
> Protestant journal is considering a series of articles by
> younger theologians under sixty called "How my Mind
> Has Changed in the Past Five Minutes." The only thing
> that is holding up the project is the problem of getting

the journal distributed fast enough. A great aim of the liberal Protestant seminary is to be so relevant that no one would suspect Protestantism had a past, or at least a worthwhile one. The point is for the seminary to become so pertinent to modern culture that the church has nothing to say to that culture.[86]

Though such passages are great fun and make an important point, they bypass the root question, namely, Are the death-of-God theologians *correct* in what they claim? *Is* God dead? The obvious incongruity in Hamilton's presence until quite recently on the Colgate Rochester theological faculty, in van Buren's retention of Episcopal ordination, etc., pales before the truth question. Nielsen never faces this problem, for he sees the difficulty simply to be a surfeit of "eccentrics" in the church, and pleads for (as the subtitle of his article puts it) "more Benedictines, please!" As a Professor of Historical Theology who highly values the corporate tradition of the historic church, he prays: "Dear Lord, we are grateful for all the individualists and gadflies you have sent us. Hermits *are* interesting, but next time may we please also have a few Benedictines to build, organize and serve the church?" But if the God of the historic church is not dead, then "gratitude" for theothanatological gadflies seems hardly appropriate; and if he is, then Nielsen's Benedictines are a positive menace.

The November 17, 1965 issue of *Christian Century* featured a section titled, "Death-of-God: Four Views," with the following explanation from the editor: "Letters constituting entries in the death-of-God debate . . . continue to crowd the editor's desk. To print them all would be impossible, so as a way out of the dilemma we present four articles which in one or another aspect seem to inculcate most of the views, mainly critical, advanced in the letters." These articles are indeed representative of the general reaction to the movement, and their common theme is the *inconsistency* of the theothanatologists: their impossible attempt to retain love, joyful optimism, the Christian ethic, or Jesus himself while giving up a transcendent God. Warren L. Moulton argues that "without our faith in the reality of God we can know little or nothing about the love which we call *agape*"; he notes that "for the joy that was set before him Christ endured the cross; with the arrival of 'optimism' and the departure of this particular joy, a central nerve is frayed"; and asks: "Can we stick by Jesus just because we like the toys in his sandbox?" [87] Larry Shiner writes: "To get rid of God and keep a 'Jesus ethic' of involvement with the present human situation is a species of absent-mindedness amazing to behold in a movement that takes its motto from Nietzsche. *He* at least knew better; he never tired of pointing out that Christianity is a whole and that one cannot give up faith in God and keep Christian morality." [88]

But as sound as these criticisms are from the standpoint of the Biblical world-view, they overlook the plain fact that the death-of-God theologians are quite willing to follow Nietzsche, if need be, in a "transvaluation of all values." Altizer, as we have seen, has already called upon radical Christians to "defy the moral law of the churches"; and van Buren, in his article for *Christian Century*'s "How I Am Making Up My Mind" series, does not mention the name of Jesus once, and defines the task of theology entirely in humanistic terms.[89] It is therefore painfully evident that the charge of inconsistency toward the Christian tradition will not move the theothanatologists to repentance; they are fully prepared to embrace "creative negation" on all fronts. The basic issue remains: Is such negation justified?

The scholarly attempts to meet this fundamental truth question have thus far issued chiefly from the theological camps the "Christian atheists" have endeavored (quite successfully) to demolish: existentialism, Whiteheadian process-philosophy, and Neo-Orthodoxy. The result is a rather painful example of the defense of vested interests. Existential theologian John Macquarrie[90] is willing to admit, with van Buren, that "our modern scheme of thought affords no place for another being, however exalted, in addition to the beings that we encounter within the world"; but he still sees as a viable alternative the Heidegger-Tillich-Robinson existential-ontological conception of God as Being itself:

> The alternative is to think of God as Being itself—Being which emerges and manifests itself in and with and through every particular being, but which is not itself

another such being, which is nothing apart from particular beings, and yet which is more beingful than any particular being, since it is the condition that there should be any such beings whatsoever.... It is Heidegger's merit that he has shown the empirical anchorage of this question in certain moods of our own human existence—moods that light up for us the wider Being within which we live and move and have our own being.[91]

Process-philosophy is made the bulwark of defense against "Christian atheism" by theological advocates of this philosophical school. Stokes claims that a program to counter "the threat of a world view which repudiates the belief in a personal God ... can best succeed with the aid of personalistic modes of thought which are informed and enriched by some of the insights of Whitehead and Hartshorne." [91] John B. Cobb, Jr., author of the Whitehead-oriented *Living Options in Protestant Theology*[93] (which does not even include orthodox Reformation theology as an option!), informs us that "once one enters the strange new world of Whitehead's vision, God becomes very much alive.... Insofar as I come existentially to experience myself in terms of the world to which Whitehead introduces us, I experience myself in God; God as in me; God as law, as love, as grace; and the whole world as grounded in him.... If Whitehead's vision should triumph in the years ahead, the death of God's would indeed turn out after all to have been only the 'eclipse of God.' " [94] Bernard Meland argues in terms of process-philosophy and comparative religion that "ultimacy and immediacies traffic together," and that "while notions of the Absolute have dissolved in our modern discourse, the vision of a *More* in experience, as a dimension that is lived rather than thought, is not unavailable." [95]

Even the Neo-Orthodox theology out of which the death-of-God theologians have carved their casket for the Infinite is presented as an answer to "Christian atheism." Langdon Gilkey, in his Crozer Lectures on the God-is-dead movement, holds that the theothanatologists are influenced solely by the "negative elements" of Neo-Orthodoxy and "not at all by the balancing positive elements." [96] On the positive side, when one looks deeply into human experience, one finds "a special kind of Void and loss," the character of which is best expressed by such terms as "ultimate," "transcendent," and "unconditioned." Here "there is either no answer at all and so despair, or, if there be an answer, it comes from beyond the creaturely." At this goint revelation puts in its claim: "Revelation is that definite mode of experience in which an answer to those ultimate questions is actually experienced, in which, that is, the reality and truth of language about God is brought home to the experiencer, in which propositions about God are 'verified.' " [97] In the Neo-Orthodox spirit, Gilkey quickly adds: "No proof here is possible; only confession and conviction based on this experience." In sum: "The 'verification' of all we say about God occurs, then, in the life of faith lived by the Christian community, and from that living experience springs the usage and the reality of its God-language." [98]

The existential-ontological, process-thinking, and Neo-Orthodox arguments against "Christian atheism" ring more and more hollow as analytical philosophy intensifies its barrage against these increasingly anachronistic theologies. Theothanatology was built over the wreckage of these positions, and in itself it has marshaled overwhelming analytical evidence of their debility. Listen to van Buren's decimation of such arguments as have just been presented:

> Along comes the knight of faith and speaks of "reality breaking in upon us!" Or he speaks to us in the name of "absolute reality," or, even more confusing, his faith is placed in "an objective reality." And here I would suggest that language has gone on a wild binge, which I think we should properly call a lost weekend.
>
> This knight of faith is presumably speaking English, and so we take him to be using words which we have learned how to use. Only see what he does with them. "Reality," which is ordinarily used to call our attention once more to our agreements about how things are, is used now to refer to what the knight of faith must surely want to say is radically the opposite of all of our ordinary understandings. Why not better say, "Unreality is breaking in upon us"?
>
> I think we can say something about what has gone wrong here. There was a time when the Absolute, God, was taken to be the cause of a great deal of what we would today call quite real phenomena, from rain and hail to death and disease. God was part of what people took to

be the network of forces and factors of everyday existence, as real and as objective as the thunderbolts he produced. But today we no longer have the same reference for the word "reality." The network of understandings to which the word points has undergone important changes. The word "reality" has taken on an empirical coloration which makes it now a bit confusing to speak of "reality breaking in upon us," unless we are referring to, for example, a sudden and unexpected visit from the police or a mother-in-law.[99]

The point van Buren cleverly makes here applies equally to existential ontologies, process philosophies, and Neo-Orthodox theologies, for all of these positions offer concepts of Deity which, being compatible with anything and everything, say precisely nothing. Macquarrie's "beingful Being" may be nothing but an animistic name for the universe (the existence of which is hardly in dispute!);[100] the God of Whitehead and Hartshorne, as worshipped by Ogden, Cobb, Meland, et al., may likewise be little more than a pantheistic projection of their personalities on an impersonal universe (even William James, whose notion of "the More" Meland appropriates, admitted that it might be only an extension of the subliminal, para-psychological life of man);[101] and Gilkey quite rightly encloses the word "verification" in quotation marks when he uses it, for Neo-Orthodoxy's experience of revelation as filling a "Void" is no more a validation of God's ontological reality than the existentialist's "moods that light up the wider Being within which we live" or the process theologian's experience of "non-objective reality."[102] In all of these cases, the source of the experience could be purely psychological, and an appeal to a more-than-human level of explanation totally without warrant.[103]

Some efforts have been made to oppose the God-is-dead ideology from the standpoint of traditional orthodox theology, but these attempts, operating from presuppositionalist or fideist orientations,[104] have had little impact. Paul Holmer of Yale, whose theology falls within the Lutheran spectrum,[105] makes the excellent points that the God-is-dead school has misinterpreted Bonhoeffer, who was no advocate of atheism, and that the theothanatologists have falsely assumed that Christianity can be modified so as to become universally acceptable to modern man while still remaining true to itself. On the latter point he writes: "The Christian idea of God has never been the coin of a very large realm. ... Theology never did have the allegiance of the intelligentsia in the West, nor did the church's other powers extend over the whole of European social life. ... The theologian must understand the world and the people in it, not to make Christianity relevant to them as much as to help them become relevant and amenable to Christianity." [106] But when he moves to a positive defense of the Christian view of God, Holmer vitiates his effectiveness by presuppositionally driving a wedge between theology (which, presumably, could remain true no matter what) and secular knowledge (whose development cannot touch theological truth): "Theology was never so much a matter of evidence that it had to change as the evidence advanced." [107]

Robert E. Fitch of the Pacific School of Religion unmercifully castigates the God-is-dead mentality, arguing that "if there is anything worse than bourgeois religiosity, it is egghead religiosity" and that "this is the Age of the Sell-Out, the Age of the Great Betrayal. We are a new Esau who has sold his spiritual birthright for a secular mess of pottage." [108] Particularly telling is Fitch's case for the permanent and culture-transcending impact of Scripture; he tells of the current wave of interest on the part of East Africans in the first published Swahili translation of *Julius Caesar,* and comments:

> Perhaps some cultural relativist would like to explain how an event in ancient Rome could have meaning almost 1,500 years later in Elizabethan England and how it could now, centuries later, be reborn in meaning in east Africa. What is striking is not just the continuity of meaning in the event but the continuity of expression in Plutarch-North-Shakespeare-Nyerere [the Swahili translator]. Our Bible can do as much. Indeed, it always has done so.[109]

But universal literary impact hardly establishes the cognitive truth of the Bible's claims, and it is the latter that the death-of-God theologians dispute. Moreover, when Fitch opposes existentialistic-experiential thinking with the argument that secular concepts and categories "yield but an erudite darkness until they are illuminated by a vision which sees this world in the light of another world," he does not move beyond the "soft" radical Cox whom he criticizes.[110] Even if Reinhold Niebuhr, with his transcendental perspective on the human predicament, accomplished more than secularist John Dewey[111] (a debatable assumption, in any case), the basic question of the *de facto existence* of the transcendent still remains. The "world seen in light of another world" is an argument subject to infinite regress, and the pragmatic effect of belief in Deity can hardly establish the independent existence of Deity. Fitch appears to operate from a presuppositional orientation which (sound though it may be) leaves death-of-God thinking basically untouched.

Representing fideistic attacks on the theothanatologists, we have Episcopal rector David R. Matlack, who speaks eloquently for most Christian believers: "Even if their assumptions were granted and their logic airtight—and this is far from the case—they would not be touching the real life experiences I believe I have had of God's grace, and the real life experiences other Christians have had."[112] Here the issue is, of course, whether Matlack's "real life experiences" and those of other believers necessarily demand the existence of a transcendent God. Suppose, as philosopher Kai Nielsen has argued in a paper written from van Buren's analytical stance, fideistic claims such as Matlack's "are in reality no claims at all because key religious words and utterances are without intelligible factual content"?[113] How does the orthodox believer (any more than the existentialist) know that his experiential "encounters" require a transcendental explanation?[114] It is the contention of "hard" death-of-God thinking that such "encounters" must be translated into purely human terms to make sense. Attempts by Christian believers to meet this issue—which lies at the very heart of the God-is-dead movement—have thus far fallen wide of the mark.

A Closer Pathological Examination

In endeavoring to strike to the root of the theothanatological problem, we shall focus attention on the theoretical underpinning which van Buren has provided for the movement. Our concern will not center on the metaphorical uses of the God-is-dead formula as employed by the "soft" radicals, since their claims that people have difficulty in believing today and that theological language lacks relevance for modern man simply highlight the perpetual need to preach the gospel more vigorously and communicate its eternal truth more effectively. Likewise, we shall spend little time on the positions of the "hard" radicals Altizer and Hamilton, for, as already noted, these thinkers, in spite of the ostensively atheistic character of their affirmations, do in fact allow for the reintroduction of Deity (Altizer's "God beyond God," Hamilton's "God of delight") at the back door even while ejecting him from the front. Cox is right when he says of Altizer, "he will have to be more precise if he's going to be taken seriously," [115] and the recent television discussion in which Oxford philosopher-theologian Ian Ramsey went to work on Hamilton showed clearly that the same charge of confused ambiguity must be leveled at him.[116] The trenchant character of God-is-dead thinking comes not from these basically emotive outcries but from van Buren's straightforward attempt to show that God-statements are meaningless unless they are translated into Man-statements. What, then, of van Buren's argument?" [117]

First, unlike most theological apponents of the death of God,[118] we readily concede the validity of van Buren's basic epistemological principle, namely, that assertions compatible with anything and everything say nothing. Contemporary analytical philosophy, in arriving at this principle, has made an inestimable contribution to epistemology, for by way of the principle, vast numbers of apparently sensible truth-claims can be readily identified as unverifiable, and time and energy can thereby be saved for intellectual pursuits capable of yielding testable conclusions. We also agree with van Buren that this verification principle[119] should be applied in the religious realm as fully as in other areas, and we find the Flew-Wisdom parable of striking value in illustrating the technical meaningless of numerous

God-claims made in the history of religions and by many religious believers today, including those Protestants addicted to Neo-Orthodoxy, existentialism, and process-philosophy.[120] The God-is-dead issue, however, depends not upon whether non-Christian religions or contemporary Protestant theologians make meaningless assertions about God's existence, but upon whether Biblical Christianity is subject to this criticism. van Buren is thus quite correct to focus attention on the New Testament picture of Jesus, and especially on his Resurrection; but it is exactly here that van Buren's analysis fails—and, ironically, proves itself to suffer from the very analytical nonsensicality it mistakenly sees in Christianity's continued affirmation of a transcendent God.

The New Testament affirmation of the existence of God (the Divine Gardener in the Flew-Wisdom parable) is not a claim standing outside the realm of empirical testability. Quite the contrary: the Gardener *entered* his garden (the world) in the person of Jesus Christ, showing himself to be such "by many infallible proofs" (Acts 1:3). Mascall illustrates with Jesus' miraculous healing of the blind man in John 9, observing that "one can hardly avoid being struck by the vivid impression of eyewitness reporting and by the extremely convincing characterization of the persons involved." [121] To drive the latter point home, Mascall renders the beggar's remarks into cockney, e.g.: "Yesterday I couldn't see a ruddy thing and now I can see orl right. Larf that one orf!" (John 9:25). The Resurrection accounts, as I have argued in detail elsewhere,[122] provide the most decisive evidence of the empirical focus of the Biblical affirmation that "God was in Christ, reconciling the world unto himself." In I Corinthians 15 the Apostle, writing in A.D. 56, explicitly states that the Christian God-claim, grounded in the Resurrection of Christ, is not compatible with anything and everything and therefore meaningless: after listing the names of eyewitnesses who had had contact with the resurrected Christ (and noting that five hundred other people had seen him, most of whom were still alive), Paul says: "If Christ has not been raised, then our preaching is in vain and your faith is in vain."

The early Christians were quite willing to subject their religious beliefs to concrete empirical test. Their faith was not blind faith; it was solidly grounded in empirical facticity.[123]

But, argues van Buren, the New Testament claims only *appear* to be of an empirical nature. When the writers speak of Jesus as God and describe his miracles, "they were saying the most that they could say about this man." The Resurrection accounts are but the final proof of how thoroughly Jesus' liberating personality changed the lives of his disciples; here we see Jesus' followers experiencing what R. M. Hare has called a "blik"—a "discernment situation" in which they place a quite new evaluation on their whole experiential world.

On looking closely at van Buren's superficially plausible interpretation, we discover that, being compatible with anything and everything, it says nothing! Consider: *any* point of evidence cited from the New Testament documents to refute van Buren (e.g., the doubting Thomas episode) will be dismissed by him as simply indicating how *powerful* the "discernment" was for the disciples. The peculiar situation therefore arises that *no* amount of evidence (including Peter's direct statement, "we did not follow cleverly devised myths when we made known to you the power and coming of our Lord Jesus Christ, but we were eyewitnesses of his majesty"!— II Pet. 1:16) could dislodge van Buren from his humanistic reduction of the Biblical narratives.

The meaninglessness of van Buren's approach will become clearer by the use of analogies drawn from nonreligious spheres. Suppose you were to say to me: "Napoleon conquered Europe in a remarkably short time with amazing military resourcefulness, and after suffering defeat and exile, he escaped and came close to overwhelming Europe once again";[124] and I were to reply, "You really are impressed by Napoleon, aren't you?" Obviously irritated, you retort: "Yes, I am impressed by Napoleon, *but* I'm trying to tell you some facts about him, and here are documents to prove what I have just said." Then I would blandly answer: "How wonderful! The very interest you show in marshaling such material shows me how great an impact Napoleon has had on you." Your frustration would be boundless, for no matter what evidence you produced, I could, following van Buren's approach, dismiss it simply as an empirical code representing a non-empirical "blik" situation.

Or suppose I were to say: "My wife studied art history and enjoys painting"; and you commented: "You really love her, don't you?" "Well, yes," I would say, "but she *does* have artistic interests. Here are her transcripts representing art courses she's taken, here are paintings she's done, and. . . ." At which point you interrupt with a sweep of the hand: "Come, come, no need to bother with that; I can recognize true love when I see it! How commendable!" My composure would be retained with great difficulty, since I would find it impossible under the circumstances to get across a genuinely factual point.

In this way van Buren endeavors to "larf orf" the empirical claims of Scripture to the existence of God in Jesus Christ; but his endeavor lands him squarely in the abyss of analytical nonsensicality where he mistakenly tries to place the Biblical witness to the supernatural. Indeed, van Buren is not even being faithful to the Wittgenstein of the *Philosophical Investigations,* whose principles he seeks to follow: for Wittgenstein saw the necessity of respecting the "language game" actually being played and the absurdity of reductionistically trying to say that a given language game really means something else. Wittgenstein asks if it is proper to assert that the sentence "The broom is in the corner" really means "The broomstick is in the corner, and the brush is in the corner, and the broomstick is attached to the brush." He answers:

> If we were to ask anyone if he meant this he would probably say that he had not thought specially of the broomstick or especially of the brush at all. And that would be the *right* answer, for he meant to speak neither of the stick nor of the brush in particular.[125]

By the same token, van Buren's reductionistic trans-

lation of the empirical language game of Biblical in-
carnation-claims into non-cognitive, ethical language is
artificial, unwarranted, and at cross-purposes with the
whole thrust of the Biblical narratives. The same is true
of the literary, urban, eschatological-mystical, and social
reductionisms of scriptural God-assertions carried on
respectively by Vahanian, Cox, Altizer, and Hamilton.
The God proclaimed by the Bible as having entered
the empirical world in Jesus is not dead, though an
obvious attempt has been made to murder him using
the lethal weapon of reductionistic, humanistic bias. But
the murder of God in the interests of Man has always
had consequences exactly the opposite of those anticipated, as our Lord indicated when he said, "Whosoever
will save his life shall lose it: and whosoever will lose
his life for my sake shall find it." It is ironic that the
theothanatologists have not learned from the experience
of Sartre's Goetz: "J'ai tué Dieu parce qu'il me séparait
des hommes et voici que sa mort m'isole encore plus
sûrement." [126]

The Case History Yields a Moral

Why have the God-is-dead theologians so easily run
into this humanistic dead-end? The answer lies in their
starting point, and a sobering moral can be drawn
therefrom. As we pointed out through primary and
secondary sources employed in the early portion of
this paper, every one of the death-of-God thinkers was
profoundly influenced by the dialectic orientation of Neo-
Orthodoxy. Alasdair MacIntyre, in his incisive critique
of Robinson's *Honest to God*, draws the connection between Neo-Orthodoxy and "Christian atheism":

> We can see the harsh dilemma of a would-be contem-
> porary theology. The theologians begin from orthodoxy,
> but the orthodoxy which has learnt from Kierkegaard
> and Barth becomes too easily a closed circle, in which
> believer speaks only to believer, in which all human con-
> tent is concealed. Turning aside from this arid in-group
> theology, the most perceptive theologians wish to translate
> what they have to say to an atheistic world. But they are
> doomed to one of two failures. Either they succeed in their
> translation: in which case what they find themselves say-
> ing has been transformed into the atheism of their hearers.

Or they fail in their translation: in which case no one
hears what they have to say but themselves.[127]

And why does the Kierkegaardian-Barthian theology
operate as a "closed circle"? Because of its basic premise that, as MacIntyre well puts it, "the Word of God cannot be identified with *any* frail human attempt to comprehend it." [128] Since the logical consequences of such
a principle are a fallible Scripture and a kenotically
limited Jesus, the Bible appears to secular man as no
different qualitatively from other human writings, and
the Incarnate Christ becomes indistinguishable from other
men. The believer thus moves in a closed circle of irrational commitment, which the unbeliever finds impossible to accept. The God of such an irrational faith has
no recourse but to become a transcendent Wholly Other,
and when analytical philosophy poses the obvious verification question as to the ontological existence of the
transcendent, no answer is possible. In the Flew-Wisdom
parable, the Gardener-God of Neo-Orthodoxy *cannot* be
discovered empirically in the garden, for his transcendence would thereby be profaned;[129] thus the garden
of the world looks as secular to the believer as to the
unbeliever, and the latter rightly asks: "Just how does
what you call an invisible, intangible, eternally elusive
gardener differ from an imaginary gardener or even
from no gardener at all?" To this, the "yes-and-no"
dialectic of Neo-Orthodoxy can say nothing whatever;
and the obvious result is the death of God. For contemporary theological thought, the Bible would be no more
erroneous if there were no God; the Resurrection of Christ
in Barth's theology would be no more unverifiable if God
did not exist; and Tillich's "Protestant principle" would
make Jesus no more kenotic if there were no "Ground
of all being." The God-assertions of mainline theology
in the twentieth century are compatible with anything
and everything, and therefore can be dispensed with as
meaningless. God dies, and only modern secular man is
left.[130]

This appalling situation—what Fitch calls the theological Sell-Out—is the direct result of a refusal to

acknowledge God's power to reveal himself without qualification here on earth. The ancient Calvinist aphorism, *finitum non capax infiniti*, has been allowed to obscure the central Biblical stress on God's incarnation and on his ability to speak the Word of truth through human words. The Bible does not present God as Rudolf Otto's transcendent, vague Wholly Other or as Tillich's indescribable Being itself, but as the God of Abraham, Isaac, and Jacob, who through the entire expanse of scriptural revelation speaks inerrant truth to men and who manifestly enters the garden of this world in Jesus Christ (cf. John 20:15). For orthodox Christianity, unafraid of a miraculous Saviour or of an inerrant Scripture, God's existence does make a difference in the world, for only on the basis of his existence is revelation explainable. Mainline Protestant theology, having lost its doctrine of revelation and inspiration in the days of liberalism and never having recovered it, now finds itself incapable of showing why God is necessary at all.

The moral, then, is simply this: Physicians of the soul will inevitably find themselves faced with the corpse of Deity if they lose their confidence in God's special revelation. The final and best evidence of God's existence lies in his Word—in the triple sense of Christ, the gospel he proclaimed, and the Scripture that infallibly conveys it. The historicity of the Resurrection, the facticity of the Biblical miracles, the internal consistency of Holy Writ and its freedom from empirical error: these must be sustained, or the God of Scripture will face away into a misty transcendence for us, too, and eventually disappear. Conversely, if we do maintain the doctrine of God's *historische* revelation through an inerrant Bible, we will find that, in an age of almost universal theological debility, we will be able to present a meaningful God to an epoch that desperately needs divine grace. The only living God is the God of the Bible, and for the sake of secular man today we had better not forget it.

Final Autopsy: A Mistaken Identity Revealed

The God-is-dead movement is a reflection and special

case of an abnormal preoccupation with Death in our time. On the popular level we have sick comedies such as *The Loved One;* on the sociological level, analyses such as *The American Way of Death;* on the psychological level, the wide acceptance of Freud's theme of the *mortido;* and on the plane of theoretical analysis revealing works such as Feifel's anthology *The Meaning of Death,* containing essays by Jung, Tillich, Kaufmann, and many others.[131]

It is interesting to note other eras when death was an overarching concern. Huizinga, in his classic *The Waning of the Middle Ages* notes how "the vision of death" embraced late medieval man, and how the dance of death, the surrealistic horrors of Hieronymous Bosch's depictions of hell, and the satanic black masses blended into a symbolic projection of a collapsing culture. Fin-de-siècle France is another illustration of the same phenomenon: J.-K. Huysmans' description in his novel *A Rebours* of a "funeral feast" in which the orchestra played dirges while guests, dressed in black, silently ate dark foods served by negresses was no less based on fact than his accounts of satanic rites in *La-Bàs;* the Parisian society of the 1880's and 1890's, living in the wake of the Franco-Prussian War, had fallen into degeneration and corruption, and the preoccupation with death and hell was the cultural equivalent of psychological sublimation.

Today's death-of-God thinking is likewise symbolic. Holy Scripture speaks of death also, but it is *man's* death upon which the Bible dwells: "The wages of sin is death, but the gift of God is eternal life through Jesus Christ our Lord" (Rom. 6:23). Scripture finds the human race, not God, in the throes of death. And when God does die, it is on the Cross, as an expiation for man's mortal disease; and God's conquest of the powers of death is evidenced in his Resurrection triumph.[132]

"The sting of death is sin," however, and from Adam on the sinner has sought above all to hide himself. Thus in our day men unwilling to face their own mortality have projected their own deserved demise upon their Maker and Redeemer. As suggested at the beginning of this essay, the theothanatological movement could provide a mystery writer with a classic case of the "wrong corpse": for when one examines the body carefully, it turns out to be, not God but *oneself*—"dead in trespasses and sins." And *this* corpse (unlike that of Deity) fully satisfied the empirical test of verifiability, as every cemetery illustrates.[133]

In romantic literature, the *Doppelgänger* motif (a character meeting himself) is employed as a device to symbolize the individual's attainment of self-awareness. Let us hope that the present autopsy, insofar as it brings a sin-sick theology to a realistic confrontation with itself, may contribute to such self-knowledge.[134] How revealing it is, for example to read William Hamilton's autobiographical description of his entrée into the death-of-God sphere at age forty: "Time was getting short and I saw I needed to make things happen." [135] When we realize the true identity of the theothanatological corpse, such a remark fits into place. It is the natural man, the builder of towers of Babel, who must "make things happen" theologically. For the essence of the scriptural gospel is that sinful man cannot make things happen in the spiritual life; the living God has made them happen in Jesus Christ, and the only true theology endeavors, above all, to remain faithful to the one who "after he had offered one sacrifice for sins for ever, sat down on the right hand of God."

And if, as Christian believers, the silence of God in our age sometimes makes us wonder in the depth of our souls if he still remains with us, let us soberly consider Sir Robert Anderson's profound observation that God's silence is a reminder that the amnesty of the Cross is still available to men: "A silent Heaven gives continuing proof that this great amnesty is still in force, and that the guiltiest of men may turn to God and find forgiveness of sins and eternal life." [136] The task then stands: to work while it is yet day, for the night cometh when no man can work. As for the nature of that work, Henry van Dyke described it well in his touching allegory *The Lost Word;* it is to proclaim to our generation the Word which has been lost through preoccupation with lesser words:

"My son, you have sinned deeper than you know. The word with which you parted so lightly is the key-word of all life and joy and peace. Without it the world has no meaning, and existence no rest, and death no refuge. It is the word that purifies love, and comforts grief, and keeps hope alive forever. It is the most precious thing that ever ear has heard, or mind has known, or heart has conceived. It is the name of Him who has given us life and breath and all things richly to enjoy; the name of Him who, though we may forget Him, never forgets us; the the name of Him who pities us as you pity your suffering child; the name of Him who, though we wander far from Him, seeks us in the wilderness, and sent His Son, even as His Son has sent me this night, to breathe again that forgotten name in the heart that is perishing without it. Listen, my son, listen with all your soul to the blessed name of God our Father." [137]

Notes

[1] We prefer the neutral term "Theothanatology" to J. Robert Nelson's "Theothanasia" (implying that the new theologians have put God to death; except for Altizer, who speaks, à la Nietzsche, of "passionately willing God's death," the death-of-God theologians regard the divine demise as a "natural" phenomenon of our time, over which one has little or no control) or "Theothanatopsis" (which conjures up the shade of William Cullen Bryant, who would have been horror-struck at this whole movement). For theothanatological bibliography, see William Hamilton's "selected list of works pertaining to the radical development in theology," in Altizer and Hamilton's *Radical Theology and the Death of God* (Indianapolis: Bobbs-Merrill, 1966), pp. 193-202; Glenn R. Wittig, "The Radical Theologians—A Bibliography," *Encounter* (Indianapolis), XXVII (Autumn, 1966), 299-316; and the "Selected Bibliography" appended to Altizer's *Toward a New Christianity: Readings in the Death of God Theology* (New York: Harcourt, Brace & World, 1967), pp. 365-74.

[2] *Time* initially described the movement in the Religion section of its October 22, 1965, issue; the Easter Cover Story in the April 8, 1966, issue deals with the question of God's existence in light of current death-of-God thinking. For *The New Yorker*'s valuable account of theothanatology in the contemporary theological scene, see note 12 below.

[3] Mack B. Stokes, "The Nontheistic Temper of the Modern Mind," *Religion in Life*, XXXIV (Spring, 1965), 245-57.

    [4] Carl F. H. Henry, *Frontiers in Modern Theology* (Chicago: Moody Press, 1966), especially pp. 33, 101, 149-50. Cf. Henry's articles, "A Reply to the God-Is-Dead Mavericks," *Christianity Today*, X (May 27, 1966), 893-97 (published in a shorter version in the June, 1966 issue of *Pageant*), and "Where Is Modern Theology Going?" *Christianity Today*, XII (March 1, 1968), 527-31.
    [5] "Why This Non-God-Talk? An Editorial," *The Christian Century*, LXXXII (December 1, 1965), 1467.
    [6] William Hamilton, "The Shape of a Radical Theology," *The Christian Century*, LXXXII (October 6, 1965), 1220. Paul van Buren, however, "expressed astonishment at Hamilton's announcement that there would soon be an organization of death-to-God theologians, with a new journal, etc., etc. Apparently there is less communication within this trinity [Altizer, Hamilton, van Buren] than is assumed" (J. Robert Nelson, "Deicide, Theothanasia, or What Do You Mean?" *The Christian Century*, LXXXII [November 17, 1965], 1415). In a later issue of *Christian Century* (LXXXIII [February 16, 1966], 223), "Penultimate" provided a satirical application blank for the "God-Is-Dead Club."
    [7] E.g., in his book, *The New Essence of Christianity* (New York: Association Press, 1961).
    [8] He continues: "One cannot deny that he left the cloister, had some doubts, stomach aches and a father. At the same time it is equally evident that he was a highly theocentric thinker ('Nothing can be more present . . . than God himself'), and that he was also what Weber and Troeltsch call an ascetic of the 'intramundane' type whose hope was in the world above—which, I take it, is not quite 'the world.' But of course Luther's asceticism and theocentrism should never keep him from being used in Protestantism as a symbol for secular theology and the God-is-dead movement. After all, Protestant theologians have a long and glorious tradition of using history, shall we say, 'freely' " (Charles M. Nielsen, "The Loneliness of Protestantism, or, More Benedictines, Please!" *The Christian Century*, LXXXII [September 15, 1965], 1121).
    [9] Cf. Montgomery, "Lutheran Hermeneutics and Hermeneutics Today," in *Aspects of Biblical Hermeneutics* ("Concordia Theological Monthly. Occasional Papers," No. 1; St. Louis, Missouri; 1966), pp. 78-108 (reprinted in Montgomery, *Crisis in Lutheran Theology* [2 vols.; Grand Rapids, Michigan: Baker Book House, 1967], I, 45-77, and in Montgomery, *In Defense of Martin Luther* [Milwaukee: Northwestern, 1970]).
    [10] Quoted in *Time's* report of the seventeenth Annual Meeting of the Evangelical Theological Society in Nashville, Tennessee, December 27-29, 1965 (*Time*, January 7, 1966, p. 70).
    [11] Cox's informal paper was titled "Second Thoughts on the Secular Society" and was delivered at the Seabury-Western Theological Seminary on January 22, 1966; further reference to this paper will be made below. I was privileged to attend the Annual Meeting of the American Society of Christian Ethics as Carl F. H. Henry's surrogate; my report of the sessions appears in *Christianity Today*, X (February 18, 1966), 538.
    [12] Quoted in an interview with Ved Mehta, "The New Theologian.

I. Ecce Homo," *The New Yorker,* XLI (November 13, 1965), 144.

[13] See especially Hamilton's "The Death of God Theology," *The Christian Scholar,* XLVIII (Spring, 1965), 27-48. (This essay has been reprinted in Altizer and Hamilton, *Radical Theology and the Death of God* [*op. cit.* in n. 1], pp. 22-50, but citations to it in the present work will follow the original pagination in *The Christian Scholar.*)

[14] Cox made this point in his unpublished lecture, "Second Thoughts on the Secular Society" (see note 11 above).

[15] Hamilton, "The Shape of a Radical Theology," *loc. cit.* The "hard" radicals have had hard things to say about their "soft" counterparts, e.g.: "Dr. Altizer considers Harvey Cox a 'phony masquerading as a member of the avantgarde,' a sociologist in theologian's clothing. Dr. Hamilton of Colgate Rochester describes *The Secular City* as pop-Barth' . . . 'Dr. Cox will keep neo-orthodoxy alive another six months,' he scoffs" (Lee E. Dirks, "The Ferment in Protestant Thinking," *The National Observer,* January 31, 1966, p. 16).

[16] Cf. his article, "Sociology of Religion in a Post-Religious Era," *The Christian Scholar,* XLVIII (Spring, 1965), 9-26.

[17] So Cox stated in his paper, "Second Thoughts on the Secular Society" (see note 11 above).

[18] Hamilton, "The Death of God Theology," pp. 32, 34.

[19] *Ibid.*, p. 34.

[20] Nelson, "Decide, Theothanasia, or What Do You Mean?" *loc. cit.*

[21] Mehta, *op. cit.,* p. 138. Gilkey of Chicago, a critic of the movement, has endeavored to compile a book of essays on the new Christian Radicalism, but Vahanian was not included among the prospective contributors. Vahanian's relative (neo-Barthian) conservativism is demonstrated in his recent article, "Swallowed Up by Godlessness" *(The Christian Century,* LXXXII [December 8, 1965], 1506), where he argues that the radical death-of-God view "not only surrenders to the secularism of our time but views it as the remedy instead of the sickness."

[22] Vahanian, *The Death of God: The Culture of Our Post-Christian Era* (New York: George Braziller, 1961), p. 228.

[23] Vahanian, *Wait Without Idols* (New York: George Braziller, 1964), pp. 31-32. Several essays in this book have been published in less complete form in journals, e.g., "The Future of Christianity in a Post-Christian Era," *The Centennial Review,* VIII (Spring, 1964), 160-73; "Beyond the Death of God: The Need of Cultural Revolution," *Dialog,* I (Autumn, 1962), 18-21.

[24] Tillich described this phenomenon as the substitution of non-ultimate concerns for the only true ultimate concern, Being itself; Voegelin refers to such idolatry as "Metastatic Gnosis" (see Montgomery, *The Shape of the Past: An Introduction to Philosophical Historiography* ["History in Christian Perspective," Vol. 1; Ann Arbor, Michigan: Edwards Bros., 1963], pp. 127-38).

[25] Vahanian, *Wait Without Idols,* p. 233.

[26] Vahanian, "The Empty Cradle," *Theology Today,* XIII (January, 1957), 526.

[27] Vahanian, *The Death of God*, p. 231.

[28] Vahanian, *Wait Without Idols*, p. 231.

[29] *Ibid.*, p. 46.

[30] Quoted in Mehta, *loc. cit.*

[31] Harvey Cox, *The Secular City: Secularization and Urbanization in Theological Perspective* (New York: Macmillan Paperbacks, 1965), p. 20. In his paper at the American Society of Christian Ethics (see note 11 above), Cox stated that a revised, hardbound edition of his book will soon appear, and that this second edition will become the basis of several translations in European languages.

[32] *Ibid.*, p. 261. Wilder's statement appears in his essay, "Art and Theological Meaning," *The New Orpheus* (New York: Sheed and Ward, 1964), p. 407.

[33] Cox, *The Secular City*, p. 266.

[34] *Ibid.*, p. 258.

[35] *Ibid.*

[36] See note 11 above and corresponding text. Cf. Cox's article, "The Place and Purpose of Theology" (*The Christian Century*, LXXXIII [January 5, 1966], 7), where he hits the "hard" death-of-God Radicals for missing the prophetic challenge of the modern revolutionary polis: "Rather than helping the prophets greet a religionless, revolutionary tomorrow, some theologians are more interested in dissecting the cadaver of yesterday's pieties."

[37] Not so incidentally, Cox approvingly quoted his Harvard acquaintances Krister Stendahl ("you can only have Neo-Orthodoxy after a good long period of liberalism") and Erik Erikson, author of the psychoanalytic study, *Young Man Luther*, whose view of the "identity crisis" makes Stendahl's point in psychological terms.

[38] Altizer, *Mircea Eliade and the Dialectic of the Sacred* (Philadelphia: Westminster Press, 1963); the book grew out of an article, "Mircea Eliade and the Recovery of the Sacred," *The Christian Scholar*, XLV (Winter, 1962), 267-89. As Hamilton notes, Altizer's book is a mixture of Eliade's views and Altizer's and therefore is "not structurally satisfactory" ("The Death of God Theology," p. 31).

[39] *Ibid.*, p. 32.

[40] Altizer, *Oriental Mysticism and Biblical Eschatology* (Philadelphia: Westminster Press, 1961). Some of the material in this book has been incorporated into Altizer's essay, "The Religious Meaning of Myth and Symbol," published in *Truth, Myth, and Symbol*, ed. Altizer, et al. (Englewood Cliffs, N.J.: Prentice-Hall, 1962), pp. 87-108.

[41] Like Toynbee, Altizer places Christianity and Mahayana Buddhism on the religious pinnacle together. Altizer's dependence on Toynbee would be a subject worth investigating.

[42] Altizer, "Nirvana and the Kingdom of God," in *New Theology No. 1*, ed. Martin E. Marty and Dean G. Peerman (New York: Macmillan Paperbacks, 1964), p. 164. This essay first appeared in the University of Chicago's *Journal of Religion*, April, 1963.

[43] Altizer, "Theology and the Death of God," *The Centennial Review*, VIII, (Spring, 1964), 130 (reprinted in Altizer and Hamilton, *Radical Theology and the Death of God* [*op. cit.* in n. 1], pp. 94-

111). It is interesting to speculate whether Jaroslav Pelikan is fully aware of the consequences of his attempts theologically to baptize Kierkegaard (*From Luther to Kierkegaard*) and Nietzsche (*Fools for Christ*).

44 Cf. Altizer, "Word and History," *Theology Today*, XXII (October, 1965), 385. The degree of current popular interest in Altizer's radicalism is indicated by the fact that the *Chicago Daily News* adapted this article for publication in its Panorama section (January 29, 1966, p. 4). The original has been reprinted in Altizer and Hamilton's *Radical Theology and the Death of God* (*op. cit.* in n. 1), pp. 120-39.

45 Altizer, review of *Christianity and the Encounter of the World Religions* by Paul Tillich, *The Christian Scholar*, XLVI (Winter, 1963), 362. Altizer and Hamilton dedicate their joint work, *Radical Theology and the Death of God*, "in memory of Paul Tillich."

46 Altizer, "Theology and the Death of God," p. 132.

47 *Ibid.* On Nietzsche vis-à-vis current thought, see the excellent article by Erich Heller, "The Importance of Nietzsche," *Encounter* (London), XXII (April, 1964), 59-66.

48 Altizer made this point in a keynote speech at a recent conference at Emory University on "America and the Future of Technology"; it was reported in *Christianity Today*, X (December 17, 1965), 1310 (cf. Altizer's letter to the Editor. commending this report: *Christianity Today*, X [May 27, 1966], 884). For Altizer's significant dependence on the theosophical visionary Blake, who, in the words of one critic, "spurns reason as well as nature and lives solely in the realm of imagination" and whose religion was "a religion of art," see Altizer's essay, "William Blake and the Role of Myth in the Radical Christian Vision," in Altizer and Hamilton, *Radical Theology and the Death of God* (*op. cit.* in n. 1), pp. 170-91. Altizer says of this essay, "Somehow I love this piece more than any other article I have published, perhaps because of my love for Blake, but thus far its readers have reacted either with silence or with a mute but somehow meaningful[!]affirmation."

49 Altizer, "Theology and the Death of God," p. 134.

50 Altizer, "The Religious Meaning of Myth and Symbol," p. 95. For a full-orbed presentation of Altizer's "Christology," see his latest work, *The Gospel of Christian Atheism* (Philadelphia: Westminster Press, 1966), especially pp. 132ff. Significantly, Altizer states that "the primary sources of this book are the writings of Blake, Hegel, and Nietzsche" (p. 29); the Bible is conspicuous by its absence from the list. Robert McAfee Brown evaluated the work as follows: "It is not a gospel . . .; it is not Christian . . .; and it is not atheism. . . . In an attempt to celebrate 'the death of God,' this book succeeds only in demonstrating the death of the 'death-of-God-theology.' "

51 Altizer, "The Religious Meaning of Myth and Symbol," *loc. cit.*

52 Quoted in a symposium-interview in *Christianity Today*, X (January 7, 1966), 374.

53 *Ibid.* The expression, "third age of the Spirit," comes from the twelfth century mystic-millennial theologian Joachim of Floris (see Montgomery, *The Shape of the Past*, p. 48). Altizer continually opts for

"the present" and for "openness to the future" stating flatly: "Of course, dialectical faith, whether in its Eastern or its Western, its mystical or its eschatological form, negates history" ("America and the Future of Technology," in Altizer and Hamilton, *Radical Theology and the Death of God* [*op. cit.* in n. 1], p. 20). As in Cox, so in Altizer we find a definite tone of anabaptist enthusiasm, with concomitant substitution of present experience and future expectation for the concrete reality of historical revelation.

[54] Altizer, "Creative Negation in Theology," *Christian Century*, LXXXII (July, 1965), 866-67. The strong influence of Hegel on Altizer is clear from such passages; Altizer accepts the (utterly unverifiable) contention of Hegelian idealistic philosophy that the Spirit, having "incarnated" itself with Jesus, thereafter works immanently in mankind. For further discussion and critique of this point, see the following essay, where Altizer's position is subjected to detailed refutation.

[55] Hamilton, "The Shape of a Radical Theology," *loc. cit.*, 1219-20. Apparently Hamilton just made it in time, for Altizer is of the opinion that "the real barrier to this kind of thinking is mainly age, because most of those under 45 do respond to it" (*Chicago Daily News*, January 29, 1966, *loc. cit*).

[56] Hamilton, *The New Essence of Christianity*, p. 55.

[57] *Ibid.*, p. 116.

[58] *Ibid.*, pp. 93-94.

[59] Nelson, "Deicide, Theothanasia, or What Do You Mean?" *loc. cit.*

[60] Hamilton, "Daring To Be the Enemy of God," *The Christian Scholar*, XLVI (Spring, 1963), 40-54; Barth's lavish appreciation of Mozart is well known. Cf. also Hamilton's earlier (1959) article, "Banished from the Land of Unity" (reprinted in Altizer and Hamilton's *Radical Theology and the Death of God* [*op. cit.* in n. 1], pp. 52-84); of it he writes today (1966): "The immersion in Dostoevsky that this essay required was the decisive influence in my transition from the neo-orthodox to the radical mode of theological thinking."

[61] Hamilton, "The Shape of a Radical Theology," p. 1220.

[62] Hamilton, "Thursday's Child: The Theologian Today and Tomorrow," *Theology Today*, XX (January, 1964), 489, 494. This essay has been reprinted in Altizer and Hamilton's *Radical Theology and the Death of God* (*op. cit.* in n. 1), pp. 86-93.

[63] Mehta, *op. cit.*, p. 142.

[64] Hamilton, "The Shape of a Radical Theology," p. 1219.

[65] Cf. the following lines in "Thursday's Child": "The theologian is sometimes inclined to suspect that Jesus Christ is best understood not as either the object or ground of faith, and not as person, event, or community, but simply as a place to be, a standpoint. That place is, of course, alongside the neighbor, being for him. This may be the meaning of Jesus' true humanity, and it may even be the meaning of his divinity, and thus of divinity itself" (p. 494).

[66] Hamilton, "The Death of God Theology," pp. 27-48.

[67] *Ibid.*, pp. 46-47. Though both Hamilton and Altizer connect the

death of God with a totally kenotic Jesus, Hamilton focuses attention on the modern awareness of God's incarnational replacement by man (thus locating God's decease in the anthropocentric nineteenth century), while Altizer stresses the original proclamation of God-becoming-man in Christ as establishing the "time" of the divine demise. They are in agreement, however, that "the nineteenth century is to radical theology what the sixteenth century was to Protestant neo-orthodoxy" and that "radical theology must finally understand the Incarnation itself as effecting the death of God" (Altizer and Hamilton, *Radical Theology and the Death of God* [op. cit. in n. 1], p. xii).

[68] Hamilton, "The Death of God Theology," p. 40.

[69] *Ibid.*, p. 41. Hamilton's subsequent loss of hope in a "God of delight" and his movement to an unqualified humanistic secularism are analyzed and critized below in "The Death of God Becomes More Deadly."

[70] Interestingly, while Hamilton was still in theological limbo, he wrote an article on Hamlet, finding portrayed there the death of a demonic idea of God: "Hamlet and Providence," *The Christian Scholar*, XLVII (Fall, 1964), 193-207.

[71] Hamilton, "The Death of God Theology," p. 46. On the motif of optimistic secularity in Hamilton's thought, see his essay, "The New Optimism—from Prufrock to Ringo," in Altizer and Hamilton, *Radical Theology and the Death of God* (op. cit. in n. 1), pp. 156-69.

[72] Quoted in an interview with Mehta, *op. cit.* (in note 2 above), p. 150. Since the above paragraph was written, prayer has become a thing of the past for Hamilton too; see below, "The Death of God Becomes More Deadly."

[73] Van Buren's thesis dealt with Calvin: *Christ in Our Place: The Substitutionary Character of Calvin's Doctrine of Reconciliation* (Grand Rapids, Michigan: Eerdmans, 1957).

[74] Van Buren, "Theology in the Context of Culture," *The Christian Century*, LXXXII (April 7, 1965), 429.

[75] *Ibid.*

[76] Interview with Mehta, *op. cit.*, p. 143.

[77] Antony Flew, "Theology and Falsification," in *New Essays in Philosophical Theology*, ed. Antony Flew and Alasdair MacIntyre (London: SCM Press, 1955), p. 96.

[78] Van Buren, "The Dissolution of the Absolute," *Religion in Life*, XXXIV (Summer, 1965), 334-42.

[79] Interview with Mehta, *op. cit.*, p. 153.

[80] *Ibid.*, p. 148.

[81] Van Buren, *The Secular Meaning of the Gospel*, p. 200.

[82] *Ibid.*, p. 134.

[83] *Ibid.*, p. 198. Parenthetically, it is worth noting that van Buren's argument is no more valid in reference to alchemy than it is in regard to theology; see Montgomery, "Cross, Constellation, and Crucible: Lutheran Astrology and Alchemy in the Age of the Reformation," *Transactions of the Royal Society of Canada*, 4th ser., I (1963), 251-70 (also published in the British periodical *Ambix, the Journal of the Society for the Study of Alchemy and Early Chemistry*, XI [June, 1963].

116   THE SUICIDE OF CHRISTIAN THEOLOGY

65-86, in French in *Revue d'Histoire et de Philosophie Religieuses*, [1966], 323-45 and in *In Defense of Martin Luther* [*op. cit.* in n. 9]).

⁵⁴ Van Buren, "Theology in the Context of Culture," p. 430.

⁵⁵ Reference will be made to Mascall's book in the next section. Any attempt to show the connections between the God-is-dead movement and the popular British radicalism represented by Robinson, Alec Vidler, et al., would carry us too far afield; see on the latter my article, "Vidler at Strasbourg," *Christianity Today*, XI (May 26, 1967), 886-87 (II. A. 2 below), and my critiques of Bishop Pike's theology in *The Sunday School Times*, CVIII, No. 18 (April 30, 1966), 311-12, 317; and No. 19 (May 7, 1966), 327-28, 343 (I. 2 above), and in *Christianity Today*, XII (February 16, 1968), 534. Warning should perhaps be given that Austin Farrer's book, *God Is Not Dead* (New York: Morehouse Barlow, 1966), does not in fact treat the God-is-dead movement; its original (British) title (*A Science of God*) was changed to capitalize on the present theothanatological stir in America.

⁵⁶ Nielsen, "The Loneliness of Protestantism," *loc. cit.*

⁵⁷ Moulton, "Apocalypse in a Casket?" *The Christian Century*, LXXXII (November 17, 1965), 1413. The false optimism of death-of-God thinking is hit particularly hard by W. M. Alexander ("Death of God or God of Death?" *The Christian Century*, LXXXIII [March 23, 1966], 363-65): he correctly observes that this optimism reflects a naive and demonic confusion of the progressivistic, perfectionistic American dream with ultimate theological truth; "Christian atheism" is thus *insufficiently* radical, for it avoids proclaiming to our cultural epoch the radically prophetic judgment that "the wages of sin is death."

⁵⁸ Shiner, "Goodbye, Death-of-God!" *The Christian Century*, LXXXII (November 17, 1965), 1418.

⁵⁹ Van Buren, "Theology in the Context of Culture," *loc. cit.*

⁶⁰ Best known for his useful survey, *Twentieth-Century Religious Thought* (London: SCM Press, 1963), which concludes with a treatment of "Existentialism and Ontology" (pp. 351 ff.); Macquarrie explicitly identifies his own position with "those philosophies of existence and being that have been developed by Martin Heidegger and other thinkers" and theologically with "the related work of men like Bultmann and Tillich" (p. 374).

⁶¹ Macquarrie, "How Can We Think of God?" *Theology Today*, XXII (July, 1965), 200-201; reprinted in *New Theology No. 3*, ed. Martin E. Marty and Dean G. Peerman (New York: Macmillan Paperbacks, 1966), pp. 40-52.

⁶² Stokes, "The Nontheistic Temper of the Modern Mind," *loc. cit.*

⁶³ Philadelphia: Westminster Press, 1962.

⁶⁴ Cobb, "From Crisis Theology to the Post-Modern World," *The Centennial Review*, VIII (Spring, 1964), 184-85. Cf. Cobb, *A Christian Natural Theology, Based on the Thought of Alfred North Whitehead* (Philadelphia: Westminster Press, 1965), *passim*.

⁶⁵ Meland, "Alternative to Absolutes," *Religion in Life*, XXXIV (Summer, 1965), 346. For further explications of process thinking in current theology, see Schubert M. Ogden, "Faith and Truth," *The Christian Century*, LXXXII (September 1, 1965), 1057-60; Norman Pittenger, "A Contemporary Trend in North American Theology:

Process-Thought and Christian Faith," *Religion in Life,* XXXIV (Autumn, 1965), 500-510; and Gene Reeves, "A Look at Contemporary American Theology," *ibid.,* pp. 511-25 (Reeves employs—with some qualification—the rubric "Christless theology" for process thinking).

[96] Gilkey, "Is God Dead?" *The Voice: Bulletin of Crozer Theological Seminary,* LVII (January, 1965), 4.

[97] Gilkey, "God Is NOT Dead," *ibid.,* pp. 9-10. That Gilkey's approach to revelation is neither that of Reformation orthodoxy (which regard the Bible as God's inerrant word) nor that of classic Neo-Orthodoxy which took Scripture, though regarded as errant, as its theological *point de départ*), becomes clear when he writes: "Our theological analysis must begin with man. If we felt sure that the divine word in Scripture was the truth, then the Bible might be our starting point" (Gilkey, "Dissolution and Reconstruction in Theology," *The Christian Century,* LXXXII [February 3, 1965], 137). But in finding his answers to the human predicament in the revelation of an unconditioned, transcendent God, Gilkey places himself in the general stream of Neo-Orthodoxy. For the latest word on Gilkey's "steadily maturing and often revised viewpoint" which grew from his "death of God" writings, see his *Naming the Whirlwind: The Renewal of God Language* (Indianapolis: Bobbs-Merrill, 1969).

[98] Gilkey, "God Is NOT Dead," p. 11.

[99] Van Buren, "The Dissolution of the Absolute," *op. cit.,* pp. 338-39.

[100] Cf. Paul Edwards, "Professor Tillich's Confusions," *Mind,* LXXIV (April, 1965), 192-214; and note the pertinence of Quine's remarks at the beginning of his essay, "On What There Is": "A curious thing about the ontological problem is its simplicity. It can be put in three Anglo-Saxon monosyllables: 'What is there?' It can be answered, moreover, in a word—'Everything' [or 'Being itself'!]—and everyone will accept this answer as true. However, this is merely to say that there is what there is. There remains room for disagreement over cases [e.g., the existence of the transcendent God of the Bible!]" (Willard van Orman Quine, *From a Logical Point of View* [2d ed.; New York: Harper Torchbooks, 1963], p. 1). Reference is also in order to the refutations of Hartshorne's ontological argument for God's existence; see *The Ontological Argument,* ed. Alvin Plantinga (Garden City, New York: Doubleday Anchor Books, 1965), especially pp. 123-80.

[101] See William James, *The Varieties of Religious Experience, passim;* and cf. *William James on Psychical Research,* ed. Gardner Murphy and Robert O. Ballou (New York: Viking Press, 1960), *passim.* Note also my "Critique of William James' *Varieties of Religious Experience,"* in my *Shape of the Past, op. cit.,* pp. 312-40.

[102] Cf. Brand Blanshard, "Critical Reflections on Karl Barth," in *Faith and the Philosophers,* ed. John Hick (New York: St. Martin's Press, 1964), pp. 159-200 (other papers in this symposium volume are also relevant to the issue); and C. B. Martin, "A Religious Way of Knowing," in *New Essays in Philosophical Theology (op. cit.,* in n. 77), pp. 76-95.

[103] This point is well made by the psychoanalyst in A. N. Prior's clever dialog, "Can Religion Be Discussed?" *(ibid.,* pp. 1-11).

[104] I have endeavored to show the fallacies of the presuppositionalist and fideist viewpoints in reference to Christian apologetics; see my articles, "The Place of Reason," *His*, XXVI (February, 1966), 8-12; (March, 1966), 13-16, 21.

[105] Cf. his book, *Theology and the Scientific Study of Religion* ("The Lutheran Studies Series," Vol. 2; Minneapolis: T. S. Denison, 1961).

[106] Holmer, "Contra the New Theologies," *The Christian Century*, LXXXII (March 17, 1965), 330-31. For Hamilton's (highly questionable) interpretation of Bonhoeffer as radical theologian, see Altizer and Hamilton, *Radical Theology and the Death of God* (*op. cit.* in n. 1), pp. 112-18.

[107] Holmer, "Contra the New Theologies," p. 332. Note also in this connection Holmer's article, "Atheism and Theism," *Lutheran World*, XIII (1966), 14-25.

[108] Fitch, "The Sell-Out, or the Well Acculturated Christian," *The Christian Century*, LXXXIII (February 16, 1966), 202.

[109] *Ibid.*, p. 203.

[110] See my text at note 37 above.

[111] So argues Fitch, *loc.cit.* in n. 15).

[112] Quoted in Dirks, *loc.cit.*

[113] Nielsen, "Can Faith Validate God-Talk?" in *New Theology No. 1* (*op. cit.* in n. 42), p. 147. This penetrating essay first appeared in the July, 1963 issue of *Theology Today*.

[114] Cf. Frederick Ferré, *Language, Logic and God* (New York: Harper & Row, 1961), chap. viii ("The Logic of Encounter"), pp. 94-104.

[115] Quoted in Dirks, *loc. cit.* Among the more blatant imprecisions in Altizer's thought are: (1) his highly debatable assumption that negation is the ideal way to fulfillment (does one, for example, create the best society or government by completely destroying the existing order and starting over, or by refining what already exists?); (2) his unbelievably naive and unrealistic identification of the basic doctrines of Christianity with those of Buddhism (on this, cf. my article, "The Christian Church in McNeill's *Rise of the West*: An Overview and Critique," *The Evangelical Quarterly*, XXXVIII [October-December, 1966], 197-218, reprinted in Montgomery, *Where Is History Going?* [Grand Rapids, Michigan: Zondervan, 1969], pp. 75-99); and (3) the utterly unverifiable, indescribable character of his "God beyond God" and of his nonobjective, fully kenotic Christ—the "Jesus of the third age of the Spirit" (is he not the Jesus of *Altizer's* spirit? certainly he is not the biblical Jesus, who is "the same yesterday, today, and forever"!).

[116] The discussion took place on Norman Ross's program, "Off the Cuff," Monday, March 28, 1965, beginning at 12:30 a.m. (channel 7, Chicago).

[117] For van Buren's position, see above the text at notes 72-84.

[118] E.g., M. C. D'Arcy, *No Absent God* ("Religious Perspectives," Vol. 6; New York: Harper & Row, 1962), chap. i, pp. 15-31; and Eric Mascall, *The Secularisation of Christianity: An Analysis and a Critique* (London: Darton, Longman & Todd, 1965), pp. 103-104. Other problems with Mascall's (nonetheless valuable) book are its strongly Anglo-

Catholic perspective (stress on natural theology, the visible church introduced as a kind of *deus ex machina* into arguments, and reference to such non-Biblical miracles as the Holy Shroud of Turin!), and a mild incorporation of the *finitum non capax infiniti* principle (p. 38), which, as we shall emphasize later, is actually one of the ideological roots of the death-of-God error.

[119] It will be observed that the principle as here stated is not identical in form with A. J. Ayer's famous verifiability criterion that played a central role in the development of Logical Positivism. Thus the philosophical attempts to break down Ayer's principle are not relevant to the present discussion even if they are held to be successful (which is by no means certain).

[120] I have developed this point in reference to Neo-Orthodox and existentialistic views of revelation in my article, "Inspiration and Inerrancy: A New Departure," *Bulletin of the Evangelical Theological Society,* VIII (Spring, 1965), 45-75 (reprinted with revisions in my *Crisis in Lutheran Theology* [2 vols.; Grand Rapids, Michigan: Baker Book House, 1967], I, 15-44, and in III. 3 below).

[121] Mascall, *op. cit.,* p. 240.

[122] Montgomery, "History & Christianity," *His,* December, 1964—March, 1965 (available as a *His* Reprint; address: 4605 Sherwood, Downers Grove, Illinois 60515, and in *Where Is History Going?, op. cit.,* pp. 37-74); and *The Shape of the Past, op. cit.,* pp. 138-45, 235-37, and *passim.*

[123] Cf. my paper, "The Theologian's Craft: A Discussion of Theory Formation and Theory Testing in Theology," published both in the *Concordia Theological Monthly,* XXXVII (February, 1966), 67-98, and in the *Journal of the American Scientific Affiliation,* XVIII (September, 1966), 65-77, 92-95, and in III. 2 below.

[124] This analogy is suggested by that remarkable apologetic tour de force by Richard Whately, *Historic Doubts Relative to Napoleon Bonaparte* (11th ed.; New York: Robert Carter, 1871).

[125] Ludwig Wittgenstein, *Philosophical Investigations,* trans. G. E. M. Anscombe (Oxford: Blackwell, 1953), Pt. I, sect. 60. Cf. George Pitcher, *The Philosophy of Wittgenstein* (Englewood Cliffs, N. J.: Prentice-Hall, 1964), chap. vii, pp. 171-87.

[126] Jean-Paul Sartre, *Le Diable et le Bon Dieu* (Paris: Gallimard, 1951), p. 237. Cf. Georges Gusdorf, "The Absence of God in the World Today," *Lutheran World,* XIII (1966), 1-13.

[127] Alasdair MacIntyre, "God and the Theologians," *Encounter* (London), XXI (September, 1963), 7. Gilkey in his Crozer Lectures (*op. cit.* in n. 96) makes the same point. Cf. Robert W. Lunk's comment in his report on the Second Drew University Consultation on Hermeneutics (April 9-11, 1964): "Neo-orthodoxy taught that God is never object but always subject, with the result that third generation neo-orthodox theologians have been forced to wrestle with the non-phenomenal character of God. They are unwilling to settle for God as noumenon (perhaps as a legacy of theologies of history, and perhaps as the result of a radical empiricism), which means that for them God does not 'appear' at all" (*Theology Today,* XXI [October, 1964], 303).

[128] MacIntyre, "God and the Theologians," p. 5 (MacIntyre's italics).

[129] Cf. Montgomery, "Karl Barth and Contemporary Theology of History," published in the *Bulletin of the Evangelical Theological Society*, VI (May, 1963), 39-49, in *The Cresset*, XXVII (November, 1963), 8-14, and in *Where Is History Going?, op. cit.*, pp. 100-117.

[130] Lack of recognition of Neo-Orthodoxy's substantive contributions to death-of-God thinking is the chief weakness in Kenneth Hamilton's *God Is Dead: The Anatomy of a Slogan* (Grand Rapids, Michigan: Eerdmans, 1966). Though Hamilton does offer a useful anatomy of the movement, he does not perform effective *surgery* on it owing to his neglect of the epistemological and revelational considerations that logically and developmentally bind theothanatology to twentieth century Protestant dialectic thought. Hamilton's article, "The Essentiality of Tradition," in *Christian Century*'s "How I Am Making Up My Mind" series (LXXXIII [June 1, 1966], 707-10), is disappointing for much the same reason: Kierkegaard, Forsyth, and Barth are placed on the side of the angels with no note of their severe epistemological failings, and orthodoxy is viewed as "always relative to an ecclesiastical tradition," instead of being understood as fidelity to a perspicuous and inerrant scriptural revelation which determines what is and what is not "authentic doctrine." Cf. in this name connection Hamilton's recent work, *What's New in Religion? A Critical Study of New Theology, New Morality, and Secular Christianity* (Grand Rapids, Michigan: Eerdmans, 1968).

[131] Herman Feifel (ed.), *The Meaning of Death* (New York: McGraw-Hill, 1965). Cf. Roger Mehl, *Le Vieillissement et la mort* (2. éd.; Paris: Presses Universitaires de France, 1962); Roger Mehl, *Notre vie et notre mort* (2. éd.; Paris: S. C. E., 1966); Vladimir Jankélévitch, *La Mort* (Paris: Flammarion, 1966); and Edgar Herzog, *Psyche and Death*, trans. David Cox and Eugene Rolfe (New York: G. P. Putnam, for the C. G. Jung Foundation, 1967).

[132] Cf. Gustaf Aulén, *Christus Victor*, trans. A. G. Hebert (New York: Macmillan, 1956).

[133] The original presentation of this essay in lecture form had to be postponed a week because of the sudden death of my wife's mother. On the day when I was scheduled to lecture on the (unempirical) death of God, I attended the overwhelmingly empirical funeral of a loved one. This was an object lesson worth pondering.

[134] Ingmar Bergman's film *The Silence* offers an analogous confrontation: "A silence has befallen us, but it is connected with the cry of the inferno. The men, the women, who have 'freed themselves' from God are not those who are happy and satisfied, who have found themselves. They are the tormented who are shown no mercy, the hungry who are not filled, the separated who cannot get away from one another. . . . Bergman in his film shows 20th century man—who does not cease in his grand technological achievements to sing his own praise and who wants to liberate himself from the tyranny of God—as he is" (Vilmos Vajta, "When God Is Silent," *Lutheran World*, XIII [1966], 60-61).

[135] Hamilton, "The Shape of a Radical Theology," *loc. cit.*, 1220.

136 Sir Robert Anderson, *The Silence of God* (8th ed.: London: Hodder and Stoughton, 1907), p. 165.

137 Henry van Dyke, *The Lost Word: A Christmas Legend of Long Ago* (New York: Scribner, 1917), pp. 87-89.

Wagering on the Death of God *

Three weeks after the publication of my book, *The 'Is God Dead?' Controversy,* in August of 1966, I received a letter from Professor Altizer in which he said: "How I wish that you had responded to my 'wager' in *The Gospel of Christian Atheism!*" The "wager" in question is posed at the end of Professor Altizer's book and constitutes his challenge to the historic Christian faith; he calls modern man to a new risk of faith—to a wager that Christ is not the same yesterday, today, and forever, that the God of orthodox Christian theism is dead, that Christ's "contemporary presence negates his previous epiphanies" and that the only genuine Christ is a "totally profane" Christ.

I did not directly treat this peculiar wager in my book. This was not because I'm not a betting man, but because I had more important things to do in the book: I agreed with Harvey Cox that Professor Altizer "will have to be more precise if he's going to be taken seriously" and I was therefore more concerned with philosophically sophisticated varieties of death-of-God thinking than with the Altizer accurately pictured by his fellow theothanatologist William Hamilton: a "dancer at a Hindu procession to the burning ghat," leaping in "corybantic exultation" about the bier of God the Father and of his historical Son.

Now, however, the opportunity has afforded itself to speak specifically to Professor Altizer's wager and to the theology (better, dystheology) that lies behind it. Hard though it will be, I shall attempt to follow E. W. Shideler's kosher advice in the July, 1966, *Theology Today,* on

* An invitational critique of the theology of Thomas J. J. Altizer, presented in dialogue with him at Rockefeller Memorial Chapel, University of Chicago, February 24, 1967, as part of the University of Chicago Student Government's 75th Anniversary Speakers Program.

"taking the death-of-God seriously." (Parenthetically, "taking x seriously" is theologically "in" this year. Example: "I cannot agree with all of Eichmann's racial theories, but surely we must take him seriously." That this analogy is not as farfetched as it seems will become evident later on.) As a writer in the October, 1966, *Journal of Religion,* puts it, better than he realizes: "We must enter the intoxicating world of Thomas J. J. Altizer." "Intoxicating" is *le mot juste,* for his views both represent and carry to their logical conclusion the hang-over conditions prevailing in Protestant theological circles since the advent of modernism, and Altizer is aiding and abetting a true "days of wine and roses" atmosphere in contemporary Christianity.

Three Roads to Religious Absurdity

Professor Altizer, a lover of mystical, intuitionist poets such as Blake, appreciates literary indirection in making a point. I therefore begin with a modern parable. Once upon a time (note the mythical cast) there was a man who thought he was dead. His concerned wife and friends sent him to the friendly neighborhood psychiatrist. The psychiatrist determined to cure him by convincing him of one fact that contradicted his belief that he was dead. The fact the psychiatrist settled on was the simple truth that dead men do not bleed, and he put the patient to work reading medical texts, observing autopsies, etc. After weeks of effort, the patient finally said, "All right, all right! You've convinced me. Dead men do not bleed." Whereupon the psychiatrist stuck him in the arm with a needle, and the blood flowed. The man looked with a contorted, ashen face and cried: "Good Lord! Dead men bleed after all!"

This parable well illustrates that if you hold unsound presuppositions with sufficient tenacity, facts will make no difference at all, and you will be able to create a world of your own, totally unrelated to reality and totally incapable of being touched by reality. Such a condition (which the philosophers call solipsistic, psychiatrists call autistically psychotic, and lawyers call insane) is tantamount to death, for connection with the living world is severed. The man in the parable not only thought he was dead; in a very real sense he *was* dead, for facts no longer meant anything to him. I think that it can be shown that Professor Altizer is in this lamentable condition and that his death-of-God theology is a projection of his own sclipsistic death on his Creator and Redeemer. Consider the three presuppositions which cut Professor Altizer off from religious reality and make it virtually impossible for him to face the facts theologically.

First, he dumps the law of contradiction on which (as Russell and Whitehead demonstrated in their monumental *Principia Mathematica*) all logical thinking is based, and substitutes for it Hegel's so-call "dialectic logic." Says Altizer in his *Gospel of Christian Atheism* (pp. 79-80): "So long as theological thinking is grounded in the logical laws of identity and contradiction it cannot apprehend a forward-moving and self-transfiguring Word. . . . Hegel . . . insisted that it is only when dialectical understanding (*Vernunft*) has negated and transcended the logical laws of pure reason (*Verstand*), that thinking can apprehend the movement of Spirit in history."

Now we could point out that Altizer, like the orthodox Marxists, has seriously misunderstood Hegelian method; as Walter Kaufmann has shown in his great edition of Hegel, the philosopher "occasionally (though not nearly as often as is generally assumed) affected what are usually called dialectic deductions. These differ greatly from case to case and are certainly not reducible to any mechanical three-step; but what many of these cases have in common is the attempt to be rigorous in some way or other that does not really lend itself to rigor." Putting it otherwise, there is simply no necessitarian progress from thesis and antithesis to synthesis, and just as the Marxist has been incapable of demonstrating such an inevitable movement in the economic realm, so Hegel and Altizer are totally unable to demonstrate it in the realm of Spirit or Word.

And it is not without significance that even Kaufmann, whose *Critique of Religion and Philosophy* has shown him to be no friend of Christianity, finds it impossible to regard Hegel as a Christian in any meaningful sense, since he forced the historic Christian message into the Procrustean bed of his philosophical immanentism. Kaufmann perceptively notes that Hegel thereby "became a precedent for theologians like Tillich and Bultmann"; and the same applies with even greater force to Altizer, who, seeing Tillich's selective biblical proof-texting of Schelling and Bultmann's free and easy use of the Bible to illustrate Heideggerian existentialism, arbitrarily picks and chooses among the resources of the Christian tradition to give dialectic immanentism a Christian coloring.

But the fundamental problem here is the utter irrationality of so-called "dialectic logic," which, as Bertrand Russell has shown, is not a "logic" at all but a disguised metaphysic. If thinking were really to be governed by dialectic standards, then we could know absolutely nothing and could not in fact state even the simplest fact. Why? Because each fact or idea could be understood only in terms of its further development in antithesis and synthesis, i.e., knowledge of any particular would be possible only in light of the whole of existent reality (Hegel's "Absolute Idea").

> Now this is all very well [comments Russell], but it is open to an initial objection. If the above argument were sound, how could knowledge ever begin? I know numbers of propositions of the form "A is the father of B," but I do not know the whole universe. If all knowledge were knowledge of the universe as a whole, there would be no knowledge. This is enough to make us suspect a mistake somewhere. . . . This illustrates an important truth, namely, that the worse your logic, the more interesting the consequences to which it gives rise.

To maintain that a "dialectic movement" or a "dynamic process" is the basic universal category is sheer absurdity, for this would mean that our very methods of investigation and our dialectic philosophy *itself* would lack any normative significance. This is the overwhelming objection both to "process" philosophies (Whitehead, Hartshorne) and to "process" theologies, whether Catholic (Teilhard de Chardin) or Protestant (John B. Cobb, Jr.), whether theistic (Pittenger) or atheistic (Altizer). In locating the origin of Western dialectic thinking in Heraclitus, Altizer unfortunately does not reflect sufficiently on the (reconstructed but genuine) Heraclitean fragment, "panta rei, ouden de menei; panta chorei, kai ouden menei" ("Everything flows and nothing abides; everything gives way and nothing stays fixed"). Out of flux, nothing but flux; out of Altizer's flux, nothing but irrational theological fluctuation.

The law of contradiction and the logical thinking based upon it are not optional. They must be employed for any meaningful thought, theological or otherwise. No Hegelian could even talk about syntheses unless he were implicitly distinguishing the components involved in them, and no process theologian could talk about higher levels of development or reaching an Omega-point unless he were in practice distinguishing stages along the way. What Professor Altizer does, of course, is what every irrationalist does: he employs logic *selectively,* when it works to his advantage, and screams "Western rationalist" at those who point to the hopeless irrationality of his general worldview.

But if Professor Altizer really wishes to employ a "credo quia absurdum" approach to life and theology, let him consider full well that modern man has a wide variety of irrational options to choose from besides his own; there are, in fact, an infinite number of irrational, unverifiable religious possibilities open at any time (we shall consider some especially juicy examples shortly). Why Altizer's brand of theological irrationality? But to answer the question, the good Professor would have to offer a reason, and that would require the acceptance of the law of non-contradiction. . . .

Altizer's second presuppositional road to religious absurdity is his conviction that there is an underlying unity of thought between Eastern mystical religion and the Christian faith: that in some sense Nirvana can be identified with the Kingdom of God and Buddha with the Christ. Here Altizer claims as his spiritual father the greatest living phenomenologist of religion, Mircea Eliade, who finds a "coincidence of opposites" *(concidentia oppositorum)* in primitive, Eastern, and Western religious experience. But here, as in so many other instances, Altizer runs while he reads and suffers the consequences.

Even theological existentialist John Macquarrie has
noted that for Eliade "Biblical religion broke out of the
cyclical framework, and revelation became not cosmic
but historical. The God of the Hebrew people is not one
who creates archetypal gestures, but one who constantly
acts irreversibly in history. This idea is carried on and
enriched in Christianity, with its recognition of the unique
event of Jesus Christ" *(Twentieth-Century Religious
Thought,* p. 222). In conversation with me a week ago
this evening, Professor Eliade made this very point about
Christianity's unique, historical focus on a "once-for-all"
incarnation of God in Christ, expressed his dissatisfaction
with Altizer's interpretation of his conjunction of opposites
(Eliade's dialectic, unlike Altizer's, is descriptive, not
normative, and involves no "higher synthesis": the sacred
and the profane exist simultaneously), and stated that,
frankly, he could not understand Altizer's theological
writings. (I was reminded of Macaulay's remark on reading Kant's *Critique of Pure Reason:*" In this day and age
it is unfortunate that one intelligent man cannot write
so that another intelligent man can understand him.")

Professor Altizer's gross inability to cut the data of
comparative religions "at the joints" (as Plato would
put it) stems from his general disrespect for historical
facts: he will not allow a given religion to speak for itself;
he insists on drawing from different and in many ways
contradictory religious traditions common sermon-
illustrations to support his predetermined Hegelian immanentism. If Professor Altizer would let the facts speak
for themselves, he would have to give up any hope of
blending Eastern and Western religion. How unfortunate
that he is incapable of appreciating the "radical dissimilarities" between Jesus' teachings and the great Indian
faiths, as set forth by such specialists as R. E. Hume,
translator of the Upanishads from the Sanscrit; and how
sad that even the latest literature in the field is unable
to break his presuppositional barriers (e.g., I. A. Sparks'
paper, "Buddha and Christ: A Functional Analysis," in
the October, 1966 issue of *Numen*; there one reads:
"Whereas the Buddha introduces a new and saving truth,
by means of which men find release, the Christ introduces

a new and saving situation, under whose conditions men are reconciled and redeemed").

The third *a priori* by which Professor Altizer separates himself from religious reality is his uncritical acceptance of scientistic biblical criticism. Altizer feels justified in wagering for a mythical, totally "profane" Jesus because everyone must recognize that "modern New Testament scholarship has for the most part dissolved the image of Jesus in the Christian tradition," leading to the acknowledgement, "if only on the basis of the Gospel accounts of his teaching, that Jesus will be present to later ages in strange and paradoxical forms" *(The Gospel of Christian Atheism,* p. 55; cf. Altizer's essays on "The Religious Meaning of Myth and Symbol" and "Word and History"). In reply we could raise the painfully obvious point that if the New Testament picture of Jesus has in fact been dissolved, then Altizer will not even be able to abstract from it a Schweitzerean apocalyptic Jesus, much less a Jesus "present to later ages in strange and paradoxical forms."

But the premise does not even need to be granted— and *must* not, if one is going to stay with the facts. The Dibelius-Bultmann *formgeschichtliche Methode* (form-critical method) which, in Professor Altizer's judgment, has "dissolved the image of Jesus" as a historical Redeemer, has itself largely been dissolved. The method depends on rationalistic presuppositions against the miraculous (e.g., Bultmann's arrogant and undemonstrable judgment that "the nexus of natural causes cannot be broken"), and it leaves the gates wide open to subjective interpretation as to which "forms" indeed underlie the New Testament materials. The method principally falls down because, as McNeile and Williams have emphasized, the time interval between the writing of the New Testament documents as we have them and the events of Jesus' life which they record is too brief to allow for communal redaction by the early church. The so-called "historical-critical method" is found, on examination, to be scientistic rather than scientific, i.e., to yield results in accord with its nonscientific assumptions rather than in accord with the objective historical materials at hand.

Criticism of this approach from outside the theological field is now quite common. Thus A. N. Sherwin-White, in his 1960-61 Sarum Lectures (*Roman Society and Roman Law in the New Testament*), contrasts the historical evidence for Tiberius Caesar with the evidence supporting Christ's life and ministry, and shows how superior the latter is to the former. Says Sherwin-White:

> It is astonishing that while Graeco-Roman historians have been growing in confidence, the twentieth-century study of the Gospel narratives, starting from no less promising material, has taken so gloomy a turn in the development of form-criticism that the more advanced exponents of it apparently maintain—so far as an amateur can understand the matter—that the historical Christ is unknowable and the history of his mission cannot be written. This seems very curious when one compares the case for the best-known contemporary of Christ, who like Christ is a well-documented figure—Tiberius Caesar.

"Astonishing" and "curious" indeed: but only if one is unacquainted with the degree to which contemporary theologians such as Altizer uncritically absorb methodological *a prioris* that keep them in principle from discovering a clear historical portrait of Jesus in the primary documents.

Will the Real Jesus Please Stand Up?

Professor Altizer's three-fold path (dialectic opposition to the laws of logic; religious syncretism; form-critical destruction of the historical Jesus) leads not to Nirvana or to the Kingdom of God, but to a "fully kenotic Word." Here is how Altizer put it in the July 7, 1965 *Christian Century*:

> Neither the Bible nor church history can be accepted as containing more than a provisional or temporary series of expressions of the Christian Word.... Not only does Christianity now have a new meaning, it has a new reality, a reality created by the epiphany of a fully kenotic Word. Such a reality cannot be wholly understood by a word of the past, not even by the word "kenosis," for the Christian Word becomes a new reality by ceasing to be itself: only by negating and thus transcending its previous expressions can the Incarnate Word be a forward-moving process.

When we cease to look back to a historical Christ and instead give ourselves to the totally hidden Christ in our secular, profane present, we will become "spiritual or apocalyptic" Christians, participating in mystic-millennial theologian Joachim of Floris' "third age of the Spirit." The Jesus of this "third age of the Spirit" is not of course to be "identified with the original historical Jesus," but "rather is known here in a new and more comprehensive and universal form" (Altizer, quoted in a symposium-interview in *Christianity Today*, January 7, 1966).

The obvious question is: Suppose we want to be "spiritual or apocalyptic" Christians, à la Altizer; how will we find the "new and more comprehensive and universal" Jesus? At first we may hope that the word "kenosis" will help us, since the word describes Christ as "emptying himself" in his Incarnation (Phil. 2:5-11). But even the most elementary exegesis of this New Testament passage shows that any resemblance between the kenotic theories of contemporary liberal theology—to say nothing of Altizer's "kenosis"—and the biblical teaching is purely coincidental. Eugene R. Fairweather, after examining the whole kenotic question in detail, concludes: "It can hardly be claimed that Kenoticism is explicitly contained in the New Testament picture of Christ; rather, it depends on a complicated deduction, involving highly debatable presuppositions. . . . The Kenotic theory does not in fact vindicate the religious meaning of the Christian Gospel. On the contrary, in the severe words of Pius XII, it 'turns the integral mystery of the Incarnation and of redemption into bloodless and empty spectres' " (see Fairweather's appendix to F. W. Beare's *Philippians*). "Bloodless and empty spectres": Pius XII had Altizer's number!

But Professor Altizer cuts himself off even from the New Testament concept of Kenosis: "Such a reality cannot be wholly understood by a word of the past, not even by the word 'kenosis,' for the Christian Word becomes a new reality by ceasing to be itself." Fine; then how do we recognize it? If today's Christ is totally hidden, if he has totally ceased to be himself, what is he? From a contradiction, anything follows. Is he then a billboard? a toasted-cheese sandwich? love (as Altizer suggests in the concluding sentence of his *Gospel of Christian Atheism*)? hate (that possibility is as open as any other)? totalitarianism? genocide?

Let us consider a few examples of the "Christs" people have found when they have given up, as has Altizer, the historical Christ of the New Testament documents. John Symonds' recent work, *Thomas Brown and the Angels* (1961), describes the 18th century Shakers in the following terms:

> The Shakers believed that Christ, whose Second Coming is foretold in *Revelation,* would appear in the form of a woman. And slowly it dawned upon them that Ann Lee, through her suffering and labouring for the lost state of mankind, had so purified and prepared herself that she had become the vehicle for this divine female spirit which the Shakers called "Mother Spirit in Christ, an emanation from the Eternal Mother." Ann's leadership of the society inevitably followed, and to her confession of sins was now made.

Ronald Knox, in his celebrated study, *Enthusiasm*, has chronicled and analyzed numerous cases of a similar kind, where the common element is a refusal to allow the historical Jesus to have any determing influence on one's "Christ of faith."

Psychiatrist T. B. Hyslop presents, as one of his *Great Abnormals* (1925), the 19th century drunkard (was he called "intoxicating"?) and religious mystic David Lazzaretti:

> He adopted a singular emblematic device—the double C, about which he was most concerned, and which stood for the first and second Christ—Christ, the son of Joseph of Nazareth, and Christ, the son of the late Joseph Lazzaretti of Arcidosso. . . . He entreated all true believers to disassociate themselves from the world by "abstaining from food, and from sexual intercourse, even in the case of married persons, who, however, if they indulged, were required to pray for at least two hours, naked, outside the bed," concluding his exhortation by declaring himself to be the "man of mystery, the new Christ, the Leader and Avenger."

In our own time we have Meher Baba, the patron saint of Sufism Reoriented, who, "through the medium of his alphabet board," prepared a book modestly titled, *God Speaks* (1955), in which we are introduced to the "true meaning" of Christ:

> Jesus of Nazareth, the Son of God, is like Mohammed,
> Zoroaster, Krishna, Rama, Buddha—the God-Man; whilst
> "Christ," like Haqiqat-e-Mohammedi, is the divine office
> of Jesus.
>   When we try to put together all the different stages
> of God in a nut-shell, five distinct stages, in the travail
> of the unconscious Paramatma to gain complete conscious-
> ness, become conspicuous.

This dynamic religious process moves from an unconscious atma (stage 1) to a glorious fifth stage in which
"atma is fully and completely conscious of the gross body,
the subtle body and the mental body," and "experiences
and *uses* the infinite power, infinite knowledge and infinite bliss of its own Paramatma state." Note how much
more vital—how much more pulsating with life this world-
view is than a stuffy old Hegelian World Spirit!

The previous examples, though bizarre, are in the general category of the inane; consider now not the silly but
the sinister consequences of "fully-hidden" Christs. In
refusing to provide any objective referent for his kenotic
Word, Altizer allows Christ to be identified with Antichrist; indeed, with Nietzsche and Blake he welcomes
such identification as a means to "the God beyond the
Christian God" (see his "Theology and the Death of God,"
in the Spring, 1964, *Centennial Review*). In this vein, Altizer calls on radical Christians to "defy the moral law
of the churches, identifying it as a satanic law of repression and heteronomous compulsion" (*Christianity
Today*, January 7, 1966).

A good example of such a philosophy in practice is
offered not by clean-cut Professor Altizer, whom a De
Paul University female public relations officer last week
described as a "living doll," but by the late Satanist, phil-
anderer, and narcotics addict Aleister Crowley, who appropriately called himself "the Great Beast." John
Symonds, in his biography of Crowley, describes his life
orientation in terms which, *mutatis mutandis,* could apply directly to Professor Altizer's views:

> To Crowley, Christ the Saviour was only the Pseudo-
> Christ. Christ's enemy was Satan; therefore the Devil is
> not so bad as he is painted. Indeed, he is a worthy ally;
> together they will make war upon Christ, and with his
> destruction the real lord of the Universe will arise. Like the

idol Baphomet which the Templars were supposed to have worshipped, he is many-faced, and upon one of his faces is carried the mask of Aleister Crowley.

Crowley was only one Satanist; the theologians of the Deutsche Christen movement in Hitler's Germany were many, and they justified genocidal activity on precisely the same grounds as Altizer justifies his opposition to traditional religious and ethical teaching: the New Age has dawned; Christ must not be conceived in New Testament terms, but in terms of the dynamic, contemporary life-process in which we are involved. For Altizer, to be sure, glorious secularity is located in the America of the 1960's, not the Germany of the 1930's (for which we fervently thank the living God!), but this is only a historical accident. The theologians and philosophers of that day (who, like Altizer, had allowed historical-critical method to destroy their confidence in the Christ of history) proceeded to de-Judaize and Aryanize Christ, so as to make him a guiding spirit of the millennial Third Reich.

As Max Weinreich points out in his monumental work, *Hitler's Professors* (1946), such distinguished theologians as Rudolf Kittel and Emanuel Hirsch were involved in these abominations and, with the same gross confusion of scientistic presuppositionalism with proper scientific method as we have observed in higher critical studies of the Bible, justified their work by "the perennial traditions of German scholarship." The final rationalization, with them as with Altizer, was the present- and future-orientation of the on going life-force which was sweeping them along. The atheistic existentialist Heidegger, whose thought has been determinative for radical Protestant theologian Rudolf Bultmann, spoke forth in no uncertain terms in 1933: "This revolution means a *complete* revolution of our German existence. . . . Heil Hitler." Prof. Dr. Wolf Meyer-Erlach, rector of the University of Jena and a theologian, wrote in the same vein in 1936: "There are still instructors and students whose eyes are turned backward, toward eternal yesterday's life. But we know that . . . the future is more potent than the past."

For these men, the "God beyond God" was indeed "where the action is"; but, as a matter of fact, the action was demonic action and their deity turned out to be no less than the Devil himself. Without a firm criterion for determining what is true and what is false religious belief—without a firm historical check on the Christ of faith—this kind of satanic error is not merely possible, but inevitable. Man is an idol-making animal, and he will build Christs to fit his own image or his most cherished dreams of egotistic autocracy when theologians are so misguided or foolish as to give him the tools for doing so.

Russian Roulette As a Religious Principle

While optimistic churchmen such as President James McCord of Princeton Seminary are joyously heralding "a whole new era in theology" characterized by Altizer's stress on the Spirit—"the God of the present" (see *Time*, August 5, 1966), Altizer himself is dimly aware of the ghastly Pandora's box his theology may be opening up. In discussing his "wager" in the closing pages of *The Gospel of Christian Atheism*, he writes:

> The contemporary Christian who bets that God is dead must do so with a full realization that he may very well be embracing a life-destroying nihilism; or, worse yet, he may simply be submitting to the darker currents of our history, passively allowing himself to be the victim of an all too human horror. No honest contemporary seeker can ever lose sight of the very real possibility that the willing of the death of God is the way to madness, dehumanization, and even to the most totalitarian form of society yet realized in history.

Yet Altizer would have us "wager" against the historic Christ and in behalf of a totally-hidden "Jesus" who can be immanently identified with any aspect of the current milieu we wish!

In ordinary life a wager involves odds, and odds are determined by the weighing of evidence. No man in his right mind will take on a wager endangering his life or the lives of others unless powerful reasons compel him to do so. But where are the odds in favor of Altizer's religious option? We have already seen that the roads leading to his kenotic Christ are utterly irrational, and that his "third age of the Spirit" is without a redeeming feature.

Even if one were to make the tragic mistake of accepting, with Altizer, the Kierkegaardian-Barthian concept of faith as a "blind leap" without objective justification, one would grievously err in embracing Altizer's position. Pascal correctly noted that even if the religious wager were conceived in non-evidential terms, one ought to opt for God, since in doing so there is everything to gain and nothing to lose (if Christ's claims are true and you refuse them, you destroy your soul; if they are false and you accept them, the worst consequence is that you live out this life in accord with the greatest moral Example the world has ever seen). But the evidence is not equal for the two alternatives; on Altizer's side it is non-existent (since his totally kenotic Christ is by definition unidentifiable and therefore indefensible), whereas the claims of the historic Christ and the support for them can be documented in primary historical records.

The scholarship which Professor Altizer displays in his writings ought in itself to show how meaningless his wager is. Consider this single example: the introductory "Bibliographical Note" to his *Gospel of Christian Atheism*, which commences with the incredible assertion: "The primary sources of this book are the writings of Blake, Hegel, and Nietzsche." Why not Edna St. Vincent Millay, Omar Khayyam, and Edgar Guest? Perhaps the essence of the Christian Gospel is to be found in those immortal, compelling, future-orientated lines of W. S. Gilbert?

> Come mighty Must!
>   Inevitable Shall!
> In thee I trust.
>   Time weaves my coronal!
> Go mocking Is!
>   Go disappointing Was!
> That I am this
>   Ye are the cursed cause!
> Yet humble second shall be first,
>   I ween;
> And dead and buried be the curst
>   Has Been!
>
> Oh weak Might Be!
>   Oh, May, Might, Could, Would, Should!
> How powerless ye
>   For evil or for good!

> In every sense
>   Your moods I cheerless call,
> Whate'er your tense
>   Ye are imperfect, all!
> Ye have decieved the trust I've shown
>   In ye!
> Away! The Mighty Must alone
>   Shall be!

How long would even an undergraduate (to say nothing of a doctoral student) last at this University if he attempted to determine the nature of the Muslim faith through such "primary sources"? Perhaps the true understanding of Napoleonic policy can be discovered in Donne, Keats, and Ayn Rand? Such an approach to the essence of the Christian Gospel—an approach that ignores and by-passes the historical documents concerning Christ—is a travesty of scholarship. Even Hegel made a half-hearted attempt to deal with the Gospel accounts (cf. Crites' "Gospel according to Hegel," *Journal of Religion,* April, 1966); Altizer sublimely floats over them in a mystic cloud of unknowing.

And what about the "primary sources" Altizer does choose? We have already discussed Hegel's illogical logic; Nietzsche went insane in his last years; and the visionary Blake, who identified art with Jesus, conversed with his dead brother and numerous other spirits and claimed that they dictated poems to him: "Thirteen years ago I lost a brother, and with his spirit I converse daily and hourly. . . . I hear his advice, and even now write from his dictate"; "I write when commanded by the Spirits and the moment I have written I see the words fly about the room in all directions. It is then published & the Spirits can read" (see Sherman Yellen, "William Blake: The Last Prophet," *International Journal of Parapsychology,* Autumn, 1966). Granting Hegel's brilliant insights, Nietzsche's penetrating criticisms, and Blake's poetic raptures, what do they necessarily have to say about the essence of Christianity or the *de facto* truth of religious claims?

But Blake's "Spirits" and Altizer's "third age of the Spirit" are indeed intimately related: they are comparable gibberish. Though they tell us much about their proponents psychologically, they tell us nothing about the subject under discussion, namely, the nature and validity of the Christian truth-claim. In fact, the more one encounters such visionary scholarship in Altizer, obfuscated as it is in an impenetrable jungle of Neo-Hegelian jargon, the more one recalls H. L. Mencken's classic description of the work of Warren Gamaliel Harding (and note the dialectic counterpoint integral to the evaluation):

> It reminds me of a string of wet sponges; it reminds me of tattered washing on the line; it reminds me of stale bean-soup, of college yells, of dogs barking idiotically through endless nights. It is so bad that a sort of grandeur creeps into it. It drags itself out of the dark abysm (I was about to write abscess!) of pish, and crawls insanely up the topmost pinnacle of posh. It is rumble and bumble. It is flap and doodle. It is balder and dash.

Altizer's "wager" is exactly this. And yet it is not even a "wager" in the gentleman's sense, involving odds and evidence. It is a suicidal game of Russian roulette, in which all chambers of the weapon are loaded against the theological gambler, and in which one's chances are 100% in favor of blowing one's eternal brains out.

The Premature Demise of a Precocious Theologian

In September, 1955, a doctoral dissertation on psychoanalyst Carl Gustav Jung's understanding of religion was submitted to the University of Chicago Divinity School faculty. The candidate concluded his study with the following testimony of faith:

> Jung's basic weakness, which proceeds out of the most basic principles of his thought, is that he is incapable of finding meaning or reality in the historical foundations of religion. . . . This writer is an Anglican who accepts the canonical authority of the Bible as well as the ecclesiastical authority of the creeds and practices of the ancient church catholic as normative standards for Christian life and belief. He believes that Christianity is nothing if it is not founded in the life and teachings of Jesus Christ, and that without its Christological foundations as normatively established by the ancient church, it cannot preserve its authentic nature. Therefore, he is forced to reject Jung's conception of Christianity as well as his conception of the figure of Christ. . . . That Jesus Christ is wholly a mythical figure arising from the deeper pro-

cesses of the collective unconscious which has artificially been engrafted by tradition into the insignificant figure of history, Jesus of Nazareth, this writer cannot in any sense accept. Jung's interpretation as it stands cannot possibly be incorporated into the classical structure of the Christian faith.

Incredibly, the author of this passage, who so precisely describes the fundamental error in current death-of-God thinking—the absorption of the historical Christ into a mythical Christ—is Thomas J. J. Altizer, the author, a decade later, of *The Gospel of Christian Atheism*.

How could such a complete *volte-face*, such an extreme counter-conversion, have occurred in so brief a time? The answer (it is a very instructive one) is that even in his earliest graduate work at the University of Chicago Divinity School, Altizer had picked up certain presuppositions that would eventually eat away the foundations of his faith in historical Christianity. His master of arts thesis on the concepts of nature and grace in Augustine's theology (June, 1951) concludes on the theme of the "Augustinian dialectic" and with the hope that "the conflicting truths which it [the problem of nature and grace] embodies may be seen to point to a higher synthesis and to the possibility of the retention of all the truths which they embody, through a dialectical synthesis that unites these contrary concepts by incorporating the truth in each." Already the requirements of clear, logical thinking are being sacrificed in the interests of a "dialectic logic."

In his doctoral work on Jung's thought, Altizer's difficulties become even more apparent. He recognizes the dangers of Jung's "innate hostility towards reason and history" (p. 250) but is fascinated by the psychoanalyst's mythico-poetic religious insights. While refusing "at any cost to accept the dissolution of reason, nature, and history which entails not only the destruction of the world-view of empirical science but of the reality of the Christian faith as well" (*ibid.*), he seeks to bring the conflicting poles of science and art together through "some form of dialectical thinking"; and the latter will necessitate a "return to the problems of Hegel, Schelling, Kierkegaard, and Nietzsche" (pp. 251-52). Altizer did not realize it, but to enter the presuppositional domain of these thinkers was in itself to give up the possibility of retaining objective truth, since in differing ways all four reject the subject-object distinction.

As a matter of fact, the Preface to Altizer's doctoral dissertation reveals an already-existing commitment which made the transition to irrational subjectivism easy for him. "Wilhelm Dilthey has taught us," he writes, that "the historian is unable to escape the vantage point of his own situation, for in the historical sciences the object of knowledge and the knowing subject are not distinct. Where there can be no clear epistemological distinction between subject and object there can be no valid goal of absolute objectivity." Precisely: if Dilthey is correct (and Altizer tragically does not doubt it), then objective knowledge of the past, *including objective knowledge of the historical Christ,* is impossible. The floodgates are open to Dilthey's principle that "the historian must himself become a participant and actor in the object of his inquiry" (p. xi), and eventually Altizer becomes just such a "participant and actor"—indeed, a godlike creator and reformulator of the Christ in the image of his own philosophical speculations.

An interesting parallel exists here between Altizer and Owen Barfield, whose book, *Saving the Appearances,* Altizer regards as "potentially one of the truly seminal works of our time" (*Journal of Bible and Religion,* October, 1964). Barfield was a close friend of C. S. Lewis, and in his Introduction to *Light on C. S Lewis* (1965) he recalls how Lewis educated him in "the fundamental 'law of thought' (contradictories cannot both be true)" as the *sine qua non* for all meaningful communication, but that he "strugglingly groped" towards the imaginative "polarity of contraries (Coleridge's 'polar logic')." How well Barfield succeeded in his unfortunate struggle against the greater mind of Lewis is clear from his philosophically untenable view that all language is naturally and fundamentally metaphorical (if this were so, the knowledge—including knowledge of language—would be impossible in principle!) and from *Saving the Appearances* (1957), which endeavors specifically to remove obstacles against contemporary appreciation of mystical anthroposophist Rudolf Steiner (p. 141). Steiner, whose teaching Barfield considers "crucial for the future of mankind" (*ibid.*), seriously held that the archetypal founder of Rosicrucianism, "Christian Rosenkreutz," sent Buddha, his closest pupil, to Mars, that Mars was purified through Buddha's deed of sacrifice, and that "the Mars-forces, now radiating peace, work into the souls of men between death and a new birth" (see his *Mission of Christian Rosenkreutz* [1950] and my Strasbourg dissertation for the degree of Docteur d'Université, mention Théologie Protestante). Steiner's Christology is almost a dead-ringer (the pun is intentional) for Altizer's:

> The Buddha stream and the Christ stream will flow into one. Only so can the Christ Mystery be truly understood. So mighty and all-pervading was the Impulse poured into the evolution of mankind that its waves surge onwards into future epochs. . . . And we are now going forward to an epoch when the Impulse will manifest in such a way that human beings will behold the Christ on the astral plane as an Ether Form.

Again loss of confidence in the historical objectivity of the Christ has led to kenotic absurdity and to sheer superstition.

Altizer's capitulation to Diltheyan historiography was in no sense necessary—and could not have been more disastrous. The application of the insights of analytical philosophy to historical thinking (Danto's *Analytical Philosophy of History*; W. H. Dray's *Philosophical Analysis and History*; etc.) has shown how unjustifiable was Dilthey's attempt to transcend the subject-object distinction. J. W. N. Watkins, in Klibansky's *La Philosophie au milieu du vingtième siècle* (Vol. III, p. 159) makes the vital point, over against the Dilthey tradition, that recent analytical work by such philosophers as Ryle "dispels the old presumption, to which Hayek, Swabey and others are still inclined, that to understand Ghengis Khan the historian must be someone very like Ghengis Khan." If one gives up historical objectivity, one perforce gives up at the same time the possibility of objective knowledge of the present (for the past is, in a very real sense, nothing but a "sloughing off" of the present); and the result is a solipsistic relativism in which even one's own existence and identity come under question.

In such a philosophical and theological bog has Professor Altizer managed to engulf himself. The remarkable thing is that he has achieved such catastrophic results in such a short time; it generally takes professional academicians a lifetime to destroy themselves as thoroughly as Professor Altizer has done in a decade. Perhaps, however (and we fervently hope for it), the next decade will display a recovery on his part no less remarkable than the collapse we have sadly documented. He is capable of it; and the lights in the Father's house still burn, awaiting the return of the Prodigal from the Hegelian far country to his baptismal and confirmation vows.

The Supreme Irony of an Archaic Radicalism
and
The Supreme Glory of an Eternally Relevant Christ

In his lecture at De Paul University six days ago, Professor Altizer stressed the continuity between his thought and mainline Protestant emphases in the 20th century, and endeavored, quite successfully, to show how his theology carried to consistent conclusions basic themes in Neo-Orthodoxy, Existentialism, and Tillichianism. What is seldom recognized, however, is the degree to which these Protestant theological positions themselves depend on the 19th century presuppositions which Professor Altizer's work so fully displays.

Nineteenth-century dialectic thinking, with its destruction of historical objectivity and the subject-object distinction, is manifest in varying but significant degrees in Barth, Bultmann, and Tillich (see my article, "Lutherische Hermeneutik—und Hermeneutik Heute," *Lutherischer Rundblick*, 1. Quartal, 1967); the 19th century "history of religion" blend of Christ with non-historical Eastern faiths came to be a vital motif in Tillich's thinking (see my article, "Tillich's Philosophy of History," in *Themelios* [1967]); the scientistic biblical criticism of the 19th century, firmly rooted in anti-miraculous, Newtonian "natural law" thinking, became an integral element in all mainline 20th-century Protestant theological scholarship (see Carl F. H. Henry's *Jesus of Nazareth: Saviour and Lord*); and the subjectivism of Kierkegaard, Blake, and Nietzsche has borne fruit in contemporary existential theologies. What Altizer has done is uncritically to pick up these 19th-century *a prioris* from his 20th-century masters, refine them, and garnish them with a liberal dose of the cultural optimism for which the 19th century has become justly infamous; he has then served them—piping hot from the fire of his personality and salted with an obscure, mystifying literary style—to men hungry for religious truth in the 20th century.

But the meal should not so much as receive mention in a theological Michelin's guide, for it is nothing but warmed-over hash. Altizer's radicalism is impossibly archaic and pre-modern, and its presuppositions, as we have been at pains to show, are discredited at every point. Altizer and his confrères in the death-of-God movement have simply demonstrated beyond all question the bankruptcy of dialectic and liberal theologies in our time, and the absolute necessity to make a fresh start.

At De Paul, Professor Altizer was perceptively asked by a member of his audience to relate his death-of-God theology to science; he declined to "engage in scientific dialogue" on the ground that he was not sufficiently acquainted with scientific thought to do so. Here the archaism of his approach was especially manifest. Ours is above all a day of scientific, empirical concern—but scientific in an open, Einsteinian way that the 19th century mind cannot even comprehend. As we rapidly approach century 21, men are looking for tangible, objective evidence on which to build their religious life, and they are not about to close off areas of possible truth because "natural laws" prohibit ("natural laws" are but generalizations dependent on objective, experiential data!). What modern man insists on above all is a verifiable base for his faith, so that he can bring some order out of the conflicting welter of religious claims. He is sick to death of verbal panaceas—of autobiography masking as theology—of the naive confusion of cultural trends with religious truth—of the theologian who hypnotizes himself by his own terminology and leaves no possible means of confirming what he says. The Delphic Oracle phase in modern theology is almost over, and in Thomas J.

Altizer you may well be seeing its last, soon-to-be extinct representative.

Into this theological vacuum the historic Christ—who is, *pace* Altizer, still the same yesterday, today, and forever—comes in maximum relevance. George Tavard's criticism of Tillich applies even more squarely to Altizer:

> Tillich is right in being skeptical of the historians' efforts to re-write the story of Jesus—but for the wrong reason. Historians cannot re-write the story because it is already written: the historical value of the New Testament is plain enough. Historians have not been able to make its reliability improbable. Tillich has simply not been radical enough in criticizing liberal theology. He has not seen that the historians who doubt the value of the records have failed to establish their point. Here, Paul Tillich remains a child of his generation, a victim of the historicism of the last century.

And when contemporary man goes to these historical records, he finds a Jesus who speaks and acts as God Incarnate, who takes the self-centeredness and self-deification of the centuries on himself at Calvary, and rises again in demonstration that he has conquered "once for all" the powers of sin and death for men in every age.

New religions come and go, but they are generally old religions in new garb (for, outside of the Gospel, there is nothing new under the sun). In Thomas J. J. Altizer you have another, albeit archaic, option presented to you in the marketplace of unverifiable metaphysical claims. Consider well before you buy! *Caveat emptor*! Recall the story of La Revellière and Talleyrand (as recounted by Duff Cooper in his biography of Talleyrand):

> La Revellière was a revolutionary of the feebler, doctrinaire, idealistic type. He bitterly hated the Christian religion and Carnot. In the place of the former he had attempted to introduce a new pseudo-philosophical fad manufactured in England called "Theophilanthropy." On one occasion he read a long paper explaining this novel system of worship to his colleagues. When he had concluded it and received the congratulations of the other Ministers, Talleyrand remarked: "For my part I have only one observation to make. Jesus Christ, in order to found His religion, was crucified and rose again—you should have tried to do as much."

To Professor Altizer I say the same: "You should have tried to do as much." Until you do, as for me and my house, we will serve the Lord—the Lord who will still rule heaven and earth when debates like this are forgotten, when we ourselves are forgotten, and our children's children are forgotten. Then, as today, men will believe, and will have every reason to believe, that the kingdoms of this world are one day to become the kingdoms of our Lord, and of his Christ; and he shall reign for ever and ever.

The Altizer-Montgomery Debate *

Altizer. From my point of view, the primary issue here tonight is: Can the Word of God, as it is present in the Bible and in those communities who give their fundamental and total allegiance to the Bible—can this Word be spoken in our time?

Now it is my persuasion that we are living in a time in which the Word of God as therein contained can no longer be spoken as a source of life and joy and that to speak the Word of God in its original or traditional form is to bind oneself to death. Indeed, from my point of view, one becomes bound to a condition of speechlessness, and is therein enslaved to the dead body of God which has been negated by God Himself in Jesus Christ. Our problem as Christians today is to speak a word of life—to speak a redemptive word which can release energy joyously and compassionately into the world. Speaking as one who comes from the South, who lives in the South, who lives indeed in what is commonly called the Bible Belt, and who has seen the servants of this form of the Word of God bind themselves to repression and be, themselves, the primary social force embodying segregation in the South, I've long since lost any hope that the spokesman of the traditional Word of God can be anything in our day but an enemy of man. Our problem today is to understand that form, that reality of the Word of Christ which is actively present in our midst. I, in

---

* A full transcription of the interchange which took place at Rockefeller Memorial Chapel of the University of Chicago, February 24, 1967.

large measure, believe it or not, share some of Professor
Montgomery's criticisms. Nevertheless, I do so with the
conviction that our situation is so erratic that nothing
but the most extravagant kinds of leaps are going to
make possible any real life and love today because ours
is a time of darkness. I do not share Professor Montgomery's rationalistic optimism. I do not share his confidence in what he calls logic in science. I don't share
his confidence in the world. Ours is indeed a world bathed
in darkness. And Christians, too, live in darkness insofar as they remain bound to past forms of the Word.
Therefore we must give ourselves to a radical quest for
a new form of the Word which is indeed hidden in our
midst. There are no obvious routes to it. There is no
rational calculus by which we can make a wager to insure
our success. We must indeed make a leap into the darkness because the only reality we know is the world of
darkness, and we mustn't delude ourselves into thinking
that we are living in the midst of light, least of all a
light which is indeed a source of darkness. Therefore
I seize upon a Blake, upon a Hegel, upon a Nietzsche,
upon numerous others as well, including the great work
of Professor Eliade. I sieze upon them because I believe
that therein we find a new vision, a new reality, a new
life which indeed reverses the words which we once knew,
the Word which we once knew. Nevertheless, I think this
reversal is in continuity with what we know about the
primary form and direction of the Christian Word, a word
that enters ever more fully into flesh, that penetrates
ever more decisively, ever more actually into the world,
and which in its very movement reverses its former expressions, therein making possible new moments of life
even though such life—in life as it may be present to
us—can only be reached by us by means of a movement
through darkness. These are very, very difficult days
to the man of faith. Theology is in an extremely critical
state. Indeed, Professor Montgomery and I, I think, share
a common conviction that what is commonly known as
Protestant neo-orthodoxy has indeed collapsed. I think
that what has collapsed is the primary form of the Christian's understanding of the Word in the world, and only

by means of a radical leap, a radical quest, can we find a Word which can be for us a source of life.

Montgomery. You seem to feel that a blind leap of faith involves two alternatives—either the traditional Christian position or the completely kenotic and hidden Christ who is manifest in some sense in the present situation. I'm sure you realize that this is not simply a matter of two alternatives. A blind leap can be made in an infinite number of directions. Now at a university such as this, there are many uncommitted students who are searching for a way out of the difficulties of our time to which you have so eloquently referred. What they want to know is: Why should the leap be made in the direction you suggest, particularly since you give no criteria whatever for the notion of a word somehow hidden in the present situation. Why a leap in that direction, rather than a leap in the direction of Meher Baba's Sufism, in the direction of the Marxist ideology, in the direction of traditional Christianity, or in any number of other directions that could be mentioned.

Altizer. Let me clarify a point here. I certainly do not intend to suggest that my own way is the only way—far from it. That would be a horrible situation.

Montgomery. Why is it a possibility at all in the present situation?

Altizer. I think it's a possibility because it attempts to understand Christ as being present in our world in a way which will fulfill His original movement into flesh.

Montgomery. May I interrupt you at this point? How can you speak in any sense about a "Christ" when you have cut yourself off from an historical Jesus? You have already pointed out that the Christ as He appears now has no necessary connection at any point with the Christ of history. Under these circumstances, how do you justify your use of the six-letter word "Christ"? With what referent are you employing this word?

Altizer. There's a misunderstanding on your part here, I think. What I assert is that the person of Jesus of Nazareth has disappeared from history. His Word is in part present to us, and we can in part truly know His Word.

Montgomery. On what basis do you make that statement?

Altizer. Which statement?

Montgomery. That His Word is still present with us and we can in some sense come into contact with it.

Altizer. Simply on the basis that it is possible critically, I believe, to ascertain something of the meaning of the original message of Jesus. I think that we cannot possibly recover the full meaning of it, but I think it is possible to recover essential dimensions of it. For example, it seems to me to be quite clear that He was an apocalyptic preacher, if you will, that He proclaimed an apocalyptic word. This can be known, and indeed, I think, has to be an essential ground of any contemporary Christian theological quest.

Montgomery. Why is His apocalyptic emphasis not an imposition on His teachings by the early Church as you would regard other aspects of His teaching?

Altizer. There's a very good reason for this, using here the basic principle that those words of His which can be ascertained as being most offensive to the early Church are most likely to be authentic. There are lots of technical problems here, of course, but I simply accept what seems to me to be the general result of modern New Testament scholarship which identifies the original message of Jesus as being apocalyptic.

Montgomery. There was probably nothing more offensive in the teachings of Jesus than His affirmation to be God incarnate, to be God in the flesh.

Altizer. I don't think there's any possibility that Jesus taught that He was God in flesh.

Montgomery. But the point is: You just said the more offensive the teaching, the more likelihood it was Jesus' original teaching.

Altizer. Offensive to the Hellenistic Church. That was the ground of the faith of the Hellenistic Church.

Montgomery. Is that right? What about Jesus' resurrection from the dead? There was nothing that irritated the Hellenistic world more.

Altizer. The Hellenistic Church: It was the church that canonized the New Testament, not the Hellenistic world.

Montgomery. You don't feel it bothered the Hellenistic Church in the slightest that Jesus' claims were the fulfillment of the Jewish Messianic claims of God incarnate?

Altizer. First of all, there never were any Jewish Messianic claims that there would be an incarnation of God. That's not Messianic. The Messiah in Jewish tradition was a human figure, not a divine figure.

Montgomery. You don't feel it was the least bit disturbing to the Hellenistic Church that Jesus claimed to be God incarnate, that He died for the sins of the world?

Altizer. These are the theological foundations of the Hellenistic Church. Of course they're primary.

Montgomery. All right. How do you distinguish the Hellenistic Church from the Jewish Church?

Altizer. One of the major distinctions is that the original primitive church was an apolcalyptic Jewish sect.

Montgomery. But you see, you're begging the question. How do we determine what was the original and primitive proclamation?

Altizer. You didn't ask that question.

Montgomery. I'm asking it now. Obviously it's integral to your argument.

Altizer. Let me put it this way. Do you doubt that Jesus was an apocalyptic teacher?

Montgomery. Not in the slightest.

Altizer. Well, then, I don't see the thrust of your question.

Montgomery. The point is that you are selecting from His teachings this particular aspect—apocalypticism—and you're arguing that it is primary because it would have been offensive to a particular group within the early church. Now, as a matter of fact, practically everything Jesus said was offensive to somebody in the early church, and this is no criterion at all for selectivity. You are arriving at the New Testament with certain presuppositions about what can be removed and absolutized. For you, apocalypticism happens to be one of these things.

Altizer. We have to remember, there is no possibility of reconciling everything in the New Testament. There's too much that is self-contradictory; so no one could say that he accepts the full authority of the New Testament. No one could say that he accepts everything that the New Testament says about Jesus or about Christ without embracing some real kind of schizophrenic madness.

Montgomery. All right, let me give you an example

of schizophrenic madness if you'd like it. At De Paul University you made the statement that the ascent into heaven is heretical, but the descent into hell is a magnificent presentation of the early, basic Christian proclamation. Now, unless I'm mistaken, textual scholars have had far more difficulty with the descent into hell in terms of its Petrine statement than they have ever had with the ascent into heaven. The ascent into heaven is presented, for example, at the end of Luke and at the beginning of the book of Acts. Now on what possible New Testament basis do you say that the descent into hell is orthodox while the ascent into heaven is heretical? This shows perfectly well that you're operating with extrinsic criteria. You're using the Bible as nothing but an opportunity for proof-texting. This is the worst kind of fundamentalistic proof-texting.

Altizer. I offer no proof-text for the descent into hell. As a matter of fact, that's a strange thing to accuse me of. I'm not aware that I've ever used a proof-text.

Montgomery. What I'm trying to find out is why you feel that the ascent into heaven is heterodox, while the descent into hell is orthodox.

Altizer. I think that we have a primary problem in ascertaining the basic, fundamental, primary meaning of the Christian faith. I do so on the basis of the understanding of the *incarnation*—on the basis and understanding that God in Christ has become flesh—that God has become manifest in the world, in time, and in space. The incarnation is a final and complete movement of God into the world.

Now, to believe in the *ascension* is to believe that God has annulled and reversed this process. One who believes in the ascension continues to cling to a preincarnate form of the word, therein refusing the reality of the incarnation. Therefore I regard it as a false form of faith, or a bad form of faith. But to believe in the *descent into hell* is to believe that Christ Himself continues to move into the depths of life and body and the world after the crucifixion. And that seems to me to be perfectly consistent with the fundamental Christian understanding of the incarnation.

Montgomery. Yes, but what ground do you have for

saying anything about the incarnation? You already said that the notion of Christ presenting Himself as God in flesh was not in the least offensive to the Hellenistic community which you feel created this New Testament situation. Under those circumstances, you've cut yourself off from making any statements about the incarnation. All you're able to talk about apparently is Jesus' apocalypticism, which was terribly offensive to the Hellenistic Church. You see, you're importing an understanding of incarnation into the situation.

Altizer. We understand the incarnation primarily not on the basis of deductions from the New Testament, but rather on the basis of an encounter with an understanding of the Word which is present in our midst in our flesh.

Montgomery. There's an article by philosopher Kai Nielsen which was reprinted in *New Theology No. 1* entitled "Can Faith Validate God-Talk?" The essence of this article is that anybody who speaks about an encounter with something has a responsibility to make sure that he is encountering something other than his own innards. What I want to know is why this is an encounter with a Word? It seems to me that it is an encounter with Altizer.

Altizer. If the Word isn't present in us, then it's nowhere.

Montgomery. Why is it present in our flesh and nowhere else?

Altizer. That is the essence of faith that the Word is here now in us redemptively as a source of life.

Montgomery. Let me present you with another faith position. This has to do with a little green man who is eating toasted cheese sandwiches and is sitting on a planet exactly two miles out of the range of the best telescope on earth. He is a figure who loves us, particularly if we eat toasted cheese sandwiches. He has a nasty habit of moving out of the range of the telescopes as they increase their range. Now let us say that I believe in this. How does this differ from your claim that you're having some sort of encounter with the kenotic Word?

Altizer. The decisive criterion is, Can you speak of it?

Montgomery. I've just spoken of it.

Altizer. Oh no, that's not speech, that's gibberish.

Montgomery. The thing that you don't seem to realize is that what you're saying is regarded as gibberish in the exact same sense because you have absolutely no criteria for affirming that you're having an encounter with any Word. You've cut yourself off from any kind of criteria. Why not an encounter with bloop or gleep?

Altizer. The decisive question here is, Can such an encounter be spoken of in such a way as to embody life and light?

Montgomery. All right, why is it life and light?

Altizer. Call it what you will, redemption or . . .

Montgomery. Why do you think it's life and light? Why isn't it darkness and damnation?

Altizer. It no doubt appears to be darkness and damnation.

Montgomery. You're not kidding! But the issue is not how it appears to you or how it appears to me, but how we can settle such a question. This is obviously of tremendous importance because people today are looking for religious answers in the situation that you've described. Now you go around talking about your encounters with a fully kenotic Word. Why should anybody listen?

Altizer. There's no reason why they should listen to me, of course. But they do have a primary obligation to listen to anything that can bring meaning to life. Now one thing they can't do—they can't find any objective, rational, scientific means of validating a Word of life. That is hopeless and demonic, I believe!

Montgomery. In that case, why are you bothering to write?

Altizer. Let's not identify all writing with objective rational analysis. If we were to do that, there would be no theology whatsoever.

Montgomery. Then you're thinking in terms of theology as a kind of poetic expression of your own approach to the universe. Is that right? Then it is essentially autobiography.

Altizer. It's autobiography in the sense that it is an attempt to witness to a reality dawning in humanity at this time.

Montgomery. Why is there a reality dawning in humanity? In the 1930's people exactly like you were convinced that reality was dawning in national socialism.

Altizer. Just a second. The majority of the people who supported the national socialists were orthodox Christians.

Montgomery. Is that right? For example, the critical theologians Kittel and Hirsch?

Altizer. I'm talking about the masses in Germany.

Montgomery. You'd have a deuce of a time demonstrating *that.*

Altizer. Just as most orthodox Christians in this country are segregationists.

Montgomery. I'm glad you bring that up again, particularly since you make reference to the South as you did at De Paul University. I think this is very important because it shows one of the basic difficulties in your thought, namely, that you confuse sociology with theology. You see a situation in the South which is a mess sociologically. And you see churches that have deviated from the historic Christian proclamation and who still claim to be in accord with it. But instead of bringing their false theology up against the historic Word and the Christ who is objectively present in history, and whose words are objectively presented in Scripture, you dump the whole business. You manifest the Hegelian dialectic in your own person in that you're tossing out baby and bath water. In Scripture it says that there is neither Jew nor Greek, neither bond nor free, and that we are all one in Christ Jesus. Thus any Christian who claims segregation to be Christian is un-Christian. The way to handle this is not to toss out the Christian faith, but to apply the Christian faith.

Moderator*. Dr. Altizer, what is the manifestation today of the energy that entered the world by virtue of God's death in Christ?

Altizer. Now this is the fundamental question with which we're dealing, of course. In a very real sense this is a question which cannot be answered objectively. It

---

* Raymond D. Fogelson, Assistant Professor of Anthropology and Social Sciences, University of Chicago.

is a question which each man is called to answer for
himself. Each man has to ask himself wherein he truly
finds a release of energy, wherein he truly finds love
and joy. Now I think that what we do have, I would
not say objectively but symbolically, is a fundamental
pattern within the tradition of the Christian faith. And
for me, as I said before, the pattern is the incarnation.
Insofar as I believe that the incarnation is a continuous
forward movement in history, I believe that we can look
to the world, the flesh, the body energy as being most
fundamentally the source of life for us. I believe that
living in the time in which we do, namely, in the time
of the death of God, everything which appears in our
transcendent horizon, or everything which is associated
with mystery or the beyond can only be a source of death,
alienation, and repression. We are called instead to a
movement of Christ in the world, actually and immediately present to us, which releases us here and now, not
in some after world, for a fulness of life which we can
only know insofar as interiorally and actually we become
open to energy wherever it will appear, whenever it may
appear. We have no clear guidelines to such a source
of light; I would only say that we have a symbolic guide-
line insofar that we can know that God is no longer manifest as God, that the Word is no longer manifest in the
form of pure or transcendent spirit, but instead is released
in the world as a source of life and energy here and
now immediately and actually to us.

   Montgomery. If I stick my finger in a light socket,
I get plenty of energy. The question is, How do I know
when it is divine, spiritual energy, and when this is simply
a device for self-shocking? It seems to me you've simply
got to answer this question. You can't allow the thing
to float off into the realm of mystical incarnational teaching when you don't even have a basis for that. When
you say that you can get some kind of symbolic indication, you ought to know that unless you have an identifiable reference there is no sense in even talking about
symbolism. If A is the symbol for B, and B is the symbol
for C, and C is the symbol for A, you don't know nothin'
about nothin' about any of 'em.

Altizer. Yes, I think that's the position of the orthodox Christian today.

Montgomery. It's also the position of the orthodox Christianity of the first century that declared that on the basis of the *de facto* resurrection of Jesus Christ from the dead, à la the Tallyrand story, they had a basis for affirming that Jesus Christ is the same yesterday, today and forever. I'm still calling for a resurrection on your part, or a deferral to the One who did rise from the dead.

Altizer. I really don't know how to reply to that, except that I can't conceivably imagine how such a question could ever be asked by a Christian.

Montgomery. It seems to me Thomas asked it.

Altizer. Yes, I think he's your model here.

Montgomery. And most good exegetes of the Gospel of John point out that it reaches its climax in Thomas' affirmation, *Ho kyrios mou kai ho theos mou* ("My Lord and my God"). The Gospel of John begins with the incarnation—the Word became flesh—and comes to its climax with Thomas' affirmation of faith. Immediately following is John's statement that these things have been written that you might have life through believing in the name of Christ. It seems to me that you've got to ask yourself whether you're going to bring your theology into line with the primitive theology of the Christian faith, or whether you're going to continue to create a religion on the basis of your own inner experience.

Altizer. Well, there's no question about that. It's the latter. But here I would say that my own inner experience is not simply my own, of course. It's whatever participation may be open to me of the body of Christ which is present today.

Montgomery. This reminds me of Harvey Cox at the Seventh Annual Meeting of the American Society of Christian Ethics held in Evanston a little over a year ago. Cox presented a paper on his "Secular City Revisited." In the course of this he said that God is where the action is. But there was somebody with some sense in the audience who said: "Wait a minute! How do you know when it's God's action and when it's the devil's action?"

And Cox gave a long answer, the essence of which was that you discover genuine action by participating in the confessing community (an answer very similar to what you've just said). Then the questioner asked: "Carl McIntire's church or your church?" Carl McIntire, for the benefit of some of the people here, is a right-wing reactionary if there ever was one—politically and in every other way. And his general approach is about as different from that of Professor Cox as you could imagine. This just shows how frequently today's theologians beg the question. If you talk about participation in the community, then the question obviously is, What community? Many communities declare that they are the body of Christ. Edgar Sheffield Brightman of Boston University used to say that the universe in which both Christian Science and Catholicism are true, would be a madhouse. Questions of this kind must be settled. You can't leave them in vague terms such as "participation in the body of Christ." You're just playing with words.

Altizer. I'm afraid there aren't any easy answers, Mr. Montgomery.

Montgomery. You don't present *any* answers. I'll listen to any old answer.

Altizer. I'd be un-Christian if I presented an answer that would satisfy you.

Montgomery. That's interesting because that's about the criticism that the early Christians received. They went around actually proclaiming something—that God had come into the world in Jesus, that He had died for people's sins, and that He had risen again for their justification. Paul cites people who saw the resurrected Christ and says that over 500 were still alive—the implication being that if you don't believe it, go and ask one of them. The early Christians were so blamed definite that they turned the world upside down. But contemporary theologians, such as yourself I'm afraid, are so indefinite that they're leaving the world in the mess in which they find it.

Moderator. Dr. Montgomery, how do we have the knowledge of persons? In what sense can we know an historical figure who has died in space and time such as Jesus or Caesar?

Montgomery. This is a very good question. The answer is that we come to know an historical figure personally as we come to know that historical figure objectively. Not the other way around. Anybody who tries to set personal knowledge over against objective knowledge is doomed to solipsism. This is evident within the New Testament itself. For example, when John the Baptist was finding difficulty in retaining his commitment to Christ (John was in Herod's hoosegow), he sent his disciples to ask Jesus: "Are you the one who was supposed to come or shall we look for another?" Jesus said: "Go back and tell John the things which you heave heard and seen, that the dead are raised, that the blind receive their sight, that the gospel is preached," etc. The point is that in order for John's personal commitment to remain as it ought to be, it was necessary for that personal commitment to be grounded referentially. The great mistake of historiographers such as Dilthey is that they attempt to impart some kind of knowledge by participation without taking seriously the objectivity of the historical facts. If you want to find out about Jesus personally, the way to do it is to go to the primary historical records. Don't go to Altizer's books, don't go to Montgomery's books, go to the books that were written by people who had personal and direct contact with Christ. That's the way to find out what the Christian faith is all about. That's the way to find out what that magnificent personal encounter with the living Christ can mean.

Altizer. Fantastic!

Moderator. Dr. Altizer, what kind of concept do you have of salvation? If God is dead, who will be the judge when the apocalypse comes, etc.?

Altizer. Of course we as a nation are people who try to do everything in our power to hide the reality of death from ourselves. I happen to believe that death is one of our most important realities with which we have to live. I think that an example of bad faith, un-Christian bad faith, in response to death is to yearn for immortality. But I think it was particularly revealing here that the question of judgment was brought up. Now first of all, of course, in terms of our tradition, it's Christ who will be the judge. But perhaps more basically than that, from my point of view, God, in dying as God in Christ, died as the alien Other. He died as that Other who can judge us from the vantage point of the infinite gulf between the Creator and the creation, that God Himself has become Christ, therein emptying Himself of that plenitude of being which separated Him infinitely from the world. So that the Christian in response to death knows full well that he is to die, knows full well that he must die, and yet, nevertheless, finally, I believe, approaches death with the conviction that therein he is finally being called to a yet deeper union with the incarnate Word, with the Word that is at the center of life and at the center of the body and death, and therein enters into a final union with that Word, not in an immortal, transcendent realm, but rather somehow finally in the center of everything that we know is life and energy.

Montgomery. Would you mind expanding on "plenitude of being"? I especially like that! It makes me think of a line in Paul Edwards' critique of Tillich's thought (*Mind,* April, 1965) in which he quotes *Alice in Wonderland.* The king meets someone on the road and says, "Has anyone gone along ahead of me?" And the other fellow says, "Nobody." And the king says, "That's impossible because I didn't see him on the road." This is an example of the hypostatizing of language. One creates reality by the use of words. This is word magic, Professor Altizer, nothing but word magic. What in thunder is plenitude of being?

Altizer. It's an established traditional theological category which you should know, sir.

Montgomery. I know the category, but I'm wondering how you can possibly justify it. Why is there a concept of plenitude of being? A long tradition from the time of neo-Platonic philosophy does not establish its *de facto* validity.

Altizer. Again I don't quite know what you're asking.

Montgomery. Just tell me what *you* mean by the plenitude of being and *justify* your use of the expression.

Altizer. Herein I mean the plenitude of being to refer to the fulness and totality of God as God, of God as Lord— a totality which isolates God as God from the creation.

Montgomery. Where does your knowledge of either God

or the creation come from so that you can define the term "plenitude of being" in this way?

Altizer. Fundamentally, of course, the doctrine of God the Creator is grounded in the Old Testament.

Montgomery. I thought that we had more or less gotten rid of the Bible as any kind of normative base for determining such questions.

Altizer. Quite to the contrary.

Montgomery. Then, of course, you have no objection to the ascent into heaven, since the ascent into heaven is the return of the Son to the Father who manifests this plenitude of being?

Altizer. You're misunderstanding everything that I say, for I speak of a divine movement from spirit to flesh, of a divine negation of spirit. And there cannot be a self-negation of spirit unless there is a prior reality of spirit to be negated.

Montgomery. How do we know that there was any prior reality of spirit?

Altizer. Only in faith.

Montgomery. Why your "plenitude" and "spirit" rather than the toasted-cheese sandwich deity that I suggested earlier?

Altizer. Because this has been spoken of and made manifest in such a way as to be believable in faith.

Montgomery. And why has it been made believable in your understanding?

Altizer. Quite simply because it's become manifest in history, in experience in such a way as to be livable, to be real.

Montgomery. So is Marxism.

Altizer. Of course, that's another question.

Montgomery. Why your "Christian atheism" rather than Marxism?

Altizer. I didn't repudiate Marxism.

Montgomery. It seems to me that the Marxists would be terribly unhappy with the understanding of the kenotic Jesus that you have presented. The Marxists would like to have such theological terminology removed—eliminated completely.

Altizer. Not at all, kenotic language is Hegelian. That's another point.

Montgomery: Yes, I pointed out, I think, in my initial critique that your concepts and language are Hegelian. But Marx, you remember, turned Hegel on his head and insisted that in any dialectic process solely material considerations would be the determining elements.

Altizer. Not in the positivistic sense.

Montgomery. Nonetheless, the determining elements in the Marxist dialectic are held to be material factors. Now if you think that's what the Old Testament is saying . . .

Altizer. I didn't say that's what the Old Testament is saying.

Montgomery. Then you would disagree with the Old Testament in that particular.

Altizer. I just repeat my former position which is that God has emptied Himself of that which He was when He was manifest to the old covenant as God.

Montgomery. Don't you see that you've made a complete circle? You're back to the God of the Old Testament emptying Himself. The point is: Can we rely upon the Old Testament in its theology? Can we trust its presentation of God?

Altizer. Of course we can. We can't understand the death of God unless we understand the God who dies. We have to go to the Old Testament for that.

Montgomery. In other words, you wouldn't find that God apart from the Old Testament?

Altizer. No.

Montgomery. And when we come to the New Testament in which Jesus affirms that God has become manifest in Him, that He will die for the sins of the world and will rise again, and then He does rise from the dead and ascend to the right hand of the Father, then . . .

Altizer. Then we have a return to Old Testament faith, a reversal of the incarnation and a regression to a preincarnate form of faith. But it's bad faith. It returns to an empty form of Old Testament faith, possible only for the Jew, not for the Christian.

Montgomery. Why did Jesus botch it so badly when it came to the whole question of the ascension?

Altizer. Jesus certainly did not teach that He would ascend into heaven.

Montgomery. Oh, really?

Altizer. Certainly not.

Montgomery. According to the primary documents (which I think have got to take a little precedence over your judgments of them nineteen centuries later), Jesus publicly ascended into heaven and the promise was given: "In the same manner in which you see Him go into heaven, He will come again from heaven." This promise is recorded in the first chapter of the book of Acts. The writer is certainly the same person who wrote the Gospel according to St. Luke. Therefore we are in the midst of the primary documents of the Christian faith. Now what's the trouble with the document at that point?

Altizer. There are innumerable problems here, of course, which I don't quite see how we can discuss. Frankly, this is a strange kind of discussion for me. I'm just not accustomed to people who take such things as being the teachings of Jesus. This is all new to me.

Montgomery. I can only conclude that nineteen and a half centuries of church history are totally new to you, which is a strange thing for a theologian to say. What I'm presenting is not Montgomeryism. This happens to be the teaching of the ecumenical creeds maintained by all orthodox Christians, Eastern Orthodox, Roman Catholic and Protestant. It is the position maintained by the Reformers, reiterated by Wesley, and on to the present time. You're the one presenting the most bizarre and aberrational form of religion imaginable and you have the gall to cloak it with the name of the Christian faith.

Moderator. Dr. Montgomery, the reason the death of God is a gospel to Altizer is because the notion of the transcendent God is such a horror. Yet you said nothing about the concept of the transcendence of God. Will you please make up this deficit? What is your notion of a transcendent God?

Montgomery. God's transcendence is presented in the ecumenical creeds which are grounded in the totality of scriptural relevation. There we learn that God is transcendent over the world, for He created it out of nothing, and He preserves it by His grace. If He were to withdraw His hand, in a moment Altizer and Montgomery and

the whole gang here would go up in smoke. In this sense
He is transcendent over His creation; it depends on Him,
but He is not limited by it. One of the great errors of
contemporary process theology—Professor Altizer has
close relations with this, as he pointed out at De Paul—
is that God is made dependent upon the creation in such
a way that the creation conditions God. Now the idea
of the creation conditioning God is a notion which simply
can't be reconciled with the biblical teaching. In the
Bible—from Genesis to Revelation—God is transcendent
over the creation, over His world, and He does with it
as He wills. That God appeared in this world in Jesus
Christ. If He hadn't appeared in Christ, we would have
very, very little knowledge of Him.

   Altizer. I'm largely in agreement with that. That is
to say, I think Dr. Montgomery has accurately spoken
of what I understand to be the transcendence of God.
But I'd like to make a further point. I think one of the interesting
things we can observe in the movement of history
(here I limit myself to Western history, specifically
to Western Christendom, herein not speaking for example
of Judaism) is that as our history has unfolded as it has
moved and we have increasingly known the transcendence
of God in ever more empty and alien forms and images.
So that by the time we come to the disintegration of
Western Christendom, which perhaps fundamentally
occurred by the time of the French Revolution, certainly
by the time of the 19th century, the fruits of which we're
living today, we reach this point when it's no longer possible
for Western man to know the transcendent God as
a source of life or joy. Instead transcendence appears
either as a wholly alien oppressive realm or as a wholly
abstract and empty realm. I think it's very interesting,
for example, that in what many regard as our greatest
American novel, *Moby Dick,* the transcendent God is
known under the image of the white whale. Or to move
to the 20th century, perhaps the most profound spokesman
of the reality of transcendence is Franz Kafka, in which
we see a wholly negative, wholly destructive, repressive,
alien form of transcendence. I would say that the only
form of transcendence which we can actually know, which
we can live, is either an alien or an empty one. It is pre-

cisely for this reason that the Christian can know the death of God as gospel, as joy, as liberation.

Montgomery. I agree that from the French Revolution on—indeed, as early as the end of the 17th century—a movement away from transcendence, meaningful transcendence, gained momentum. But the answer to this is not the death of God. The answer is to go to Jesus Christ— that point in human history when God enters our realm so that we can experience Him. If one looks elsewhere in trying to solve this problem, he gets absolutely nowhere. And that's what contemporary Protestant theology is demonstrating. Karl Barth attempts to find God in the realm of *Geschichte* ("supra-history") rather than *Historie* (ordinary history), and as a result he gets exactly nowhere. It's very difficult to identify resurrections or even poker games in *Geschichte!* This is a realm of "meta-history" for which no criteria seem to exist. Rudolf Bultmann attempted to find God in internal experience, but it's very difficult to distinguish the Holy Spirit from stomach trouble, as Professor Altizer has so well demonstrated. Paul Tillich attempted to solve this problem in the realm of religious symbolism. Professor Altizer reflects this also, having nothing but symbolic statements made about God. But if everything is symbolic, you've gotten nowhere. Finally we come to the death of God movement at which point no statements are made about the transcendent at all. This reminds me of what Wittgenstein talked about when he said that the proper function of philosophy is to show the fly the way out of the fly bottle. Professor Altizer is flying around in this fly bottle along with most of contemporary Protestant theology. The fly bottle was created when Protestant theology lost its confidence in the historical records concerning the life and ministry of Jesus Christ. The only way out of this is the way the contemporary theologian got into it. He must come to see that it's possible to deal with these records and find a Jesus who is both God and man there. Then he can see the transcendent God manifest in the human situation. And seeing this, he has his entrée to the transcendent.

Moderator. Dr. Montgomery, how do you really feel that Altizer has contradicted the historical Jesus?

Montgomery. It would require an evening to answer that. The point is—and I think this became quite clear in the exchange that we had earlier—Professor Altizer abstracts from the New Testament documents those elements in Jesus' teachings which fit with the neo-Hegelian immanent spirit which is expanding in the world and creating dialectically the fulfillment which Altizer looks for. For example, he is able to take the notion of Jesus as an eschatological figure. He has no trouble with this at all. But whenever he comes across material in Jesus' teachings which doesn't go along with this, then that material is immediately transferred to the realm of the incredible. This is a deuce of a way of finding out what Jesus' teachings actually are. In history one has to put oneself at the disposal of the records to allow the records to speak to the individual. One cannot stand over the records with the kind of arbitrary critical selectivity that's being used here. The result of this is always that you get historical figures that are simply mirror images of yourself. What we get here is not an historical Jesus, nor an objective Jesus. What we get here is a Jesus who fits with remarkable precision the theological presuppositions Professor Altizer brings to the investigation to begin with. So we learn nothing.

Altizer. I would simply like to ask, do you really believe it's possible to construct a theological position which accepts the full authority of the Bible or of the New Testament and which does not rest inevitably upon the negation of certain material present in the New Testament?

Montgomery. Not only do I think it's possible, I don't even have to do it. That's been done again and again in the history of the church. You can take Augustine, you can take . . .

Altizer. Has it been done by anyone since the dawn of the modern historical consciousness?

Montgomery. I would say yes, very definitely.

Altizer. For example?

Montgomery. Well, I hate to cite a theologian of my own tradition, but Franz Pieper's *Christian Dogmatics* is an example of this sort of thing. If you'd like something in a more literary vein, you can take the writings of C.

S. Lewis. You'll find in the writings of C. S. Lewis a comprehensive body of biblical teaching. Lewis doesn't stand over Scripture and pick and choose.

Altizer. Yes, he does. He certainly does.

Montgomery. For example?

Altizer. For example, the apocalyptic Jesus is absent from Lewis.

Montgomery. I wouldn't say He was absent if I wanted to take into account some of Lewis' most important writings, his children's stories, for example—the Narnia Chronicles. In the seventh and final Narnia book, *The Last Battle*, is an apocalypticism that transcends anything that a professional Protestant theologian has done in the 20th century. Remember that tremendous passage where "the farther in you go the larger it becomes—"

Altizer. I have to confess my ignorance. I haven't read them, but I shall.

Montgomery. You ought to. You ought to give them to your children to read. They're magnificent.

Moderator. Dr. Altizer, why is it just now at this time in history that the death of God has broken in upon the consciousness of the corporate Christian body? If this process is going on and on, why is it that it's at this particular junction in history? Why not 100 years from now, another millennium or something?

Altizer. By "right now" I really mean a period of, say, 200 years; I don't mean 1967. It's a gradual thing, of course. I think, however, that there is one fundamental answer to this question. I really think that, historically speaking, what underlies our time, insofar as ours is a time of the death of God, is the collapse of Christendom. This is seen in the breakdown of our traditional Christian culture and society, the breakdown of the Church as the dominant bearer of culture, etc. etc. This is time in which traditional Christian norms are no longer decisively operative throughout the human community or throughout interior experience. Christendom evolved, in a certain sense, a form of faith or of religion or of belief which could partially absorb the reality of Christ, but nevertheless make possible a God language perpetuating a preincarnate form of Christ. Once that breaks down, then in a certain sense there is no barrier between man and the reality of the death of God. That's one explanation. I do think that what we call the death of God is integrally an expression of the collapse of Christendom. But there are many other ramifications to this.

Montgomery. You feel the death of God is a positive phenomenon and therefore the 19th century appearance of this and the 20th century reinforcement of it are definitely a revelatory kind of experience?

Altizer. Yes, yes.

Montgomery. Doesn't this suffer from that famous old fallacy of *consensus gentium*—that because things are going on, because people happen to take a particular point of view, that point of view is necessarily a good one. Why shouldn't we pick the 13th century as revelatory? It seems to me I once read an interesting Thomist work entitled "The Greatest of Centuries." Of course, this turned out to be the 13th century since it was the century of Thomas Aquinas. People such as I in the Reformation tradition tend to glorify the 16th century, the Reformation era. Isn't there a . . .

Altizer. It's not humanly possible to live in any century but our own.

Montgomery. You mean that anything which happens to go on in our century is *ipso facto* an example of the Spirit operating?

Altizer. Not necessarily. But this is our reality. This is our world. We can't live in another world. We have to live in the 20th century.

Montgomery. I agree definitely. The question is: On what in the 20th century ought a positive evaluation to be placed? And on what in the 20th century ought a negative evaluation to be placed?

Altizer. Granted. That's the crucial question. I think I've made my choice. I'm not disguising it, am I?

Montgomery. I'm not questioning that you made a choice. I want to know why one should choose as you have in regard to the phenomena of the 20th century. Why, for example, should you choose in the direction of the death of God phenomena as you see them in the 20th century and choose against that which is held by those historic Christian churches still maintaining the faith once delivered to the saints?

Altizer. I frankly don't know of any such churches, to be perfectly honest with you.

Montgomery. I suggest that you move north. Maybe that's the answer!

Moderator. Dr. Montgomery, if you attack Altizer for having a faith which is unverifiable empirically, please state how the faith which you hold can be empirically verifiable for our grandsons.

Montgomery. The answer to this is simply the answer that is provided by the early Christian proclaimers of the gospel. They had personal, empirical contact with Jesus. They found that this Jesus was not simply a man. He was more than this, both in what He said and in what He did. He forgave sins, for example. People said to Him, "Who can forgive sins but God only?" And He didn't say, "Oops! You're quite right. It was a slip." He identified Himself with the eternal God in the forgiving of sins. He performed miracles. He rose again from the dead. The *New Testament* writers had that kind of personal, empirical contact with Jesus. We have documents reporting this, and these documents are primary documents. They were in circulation when people were still alive who had had contact with these events. Many of those people were very hostile in their attitude toward the Christian faith. They would have destroyed this thing if it could have been destroyed, just as many false messiahs fell by the wayside. Theudas, who wanted to divide the Jordan River, was one example of this kind. Under these circumstances, we have here the empirical testimony of those who saw Christ manifest His deity by rising from the dead, conquering the powers of death. Orthodox Christians, whatever their denominational connection, believe that this Christ who rose from the dead is exactly who He said He was. Certainly He was in a better position to make statements on the subject than we are. That's an empirical base which is solid. Now it isn't 100% certain, as no historical knowledge is. But neither is any knowledge of your present. You base your understanding of the world on your uncertain empirical contacts in the present. And you have to act on this basis.

The evidence in this case is remarkable. It's the kind of evidence that, for a person who will consider it seriously. points in a definite direction. As Pascal said, there is enough evidence to convince anybody who is not set against it. But there is not so much evidence that a person can be forced into believing it if he simply will not.

Moderator. Dr. Altizer, does the Jewish theologian Rubenstein believe God died in Jesus? If not, when does he believe God died? If he believes God died in Jesus, has he left the Jewish stance before he joined the God is dead movement?

Altizer. I don't believe this is a good question to choose. Who am I to speak for Dr. Rubenstein? I know him very well, and I've read many of his things. He does not believe that God died in Jesus. He's a Jew. But so what? If he does not believe God died in Jesus, then when does he believe God died? Rubenstein is grounded in the Cabala—in the Jewish mystical tradition. In a certain sense he believes that God died in becoming the Creator. but this is a technical point. I would say, read his book *After Auschwitz.* It's a wonderful book. I'm no one to speak for his position. He's a very clear, forceful writer. A person who reads his book will have no trouble getting Rubenstein's position.

Montgomery. I'd be very interested sometime to hear a dialogue between the two of you about whether God died in Jesus or whether he didn't.

Altizer. We've had many battles.

Montgomery. The problem of verifiability would come out with agonizing clarity in a discussion like that because neither of you would be able to say anything.

Moderator. On that ecumenical note we close!

The Death of God
Becomes More Deadly

In my book *The 'Is God Dead?' Controversy,* which was published in August, 1966, and treats the theonthanatological movement as of June 5 of that year, I placed William Hamilton to the left of Altizer but to the right of van Buren. On October 28, 1966, it became evident that Hamilton's former Colgate-Rochester colleague Charles M. Nielsen had not been exaggerating when he cynically

wrote of the death-of-God theology: "So powerful is the
thrust toward novelty that a famous Protestant journal
is considering a series of articles by younger theologians
under sixty called 'How My Mind Has Changed in the
Past Five Minutes'" (*The Christian Century,* Sept. 15,
1965).

At a program on the radical theology sponsored by
the University of Michigan's Office of Religious Affairs,
Hamilton gave a position paper in question-and-answer
form, and the answers quite plainly showed how rapidly
his mind had changed in the last few months (if not minutes). The direction of change was—predictably—to
the left, and now Hamilton stands with van Buren at
the radical extremity of the God-is-dead movement. Having presented a critique of theothanatology in the same
University Lecture Series a week earlier (October 21),
I was privileged to engage in close study of Hamilton's
position paper, and its interest is such as to warrant comment here.*

My original basis for considering Hamilton less radical
than van Buren was his stress on the Christian as "both
a waiting man and a praying man": though the "God
of necessity" (i.e., the traditional God required by believers to "explain" aspects of their world of experience)
was dead, Hamilton continued to hope and pray for the
possible epiphany of a "God of delight"—a God not needed
but perhaps discoverable by modern secular man in the
freedom of his emancipation from old loyalties. Now Hamilton has closed this door; says he: "I wouldn't put things
in this way now. . . . In place, in a way, of 'waiting
for God' is the interest in the development of new approaches, godless approaches, to the sacred" (question
30).

What approaches—now that the "death of God does
not refer to a disappearance of a psychological capacity,"
and "the God in the phrase 'I believe in God, Father
Almighty, maker of heaven and earth' . . . is no more"
(question 1), and "doing without God means doing without
eternal life" (questions 13, 16, 17)? The new thrusts of

---

* Hamilton's paper has since been published in *The Death of God
Debate,* ed. Jackson Lee Ice and John J. Carey (Philadelphia: Westminster Press, 1967), pp. 213-41.

Hamilton's "Christian humanism" (question 4) are (bald-
ly stated) *Society, Sex,* and the *Simple Jesus.* Society:
"What once was done by God is done by social change,
politics, even revolution" (question 9). Sex: "May it not
be that the experience of sex can become a kind of sacred
event for some today?" Hamilton answers by quoting
a rococo passage from *The Scarlet Letter* and commenting, "Here is an astonishing event—the idea of a sexual
relationship outside of marriage, in the midst of Puritan
New England, possessing a sacredness that does not seem
to require the idea of God" (question 16).

But, admits Hamilton, this attempt to find Jesus "concealed in the struggle for truth, justice, or 'beauty' is
unstable unless one sees that it must be based on the
New Testament picture" of Jesus (question 10). "I take
it," he continues, "that Bornkamm's *Jesus of Nazareth*
can stand as a statement of a consensus of what can
be known." Here is immediately raised "the most important theological question that can be asked of us," namely,
"Can you really maintain a loyalty to Jesus without a
loyalty to God?" (question 11). Hamilton's answer is
of such consequence that it deserves to be quoted at
length:

"Professor Altizer solves the problem more readily
than I by his apocalyptic definition of Jesus, more Blakean
than biblical, as the one who is born out of God's death.
I am not yet ready to give up *sola scriptura* [!], and
thus my answer must be more complex and tentative. . . .
Early in the nineteenth century, we had to face, under
the early impact of historical criticism, both that Jesus
was firmly committed to demon-possession as the meaning of mental and physical illness, and that we were not
so committed and needn't be. But obedience to Jesus
was not destroyed. Later, at the time of Darwinian controversy, we had to face another instance of Jesus' full participation in the thought forms of his day—the three-story,
primitive cosmology. But we do not go to the Bible for
science, we were rightly told, and obedience to Jesus
was not hurt. At the close of the century we had to face
an even more disturbing fact—the fact brought before
us by Weiss and Schweitzer that Jesus was completely
committed to the apocalyptic views of the Judaism of his

day. . . . If Jesus' demonology and cosmology and eschatology were taken as first-century views, appropriate then,
not so now, needing reinterpretation and understanding
but not literal assent, what is inherently different about
Jesus' *theology*?"

The significance of this argument for the current theological situation cannot be overestimated, for it explicitly
maps the progressive demise of Christology through the
consistent application of rationalistic biblical criticism.
For over a century, orthodox Christians have vainly reminded their liberal confrères of the Reformers' conviction that the "material principle" (the Gospel of Christ)
cannot possibly survive apart from the "formal principle"
(divinely inspired Scripture). "Fiddlesticks!" has been
the reply: *"Of course* we can distinguish the true theological core of Scripture and the central message of Jesus
from the biblical thought-forms of the ancient Near East."
But in point of fact, as Hamilton well shows, the stripping
of the cultural thought-forms from the "true" teaching
of Scripture is like peeling an onion: when finished, you
have no teaching at all, only tears (unless you happen
to be a constitutional optimist like Hamilton, who finds
mankind a satisfactory God-substitute).

Either Jesus' total teachings are taken as God's word
(including his full trust in Scripture as divine revelation)
or, as Luther well put it, "everyone makes a hole in
it wherever it pleases him to poke his snout, and follows
his own opinions, interpreting and twisting Scripture any
way he pleases." The Bible has become just such a "wax
nose" today, so that even a death-of-God theologian claims
to follow *sola scriptura.* This is the inevitable outcome
of rationalistic biblical criticism that refuses to distinguish between straight-forward grammatical-historical
explication of the biblical message and presuppositional
judgment upon it. Has the time perhaps come for the
Church to recognize that aprioristic biblical criticism has
brought theology to the bier of Deity?

Otto Piper of Princeton, in reviewing Bornkamm's
Jesus of Nazareth, saw what few others had seen but
what is perfectly demonstrated by the death-of-God
school: "The theologian has already arrived at the knowledge of the religious truth before he opened his New Testa-

ment, and consequently everything in the Gospels that is not fit to illustrate this truth is *a priori* doomed to be rejected" *(Interpretation,* October, 1961).

Altizer and Rome

The Death-of-God movement displays less and less vitality with each passing month. It would seem that this quasi-religious phenomenon, centering as it does on the motif of mortality, is itself experiencing death-throes.

An oblique indicator that the cry "God is dead" is losing its force is the appearance of an anthology of "Readings in the Death of God Theology" *(Toward a New Christianity,* edited by Thomas J. J. Altizer). This volume—though it conveniently omits bibliographic reference to the Altizer-Montgomery dialogue at the University of Chicago, which certainly marks at least one step in the decline of theothanatology—suggests that this "radical" movement has already reached the unenviable bourgeois stage of collected "readings."

But an even more direct evidence that death-of-God is dying was provided on June 21, 1967, when Professor Altizer addressed a philosophy workshop at The Catholic University of America on "The Problem of God in Contemporary Thought." Having found his position roundly rejected by virtually all strata of Protestant thought, Altizer emphatically stated that if there proves to be no possibility that Roman Catholic theology will move in the direction of his "totally christocentric" form of faith and the dialectical self-negation of God, then "I for one will be reluctantly forced to concede that an atheistic or death of God theology is a destructive aberration." Quite a concession!

What has convinced Altizer that he should now put all his atheological eggs in a Roman Catholic basket? The answer is not hard to find, and it is an exceedingly instructive one for those Christians recently celebrating the 450th anniversary of the Reformation.

Let us begin by recalling the essence of Altizer's position: his affirmation of God's death is a variant of archaic nineteenth century Hegelianism. He begins by rejecting the law of non-contradiction (on which all logical thinking

is based) and substitutes for it Hegel's so-called "dialectic logic" of perpetual thesis, antithesis, and synthesis,
whereby religious truth undergoes self-negation and thus
progressively rises to higher and higher levels, issuing
out in a "God beyond God" and a "fully kenotic Word."
This totally hidden Christ (which must not be "identified
with the original historical Jesus") is encountered in the
secular, profane present and even more fully in the apocalyptic "third age of the Spirit" growing in the crucible
of today's secularism. (See my *The 'Is God Dead?' Controversy* [Zondervan, 1966] which appears as a chapter
in Bernard Murchland's *The Meaning of the Death of
God* [Random House, 1967], and in the present section
as the essay titled "Morticians of the Absolute.")

At Catholic University Altizer effortlessly related these
views to contemporary thinking in the Roman church.
In contrast to historic Protestantism, which relies on the
Bible as God's sole and final revelation of truth, the modern Catholic thinker—whose greatest model is provided
by the evolutionary theology of Teilhard de Chardin—conceives of a dynamic or evolving Christ. This Christ is
progressively manifested in the growth of his Body, the
Church—an organic development inseparable from the
total body of humanity. "Once we are liberated from
the root idea that the biblical and apostolic images of
God have an absolute and eternal authority, then"—
Altizer underscored the lesson for modern Catholics—"we
can become open to the possibility that everything which
orthodox Christianity has known as God is but a particular
stage of God's self-manifestation, and must in turn be
transcended by the forward movement of God Himself."

Doubtless Altizer goes too far in his endeavor to create
a one-to-one correlation between Rome's world-view and
process-thought. Aristotelain logic, St. Thomas's passion
for objective, final truth, and the respect given through
the centuries to the inerrant Scriptures and creedal verities are too much a part of Rome's life to be brushed
lightly aside. But Altizer is not mistaken when he points
up the extent to which evolutionary, process thinking influences the contemporary Catholic mind.

Karl Adam, in his classic *The Spirit of Catholicism*
argued that true Catholic Christianity must not be seen

in the "embryonic" state (its original biblical documents) but rather in its "progressive unfolding," even as the oak must be seen not as an acorn but in its full maturity. Today many Catholics regard their church as a living organism that, as the extension of Christ's incarnation, can creatively reshape its past: "reinterpreting" past pronouncements such as *extra ecclesiam nulla salus* so as to give them totally new force. Once the Magisterium does reinterpret a past teaching, then all previous authoritative expressions of the teaching are held to carry this meaning: the past is rewritten in terms of the dynamic, living present. (See my book, *Ecumenicity, Evangelicals, and Rome* [Zondervan, 1969].)

To the Reformation Protestant, this procedure invariably suggests both the Marxist (*dialectic,* note well) rewriting of history and George Orwell's *1984,* where Winston, the citizen of a totalitarian world in which truth is continually "evolved" and "redefined," comes to realize that his society has fallen into the epistemological hell of solipsism. The Protestant knows well—or ought to know well—that unless an objective Word from God stands over against the Church, judging it and proclaiming grace to it, the Church invariably deifies itself, thereby engaging in the worst kind of idolatry. When any corporate body lacking a clear external standard of truth grows in strength, it strives to become a standard to itself, a law to itself: a Leviathan, the "mortal god" described by Hobbes. Solovyov, in his *Short Story of Antichrist (Christianity Today,* Jan. 29, 1965), well showed that where objective revelational truth ceases to provide a firm criterion of action, no church has the holiness to withstand the blandishments of antichristic power.

From all sides today efforts are being made to unite Christendom ecumenically on the basis of vague dreams of evolving, process truth (a particularly unfortunate example being the writings of Charles J. Curtis, who employs Söderblom as a bridge to join Protestant with Catholic à la Whiteheadian process-thought). Altizer delineated the issue precisely when he asserted at Catholic University: "Any genuine evolutionary understanding of God is incompatible with the idea of an original deposit of faith which is absolute and given or unchanging."

Here is the watershed: *Was* God in Christ, objectively reconciling the world unto himself? *Did* he "once in the end of the world [appear] to put away sin by the sacrifice of himself" (Heb. 9:26)? *Has* God spoken with absolute finality in the Holy Scriptures, which testify of Christ? If so, process-theology in all its forms must receive the kiss of death. For only the Christ of Scripture, who is the same yesterday, today, and forever, can offer Church and society a genuine Resurrection and Life.

6.

Theological Education Today

On Taking a
European Theological Doctorate

The morning mail at 3, blvd Gambetta, Strasbourg, brought the latest issue of the new Lutheran theological journal *Dialog*. In an editorial entitled, "A Theology of Rediscovery," Roy A. Harrisville of Luther Seminary, St. Paul, Minnesota, informed readers that the "boredom" of Lutheran orthodoxy was being replaced by a "new posture"—characterized by such views as that "there is a demonstrable parallel between Bultmann's method and Luther's concentration of the gospel in the single theme of justification" *(Dialog*, Summer, 1963, pp. 188-90).

This kind of reasoning was no surprise, for I had encountered similar utterances in earlier issues of this journal which consistently tries to lift American Lutheranism out of its "boring" biblical orthodoxy into the mainstream of "contemporary" theological thought (i.e., that contemporary theology which, with Harrisville, "admits to the discrepancies and the broken connections in Scripture"). What did surprise and amuse me was the assertion that "this concern for the contemporary manifested itself in a streaming to the universities of Europe. . . . One by one, the so-called 'Young Turks' went to Basel, to Heidelberg, to Marburg, to Tübingen, to the universities of England and France." The obvious implication was that merely to drink the heady wine of European theology was to be forever cured of reactionary views of plenary inspiration and Reformation orthodoxy. I found this implication especially bizarre because I was then engaged in writing a dissertation for the degree of *Docteur de l'Université, mention Théologie Protestante*, at Schweitzer's alma mater, the historic University of Strasbourg. To suggest that European theological study and historic Protestant conservatism were incompatible seemed a serious misunderstanding of the nature of the European

academic atmosphere. This "Young Turk" thus felt a
strong desire to dethrone a stereotype by offering a closer
look at the European doctoral experience.

Why Europe?

Doubtless theological "boredom" in the States has
driven students to Europe. None except the intellectually
lazy care for the seminary or graduate school where students must conform to their professors' views. But where
today on the American scene is such orthodoxy enforced?
Not, I should say from personal experience, in the doctrinally orthodox seminaries, but rather in the very institutions claiming to offer "theologies of rediscovery."
While serving as a faculty member in a theological school
of a large American university, I discovered to my dismay
that able doctoral students in that school often spent long
years attempting to complete their work, only to be eliminated from the program because their theological "attitudes" did not fit the prevalent modes of thinking or
methodologies. Encouragement was ostensibly given to
engage freely in "constructive theology," but such "construction" was not really a "free" activity, because it
implied that the great confessional documents of the historic Church, and even the Scriptures on which they are
founded, stand always in need of reconstruction. I also
noted that at this same university the theological school
was often viewed with less than respect by the non-theological faculties, because it was evident that a doctorate
in theology meant not so much a superior level of academic attainment as an achievement in learning how to
manipulate currently accepted conceptual patterns and
"in-group" terminology.

Faced with such an atmosphere, I took my Ph.D. in
a non-theological field and looked to one of my own denominational seminaries as a more satisfactory possibility for the Th.D. However, the latter situation manifested
the same kind of "inverse orthodoxy": to display a non-
conservative doctrinal position was to exemplify "academic freedom," whereas to affirm biblical evangelical-
ism was to betray "poor scholarship." After a summer
program in which I received professorial criticism for
a subsequently published paper asserting the historical

as well as theological soundness of John's Gospel, I determined that a Th.D. from such an institution would
represent conformity to a viewpoint rather than scholarly
achievement.

At this point, I recalled two or three European theological professors under whom I had studied during their
visits to American seminaries; these men differed from
their average American counterparts not so much in doctrine as in their attitude toward the nature of theological
study. Whatever their personal religious position, they
respected the views of the individual student. They demanded of him not conformity to their beliefs but sound
scholarship in clarifying and defending his beliefs. This
was in refreshing contrast to the approach taken by a
professor of church history under whom I studied, who
began the year by saying, "We are going to remold you
here in seminary...." My thoughts thus turned to
Europe. "Boredom" with theological conformity did enter
the picture; but it was the exact reverse of the straw-man
boredom referred to by Harrisville. I was bored with
a conformity imposed by so-called "theologies of rediscovery," which say in essence: "Be as free in your theological thought as you wish—as long as you don't try
to embrace orthodoxy." For me a theological doctorate
had to represent scholarship and not sycophancy. This
was my "Young Turkism."

Professorial Tone at Strasbourg

My first insight into the character of a European doctoral program came when I applied for the program.
There were no "fill-in-the-blanks" forms, no psychological
aptitude tests. Application was by personal letter, accompanied by proof of degrees held and examples of already
published works. The *Faculté de Théologie Protestante*
wished to be satisfied on two counts only: first, that the
candidate had an original and significant doctoral topic
he wished to pursue; and second, that he was capable
of pursuing it. Administrative safeguards of course exist:
the foreign student must, by French law, evidence academic achievement equivalent to the old *licence en Théologie Protestante*—that is, he must have the theological
competence of the French doctoral student who has com-

pleted all course work, written examinations, and the minor thesis for the so-called "state doctorate." But the entire admissions procedure has the ring of scholarship, not the smell of administrative minutiae. Even the physical arrangements at the university uphold this impression: the secretariat of the faculty, where official *inscription* is made, is a dingy office in a building separate from the *Palais Universitaire*, where the attractive faculty offices are situated. How unlike the average American institution, in which the "administration" possesses the visible signs of power while faculty offices display clear evidence of subordinate status!

What were faculty members like? Were they cold, dogmatic rationalists—radical negative critics of Scripture and creeds—promoters of "theological rediscovery"? Doubtless, examples of these stereotypes can be found in European theological schools. However, I had no professor of this kind at Strasbourg. It was impossible to compartmentalize the faculty; no one was a "Bultmannian," a "Barthian," or a "Bonhoefferian." In general, the tone was more Barthian than anything else; but the overriding impression conveyed by faculty members was that the search for theological truth can never be limited to the categories of a single modern school of thought.

The perspective was thoroughly academic and thoroughly historical. Flanking the entrance to the Library of the Faculty was a glass bookcase containing the publications of its members, which represented a wide gamut of approaches and judgments and testified to the principle that scholarship, not ideological conformity, should characterize the true graduate faculty in theology as in any other subject. The historical emphasis—natural in a faculty out of which the university itself arose during the Protestant Reformation—prevented the substitution of facile novelties for serious analyses of theological problems. The creeds of the Reformation and the work of the Orthodox fathers were listened to—not passed over in haste in an effort to reach the twentieth century as quickly as possible. Dean François Wendel, in a course on the Christology of the Reformation, spent more time in the seventeenth century (the "Age of Protestant Orthodoxy") than in the sixteenth, even though Wendel is one of the greatest living Calvin scholars. Roger Mehl's course in the Augsburg Confession frequently pointed out how Barth has to his detriment moved away from Reformation doctrine. I was often reminded of Paul Tillich's famous remark that the European theologian, unlike the American, when faced with a theological problem asks first, "What has been thought on the question through church history?" Such an approach is a valuable corrective to the popular notion today that nineteen and a half centuries of Christian history have been but an inadequate prelude to the theological innovations of our generation.

The faculty members assuredly did not hold the verbal inspiration view of Scripture, and often it became evident that they confused this position with the Roman Catholic, Tridentine dictation-theory. But never was there the slightest attempt to ridicule plenary inspiration or to force conformity to another view. Indeed, I am firmly convinced that because scholarship and not presuppositionalism is the determinative factor in the theological atmosphere at Strasbourg, its faculty members would be hospitable to the orthodox view if it were consistently represented today by scholarship on the level of that of Theodor Zahn or B. B. Warfield. This is saying a great deal, for few American theological faculties would be psychologically capable of embracing biblical orthodoxy regardless of the force of its presentation, simply because conformity to the prevalent view, not scholarly objectivity, so often seems the overriding consideration.

A theological faculty usually sets the tone for its students. Have not many of us suffered from the indefinable student tensions in a seminary where the faculty, unsure of itself because of the unacademic nature of much of its work, overcompensates for inferiority feelings through heavy assignments and through preoccupation with the minutiae of course requirements and "hours" for graduation? At Strasbourg, the Protestant Theological Faculty, as the founding faculty of the university and as a faculty comparable to the others in scholarly productivity and academic standards, found no need to question its *raison d'être*. Therefore the students also could relax and study theology for its own sake—not for the sake of "proving" something by accumulating course hours. Indeed, since there the attainment of degrees is based upon written examinations, the production of a thesis, and oral defense of the thesis, one must think of actual mastery of the subject, not of mechanical acquisition of "grade points." The program for the present *licence* (much like our S.T.M., but required of all candidates for ordination in the state Lutheran Church in the Alsace) is thus rigorous, but the students find themselves in such a "permissive" environment that they show few signs of student neurosis. Quite the contrary; I have seldom met a more irrepressible group in or out of the theological circles. I remember well the evening we sang Negro spirituals in the single students' subsidized residence, and the cartoon on the front cover of one issue of the student paper, showing a dancing figure with the caption: *"Vive le Yé Yé théologique—David twistait devant l'Arche!"*

Granted that many students, especially on the *license* level, find it difficult to secure a firm theological orientation in such a non-regimented environment, nevertheless the truly open-minded faculty attitude, coupled with insistence upon a solidly grounded historical program of studied—including mastery of the original languages of Scripture—helps the students arrive at confessional solidity. Certainly no faculty prejudice creates the barrier to orthodoxy that is the most unfortunate aspect of American seminary life. It was evident how much a plenary inspirationist could accomplish on a faculty such as that at Strasbourg; and it is noteworthy that the *Groupes Bibliques Universitaires* (the French equivalent of IVCF) have a potentially open field among seminary students.

Because I was encouraged to work in complete independence, I became so engrossed in the subject of my thesis that a three-volume, 950-page work resulted. The necessity of consulting primary documents of the Reformation era led me to manuscript collections in five countries and to conversations with theological specialists such as Heinrich Bornkamm of Heidelberg. On completion, the thesis was presented and defended in a public examination before a traditional jury of three members of the *Faculté:* Dean Wendel as *Président,* accompanied by Pierre Burgelin, the Rousseau authority and urbane philosophy professor from Paris, and René Voeltzel, the author of works on seventeenth-century theology and on twentieth-century religious pedagogy. During this three hour French-language defense, two things became evident: though on many theological issues the jury and I disagreed their concern was simply that I be able to defend the scholarship of my position; and though the four of us did not always see eye to eye, we thoroughly enjoyed the dialogue.

Thus from my European experience I carried home this ideal of true "dialogue," which by no means necessitates the "theological rediscoveries" of Harrisville's "Young Turks." Mention of Strasbourg will always conjure before me the image of its medieval cathedral, rose-pink at dusk, where in the late sixteenth century Jakob Andreae preached acceptance of the Formula of Concord. That orthodox confession, it will be remembered, opens with the words: "We believe, teach, and confess that the prophetic and apostolic writings of the Old and New Testaments are the only rule and norm according to which all doctrines and teachers alike must be appraised and judged."

Bibliographical Bigotry

As confessional Protestant*—as one who believes in the evangel of Christ's atoning death and historical resurrection and in the veracious presentation of God's saving message through a totally reliable Scripture—I am supposed to be a bigot.

Theological conservatives are expected to be closed-minded, authoritarian types who obnoxiously endeavor to ram their narrow dogmas down people's gullets. More specifically, confessional bigotry is supposed to display itself in a refusal on the part of the orthodox to come into contact with ideas contradictory to their own. The conservative is expected to react like the (apocryphal) caliph who burned the Alexandrian Library: the books, he said, either disagreed with the Koran, and were there-

---

* For a fuller discussion of the meaning of this expression, see my contributions to *Spectrum of Protestant Beliefs*, ed. Robert Campbell, O.P. (Bruce, 1968).

fore heretical, or agreed with the Koran, and were therefore superfluous.

This equating of orthodoxy and bigotry has disturbed me more and more as I have had opportunity to become acquainted in depth with schools and individuals of "conservative" and "liberal" persuasion. My overwhelming impression has been the exact opposite of the stereotype: The orthodox have been wonderfully broad and liberal (in the original sense of "open to all truth"), and the self-styled "liberals" have been exceedingly illiberal.

An example or two may be useful. A year ago my seminary had a dialogue on the historicity of Christ's resurrection; we invited a Roman Catholic theologian, an Episcopalian of existentialist-linguistic leanings (Jules Moreau of Seabury-Western), and William Hordern of Garrett (author of the mediating *Case for a New Reformation Theology*) to participate with Dean Kantzer, Carl F. H. Henry, and myself (see "Faith, History, and the Resurrection," *Christianity Today*, March 26, 1965*). But in the eight years I spent on the faculties of three institutions that would certainly not call themselves "conservative," I cannot remember one occasion when a dialogue took place with a comparable representation of orthodox and liberal participants; indeed I can recall only one dialogue when a conservative was present at all.

My own seminary has separate courses on Kierkegaard, Barth, Bultmann, Bonhoeffer and Thielicke, Kant, Nietzsche, Heidegger, and Sartre; we would consider it a disgrace not to bring our students into contact with these thinkers. But I have yet to find the "liberal" seminary that offers courses on Machen, Berkouwer, Carnell, *et al.*—or that gives its students any realistic contact with their viewpoints.

An acid test of ideological bigotry lies in the field of bibliography; what people put in their libraries and what they read and recommend to be read tells us more about their liberality of mind than almost anything else.

When on the faculty of the University of Chicago Divinity School, I therefore found particularly revealing a comparison of library holdings with Wilbur Smith's standard,

---

* Reprinted in my recent book, *Where Is History Going?* (Zondervan, 1969).

authoritative *Preliminary Bibliography for the Study of Biblical Prophecy* (1952). The divinity school made a very poor showing in the field of biblical eschatology, owing apparently to the indifference of faculty members to this aspect of scriptural teaching or to the incompatibility between miraculous fulfillment of prophecy and their own theological viewpoints (cf. my paper, "A Normative Approach to the Acquisition Problem in the Theological Seminary Library," *American Theological Library Association Proceedings*, XVI [1962], 65-69).

Such a comparison was only suggestive, and it has recently led me on to a close examination of two of the most widely used recommended booklists published by seminaries lacking an orthodox confessional orientation: *A Basic Bibliography for Ministers, Selected and Annotated by the Faculty of Union Theological Seminary, New York City* (2d ed., 1960), and *Theological Bibliographies: Essential Books for a Minister's Library*, published as the September, 1963, issue of the *Andover Newton Quarterly* and prepared by its faculty. I was interested to discover what kind of openness to worthy conservative publications such lists displayed.

First, I prepared a checklist of orthodox scholars whose contributions to theological learning could not be gainsaid. This list was built up from Carl F. H. Henry's *Contemporary Evangelical Thought*, the basic bibliographical guide to twentieth-century scholarship by orthodox Protestants, and consisted of twenty-seven specialists in exegetical theology (men like O. T. Allis, Robert Dick Wilson, Edward Young, G. Ch. Aalders, Theodor Zahn, A. T. Robertson, J. G. Machen, H. E. Dana, J. R. Mantey, R. C. H. Lenski, W. F. Arndt, Merrill Tenney, W. C. Robinson, F. F. Bruce, Leon Morris) and thirty in dogmatics and philosophy of religion (Orr, Warfield, Bavinck, Berkhof, Chafer, Pieper, Walther, J. T. Mueller, Sasse, Van Til, Cailliet, C. S. Lewis, Gordon Clark, Ramm, Packer, Carnell, Berkouwer, and others).

Then I compared this checklist with the Old Testament, New Testament, and systematic theology sections of the Union and Andover Newton recommended bibliographies for pastors. Here are the "liberal" results:

1. The Union Seminary list does not include a single

one of the conservatives either among its fifty-six citations in systematic theology (the only strictly orthodox inclusion is Calvin's *Institutes*!) or among its 163 citations in the Old Testament and New Testament areas (the closest are Kenyon, Albright, Cullmann, V. Taylor, Metzger—but Metzger is cited only for his *Introduction to the Apocrypha,* which receives no asterisk, as compared with Pfeiffer's *Apocrypha,* which does—and Davis's *Dictionary of the Bible,* but only in the Gehman revision).

2. Andover Newton does cite seven conservatives. This is little improvement, however, for its list is almost three times the size of Union's. Among 149 books in systematic theology, only Berkouwer, Cailliet, and Carnell are cited; and among 423 listings in biblical fields, the only "idea" book by an orthodox theologian is Machen's *Origin of Paul's Religion,* and that receives no asterisk.

Now we begin to appreciate Ambrose Bierce's definition of a bigot: "one who is obstinately and zealously attached to an opinion that you do not entertain." And why this "liberal" bigotry?

G. K. Chesterton suggested the answer in his classic, *Orthodoxy:* The religious "liberal," having no firm anchor in eternity, builds his world-view on the shifting sands of the *Zeitgeist;* his theology is inherently unstable and he knows it. He therefore resents, vainly tries to ignore, and subjects to ridicule and calumny the orthodox believer, who claims to have an unchanging and certain message.

Defensiveness and illiberality are thus concomitants of theological liberalism, whatever its form. Only the man who trusts fully in Christ and his Word can be truly liberal, for only he has nothing to fear.

7.

Why Churches Decline

Some American visitors to Europe return home with sad accounts of gastric disturbances, while others seem to thrive on unfamiliar cuisine. But hardly a single Christian traveler on the Continent or in Great Britain comes home unshaken by the low church attendance in virtually all European countries. My wife and I were saddened by this phenomenon during our year in the great Reformation city of Strasbourg; as we participated in the ancient liturgy and were blessed by the Christocentric messages delivered at the Lutheran Eglise St. Thomas—whose history stretches back to the ninth century—we sometimes found ourselves among only fifty or seventy-five worshipers.

Why this pitiful state of affairs? Recently a French sociologist has gone to work on the problem, and his far from tautological conclusions warrant careful consideration by the theological community. The sociologist is Professor Francçis-G. Dreyfus of the Faculty of Letters and the Institute of Political Science at the University of Strasbourg, and his analysis of church decline is summarized in an article titled, "Secularization in Alsatian Protestantism Since the Nineteenth Century," appearing in a recent issue of the *Revue d'Histoire et de Philosophie Religieuses* (Vol. 45, No. 2).

Dreyfus begins with a careful presentation of the church situation in the Alsace. In spite of general population increases from 1800 to the present, and in spite of the enlargement of Roman Catholic communicant membership, Alsatian Protestantism has shown no appreciable growth: there were 210,000 Protestants in 1820, 247,000 in 1871 (when, as a result of the Franco-Prussian War, the Alsace was annexed to Germany), and only 242,000 in 1954.

These statistical phenomena pose a genuine interpretative challenge, and Dreyfus reaches solid ground by analyzing an invaluable survey of Alsatian church life carried out in 1851 by the Lutheran state church. The replies to the questionnaires are still preserved in the National Archives, and they give minute data on the condition of the parishes—data that frequently reveal far more than the pastors or laity of the time could have imagined.

Typical, for example, are the comments of the pastors at Colmar and at Sainte-Marie-aux-Mines: "With some honorable exceptions, the poor class is too demanding, not sufficiently grateful, crude, and for the most part drunk and lazy." "The working class constitutes the majority of the Protestant parish, and on the whole it lacks industriousness. But, happily, we also have a solid bourgeoisie which is the pillar of the church."

From such clear and striking comments as these, Dreyfus soundly concludes that one of the major reasons for the decline of Alsatian Protestantism in modern times has been the indifference of the Church to the industrial revolution and to the working classes that arose as part of that great social movement. Just as during the Old Regime the Roman church lost its influence over the great mass of French Catholics by identifying with the rank and privileges of the nobility, so during the urban-industrial revolution of the last century and a half, Protestant Christianity has made the equally tragic mistake of identifying with the status quo. Ignoring "the signs of the times," it has pharisaically passed by on the other side when vast numbers of people have desperately needed its ministrations.

But important as was this social factor, another consideration had an even greater part in the decline of Alsatian Protestantism. States Dreyfus: "We must underscore the very great role played by Protestant thought itself," specifically the impact of "rationalism," "liberalism," and "latitudinarianism of doctrine"—and "it seems clear that this considerable influence enjoyed by liberalism is not peculiar to Protestant Alsace; one encounters it in most of the Protestant regions of Europe." Illustrating from questionnaire data and from other primary sources, Dreyfus shows that (in the words of a Pfaffenhoffen pastor), "from the middle of the eighteenth century, the Protestant church seems to have slept; it appears to have forgotten the confessional writings upon which its pastors took their ordination vows."

By 1860, the majority of the professors on the Protestant Theological Faculty of the University of Strasbourg had become liberals, and (as is the invariable pattern) the decline then began in earnest. Typical of the church situation was Pastor Nied's beginning-of-term address for the Protestant Seminary in 1868; his subject was "Preparation for the Holy Ministry," and not once does the name of Jesus appear in it. Dreyfus notes that where German rationalistic theology had the most influence, the Alsatian church suffered most. Today, in the wake of two world wars, there is little unreconstructed liberalism left in the Alsace, and the Protestant Theological Faculty is again confessionally Lutheran; but the damage has been done, and the common man in the Alsace, hostile to religion without knowing why, is the chief victim.

Though Dreyfus's study of church decline is limited to the Alsace, the wider significance of his investigation can hardly be missed. Observation of the Church in the modern era—whether on the European continent or in England or in the United States—would seem to elevate Dreyfus's two causal explanations for Alsatian church decline to the level of ecclesiological laws: doctrinal liberalism and social conservatism are two best ways to insure the secularization of the Church.

In our own land, what has been the effect of our middle-class, white-only churches, striving to delay social progress and to ignore the existence of great masses of people? The result has been that social progress has come anyway, spearheaded by those who do not represent evangelical Christendom, and untold numbers in minority groups have been permanently alienated from the historic Gospel. The unregenerate man has an instinctive ability to identify bad trees by their bad fruit.

And what has been the result of the weakening of biblical and doctrinal authority in U.S. churches? Indifference on the part of the unbeliever to the Church's appeals. It is not for nothing that the most theologically conservative Protestant bodies (e.g., the Southern Baptists and the Missouri Lutherans) have been the most energetic and have had the greatest growth rates—nor that Unitarian seminaries hobble along from year to year heavily endowed but virtually empty. Unregenerate man also knows instinctively that liberal religion is man-made and therefore incapable of rising from puerile good advice to transcendental Good News.

Want to arrest the secularization of the Church? Try an *unqualified* biblical message, directed to *all* those for whom the Lord of glory died.

PART TWO

Reporting and Reviewing

A. The Theologian as Reporter

1.

Barth in Chicago

As a former member of the faculty of the University of Chicago Divinity School, I attended the Barth lectures and discussions (April 23-27, 1962) with considerable theological anticipation, and came away ambivalently moved.

On the positive side, Barth may well be credited with the strongest, clearest presentation of the Christian gospel that has been given at the University of Chicago in its entire history. Without apology or sophisticated semanticizing, Barth preached a kerygmatic, objectively christocentric message of God's gracious acceptance of sinful man through the death and resurrection of his Son. Such a message could not have been in more marked contrast to the "Chicago School of Theology" which, early in the history of the University, made its Divinity School famous by its socio-historical method of interpreting the Christian religion. The method was developed chiefly by Shailer Mathews, Shirley Jackson Case, G. B. Smith, and J. M. P. Smith, and the essence of the approach, as described by a present-day member of the Divinity School faculty, Bernard Meland, was the conviction that "religion is pre-eminently a phenomenon of the social experience within a given cultural period." To Barth, as every page of his *Kirchliche Dogmatik* eloquently testifies, Christianity must never be treated as a "religion" in this sense—for it is not ultimately the product of man's social experience, but the result of the revelatory activity of God's Word. In reply to a discussion question from Schubert Ogden of SMU (now himself at Chicago), Barth asserted: "One of my primary intentions has always been to declare the independence of theology from philosophy, including religion." Into a theological atmosphere still influenced by the confusion of special with general revelation, Barth appeared like George Fox *redivivus*, crying, "Woe to the bloody city of Chicago!"

Unfortunately, however, much of the effectiveness of Barth's proclamation appeared to be vitiated by his long-standing disregard for adequate epistemological foundations for theology. The problem here was pointed up by Jakob Petuchowski of Hebrew Union College, who asked in all sincerity if the presentation of the Christian gospel to the Jew does not require the very involvement in textual and historical considerations which Barth tends to disregard as irrelevant to the central proclamation of Christ. The issue became even more painfully evident when Edward John Carnell, the neo-evangelical apologist, directed to Barth the question: "How does Dr. Barth harmonize his appeal to Scripture as the objective Word of God with his admission that Scripture is sullied by errors, theological as well as historical or factual?" Barth quite rightly disallowed the use of the term "sullied" in reference to his position, but he did not meet the crux of the question—namely the matter of alleged "theological errors" in Scripture.

That Barth freely recognizes such was illustrated in his answer to another of Carnell's queries. Carnell questioned Barth's refusal to assert the ontological existence of the devil, and quoted Billy Sunday's well-known comment: "For two reasons I believe the devil exists: first, because the Bible says so, and second, because I've done business with him." Barth countered by saying (and this drew applause—especially from the Divinity School contingent) that the attitude of Jesus and the Gospel writers to the existence of the devil is not to be considered sufficient reason for our affirming it. Yet, not twenty minutes later, Barth gave a minutely detailed (and impeccable) analysis of the precise meaning of *hypotassesthai* in Romans 13:5, and indicated that "willing involvement in the orders of society" is made binding on the Christian by the passage. But why bother to milk any New Testament word for its full theological import if the unwavering position of the Gospels with regard to the ontology of the demonic can be discounted? Likewise, in his concluding lecture, dealing with the Holy Spirit, Barth offered no test for the Spirit's presence except the vague idea of "human freedom," for "the *pneuma* moves where it wills"; yet—to use a physical analogy—it is vital to be able objectively to distinguish an atmosphere penetrated by CO_2 from one polluted by CO! Perceptive non-Christian seekers after truth in the academic audience at Chicago could not help concluding that ultimately it is Barth's personal preferences that determine theological truth for him—and thus that they had every right to consider "his" theology as but one option among the numerous conflicting claims of our time—from Alan Watts' Zen to Sartre's existentialism.

Barth's lectures at Chicago had the same strength and weakness as his epochal Romans Commentary of 1919: powerful proclamation, but refusal to justify epistemologically the source of the proclamation. But at a time when there is a dearth even of courageous kerygmatic proclamation, Barth's efforts should not be devaluated. The Mozart anthem chosen for the Barth convocation had a fitting text: *"Laudate Dominum, quoniam confirmata est supernos misericordia ejus, et veritas Domini manet in aeternum."*

2.

Vidler at Strasbourg

The manifesto of contemporary radical theology in England is not so much the Bishop of Woolwich's *Honest to God* (which is regarded as painfully superficial even by the theological community that shares its views) but the volume *Soundings: Essays concerning Christian Understanding,* edited by A. R. Vidler. It was almost inevitable that when Pike took a "sabbatical" for theological study in England, he spent it at Cambridge in close touch with Vidler (cf. my analyses of Pike's theology in the *Sunday School Times,* April 30 and May 7, 1966*). There is little doubt that Dr. Vidler has succeeded admirably in his cherished purpose of serving as a midwife to the radical theology of the day.

It was therefore with considerable interest that I, together with the students now participating in Trinity Evangelical Divinity School's annual European Program at the *Faculté de Théologie Protestante* of the University of Strasbourg, attended Dr. Vidler's recent presentation on "Church and Society in England, 1900-1950." The lecture-and-discussion session took place on April 14, 1967, under the sponsorship of the University's *Centre de Recherches d'Histoire des Religions.* The fifty or so students and professors who turned out for the two-hour session found Dr. Vidler a paradoxically engaging fellow: with white eyebrows, mustache, and goatee, he looked from the neck up like a sophisticated Santa Claus; with white tie and black shirt, he looked from the neck down like a sophisticated Chicago gangster. Perceptive listeners to his talk found the same odd combination of the positive and the negative in his remarks.

Vidler's lecture was frankly autobiographical. Born in a thirteenth-century house in Rye, Sussex, at the turn of the century. Vidler recalled Henry James's home in one direction and slums in the other. For the socially con-

---

* Reprinted in the present volume in I. 2.

servative church of the day, poverty was simply taken for granted as a concomitant of the natural order: it could and should be mitigated through charity, but to attempt to root it out by way of radical social programs went beyond the vision of clergy and laity. At preparatory school in 1910, Vidler encountered only one professed political liberal out of 100 boys (quite naturally, the boys followed their fathers' viewpoints). Vidler became "quite religious" in these vital pre-university years—"too religious" he now thinks; never did he consider that his Anglican high-churchmanship had anything to do with politics or society.

In 1919, Vidler entered Cambridge, and while he was an undergraduate his eyes were opened to many of England's great social and political needs. Under the influence of S. C. Carpenter (a theologian and Christian socialist of the Gore and *Lux Mundi* school) and Muggeridge *père* and *fils*, he became a convinced socialist. On graduation in 1921, he went to Wells, Somerset, for theological training; but finding it hopelessly conservative (paralleling Anthony Trollope's Barchester), he soon withdrew and obtained a "title" to a mining parish in Newcastle-on-Tyne. There 10,000 people lived in miserable slums, and the rector was a political conservative who worked there only from a sense of duty. Vidler, however, was soon involved in political activity; sometimes after the Sunday evening service he would dash off to a Labor Party meeting to speak (and now he recalls the latter meetings as often more exhilarating than the former).

Later Vidler moved to a Birmingham parish, was temporarily drawn into Eric Gill's orbit (society should return to handicraft; the invention of the internal combustion engine was an incalculable tragedy), but soon had his views tempered by the writings of Reinhold Niebuhr. Chiefly owing to Niebuhr, Vidler gave up "all naive, Sermon-on-the-Mount idealism." Now he saw that one could not appeal to man's "better nature" to achieve social goals but that the will-to-power, especially in collective activity, necessitates action in terms of the lesser of evils. Politics is the art of the possible, and appeals should be made not to principles but to the exigencies of the concrete situation.

Eventually, Vidler came to entertain thoughts of a "social faith" for all of Great Britain. Naturally this faith could not be distinctively Christian, since only a small number of citizens are committed to Christianity; perhaps it could take the shape of a neo-Utilitarianism. Discussions along this line went on in a private group called "The Moot," whose leading figure was sociologist Karl Mannheim, and which included T. S. Eliot, Walter Moberly, Dr. John Baillie, and other notables of varying persuasions. Though it ceased to exist after Mannheim's death in 1947, this group prefigured, as Vidler sees it, the concerns of such contemporary organizations as the Evangelical Academies in Germany and—most particularly—the Ecumenical Institute in Switzerland.

In the most penetrating critique of Vidler's *Soundings* to date—E. L. Mascall's *Up and Down in Adria* (Faith Press, 7 Tufton St., London SW 1)—the author writes: "My first criticism . . . is that, taking it in its overall character, it has misunderstood the function of the Christian theologian *vis-à-vis* the contemporary world." This criticism precisely applies to Dr. Vidler's Strasbourg lecture, for he unabashedly set aside Christ's Great Commission in favor of a program of generalized, secularized social amelioration. One fully empathizes with Vidler's disgust for the socially indifferent church-life of his youth; but how much greater a tragedy it is that he has aided and abetted a pendulum-swing in the opposite direction that leaves man with no clear hope for the next world and no solid grounding for his social action in the present.

The discussion period following the lecture underscored the impotence of Dr. Vidler's approach. Questioned on his assertion in *Soundings* that "there is still in the tolerant, pluralist, democratic kind of society which we now have and want to maintain and strengthen—value and validity in the idea of a national church," Vidler reaffirmed his belief that a reconstituted form of established church—oriented not to "evangelism and piety" but to "the whole life of the nation"—could "witness to a transcendent Authority over the state."

Two of my Trinity students raised serious objection to such a program on the ground that a church drawn into the communal, secular orbit of the state is in the worst possible position to speak prophetically to the state—as the Church of England so well illustrates. Moreover, by cutting himself off from the moorings of scriptural revelation, Vidler eliminates the very possibility of establishing any clear view of the transcendent God and any definite expression of his will for man socially and ethically. Thus social action becomes a chameleonic reflection of the secular situation itself, and the church is powerless to deal with those totalitarian threats to man's very existence that appear on every hand with increasing intensity in the modern world.

Why is Dr. Vidler always the midwife and never the mother? Is it because to bring forth genuine theological life, one needs seed—the seed of the Word of God? That seed is sure to produce fruit both in temporal society and in the eternal Kingdom: some thirtyfold, some sixtyfold, some an hundredfold.

3.

Kirchentag 1967

After five days of whooping at the thirteenth annual German Protestant "Church Day," I made a solemn vow over my Wienerschnitzel: never would I attend another ecumenical clambake (to change the gastronomic figure). Naturally this was a precipitous vow, and as the effect of the Kirchentag wears off in a few months, I shall doubtless find myself panting at a registration booth for the next extravaganza.

For the time being, however, the Kirchentag has given me more than I can take. During the multitudinous sessions in Hannover from June 21 to 25, 1967 (for news coverage, see the July 21, 1967 issue of *Christianity Today*), I kept recalling Alice's experience with the Cheshire cat who gave her advice and then faded away except for a smile. "I have often seen a cat without a grin," mused Alice, "but a grin without a cat! That's surely the strangest thing I've ever seen!" The Kirchentag was precisely such a phenomenon, and it well represented the German theological scene: a reassuring smile of piety and churchiness without any substantive biblical or theological foundations.

My negative response was not based on externals, though these certainly helped. Participants were engulfed by an appalling circus-like atmosphere in which venders hawked badges, buttons, souvenirs, books by the speakers, and food. Everywhere there were banners, flags, and uniforms (members of youth organizations directed the human traffic—some 30,000 people in attendance each day), uncomfortably suggesting the mass rallies of the National Socialist era and the classic line in the film version of *Is Paris Burning?:* "Les allemands aiment beaucoup les uniformes." And there was the lack of foresight that put Friday evening's boring "Social World Peace" session (with Niemöller and Visser 't Hooft) into much too large an auditorium, while numerous eager people were turned away from simultaneous musical sessions (Negro spirituals, gospel songs) and Helmut Thielicke's preaching.

All this I could tolerate. What I could not take was the ideological atmosphere—the heart-rending contrast between spiritually hungry laymen (many brought up in centers of dynamic evangelical piety) and Olympian theologians (whose mini-beliefs leave the German church without any substantial biblical or confessional underpinnings).

It was precisely this ideological tone that led to the (unsuccessful) boycotting of this year's Kirchentag by the two major conservative "protest" movements in Germany: the broadly evangelical "No Other Gospel" group and the more distinctively Lutheran Kirchliche Sammlung. For pastors and laymen in these loosely organized movements, participation in the union activities of the Kirchentag, which included ecumenical communion services, was tacit admission that the liberal and radical theologians offer a legitimate option in German church life.

Perhaps the protest movements were at fault for not actively defending historic Christianity at the Kirchentag. But they were right in predicting the character of the Church Day. True, there were some stellar speakers, such as distinguished physicist C. F. von Weizsacker (author of *History of Nature*) and U.N. leader Ralph Bunche. But the strictly theological presentations were at best mediating and at worst out-and-out heretical. It was quite significant that the most orthodox systematician on the program, Wolfhart Pannenberg of Mainz who, in spite of his critical approach to the Bible, holds to a fully historical resurrection of Christ and has struck decisive blows at Bultmannian and post-Bultmannian existentializing of the Gospel, was scheduled late in the afternoon and drew weak and sporadic clapping from a relatively small audience.

In sharp contrast, the prime-time morning lecture by Ernest Käsemann pulled in a gigantic crowd, including many young people (over half the full-time Kirchentag registrants were 17- to 35-year-olds) whose frenetic clapping demonstrated that, even if they didn't understand Käsemann, they regarded him as a hero-radical. Käsemann, who in Kirchentag discussions categorically refused to commit himself on the question whether the empty tomb was in fact empty, is one of Bultmann's most prominent disciples. Although he wishes to go beyond Bultmann's minimal "thatness" of the historical Jesus, he accepts Bultmann's enmeshing of biblical event with the interpreter's situation (the "hermeneutical circle"), castigates the fundamental tenet of confessional ortho-doxy that the Gospel is nothing less than objective truth, and encourages Christians to "test the spirits even with-in Scripture itself" (*Exegetische Versuche und Besin-nungen*, I² [1960], 232f.; see my *Crisis in Lutheran The-ology*, [Baker, 1967], Vol. 1).

Morning Bible studies, led for example by post-Bult-mannian popularizer Heinz Zahrnt (*Es begann mit Jesus von Nazareth*), were largely a farce—and drew minus-cule attendance in comparison with the "Politics" ses-sions (significantly, the only sessions with simultaneous translation into French and English). The study I at-tended was incredible. We began by singing "We Shall Overcome." The text—Ephesians 1, with its stress on remission of sins through Christ's blood (v. 7), appropria-tion of this by faith in him (v. 15), and his glorious res-urrection and ascension (v. 20)—became nothing but a pretext for asking the question: In our time, what are the liberating events for which we give thanks, and the lib-erating tasks which we face? Not a single participant mentioned the proclamation of the Gospel or its effects (e.g., on the Aucas); we were treated to such examples as black power, potential reconciliation with Red China (leading a wild-eyed Canadian to rant about the "murder-ing" of North Vietnamese by the United States), and (I kid you not) the increased use of fertilizer by uncivil-ized peoples who previously resisted its introduction!

The final Kirchentag assembly, attended by 75,000, featured WCC General Secretary Eugene Carson Blake. In a simplistic message translated sentence by sentence into German, Blake well summed up the entire week. He obliquely slapped the confessional movements ("it is a scandal that in Germany one confession is so unchari-table to another")—drawing applause for it and re-iterated *ad nauseam* his theme: "You cannot hear the Word of God without your brother." True, said he, the Word and belief in it are at the heart of the Church; but you cannot even understand the Word unless you are in ecumenical relationship with other Christians. The proof-text given for this ghastly inversion of biblical teaching (the community has priority over the Word) was "where two or three are gathered, I am in the midst"!

The sign of the Kirchentag was the Crusader's cross, representing the spread of the Gospel to the four corners of the earth. Speakers frequently appealed to Luther's name and to the grand tradition of the Reformation. The hymnody of the sixteenth and seventeenth centuries, used in juxtaposition with tasteful and striking contemporary musical settings, provided a stirring reminder of the theological resources of the historic Christian faith. What a pity that all this lay on the surface. What a tragedy to see the smile without the cat.

4.

Fresh Spirit
in Continental Theology

Street barricades. Alternate singing of the *Internationale* and the *Marseillaise* on the Champs-Élysées. Near-total paralysis of the economy. Near-anarchy everywhere. This was Paris during the already historic "days of May," 1968.

For church history, a Paris Congress of Evangelical Theology attended by 140 theologically sophisticated persons from the French-speaking areas of Europe may be no less significant. The meeting, projected in February by a committee of stellar French theologians and pastors, was providentially scheduled for the days immediately following the end of the three-week general strike that reduced transportation and communication to zero.

Organizers made the aim clear: to affirm to Christians and the general public "the sovereign authority of the Bible as the Word of God. After the assaults of Modernism at the end of the last century, currents of still another New Theology are now disturbing the minds of many. The Congress will be a reminder that there is only one Gospel, and that to believe it and to preach it does not presuppose either ignorance or obscurantism."

The three intensive days focused on the necessity of an unadulterated biblical theology and the relevance to the problems of our day that results only when such a message is proclaimed. The Paris congress came like a fresh breeze in a Europe where for a century theology has been characterized by rationalistic dogmatism and the changing fashions of the German professorial caste. It was as if the spirit of the Monods, d'Aubigné, and Gaussen—those firebrands of early nineteenth-century orthodoxy—was once again animating the life of the Church.

In the opening address, General Secretary Pierre Marcel of the French Bible Society argued that the post-

Bultmann "new hermeneutic" is by no means new, since it rests squarely on rationalistic presuppositions expressed (more clearly) by Semler in the eighteenth century. For the critical interpreter past or present, "the Holy Spirit is dead," since the Bible is a product of its human authors and not, as it claims for itself, the work of a single Divine Author. The result: a "pathological state of jesiology" where the interpreter, caught by his own debilitating humanistic presuppositions, speaks only of "Pauline thought," "Petrine thought," and, by extension, "Jesine thought"—never of the Word of God. Marcel said reports he receives from all parts of the world show beyond question that the Bible is "not merely the opinions of human writers, for whenever it is placed in men's hands, regardless of their cultural diversities, it speaks to them, and it speaks the same unequivocal message."

Henri Blocher, young, dynamic professor at the new government-approved Faculty of Evangelical Theology at Vaux, presented the concept of myth developed by Eliade, Ricour, and Gusdorf, then demonstrated that on no single count could the New Testament message, centering on the death and resurrection of Christ, be regarded as mythical. The Bible's stress on historical localization (versus the timeless quality of myth), on removal of the sacred-profane distinction, on salvation once-for-all accomplished in Christ (versus the "eternal return"), and on the specific power of the Gospel to free men from ritualistic myth—all this demands that man's fall and Christ's redemptive work be faced as historically true, he said. "The natural man prefers myth to history because he can thereby avoid facing his own historical responsibility for sin."

Rector Hans Rohrbach of the University of Mainz, a mathematician, said today's biblical critics assume that science is still operating in closed nineteenth-century categories that exclude the miraculous, a view that fell by the wayside in the Einstein revolution. And they erroneously assume that the Bible presents a primitive three-story cosmology. Rohrbach told how he found the reality of the biblical world-view and personal salvation in Christ during the chaos of Germany as the war ended.

Professor Frank Michaëli of the Protestant Theological Faculty at Paris stressed the amazing relevance of the Old Testament in terms of re-establishment of the State of Israel, progress in biblical archaeology, and rediscovery of a unified Old Testament theology after years of efforts to fragment its message.

Marc Lods, dean of the Theological Faculty, and Editor René Lovy of *Positions Luthériennes* agreed that neither the Church Fathers nor the Reformers would allow any other authority than Holy Scripture as the ultimate norm in the Church. Lods asserted that in spite of the cultural diversity among patristic writers spanning seven centuries, "none of them allowed any other final authority than Scripture."

Professor Jacques Ellul of the Law Faculty at Bordeaux posed again Jesus' question, "When the Son of Man comes, will he find faith on the earth?" Ellul said we have no guarantee of any given amount of faith or church success, or of personal well-being. We are guaranteed only his Coming.

"We are tempted to be conformed to this world in our theology and in our lives," he said. "It's up to us to give the full evidence that God is alive before the bar of this world. We cannot live in the past, not even in our great confessional traditions. We must help society out of the secularistic prison it has made for itself, and this is only possible when the authenticity of Christianity is seen in the authenticity of our faith."

This idea of relevance was reinforced by Walter Martin of the United States, who drew rapt attention as he presented Christian Research Institute's ideas for dissemination of theological and apologetic insights through world-wide computer networks.

Underlying all such evidences of the supreme vitality of orthodox theology was the congress theme, repeated in magnificent French hymnody: "Thy Word, Lord, is our strength and our life; the torch that illumines the darkness of our path; the sun that enlightens our way."

5.

France in Flame

Very rarely is one given the ambiguous privilege of experiencing a revolution personally. For the theologian, such times are especially valuable, since in the absence of actual revolutionary conditions, it is easy to content oneself with a smug quoting of Romans 13, as if this single passage presented all the Bible has to say on (i.e., against!) political action. Werner Elert, in his *Christian Ethos*, noted on the basis of his experiences in Germany during the nightmare of World War II that both those Christians who support and those who reject the political status quo do so in a crisis of conscience, for God's Word stands in judgment not only on irresponsible change but also on the irresponsible exercise of power by the establishment. The turmoil of May and June, 1968, in France has indeed reinforced this interpretation for sensitive Christian participants in the drama of revolution, counterrevolution, general strike, and election upheaval.

The outline of events during and after the historic "days of May" is now quite plain. *Paris Match* of June 29 and July 6, 1968 gave a superb retrospective coverage of the revolutionary period in terms of "eight episodes": (1) The student uprising at Nanterre, which under the aegis of wild-eyed sociology student David Cohn-Bendit grew so large that the university had to be closed. (2) The transfer of the revolutionary spirit from the youngest to the oldest French university: the start of organized resistance by students at the Sorbonne, followed by police intervention (a supreme tactical error on the part of the dean, who requested aid despite a centuries-old tacit agreement that town must not interfere with gown) and, as a consequence, thousands of students demonstrating in the streets, barricades, the burning of automobiles, the introduction of tear gas by the authorities, and uncontrolled fighting. (3) First Minister Pompidou offered concessions to the Paris students, but these came too little and too late. (4) The French workers, following the student example (though suspicious of them as future "bourgeoisie"), declared a massive general strike to protest the status quo. Soon nine million Frenchmen were on strike, almost totally paralyzing the French economy. (5) De Gaulle stepped in to announce a referendum, but, again, events had gone too far. Demonstrations choked the streets, and the workers refused to accept the negotiations between their union bosses and the state. It appeared that de Gaulle's government would surely fall. (6) After a secret trip to confirm the army's support in case of a left-wing coup, de Gaulle delivered a master stroke: he legally dissolved the General Assembly, thus calling for new elections and forcing everyone to cease striking in order to make them possible. The immediate result: massive counter-demonstrations in support of the General. (7) A final "night of flames"—the last desperate move of the anarchial spirits. (8) The self-imposed exit of students from physical control of the Sorbonne, and the commencement of electioneering.—And then: a stupefying victory at the polls for de Gaulle's party, with a loss by the leftist opposition of half its former power in the Assembly.

What were the motivating elements in this amazing series of events? Who was "morally right" and who "wrong"? Predictably, simplistic interpretations have not been lacking. After having just made it in and out of Paris to deliver my biweekly courses at the Lutheran Study Center at Châtenay—and having seen the frenzy, the fighting, the hopes and the fears in the Latin Quarter—I returned to Strasbourg to hear the pastor of perhaps the most active evangelical church in France argue from the pulpit that social chaos is the devil's work and that the government represents order, stability, and (presumably) divine approval.

Now it is certainly true that the student rebels were an unwashed, disorderly, generally irreligious group and that their idealism was often incredibly naive (for example, the motto plastered on walls everywhere, *Tout est possible*—"Everything is possible"). It is also true that anarchists and Maoists tried to turn the days of May to their own evil purposes. But these facts do not touch other, more basic considerations.

De Gaulle, in spite of his unarguable assets as the French head of state, suffered from a clear case of Messianic complex. He was not able to distinguish his own ideas from the "will of the people," and, indeed, regarded the French as sheep needing to be led by himself as shepherd. That leading was in the direction of a disastrous foreign policy (the Force de frappe, the Quebec incident, anti-Americanism, and so on), and a woeful neglect of internal economic and educational reform. (Only 16 percent of college-age persons go to university in France, as compared with 44 percent in the United States. In terms of number of telephones, TV sets, and kilowatt-hours of energy used per person, France is today far closer to reactionary Spain than to progressive, industrially developed Sweden.) And Gaullism threw its weight around in a most nondemocratic way: while the bourgeois Communist party in France (to the irritation of international, orthodox Communism) has consistently taken a stand for democratic procedures, Gaullists have managed all TV news, and, in Strasbourg during the chaos, nearly succeeded (with the active support of the Gaullist secretary of state for the interior) in burning down the Palais Universitaire to "clean out the Communists"!

The biblical Gospel most certainly condemns irresponsible opposition to constituted authority. But—and this is a fact consistently forgotten by well-meaning conservative Christians who confuse political with theological conservatism—Scripture *also* opposes totalitarianism, whatever its political garb (left *or right*). Freedom of decision is vital to the free course of gospel proclamation (John 7:17), and the arbitrary removal of such freedom in one area soon leads to its removal in others. "Power corrupts," shrewdly observed Lord Acton, "and absolute power tends to corrupt absolutely." The fathers of our American Revolution—even when not themselves Christian—saw this clearly, and they are our benefactors both politically and religiously today.

How then de Gaulle's ensuing election triumph? Some quoted Emile Ollivier: "When one has lived much history, one is not surprised at any inconsistency." But J.-J. Servan-Schreiber, the most astute of France's young political analysts, saw the true picture: in the face of demonstrably impotent leftist party options, de Gaulle's new party slate was ironically in the best position to enact the reforms the electorate had demanded by three weeks of revolution; the election, in other words, gave the General his last chance to democratize (*L'Express*, 1-7 July, 1968, p. 39).

The natural man, said Luther on the basis of Romans 7, perpetually swings between extremes. Let us hope that between anarchy and messianism, la belle France can find her way to genuine political and economic freedom whose exercise will make the freedom of Christ more readily comprehensible to her citizens and her friends.

6.

Marcuse

To the dismay of my friends and the infuriation of my enemies, I was privileged to spend the winter quarter of the 1969-70 school year in La Jolla ("the jewel of the sea") as Honorary Fellow of Revelle College, University of California at San Diego. Meanwhile, most of the U.S. and Europe was suffering from weather. Doubtless this should have brought on pangs of conscience, but so powerful was the old Adamic nature that I experienced no more than an occasional twinge of guilt-feelings.

The glorious climate was only one of the positive features. Opportunity was provided to renew acquaintance with an old nemesis: Avrum Stroll, now head of UCSD's Philosophy Department; when in 1963 he was on the faculty of the University of British Columbia and delivered lectures against the historical foundations of Christianity, I was invited to that campus to present the other side (see my recent work, *Where Is History Going?*, chaps. ii and iii). But even more stimulating was the experience of operating in a university atmosphere across which continually fell the shadow of Herbert Marcuse.

Who is Marcuse? For European students and intellectuals, the question would be superfluous. During the revolutionary "days of May," 1968, in France, Marcuse's neo-Marxist theories were basic sustenance for a remarkable variety of radical movements. The same has been true in other European countries; indeed, more than any other contemporary, Marcuse serves as the theoretician of student revolt. His lesser fame on the U.S. student scene is due not to disagreement with his ideas, but to the difficulty American student radicals encounter in reading Germanic philosophical prose; they operate with his ideas, but obtain them in pre-digested (or better, reader's digest-ed?) form.

Marcuse himself displays anything but the now-generation image. He is seventy-one and retired from

210 THE SUICIDE OF CHRISTIAN THEOLOGY

his philosophy professorship in 1970. (He has taught on yearly contract since reaching the compulsory retirement age; the University has refused to be intimidated by such pressure groups as the American Legion, who tried to buy his contract to get rid of him.) His heavy German accent reminds one more of dull 19th century teutonic speculation than explosive 20th century revolution. But he is a most energetic proponent of radicalism, and his ideas have far-reaching impact.

What is the essence of his position? It can perhaps best be understood in terms of the two "evils" against which he continually jousts: tolerance and objectivity. Western society holds forth the ideals of tolerance (equal opportunity for opposing viewpoints) and objective truth (competing claims must be arbitrated by factual evidence). But, argues Marcuse, these ideals are fatuous and hypocritical, since Western society is already committed to a "totalitarian" capitalism which feeds upon itself, creating a frame of reference which automatically weakens the force of all opposition to the status quo and justifies this in the name of pseudo-objectivity.

Here is how Marcuse puts it in his seminal essay, "Repressive Tolerance": "When a magazine prints side by side a negative and a positive report on the FBI, it fulfills honestly the requirements of objectivity: however, the chances are that the positive wins because the image of the institution is deeply engraved in the mind of the people . . . . The tolerance expressed in such impartiality serves to minimize or even absolve prevailing intolerance and suppression . . . . This kind of objectivity is false, and this kind of tolerance inhuman. And if it is necessary to break the established universe of meaning (and the practice enclosed in this universe) in order to enable man to find out what is true and false, this deceptive impartiality would have to be abandoned" (*A Critique of Pure Tolerance*, by Wolff, Moore, and Marcuse [1965], p. 98).

Marcuse never tires of rapping the scientific attempt to get at objective truth by investigating particular facts; in line with the Hegelian dialectic he always declares that "it is the whole which determines the truth" (*ibid.*, p. 97). The objective ideal of the university "induces thought to be satisfied with the facts, to renounce any transgression beyond them, and to bow to the given state of affairs" (*Reason and Revolution* [1960], p. 27). The only proper approach is to begin dialectically, employ one's energies to "break the established universe of meaning," and thereby achieve a higher synthesis: a non-repressive society.

It is not difficult to understand the appeal of such a revolutionary viewpoint to students convinced that present society is so corrupt that even its best ideals are a mockery. But Marcuse's position is fraught with jocular ironies that appear lost both on him and on his followers (a sense of humor not being exactly their strong point). For example: If American society is so impossibly repressive, how does it happen that the platform from which Marcuse fires his antitheses against the status quo is a professorship in a state university—a university supported by the public funds of Reagen's California (which can hardly be considered a hot-bed of leftism)?

And if "the whole determines the truth," just *whose* whole are we talking about? Marcuse is so convinced of his dialectic philosophy of total existence that he wishes to repress contrary viewpoints. Yet this is precisely the approach of the radical right to *Marcuse's* ideas—as when the American Legion endeavored to remove him from his professorial chair! Doesn't this perhaps suggest that, even though tolerance and objectivity are often misused in our society, those who give up these ideals and attempt to enforce their views of "total reality" on others institute the rule of might-makes-right and lose all possibility of distinguishing truth from error?

Bertrand Russell rightly lambasted Hegel's claim that truth is predicated on his dialectic philosophy of universal reality: "If the above argument were sound, how could knowledge ever begin? I know numbers of propositions of the form 'A is the father of B,' but I do not know the whole universe. . . . This illustrates an important truth, namely, that the worse your logic, the more interesting the consequences to which it gives rise" (*A History of Western Philosophy*, pp. 745-46).

Theological presuppositionalists might also take heed at this point: if particular factual evidence doesn't determine the truth of a world-view, what does? Why assume Christian holism rather than revolutionary holism?

At the root of Marcuse's difficulties—and the same is true of revolutionaries in general—lies a hopelessly naive view of human nature: the present "repressive" society was created by bad guys, whereas we—the good guys—can remedy the difficulty. But history shows that revolutionary regimes are frequently more repressive and unfree than the societies they overthrow. Why? Because "*all* have sinned and come short of the glory of God"— and this includes revolutionaries as well as non-revolutionaries. All of us need God's offer of pardoning grace for individual and societal transformation. The starting point is the particular fact of Incarnation. At the cross and the open tomb the way is opened from concrete fact to universal truth, from the repressiveness of sin to resurrection and life.

7.

Freedom and the Gospel

My United States passport suggests not so much a peripatetic theologian as an active Agent 007. In 1964 the self-styled "Deutsche Demokratische Republik" gleefully stamped its multicolored visa into my passport on the occasion of a personal study trip into East Germany; in the summer of 1966, a second and even more gaudy DDR visa was added when I took the members of the Trinity Evangelical Divinity School's European Program into East German Luther country.

As a political and social liberal who is convinced that his views in these areas are fully compatible with theological conservatism, I receive a certain perverse pleasure from the contradictory state of my passport: it contains visas from a country which for us does not exist as a political entity. But East Germany has a very real existence, and contact with it offers a sobering corrective to loose thinking about the relation between the Gospel and political freedom. Personal experiences are a dangerous form of argument, but I shall run the risk.

My 1964 pilgrimage took me to the partially extant Erfurt cloister where Luther had lived as a monk, flagellated himself in a vain effort to become right with God, and felt the hopelessness of all attempts at self-salvation; next to the former cloister (now a small Protestant practical seminary) are ramshackle church offices, testifying only too well to the economic plight of the church in a religiously hostile state. In 1966, the hospital across the street from the cloister sported a large propaganda sign reading: "Fight U.S. Aggression in Viet Nam. Give Blood."

Not even the small towns are free from disfiguring political mottoes—far more sinister than those that prompted the parody on Joyce Kilmer, "I think that I shall never see / A billboard lovely as a tree." On my first trip to East Germany I said to a prominent theologian: "I see many signs proclaiming *Freiheit* (freedom) here." "Yes," he replied, "and that's the only place you'll find

Freiheit here—on the signs. I hope you can come back someday and bring genuine *Freiheit* with you." I came back; but *Freiheit* was little closer than before.

The Wittenberg Schloss, on whose church door Luther posted his Ninety-Five Theses, now also serves as a cultural museum (with bi-lingual German and Russian plaques) and provides meeting rooms for a Communist youth organization. The regime brashly appropriates Luther—as one who smashed medieval church authority and prepared the way for the modern secular era. Objective history is of little consequence to an ideology that in principle allows the end to justify the means.

Both trips to East Germany yielded an unforgettable gallery of faces: the young couple who in 1964 insisted on buying me Russian "champagne" at the Wartburg Castle, lambasted Walter Ulbricht, and said that I could not imagine how bad the restrictions of freedom really were (cf. my article, "A Day in East German Luther Country," *Christian Herald*, June, 1965); an official chauffeur who wistfully spoke of his desire to travel beyond the confines of Eastern Europe; a waiter who told me that I must be sure to "look in the corners" while in the DDR and that he personally yearned for unmanaged news and a true view of America; a graduate student who sought an honest picture of the U.S. racial situation; a citizen of Wittenberg who insisted that I not get the impression that "we are all Communists here"; a Christian believer who described the economic and personal sufferings of his countrymen and of his own family and longed for better days; etc., etc.

My students were particularly struck by the general tone of life in the East: the deadness and abnormal silence of the towns and cities and the subdued if not hopeless faces of the people. Even the children seemed listless. To move across the mined and pill-box controlled borders from East to West was like entering a different world. Leipzig and Munich could not be more different in vitality, warmth, and *joie de vivre*. It is no exaggeration to say that in East Germany vast numbers of people have been reduced from living to mere existing.

What are the theological implications of this sad political situation? In general, there must be a rejection of the incredible naïveté that has typified whitewashings of East German Communism by many American religious liberals, and that has also characterized the neutralist judgments of Karl Barth on the East German situation. In point of fact, the DDR is a political abomination and deserves no more commendation than Papa Doc's rule in Haiti.

But it is not just the theologically liberal and neo-orthodox who tend to cry peace, peace, when there is no peace. Advocates of a strict Reformation theology have more than once allowed the principle of the *Schöpfungs-ordnungen* (Orders of Creation) to justify the political status quo, and Romans 13 has been falsely employed as a charter of political indifferentism. Some theological con-servatives have even had difficulty in rationalizing the American Revolution, since revolution for the sake of free-dom seems incompatible with "subjection to the higher powers."

As confessional Christians we need to reappropriate the biblical insight into the essentiality of freedom. The very proclamation of the Gospel requires the freedom to decide for or against it; and where human restrictions are placed on man's free choice, the result is a closing-off of the way of salvation. Historically the "free churches" have seen this truth most clearly, for they have recognized that to force religious values on a people through state influence is actually to cut men off from the Gospel. How much more is this the case when a regime restricts free will in the interests of an anti-Christian religion!

We are indeed to render unto Caesar the things that are Caesar's, but freedom of choice is not one of them; it is a divine gift, and no government has the right to remove it, this was the persuasion of the Christians who supported the American Revolution (they did not need a deistic "natural rights" theory to ground their action); and their biblical conviction should be ours as we en-deavor to evaluate present-day Communist rule.

All forms of totalitarianism approach in principle the thought-control that is described by Orwell in *1984*, and we must work and pray for the liberation of peoples whose lives are reduced to a sub-human level through the removal of their decision-making powers.

Although the "American way of life" and the Gospel
are separate, distinct, and not infrequently at odds, freedom and the Gospel are intimately bound together, since
the former is a condition of the latter (Rev. 3:20) and the
latter is essential to the full manifestation of the former
(John 8:31-36). Julia Ward Howe was not a bad theologian
when she juxtaposed the two poetically: "As He died to
make men holy, let us die to make men free."

8.

Dissecting 'Courage'

Surprisingly, no one quoted Pericles' Oration on the Athenian Dead: "The secret of freedom is courage." But there was no lack of other citations, examples, and approaches offered by speakers of wildly conflicting viewpoints at the symposium on "An Anatomy of Courage" held November 9, 1968 at Roman Catholic Barat College in the northshore Chicago suburb of Lake Forest.

In an electrically charged atmosphere of fundamental disagreement, famed conservative Russell Kirk asserted that courage was impossible apart from commitment to the transcendent; Staughton Lynd, radical pacifist and spearhead of the "Mississippi Freedom Schools," ignored the transcendent and spoke of courage as an "elemental" phenomenon to be realized in social action, not in "academic discourse" or in the kind of "afternoon symposia" Barat had organized; Michael Novak of the faculty of the State University of New York, a vocal opponent of American involvement in Vietnam (co-author with McAfee Brown of *Vietnam: Crisis of Conscience*) and Roman Catholic existential death-of-Goder, denied the existence of the transcendent realm entirely, claimed that all value-systems are competing myths, and set his own version of Tillich's "courage to be" ("in creative existential despair we can pull ourselves up by our own bootstraps") over against the "basic American myth of happiness"; Chicago *assemblage* artist Harry Bouras assembled a concept of "initiative" courage (derived from dynamic action, vs. the common artistic variety of passive, "responsive" courage); and, finally, Bruno Bettelheim, professor of psychology and psychiatry at the University of Chicago, and personal survivor of German concentration camps, castigated the liberals on the program for their naive conviction that they were "on the side of the angels" (" 'We shall overcome' gives me the creeps," he said), argued that courage is seldom more than the projection of the hero's inadequacy-feelings, and called for a "moving

ahead of human evolution by the intellectual activity of
the mind." Bettelheim even took issue with a relatively
mild introductory remark by Barat philosophy professor
Hollenhorst: "Knowledge without courage is useless";
countered Bettelheim: "Courage without knowledge leads
us into the most abominable messes."

The fundamental cleavage at the symposium was ex-
hibited at the level of methodology: the "conservatives"
relied on intellectual argumentation, while the "liberals"
endeavored to win the audience through existential-
emotional appeal. Thus Kirk employed Burke, Joad, Car-
lyle, Stevenson, Graves, Newman, Waugh, Bernard of
Chartres, Shaw, and C. S. Lewis in a high-flying defense
of transcendent, communal values; and Bettelheim performed a veritable biopsy on the Northern civil rights
workers in the south and the demonstrators during the
Chicago Democratic Convention ("They have not been
able to put themselves in the place of the poor southern
white or the Chicago policeman; instead of seeing their
opponents as basically like themselves, they compensate
for their own shaky identity by a posture of superior righteousness; therefore they compound the social problem instead of solving it").

In contrast, Lynd affirmed the non-articulate, personal
dimension of liberal social action: his presentation consisted of examples of people "from whom he had received
courage"—such people as Bob Moses, who "hated to go
up on a platform, and when he did, *he* would ask the *audience* questions"; Father Beregan, just sentenced for destroying selective service files; and other jailed workers,
one of whom poeticized: "We swim in muddy waters, finding our way." In the same vein, Novak set forth a remarkable series of delphic-oracle-like emotive judgments: "It
is more important to be a decent human being than a
Catholic believer." "American industrial and militaristic
society crushes our emotions (contrast European reactions in a traffic jam) and is preparing now for new
Vietnams." "Military spending is not even debated in Congress." "Our give-away programs are geared to help the
upper classes, not the underprivileged." "By using black
to symbolize sin in parochial schools, we condition our
children to racism." "We are incurably optimistic: the

word 'up' occurs more in American than in British English." "The whole purpose of suburbs is to avoid confrontation with misery."

Novak and Lynd shrewdly criticized Bettelheim for
"intellectual utopianism" and "psychological reductionism," but their own retreat into the emotional, existential
realm hardly satisfied the desire of the audience to discover the meaning of true courage. At least Bettelheim
was willing to question the sacred cows of "self-evident"
liberal social action, though he was not able to offer a
way to the "rare 3 A.M. courage" that Napoleon valued
above all other kinds. The University of Chicago ortho-
genist penetratingly analyzed the problem as getting the
lion and the lamb in human nature to lie down together,
since "courage"—not just etymologically—centers on the
heart (Latin, *cor*). But how? In a reference to Luther
at Worms, Bettelheim argued that courage does not depend on anything but the necessity of our own inner being:
"I can do no other." But Luther himself engaged in an
even deeper depth analysis when he said on that occasion:
"My conscience has been captured by the Word of God."

9.
Theological Expo 69

Most visitors to Montreal were frantically absorbed in Expo 67's encore: Act II of the international exhibition "Man and His World," offering the public a bewildering kaleidoscope of human values and dysvalues. Across town at Loyola of Montreal, another international conclave was taking place, minuscule in comparative numbers but presumably of far more lofty significance, inasmuch as its official theme was "vertical"—the things of God rather than the things of man.

For the sixth consecutive year Loyola was holding its "Contemporary Theology Institute." The subject could not have been more basic ("The Structure of Theology") or the essayists' lineup more promising (Lonergan, Moltmann, Ogden, Rahner, Wingren). Despite high registration fees and the disappointing last-minute non-attendance of Moltmann and Rahner because of illness (in the former case, relatively mild; in the latter, extremely severe), more than 250 selected participants arrived—hailing from as far away as France, Australia, and Japan.

Though Roman Catholics understandably predominated, Protestant attendance was considerable and the Jewish voice was represented (e.g., by Samuel Sandmel of Hebrew Union College). A high proportion of registrants were professional theologians, as evidenced by the autograph party in which participants, including the undersigned, offered their books to one another in an orgy of collective narcissism. The only significant missing element in the total picture was the Student Radical; when one buttonholed crusty Father Lonergan and offered to "make a statement and find out what the people really want," he was told to "go conduct your own conference."

Each of the major essayists in the five-day institute had a full day at his disposal. Gustaf Wingren, Anders Nygren's successor as professor of systematic theology at Lund, led off; and Bernard Lonergan of the Gregorian University, Rome, followed him. It was a happy choice,

since only Wingren and Lonergan not only stayed reasonably close to the subject (unlike Moltmann) but also consciously endeavored to give methodological expression to
their respective confessional commitments (unlike Ogden
and Rahner). (The papers of Moltmann and Rahner were
read for them.)

Wingren entitled his presentations "The Structure of
Protestant European Theology Today—A Critical Approach." The accent was indeed on criticism, along the
lines of his book *Theology in Conflict,* about which he said:
"It has not yet been read seriously by anyone except those
who are already supporters of Barth, Bultmann, and Nygren." As a specialist in Irenaeus's understanding of the
recapitulation of creation in Christ and Luther's doctrine
of creative vocation, Wingren expressed particular revul-
sion toward the neo-orthodox theological method that ab-
sorbs the first article of the Creed (creation) into the second (redemption) and thereby splits church and world.
"The modern negation of the belief in creation," Wingren
declared unqualifiedly, "has Karl Barth as its spiritual
father." But the demise of neo-orthodoxy has not provided
the necessary counteractive. Now we write "large expen-
sive books about topics without importance and slim occasional volumes about vital topics"—as if medical
specialists were writing tomes on the Black Death and
blood-letting while general practitioners produced pamph-
lets on cancer and polio.

What is needed, stressed Wingren, is the true biblical
perspective on creation, such as is offered today by
Harald Riesenfeld or K. E. Lögstrup. The latter refuses
to be drawn into theologies of revolution that place change-
for-its-own-sake in first position but "his voice of course
is not heard in the flow of words from Geneva: it does
not blend with the chorus." Lögstrup has rightly hit the
Kierkegaardian "hatred of everything that smacks of everyday life." The answer, for Wingren, is a return to the
biblical message of joy in the creation as redeemed by
Christ's incarnation. The Church must display "the joy
she possesses. Present-day life has so little joy that one
is surprised to come across it." How is this biblical joy
justifed methodologically? For an anti-Barthian paper,
the response was disquietingly Barthian: self-authenticat-

ing faith. Concluded Wingren: "The authority of the message does not receive any support from science. . . . Otherwise faith would no longer be faith."

While Wingren spoke of recapitulating creation, Lonergan recapitulated Lonergan. His papers did little more than summarize the thesis of his major work, *Insight*, in which an effort is made to give our time what St. Thomas gave his: a synthesis of philosophy and theology. Lonergan builds from today's natural and social sciences rather than from Aristotelian assumptions, and is convinced that one is thereby led to a "transcendental method," since insight lies at the source of the patterns employed in all cognitive enterprises. How does one learn this method so as to attain the theological realm? Not from books; it is something "each one, ultimately, has to do in himself and for himself." In self-transcendence man achieves authenticity; we "become actuality when we fall in love," and only "being in love with God is love in an unrestricted fashion." Insight, then, is the key to theological method. "Later revision of this notion," stated Lonergan with somewhat unscientific confidence, "is actually not possible. . . . There is then a rock on which one can build." In spite of the typical Roman Catholic synergism inherent in this position, observers were amused to discover a rock that evidently was neither Christ nor Peter!

Schubert Ogden, the University of Chicago process-theologian, delivered his papers on Bultmann's eighty-fifth birthday, and characteristically dedicated them to him. For Ogden, who readily admitted in a question period that he was "applying Schleiermacher and the nineteenth century to new situations" and was "proud of it," Christian theology "cannot be made intelligible by way of its own claims." Theology proper must be approached both by way of the universal human characteristic of faith (all men consent, either authentically or inauthentically, to existence) and by philosophical theology—more specifically, Whitehead and Hartshorne's "neo-classical theism," in which one argues ontologically for God's existence and (in opposition to classical theism) " 'God' and the 'world' are correlative terms."

Lonergan, quite readily perceiving the drift of Ogden's

method, queried: "Do you see any differences between philosophical and theological conceptions of God?" The inevitable nineteenth-century answer came back: "No." "Unitarianism, then?" responded Lonergan. To this Ogden offered the awkward rejoinder that "the Trinity is not a specifically Christian idea." Some participants rightly thought it curious, under these circumstances, that all men by natural religiosity were not trinitarians! Wingren astutely commented that Ogden had built his methodological house without regard to the furniture of revelation; the resulting edifice now has no apertures large enough to get the furniture in!

The absence of Moltmann and Rahner and the reading of their papers by surrogates naturally dampened meaningful discussion of their theological approaches. In the case of Moltmann, the problem was further aggravated by a non-methodological paper: a treatment of the theology of the Cross, over against Moltmann's critics who have said that the Cross was swallowed up by the Telos in his *Theology of Hope*. But Moltmann's methods were implicitly reflected in the paper: for example, in his blithe assertion that "unfortunately" Luke 23:46 has been used to interpret Jesus' death, whereas Mark 15:34 is the true tradition and should have provided the Church's interpretation. Moltmann's stand-in, Father Gerald O'Collins of Australia, who knows him well, admitted that Moltmann employs the Bible very selectively; for example, much influenced by Käsemann's rejection of the Fourth Gospel, Moltmann makes not a reference to that biblical book in *The Theology of Hope*.

Father Rahner's essays, though written specifically for the institute, offered little opportunity for discussion, since they rang the changes on the inexpressible character of all true theology. Theology is transcendental, and its knowing subject is antecedent to all knowledge of particular facts (à la classical idealism); yet theology reflects the radical historicity of everything and cannot therefore set itself up as absolute (à la modern existentialism). Where does this lead? To a *reduction in mysterium*, wherein we discover that all mysteries reduce to the mystery of God himself. "Man must engage in self-abandonment to mystery." Indeed, "God is mystery forever, even in the beatific vision." At the outset of his presentations, Rahner noted that for him "linguistic philosophy is a book with seven seals." This he effectively illustrated by making assertion after assertion whose validity could hardly be established even in principle. Linguistic philosophy has frequently noted that true believers in the ineffability of their disciplines should be really consistent and stop talking.

Although there was much talk about proper theological method at Montreal, epistemological issues had a way of being skirted. Either good theology was offered without adequate support (Wingren) or bad theology was presented as philosophically respectable (Ogden). And instead of God at center, man assumed the dominant role: man's insight (Lonergan), man's critical dominance over God's revelation (Moltmann), man's loquaciousness in the face of God's alleged ineffability (Rahner). "Man and His World" could have been the theme here too. Many at the institute longed for an epistemologically sound analysis of a different theme: "God and *His* World."

B. The Theologian as Reviewer

1.

Georgia Harkness

Beliefs That Count, *by Georgia Harkness (Abingdon, 1961, 125 pp.).*

It is the conviction of many that American popular theology has in recent years been moving more and more in the conservative direction. The questionable character of this generalization is well illustrated by Georgia Harkness' latest book, which contains such statements as: "The Bible is not in every word an infallible revelation of God, but a record made through human instruments" (p. 50); and "Biblical scholars no longer believe that the Gospels are exact accounts of the words of Jesus, since these writings were compiled forty to seventy years after his death and thus reflect only the memories and interpretations of the early church" (p. 28). The Christology of the volume is generally of an imitative nature, and the theological criterion of truth employed throughout the book appears to be a rather naive *consensus gentium* (e.g.: "We come now to say a few words about the disputed subject, the reality of hell and the possibility of everlasting punishment meted out by God. Here opinions differ greatly among Christians, and anything we say must be tentative" —p. 114).

The book achieves its purpose as a commentary on certain episcopal affirmations read at the Methodist General Conference in 1952, and underscores the fact that American Methodism still has much to learn both from the evangelical beliefs of the Wesleys and from the solid Reformation scholarship of such contemporary English Methodists as Philip S. Watson.

2.

Martin Marty

The Outbursts That Await Us: Three Essays on Religion and Culture in the United States, *by Arthur Hertzberg, Martin E. Marty, and Joseph N. Moody (Macmillan, 1963, 181 pp.), and* Second Chance for American Protestants, *by Martin E. Marty (Harper & Row, 1963, 175 pp.).*

A single, exceedingly important contemporary problem provides the backdrop and immediate occasion for these two works: the increasing tension between religion and society in America, as evidenced by the Supreme Court decision in June of 1962 (*Engle* vs. *Vitale)* forbidding the use of the so-called Regents' Prayer in the public schools of New York State. In *The Outbursts That Await Us,* sophisticated theological representatives of Protestantism, Roman Catholicism, and Judaism present their reactions to an apparently growing "secularism" in the United States; in *Second Chance for American Protestants,* one of these writers virtually sets forth a theology for the new age in which the Reformation faith can less and less rely upon support from its social environment.

At first glance the alignments appear incongruous: Hertzberg and Marty are far closer to each other on the basic issue than are Moody and Marty. To Moody, representing enlightened American Catholicism, the Supreme Court decision marked a tragic decline in the generalized Christian values characteristic of American life; but to Rabbi Hertzberg and to the Lutheran Church-Missouri Synod's Rev. Dr. Marty, *Engle* vs. *Vitale* can by no means be regarded as a tragedy. Hertzberg sees the court decision as a consistent attempt to separate church and state on the basis of the First Amendment, and as a Jew he rejoices to see that "only in America" Jews are finding a land in which religious "establishment"—even in general sociological terms—is less and less allowed to discriminate against minorities. He suggests darkly that the Roman Catholic reaction to the Supreme Court decision was motivated not simply by natural-law doctrine, but more especially by "the great problem of the future financing of the parochial schools"! Marty regards the court action as a clear indicator that the days of "placed," secure, safe Protestantism in America are over, and that now, like Abraham and the saints described in the eleventh chapter of Hebrews, American Christians will have to seek "a better country, that is, a heavenly one"; no longer will they be able to rely on the culture to support a polite and innocuous faith—their "second chance" lies solely in "drawing on resources not wholly captive to this environment," namely, the resources of God's Word.

This reviewer finds the Marty thesis solidly biblical and eminently relevant to the present cultural situation. Evangelicals especially should ponder the fact that the most articulate Protestant objections to the *Engle* vs. *Vitale* decision came from theologians of the stamp of Bishop James Pike, John C. Bennett, and Reinhold Niebuhr; Niebuhr characteristically asserted that "the prayer seemed to be a model of accommodation to the pluralistic nature of our society." In point of fact, the Gospel cannot be pluralized or accommodated without distortion, and the clear Reformation distinction between Law and Gospel has as its proper corollary a clear distinction between politics and religion.

The present review was originally written on shipboard in the mid-Atlantic, and the "displaced" nature of the environment was quite hospitable for analyzing a proposal for "displaced" vs. "placed" Christianity. Two events aboard ship added weight to Marty's argument. The first was the front-page news article in Cunard's *Ocean Times* informing passengers that the Supreme Court had banned as unconstitutional any required use of the Lord's Prayer or devotional Bible reading in public schools; thus Marty's prophecy was further validated, and Christian believers should be thankful that they now have no other recourse than to introduce young people to Christ through solid church teaching—that they can no longer lamely rely upon generalized moralistic "Bible reading" in the public schools to do a poor-at-best job for then. Second was the marked contrast between the "official," "established" Sunday worship service (Anglican Morning Prayer, with lengthy petitions for the Queen, conducted with painful self-consciousness by a Ship's Officer and attended by a pluralistic, equally uncomfortable congregation), and an almost spontaneous witness-by-songfest initiated by an anonymous passenger with a fine voice who played such numbers as "How Great Thou Art" on the lounge piano and soon had a crowd around him. In a pluralistic post-Christendom, believers had better wake up to the absolute necessity of serving as lights of the world by living and preaching the Gospel, not by expecting any form of generalized social or official establishment to do it for them.

3.

Gustaf Wingren

Gospel and Church, *by Gustaf Wingren, trans-lated by Ross Mackenzie (Fortress, 1964, 271 pp.).*

Two exceedingly important reasons should impel con-fessional Christians to acquaint themselves in depth with Gustaf Wingren, Anders Nygren's successor as professor of systematic theology at Lund. First, he gives the sacrosanct giants of contemporary theology the kind of merciless drubbing they deserve for their unbiblical emphases; in this he performs a great service, since the same criticisms expressed by consistent conservatives are either ignored or treated as hopeless obscurantism by the theological establishment. Thus Wingren's *Theology in Conflict,* the negative backdrop for his positive construction in *Creation and Law, The Living Word,* and *Gospel and Church,* pulls no punches: the Lundensian theology of Nygren is rapped for its philosophical for-malism; Barthian neo-orthodoxy is characterized as a system "totally foreign to the Bible" for its refusal to recognize the ontological reality of sin and for its christo-centric unitarianism; and Bultmann is hit unsparingly for his egocentric existentialism. In *Creation and Law* and *Gospel and Church,* Cullmann as well receives severe criticism, since his *Heilsgeschichte* theology "never re-lates the biblical revelation to the man who hears it."

In the second place, Wingren offers a strikingly attrac-tive theology of his own—a theology at once biblical and Lutheran in content, yet fully contemporary in treatment. The significance of such an endeavor for English-speaking Protestants lies chiefly in the fact that the only con-fessional choices before them so often seem to be the rigid extremes of Arminianism and Calvinism; Wingren points to an option that neither permits anthropocentric works-righteousness nor encourages the hyper-theocentrism from which Barth's errors sprang.

Wingren's basic contention, which runs through all four of his volumes, is that modern theology errs by not reading the totality of Scripture as it was intended: first, creation and law; then, Gospel and Church. He roundly condemns Barth's attempt to reverse the order of law-Gospel to Gospel-law, and thereby to absorb all theology into a legalistic Christology. Wingren pleads for a genuinely trinitarian hermeneutic, which he finds rooted in patristic theology (cf. his *Man and the Incarnation: A Study in the Biblical Theology of Irenaeus*) and in primitive Lutheranism (cf. his *Luther on Vocation*). The law in Scripture is the starting point for theology, not because it reveals a covenantal polity but because it is a perspicuous expression of the natural law that orders man's life, condemns him as sinner before God, and drives him to Gospel and Church. As Wingren has argued elsewhere in reference to Calvinistic legalism: "The weakness of the Reformed position undoubtedly lies even today in its difficulties in expressing the inner unity between the gospel and the church" (*Studia Theologica,* XVII [1963], 88). It is this inner unity that Wingren does so much to clarify.

4.

James A. Pike

What Is This Treasure, *by James A. Pike (Harper and Row, 1966, 90 pp.).*

Whatever else may be said of Bishop Pike, no one will say he was non-controversial. His prolific writings placed him in the maelstrom of contemporary social dialogue *(The Church, Politics, and Society; Beyond the Law; Teen-Agers and Sex;* and so on); the Blake-Pike proposal made him famous in American ecumenical discussion; and his theological radicalism ("There are several phrases in the Creeds that I cannot affirm as literal prose sentences, but I can certainly sing them") involved him in three heresy charges all dismissed by his fellow Episcopal bishops. In the February 22, 1966, issue of *Look* magazine, Pike—whose religious peregrination took him through Roman Catholicism, agnosticism, neo-orthodoxy, and Anglican neo-liberalism—was described as a bishop "searching for a space-age God." Then visiting his confrère Bishop John A. T. Robinson in England, Pike told *Look* that he had "jettisoned the Trinity, the Virgin Birth and the Incarnation," and said of those who had made the latest heresy charge against him: "If they only knew what I had in my briefcase." This was the manuscript of *What Is This Treasure,* and now the eager theological public—properly prepared by the Bishop of Woolwich and the death-of-God school—can examine Pike's portfolio for themselves. Was it Pike's peak?

We are told that *"What Is This Treasure* opens wide the door left ajar by *A Time for Christian Candor"* and informs us of "what to keep—not what to throw out—to make today's church more vital." Both books have as their theme II Corinthians 4:7a ("we have this treasure in earthen vessels"), and Pike's aim is to distinguish between the treasure and the vessels. The Bishop's conclusion displays him, not as an original thinker but as a poor man's Tillich: only "God, the Ultimate Ground of all being" is the treasure, and all earthly expressions (including Jesus. Scripture. all doctrines and creeds) are but fallible and conditioned vessels. "The answer is more belief. fewer beliefs." Thus Pike eviscerates the New Testament treasure (for Paul, the Gospel of Christ):

> "I am the Way, the Truth, and the Life," we read in the Fourth Gospel (14.6). While, as we have already seen, the negative conclusion of the sentence ("No one cometh to the Father but by me") won't do, the opening clause beautifully reflects the experience of the early Christian community of the role of Jesus in their lives. To sum up, in Him they saw what a man is to be; and since Jesus was Himself fully this, they saw showing through Him the fullness of God as Truth (which in good measure we can see also through Socrates and Buddha as "free and open" men) and, certainly as important, as Love [p. 80].

In this way the Bishop of California stood in judgment upon Scripture, upon its apostolic authorship—and upon "the Shepherd and Bishop" of his soul (I Pet. 2:25). By arrogating the right of final spiritual judgment to himself. Pike's pilgrimage ironically brought him to a caricature of his starting point. His favorite verse ends "that the excellency of the power may be of God, and not oɩ us." The bishop, however, by refusing to allow God to reveal himself adequately, elevated himself to the powerful role of arbiter of revelation. Finally only he himself was left to speak *ex cathedra*.

5.

Fredrick Herzog

Understanding God: The Key Issue in Present-Day Protestant Thought, *by Fredrick Herzog (Scribner, 1966, 191 pp.).*

Even the most theologically unsophisticated layman is aware of the bewildering revolution going on in current Protestant thought. Death-of-God theologians Altizer and Hamilton, situation ethicists Fletcher and Rhymes, and popular advocates of a secular Christianity such as Robinson and Pike have made the national news media with increasing frequency. Clearly, in spite of all the hoopla, these new emphases reflect vitally important underlying shifts in Protestant theological orientation. Professor Herzog of the Duke Divinity School has written his first book in an endeavor to understand, interpret, and constructively criticize the theological roots of the current radical theology. His approach has four foci: the problem of God (as raised by the theothanatologists); the post-Bultmannian "New Quest" (James M. Robinson, et al.); the related problem of acquiring a "historico-ontological hermeneutic" (Fuchs, Ebeling), illustrated especially by the interpretation of the Fourth Gospel; and the ethical issue as displayed in nonviolence and the new morality. In a concluding chapter, Herzog seeks to pull the four strands together, thereby expressing the present-day task of systematic theology": "In the diakonic word and the diakonic deed Jesus' words take on new meaning today. . . . Perhaps we are seeking for a new articulation of the Name we have known all along."

Bewildered we are, but this book is not going to reduce the confusion; if anything, it is going to increase it. The reason is not primarily its technical and scholarly flaws (its discussion of the post-Bultmannian New Quest with no mention at all of Conzelmann or Käsemann, mere *en passant* reference to Bornkamm, and woefully inadequate treatment of Pannenberg); the difficulty chiefly lies in the fact that the author has become so mesmerized by the jargon of contemporary theology that he allows verbal formulations to substitute for clear thinking.

Had Herzog confronted in depth (instead of relegating to footnotes) theologians such as John Hick and Ian Ramsey, who have been applying the insights of analytical philosophy to contemporary theological problems, he might have been able to find his way out of the semantic thicket of unrecognized metaphysical *a priori* that vitiates most mainline theological investigation today. Similar benefits would have accrued if the author had entered into meaningful dialogue with orthodox theologians, whether Anglo-Catholic or evangelical. Both the analytical and the orthodox theologians would have reminded Herzog that until modern theology faces the epistemological issue—the basic question as to how one validates theological assertions—it will forever wander in a speculative labyrinth.

Particularly irritating to a Lincoln lover and a *docteur* of the University of Strasbourg is the author's prefatory statement that Jean-Fréderic Oberlin "looked over the author's shoulder" and Lincoln's "abiding influence" presided over him as he wrote. I doubt if the vague Christology and the vaguer bibliology of *Understanding God* would have appealed to either.

6.

E. Schillebeeckx

God the Future of Man, *by E. Schillebeeckx, O. P., translated by N. D. Smith (Sheed and Ward, 1968, xii, 207 pp.).*

Query: Is the change in posture of the post-Vatican II Roman Church a good thing? Answer of most Protestants: Definitely—there is now less superstition, less use of Latin, more toleration, etc.

But, though we naively dislike facing it, ecclesiastical changes in a sinful world invariably produce gray, not lily white or jet black. Even the Roman Church (in spite of Bishop Sheen's famous appearance in a cowboy hat) cannot be regarded as an old western movie, with the good guys clearly separated from the heavies. A practical example is Dominican Robert Campbell's survey of Roman Catholic youngsters entering De Paul University as freshmen: whereas five years ago 90% held that Christ is God and 73% that extramarital intercourse is wrong, this year only 64% believed in Christ's deity and less than half (47%) would condemn extramarital sex relations (see Campbell's book, *Spectrum of Catholics Attitudes* [Bruce]).

An equally jolting example of the negative side of current Roman Catholic change is the work of the Dutch theologian Schillebeeckx, whose influence on the controversial new "Dutch Catechism" has been very strong, and who is endeavoring to substitute existential for Thomistic categories of interpretation in such areas as sacramental theology (a perfect example of getting rid of one devil and thereby opening the door for seven others). *God the Future of Man* is the product of the author's 1967 lecture tour in the U.S., and further develops his ideas vis-à-vis American radical theology and the new hermeneutic.

In an essay in volume one of my *Crisis in Lutheran Theology* (Baker, 1967), I treated the question as to whether the new hermeneutic of post-Bultmannians Ebeling, Fuchs, Käsemann, et al. ought (as they claim) to be identified with the hermeneutic of the Reformers. My judgment was exactly the opposite: the new hermeneutic is the inverse of the Reformers' conviction that Scripture is objectively, propositionally, and perspicuously God's Word; it was the Roman Catholics who insisted on a "hermeneutical circle" that made the scriptural text dependent on the context (*traditio*) of the interpreter. Schillebeeckx cheerfully agrees: "Man can never escape from this circle, because he can never establish once and for all the truth or the content of the word of God" (p. 8).

Faced with the death-of-God thinking of Hamilton, Altizer, and van Buren, and the epistemological question their work has raised, Schillebeeckx can only offer a future-directed existential experience of God: as to "the 'verification principle' . . . all that we Christians can say, in the light of our faith in God as our future, is that faith is not based on what is empirically and objectively verifiable, but comes under the category of human existential possibility" (p. 182). This answer is especially ironic when we remember that it was in part the unverifiable identification of truth with subjective immanence that led the death-of-Goders to deny objective divine transcendence in the first place.

Schillebeeckx, in obvious dependence on Ernst Bloch and Jürgen Moltmann, gives himself—and theology—up to the future. God is not the "wholly New"; "the Christian leaves the future much more open than the Marxist"; "the Christian cannot formulate the content of this promise in a positive way"; "the message which Christianity brings to the secular world is this—humanity is possible!" (pp. 181-193). The author cautions his readers not to forget "the biblical basis of this so-called new idea of God" (p. 188), but in light of Schillebeeckx's prior commitment to the "hermeneutical circle," what objective check can the scriptural text possibly have on a new God of futurity?

Is Rome becoming the elephants' graveyard for Protestant heresies?

7.

Robert M. Grant

The Apostolic Fathers: A New Translation and Commentary. *Vol. 1*: An Introduction, *by Robert M. Grant (Thomas Nelson, 1964, 200 pp.)*.

English readers are here introduced to a projected six-volume translation of the Apostolic Fathers, of which Volume 2 will contain First and Second Clement (ed. Grant and H. H. Graham of Virginia Theological Seminary), Volume 3, the Didache and Barnabas (ed. R. A. Kraft of Manchester), Volume 4, Ignatius of Antioch (ed. Grant), Volume 5, Polycarp, the Martyrdom of Polycarp, and the Fragment of Papias (ed. W. R. Schoedel of Brown), and Volume 6, Hermas (ed. G. F. Snyder of Bethany Biblical Seminary).

Volume 1, by the general editor of the series and my former colleague on the University of Chicago Divinity School faculty, Robert M. Grant, might appear to be an objective background essay introducing the patristic texts which subsequent volumes will supply in translation. Unhappily, however, this is far from the case. Grant's *Introduction* is a piece of special pleading for a particular approach to the Fathers in relation to the New Testament. The Reformers' question, "Is true Christianity to be found in an ongoing, continuous tradition or in a book [the Bible] which provides a permanent norm?" is posed at the outset (p. 2), and Grant, opting for the former, resoundly raps the Reformers for holding to the latter. For him, no qualitative line can be drawn between the canonical New Testament and the writings of the Apostolic Fathers. Thus Grant adds to the mass of current literature which opposes Sola Scriptura by subsuming it under the general rubric of Tradition—a position whose ecumenical overtones are not difficult to see. Doubtless we should not be surprised at Grant's theological stance when we recall that Frederick W. Danker, himself hardly a thoroughgoing conservative, wrote of Grant's *A Historical Introduction to the New Testament* (1964): "This introduction to the New

Testament might well be titled 'An Agnostic's Credo,' for one of its primary objectives is to demonstrate that there is much that we do not know about the historical circumstances surrounding the contents and the publication of the New Testament documents" (*Christian Century*, May 20, 1964).

Though there are values in Grant's patristic introduction (e.g., a useful history of the interpretations of the Apostolic Fathers across the centuries, with bibliographical data on the discoveries of their various writings), the discriminating reader owes it to himself to study this book in the light of such a treatment of canonicity as is provided by R. Laird Harris' *Inspiration and Canonicity of the Bible* (1957), where it is decisively shown (chap. xi: "The Patristic Test of Canonicity") that "the authors who are closest to the apostles make much of the fact that the apostles are far above them." Moreover, in contact with standard patrological reference works (Quasten, Altaner, Cayré, et al.), one soon begins to question the necessity of yet another introduction to the Apostolic Fathers; but perhaps the translations in subsequent volumes of Grant's series will provide *post hoc* justification for his book.

8.

G. Ernest Wright

The Challenge of Israel's Faith, *by G. Ernest Wright (University of Chicago Press, 1944, 108 pp.).*

The Challenge of Israel's Faith, a slim volume of a little over one hundred pages, is G. Ernest Wright's attempt to clarify some of the major doctrines of Old Testament theology for the benefit of the mid-twentieth century reader. In his Foreword Wright says, "My concern in these pages . . . is not with the history of Israelite religion but rather with the central propositions of Israelite faith." The book was first published in 1944, and has undergone several impressions; its author has come to be recognized as one of the foremost Protestant scholars in America—and one of the leading lights in the new "biblical theology" movement. In the interests of brevity, I shall here subordinate exposition to criticism, and shall follow the (somewhat arbitrary) approach of dealing with one main positive and one main negative feature of each chapter or section of Wright's treatise. I shall then conclude with a few general comments on the book as a whole.

Chapter I. "Thus Saith the Lord": The Eternal in the Temporal

The first chapter in *The Challenge of Israel's Faith* appropriately deals with the divine character of the Old Testament Scriptures. Professor Wright attempts to determine in what sense we may consider Scripture as "God's Word."

On the positive side we commend Wright for his criticism of the almost completely descriptive Biblical studies carried on today (linguistic, literary, historical studies), which have neglected the basic issue of the dynamic, vital message presented by such Biblical figures as the prophets. Wright says: "Scripture is of little value, except for antiquarian purposes, unless it affords the readers a quickening of spirit, a searching of heart, and a cleansing of soul" (p. 5).

However, we object to the distinction Wright makes between the "words" of Scripture and the "Word behind the words" (pp. 12-13). Wright makes this distinction (which, incidentally, is not made by the Scripture itself!) because he accepts the presence of "absurdities" (p. 7) and "inconsistencies" (p. 9) in the Bible. He does not consider the force of such Biblical statements as II Tim. 3:16, Matt. 5:18, II Pet. 1:21, and Deut. 4:2. Because Wright feels compelled to distinguish "between what is God's Word and what is man's word" (p. 9), he must find an epistemological test to which he can submit passages of the Bible. The test he offers for our consideration is that of *conscience* (p. 12). "Those tremendous words from Isaiah are authoritative in that . . . they strike some kindred note within us which says, "This is true!' " (p. 12). Wright attributes this view to both Luther and Calvin (pp. 11-12). However, we hasten to point out that conscience is no adequate epistemological test by which to determine the divine, authoritative Word of God. Conscience is subjective, and its specific judgments may be culturally determined, as anthropologists such as Ruth Benedict and Margaret Mead have shown. Even the consciences of Christians can be dulled (e.g. I Tim. 1:19). Philosophically, subjectiveness of the sort advocated by Wright in dealing with the Scriptures leads straight to *relativism*, for each man has the final say as to what portions of the Bible manifest "the Word behind the words" and which ones do not. If the Scriptures are not objectively true (apart from the judgment of conscience) we have no solid basis of Revelation from which to draw our doctrinal statements or our homiletical exhortations. Furthermore, we criticize Wright for attributing his epistemological position to the Reformers. Both Luther and Calvin (whatever Luther's idiosyncrasies on the content of the Canon) believed the Canonical Scriptures to be objectively inspired. Readers of Reu's *Luther and the Scriptures* will receive a far different impression than Wright gives concerning Luther's view of the Scriptures; and a perusal of Chapter I of the *Westminster Confession of Faith* will indicate the true nature of the Calvinistic position on Holy Writ—a position which Calvin directly influenced. The Reformers were not Old Testament prophets nor New Testament apostles; they did not reveal new truth to be checked against human conscience for verification; their role was rather to bring men back to the truths already revealed once for all in Scripture. They asked that their teachings be checked against the *objective truth* of the Bible (contrast what Wright says on p. 46). If we today forget the unique character of the work which the prophets and apostles did, we do so at our own peril. We are not to judge the truth value of what God has already revealed through them. Like the Reformers we are to preach what *has* been revealed, and appeal, not to conscience, but to Holy Writ itself for validation of our message.

Chapter II. "Choose You This Day": The Meaning of History

The second chapter of Wright's book deals with the interesting subject, Philosophy of History, about which we hear a great deal these days. Wright is concerned chiefly with the philosophy of history presented by the Old Testament prophets.

This chapter rightly points out that the prophets were not "preachers concerned only with individual piety or the 'spiritual glow,' " nor philosophers who stood on the side-lines and theorized about the events of their times. We agree (and see a real application for today's pastor) in the "two conditions" which Wright sets forth for truly understanding the prophets: that "we be willing to stand with them at their point of vantage . . . and experience the challenge and immediacy of the will of God for that moment" (p. 29); and that we endeavor to do the same for *our own* critical moment of history.

Yet we see manifested in this chapter a tendency which will become more evident as we proceed: a tendency to reduce the extent of God's direct intervention into the Old Testament scene. We refer to such rationalizations as the attempt to explain manna as "a honey-like substance which still drops from tamarisk trees in Sinai" (p. 22). Just as in the case of the kenosis theory (which attempts to reduce Christ's omniscience beyond the clear assertions of the New Testament), there is no logical stopping point for this type of rationalizing. The Scripture does make clear that God often works through the laws He has established; but it just as clearly shows that in Biblical times He frequently cut through these laws and directly intervened in the affairs of men. Once we begin to try to explain away the Biblical accounts of God's direct intervention in history, where should we stop? Perhaps we should view the Incarnation (as some neo-orthodox theologians do) as primarily an immanent phenomenon! Or perhaps we should be consistent and speak (as the modernists did) of a "spiritual" Resurrection of Christ—rather than a physical, bodily, truly miraculous one. Obversely, it should be emphasized that if God did *in fact* intervene objectively in history in the person of Christ, there is no logical reason (only an emotional one—dislike of the miraculous) for trying to explain away His miraculous interventions in Old Testament times.—And ironically enough, Wright criticizes *others* for Deistic tendencies (pp. 54-55)!

Chapter III. "Obey My Voice": A Chapter of Terminology

Here Professor Wright makes several excellent clarifications of the meaning of concepts vital to the theology of the Old Testament. His apologetic arguments against those who set the New Testament "loving Father" against the Old Testament "God of wrath" are excellent (see especially p. 47). His discussion of the meaning of "fear" in the Old Testament is likewise valuable apologetically (p. 40).

From the negative side, we find Wright both criticizing Biblical rationalism and engaging in it himself! He says: "The Biblical study of the last century failed us. Its methods and argument were basically valid, but its proclamation of the saving faith was diluted in the waters of overconfident rationalism" (p. 47). Yet only a few pages before this, Wright goes against one of the foremost canons of literary criticism (even criticism of secular writings): that of always giving the benefit of the doubt

to the text as it stands. He states as *fact* (not hypothesis
or even theory) the view that Ps. 51 is not a unity—and
devotes a whole paragraph to the point (pp. 43-44). Yet
Franz Delitzsch (*Biblical Commentary on the Psalms,*
1888, Vol. II, p. 164) says, "The prayer: *build Thou the
walls of Jerusalem* is not unsuitable in David's mouth."
Wright should see that he is here (and elsewhere) committing the same sort of judgmental error against Holy
Scripture that the 19th century rationalists committed.

Chapter IV. "For I Am Thy God": The Living and Anthropomorphic God

This chapter, in my opinion, constitutes one of the
most magnificent in this little book. Wright's discussion
of the characteristics of the God of the Old Testament
is invaluable—especially for its criticism of false approaches to God present in our day. Modern liberal
mysticism of the Schleiermacher variety is contrasted
with the prophetic emphasis (pp. 49-53). Those who want
ethics without theology are criticized (pp. 53-54). Likewise
those who would depersonalize God (pp. 54-55). The sac-
rilegiously intimate sort of praying practised by many
today is contrasted with God's holiness (separateness),
as set forth in the Old Testament (pp. 56-57). Morality
apart from God is condemned (pp. 57-59). The "concordance method" of Bible study is seen to be inadequate
for discovering the grace or love of God in the Old Testament (pp. 59-62). Our present-day fetish of "tolerance"
is contrasted with the concept of the "jealous God" of
Scripture (pp. 62-65). Lastly, the anthropomorphic picture
of God in the Old Testament is cogently defended (pp.
65-67).

Yet in this very matter of Scriptural anthropomorphism we can see the difficulties which Wright faces in
trying to find the "Word behind the words" of Scripture
by means of the criterion of conscience. We read (p.
67): "Of course, there are crude extremes of anthropomorphism into which no intelligent man can go. . . . The
old bibliolatry is gone, and one cannot blindly and credu-
lously accept something merely because it is in the Bible
without considering its temporal and eternal validity (cf.

chap. i)." We might ask Professor Wright how he goes about distinguishing "crude" from non-crude anthropomorphism (*de gustibus non est disputandum*), but an even more important question which should be asked him is the following: What gives us the overweening confidence that we can judge which things in Holy Writ have "temporal and eternal validity" and which ones do not? Christ validated the authority of the most disputed portion of the Old Testament Scripture when he said, "Till heaven and earth pass, one jot or one tittle shall in no wise pass from the law, till all be fulfilled"; did he give any equivalent validation for our ability to judge the truth-value of Scripture? I must confess that I find no New Testament passage which says that He did. And if He did not, it impresses me as presumption of the highest order that we should set ourselves up as judges of the "temporal and eternal validity" of God-breathed Scripture (II Tim. 3:16; II Pet. 1:21).

Chapter V. "Ye Shall Be My People": The Covenanted Community

This chapter, as its title indicates, treats the extremely important theological concept of the Covenant, as seen in the relationship between God and the Israelites in the Old Testament. In discussing the Covenant, Wright effectively deals with several current misconceptions about Israelite faith. For example, he says concerning individualism and collectivism among the Hebrews: "Individualism appears for the first time, we are told, in the writings of Jeremiah and Ezekiel. . . . This attempt to place the beginning of individualism in the Old Testament during the Exile is always made with the implication that the pre-Exile collectivism is inferior to post-Exilic individualism. Such an idea could only arise in an age like ours when the true nature of man in his relation to society is forgotten" (p. 79). We also find in this chapter the very important observation that the saving of a civilization or preservation of status quo was not the summum bonum in the eyes of an Old Testament prophet (pp. 70-71).

One of the unfortunate characteristics of the Calvinistic

theological system has always been its overemphasis of the importance and application of the Covenant idea in Scripture; the very term "covenant theology" is a witness to the importance which Presbyterian and Reformed theologians have attached to this concept in their theological activity. It seems to me that in this chapter Professor Wright betrays the influence of his background by over-extending the application of the Covenant in Scripture. He says on the one hand: "The ultimate ground of the covenant is in the sovereign will of God. It is he who has initiated the pact" (p. 78); yet he does not seem to recognize the uniqueness of God's Covenant with the Israelites. Historically, there is no evidence that God entered into a pact with any other people, but Wright speaks approvingly of the English Puritans and the Scottish "Covenanters" who "are well known for the covenants with which *they* bound both individuals and nation to God" (p. 81, italics mine). Note who did the "binding" in this case. One of the gravest faults of Calvinism has been its readiness to put God in a covenant relationship with their own national or cultural groups. The result of such attempts is generally legalism, bigotry, and intolerance—due to the creation of an in-group and the attributing of divine sanction to it (cf. the Anglo-Israelite movement). Probably Wright's conception of Scripture influences him here; for if the Old Testament is tainted by human error, and often historically unreliable (note Wright's uncritical acceptance of the documentary hypothesis, p. 72; cf. John 5:46, 47), then why can't we "assume," as the Israelites did, that God is in a covenant relationship with us? However, the Pentateuch, as its stands, maintains that God did *in fact* establish a unique Covenant with Israel at Sinai; if the Canon of Revelation is closed, we have no right to assume that God has created or will create this sort of covenant relationship with other nations—including our own. God's only Covenant today is with believers in His Son—and note that Lutheran theology rightly sees Christ's atonement to be of universal application, not merely limited to the elect as the Calvinist believes.

Chapter VI. "Behold, the Days Come": The Outcome of History

Professor Wright's final chapter deals with the eschatology of the Old Testament. The value of the chapter again lies in the fact that the author refutes several modern misconceptions about the subject under discussion. We need only note one example: Wright's magnificant rebuttal of the "utopia without judgment" hope expressed by many religious liberals. Wright blasts (and rightly so) those who would identify the Kingdom of God with the present world order—or with a political ideology such as democracy.

On the other hand, we find a strange paradox: in contrast to Wright's overweening confidence and presumption in deciding which portions of Scripture are God's Word and which are man's words, we see him manifest real humility when faced with the coming New Heaven and New Earth: "We cannot form any rational conception of it . . . . No man can be certain as to the details of the future order; and the more dogmatic he attempts to be about them, the more he reduces his position to absurdity. The idea of the resurrection of the body, for example, can scarcely be more than a symbol of a deep truth to which a finite mind with finite language can hardly give adequate expression" (pp. 97-98). We wish only that Wright were more consistent. If God's plans for the end of the age are beyond his attempts to criticize them rationally, why does he think that he can judge rationally the "temporal and eternal validity" (p. 67) of God's written Revelation to man—especially in view of the numerous New Testament references to the nature of inspiration?

Conclusion

The Challenge of Israel's Faith contains much valuable material, especially of an apologetic character. Moreover, it is an eloquent testimony to the value of Old Testament studies for the minister and prospective minister (see specifically the Postscript). It contains little new material (conservatives have long argued for many of the points Wright makes), but the book should have a salutary effect on religious liberals, by forcing them further to the right theologically.

However, because of its weak view of the inspiration of Scripture, and its inadequate epistemological test for determining what is God's Word, the book suffers from the same grave difficulty that most neo-orthodox writings have today: no solid foundation for the theological statements made. We are glad that Wright's "conscience" leads him back toward orthodoxy, but let us not forget that the conscience of 19th and early 20th century liberal scholarship seemed to lead in the opposite direction.

PART THREE

Reconstructing

1.

Is Man His Own God? *

Currently making the rounds on American college campuses is the question, "How are you going to recognize God when you get to heaven?" Answer: "By the big 'G' on his sweatshirt." This litany has more metaphysical profundity than meets the eye, for it reflects the contemporary philosophical dilemma as to the meaningfulness of God-language—a dilemma to which we shall be addressing ourselves shortly. But it is essential to make one basic point at the very outset: in the philosophy of life of every person without exception, someone or something is invested with the sweatshirt lettered "G." There are no atheists; everyone has his god. In the language of Paul Tillich (who was ironically called an atheist by some of his less perceptive critics), all of us have our "ultimate concerns," and the sad thing is that so few of them are truly ultimate or worthy of worship. As one of William James' "twice-born" (having come to Christian belief as an adult), I am especially concerned that idols be properly identified and the true owner of the cosmic sweatshirt wear it. As a modest contribution to that end, we shall first consider how much ultimacy ought to be attributed to three prominent alternatives to biblical theism, and then devote ourselves to the crucial arguments in behalf of the Christian view of God.

The Unreality of Major Non-Theistic Positions

Pantheism à la Spinoza

I recall but one occasion when my old Greek professor

_____

* An invitational presentation at DePaul University, Chicago, February 5, 1969, in debate with humanist Julian J. Steen, dean of the Chicago School for Adults. The debate was sponsored by DePaul's theology department; Professor Robert Campbell, O.P. served as moderator. This same essay was also presented at Harvard University on February 14, 1969, as one of a series of "Christian Contemporary Thought Lectures."

at Cornell was drawn into a religious discussion, and—in a state of obvious discomfort—he defended his unorthodoxy somewhat as follows: "But do not conclude that I am an atheist. Far from it. For me the universe as a whole, with all its mystery, is God, and I reverence it." This viewpoint (which can, of course, be stated in many different ways) has perhaps best been set forth and defended by Spinoza. In Part One of his *Ethics*, the philosopher endeavors to show that the universe is a single, all-embracing unity and that that unity is God. This is proved by the fact that the universe obviously consists of some thing—Spinoza calls it Substance—and this Substance "is in itself and is conceived through itself"; now since God is properly defined as "a being absolutely infinite" and Substance is infinite and unique, it follows that Substance is God.

The fallacy in this piece of geometrically-modeled legerdemain has been well stated by C. E. M. Joad in his *Guide to Philosophy*: "If we assume that Substance in the original definition means simply 'all that there is,' then the initial definition contains within itself the conclusion. Such a conclusion is not worth proving. It is, indeed, merely a tautology—that is to say, an asserting of the same thing in two different ways." Pantheism, in other words (and this applies equally to all forms of it, whether derived from Spinoza or not), is neither true nor false; it is something much worse, viz., entirely trivial. We had little doubt that the universe was here anyway; by giving it a new name ("God") we explain nothing. We actually commit the venerable intellectual sin of Word Magic, wherein the naming of something is supposed to give added power either to the thing named or to the semantic magician himself.

Humanism

If the universe cannot be meaningfully deified, why not man himself? Can we not regard as strictly literal the question posed in the title of this presentation, "Is Man His Own God?" and answer it affirmatively? For the humanist, man is himself the proper "ultimate concern," and human values are the only eternal verities.

But which "human values" do we mean? Anthropolo-

gists such as Ruth Benedict have discovered a most bewildering variety of human value systems, styles of life,
and ethical norms. And what is worse, these morals and
mores are often entirely incompatible. Some peoples reverence their parents and others eat them. Among cannibals it is doubtless both good ethics and good table man-
ners to clean your plate.

How is the humanist going to decide among these
competing value systems? He has no absolute vantage
point from which to view the ethical battle in the human
arena. He is in the arena himself; or, to use beatnik poet
Kerouac's expression, he is "on the road"—not in a
house by the side of the road where he can watch the
world go by and arbitrate it. All value systems that arise
from within the human context are necessarily conditioned by it and are therefore relative. Out of flux, nothing
but flux. As Wittgenstein correctly observed in the *Tractatus Logico-Philosophicus*: "If there is any value that
does have value, it must lie outside the whole sphere of
what happens and is the case . . . . Ethics is transcendental."

Yet a transcendental perspective is exactly what the
humanist does not have. He is therefore left to *consensus
gentium* (majority values), cultural totalitarianism (the
values of one's own society) or sheer authoritarianism
(*my* values, not yours). But, sad to say, fifty million
Frenchmen *can* be wrong; the ethical perspective of an
entire society can be cruelly immoral; and the individual
who considers himself the true barometer to moral worth
may simply be suffering from overactive glands or an
advanced stage of messianic complex.

To establish absolute ethical values for human action
is both logically and practically impossible apart from
transcendence. To move the world Archimedes rightly
noted that he would need a fulcrum outside the world. The
assassination of biblical revelation in the 18th century left
man without a clear conception of or confidence in God,
and God's resultant death in the 19th century (in the work
of Nietzsche and others) set the stage for the dehuman-
ization of man in the 20th. Nietzsche recognized full well
that apart from God only man remains to establish his
own value; and the stronger has every right under such

conditions to impose his self-centered value system on the weaker—and eliminate him if he does not learn his lessons well. The anti-Semitism of the deists of the 18th century Enlightenment (as definitively researched by Arthur Hertzberg in his 1968 publication, *The French Enlightenment and the Jews*), the Nietzschean transvaluation of values, will-to-power, and antichristic treatment of the weak, and the National Socialist extermination of racial and political minorities demonstrate only too clearly what happens when man becomes the measure of all things. It is curious that humanists presently (and commendably) striving for racial equality in this country do not ask themselves why, in any absolute sense, their goals are more justifiable than the genocide practiced by an equally passionate and idealistic generation of young people in the Germany of the 1930s and 1940s. As for me, I'm for absolute racial justice, and I'm unwilling to see it—or any comparable value—left at the mercy of relativistic humanism. If man is his own god, then religion is *really* in trouble. Personally, I'd be willing to join a Man-is-dead movement!

Agnosticism

High on the popularity poll of non-theistic ultimate concerns today is agnosticism. What is seldom recognized, however, by either its advocates or its opponents, is that the term agnosticism embraces two very different positions. The first might be called "hard-boiled" agnosticism: "I know that I am unable to know that there is a God"; the second, "soft-boiled" agnosticism: "I am not sure whether knowledge of God is possible."

Little time should be spent on hard-boiled agnosticism, since it is tantamount to traditional atheism, and suffers from its basic fallacy: it presumes that one can (apart from any revelation of God, to be sure!) know the universe so well that one can assert the non-existence of God or the non-existence of compelling evidence for his existence. But such comprehensive knowledge of the universe would require either (a) revelation, which is excluded on principle, or (b) divine powers of observation on the part of the atheist or hard-boiled agnostic. In the latter case, atheism and the extreme agnostic position become self-defeating, since the unbeliever perforce creates a god by deifying himself.

As for soft-boiled agnosticism, it is highly commendable *if actually practiced* (which is very seldom). A genuine agnostic of this school will of course bend every effort to see whether in fact evidence does exist in behalf of theistic claims. His view of the universe is open-ended; he is a passionate seeker for truth; and he recognizes that his best energies must be put to this quest, since one's happiness in this world, to say nothing about one's eternal destiny in the next, is directly at stake if God in fact exists and makes demands on his creatures. The true agnostic, then, might be thought of as a person in this room who was not sure whether or not to believe a report that a bomb was planted in the building and would go off in two hours. Because of the cruciality of the *possibility,* he would not sit here in blasé indifference (the usual agnostic posture), but would clear the room and engage in a most diligent search of the premises to determine whether concrete evidence supported the claim or not.

It is now our task to perform a brief, but hopefully constructive, check of the universal premises to see if divine power is there revealed.

The Reality of the Biblical God

Where to look for the footprints of Deity? Virtually anywhere but in the arguments of some modern theologians, clerics, and mystics, of whom it might well be said: "With friends like that God doesn't need any enemies." I refer, for example, to those Anglican canons who parachuted from the top of St. Paul's Cathedral, to "bring the young people back to the church" (eliciting the remark in *Esquire* magazine: "If God isn't dead, maybe he wishes he were"); or the Protestant-Roman Catholic-Jewish death-of-God school; or Aldous Huxley's World Controller, who declared in *Brave New World* that God now "manifests himself as an absence; as though he weren't there at all." Once having stated this small *caveat,* however, not even the sky is the evidential limit. As Jacques Maritain so well expressed it in *Approaches to God:* "There is not just one way to God, as there is to an oasis across the desert or to a new mathematical idea across the breadth of the science of number. For man there are as many ways of approach to God as there are wanderings on the earth or paths to his own heart." We shall consider four such pathways.

God and the World

In his famous 1948 BBC debate with Bertrand Russell, the great historian of philosophy F. C. Copleston succinctly stated the fundamental "argument from contingency" for God's existence:

> First of all, I should say, we know that there are at least some beings in the world which do not contain in themselves the reason for their existence. For example, I depend on my parents, and now on the air, and on food, and so on. Now, secondly, the world is simply the real or imagined totality or aggregate of individual objects, none of which contain in themselves alone the reason for their existence. There isn't any world distinct from the objects which form it, any more than the human race is something apart from the members. Therefore, I should say, since objects or events exist, and since no object of experience contains within itself the reason of its existence, this reason, the totality of objects, must have a reason external to itself. That reason must be an existent being. Well, this being is either itself the reason for its own existence, or it is not. If it is, well and good. If it is not, then we must proceed farther. But if we proceed to infinity in that sense, then there's no explanation of existence at all. So, I should say, in order to explain existence we must come to a being which contains within itself the reason for its existence, that is to say, which cannot not-exist.

This argument is not only regarded by most philosophical advocates of theism as the keystone of the so-called "classic proofs" of God's existence; it is today reinforced by a most impressive battery of evidence from the physical sciences. For example (one may on the point consult the engineering publications of University of Michigan professor Gordon J. Van Wylen), the second law of thermodynamics states that for irreversible processes in any closed system left to itself, the entropy (loss of available heat energy) will increase with time; thus the universe, viewed as such a system, is moving to the condition of maximum entropy (heat death); *but* (and this is the significant aspect of the matter for our purposes)

if the irreversible process had begun an infinite time ago—
if, in other words, the universe were uncreated and eternal—the earth would *already* have reached maximum entropy; and since this is not the case, we are driven to the
conclusion that the universe is indeed contingent and
finite, and requires a creative force from the outside to
have brought it into existence.

It should be carefully noted that this *a posteriori* argument from contingency is empirically grounded in testable experience; it is neither a disguised form of the
highly questionable ontological argument, which asserts
a priori that God's essence establishes his existence, nor
an attempt at allegedly "synthetic *a priori*" reasoning.
And unlike the "causal argument," it does not gratuitously presuppose an unalterable cause-and-effect structure in the universe (a very doubtful assumption in light
of Einsteinian physics and the Heisenberg uncertainty
principle which requires us to give serious consideration
to all event-claims, even those "miraculously uncaused").

But what about the standard rebuttal: "You just beg
the question; now tell us why God exists"? Though this
question evidently started Bertrand Russell on the down-
hill slide into intellectual anticlericalism at an early age,
it is not especially profound. We have just seen some of
the evidence for the contingency of the universe we live
in; to regard this world as eternal is out of the question.
But to regard its creator as likewise contingent ("Who
created *him?*") *would* beg the question, for it would force
us to pose the very same query again—and again. Only
by stopping with a God who is the final answer to the
series do we *avoid* begging the question—and only then
do we offer any adequate account for the contingent
universe with which we began. Moreover, the "why
God?" question suffers an acute case both of artificiality
and of absurdity, as philosopher Plantinga has shown in
his essay on "Necessary Being" (in his *Faith and Philosophy* [1964]):

> We should note that the question "Why does God
> exist?" never does, in fact, arise. Those who do not be-
> lieve that God exists will not, of course, ask *why* He
> exists. But neither do believers ask that question. Outside
> of theism, so to speak, the question is nonsensical, and in-

side of theism, the question is never asked. . . .

Now it becomes clear that it is absurd to ask why God exists. To ask that question is to presuppose that God does exist; but it is a necessary truth that if He does, He has no cause. And it is also a necessary truth that if He has no cause, then there is no answer to a question asking for His causal conditions. The question "Why does God exist?" is, therefore, an absurdity.

God and Personhood

Robert Benchley tells of the disastrous college biology course in which he spent the term meticulously drawing in his lab manual the image of his own eyelash as it fell across the microscopic field. The catastrophe occurred because he lost track of the necessary distinction between himself as subject (his subjectivity) and the external object to be observed (the objectivity of the outside world). Such results and others no less dire are inevitable when one engages in what Whitehead well termed "extreme objectivism"—an objectivism which even objectifies the subject. A person is an "irreducible I": he can never be fully comprehended as an object. No matter how complete a list you make of your own characteristics—or of the characteristics of that stunning coed you are dating—you and the coed *transcend* the list. Persons are grounded in the clay of the contingent world we discussed above, but at the same time they transcend it; human personhood warrants the designation "semi-transcendent." This semi-transcendent, irreducible character of the human person is the quality that has escaped (and logically must escape) the behaviorist who always treats his subjects as objects; it is to the credit of contemporary psychological (especially psychoanalytic) thought that efforts are now made to get beyond such hyper-objectivism. Indeed, in those cases where human subjectivity and freewill are consistently denied, the deterministic objectivist loses all right to claim volitional action and purpose as an experimenter. His refusal to recognize the "semi-transcendent I" finally results in his own epistemological evaporation.

Now, as philosophical theologians such as Ian Ramsey have shown in considerable detail in recent years, the partial transcendence of the human subject establishes both the possibility of metaphysical assertions and the legitimacy of God-language. We cannot meaningfully talk about the universe around us without presupposing our own subjectivity, and the partial transcendence we possess demands an unqualifiedly transcendent integrating subjectivity to make it meaningful. As Ramsey puts it in an essay in his *Prospect for Metaphysics* (1961): "Just as 'I' acts as an integrator word for all kinds of scientific and other descriptive assertions about myself, 'I exist' being a sort of conceptual presupposition for them all, so also may 'God' be regarded as a contextual presupposition for the Universe."

This perspective sheds considerable light on two fundamental problems raised by theistic belief: the existence of evil and the question of meaningful God-talk (the problem of the "sweatshirt," as alluded to at the outset of this presentation). Opponents of theism have perennially argued that the natural and moral evils in the universe make the idea of an omnipotent and perfectly good God irrational. But if subjectivity (and its correlative, freewill) must be presupposed on the level of human action, and if God's character as fully transcendent divine Subject serves to make human volition meaningful, then the existence of freewill in itself provides a legitimate explanation of evil. To create personalities without genuine freewill would not have been to create persons at all; and freewill means the genuine possibility of wrong decision, i.e., the creation of evil by God's creatures (whether wide-ranging natural and moral evil by fallen angels or limited chaos on earth by fallen mankind). As for the argument that a good God should have created only those beings he would foresee as choosing the right—or that he should certainly eliminate the effects of his creatures' evil decisions, the obvious answer is (as Plantinga develops it with great logical rigor in his *God and Other Minds* [1967]) that this would be tantamount to not giving freewill at all. To create only those who "must" (in any sense) choose good is to create automata; and to whisk away evil effects as they are produced is to whisk away evil itself, for an act and its consequences are bound together. C. S. Lewis has noted that God's love enters into this issue as well, since the biblical God created man out

of love, and genuine human love is impossible without
freewill—without the free possibility of accepting love or
rejecting it. Just as a boy who offers himself and his love
to a girl must count on the real possibility of rejection,
so when God originated a creative work that made genuine love possible, it by definition entailed the concomitant
possibility of the evil rejection of his love by his creatures.

By the "sweatshirt" problem we refer to an objection
to theism posed by such analytical philosophers as Kai
Nielsen and Antony Flew, who claim that God's very
uniqueness makes it irrational to say anything about him:
since, in the absence of any perfect analogy, he must
always be described in negatives, God-talk becomes totally meaningless. The sweatshirt with the big "G," we
are told, is necessarily empty. But again note how the
understanding of God as transcendent integrating Subject in relation to semi-transcendent human subjects
clears the air. Human persons are *likewise* unique—no
person is just like another, and the very meaning of "subject" and individual "freewill" entails this irreducible
uniqueness. To call God-talk meaningless, then, is at the
same time to render man-talk nonsensical! Conversely,
if we once accept what is involved in the concept of human subjective existence (and how can we avoid it?)
then we simultaneously open the gate to meaningful God-
talk. As Ramsey neatly suggests, "We might perhaps then
say that we are as certain of God as we are of ourselves."

However, it would be conceding far too much if we
were to allow that talk about God involves only negatives—the so-called "death by a thousand qualifications."
Here we find ourselves immediately drawn into discussion
of

God in Christ

The following parable, formulated by philosophers
Flew and Wisdom, is a good statement of the view that
God-claims are too vague to be sensible and offer no
adequate empirical evidence in their behalf:

> Once a time two explorers came upon a clearing in the
> jungle. In the clearing were growing many flowers and
> many weeds. One explorer says, "Some gardener must

tend this plot." The other disagrees, "There is no gardener." So they pitch their tents and set a watch. No gardener is ever seen. "But perhaps he is an invisible gardener." So they set up a barbed-wire fence. They electrify it.
They patrol with bloodhounds. (For they remember how
H. G. Wells' *The Invisible Man* could be both smelt and
touched though he could not be seen.) But no shrieks ever
suggest that some intruder has received a shock. No movements of the wire ever betray an invisible climber. The
bloodhounds never give cry. Yet still the Believer is not
convinced. "But there is a gardener, invisible, intangible,
insensible to electric shocks, a gardener who has no scent
and makes no sound, a gardener who comes secretly to
look after the garden which he loves." At last the Sceptic
despairs, "But what remains of your original assertion?
Just how does what you call an invisible, intangible, eternally elusive gardener differ from an imaginary gardener
or even from no gardener at all?"

This parable may echo the religious claims of many
sincere people, but it has little to do with the Christian
affirmation of God. Why? Because central to the Christian position is the historically grounded assertion that
the Gardener entered the garden: God actually appeared
in the empirical world in Jesus Christ and fully manifested his deity through miraculous acts in general and
his resurrection from the dead in particular. Christian
talk about God therefore becomes in the most rigorous
sense affirmative, for when asked to "define God" or
"tell us what he looks like," the Christian simply points
to Christ. Dr. Jowett was supposed to have been asked
by an effusive young lady, "Do tell me—what do you
think about God?" and his reply was: "That, my dear
young lady, is a very unimportant question; the only thing
that signifies is what he thinks about me." The Christian
knows what God thinks about him—and the human race;
he knows what God's eternal value system is (and how
desperately the human race needs that knowledge, as we
saw in our discussion of humanism!); and he knows that
in spite of man's self-centered trampling of God's values,
God's love has reached down to earth. How does he know
this? Because God tells him this in Christ.

Now it cannot be stressed too strongly that this claim
to divine intervention in history is solidly grounded in
historical evidence. The textual case for the New Testament documents which record Christ's divine utter-

ances and acts is so excellent that Sir Fredric G. Kenyon, director and principal librarian of the British Museum, could write in 1940 in *The Bible and Archaeology*: "Both the *authenticity* and the *general integrity* of the books of the New Testament may be regarded as finally established" (Kenyon's italics). The world's foremost living biblical archeologist, W. F. Albright of Johns Hopkins University, has identified the New Testament materials as primary source documents for the life of Jesus, dating all of them (including John's Gospel) "between the forties and the eighties of the first century A.D. (very probably sometime between about 50 and 75 A.D.)" (interview in *Christianity Today*, January 18, 1963). The New Testament writers claim eyewitness contact with the events of Jesus' career, and describe his death and post-resurrection appearances in minute detail. In A.D. 56, for example, Paul wrote (I Cor. 15) that over five hundred people had seen the risen Jesus and that most were still alive. The New Testament writers explicitly affirm that they are presenting historical facts, not religious fables; writes Peter (II Pet. 1:16): "We have not followed cunningly devised myths when we made known to you the power and coming of our Lord Jesus Christ, but were eyewitnesses of his majesty." And if deception and fabrication were here involved, why didn't the numerous religious enemies of the early Christians blast the whole business? F. F. Bruce of the University of Manchester has shrewdly observed in his book, *The New Testament Documents* (5th ed., 1960), that if the early proclaimers of Christ's deity had had any tendency to depart from the facts, the presence of hostile witnesses in the audience would have served as a most powerful corrective.

The central attestation for Jesus' deity is his resurrection, and to deny its facticity isn't easy. To oppose it on historical grounds is so difficult that, if one succeeds, the victory is entirely Pyrrhic: any argument that will impugn the New Testament documents will at the same time remove confidence from virtually all other ancient, and numerous modern, historical sources; the result, then, is a general (and entirely unacceptable) historiographical solipsism. To oppose the resurrection on the ground that miracles do not occur is, as we have noted

earlier, both philosophically and scientifically irresponsible: philosophically, because no one below the status of
a god could know the universe so well as to eliminate
miracles *a priori;* and scientifically, because in the age
of Einsteinian physics (so different from the world of
Newtonian absolutes in which Hume formulated his classic anti-miraculous argument) the universe has opened up
to all possibilities, "any attempt to state a 'universal law
of causation' must prove futile" (logician Max Black),
and only a careful consideration of the empirical testimony for a miraculous event can determine whether in
fact it has or has not occurred.

Success in opposing the evidence for Christ's resurrection is so hard to come by that some objectors to
Christian theism (e.g. humanist Corliss Lamont) are reduced to arguing that the event is trivial. "Even if Christ
rose from the dead, would that prove his claims? And
would it necessarily mean anything for us?" In a recent
public discussion following a lecture I delivered at Roose-
velt University, I was informed by a philosophy professor
that Christ's conquest of death was no more significant
qualitatively than a medical victory over pattern baldness. To which I offered the inevitable reply: "A knock
comes at the door. It's the faculty secretary with the
message that your wife and children have just been
killed in a traffic accident. Your comment would of course
be: 'Oh well, what's death? Just like pattern baldness'."
In point of fact, we all recognize the overarching significance of death, and a very large proportion of our individual and societal energies are expended in trying to
postpone it (medicine), indirectly overcome it (familial,
vocational, and artistic achievement), ignore it (escap-
ist entertainment), or kid ourselves about it (funeral
practices). Whether we look to anthropological evidence,
psychoanalytic studies (E. Herzog's *Psyche and Death*
[1967]), philosophical treatments (Jacques Choron's
Death and Western Thought [1963]), or literary expressions of the human dilemma (Camus' *La Peste*), the reality of the problem of death for all mankind is displayed
with appalling clarity. If Christ did in fact conquer this
most basic of all human enemies and claimed on the
basis of it to be God incarnate, able to give eternal life

to those who believe in him, it would be sheer madness
not to take with full seriousness the biblical affirmation
that "God was in Christ, reconciling the world unto himself."

God and Human Experience

Contemplation of the centrality of death and man's
quest for immortality vis-à-vis the God question leads us
quite naturally to a striking new book which treats the
existence of God from the standpoint of man's sociological experience. I refer to *A Rumor of Angels: Modern
Society and the Rediscovery of the Supernatural* (1969)
by Peter Berger, a professor of sociology at the New
School for Social Research. Berger argues that such human experiences as hope in the face of death and the
conviction that there must be a retribution transcending
inadequate human justice for the commission of monstrous evil in this life are most sensibly explained in terms
of God's existence. Other analogous empirical pointers
to the existence of the transcendent are man's affirmation
of societal ordering (cf. Voegelin's *Order and History*) and
unshakeable conviction that such ordering extends to the
universe as a whole (cf. the reassurance given by moth-
ers to their frightened children since the world began,
"Everything is all right"); man's humor, reflecting his
basic awareness that a radical discrepancy exists between life as he lives it (in finitude) and life as it ought
to be (in transcendent rightness); and man's play experiences—his brief transmigrations out of time into
realms where finitude is momentarily transcended:

> Some little girls are playing hopscotch in the park. They
> are completely intent on their game, closed to the world
> outside it, happy in their concentration. Time has stood
> still for them—or, more accurately, it has been collapsed
> into the movements of the game. The outside world has,
> for the duration of the game, ceased to exist. And, by impli-
> cation (since the little girls may not be very conscious of
> this), pain and death, which are the law of that world,
> have also ceased to exist. Even the adult observer of this
> scene, who is perhaps all too conscious of pain and death,
> is momentarily drawn into the beatific immunity.
>
> In the playing of adults, at least on certain occasions,
> the suspension of time and of the "serious" world in which
> people suffer and die becomes explicit. Just before the

Soviet troops occupied Vienna in 1945, the Vienna Phil-
harmonic gave one of its scheduled concerts. There was
fighting in the immediate proximity of the city, and the
concertgoers could hear the rumbling of the guns in the
distance.... It was ... an affirmation of the ultimate
triumph of all human gestures of creative beauty over the
gestures of destruction, and even over the ugliness of war
and death....

All men have experienced the deathlessness of childhood and we may assume that, even if only once or twice,
all men have experienced transcendent joy in adulthood.
Under the aspect of inductive faith, religion is the final
vindication of childhood and of joy, and of all gestures that
replicate these.

Professor Berger's arguments carry us from the low-
lands of sociology to the heights of philosophical ontology for they conjoin with a very important passage in
Norman Malcolm's classic essay on Anselm's ontological
proof of God's existence (*Philosophical Review*, January,
1960). Asks Malcolm: Why have human beings formed the
concept of "a being a greater than which cannot be conceived"? This is his suggested answer, based, as are
Berger's arguments, on "an understanding of the phenomena of human life:"

There is the phenomenon of feeling guilt for something
that one has done or thought or felt or for a disposition
that one has. One wants to be free of this guilt. But sometimes the guilt is felt to be so great that one is sure that
nothing one could do oneself, nor any forgiveness by
another human being, would remove it. One feels a guilt
that is beyond all measure, a guilt "a greater than which
cannot be conceived." Paradoxically, it would seem, one
nevertheless has an intense desire to have this incomparable guilt removed. One requires a forgiveness that is beyond all measure, a forgiveness "a greater than which cannot be conceived." Out of such a storm in the soul, I am
suggesting, there arises the conception of a forgiving
mercy that is limitless, beyond all measure.

The experiences of death, judgment, order, humor,
play, and guilt point beyond themselves—as does the very
"I" who is conscious of them—and the direction of the
signpost is to a Cross where the transcendent God offered
"forgiving mercy that is limitless, beyond all measure."
In the words of the Apostle (Rom. 4:25), he was "delivered for our offences and was raised again for our

justification." Is man his own God? No, for man could never attain such limitless mercy. But God became man to offer that mercy, which no one could buy at any price, as a free gift. The evidence of God's existence and of his gift is more than compelling, but those who insist that they have no need of him or it will always find ways to discount the offer. As Pascal trenchantly observed (*Pensées,* No. 430): "Il y a assez de lumière pour ceux qui ne désirent que de voir, et assez d'obscurité pour ceux qui ont une disposition contraire." This statement is, of course, but a corollary of Jesus' words (Matt. 9:13; 18:3): "I am not come to call the righteous, but sinners to repentance. Except you be converted and become as little children, you shall not enter into the kingdom of heaven."

2.

*The Theologian's Craft: A Discussion of Theory Formation and Theory Testing in Theology**

What is it to "do theology?" Numerous conflicting and inadequate answers (e.g., Bultmannian existentialism, the post-Bultmannian "New Hermaneutic") hold the field today; these have in common a basic misunderstanding as to the relation of theological theorizing to theory construction in other fields of knowledge, and a fundamental misconception in regard to the proper way of confirming or disconfirming theological judgments. In this essay, a detailed comparison between scientific and theological methodologies is set forth, and the artistic and sacred dimensions of theological theorizing are explicated by way of an original structural model suggested by Wittgensteinian philosophical and linguistic analysis.

Scientists are generally at a loss to know precisely what theologians *do.* Mailmen deliver letters; bartenders serve numerous varieties of firewater; otorhinolaryngologists concern themselves with ears, noses, and throats: but what exactly do theologians endeavor to accomplish? The aura of mystery surrounding theological activity troubles not merely the scientist, who generally has a clear-eyed view of his own professional function, but also the so-called "average man," who, though his awareness of his own role in life may be exceedingly vague, is even more troubled by the peculiarities of "religious" vocations. The wry comment of the parishioner, "We take care of pastor in this life and he takes care of us in the next," well illustrates the gulf that, in general, seems to separate theological activity from the meaningful work of the world.

* An invitational paper presented August 24, 1965, at the 20th Annual Convention of the American Scientific Affiliation, convened at The King's College, Briarcliff Manor, New York.
Notes for this section, pages 300-313.

A theologian of course theologizes, i.e., he does theology. But the tautological character of this statement requires us to press on: What is it to "do theology"? Etymologically, as everyone knows, "theology" involves a "speaking-of-God," and this expression should be regarded very carefully, for its double meaning suggests the source of difficulty in understanding the theologian's craft: theology speaks *about* God (the objective genitive of the grammarians), but only because of "God's speaking" to man (the subjective genitive); it is the active presence of the Numinous in the work of theology that renders its task so strange to those who look upon it from the outside. But leaving aside (for the moment only!) the active numinosity in theological endeavor, and concentrating on the object of theological research, we can say very simply that the theologian[1] is one who engages in forming and testing theories concerning the Divine.

Our task in this paper is thus the clarification of what it properly means to form and to test theological theories; and it is hoped that the result will aid both the non-theologian (particularly the scientist) to understand and to appreciate better the nature of theological endeavor, and the theologian himself to keep his methodological sights correctly focused. The center of attention will be neither the historical circumstances attending theological theorizing[2] nor the psychological factors relating to theological discovery[3]—interesting as these subjects are. We shall hold ourselves quite closely to the fundamental realm of theological prolegomena, and seek to discover the nature of the operations that make theology theology. As the reader enters the rarified air of this domain, he is warned to prepare himself for innovation and ground-breaking; it is the writer's conviction that precisely here lie the basic sources of error in much contemporary theological thinking, as well as the relatively untapped resources for theological recovery in our time.

Through a Welter of Confusion

Any attempt to get at the nature of theological theorizing runs the immediate danger of being bogged down in a morass of conflicting interpretations of theological activity. On the one hand, the student of the subject is

faced with dogmatically simplistic and pejorative definitions, such as that of Princeton philosopher Walter Kaufmann:

> First, theology is of necessity denominational. Second,
> theology is essentially a defensive maneuver. Third, it is
> almost always time-bound and dated quickly.
>   Theology is the systematic attempt to pour the newest
> wine into the old skins of a denomination.[4]

To which it may be replied: First, even if all theologians were members of denominations (which is not the
case), this would not make theology "denominational"—
any more than the (fallacious) assumption that all physicians are members of state medical societies would make
medicine political. Secondly, the defense of the faith
(technically: apologetics) is but one of the tasks of systematic theology, not the whole or even the center of it.
Thirdly, one needs a firm criterion of obsolescence in
order to assert that theology is "time-bound"—but the
secularist is, *ex hypothesi*, in the worst possible position
to establish such a criterion. Finally: to define theological
theorizing à la Kaufmann one must gratuitously assume
that its content (wine) is forever new and changing, that
its interpretative categories (skins) are old and denominational, and that the theorizing process (the pouring) requires no special examination. None of these assumptions,
however, is credible enough to warrant pursuing.

Alongside of simplistically objective definitions of theological activity, one encounters existentially subjective
descriptions of the theologian's work. In his Cambridge
University Stanton Lectures on "Theological Explanation," G. F. Woods asserts, in partial dependence on
Tillich:

> The first sense of theological explanation is the ulti-
> mate personal being which is the real ground of the world.
> The second sense is the act of seeking an explanation of
> what is ultimate, both through our own efforts to make it
> plain and through its own endeavours to make itself plain
> to us. The third sense is the act of using ultimate personal
> being as an explanation of the world in which we live.
> These manifold acts of explanation take place on particu-
> lar occasions and are markedly influenced by the circum-
> stances of the day, particularly by the methods of explana-
> tion which happen to be dominant at the time. But,
> throughout the confused series of particular acts of expla-

nation, there is the perpetual trend towards the use of explanatory terms derived from our own being. What we are is the source of all our methods of seeking to explain the actual world.[5]

Here one must unkindly lay stress on the author's phrase "the confused series of particular acts of explanation," for confusion does indeed reign in any theological enterprise where "our own (existential-ontological) being," constitutes the center of the stage. As Carnap showed the analytical nonsensicality of Heidegger's "non-being," so A. C. Garnett has pointed up the unverifiable nonsense involved in "being"-assertions as theological starting-points.[6]

A third major variety of metatheological explanation is illustrated in William Hordern's book, *Speaking of God*, which endeavors to create a bridge between current "ordinary-language philosophy" and theology. Here Hordern, by an exceedingly unfortunate substitution of the later Wittgenstein for the earlier Wittgenstein, leaves the fundamental problem of theological verification aside and attempts to describe theology as a unique, *sui generis* "language game":

> Instead of thinking of theology as the queen of the sciences, can we think of it as the Olympic Games? . . . The Olympic Committee does not legislate the rules of ice hockey, and much less does it train a hockey player how to play hockey. But ice hockey takes its place within the total pattern of the Olympics, and its players must meet the Olympic standard. . . .
>
> By analogy, natural science and other language games are separate and independent, with their own questions, rules, methods of verification, and ways of giving answers. . . . [The] Christian faith cannot answer scientific questions any more than the Olympic Committee can tell a hockey player how to shoot the puck. . . .
>
> Theology, as the Olympics of life. . . . does not pretend to be a superscientific system with answers to all questions left unanswered by science. It is concerned with another kind of question than is science. It does not offer a systematic explanation of the universe; it is a means whereby man is enabled to live his life with a sense of purpose, direction, and integrity.[7]

Such an approach places theology in a mystical cloud of unknowing, and lifts the Mt. Olympus of theology off of the earth entirely.[8] Since theology, in Hordern's view, "cannot answer scientific questions," its axiological ship passes in the night the cognitive vessel of the scientific disciplines, and neither can communicate with the other. Moreover, and most important, the theological "language game" is without external verification, so its theories do not have to be accepted as "Olympic rules" by anyone who is not theologically inclined. It is too bad that Hordern did not see the point behind Wittgenstein's concern that his *Tractatus Logico-Philosophicus* be published along with his *Philosophical Investigations:* the latter, without the former, provides no answer whatever to the fundamental question: how do you know if a "language game" (e.g., theological theorizing) represents reality at all?"

In light of fallaciously objectivistic, existentially subjectivistic, and etherially olympian descriptions of theological activity, is it any wonder that tongue-in-cheek humor not infrequently captures the special-pleading character of contemporary theological theorizing? The January 15, 1965, issue of *Christianity Today* carries Lawing's cartoon of Moses' return from Mt. Sinai with the Commandments; a sly Israelite meets him with the suggestion, "Aaron said perhaps you'd let us condense them to 'act responsibly in love.'" Here Bishop Robinson's theological theory as to the "real" meaning of the Commandments is lampooned: the sick humor lies in the fact that the Israelite (probably) and Robinson (certainly) lack awareness of the degree to which cultural conformity and personal preference dictate the content of their theological constructions.

How can we gain clarity in this vital area? Let us, for the moment, step outside of the theological realm and examine the essential nature of theories by way of the discipline in which they have been most thoroughly discussed: the field of science. Here we can gain our bearings and find an immediate and meaningful entrée to the larger question of theological theory formation and testing.

Theory Construction in Science

Though there have been many theories as to the exact nature of scientific theories, a general convergence and agreement among them is not hard to find. Popper uses

Wittgenstein's analogy of the Net: "Theories are nets cast to catch what we call 'the world': to rationalize, to explain, and to master it. We endeavor to make the mesh ever finer and finer." [10] Comments Leonard Nash of Harvard: "He who realizes the existence of such a conceptual fabric, and is capable of lifting it, carries with it all its cords, all the colligative relations it accommodates." [11] The use of an image (the net) to illustrate the nature of scientific theory construction points to an especially vital element in such theories: the employment of "models"—representations that carry "epistemological vividness." [12] So, in speaking of the discovery that "light travels in straight lines," Stephen Toulmin notes that "a vital part of the discovery is the very possibility of drawing 'pictures' of the optical state-of-affairs to be expected in given circumstances—or rather, the possibility of drawing them in a way that *fits the facts.*" [13]

To concretize these abstract remarks on scientific theorizing, let us consider a dramatic and very recent case of successful theory-building: the 1962 Nobel Prize discovery, by James Watson and Francis Crick, of the molecular structure of DNA (the nucleic acid bearing the blueprint of heredity).

> Watson was convinced by reasons based upon genetics that [the] structure could only be built around two spirals arranged "in a certain way." The answer lay in this "certain way."
>
> The only way of representing the three-dimensional structure of an invisible molecule is to replace atoms or groups of atoms by spheres and then build a model of the molecule.
>
> This is exactly what Crick and Watson did, tirelessly attempting to arrange the two spirals. To quote the expression used by one of them, all of their models were "frightful," and quite inadequate to cope with DNA's known qualities ("You couldn't hang anything on these spirals"). . . .
>
> Then came the famous "spiral night." Crick was working late in a laboratory upstairs. On the ground floor, Watson also was going over a list of possible solutions. That night Crick had a revelation, a solution whispered to him by his intuition: there were only two spirals, they were symmetrical, and they coiled in opposite directions, one from "top to bottom" and the other from "bot-

tom to top" (this hypothesis also reflected certain laws of crystallography).

Crick raced downstairs—it was a spiral staircase—and enthusiastically explained his theory to Watson. Watson received it calmly: it sounded simple to him, much too simple. Then, mentally, he built a spiral form based on this idea, and all the various chemical, biological and physical requirements he put forward were met by it. Now he too was excited; he paced up and down the laboratory, repeating: "It must be true, it must be true." [14]

This lively description of the key point[15] in the discovery of DNA's molecular structure drives home several basic truths about scientific theorizing—truths expressed formally in the definitions previously cited. First, theories do not create facts; rather, they attempt to relate existent facts properly. The DNA molecular model is a "net" thrown to catch the "world" of "chemical, biological and physical requirements" demanded by empirical facticity. The theory maker must never suppose that he is building reality; his task is the fascinating but more humble one of shaping a "conceptual fabric" that, with "epistemological vividness," will correctly mirror the world of substantive reality.[16]

The DNA discovery illustrates, moreover, that theories in science are not formed "either by deductive argument from the experimental data alone, or by the type of logic-book 'induction' on which philosophers have so often concentrated, or indeed by any method for which formal rules could be given."[17] Writers such as Braithwaite have effectively argued the case for the indispensable role of deductive reasoning in scientific explanation; but Braithwaite's concluding paragraphs stress the inductivist side of the coin: "Man proposes a system of hypotheses: Nature disposes of its truth or falsity. Man invents a scientific system, and then discovers whether or not it accords with observed fact."[18] G. H. von Wright has logically demonstrated that "if we wish to call reasoned policies *better* than not-reasoned ones, it follows . . . that induction is of necessity the *best* way";[19] yet the appealing ghost of Francis Bacon's pure inductivism in science has been laid by such philosophers of science as Joseph Agassi,[20] and as the history of scientific discovery shows beyond question, the great advances in theory have not arisen through static, formalistic induction.[21] Rather than making invidious comparisons between deduction and induction in scientific theory formation, we should see these operations as complementary.[22] Instead of seeking monolithic explanation of scientific method, let us, with Max Black, "think of science as a concrescence, a growing together of variable, interacting, mutually reinforcing factors contributing to a development organic in character."[23] Nash provides the following helpful diagram, illustrating how scientific knowledge is generated by endless cyclical renewal:[24]

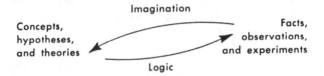

The essential place of "imagination" in scientific theorizing has been greatly stressed by Einstein; and its role can perhaps best be seen by introducing, alongside induction and deduction—as, in fact, the connecting link between them—Peirce's concept of "retroduction" or "abduction," based upon Aristotle's ἀπαγωγή type inference.[25] "Abduction," writes Peirce, "consists in studying facts and devising a theory to explain them.... Deduction proves that something *must* be; Induction shows that something *actually is* operative; Abduction merely suggests that something *may be*."[26] N. R. Hanson has well illustrated the centrality of such "retroductive" reasoning to scientific theorizing; consider Hanson's ambiguous "bird-antelope":

Were this flashed on to a screen I might say "It has four feathers." I may be wrong: that number of wiggly lines on the figure is other than four is a conceptual possibility. "It has four feathers" is thus falsifiable, empirical. It is an observation statement. To determine its truth we need only put the figure on the screen again and count the lines.

The statement that the figure is of a bird, however, is not falsifiable in the same sense. Its negation does not represent the same conceptual possibility, for it concerns not an observational detail but the very pattern which makes those details intelligible. One could not even say "It has four feathers" and be wrong about it, if it was not a feathered object. I can show you your error if you say "four feathers." But I cannot thus disclose your "error" in saying of the bird-antelope that it is a bird (instead of an antelope).

Pattern statements are different from detail statements. They are not inductive summaries of detail statements. Still the statement, "It's a bird" is truly empirical. Had birds been different, or had the bird-antelope been drawn differently, "It's a bird" might not have been true. In some sense it is true. If the detail statements are empirical, the pattern statements which give them sense are also empirical—though not in the same way. To deny a detail statement is to do something within the pattern. To deny a pattern statement is to attack the conceptual framework itself, and this denial cannot function in the same way. . . .

Physical theories provide patterns within which data appear intelligible. They constitute a "conceptual Gestalt." A theory is not pieced together from observed phenomena; it is rather what makes it possible to observe phenomena as being of a certain sort, and as related to other phenomena. Theories put phenomena into systems. They are built up in "reverse"—retroductively. A theory is a cluster of conclusions in search of a premise. From the observed properties of phenomena the physicist reasons his way towards a keystone idea from which the properties are explicable as a matter of course.[27]

Watson and Crick's discovery of the molecular structure of DNA clearly displays the centrality of retroductive inference in scientific theory formation: they sought a "conceptual Gestalt" which would render intelligible the genetic and crystallographic data; and their resultant theory of two symmetrical spirals was successful precisely because it constituted a "keystone idea" from which the various physical, chemical, and biological characteristics of the molecule were "explicable as a matter of course."

It is particularly important to note that the validity of a scientific theory depends squarely upon its applicability as a "conceptual Gestalt"; experimental confirmation through predictive success is of secondary importance and is often, of necessity, dispensed with entirely. In paleobiology, for example, experimental prediction is ruled out by the very nature of the subject matter; and in astrophysics and cosmological theory predictive experiments are seldom able to be formulated. Watson could say of the DNA spiral theory. "It must be true," though several years would elapse before X-ray diffraction patterns of the molecule would become available, for his theory provided a full-scale ordering of the relevant data.

> Galileo knew he had succeeded when the constant acceleration hypothesis patterned the diverse phenomena he had encountered for thirty years. His reasoned advance from insight to insight culminated in an ultimate physical *explicans*. Further deductions were merely confirmatory; he could have left them to any of his students—Viviani or Toricelli. Even had verification of these further predictions eluded seventeenth-century science, this would not have prevented Galileo from embracing the constant acceleration hypothesis, any more than Copernicus and Kepler were prevented from embracing heliocentrism by the lack of a telescope with which to observe Venus' phases. Kepler needed no new observations to realize that the ellipse covered all observed positions. Newton required no predictions from his gravitation hypothesis to be confident that this really did explain Kepler's three laws and a variety of other given data.[28]

The Scientific Level in Theological Theorizing

We have found that scientific theories are conceptual Gestalts, built up retroductively through imaginative attempts to render phenomena intelligible. What relevance does this have for understanding the theologian's labors? Can any application be made to the field of theology? Is not theology a unique realm of the "spirit," unscientific by its very nature? To bring Tertullian's famous question up to date: "What has the Institute of Advanced Study to do with Jerusalem, the Laboratory with the Church?"

The answer to this last question is not "Nothing," but "Everything." Though theology is evidently something *more* than science (precisely what the "more" consists of, we shall see later), it is certainly not anything *less*. I say this, let it be noted, not simply in reference to the fact that any theology can be an object of descriptive, scientific study by specialists in the history, philosophy, or psychology of religion.[29] This is of course true in the case of all the world religions; but Christianity is unique in claiming intrinsic, not merely extrinsic, connection with the empirical reality which is the subject of scientific investigation. Christianity is a *historical* religion— historical in the very special sense that its entire revelational content is wedded to historical manifestations of Divine power. The pivot of Christian theology is the biblical affirmation that ὁ Λόγος σάρξ ἐγένετο (John 1:14): God Himself came to earth—entered man's empirical sphere—in Jesus Christ, and the revelation of God in the history of Israel served as a pointer to Messiah's coming, and His revelation in the Apostolic community displayed the power of Christ's Spirit.[30] From the first verse of the Bible to the last God's *contact* with man's world is affirmed. And throughout Scripture human testimony to objective, empirical encounter with God is presented in the strongest terms.[31] Christian theology thus has no fear of scientific, empirical investigation;[32] quite the contrary, the historical nature of the Christian faith—as distinguished from the subjective, existential character of the other world religions[33]—demands objective, scientific theologizing.

Hence we should expect, Barth notwithstanding,[34] that theological theories whatever suprascientific characteristics they may have, will most definitely display the full range of properties of scientific theories. The theological theorist, like his scientific counterpart, will endeavor to formulate conceptual Gestalts—"networks" of ideas capable of rendering his data intelligible. He will employ "models" to achieve epistemological vividness. He will utilize all three types of inference (inductive, deductive, retroductive) in his theory making, but, again like the scientist, he will find himself most usually dependent upon the imaginative operation of retroduction,

Little more than superficial naiveté lies at the basis of the popular opinion that science and theology are in methodological conflict because the former "employs inductive reasoning" while the latter "operates deductively!" In point of fact, both generally proceed retroductively, and neither is less concerned than the other about the concrete verification of its inferences.

And how does verification take place? In science we have seen that the success of a theory depends upon its ability, as Toulmin says, to "fit the facts." The same is true in theology. Ian Ramsey—though he does not see that theology exactly parallels science here—introduces a valuable analogy when he writes that "the theological model works . . . like the fitting of a boot or a shoe."

> In other words, we have a particular doctrine which, like a preferred and selected shoe, starts by appearing to meet our empirical needs. But on closer fitting to the phenomena the shoe may pinch. When tested against future slush and rain it may be proven to be not altogether watertight or it may be comfortable—yet it must not be too comfortable. In this way, the test of a shoe is measured by its ability to match a wide range of phenomena, by its overall success in meeting a variety of needs. Here is what I might call the method of empirical fit which is displayed by theological theorizing.[35]

This is precisely the verifying test that we have encountered in our discussion of scientific theories; the Watson-Crick spiral theory was just such a "shoe" whose adequacy depended squarely upon its ability to "fit" the relevant physical, chemical, and biological characteristics of the DNA molecule. Neither Watson and Crick, nor the great scientific theorists of past ages (we have already referred to Galileo, Copernicus, Kepler, and Newton) achieved their primary success in theory construction through the predictive character of their formulations: both in science and in theology, it is "fit," not "future," that lies at the heart of successful theorizing.[36]

But clearly scientific and theological theories are not identical! Where do the differences lie? One important difference (we leave others until later) is pointed up by Ramsey's "shoe" analogy. This analogy immediately raises two basic questions about theorizing: first and most obvious, How do you make the shoe (the theory or model)? but second, and even more fundamental, What foot (data) do you try to fit? In science, the "foot"— the irreducible stuff which theorizing attempts to grasp in its net—is the natural world, and this includes every phenomenal manifestation in the universe. Science knows no investigative boundaries; its limits are imposed not by the stuff with which it is permitted to deal, but by the manner in which it can treat its data. *Ex hypothesi,* science is methodologically capable of studying the world in an *objective* manner only: it can examine anything that touches human experience, but it can never, qua science, "get inside" its subject matter; it always stands outside and describes. This is, of course, both the glory and the pathos of science: it can analyze everything, but it is prevented from experiencing the heart of anything.

On the objective, scientific level, however, theology has no greater advantage; it likewise stands outside its data and analyzes. But what precisely does it analyze? What are the *Gegenstände* of theological theorizing—the "simples" that the theologian attempts to render intelligible through his conceptual Gestalts? In general, for Christian theology, the "foot to be shod" is revelational experience. Theological theories endeavor to "fit the facts" of such experience; theology on this level is thus one segment of scientific activity as a whole—that segment concerned with revelational, as opposed to non-revelational, phenomena. Jean Racette, in dependence upon the great contemporary Jesuit philosopher-theologian Bernard Lonergan, puts it succinctly and well:

> La théologie n'est pas une science ou une sagesse quelconque. Elle est la science du sacré et du révélé. Elle est une démarche de l'intelligence éclairée par la foi. Elle est une refléxion systématique sur un donné reconnu et accepté comme révélé, et donc comme vrai.[37]

However, the expression "revelational experience" is manifestly ambiguous. What does it signify? This question, without a doubt, is of paramount importance for the entire theological task, since a false step here will tragically weaken the entire process of theological theorizing—either by emasculation (if one excludes from purview genuine revelational data), or by adulteration (if one mixes non-revelational considerations with the truly revelational subject matter). And, ironically, it is exactly at this point that Christian theology has all too often trumpeted forth an uncertain sound—or, worse, a positive discord! To change the metaphor, the theologian has not infrequently played the role of a blind cobbler, trying to make shoes without knowing what kind of foot he is shoeing; at other times, he appears as a bungling apprentice, busily preparing what should be dainty slippers for Queen Revelation when in fact he is putting together clod-hoppers to fit Lumberjack U. (for Unregenerate) Religiosity!

Through Christian history, the "revelational experience" which yields the proper data for theological theorizing has been understood as having either a *single* source or *multiple* sources. Traditional multiple source positions include Roman Catholicism, Greek Orthodoxy, and Anglo-Catholicism (all holding that the Bible and church tradition constitute valid revelational sources), and various sects having sacred books which they use alongside of the Bible as sources of data for theologizing (e.g., Mormonism, with its *Book of Mormon;* Christian Science, with Mrs. Eddy's *Science and Health*). Multiple source approaches also constitute the epistemological core of most avant-garde mainline Protestant theological positions today: a combination of biblical insight, church teaching, and personal religious experience is supposed to provide the fund from which systematic theology should draw its data for doctrinal theorizing. For Paul Tillich, the "survey of the sources of systematic theology has shown their almost unlimited richness: Bible, church history, history of religion and culture." [38] For advocates of the post-Bultmannian "New Hermeneutic" (such as Ernst Fuchs and Gerhard Ebeling), systematic theology has as its subject matter "the word event itself, in which the reality of man comes true," and by "word event" is meant "the event of interpretation";[39] thus theology has its source in a polar dialectic of biblical text and situational interpretation. Heinrich Ott, for all his differences with Fuchs, expresses essentially the same dual-source, dialectic approach when he finds the subject matter of theology in "the Christ event, the reality of revelation and of believing" [10] and proposes that "dogmatics is simply to unfold thoughtfully without presupposing any philosophical schema the meaning-content experienced in believing from within the experience itself";[11] systematic theology thus serves as a "hermeneutical arch that reaches from the text to the contemporary sermon." [12]

All multiple-source views of the subject matter of theology are, however, unstable. They tend to give preference to one source rather than to another, or to seek some single, more fundamental source lying behind the multiple sources already accepted. Among the sects, the Bible has been virtually swallowed up by whatever special "sacred book" has been put alongside of it;[13] tradition has been more determinative than biblical teaching in the theological development of Greek Orthodoxy and Roman Catholicism; and the "New Hermeneutic" seems incapable of withstanding the old Bultmannian gravitational pull away from the biblical text toward the other dialectic pole of contemporary existential interpretation. In the "New Shape" Roman Catholicism of Karl Rahner, Küng, et al., a conscious attempt is being made to get behind the dualism of scripture and tradition through affirming a unity of "Holy Writ and Holy Church";[14] yet such a dialectic, like that of the Protestant "New Hermeneutic," does not escape the charge of question-begging. This is the essential, insurmountable difficulty in all multiple-source approaches to theological theorizing. They leave unanswered the question of *final* authority. What do we do as Roman Catholics when Holy Writ and Holy Church *disagree*? What do we do as Tillichians when church history, the Bible and the history of culture are not in accord? Obviously, one must either frankly admit that one source is final, or establish a criterion of judgment over all previously accepted sources—which criterion becomes, *ex hypothesi*, the final source! Multiple source approaches to the subject matter of theology thus logically—whether one likes it or not—reduce to single source interpretations.[15]

If theology must ultimately admit that there is but a single "foot" which its doctrinal theories are to fit, the question becomes one of identifying that foot. The numerous identifications through Christian history contract upon examination, to four: Reason, the Church, Christian Experience, and Scriptural Revelation. During the eighteenth-century "Enlightenment" it was contended that the "natural light of Reason," not any alleged sacred writing or "special revelation," constitutes the final source of valid theological data.[46] Unhappily, however, pure reason (i.e., formal logic) is tautologous and cannot impart any factual data about existent things, whether theological or otherwise;[47] and "reason" understood as "nature" can yield atheistic ideologies almost as easily as deistic theologies.[48] In Romanism, the Church becomes the court of last resort for determining what are or what are not genuine data for theologizing. But the argument that this is necessary because even an infallible Bible requires an infallible interpreter suffers from the fallacy of infinite regress; one can always ask, Then how can the Church itself function without a higher-level interpreter? Moreover, no Divine mandate can be produced to justify the authority of the Church as interpreter of Scripture.[49]

Christian Experience is the most widely accepted Protestant answer to the question of the source of data for theological theorizing. For the unreconstructed Modernism of the Schleiermacher-Ritschl-Fosdick era, "constructive (i.e., subjective) religious empiricism" was expected to yield doctrinal reconstructions in accord with the needs of contemporary man. As a matter of fact, however, such a methodology yielded only the results permitted by the experiential a priori of the particular theological investigator.[50] Bultmannian existentialism and the post-Bultmannian theologies stemming from his paramount concern with "existential self-understanding"[51] are actually "experience" theologies also: for them the current situation of the theologian, not an objectively unchanging biblical message, is the determinative factor in theological activity. In the same general class fall many of the recent attempts to interrelate theology and "ordinary language philosophy": Ramsey's concern with theological theories in relation to "our empirical needs";[52] Hick's interpretation of theological dogmas as "the basic convictions which directly transcribe Christian experience";[53] etc.

The absolutizing of religious experience commits the "naturalistic fallacy" (sometimes unkindly called the "sociologist's fallacy"): it assumes that the "isness" of the believer's "existential encounter" constitutes an "oughtness." No answer whatever is given to the vital question: How is one to know that the divine and not the demonic is operating in the given experience? Paul Tillich argues with irrefutable cogency that "insight into the human situation destroys every theology which makes experience an independent source instead of a dependent medium of systematic theology." [54] Surely the psychoanalytic discoveries of the twentieth century should give us pause before we commit ourselves to the transparent purity of man's existential life!

> The analogy from human "encounters" suggests that at least some of the experiences which are held to be "encounter with God" really are subjectively produced; can the mere claim that the experiences are "self-verifying" rule out the uncomfortable suspicion that, when dissociated from any empirical personality, they all may be only illusion? [55]

What is clearly needed is an objective check on existential experience — in other words, a source of theological data outside of it, by which to judge it. [56]

Thus we arrive at the Bible[57]—the source by which Reason, Church, and Religious Experience can and must be evaluated theologically. We reach this point not simply by process of elimination, but more especially because only Scripture can be validated as a genuine source of theological truth. [58] It is the biblical message alone that provides the irreducible *Gegenstände* for theological theorizing—the "foot" which all theological theories must "fit." In the words of the Reformation axiom, "Quod non est biblicum, non est theologicum." The Christian theologian, like the scientist, faces a "given": he endeavors, not to create his data, but to provide conceptual Gestalts for rendering them intelligible and interrelating them properly. What Nature is to the scientific theorizer, the Bible is to the theologian. Franz Pieper astutely argued this parallel as follows:

> If we would escape the deceptions which are involved in the attempts to construct a human system of theology,

we must ever bear in mind that in theology we deal with given and unalterable facts, which human reasoning and the alleged needs of the "system" cannot change in the least. There is, as has been pointed out, an analogy here between natural history and theology. Natural history studies the observable data in the realm of nature; its business is to observe the facts. All human knowledge of natural phenomena extends only so far as man's observation and experience of the given facts extends. The true scientist does not determine the nature and characteristics of plants and animals according to a preconceived and hypothetical system. . . .

This matter has been aptly illustrated by contrasting railroad systems and mountain systems. A railroad system is conceived in the mind of the builders before it exists; its construction follows the blueprint drawn up by the engineers. The mountain system, on the other hand, does not follow our blueprints. We can only report our findings regarding its characteristics, the relation of the different mountain ranges to each other, etc., as we find them. The theologian is dealing with a fixed and unchangeable fact, the Word of God which Christ gave His Church through His Apostles and Prophets.[59]

To be sure, the affirmation that Holy Scripture is the sole source of data for theological theorizing poses questions requiring serious attention. Specifically: (1) Is the Bible an inerrantly reliable source of revelational data? (2) Is the Bible self-interpreting? (3) Does the Bible provide the norms as well as the subject matter for theological theory construction? We cannot hope to discuss any one of these questions fully here, but we can indicate the central considerations which demand affirmative answers in each case.

Elsewhere[60] I have attempted to show that any view of biblical inspiration that rejects the inerrancy of Scripture is not merely incorrect, but in fact *meaningless* from the standpoint both of philosophical and of theological analysis. Anti-inerrancy inspiration positions are based upon dualistic and existentialistic presuppositions that are incapable of being confirmed or disconfirmed (thus their analytically meaningless character), and they fly directly in the face of the scriptural epistemology itself, which firmly joins "spiritual" truth to historical, empirical facticity and regards *all* words spoken by inspiration of God as carrying their Author's guarantee of veracity. More-

over, if in some sense Scripture were not unqualifiedly
a reliable source of theological truth, what criteria could
possibly distinguish the wheat from the chaff? Not the
Scripture itself (by definition), and not anything outside
of it (for the "outside" factors would then become revelation, and we have already seen that extra-biblical
revelation-claims are incapable of validation)!

This latter point also applies to the question of the
self-interpreting nature of the Bible: Were the Scripture
not self-interpreting, then a "higher" revelation would
be needed to provide interpretative canons for it; but
such a Bible-to-the-second-power cannot be shown to exist.
And, indeed, there is no reason to feel that one should
exist. If God inspired the Scripture, then its self-interpreting perspicuity is established. The Reformers soundly
argued that "the clarity of Scripture is demanded by
its inspiration. God is able to speak clearly, for He is
the master of language and words."[61] True, "there
are many impenetrable mysteries in Scripture which are
unclear in that they cannot be grasped by human intellect,
but these mysteries have been recorded in Scripture in
obscure or ambiguous language."[62] Present-day specialists in biblical hermeneutics who have been trained
in general literary interpretation make every effort to
impress upon their students and readers that the Bible
must be approached objectively and allowed to interpret
itself. Thus Robert Traina writes in the Introduction to
his superlative manual, *Methodical Bible Study: A New
Approach to Hermeneutics:*

> Now the Scriptures are distinct from the interpreter and
> are not an integral part of him. If the truths of the Bible
> already resided in man, there would be no need for the
> Bible and this manual would be superfluous. But the fact
> is that *the Bible is an objective body of literature* which
> exists because man needs to know certain truths which
> he himself cannot know and which must come to him
> from without. Consequently, if he is to discover the truths
> which reside in this objective body of literature, he must
> utilize an approach which corresponds in nature with it,
> that is, an *objective* approach.[63]

Such an hermeneutic approach has been explicitly
adopted by the great systematic theologians, past[64] and
present,[65] and *must* be presupposed in theological theor-

izing if one is to avoid exegeting and systematizing one's own subjective opinions and desires instead of God's Word. The "circularity principle" of Bultmann and his former disciples[66] gives carte blanche to this latter error and invariably destroys the possibility of sound theological theorizing; as I have written elsewhere:

> When Bultmann argues that not only historical method but also existential "life-relation" must be presupposed in exegesis, he blurs the aim of objectivity which is essential to all proper literary and historical study. Following Dilthey as well as the general stream of philosophical existentialism, Bultmann attempts to "cut under the subject-object distinction"; he claims that "for historical understanding, the schema of subject and object has validity for natural science is invalid." But in fact the subject-object distinction is of crucial importance in history as well as in natural science, and only by aiming to discover the objective concern of the text (rather than blending it with the subjective concern of the exegete) can successful exegesis take place.[67]

But does the Bible *per se* yield the norms, or only the subject matter, for theological theorizing? Not only from existentially orientated Bultmannians and post-Bultmannian advocates of the "New Hermeneutic," but also from Paul Tillich, who has valiantly endeavored to stiffen theological existentialism by means of ontology, we receive the negative reply that Scripture cannot in itself supply absolute norms for theological construction. After noting the variety of norms employed through church history for imparting significance levels to biblical data, Tillich asserts: "The Bible as such has never been the norm of systematic theology. The norm has been a principle derived from the Bible in an encounter between Bible and church."[68] Now we readily grant that church history presents a number of different normative approaches to Holy Writ: the early Greek church's stress on the Logos as the light shining in the darkness of man's mortality,[69] the sacramental Christology of the Western church in the Middle Ages, the Reformation emphasis on God's gracious forgiveness of sin, Protestant Modernism's concern with social amelioration, Tillich's own concentration on Christ as the New Being, etc. But are we, à la Tillich, to commit the naturalistic fallacy and assume that because varied judgments on the norm of biblical theology *have* existed, they *should* have existed? or that the various historical judgments on the norm have been equally valid, simply because they have met the needs of the time? or that Scripture does not in fact provide its own absolute norms for unifying its content? Tillich's dialectic "encounter between Bible and church" as the source of norms inevitably degenerates to historical relativism, leaving his own norm without justification along with the others.

In point of fact, one can readily detect unsound theological norms (e.g., Modernism's "social gospel") by virtue of their inability to give biblical force to central scriptural teachings, and by their unwarranted elevation of secondary (or even unbiblical) emphases to primary position. In other words, Scripture *does* very definitely supply "weighting factors" for its own teachings. Moreover, the majority of norms displayed in the history of orthodox theology have not really been as divergent as Tillich's discussion implies: most often they have displayed complementary facets of the overarching biblical message that "God was in Christ, reconciling the world unto Himself." Scripture itself makes this Christocentric teaching primary and ranges its other teachings in objective relation to it; and a sinful church learns the fact not through its historical "encounters" (which are always tainted), but from the perspicuous text of Holy Writ. Only Scripture is capable of truly interpreting Scripture; and only Scripture is able to provide the norm-structure for its interpretation and for the construction of theological doctrine based upon its inerrantly inspired content.

Terminating, then, our discussion of the scientific level of theological theorizing, we must reaffirm the fundamental thesis for which proof has been marshalled *in extenso:* science and theology form and test their respective theories in the same way; the scientific theorizer attempts objectively to formulate conceptual Gestalts (hypotheses, theories, laws) capable of rendering Nature intelligible, and the theologian endeavors to provide conceptual Gestalts (doctrines, dogmas) [70] which will "fit the facts" and properly reflect the norms of Holy Scripture. A tabular summary will perhaps offer the best conclusion to the rather involved discussion preceding it, as well as the best background for what is to follow.

	SCIENCE	THEOLOGY
THE DATA (Epistemological certainty presupposed)	Nature	The Bible
CONCEPTUAL GESTALTS	Laws	Ecumenical Creeds (e.g., the Apostles' Creed) and historic Confessions (e.g., the Augsburg Confession)
(In order of decreasing certainty)[71]	Theories	Theological systems (e.g., Calvin's *Institutes*)
	Hypotheses	Theological proposals (e.g., Gustaf Aulen's *Christus Victor*)[72]

The Artistic and Sacral Levels in Theological Theorizing

A recent article describing the sorry Spiritualist phase at the end of Sir Arthur Conan Doyle's distinguished career concludes with this thought-provoking evaluation:

> He was ill suited by personal temperament and life experience to become a religious philosopher. His natural sympathies were located in the outer rather than the inner life of man, as seen in his power to describe actions in his literature and his failure to portray character. Thus he was continually drawn towards the appearance of an event, its overt significance, but denied the ability to perceive its inner meaning.[73]

Leaving aside the disputable point (to which no addict of Sherlock Holmes could possibly agree!) that Doyle was a poor delineator of character, one finds here an exceedingly important reminder that the theological realm requires something more of investigators than scientific objectivity alone: it demands "the ability to perceive inner meaning." What is involved in this "inner meaning," and what connection does it have with theological theorizing?

A powerful hint toward an answer is provided in Luther's description of his theological method, which he characteristically drew from Scripture itself:

Let me show you a right method for studying theology,
the one that I have used. If you adopt it, you will become
so learned that if it were necessary, you yourself would
be qualified to produce books just as good as those of the
Fathers and the church councils. Even as I dare to be so
bold in God as to pride myself, without arrogance or lying,
as not being greatly behind some of the Fathers in the
matter of making books; as to my life, I am far from
being their equal. This method is the one which the pious
king David teaches in the 119th Psalm and which, no
doubt, was practiced by all the Patriarchs and Prophets.
In the 119th Psalm you will find three rules which are
abundantly expounded throughout the entire Psalm. They
are called: *Oratio, Meditatio, Tentatio.*[74]

By *Meditatio,* Luther meant the reading, study, and
contemplation of the Bible (i.e., very much what we have
spoken of in our foregoing discussion of the objective aspect of theological methodology); by *Tentatio,* he
meant internal and external temptation—what we today
would doubtless call subjective, experiential involvement;
and by *Oratio* ("prayer"), the vertical contact with the
Holy One, without which all theologizing is ultimately
futile. Much the same threefold approach to theology is
suggested by the treatment of the concept of faith in classical Protestant orthodoxy: faith involves *Notitia* ("knowledge"—the objective, scientific element), *Assensus*
("assent"—the subjective element), and *Fiducia* ("trust/
confidence"—the vertical, regenerating relation with the
Living God).[75] Quenstedt grounds this analysis of faith
in John 14:10-12. He notes that "heretics can have the
first, the second the orthodox alone, the third the regenerate; and therefore the latter always includes the former, but this order cannot be reversed."[76] Theology,
like the faith to which it gives systematic expression,
has objective, subjective, and divine levels, no one of
which can be disregarded. Having discussed the scientific
base in theological theorizing, let us now focus attention
on the second, or artistic, level of theological activity.

The Theologian As Artist. John Ciardi, in his excellent
introduction to literary criticism, *How Does a Poem
Mean?,* quotes the following passage from Dickens'
Hard Times:

"Bitzer," said Thomas Gradgrind, "your definition of
a horse."

"Quadruped. Gramnivorous. Forty teeth, namely twenty-four grinders, four eye-teeth, and twelve incisive. Sheds coat in the spring; in marshy countries sheds hoofs too. Hoofs hard, but requiring to be shod with iron. Age known by marks in mouth." Thus (and much more) Bitzer.

"Now girl number twenty," said Mr. Gradgrind, "you know what a horse is."

Ciardi quite rightly points out that, after having heard this learned description, "girl number twenty" knew "what a horse is" only in a very special and limited way: she knew horses in a formal, objective, scientific manner, but not at all in a personal, experiential way—not in the way in which a poet or an artist endeavors to convey knowledge. In the same vein, Peter Winch argues for the legitimate, and indeed necessary, inclusion of subjective involvement in the work of the social scientist; over against psychological behaviorism he asks the rhetorical question: "Would it be intelligent to try to explain how Romeo's love for Juliet enters into his behaviour in the same terms as we might want to apply to the rat whose sexual excitement makes him run across an electrically charged grid to reach his mate?" [77] Theorizing in the humanities or social sciences requires more than scientific objectivity; it also demands "the language of experience" [78]—"grasping the *point* or *meaning* of what is being done or said." [79]

Is this also true of theology? We have justified the scientific character of theological theorizing by pointing to the empirical, objective nature of God's historical revelation in Holy Scripture; now we must make the equally important point that, by virtue of its historical character, the biblical revelation lies also in the realm of the social sciences and humanities. Because God revealed Himself in history, and the Bible—the source of all true theological Gestalts—is a historical document, theological theories must partake of the dual science-art character of historical methodology. The historian cannot stop with an external, objective examination of facts and records; as Benedetto Croce and R. G. Collingwood have so well shown, he must relive the past in imagination—re-enact it by entering into its very heart. [80] As Jakob Burckhardt's *Civilization of the Renaissance in Italy* and Johan

Huizinga's *Waning of the Middle Ages* magnificently de-
lineate their respective historical epochs by cutting to
the essence of them, so theological constructions must
meet Ernst Cassirer's standard for every "science of culture": they must teach us "to interpret symbols in order
to decipher their latent meaning, to make visible again
the life from which they originally came into being." [81]

We cannot enter here into the problem of the logical
status of subjective artistic assertions;[82] suffice it to
say, as has been effectively shown by Ian Ramsey and
others, that such judgments follow from the independent,
irreducible nature of the "I," which is in fact presupposed
in all statements about the world—including scientific
statements.[83] What we do wish to emphasize is the
necessity of incorporating the artistic element into all theological theories, in order to avoid a depersonalization
of theology and the concomitant freezing of biblical doctrine. Concretely, all valid theological theories must be
set within the "invisible quotation marks" of belief,[84]
must represent the personal, inner involvement of the
theologian with Holy Scripture, and must convey a
genuine reliving and re-enactment of historical revelation.

The presence or absence of such artistic criteria as
these is to be determined not by formulae, but by individual sensitivity on the part of theologian and Christian
believer. Yet the artistic factor is no less real because
of that. Just as sensitive social scientist can recognize
the greatness of William James' *Varieties of Religious
Experience* as compared with pedestrian monographs on
the same subject, and the sensitive literary critic has no
doubt as to Milton's stature among epic poets, so the Christian who is in tune with Scripture can readily distinguish
between theological theorizing that cuts to the heart of
biblical revelation and theological theories that (scientifically correct as they may be) operate on a superficial
level. Luther's insistence in presenting the doctrine of the
Fall of man that "you should read the story of the Fall
as if it happened yesterday, and to you" has this requisite
inner quality,[85] as does such a creedal statement as
the following, extracted from Johann Valentin Andreae's
Christianopolis of 1619:

Credimus toto corde in Iesum Christum,[86] Dei & Mariae filium, coaequalem patri, consimilem nobis, Redemptorem, duabus naturis personaliter unitum & utrisque communicantem, Prophetam, Regem, & Sacerdotem nostrum, cujus lex gratia, cujus sceptrum pacis, cujus Crucis est sacr[i]ficium.	We believe with our whole heart in Jesus Christ, the Son of God and Mary, coequal with the Father yet like us, our Redeemer, united as to personality in two natures and communicating in both, our Prophet, King, and Priest, whose law is grace, whose scepter is that of peace, whose sacrifice, that of the cross.[87]

The Theologian and the Holy. In common with science, theology formulates its theories with a view to the objective fitting of facts (in this case, the facts of Scripture); in common with the arts, theology seeks by its theoretical formulations to enter personally into the heart of reality (God's revelation in the Bible). But theology is more than science or art, for it possesses a dimension unique to itself: the realm of the Holy. By this expression we do not refer merely to the "Numinous" quality of religion as analyzed by Rudolf Otto in his epochal work, *The Idea of the Holy;* we refer specifically to the unfathomable nature of the God of Scripture, whose ways are not our ways and whose thoughts are not our thoughts (Isa. 55:8), and who demands of the theologian as of Moses, "Draw not nigh hither: put off thy shoes from off thy feet, for the place whereon thou standest is holy ground" (Ex. 3:5; cf. Acts 7:33). Lack of recognition of the distance between sinful man and sinless God or blindness to the absolute necessity of relying upon His Holy Spirit in theologizing will vitiate efforts in this realm, even though the scientific and artist requirements are fully met. Without *Fiducia*, *Notitia* and *Assensus* are like sounding brass and tinkling cymbal. O. K. Bouwsma makes this point well in his unpublished allegory, "Adventure in Verification," where his hero encounters difficulties in determining how Zeus makes Olympus quake:

At a meeting of the P.L.B., the Pan-Hellenic Learning Bust, an annual affair at which the feasters eat each other's work, he confided to fellow-ravishers that at the time he was considering his confrontation with the Makers of Fact or the News, on Mt. Olympus, the difficulty that bothered him most was not the matter of protocol but that of language. It wasn't that, as he anticipated, they, the interviewed divinities, would not understand him—they are adept in understanding four-hundred and twenty-six languages—but that he would not understand them. . . .

He went down the mountain disappointed. . . . When he got home he wrote an account of his adventure, in order that the future of verification might not lose the benefit of his effort. His own adventure he described as one of weak verification due to sand, quicksand, too quick for the hour-glass. It never occurred to him that, not quick sand, but vanity was the condition which led to his having his eyes fixed on his own good name in the bark of the tree when they should have been fixed on Zeus who made Great Olympus shake, not by waving his ambrosial locks, nor by stamping his foot, nor by a crow-bar, nor by a cough but in his own sweet way.[88]

How many theological theorizers have failed in their herculean labors as a result of vanity—as a result of fixing their eyes on themselves "when they should have been fixed on Zeus who made Great Olympus shake"!

In what way is the dimension of the "Sacred" conveyed in theological theory construction? Essentially, by the admission that (in Bouwsma's phrase) we do not fully understand Zeus' language. That is to say, the theological theorist must always indicate in the statement of his doctrines the limited character of them—the fact that ultimately God works "in his own sweet way" (in the double sense of the phrase!). Michael Foster, by his stress on the irreducible mystery in all sound theological judgments,[89] and Willem Zuurdeeg, with his emphasis on the "convictional" nature of theological assertions,[90] endeavor (albeit by overemphasizing a good thing) to drive this point home. The best analysis of the problem, however, comes from Ian Ramsey, who observes the linguistically "odd" character of genuine theological affirmations. These consist of models taken from experience, so qualified to indicate their sacral (logically "odd") character. Such "qualified models" can be found throughout the range of Christian doctrine, e.g., in the phrases "first cause," "infinite wisdom," "eternal purpose" (where the qualifiying adjective in each case points the empirically grounded noun in the direction of the sacral, so as to reduce anthropomorphism and increase awareness of God's "otherness"). Another example is "creation *ex nihilo*" where "*ex nihilo*" is the sacral qualifier:

> In all the "creation" stories we have told, there has
> always been *something* from which the "creation" was
> effected; there have always been causal predecessors.
> So that "creation" *ex nihilo* is on the face of it a scandal:
> and the point of the scandal is to insist that when the phrase
> has been given its appropriate empirical anchorage, any
> label, suited to that situation, must have a logical be-
> haviour which, from the standpoint of down-to-earth "crea-
> tion" language, is odd. When creation *ex nihilo* as a quali-
> fied model evokes a characteristically religious situation—
> a sense of creaturely dependence—it further claims for
> the word "God," which is then posited in relation to such
> a situation, that it caps all causal stories and presides over
> and "completes" all the language of all created things.
> It places "God" as a "key" word for the universe of
> "creatures." [91]

Ramsey's assertion here that the "odd" qualifier, conveying the sacral dimension, can be "any label, suited
to that situation," reminds us again of the single source
for all sound theological theorizing: Holy Scripture. Only
the Bible can serve as an adequate guide for determining
what sacral qualifiers are "suitable" to given doctrinal
formulations.[92] On this note the present section of the
essay can properly be concluded: Sacred Scripture offers
the sole criterion for testing the scientific, the artistic,
and the sacral health of theological theories. Does a given
theory represent objective truth? Does it incorporate the
proper kind of subjective involvement? Does it adequately preserve the sacred dimension? To all three of
these questions *sola Scriptura* holds the answers.

The Structure of Theological Theories

Theory formation and testing in theology have now
been analyzed from the points-of-view of science, art, and
the holy. One final question remains—and it is, if possible,
the most consequential of all: How do the three methodological aspects of theology relate to each other? Analysis
has now been completed; what about synthesis? So important is the synthetic problem that to neglect it or to
embrace a false solution to it is to insure failure in theological theorizing, no matter how honorable one's motives
and impeccable one's procedures in other respects.

Let us clear the air by making explicit a fundamental

principle to which we have already arrived by implication.
We have seen, from clear scriptural evidence, that each
of the three methodological aspects of theology is absolutely essential. Neither the scientific, nor the artistic,
nor the sacral element can be removed from theological
theorizing without destroying the possibility of results in
harmony with God's Word. Thus we can legitimately
expect to find deleterious theological climates wherever,
in church history or in the present, reductionism is permitted with reference to one or more of the three methodological elements. The following table will indicate the unfortunate end products of the six possible methodological
reductionisms:

REDUCTION OF	INTO	PRODUCES
1. Artistic & Sacral	Scientific	Dead Orthodoxy
2. Scientific & Sacral	Artistic	Pietism
3. Scientific & Artistic	Sacral	Mysticism
4. Sacral	Scientific & Artistic	Anthropocentrism
5. Artistic	Scientific & Sacral	"Theology of Glory" [93]
6. Scientific	Artistic & Sacral	Existentialism

In terms of this scheme, many of the unfortunate examples of contemporary theological theorizing already referred to in this paper (G. F. Woods' subjectivism,
Hordern's Olympic Game thinking, Bultmannian and
"post-Bultmannian" obliteration of the subject-object distinction, etc.) become more understandable: our age is
particularly prone to reductionism; (6), which eliminates
the scientific element from theology, and produces wooly-
minded, unverifiable existentialisms that readily pass into
the realm of analytic meaninglessness. But let us not lose
perspective; this methodological sin, heinous as it is, is
only one of several committed through Christian history,
and we must link together the scientific, the artistic, and
the sacral elements in theology so that *none* of the six
methodological blunders will be permitted.

How shall the elements be related? Certainly not in
dialectical fashion,[94] for (as we pointed out earlier) a
polar dialectic is an open invitation to reductionism, since,
as pressure is brought to bear on theology from the sinful

cultural situation, the theologian can readily and almost imperceptibly slide from one pole to another, avoiding the serious demands of each. (It is this dialectic approach, so hospitable to Neo-Orthodox and existentialist viewpoints, that has permitted contemporary theology, under pressure from "scientific" critics of the Bible, to avoid the basic issue of the historical and scientific authority of Holy Writ.) And not by an attempt to find a pivot in man's faculties (e.g., Lonergan's striking "insight" motif [95]) by which the several methodological levels can be tied together, for such a pivot will inevitably shift the focus of theology from the God of Scripture to sinful man. Rather, we must structure the scientific, the artistic, and the sacral factors in theology so that they have a theocentric, Cross-centered focus, and so that the objective provides an epistemological check on the artistic, and the artistic serves as an entrée to the sacral. Consider, then, this structural model of theological explanation:

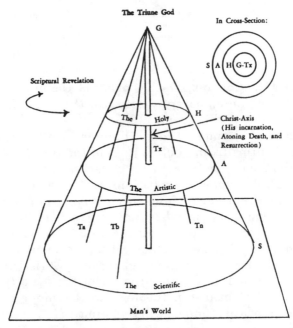

The cone represents God's revelation to man as expressed in Holy Scripture. This revelation, as we have seen, consists of irreducible, objective facts (the scientific level), to which subjective commitment must be made (the artistic level), and over which the divine majesty hovers in grace and judgment (the sacral level). The truths of which God's revelation is composed are legion (T_a, T_b, ... T_n), but they all center upon the great truth which serves as the axis and focal point of the revelation as a whole: the Word become flesh, who died for the sins of the world and rose again for its justification T_x). The task of systematic theology is to take the truths of revelation as discovered by the exegete, work out their proper relation to the focal center and to each other (in the model, these relations are represented by the distances between T_a, T_b, and T_x), and construct doctrinal formulations that "fit" the revelational truths in their mutual relations. In terms of the model, theological theories can be conceived of as cellophane tubes constructed to fit with maximum transparency the truths of revelation; the theologian will endeavor continually to "tighten" them so that they will most accurately capture the essence of biblical truth.

The theological theorist builds his cellophane tubes from bottom to top: he starts in the realm of objective facticity, employing the full range of scientific skill to set forth revelational truth; and he makes every effort not to vitiate his results by reading his own subjective interests into them.[96]

But as he climbs, he inevitably (because of the personal center of biblical truth) reaches a point where he must involve himself subjectively in his material in order to get at the heart of it; here he passes into what we have called the artistic level, where the semi-transcendent, subjective "I" cannot be ignored. Still he climbs, and eventually—if he is a theologian worthy of the name—he finds that his theory construction has brought him into the realm of the Sacred, where both the impersonal "it" of science and the subjective "I" of the humanities stand on holy ground, in the presence of the living God.

A concrete illustration may be of value here. The doctrine of the Trinity is a theological theory, since the term is not given as a revelational fact. In formulating this theory, the theologian commences by objectively analyzing the biblical data concerning the relations among God the Father, Jesus Christ, and the Holy Spirit—but especially in reference to the character of Jesus Christ, the focal center of theology.[97] He finds that Jesus fully identifies Himself with the Father through His words (e.g., forgiving sin), acts (e.g., miracles), and specific claims ("I and the Father are one"; "he who has seen Me has seen the Father"; etc.), and that He attests His claim to Deity through His resurrection.[98] The theologian discovers, moreover, that this same Jesus asserts that the Holy Spirit is "another of the same kind" (ἄλλον παράκλητον) as Himself,[99] and that in His final charge to His disciples He places Father, Son, and Holy Spirit on precisely the same level.[100] At the same time, the personal identities of Father, Son and Holy Spirit are manifestly evident in Holy Writ, though God is "One" to all the biblical writers. Conclusion: the God of the Bible is (in the words of the Athanasian Creed) "one God in Trinity and Trinity in Unity." The paradoxical character of this theological theory should not disturb us, for it is a conceptual Gestalt demanded by the data; the more "rational" (better: rationalistic) theories of unitarianism and modalism pervert the biblical facts in the interests of a superimposed logical consistency. The orthodox theologian properly and humbly subordinates his theory to the data, as the physical scientist does in formulating the paradoxical "wave-particle" theory to account for the ostensibly contradictory properties of subatomic phenomena:

> Quantum physicists agree that subatomic entities are a mixture of wave properties (W), particle properties (P), and quantum properties (h). High-speed electrons, when shot through a nickel crystal or a metallic film (as fast cathode-rays or even B-rays), diffract like X-rays. In principle, the B-ray is just like the sunlight used in a double-slit or bi-prism experiment. Diffraction is a criterion of wave-like behaviour in substances; all classical wave theory rests on this. Besides this behaviour, however, electrons have long been thought of as electrically charged particles. A transverse magnetic field will deflect an electron beam and its diffraction pattern. Only particles behave in this manner; all classical electromagnetic theory depends upon this. To explain all the evidence electrons must be both particulate and undulatory. An electron is a PWh.[101]

To be sure, the conception of the Trinity in Scripture

is not fully or even principally comprehended by an abstract formula. Though on the scientific level "Trinity" is methodologically analogous to "PWh," the comparison ceases when we rise higher. "PWh" is impersonal, but the Trinity is intensely personal and touches the life of the theologian at its very center. Thus in explaining the Trinitarian articles of the Apostles' Creed, Luther reiterates the subjective, "for me" character of the doctrine: "I believe that God has made me . . . . I believe that Jesus Christ, true God, begotten of the Father from eternity, and also true man, born of the Virgin Mary, is my Lord . . . . I believe that . . . the Holy Ghost has called me by the Gospel, enlightened me with His gifts, sanctified and kept me in the true faith." [102] Moreover, as the theologian contemplates the Trinitarian character of Holy Scripture, he is caught up in wonder and amazement, finding himself transported to the very gates of glory; with the Athanasian Creed, therefore, he must express by sacral qualifiers the "otherness" of superlative truth: "The Father uncreate, the Son uncreate: and the Holy Ghost uncreate. The Father incomprehensible, the Son incomprehensible: and the Holy Ghost incomprehensible. The Father eternal, the Son eternal: and the Holy Ghost eternal." [103]

Lost in wonder, then, does theological theorizing find its fulfilment. Commencing in the hard-headed realm of science, moving upward into the dynamic sphere of artistic involvement, it issues forth into a land where words can do little more than guard the burning bush from profanation. Here one can perhaps glimpse theology as its Divine Subject sees it: not as man's feeble attempts to grasp eternal verities, but as a cone of illumination coming down from the Father of lights (Jas. 1:17)—a cone whose sacral level brightens the artistic, and the artistic, the scientific level below it. The truly great theologian, like Aquinas, will conclude his labors with the cry: "I can do no more; such things have been revealed to me that everything I have written seems to me rubbish." [104] In the final analysis, the theologian must say of his theologizing what the great Wittgenstein said of his philosophizing:

My propositions serve as elucidations in the following

way: anyone who understands me eventually recognizes them as senseless, when he has used them—as steps—to climb up beyond them. (He must, so to speak, throw away the ladder after he has climbed up it.)

He must transcend these propositions, and then he will see the world aright.[105]

Notes

[1] It will be observed that in this essay the term "theologian" is being used in the strict sense of "systematic theologian" or "dogmatician," not in the more general and perfectly legitimate sense of "professor on the theological faculty" (a category including exegetes ["biblical theologians"], church historians, homileticians, etc., etc.).

[2] Fascinating studies of this nature are suggested by Etienne Gilson's *History of Christian Philosophy in the Middle Ages* (New York: Random House, 1955). Much needs to be done in the historical study of classical Protestant theological methodologies—e.g., the "analytic" and "synthetic" methods employed by dogmaticians of the 16th and 17th centuries.

[3] A work along the lines of Rosamond E. M. Harding's *An Anatomy of Inspiration and an Essay on the Creative Mood* (3d ed.; Cambridge, England: W. Heffer, 1948) would be an exceedingly valuable addition to the literature of theology.

[4] Walter Kaufmann, *Critique of Religion and Philosophy* (Garden City, New York: Doubleday Anchor Books, 1961), p. 221 (para. 57).

[5] G. F. Woods, *Theological Explanation: A Study of the Meaning and Means of Explaining in Science, History, and Theology, Based upon the Stanton Lectures Delivered in the University of Cambridge, 1953-1956* (Digswell Place, Welwyn: James Nisbet, 1958), p. 151.

[6] Cf. John Macquarrie, *Twentieth-Century Religious Thought: the Frontiers of Philosophy and Theology, 1900-1960* (London: SCM Press, 1963), pp. 274-75. Unhappily, Macquarrie does not personally take Garnett's critique to heart—or he would modify his own existentially-orientated theology!

[7] William Hordern, *Speaking of God: the Nature and Purpose of Theological Language* (New York: Macmillan, 1964), pp. 86-89.

[8] The Christian "Mt. Olympus," as Wittgenstein's student O. K. Bouwsma has well shown in his unpublished essay, "Adventure in Verification," is firmly embedded in the earth, and is indeed subjected to verifiability tests.

[9] Cf. C. B. Daly, "New Light on Wittgenstein," *Philosophical Studies* [St. Patrick's College, Maynooth, Ireland], X (1960), 46-49.

[10] Karl R. Popper, *The Logic of Scientific Discovery* (2d ed.; Lon-

don: Hutchinson, 1959), p. 59. For Wittgenstein's presentation of the
"net" analogy, see his *Tractatus Logico-Philosophicus*, 6.341-6.35. My
former professor Max Black, in his exceedingly valuable work, *A Companion to Wittgenstein's 'Tractatus'* (Ithaca, New York: Cornell University Press, 1964), pp. 347-61, finds difficulties in the network analogy, but concludes: "According to the view I have been presenting the
principles of mechanics are neither empirical generalizations, nor *a
priori* truths. Taken together, they constitute an abstract scheme of explanation, within whose framework specific laws of *predetermined* form
can be formulated and tested. If I am correct, Wittgenstein's central
idea in his discussion of the philosophy of science has thus been vindicated." On Popper's approach to scientific theorizing, see Thomas H.
Leith's unpublished Boston University Ph.D. dissertation, "Popper's
Views of Theory Formation Compared with the Development of Post-
Relativistic Cosmological Models," and Leith's article, "Some Presuppositions in the Philosophy of Science," *Journal of the American Scientific Affiliation*, XVII (March, 1965), 8-15.

[11] Leonard K. Nash, *The Nature of the Natural Sciences* (Boston:
Little, Brown, 1963), p. 61. Cf. Commissioner Tarquin's philosophy of
scientific crime detection: "The trick is to surround it [the total crime
situation] and then pull it all together" (Sebastien Japrisot, *Compartiment Tueurs* [Paris: Editions Denoël, 1962], chap. i).

[12] The expression is Frederick Ferré's; see his article, "Mapping
the Logic of Models in Science and Theology," *The Christian Scholar*,
XLVI (Spring, 1963), 12-15. I am not happy with certain interpretations
in this article (e.g., the author's distinction between theories and models;
his belief that scientific theories, unlike theological theories, can exist
without models), but in general the article deserves the highest commendation for its incisive wrestling with an exceedingly important
methodological issue.

[13] Stephen Toulmin, *The Philosophy of Science* (London: Hutchinson University Library, 1953), p. 28 (Toulmin's italics). Cf. also Toulmin's more recent work, *Foresight and Understanding: An Enquiry into
the Aims of Science* (Bloomington: Indiana University Press, 1961),
passim; and Max Black's *Models and Metaphors: Studies in Language
and Philosophy* (Ithaca, New York: Cornell University Press, 1962),
passim.

[14] Roger Louis, "A Team of Experimenters: The Men Who Discovered DNA," *Réalités*, No. 154 (September, 1963), 45-46.

[15] The process of discovery in the case of DNA can be traced back
directly to Max Perutz's labors as early as 1936, and the Watson-Crick
theory took several years to be collaterally confirmed by Maurice Wilkins, Perutz, and John Kendrew. All five were joint recipients of Nobel
prizes (chemistry and medicine) in 1962. For a recent technical overview of the state of research in the DNA area, see Duane T. Gish,
"DNA, RNA and Protein Biosynthesis and Implications for Evolutionary
Theory," *Journal of the American Scientific Affiliation*, XVII (March,
1965), 2-7.

[16] Cf. the basic distinction made by Wittgenstein between "objects"
or "things" ("Der Gegenstand ist einfach"—*Tractatus Logico-Philoso-*

phicus, 2.02) and "facts" ("Was der Fall ist, die Tatsache, ist das Bestehen von Sachverhalten. Der Sachverhalt ist eine Verbindung von Gegenständen [Sachen, Dingen]" — 2.0, 2.01). Of course, theories can themselves become the substantive grist for the mill of higher level theory, but this in no way lessens the need to distinguish sharply between that which is to be explained (*explicandum*) and that which does the explaining (*explicans*).

[17] Toulmin, *The Philosophy of Science,* p. 43.

[18] R. B. Braithwaite, *Scientific Explanation: A Study of the Function of Theory, Probability and Law in Science* (Cambridge: Cambridge University Press, 1955), p. 368. Braithwaite, it should be noted, is a much more helpful guide in the realm of scientific explanation than he is in the field of theological analysis; in his book, *An Empiricist View of the Nature of Religious Belief* (Cambridge: Cambridge University Press, 1955), he argues the position, grossly inapplicable to the Christian faith, that religious affirmations are meaningful only ethically, not cognitively.

[19] Georg Henrik von Wright, *The Logical Problem of Induction* (2d ed.; Oxford: Blackwell, 1957), p. 174.

[20] Joseph Agassi, *Towards an Historiography of Science* ("History and Theory Beihefte," 2; The Hague: Mouton, 1963).

[21] Kepler's discovery of Mars' orbit is a particularly good illustration. On the influence of Kepler's Reformation theology upon his scientific labors, see my essay, "Cross, Constellation, and Crucible: Lutheran Astrology and Alchemy in the Age of the Reformation," *Transactions of the Royal Society of Canada,* 4th ser., I (1963), 251-70 (also published in the British periodical *Ambix, the Journal of the Society for the Study of Alchemy and Early Chemistry,* XI [June, 1963]; 65-86; in French in *Revue d'Histoire et de Philosophie Religieuses,* No. 4 [1966] 323-45; and in my *In Defense of Martin Luther* [Milwaukee: Northwestern, 1970]). Cf. W. Pauli, "The Influence of Archetypal Ideas on the Scientific Theories of Kepler," in C. G. Jung and W. Pauli's *The Interpretation of Nature and the Psyche,* trans. Hull and Silz ("Bollingen Series," 51; New York: Pantheon Books, 1955), pp. 147 ff.

[22] See Arthur Pap's chapter on "Deductive & Inductive Inference" in his posthumously published work, *An Introduction to the Philosophy of Science,* with an Epilogue by Brand Blanshard (Glencoe, Ill.: Free Press, 1962), pp. 139-50.

[23] Max Black, "The Definition of Scientific Method," in his *Problems of Analysis: Philosophical Essays* (London: Routledge & Kegan Paul, 1954,) p. 23.

[24] Nash, *op. cit.,* p. 324.

[25] Aristotle, *Prior Analytics,* ii. 25; cf. *Posterior Analytics,* ii. 19.

[26] C. S. Peirce, *Collected Papers,* Harvard ed., V, para. 146, 171. It should go without saying that acceptance of the Peirce-Aristotle retroduction concept in no way commits one to Peirce's pragmatic philosophy; I myself have argued strongly against pragmatic epistemologies in my book, *The Shape of the Past: An Introduction to Philosophical Historiography* ("History in Christian Perspective," I; Ann Arbor, Michigan: Edwards Brothers, 1963), pp. 320-29.

[27] N. R. Hanson, *Patterns of Discovery: An Inquiry into the Con-*

ceptual Foundations of Science (Cambridge: Cambridge University Press, 1958), pp. 87-90; Hanson, following Peirce, illustrates retroductive inference by the classic case of Kepler's theorizing to an elliptical orbit for Mars. With the "bird-antelope," cf. Wittgenstein's detailed philosophical analysis of the psychologist Jastrow's ambiguous "duck-rabbit" (*Philosophical Investigations,* ed. Anscombe and Rhees [New York: Macmillan, 1953], II. xi. 194 ff).

[28] Hanson, *op. cit.,* pp. 89-90. Readers of the present essay who wish to delve further into the nature of scientific theorizing are encouraged to consult J. O. Wisdom's bibliographical article, "The Methodology of Natural Science: Publications in English," *La Philosophie au milieu du vingtième siècle,* ed. Raymond Klibansky (4 vols.; 2d ed.; Firenze: La Nuova Italia Editrice, 1961-1962), I, 164-83.

[29] It is John A. Hutchison's great mistake that he stops here in analyzing the scientific aspect of Christian theology, thereby leaving his reader with the impression that the Christian religion is no more capable of objective validation than are any of the other competing world faiths (*Language and Faith; Studies in Sign Symbol, and Meaning* [Philadelphia: Westminster Press, 1963], especially pp. 244-47, 293).

[30] I made this point *in extenso* in the apologetic lectures I delivered at the University of British Columbia on January 29 and 30, 1963; these have been published in a slightly abridged version as a series of four articles under the general title "History and Christianity," in *His,* December, 1964—March, 1965; the lectures are now available in original form in my *Where Is History Going?* (Grand Rapids, Mich.: Zondervan, 1969), chaps. ii-iii.

[31] See, for example, the accounts of Gideon and the fleece (Judges 6), Elijah on Mount Carmel (I Kings 18), and the primary-source testimonies to empirical contact with the risen Christ (Lk. 24:36-43; Jn. 20:25-28; cf. I Jn. 1:1-4).

[32] To King Agrippa Paul thus defended the empirical facticity of Christ's fulfilment of prophecy and resurrection: "I am speaking the sober truth. For the king knows about these things, and to him I speak freely; for I am persuaded that none of these things has escaped his notice, for this was not done in a corner" (Acts 26:25-26). Peter's Pentecost sermon contains the significant lines: "Men of Israel, hear these words: Jesus of Nazareth, a man attested to you by God with mighty works and wonders and signs which God did through him in your midst, as you yourselves know..." (Acts 2:22; cf. F. F. Bruce, *The New Testament Documents: Are They Reliable?* [5th ed.; London: Inter-Varsity Fellowship, 1960], pp. 45-46).

[33] It might seem that such a general statement would not apply to Islam; however, see my article, "The Apologetic Approach of Muhammed Ali and Its Implications for Christian Apologetics," *Muslim World,* LI (April, 1961), 111-22 (see author's "Corrigendum" in the July, 1961 *Muslim World*). No world religion other than Christianity stakes its life on the objective historical facticity of its claims; only the Christian faith dares to make such an assertion as Paul's: "If Christ has not been raised, then our preaching is in vain and your faith is in vain" (I Cor. 15:14).

[34] At the outset of his *Kirchliche Dogmatik,* Barth argues: "If

theology allows itself to be called or calls itself a science, it cannot at the same time take over the obligation to submit to measurement by the canons valid for other sciences" (I/1, chap. i. sec. 1). This unwarranted opposition between theology and science directly relates to Barth's scripturally illegitimate distinction between "salvation history" *(Heilsgeschichte)* and ordinary history *(Historie)*, to his unqualified rejection of natural revelation, and to the church-directed, anti-apologetic thrust of his entire theology. I have maintained elsewhere that Barth's fundamental difficulties here stem from his over-reaction to Protestant modernism and to his fear of subjecting the Christian faith to the secular examination for which John 1:14 constitutes a specific mandate ("Karl Barth and Contemporary Theology of History," *Bulletin of the Evangelical Theological Society,* VI [May, 1963], 39-49-; reprinted in *Where Is History Going?* [*op. cit.* in n. 30], chap. v). Gordon H. Clark, in his excellent work, *Karl Barth's Theological Method* (Philadelphia: Presbyterian and Reformed Publishing Co., 1963), chap. iii, points up Barth's irrationalistic tendencies, and correctly notes that in citing and arguing against Heinrich Scholz's six scientific norms *(K.D., loc. cit.),* Barth is in actuality opposing the straw man of nineteenth-century Scientism (Scientific Positivism), not genuine scientific method. Unfortunately, Barth has never cared for science (Henri Bouillard, in his *Genèse et Evolution,* reports that even as a boy Barth disliked physics and mathematics); and his *Church Dogmatics* suffers for it on almost every page.

[35] Ian T. Ramsey, *Models and Mystery* (London: Oxford University Press 1964), p. 17

[36] Ramsey *(ibid.)* perpetuates a common fallacy when he asserts that theological models differ from scientific models in that the letter must generate experimentally verifiable deductions.

[37] Jean Racette, "La Méthode en théologie: Le cours du P. Lonergan au 'Theology Institute' de Toronto" (*Sciences Ecclésiastiques,* XV (Mai-Septembre 1963), 293.

[38] Paul Tillich, *Systematic Theology* (2 vols.; Chicago: University of Chicago Press, 1951), I, 40.

[39] Gerhard Ebeling, *Theologie und Verkündigung; Ein Gespräch mit Rudolf Bultmann* ("Hermeneutische Untersuchungen zur Theologie," 1; Tübingen: J. C. B. Mohr, 1962), pp. 14-15. Cf. James M. Robinson and John B. Cobb, Jr. (eds.), *The New Hermeneutic* ("New Frontiers in Theology," 2; New York: Harper, 1964), *passim.*

[40] Heinrich Ott, "Was ist systematische Theologie?," *Zeitschrift für Theologie und Kirche,* Beiheft 2 (1961), pp. 19-46, sec. iii. Ott simultaneously regards "the gospel of Christ" as the subject matter of theology, and here also the dialectic operates: "The Christ event encounters us through the gospel of Christ, but the gospel is encountered through the Gospels and witnesses that are not yet and never will be the gospel itself. What is actually spoken is only the gospel *according to . . . .* the gospel according to Matthew, according to Mark, according to Luke, according to John, but also according to Paul, and why not also, dependent on those and secondarily, the gospel according to Martin Luther, Calvin, Rudolf Bultmann, or Karl Barth?"

[41] *Ibid.*, sec. v.

[42] *Ibid.*, sec. iii. Cf. James M. Robinson and John B. Cobb, Jr. (eds.), *The Later Heidegger and Theology* ("New Frontiers in Theology," 1; New York: Harper, 1963), *passim.*

[43] A point brought out with particular force in J. K. Van Baalen's fine work, *The Chaos of the Cults* (Grand Rapids, Mich.: Eerdmans, 1955), which has gone through a number of editions.

[44] On this trend, see especially George H. Tavard, who argues that "the authority of the Church's tradition and that of Scripture are not two, but one" (*Holy Writ or Holy Church* [New York: Harper, 1959], p. 244).

[45] Cf. W. N. Clarke's critique of philosopher Paul Weiss' *Modes of Being,* which conceives the universe as having four ultimate dimensions of being: the Weissian system "leaves unto ched the . . . fundamental and, for a metaphysician, unavoidable problem of the ultimate origin or source of existence and the ultimate principle of unity of this whole with its four irreducible modes" *(Yale Review,* September, 1958). Cf. my review of Weiss' *History: Written and Lived* in *Christianity Today,* VII (July 19, 1963), 43-44; reprinted in *Where Is History Going?* [op. cit.* in n. 30], appendix E.

[46] See, for the most influential American example of this approach, Thomas Paine's *Age of Reason,* especially Pt. 2.

[47] Whitehead and Russell, in their great *Principia Mathematica,* showed that this is the case both for formal logic and for mathematics—and that the latter is a special case of the former.

[48] Joseph Lewis' *The Tyranny of God* (New York: The Freethought Press Association, 1921) is a popular example of an atheism built on the natural evils in the world; here the "Nature" which pointed Paine unmistakably (he thought) to a beneficent Creator points Lewis to a universe having no God at all.

[49] See my essay, "The Petrine Theory Evaluated by Philology and Logic," in my *Shape of the Past (op. cit.* in n. 26), pp. 351-57.

[50] I have demonstrated this in detail in my essay, "Constructive Religious Empiricism: An Analysis and Criticism," *ibid.,* pp. 257-311.

[51] See especially Bultmann's essay, "The Task and the History of New Testament Theology," included as an Epilogue to his *Theology of the New Testament,* trans. Kendrick Grobel (2 vols.; London: SCM Press, 1955), II, 241.

[52] See above, the quotation corresponding to n. 35. I suspect that Ramsey's overstress on religious experience, combined with relatively little emphasis on biblical authority, is an underlying factor in his defense of F. D. Maurice's uncertainty about the doctrine of eternal punishment (see Ramsey's *On Being Sure in Religion* [London: University of London-Athlone Press, 1963], especially chap. i).

[53] John Hick, *Faith and Knowledge* (Ithaca, New York: Cornell University Press, 1957), p. 198. For Hick, the "catalyst of faith"—the means of theological structuring the "apperceiving mass" of experience—is "the person of Jesus Christ" (p. 196). But this Christ is not seen in the context of a fully reliable biblical revelation. Thus, in his article "Theology and Verification," Hick can make the amazing statement:

"I will only express my personal opinion that the logic of the New Testament as a whole, though admittedly not always its explicit content, leads to a belief in ultimate universal salvation" (*Theology Today*, XVII [April, 1960]. 31). In regard to the existence of God, Hick holds the experiential view that "the important question is not whether the existence of God can be demonstrated but whether . . . faith-awareness of God is a mode of cognition which can properly be trusted and in terms of which it is rational to live" (*The Existence of God*, ed. John Hick [New York: Macmillan, 1964], p. 19).

54 See his full-scale treatment of this issue, *op cit.*, pp. 40-46).

55 Frederick Ferré, *Language, Logic and God* (New York: Harper, 1961), p. 104; Ferré's entire chapter on "The Logic of Encounter" (pp. 94-104) is a masterly critique of much of the wooly "I-Thou," existential-encounter theology popular today.

56 The foregoing criticisms, it is well to point out, also apply to those theologies which attempt to make a "living Christ" (as distinct from the Christ of Scripture) the source of theological theorizing. Such a "living Christ," if He is not known through Scripture, is necessarily known through extra-biblical experience. But, in the latter case, how can one be sure that his "Christ of experience" is the *real* Christ and not a projection of personal or corporate religious needs and desires? The dangers of idolatry here are overwhelming.

57 Limitations of space prevent us from dealing with the question of extra-biblical scriptures which claim to provide the ultimate interpretation of the Bible or revelational data superior to it (e.g., the *Book of Mormon*). Interested readers are referred to Van Baalen (*op. cit.* in n. 43), where the unverifiable nature of these claims is made patent, and where specific refutation of many of them is given.

58 In my *Shape of the Past* (*op. cit.* in n. 26, pp. 138-39), I have summarized what I believe to be the crux validation: "1. On the basis of accepted principles of textual and historical analysis, the Gospel records are found to be trustworthy historical documents—primary source evidence for the life of Christ. 2. In these records, Jesus exercises divine prerogatives and claims to be God in human flesh; and He rests His claims on His forthcoming resurrection. 3. In all four Gospels, Christ's bodily resurrection is described in minute detail; Christ's resurrection evidences His deity. 4. The fact of the resurrection cannot be discounted on *a priori*, philosophical grounds; miracles are impossible only if one so defines them—but such definition rules out proper historical investigation. 5. If Christ is God, then He speaks the truth concerning the absolute divine authority of the Old Testament and of the soon-to-be-written New Testament."

59 Franz Pieper, *Christian Dogmatics*, trans, and edd. T. Engelder, J. T. Mueller, and W. W. F. Albrecht (4 vols.; St. Louis, Mo.: Concordia, 1950-1957), I, 142-43.

60 John Warwick Montgomery, "Inspiration and Inerrancy: A New Departure," *Bulletin of the Evangelical Theological Society*, VIII (Spring, 1965); reprinted in my *Crisis in Lutheran Theology* (2 vols.; Grand Rapids, Mich.: Baker, 1967), I, chap. i, and in the present volume in III. 3.

[61] Robert Preus, *The Inspiration of Scripture: A Study of the Theology of the Seventeenth Century Lutheran Dogmaticians* (Edinburgh: Oliver and Boyd, 1957), p. 159.

[62] *Ibid.*, p. 157.

[63] Introduction, sec. C. 2. a. (p. 7); Traina's italics. This book was first published in 1952 and is available from the Biblical Seminary in New York. Serious application of its principles offers perhaps the best counteractive to such absurdly superficial judgments as Kaufmann's remark on "the overt ambiguity of the Scriptures" (*op. cit.* in n. 5, p. 227): "In no case can a theology really do justice to the Scriptures because it refuses to take into account their heterogeneity and their deep differences."

[64] E.g., the classical Lutheran dogmatician Johann Gerhard (1582-1637), in his *Loci Theologici*, ed. Preuss-Frank, I, 237-40.

[65] E.g., my esteemed colleague, J. Oliver Buswell, Jr., in his epochal work, *A Systematic Theology of the Christian Religion* (2 vols.; Grand Rapids, Mich.: Zondervan, 1962-1963), I, 24-25. Edward John Carnell has rightly praised Buswell for his "repeated insistence that a univocal meaning unites the mind of God with the mind of a Christian. The defense of univocal meaning implies a forthright rejection of all species of theology, ancient or modern, that either openly assert or tacitly consent to the hypothesis that truth signifies one thing for God (because he is almighty) and another for a Christian (because he is merely human)" (*Christianity Today*, IX, [February 26, 1965], 40).

[66] Heinrich Ott defends the "hermeneutical circle" as strongly as does Bultmann; see Ott's "Was ist systematische Theologie?" (*op. cit.*), sec. ii. The "hermeneutical circle" approach is, of course, an outgrowth and corollary of Heideggerian existentialism.

[67] John Warwick Montgomery, "The Fourth Gospel Yesterday and Today," *Concordia Theological Monthly*, XXXIV [April, 1963], 204; reprinted in the present volume in III. 5.

[68] Tillich, *op. cit.*, pp. 50-51.

[69] Cf. Jaroslav Pelikan's *The Light of the World: A Basic Image in Early Christian Thought* (New York: Harper, 1962), and *The Shape of Death: Life, Death, and Immortality in the Early Fathers* (New York: Abingdon, 1961).

[70] Hick (*Faith and Knowledge*, pp. 198 ff.) distinguishes between "dogmas" and "doctrines": the former "define the religion in question by pointing to the area of primary religious experiences from which it has arisen" (example: The Apostles' Creed), while the latter are "the propositions officially accepted as interpreting [the religion's] dogmas and as relating them together in a coherent system of thought." This is a useful distinction in practice, but Hick errs at several points in developing it: (1) Not "religious experiences" but the Holy Scriptures are the proper source of data from which Christian dogmas are developed (see text above at n. 53). (2) Doctrinal systems are not to be built upon "dogmatic foundations"; doctrines, no less than dogmas, are Gestalts that conceptualize *biblical* data. (3) The difference between dogmas and doctrines does not lie in the "fixed and unchangeable" character of the former as contrasted with the variable nature of the latter

(*both* are theoretically alterable for only scripture is inerrant), nor in the fact that dogmas are formulated by "a descriptive and empirical process" while the construction of doctrines is "speculative in method," involving "philosophical thinking" (*both* are Wittgensteinian "nets" to catch Scripture—not descriptive assertions *or* philosophical speculations). In actuality, the distinction between dogmas and doctrines is *quantitative*: the former are more stable because they are based on a greater wealth of biblical evidence, whereas the latter express theological convictions for which less scriptural support can be adduced. It follows that no strict or absolute line can be drawn between dogmas and doctrines, or between heresy (the rejection of orthodox dogma) and heterodoxy (the rejection of orthodox doctrine). Christian churches, in formulating tests of fellowship, should proceed with great care so as to avoid twin errors of laxity (stemming from an insufficiently defined or enforced dogmatic-doctrinal position) and bigotry (the bruising of consciences through required subscription to biblically doubtful doctrines). Thomas Campbell's rule remains the best guide: "Where the Scriptures speak, we speak; where the Scriptures are silent, we are silent."

[71] *Absolute* certainty, both in science and in theology, rests only with the data (for the former, natural phenomena; for the latter, scriptural affirmations). All conceptualizations on the basis of these data lack ultimate certainty (in science the Einsteinian revolution helped to make this clear), but some formulations are so well attested by the data that they acquire a practically (though not a theoretically) "certain" status; in science we call such Gestalts "laws," in theology, "creeds" and "confessions." Just as a denial of scientific laws removes one from the scientific community (cf. modern alchemists such as Tiffereau and Jullivet-Castelot), so denial of creeds and confessions results in one's separation from ecclesiastical circles. Scientific hypotheses and theological proposals, however, are never proper tests of "fellowship," for they lie, by definition, in the realm of open questions—which, hopefully, more investigation will either raise to a higher status or cause to be discarded. Scientific "theories" (in the narrow sense) and theological systems occupy an intermediate position between laws/creeds-confessions and hypotheses/theological proposals; thus although they are not generally made the basis of *formal* tests of fellowship they often have that function on an informal (social or psychological) level (cf. the negative reception in scientific circles of Immanuel Velikovsky's catastrophism).

It is, of course, possible to develop a more extensive classification of conceptual Gestalts in Science and theology (since only *quantitative* differences exist among the respective levels), but the above scheme appears to be the most generally useful; in Roman Catholic dogmatics, at least ten "theological grades of certainty" are distinguished, from "immediately revealed truths" to "tolerated opinion" (see Ludwig Ott, *Fundamentals of Catholic Dogma*, trans. Patrick Lynch and ed. James Bastible [2d ed.; St. Louis, Mo.: Herder, 1958], pp. 9-10 para. 8).

[72] On the "Christus Victor" atonement motif, set forth in historical context in Aulén's book of that title (English translation by A. G. Hebert published by Macmillan of New York in 1956), see the Appendix to my

Chytraeus on Sacrifice: A Reformation Treatise in Biblical Theology (St. Louis, Mo.: Concordia, 1962), pp. 139-46, where I compare the Aulén approach with Anselm's "Latin doctrine" of the atonement and with Abelard's "subjective view."

[73] Sherman Yellen, "Sir Arthur Conan Doyle: Sherlock Holmes in Spiritland," *International Journal of Parapsychology,* VII (Winter, 1965), 54.

[74] This passage appears in the Preface to the German section of the first edition of Luther's collected writings (Wittenberg, 1539). For an excellent discussion of it, see Pieper, *op. cit.,* I, 186-90.

[75] A particularly attractive presentation of this threefold conception of faith is given by Johann Gerhard (*op. cit.* in n. 64), III, 354 ff. A similar treatment can be found in Martin Chemnitz's *Loci Theologici,* II, 270.

[76] Johann Andreas Quenstedt (1617-1688), *Theologia didactico-polemica,* IV, 282. For Quenstedt, as for many of the other classical Protestant dogmaticians, both *Notitia* and *Assensus* pertain to the intellect, and *Fiducia* to the will; however, *assensus* is better regarded as bridging the gap between intellect and will, for, as Chemnitz correctly asserts, it involves "not merely a general assent, but that by which each one determines with firm persuasion, which Paul calls assurance (πληροφορία, Heb. 10:22), that the universal promise belongs privately, individually, and specifically to him, and that he also is included in the general promise" (*loc. cit.*).

[77] Peter Winch, *The Idea of a Social Science and Its Relation to Philosophy* (London: Routledge & Kegan Paul, 1958), p. 77.

[78] John Ciardi, "How Does a Poem Mean?", in *An Introduction to Literature,* ed. Gordon N. Ray (Boston: Houghton Mifflin, 1959), p. 666.

[79] Winch, *op. cit.,* p. 115. Winch illustrates with Wittgenstein's hypothetical society where the people sold their wood by piling the timber "in heaps of arbitrary, varying height and then sold it at a price proportionate to the area covered by the piles. And what if they even justified this with the words: 'Of course, if you buy more timber, you must pay more'?" (*Remarks on the Foundations of Mathematics* [Oxford: Blackwell, 1956], pp. 142 ff.). To *understand* such behavior, notes Winch, requires much more than the formulation of statistical laws concerning it. ("Understanding" is here used, let it be noted, not in an abstract, purely cerebral way, but in Max Weber's sense of *Verstehen*—"empathic comprehension"; see Talcott Parsons, "Unity and Diversity in the Modern Intellectual Disciplines: The Role of the Social Sciences," *Daedalus: Journal of the American Academy of Arts and Sciences,* XCIV [Winter, 1965], 59 ff.)

[80] On the historical philosophies of Croce and Collingwood, see my *Shape of the Past* (*op. cit.* in n. 26), pp. 90 ff. Crime detection, like history, is both a science and an art; thus Commissioner Tarquin (see above n. 11) also recommends in the investigation of a woman's murder: "Put yourself inside this woman's skin, get to know her better than she knew herself, become her twin. Get to understand her from the inside out, if you see what I mean" (Japrisot, *op. cit.,* chap. iii).

[81] Ernst Cassirer, *The Logic of the Humanities,* trans. C. S. Howe

(New Haven, Conn.: Yale University Press, 1961), p. 158.

[82] A good beginning can be made with Virgil C. Aldrich's *Philosophy of Art* (Engelwood Cliffs, N.J.: Prentice-Hall, 1963).

[83] "In every situation, when 'I' and 'me' have been distinguished. 'I' cannot be given an exhaustive 'objective' analysis without denying ourselves in fact, or without supposing that the subject-object relation in the construction of language is merely subject-predicate, which seems a quite unnecessary, indeed a quite disastrous, assumption. It is what Whitehead calls 'extreme objectivism' which even objectifies the subject" (Ian T. Ramsey, *Miracles; an Exercise in Logical Mapwork. An Inaugural Lecture delivered before the University of Oxford on 7 December 1951* [Oxford: Clarendon Press, 1952], p. 15). Cf. Karl Heim, *Christian Faith and Natural Science*, trans N. Horton Smith (New York: Harper Torchbooks, 1957), *passim.*

[84] Ramsey, *Models and Mystery*, p. 27: "There can—and it is a logical 'can'—be no objects without a subject which cannot itself be reducible to objects. The ideal of logical completion is never a third-person assertion; it is first-person assertion. *He does X* necessarily carries with it a pair of invisible quotation marks, so that it is to be set in some such frame as 'I am saying...', and without this wider frame the third-person assertion is logically incomplete."

[85] Cf. my article, "The Cause and Cure of Sin," *Resource*, III (February, 1962), 2-4.

[86] "Credimus in" followed by the accusative is the Latin equivalent of Greek πιστεύομεν εἰς ..., signifying the highest level of faith (*Fiducia*, confidence). Andreae's Creed thus reaches beyond assent to trust, as must all genuine Christian doctrinal affirmations.

[87] For the full text of this Creed, with accompanying English translation and detailed analysis, see my dissertation for the degree of Docteur de l 'Université, mention Théologie Protestante: "Cross and Crucible: Johann Valentin Andreae's *Chymical Wedding*" (3 vols.; University of Strasbourg, France, 1964), I, 272 ff. As a contemporary example of a theological system manifesting biblically sound artistic-subjective quality throughout, I particularly recommend the late Erlangen professor Werner Elert's *An Outline of Christian Doctrine*, trans. C. M. Jacobs (Philadelphia: United Lutheran Publication House, 1927).

[88] Bouwsma, (*op. cit.* in n. 8), pp. 8, 10.

[89] Michael B. Foster, *Mystery and Philosophy* (London: SCM Press, 1957).

[90] Willem F. Zuurdeeg, *An Analytical Philosophy of Religion* (New York: Abingdon, 1958).

[91] Ian T. Ramsey, *Religious Language: An Empirical Placing of Theological Phrases* (London: SCM Press. 1957), p. 73.

[92] Unhappily, as we have seen (the text at nn. 35 and 52), Ramsey makes "religious experience" rather than Holy Writ his touchstone for confirming or disconfirming theological models and their qualifiers.

[93] Luther used the expression *Theologia gloriae* to characterize the presumptive, god-like attempts of late medieval scholastic theologians to embrace all reality in their systems; his own approach he designated

simply as a *Theologia crucis* ("Theology of the Cross"); see Philip S. Watson, *Let God Be God! An Interpretation of the Theology of Martin Luther* (London: Epworth Press, 1947), p. 78. The scholastics erred through neglecting the *Tentatio* element requisite to the theologian's activity; their impossible endeavor to theologize from as it were, the perspective of God's throne would not have come about if they had retained awareness of their own subjective involvement in the theological task.

[94] E.g., "in the tension between analysis and existentialism" (Walter Kaufmann's philosophical maxim, characteristically endorsed by Willem F. Zuurdeeg in his article, "The Implications of Analytical Philosophy for Theology," *Journal of Bible and Religion*, XXIX[July, 1961], 210). In point of fact, only a solid analytical *base* can keep existential affirmations from dribbling off into unverifiable nonsensicality; thus not a "tension" but a *structure* is required for the proper relating of objective analysis and subjective-sacral existentialism. No better illustration of this exists than Wittgenstein's arrival at "das Mystische" at the end of his *Tractatus Logico-Philosophicus*, and the manner in which this work of logical analysis prepared the ground for his later *Philosophical Investigations.*

[95] Bernard J. F. Lonergan, S. J., *Insight: A Study of Human Understanding* (London: Longmans, 1958), *passim.* The Autumn, 1964, number of the Saint Xavier College quarterly *Continuum* is a Festschrift entirely devoted to the exceedingly important work of this Wittgenstein-like professor at Rome's Gregorian University. In matters of theological methodology, Lonergan is far more worth reading than most contemporary Protestant writers on the subject, since he is well aware of the debilitating effect of current existentialism on theological method, and is thoroughly versed in post-Einsteinian scientific theory. Cf. Lonergan's review of Johannes Beumers *Theologie als Glaubensverständnis*, in *Gregorianum*, XXXV [1954], 630-48; and see also the accounts of Lonergan's institute on theological methodology held in July, 1962, at Regis College, Toronto (*Sciences Ecclésiastiques*, XV, 291-93 [*op. cit.* in n. 37], and F. E. Crowe, "On the Method of Theology," *Theological Studies*, XXIII[1962], 637-42).

[96] The mingling of the subjective with the objective is deadly to any scientific theorizing. Theologians who would disregard this fact in their eagerness to existentialize Christian theology might ponder the following quotation from Rupert T. Gould's *Enigmas* (New Hyde Park, N.Y.: University Books, 1965), p. 321: "A novel and interesting theory respecting the origin—wholly, or in part—of Schiaparelli's (Martian) 'canals' was communicated to me in November, 1944, by Dr. G. S. Brock, F.R.S.E. He draws attention to the possibility that some or all of the appearances which the Italian astronomer believed that he had discovered on the Martian disc were actually situated *in the lens of his own eye,* and were symptomatic of incipient cataract.

"It is undoubtedly true that in certain conditions of lighting an image of the lens of the eye (together with any defects which this may have) can be projected on to the object which its owner is observing. Dr. Brock informs me that this fact was first announced by an Austrian scientist c.1842, but was afterwards lost sight of in consequence of Helmholtz' invention of the ophthalmoscope some ten years later. He considers it quite possible that some, at least, of Schiaparelli's 'canals' were caused by light from Mars, reflected from his retina, causing defects in the lens of his eye to be apparently projected on to the planet's disc—and, not improbably, blended with markings actually existing there" (italics Gould's). Whether or not this explanation of the famed "canals" of Mars is sound, it should give pause to contemporary theologians; for not a few of the theological theories of our day reflect the inner life of their proponents far more than the objective revealed truth of Holy Writ.

[97] Historically, as is well known, the Church arrived at its Trinitarian doctrine primarily through just such reflection on the christological problem of Jesus' relation to the Father.

[98] See Jn. 2:18-22, and cf. my *Shape of the Past* (*op. cit.* in n. 26), pp. 138-45. What in our structural model we have called the "Christ-axis" thus becomes the epistemological support for the entire theological endeavor.

[99] Jn. 14:16; ἄλλος is sharply distinguished in the Greek from ἕτερος ("another of a different kind")—cf. Gal. 1:6.

[100] Mt. 28:19

[101] Hanson (*op. cit.* in n. 27), p. 144. Cf. Jean E. Charon, *La Connaissance de l' Univers* (Paris: Editions du Seuil, 1963), *passim*. Lutheran theology has always cautioned against violating revelational paradox, while Roman Catholic and Calvinist theologies have emphasized the need of achieving maximum rational consistency in doctrinal construction; the above parallel between the Trinity and PWh illustrates the complementary truth in the two views: the theologian must always strive for rationality in his theorizing, but he must sacrifice this ideal to the accurate "fitting of the facts" when the latter do not perit logically consistent formulation. Reason properly has a ministerial, not a magisterial role in theology.

[102] Luther, *The Small Catechism*, Arts. 1, 2, and 3 of the Creed.

[103] Cf. Ramsey, *Religious Language*, pp. 174-79.

[104] Cf. Jacques Maritain, *St. Thomas Aquinas* (London: Sheed, 1931), pp. 44-46, 51. The eminent Jesuit philosopher Frederick Copleston writes: "The Christian recognizes in the human nature of Christ the perfect expression in human terms of the incomprehensible Godhead, and he learns from Christ how to think about God. But at the same time it is certainly no part of the Christian religion to say that God in Himself can be adequately comprehended by the human mind. And that He cannot be so comprehended seems to me to be at once a truth vital to religion, in the sense that it prevents us from degrading the idea of God and turning Him into an idol, and a truth which follows necessarily from the fact that our natural knowledge begins with sense-experience. For my own part, I find the thought that the reality, the 'objective meaning,' far exceeds in richness the reach of our analogical concepts the very reverse of depressing. St. Paul tells us that we see through a glass darkly, and the effect of a little linguistic analysis is to illuminate the truth of this statement" (*Contemporary Philosophy: Studies of Logical*

Positivism and Existentialism [London: Burns & Oates, 1956], pp. 101-102).

[105] *Tractatus Logico-Philosophicus,* 6.54. On the famous concluding assertion (7.0) that immediately follows, Foster (*op. cit.* in n. 89, p. 28), perceptively comments: "When Zechariah says 'Be silent all flesh before the Lord,' this is not wholly different from Wittgenstein's 'Whereof one cannot speak, thereof one must be silent'."

3.

Biblical Authority

Inspiration and Infallibility:
A New Departure

"If I have told you earthly things, and ye believe
not, how shall ye believe, if I tell you of heavenly things?"
(John 3:12)

In his classic work, *The Progress of Dogma,* James
Orr contended that the Christian Church, in each great
epoch of its history, has been forced to come to grips
with one particular doctrine of crucial significance both
for that day and for the subsequent history of the
Church.[1] In the Patristic era, the issue was the relation
of the persons of the Godhead, and particularly the christological problem of Jesus' character; the Ecumenical
Creeds represent the success of Orthodox, Trinitarian
theology over against numerous christological heresies,
any one of which could have permanently destroyed the
Christian faith. Medieval Christianity faced the issue of
the meaning of Christ's atonement, and Anselm's "Latin
doctrine," in spite of its scholastic inadequacies, gave
solid expression to biblical salvation-history as represented by the Epistle to the Hebrews. In the Reformation
Era, the overarching doctrinal problem facing the Church
was the application of redemption in justification;
Luther's stand for *sola gratia, sola fide* arrested an anthropocentric trend which could have turned the Christian
faith into little more than pagan religiosity.

And contemporary Christianity? What great doctrinal
issue does the modern Church face? Writing just before
the turn of the present century, Orr thought that he could
see in Eschatology the unique doctrinal challenge for
modern Christianity. Subsequent events, however, have
proven this judgment wrong: the doctrinal problem which,
above all others, demands resolution in the modern
Church is that of the authority of Holy Scripture. All
other issues of belief today pale before this issue, and

Notes for this section, pages 349-55.

indeed root in it; for example, ecumenical discussions, if they are doctrinal in nature, eventually and inevitably reach the question of religious authority—what is the final determinant of doctrinal truth, and how fully can the Bible be relied upon to establish truth in theological dialog? As the Patristic age faced a *christological* watershed, as the Medieval and Reformation churches confronted *soteriological* crises, so the contemporary Church finds itself grappling with the great *epistemological* question in Christian dogmatics.[2] And, let it be noted with care: just as the Church in former times could have permanently crippled its posterity through superficial or misleading answers to the root-questions then at issue, so we today have an equal obligation to deal responsibly with the Scripture issue. If we do not, future generations of theologians may find that no criterion remains by which to solve any subsequent doctrinal problems, and the theologians of the twentieth century will have gained the dubious distinction of having made their discipline (and the Church which looks to it for its doctrinal guidance) totally irrelevant.

The Ostensible Nature of the Issue

To the unsophisticated observer of the twentieth-century theological scene, it might seem that the present epistemological issue in theology is simply whether the Bible is inspired or not. (Later we shall be reminded that the unsophisticated, like children, often have disarming insight.) However, those who are dissatisfied with the traditional formulations of the Scripture doctrine argue in the strongest terms that the real issue is not whether the Bible is inspired or not, but the *character* and *extent* of inspiration. The claim is made that a non-traditional approach to biblical authority in no way denies the existence of inspiration; it merely defines more closely what is meant by inspiration and how far such inspiration extends in Holy Writ.

Thus it is held that Scripture is inspired as a theological norm—as God's authoritative message in matters spiritual—but that in matters historical and scientific we must recognize the human, fallible element in the biblical witness. "So," writes Roy A. Harrisville of Luther Seminary, "we admit to the discrepancies and the broken connections in Scripture, we let them stand just as they are— this is part of what it means that faith has its sphere in this world and not in some cloud cuckoo-land." [3] And the editors of *Dialog,* in a recent issue devoted to "Scripture and Tradition," are willing (albeit grudgingly) to continue the use of the expression "Scripture is inspired" if by it is meant that "Scripture is God's absolutely authoritative and authorized fundamental witness to a revelation"—as long as no attempt is made to apply such inspiration to "an inerrancy of the 'parts,' of the historical and scientific opinions of the biblical authors."[4] In a subsequent issue of *Dialog,* the Lutheran Church-Missouri Synod's *Report of the Commission on Theology and Church Relations* ("A Study Document on Revelation, Inspiration, Inerrancy," 1964) is criticized for not labeling as erroneous the *Brief Statement's* inclusion of the historical and scientific data of the Bible in its definition of inspiration.[5] A more esoteric expression of the same general view is that the Bible is totally inspired— indeed, infallibly inspired—but that such inspiration does not necessarily produce inerrant results in matters historical or scientific, since God's word infallibly accomplishes only what He *intends* it to accomplish (i.e., the revelation of *theological* truths, not the imparting of historic or scientific absolutes).

In sum, then, the present controversy over biblical authority ostensibly centers on a split between inspiration and inerrancy. It is claimed that the former can and should be held without the latter. Not only will the Christian no longer have to defend the Bible against scientific and historical criticism, but he will be freed to enter more fully into a purely faith-relationship with Jesus Christ.

> In the last analysis, a rejection of the doctrine of inerrancy involves primarily a mental readjustment. Nothing basic is lost. In fact, when all the evidence is examined, those essential elements which the advocates of the doctrine of inerrancy have cherished and sought to protect are more firmly supported than ever before. Scripture is the product of inspiration and it is the indispensable source for coming to know God's claim upon us and his will for us.[6]

The contention of the present writer, over against these above-expressed views, is that inspiration and inerrancy cannot be separated—that like "love" and "marriage" in the musical production of Wilder's *Our Town*, "you can't have one without the other." This traditional position may seem on the surface to necessitate a traditional defense of it, along the lines of the vast number of admittedly drab works on the subject produced by "fundamentalists" since the days of the Scopes evolution trial. However, nothing could be farther from the truth. Note carefully that I have not said merely (as others have said) that inspiration and inerrancy *should* not be separated (i.e., that they *can* be separated but for various biblical and theological reasons *ought* not to be), but rather that scriptural inspiration and inerrancy *cannot* exist apart from each other (i.e., that to separate them results not just in error, but in plain and simple *meaninglessness*). I am convinced that the dullness and sameness in standard orthodox defenses of biblical inerrancy point to an impasse in previous thinking on the subject— and constitute a demand for ground-breaking along different lines. By way of certain new techniques derived from the realm of analytical philosophy, I believe that one can see exactly where the central difficulty lies in the present-day attempt to dichotomize inspiration and inerrancy. The result of this investigation will, it is believed, leave the reader with but two meaningful alternatives: a Bible which is both inspired and inerrant (or better, inerrant because it is inspired), or a Bible which is no different qualitatively from other books.[7] The superficially attractive half-way house of an inspired, non-inerrant Bible will be seen to evaporate in the mist— as a concept having neither philosophical nor theological, but only emotive, significance.

The Peculiarity of the Issue

The contemporary advocates of an inspired but non-inerrant view of the Bible appeal constantly to the pressure of recent scholarship as justifying and indeed demanding their viewpoint. A recent letter from a well-known Professor of New Testament Interpretation took me to task for my biblical position on the ground that "a new era of biblical theology began to dawn some twenty-five years ago; and, I believe, any biblical matters cannot ignore what has happened in this field." Warren A. Quanbeck of Luther Seminary has recently argued in more explicit terms that inerrancy was unable to survive the onslaughts of modern historical and scientific scholarship:

> Theologians read the Bible as a collection of revealed propositions unfolding the truth about God, the world, and man. Because the Holy Spirit was the real author of Scripture, every proposition in it was guaranteed infallible and inerrant, not only in spiritual, but in secular matters.
>
> Because of this insistence on the Bible's inerrancy in historical and scientific matters, the blows struck by studies in historical and natural science were crushing in their force. When men approached the Bible as a collection of historical books they saw plainly the human character of its writers and their obvious dependence upon the sources of information available in their day. They recognized also that the scientific outlook of the writers was that of their time, and could not be a substitute for present-day scientific investigation and experiment. When theologians insisted that the religious message of the Bible stood or fell with its scientific and historical information they assumed an impossible apologetic task.[8]

The strangeness in this line of argumentation lies in two principal considerations: (1) The alleged factual errors and internal contradictions in Scripture which are currently cited to demonstrate the impossibly archaic nature of the inerrancy view are themselves impossibly archaic in a high proportion of instances; and (2) the most recent scholarly investigations and intellectual trends bearing on the validity of biblical data have never been more hospitable to inerrancy claims. Let us consider, in this connection, the recent series of anti-inerrancy arguments adduced by Robert Scharlemann:

> Unless one makes all sorts of special qualifications for the term "error," this statement [that "the scientist can accept the entire Bible as God's inspired Word for it is inerrant"] can simply not be supported by an examination of the Bible itself. Let me cite two examples which, since they are not from the area of "science," are likely to be less provocative.
>
> A reporter could ask the question, "Was the Greek word *houtos* the first or last word in the superscription on the

cross at Jesus' crucifixion?" From Luke (23:38) he would receive the reply, "It was the last." From Matthew (27:37) he would receive the reply, "It was the first." By any normal definition of error, either Matthew or Luke is in error concerning this reportorial matter; perhaps both of them are.

A second example is the classical one. Matthew 27:9 ascribes to Jeremiah a quotation which is actually found in Zechariah.

These are not isolated cases. Numerous examples can be found if one is interested in hunting for them. When was Jesus crucified? According to Matthew, Mark, and Luke it was on the 15th of Nisan; according to John it was on the 14th of Nisan. At least one of them must be in error. Unless one so defines "error" that it does not really mean an error in the normal sense; or unless one holds to the word "inerrancy" with a sort of blind dogmatism, the assertion that the Bible is inerrant, "that is, contains no error," simply cannot be supported by the Biblical evidence itself.[9]

This account of representative "contradictions" derives in no sense from modern scholarship; the alleged discrepancies have been recognized for centuries and have been dealt with in a variety of effective ways. Haley, in his great work on supposed biblical contradictions, stated in 1874 what had been obvious to readers of the superscriptions since the accounts were originally set down: "It is altogether improbable that three inscriptions, in three different languages, should correspond word for word"; [10] and in reference to the Zechariah quotation in Matthew, he presents two perfectly reasonable ways of dealing with the problem, both of which are derived from earlier scholarship:

According to the Jewish writers, Jeremiah was reckoned the first of the prophets, and was placed first in the book of the prophets; thus, Jeremiah, Ezekiel, Isaiah, etc. Matthew, in quoting this book, may have quoted it under the name which stood *first* in it; that is, instead of saying, "by the Prophets," he may have said, "by Jeremy the prophet," since *he* headed the list.

Or, the difficulty may have arisen from abridgment of the names. In the Greek, Jeremiah, instead of being written in full, might stand thus, "Iriou;" Zechariah thus, "Zriou." By the mere change of Z into I [i.e., by later scribal copyists], the mistake would be made. The Syriac Peshito and several MSS. have simply, "by the prophet." [11]

Alleged contradictions of this kind were in fact, more than adequately handled by such orthodox fathers of the Reformation era as Andreas Althamer.[12] As for the 14th Nisan-15th Nisan crucifixion difficulty, which has also had much attention through Christian history, the most recent biblical scholarship has provided what may well be the final answer to the problem: A. Jaubert, a French specialist on the Dead Sea Scrolls, has shown that two calendars were employed in first-century Palestine (the official lunar calendar and a Jubilees-Qumran calendar) and that there is every reason to believe that the double dating in the Gospel accounts of the crucifixion, far from being a contradiction, simply reflects these two calendar systems.[13]

In point of fact, as Jaubert's investigations illustrate, the present climate of research is more hospitable to an inerrancy approach than was the nineteenth century or the early decades of the twentieth. Archeological work daily confirms biblical history in ways which liberal criticism would have regarded as patently impossible a few decades ago.[14] The Einsteinian-relativistic reinterpretation of "natural law" has dealt a death-blow to Hume's arguments against the miraculous and has removed the rational possibility of using antimiraculous presuppositions for dehistoricizing such biblical accounts as Jonah-and-the-Leviathan.[15] The collapse of form-critical techniques in Homeric and other classical literary criticism, and the presently recognized debility of that approach even in the literary study of English ballads, has raised overwhelming doubts as to the whole presuppositional substructure of the Dibelius-Bultmann approach to the New Testament documents.[16] All in all, the traditional position on inspiration is able to command more respect today than it has during any generation since the advent of rationalistic higher criticism.

However, there is obviously something to the claim that "a new era of biblical theology began to dawn some twenty-five years ago"—an era which, in spite of developments such as those just described, could not tolerate plenary inspirationism. What has constituted the enormous pressure against the inerrancy view? Why have contemporary theologians found it necessary to ridicule the position and to treat it as a hopelessly outmoded one, in spite of such formidable proponents of it as the philosopher Gordon Clark, the theologian Edward John Carnell, and the New Testament lexicographer W. F. Arndt? Why have such considerations as archeological findings and classical scholarship not moved the mainstream theologians in the direction of plenary inspiration? The answer is most definitely *not* (in spite of loud protests continually voiced) the weight of new factual evidence against an inerrant Bible. Such "evidence" simply does not exist; as we have noted and illustrated, the contemporary critic of an inerrant Scripture is still citing alleged discrepancies and supposed scientific objections which have been adequately dealt with over and over again.[17] *The issue is not empirical; it is philosophical* That is to say, there has been an alteration in the philosophical Zeitgeist which, apart from the question of particular factual evidence, makes scriptural inerrancy offensive to much of contemporary theological thought. What precisely is this new element in the current climate of theological opinion?

A hint of an answer is provided by Rupert E. Davies in his attempt to refute John Wenham's inerrancy position. Writes Davies:

> I cannot believe that truths which go away into mystery can be expressed once for all in propositional form; and the Bible never claims that they can. Its purpose is to draw attention in many different ways to the saving Acts of God.[18]

Here a suggestion is made that the Bible deals with a different kind of subject-matter than is capable of being expressed propositionally. Biblical truth is not propositional and static, but dynamic and active; its focus is on acts, not assertions.

For the late A. G. Hebert, one of the prime modern opponents of plenary inspiration, the "propositional" view of biblical truth is a relatively recent and unfortunate result of applying scientific categories in the religious sphere.

> The doctrine of Inerrancy was not very harmful in an age which thought of "truth" primarily as belonging to the revelation of God and of the eternal meaning of man's life. The Bible was regarded as teaching chiefly

spiritual truths about God and man. It was otherwise
when the "scientific age" had begun; truth was now commonly understood as the matter-of-fact truth of observable
phenomena, and so great a man as Locke could make the
outrageous statement that the existence of God was as
certain as the propositions of geometry. The Inerrancy
of the Bible was understood as guaranteeing the literal
exactness of its every statement. This is the Fundamentalism which has been a potent cause of modern unbelief.
This materialistic Inerrancy needs to be carefully distinguished from the theological and religious Inerrancy in
which earlier ages believed.[19]

Even if one leaves aside the minor fallacies in this
statement (e.g., the confusion of geometry with observable phenomena),[20] one cannot accept the historical explanation of the inerrancy position here presented.
Throughout the history of the Church there has been continual concern to maintain and defend the total factual
reliability of the Bible. To take only one prominent example, St. Augustine, by all odds the most important theologian of the Patristic age, argued with vehemence for
an inerrant Bible. As the definitive study of his biblical
position asserts:

> There is no point of doctrine more plainly asserted or
> more vigorously defended by St. Augustine, than the ab-
> sence of falsehood and error from the divine Scriptures.
> ... Indeed inerrancy is so intimately bound up with in-
> spiration that an inspired book cannot assert what is
> not true .... It is impossible for Scripture to contain con-
> tradictory statements. One book of Scripture cannot con-
> tradict another, nor can the same author contradict
> himself.[21]

From earliest times the Church was concerned with
the propositional accuracy of the biblical text, for such
a concern followed directly from the Church's commitment to the inspiration of Scripture. Actually, the so-called
"dynamic," non-propositional view of truth has its origin
not in pre-scientific times, but in very recent thinking.

The source of this essentially new approach to the
nature of biblical truth, over against traditional plenary
inspiration, will become more evident if we look closely
at a typical recent expression of it. Let us hear Warren
Quanbeck's "re-examination of theological presuppositions":

> Since human language is always relative, being condi-
> tioned by its historical development and usage, there can
> be no absolute expression of the truth even in the language
> of theology. Truth is made known in Jesus Christ, who
> is God's Word, his address to mankind. Christ is the only
> absolute. Theological statements, which have an instru-
> mental function, find their meaning in relation to him;
> they do not contain the truth nor give adequate expression
> to it. At best they point to Jesus Christ as the one in whom
> one may know the truth. Truth is not a matter of intel-
> lection only, but of obedient discipleship. Only by "abiding
> in Christ" can one know the truth.[22]

To any historian of philosophy, the antecedents of this
view are obvious—and they lie not in the realm of biblical/
theological presuppositions, as Quanbeck and other adherents of this position believe, but in the realm of philosophical apriori. The idea that "there can be no absolute
expression of the truth" in propositional form has clear
alignment with the venerable philosophical position known
as *metaphysical dualism*, which in one form or other has
always claimed that the Absolute cannot be fully manifested in the phenomenal world. From Plato's separation
of the world of ideas from the world of things and the
soul from the body, to the medieval "realists" with their
split between universals and particulars, through the Reformation Calvinists' conviction that *finitum non capax infiniti,* to the modern idealism of Kant and Hegel, we see
this same conviction in various semantic garbs. It is this
absolute separation of eternity and time that lies at the
basis of the contemporary theological split between *Ge-
shichte* and *Historie,* as I have indicated elsewhere;[23]
and it is most definitely the same aprioristic dualism that
motivates much of contemporary theology in its refusal
to allow the Eternal to express Himself in absolutely veracious biblical propositions.

But metaphysical dualism is only the minor element
in the anti-inerrancy position take by Quanbeck and others. "Truth," he writes, "is not a matter of intellection
only, but of obedient discipleship" and "Christ is the only
absolute." Here we see the redefinition of truth in *personal,* as opposed to propositional, terms. Truth is arrived
at not through words or through investigation, but "only
by 'abiding in Christ.' " Martin Scharlemann, in an unpub-

lished paper presenting this same general approach to biblical inspiration, concludes: "In a very real sense, therefore, it is impossible to speak of revelation as an objective reality, independent of personal reaction on the part of him to whom a disclosure is made .... Knowledge is not a matter of acquiring information but of being confronted with God Himself as He is revealed in His Son." [24] Such terminology and conceptual content point unmistakably to the *existentialist movement* in modern philosophy, which, stemming from Kierkegaard, has affirmed that "truth is subjectivity" and that "existence," as manifested in personal relationships, precedes and surpasses in quality "essence," i.e., formal, propositional assertions or descriptions concerning reality.[25] In the hands of its most influential contemporary Protestant advocate, Rudolf Bultmann, existentialist theology claims to "cut under the subject-object distinction" [26] so as to arrive at a "dynamic" view of biblical truth untrammeled by questions of propositional facticity or objective validity.

No philosophy has so captured the minds and hearts of the contemporary world as existentialism; for how can one listen to "propositional" assertions of "objective" ideals when the West has barely survived two terrible self-created holocausts and seems bent on nuclear self-destruction? Only in personal existential relationships does any hope seem to lie. So speaks the average member of the Western intelligentsia; and, as has happened not a few times in the history of theology, the professional theologian does him one better: in religious life as well, truth can only be found in personality (Christ), and one should discard as irrelevant and harmful excess baggage the traditional view that Scripture offers propositionally objective truth to man. Thus the cultural pressure to existentialism, combined with a powerful tradition of metaphysical dualism,[27] impels much of modern theology to reject inerrancy. Modernity is indeed the source of the new approach to Scripture; but it is not a modernity characterized by new discoveries of empirical fact which have forced modifications of traditional thinking. Rather, it is a modernity of philosophical Zeitgeist.

Bultmann has argued, in defense of his use of existentialistic categories in interpreting biblical data, that existentialism is really not an alien philosophy, but a heuristic methodology that does not commit one to extra-biblical positions. It is almost universally agreed, however, both by professional philosophers and by lay interpreters of existentialism, that this viewpoint does indeed constitute a philosophy, and that its presuppositions (e.g., "existence precedes essence," "the objective-subjective distinction must be transcended," "truth is found only in personal encounter," etc.) can and must be subjected to philosophical analysis and criticism. Such a process of critical analysis has been going on now for some years, and the results have been devastatingly negative for the existentialist position. Indeed, faced with the blistering criticism directed against existentialism by analytical philosophy in particular, contemporary thought is now beginning to move away from Albert Camus' dread city of Oran into more congenial philosophical habitats.

It is now our task to apply the techniques of analytic philosophy to the anti-inerrancy position on Scripture that derives from an existentialistic-dualistic *Weltanschauung*. In doing so, we shall discover, possibly to our amazement, that contemporary theological denials of inerrancy necessarily tie themselves to philosophical stars which are rapidly burning out.

The Meaninglessness of Existentialistic and Dualistic Affirmations

We shall commence our critical task with an examination of analytical technique in general and its application to existentialism and dualism in particular. The relevance of the following discussion to the inerrancy issue will become evident in the subsequent sections of the paper.

While theologians of the last two decades have been especially concerned with the epistemological problem of biblical authority, contemporary philosophy (particularly in England) has likewise focused attention on central epistemological issues. Faced with the welter of conflicting philosophical and theological world-views propounded through the centuries, twentieth-century analytical philosophers have attempted to cut back to the basic question: How can truth-claims be verified? In a brief paper such as this, it would be impossible to discuss the history of this analytical movement, arising from the pioneering *Principia Mathematica* of Russell and Whitehead, extending through the "logical atomism" of Wittgenstein's amazing *Tractatus Logico-Philosophicus*, and culminating in the (misnamed) "logical positivism" of von Mises and the "linguistic analysis" or "ordinary language philosophy" of the later Wittgenstein and Ryle.[28] But, in very general terms, the conclusions of these analytical thinkers can be summarized in regard to the problem of verifiability.

> The criterion which we use to test the genuineness of apparent statements of fact is the criterion of verifiability. We say that a sentence is factually significant to any given person, if, and only if, he knows how to verify the proposition which it purports to express—that is, if he knows what observations would lead him, under certain conditions, to accept the proposition as being true, or reject it as being false.[29]

This "Verifiability Criterion of Meaning" arose from the discovery (set forth by Whitehead and Russell in the *Principia*) that assertions in mathematics and deductive logic are tautologous, i.e., they state nothing factual about the world, but follow from the apriori assumptions of the deductive system. Such "analytic" sentences can be verified without recourse to the world of fact, since they say nothing about the world; but other assertions (non-tautological, or "synthetic" affirmations) must be tested by the data of the real world if we are to discover their truth or falsity.

Thus any propositions, upon inspection, will fall into one of the following categories: (1) Analytic sentences, which are true or false solely by virtue of their logical form, *ex hypothesi*. Such assertions, though essential to thought and potentially meaningful, are often termed "trivial," since they never provide information about the world of experience. Example: "All husbands are married," whose truth follows entirely from the definition of the word "husband." (2) Synthetic sentences, which are true or false according to the application of the Verifiability Criterion set forth above. Such sentences are sometimes termed "informative," because they do potentially give information about the world. Example: "Jesus died at Jerusalem," which can be tested through an examination of historical evidence. (3) Meaningless sentences, embracing all affirmations which are neither analytic nor synthetic. Such sentences are incapable of testing, for they neither express tautological judgments (they are not statements whose truth depends on their logical form) nor do they affirm anything about the real world which is testable by investigating the world. Example: the philosopher F. H. Bradley's claim that "the Absolute enters into, but is itself incapable of, evolution and progress." Such a statement is clearly not tautologous, for it is not deduced from the aprioris of logic, nor is it capable of any test which could conceivably determine its truth or falsity. Thus it is meaningless, or nonsensical (in the technical meaning of "nonsense," i.e., without verifiable sense).

The importance of the analytic approach to questions of truth and falsity cannot be overestimated. As a result of its application, vast areas of philosophical speculation and argument have been shown to lie in a never-never land of meaninglessness—a land where discussion could continue forever without any possibility of arriving at truth or falsity. The analysts have successfully cleared the philosophical air of numerous positions about which discussion of truth-value is a waste of time, because their verifiability is impossible in any case.[30]

It should be emphasized, however, that "category three" statements are meaningless only in the special sense of non-verifiability. When Ayer speaks of the analytical "elimination of metaphysics," one should not conclude that non-testable philosophical or religious assertions do not deserve study. They do: but only from a historical or psychological viewpoint. Such statements as "The Absolute enters into evolution and progress," while not telling us anything about logic or about the constitution of the world, does tell us something (a great deal, in fact) about its formulator, Bradley, and about the history of philosophical ideology. Wittgenstein illustrates the matter well by one of his typically striking parables:

> Imagine that there is a town in which the policemen are required to obtain information from each inhabitant, e.g. his age, where he came from, and what work he does.

A record is kept of this information and some use is made of it. Occasionally when a policeman questions an inhabitant he discovers that the latter does not do *any* work. The policeman enters this fact on the record, because *this too* is a useful piece of information about the man! [31]

Malcolm, who relates the parable, comments: "The application of the parable is, I think, that if you do not understand a statement, then to discover that it has no verification is an important piece of information about it and makes you understand it better. That is to say, you understand it *better*; you do not find out that there is nothing to understand." Thus analytical philosophy does not, *pace* its detractors, attempt to silence all discussion of non-verifiable matters; rather, it attempts to limit discussions only to the "understandable" aspects of these matters: namely, to the emotive considerations represented by metaphysical assertions. It is in light of this qualification that we must interpret Wittgenstein's two great assertions, which have so powerfully influenced all subsequent analytical work:

Alles, was überhaupt gedacht werden kann, kann klar gedacht werden.
Alles, was sich aussprechen laesst, laesst sich klar aussprechen.

Wovon man nicht sprechen kann, darüber muss man schweigen.

Everything that can be thought at all can be thought clearly.
Everything that can be put into words can be put clearly.

Whereof one cannot speak, thereof one must be silent.[32]

Now in practice how does the Verifiability Principle achieve this desirable limitation of speech to what can be said meaningfully and clearly? Let us consider several examples, which will progressively move us into the philosophical-theological application of analytical technique.

(A) "There are angels living on the planet Uranus." [33] This might seem, on the surface, to be a meaningless proposition, for no present test of verifiability exists by which the truth or falsity of the claim can be determined.

However (on the assumption that angels are visible creatures), a test can be conceived; it would involve the use of space craft to make the journey to Uranus, whereby, through direct observation, the proposition could be tested as to its truth-value. Thus the proposition, being hypothetically testable, is meaningful. However, let it be noted well, if "angels" are defined in such a way that there is no conceivable way of determining their presence even if one succeeds in arriving at their habitat, then proposition (A) would indeed be meaningless (except as an emotive assertion, such as "I like angels"). Consider Antony Flew's parable, developed from a tale told by John Wisdom:

> Once upon a time two explorers came upon a clearing in the jungle. In the clearing were growing many flowers and many weeds. One explorer says, "Some gardener must tend this plot." The other disagrees, "There is no gardener." So they pitch their tents and set a watch. No gardener is ever seen. "But perhaps he is an invisible gardener." So they set up a barbed-wire fence. They electrify it. They patrol with blood hounds. (For they remember how H. G. Wells' *The Invisible Man* could be both smelt and touched though he could not be seen.) But no shrieks ever suggest that some intruder has received a shock. No movements of the wire ever betray an invisible climber. The bloodhounds never give cry. Yet still the Believer is not convinced. "But there is a gardener, invisible, intangible, insensible to electric shocks, a gardener who has no scent and makes no sound, a gardener who comes secretly to look after the garden which he loves." At last the Sceptic despairs, "But what remains of your original assertion? Just how does what you call an invisible, intangible, eternally elusive gardener differ from an imaginary gardener or even from no gardener at all?" [34]

This parable shows with utmost clarity how meaningless are religious assertions which are removed entirely from the realm of testability. Is not one of the most fundamental reasons for the strength of the Christian proclamation that "God was *in Christ*"--since apart from God's revelation of Himself in our midst, we could never know with certainty whether the garden of this world had a loving Gardener at all? But more of this later.

(B) "The world was created in 4004 B.C., but with built-in evidence for radiocarbon dating, fossil evidence, etc., indicating millions of years of prior developmental growth." This assertion, made by some well-meaning Christian believers, is a nonsensical proposition.[35] Why? Because it excludes all possible testability. *Any* alleged scientific fact marshalled against 4004 B.C. creation is, by the nature of the original proposition, discounted as having been built into the universe at its creation. Moreover, the statement is reconcilable with an infinte number of parallel assertions, such as "The world was created ten years ago (or ten minutes ago) with a built-in history." Such assertions as (B) are really no different from meaningless cosmological affirmations of the type: "The universe is continually increasing in size at a uniform rate" (obviously, in such a case, our instruments of measurement would *also* be increasing in size uniformly, and would not therefore be capable of yielding any evidence of the increase!). The Christian can take comfort that *his* God is not like Descartes' "Evil Genius" —that He does not introduce deceptive elements into His universe, thereby driving His creatures to meaningless affirmations about the world.

(C) "The resurrection of Christ, though an historical event in the full sense of the term (*Geschichte* and *Historie*), nonetheless cannot be verified by the methods of objective historical scholarship; it is evident only to the eyes of faith." This position, developed by Karl Barth and emphasized in his 1952 debate with Bultmann, is revealed as meaningless when placed under the searchlight of the Verifiability Principle. For how could one possibly know if Christ's resurrection (or any other event) was in fact historical if it could not be tested by the ordinary methods of historical investigation? As a parallel, consider the following argument: "In my backyard is an orange hippopotamus. He is really there, but his presence cannot be tested by any techniques employed to show the existence of the other things in my backyard." Such a claim is nonsense. Either the hippopotamus is there, or he isn't; and if no empirical test will show that he is, then one must conclude that assertions concerning his existence are meaningless. Likewise, if Christ's resurrection really occurred in history (*Historie*), then historical investigation will indicate it; if not, then one must give up any meaningful claim to the resurrection as a *his-*

torisch event. Either the Orthodox theologians are right, or Bultmann is right; no meaningful middle-ground exists.

But, it is argued, can we not speak of Christ's resurrection, virgin birth, and other such religious events on the level of *Geschichte,* "metahistory," or "suprahistory"? It is exactly here that we encounter the *dualistic* tradition which, as already noted, constitutes one of the two essential elements in the contemporary anti-inerrancy view of the Bible. What about this eminent tradition of metaphysical Dualism that serves as the most extensive "footnote to Plato" in Western thought? Should we not think of the Absolute apart from earthly flux—God as Otto's "Wholly Other" or as Tillich's "Ultimate Concern," never fully identified with institutions, persons, books, or events in this world? Is it not of tremendous value to hold, with Plato and the medieval realists, that the phenomenal world can never dim the beauties of the eternal world of Ideas, and to affirm with Tillich that the "truth of faith" cannot be "judged by any other kind of truth, whether scientific, historical or philosophical"?[36] The answer is simply that, whatever the supposed advantages of metaphysical or theological dualism, and however praiseworthy the motives leading to such dualisms, their result is analytical meaninglessness. Why? Because, by definition, insofar as any statement about the "Absolute" or "God" does not touch the world of human experience, to that extent it cannot be verified in any sensible way. Thus have the analytical philosophers devastatingly criticized the metaphysical affirmations of the modern philosophical tradition represented by Hegel and Kant; and thus do the theological dualists on the contemporary scene fall under the critical axe of the same verifiability test. If, for example, the claim is made that Christ rose from the dead, but in the suprahistorical realm of *Geschichte,* not in the empirical realm of *Historie,* one has every right to ask: "What precisely do you *mean* by the realm of *Geschichte* and how do you know anything—much less a resurrection—goes on there?" A supra-experiential realm is, *ex hypothesi,* untestable, and therefore, like my orange hippopotamus mentioned earlier, irrelevant as a theological concept. It may (and does) tell us much about the theologians who rely upon it (particularly, that they fervently wish to avoid criticism from secular historians!), but it tells us nothing whatever about the truth-value of alleged events of a *geschichtliche* character. We know (or can know) whether a resurrection occurred in this world, and we know (or can know) whether God was incarnated in this world; but about a realm beyond all human testability, we can know nothing. To theological dualisms, Wittgenstein's final proposition has precise applicability: "Whereof one cannot speak, thereof one must be silent."

Existential affirmations, however, would seem to fall within the sphere of verifiable meaning, since they (unlike dualistic assertions) treat of "existence" rather than of "essence." What of this area of modern philosophy, which forms an even more important element than Dualism in the make-up of anti-inerrancy views of Scripture?

One must understand, first of all, that the assertions of Existentialism are not simply statements about verifiable, existent things or events; rather, they are specialized philosophical claims about the nature of man's existence in the universe, i.e., they are genuinely metaphysical affirmations. Consider such basic tenets of the existentialist world-view as the following: "Truth cannot be found in abstract propositions." "Truth is discovered in responsible decision." "Personal encounter is the only sure avenue to truth." "The subject-object distinction must be transcended." [37] Such beliefs as these are very definitely claims as to the nature of the world and of man's relationship to it, and as such deserve analytical inspection in the same way as other truth-claims.

And what is the result when existentialist affirmations are subjected to verifiability tests? An excellent illustration has been provided in Rudolf Carnap's examination of the following typical argument in Heidegger's *Was Ist Metaphysik?*:

> What is to be investigated is being only and—*nothing* else; being alone and further—*nothing;* solely being, and beyond being—*nothing. What about this Nothing?* ... *Does the Nothing exist only because the Not, i.e., the Negation, exists? Or is it the other way around? Does Negation and the Not exist only because the Nothing exists?* ... We assert: *the Nothing is prior to the Not and the Negation* .... Where do we seek the Nothing? How do

> we find the Nothing? . . . We know the Nothing . . . .
> *Anxiety reveals the Nothing* . . . . That for which and be-
> cause of which we were anxious, was "really"—nothing.
> Indeed: the Nothing itself—as such—was present . . . .
> *What about this Nothing?—The Nothing itself nothings.*

This argument, asserting the primacy of existence ("the
Nothing") over essence ("the Negation and the Not")
and the necessity of embracing it through personal recognition of estrangement ("anxiety"), is shown by Carnap
to consist of analytically meaningless "pseudo-state-
ments," whose "non-sensicality is not obvious at first
glance, because one is easily deceived by the analogy
with . . . meaningful sentences." To assert that "the rain
rains" is meaningful; but to argue that "the Nothing
nothings" is something else again! "Even if it were ad-
missible to introduce 'nothing' as a name or description
of an entity, still the existence of this entity would be
denied in its very definition, whereas [Heidegger] goes
on to affirm its existence." [38] In point of fact, all the
basic metaphysical affirmations of Existentialism, in pur-
porting to unfold the very heart of existent reality, over-
reach themselves and arrive not at reality but at nonsense.

The fundamental cause of meaninglessness in Existentialism lies in its convictions that the subject-object distinction must be overcome and that "I-thou" personal
encounter must be substituted for propositional truth. One
can certainly appreciate the historical factors that gave
rise to these affirmations: the breakdown of idealistic
philosophy, the coldness of "dead-orthodox" theology
(cf. Kierkegaard's *Attack upon "Christendom"*), the depersonalization of Western man in modern technological,
scientific society, and the anxieties produced by decades
of hot and cold wars. But appreciation of existentialist
motives must not obscure the fundamental fact that
meaningful thought absolutely requires the subject-object
distinction, and that questions of truth cannot even be
formulated apart from propositions. "Bohr has emphasized the fact that the observer and his instruments must
be presupposed in any investigation, so that the instruments are not part of the phenomenon described but are
used." [39] The absolute necessity of the subject-object

distinction is the source of the riotous humor in Robert Benchley's story of his experience in a college biology course: he spent the term carefully drawing the image of his own eyelash as it fell across the microscopic field! If in any investigation—whether in science or in theology—the observer loses the distinction between himself and his subject matter, the result is complete chaos: not a "transcending of the subject-object barrier," but a necessary fall into pure subjectivity. The more perceptive existentialists have indeed seen this; Sartre, for example, asserts that what all existentialists, atheistic and Christian, "have in common is that they think that existence precedes essence, or, if you prefer, that subjectivity must be the starting point." [40] Such subjectivity, however, is utterly non-testable; and utterances concerning "estrangement," "existential anxiety," and "nothingness" stand outside of meaningful discourse. [41]

Like logic itself, both the subject-object distinction and propositional thinking must be presupposed in all sensible investigations. Why? Because to argue against their necessity is to employ them already! When one asserts: "Personal encounters, not propositions, yield truth," one is in fact stating a proposition (though a meaningless one), and is implying that there is sufficient distinction between "truth" and those who claim to possess it to warrant a clarifying statement on the subject! Existentialism's passionate attempt to dissolve subject-object boundaries and to escape from propositions about reality to reality itself is thus bound to fail and necessarily to arrive at nonsense. Of objective propositional truth, as of logic itself, one must say what Emerson said of Brahma: "When me they fly, I am the wings." [42]

The Analytical Meaninglessness of a "Non-Inerrant Inspired Scripture"

Our study to this point has yielded the following conclusions: (1) Biblical inerrancy is under severe attack in our time not because of the discovery of empirical data militating against the view, but because of the climate of philosophical opinion presently conditioning Protestant theology. (2) The current theological Zeitgeist, as pertains to the issue of biblical authority, is governed by existen-

tialistic and dualistic aprioris. (3) The fundamental
axioms of both Dualism and Existentialism are analytically meaningless. From these conclusions, it is but a short
step to the central claim of this paper: that the current
attempt to maintain a divinely inspired but non-inerrant
Bible is as analytically nonsensical as are the dualistic
and existential assumptions upon which the attempt rests.
We shall proceed to make this point through an examination of four major anti-inerrancy inspiration-claims; these
four positions, it is believed, cover the gamut of non-
verbal-inspiration views in contemporary Protestantism.

(I.) "Holy Scripture is inspired, not in conveying inerrant propositions about God and the world, but in acting
as a vehicle for true Christian existential experience."
This is, in substance, the position taken by Bultmann
and by those who follow in his train. For Bultmann, "self-
understanding of one's existence" arises from the
kerygma of the primitive church; for the "post-Bultmannians," who, like Günther Bornkamm, Käsemann,
Fuchs, and Ebeling, are engaged in a "new quest of the
historical Jesus," this "self-understanding" arises from
a correlation between our personal existential situation
and Jesus' own self-understanding of *His* existence.[43]
But both Bultmann and his former disciples accept in
general the same critical presuppositions and existential
aprioris; for both, inerrancy is a hopeless, pre-existential
identification of truth with propositions instead of with
vital existential experience.

This approach to biblical inspiration is seen, on
analysis, to be completely unverifiable and therefore nonsensical. For what is meant by "Christian existential experience"? And what gives one any reason to suppose
that the Bible will serve instrumentally in promoting it?
To determine what "Christian existential experience" is,
one would have to define it in propositional terms (but
"propositions" are ruled out in the original statement
of the view!), and one would have to set up criteria for
distinguishing truly salvatory experience from non-
salvatory experience, and the Bible from other, non-
existentially pregnant religious works (but all objective
tests are ruled out by the existential refusal to employ
the objective-subjective distinction!). Thus one is left in

a morass of untestable subjectivity.

C. B. Martin, in discussing this problem of "a religious way of knowing," asks how one can know whether someone has a direct experience of God—or how the believer himself can know if he has this direct experience. Martin correctly points out that the claim to immediate existential experience on a believer's part is not analogous to experience claims in general, and is *per se* analytically meaningless.

> In the case of knowing a blue sky in Naples, one can look at street signs and maps in order to be sure that this is the really blue sky in question. It is only when one comes to such a case as knowing God that the society of tests and check-up procedures that surround other instances of knowing, completely vanishes. What is put in the place of these tests and checking procedures is an immediacy of knowledge that is supposed to carry its own guarantee.[44]

In actuality, however, "tests and checking procedures" for truly Christian existential experience have not "vanished"; they have been obliterated by those who refuse to take the objective fact of an inerrant Bible seriously. It is only a Bible capable of standing the acid test of objective verifiability that will provide the "map" of God's blue sky of religious truth. And apart from such a map, the domain of immediate religious experience will forever remain a *terra incognita* of confusion and meaninglessness.

(II.) "Holy Scripture is inspired, not in its scientific or historical statements, but in the theological truths it conveys." Relatively few Lutherans on the American scene are prepared to move fully into the Bultmannian position on Scripture represented by anti-inerrancy argument (I.). The more usual approach among American Lutheran theologians who would bring the Church out of "captivity" to verbal inspirationism is to argue for a distinction between the religious and the non-religious content of the Bible: the former is indeed inspired and fully reliable, while the latter is subject to the human fallibility which besets all of man's undertakings.[45]

The problem here is twofold: first, how do we distinguish the religious from the historical-scientific (including the sociological and the moral!) element in the

Scriptures? And, second, how do we show that the "theological" affirmations of the Bible are indeed inspired of God? The first of these questions we postpone temporarily—for consideration in the next section of this paper, where it will be shown that a dichotomy between "sacred" and "secular" is antithetical to the very heart of the Biblical faith. The second question alone, however, sufficiently reveals the meaninglessness of anti-inerrancy argument (II.). For here, obviously, one again encounters Dualism: a split between eternity (the theological element in the Bible: the *Heilsgeschichte*) and time (the scientific-historical content of Scripture: *Historie*).

An effort is being made to free the Bible from secular criticism; in effect, the proponents of this view argue, "It doesn't matter what historical and scientific errors, or what internal contradictions, are discovered in the Bible; its theological truth stands firm!" But note well: every theological "truth," to the extent of its isolation from empirical reality, becomes unverifiable and therefore meaningless. As one approaches the realm of idealistic "Absolutes," refutability does indeed become less and less possible, but this chimerical advantage is achieved by the corresponding loss of meaningful relevance. The (theoretical) possibility of proving a claim *wrong* is the *sine qua non* for the claim's meaningfulness, since those assertions which are so separated from the world that they are devoid of testability are a waste of time to discuss, except in psychological or sociological terms. The theologian who pleads for a "theologically inspired," historically errant Bible pleads a meaningless case, for insofar as theological truths are removed from the world of testable experience, nothing at all can be said of their truth-value. Like the "eternal truths" of Tantrism, such "theological truths" of Christianity might as well remain unexpressed. In avoiding the necessary offense of defending the Bible's historical and scientific content, the dualistic theologians have succeeded in rendering the Bible utterly irrelevant.

It should, moreover, be a sobering thought to those who have accepted the above-described dualistic approach in principle to be reminded that, carried to its logical conclusion, such dualism will eventually necessi-

tate the denial of infallibility *even to the "theological"
content of Scripture.* Why? because the "theological,"
just like the "historical-scientific," element of the Bible
was conveyed to human agents (the biblical writers) and
therefore (on the dualistic apriori) must also have been
touched by human fallibility. Martin Scharlemann over-
looks this point completely when he argues:

> The very limitations of the individual authors in terms
> of language, geographical, historical, and literary knowl-
> edge testify to the specifics of divine revelation. This is
> part of the "scandal" of the Bible. An insistence on its
> "inerrancy" is often an attempt to remove this obstacle.
> The use of the term almost invariably results in a docetic
> view of the Bible and so tends to overlook the fact that our
> Sacred Scriptures are both divine and human docu-
> ments.[46]

Actually, if one is to avoid all "docetism," the inevitable conclusion is that even in its theological affirmations
the Bible is touched by the fallibility of its human writers
(or perhaps *especially* in its theological affirmations,
since these evidently constitute the major part of the
Bible??).

Paul Tillich does not blink at the consequences of such
a consistent (though, as we have seen, meaningless!) dualism; for him, *everything* in the Bible must in theory at
least stand under judgment. Nothing on earth can be identified fully with Being Itself which constitutes the only
true "ultimate concern." This is Tillich's "Protestant
principle": "The only infallible truth of faith, the one
in which the ultimate itself is unconditionally manifest,
is that any truth of faith stands under a yes-or-no judgment." [47] Thus the Bible loses even theologically normative force; and what then constitutes the basis of "yes-or-
no judgment" in religion? Clearly, as Professor Gordon
Clark has argued in reference to Barth's theology, one
must then accept as a norm or canon, "something or
other external to the Bible"; and "since this external
norm cannot be a wordless revelation, for a wordless
revelation cannot give us the necessary information, it
must be secular science, history, or anthropology." [48]
The result is a reduction of special revelation to a vague
and secularistic "natural revelation," which lands us
again in the hopeless maze of unreconstructed Modern-

ism. From the heights of the Unconditioned we are plummeted to the depths of a world lacking any inspired word from God. Such is the inevitable effect of analytically nonsensical revelational dualisms.

(III.) "Holy Scripture is inspired, not as a conveyer of infallible information, but insofar as it testifies to the person of Our Lord and Savior Jesus Christ." Tillich himself employs this approach when he identifies (but symbolically only, to be sure) the "yes-or-no judgment" on all things human with "the Cross of the Christ." But it is especially the contemporary Lutheran anti-inerrantists who present argument (III.), since they—in spite of Reu's impeccable historical case[49]—hold that Luther himself took this position. Writes M. Scharlemann: Biblical "knowledge is not a matter of acquiring information but of being confronted with God Himself as He is revealed in His Son." [50] Robert Schultz expresses his "hope that Lutheran theologians generally will move back through the accumulated traditions of verbal inspiration and re-appropriate Luther's dynamic insight that the Scripture is that which teaches Christ." [51]

Argument (III.) incorporates the existential element from argument (I.) and the dualistic element from argument (II.)—thus acquiring a double dose of analytical meaninglessness. The argument must be regarded as dualistic if it is not to avoid condemnation for simple circularity: the "Jesus Christ" spoken of must be a *geschichtlicher* "Christ of faith," not a *historischer* "Jesus of history," for the latter would be describable propositionally and subject to inerrancy tests—which obviously would defeat the whole point of the argument. The idea here, as in argument (II.), is to raise biblical inspiration beyond the level of historical, scientific judgment by focusing it upon a Christ-figure who stands above the realm of verifiability. But, as emphasized in analyzing argument (II.), such supra-empirical claims by definition pass into irrelevant nonsense; and, as we shall see in the next section of this paper, a "Christ" of this kind is theologically nonsensical as well, for the biblical Christ entered fully into the empirical sphere, subjecting Himself to the full "offense" of verifiability.

The existential side of argument (III.) is pointed up

in its anti-"informational" character; scriptural inspiration allegedly leads to confrontation with Christ, not to theological data. But, as we saw in our discussion of argument (I.), meaningful "confrontation" is possible only on the basis of verifiable data—for otherwise, there is no way of knowing whether one has engaged in a real confrontation at all! Particularly in the realm of religion it is desperately important to know the difference (to speak irreverently but precisely) between Christ-in-the-heart and heartburn. Apart from an objectively reliable, inerrant biblical description of Christ, the result is always, on the part of sinful man, the creation of subjective Christs to fit one's needs. This has, in fact, been the tragic history of twentieth-century theology: the creation of God in our philosophical or cultural image instead of the straightforward acceptance of His portrait of us and of His salvation for us as presented in Holy Writ.[52]

Schultz is, we fear, unaware of the ghastly implications of his position when he expresses the hope "that Lutherans will once again find themselves bound to all in Scripture and tradition that teaches Christ, compelled to change all that is contrary to Christ, free to use creatively everything that does not matter, as well as to create new tradition."[53] What, we ask, will serve as the criterion for determining what in Scripture is "contrary to Christ" and "does not matter"? for setting the pattern of scriptural "change"? for the "creative use" of the "unimportant" in the Bible? Obviously not the biblical Christ Himself, who was concerned about the inerrancy even of scriptural jots and tittles! The theological criterion has clearly become an existential Christ-in-the-heart, who, because of his nonpropositional, analytically indefinable character, can take on, chameleonlike, the qualities of his spokesman. Perhaps we are not as far away as we think from the *Deutsche Christen* of the Third Reich, whose "Christ" conveniently supported all aspects of their demonic ideology? It is well not to forget that from analytical meaninglessness, as from logical contradiction, *anything* can be "deduced," depending on the predilections, conscious or unconscious, of the deducer.

(IV.) "Holy Scripture *is* inerrant, but in its intent—in its dynamic ability to fulfil God's purposes—not in its

static accord with objective scientific or historical fact."
Here we consider an argument which would not deserve
attention were it not for its deceptive quality. Argument
(IV.) in reality says nothing which has not already been
expressed more directly in the preceding three arguments. However, it conceals its analytic meaninglessness
under the guise of the word "intent."

The question, of course, is not whether the Bible infallibly or inerrantly achieves the purposes for which God
intended it; the orthodox Christian would be the last to
deny this. The question is simply: How does one determine
God's intent? Only two answers are possible: from an
inerrant revelation, or from a source or sources external
to special revelation. The former answer is hardly what
the proponent of argument (IV.) wants; his purpose in
stating the argument is to move away from propositional
inerrancy to an "inerrancy" which will focus on "theological" considerations, or on "existential experience,"
or on "personal encounter with Christ"—i.e., on the existential-dualistic affirmations of arguments (I.), (II.),
and (III.). Scripture is "inerrant" only when it achieves
the purpose which *he* (the non-plenary inspirationist) accepts as appropriate to it.

Thus, again, we encounter the analytical nonsense of
Dualism and Existentialism, and the subtle importation
of non-revelational considerations by which revelation is
judged. In point of fact, only God's Word is capable of
indicating God's intent; and if this Word is not propositionally inerrant and perspicuous, man will never know
the Divine intent in general—to say nothing of His intent
as regards Holy Writ itself! But a study of the totality
of Scripture confirms the historic claim of the Church
that God intended by His special revelation to convey
the truth of Christ within the solid framework of, and
confirmed by, the entire truth of an infallibly inspired
Bible.[54]

In our discussion of arguments (III.) and (IV.), we
have referred in passing to Christ's view of the Bible
and the Bible's own attitude toward itself. These references lead us quite naturally to a theological evaluation
of non-inerrancy views of scriptural inspiration. We have
found that analytically such views are nonsensical; it

now remains for us to see that from the standpoint of biblical theology also they are without any genuine meaning.

The Theological Meaninglessness of a "Non-Inerrant Inspired Scripture"

Advocates of the anti-inerrancy positions discussed in the preceding sections of this paper are united in their contention that the Bible itself, and Christ its Lord, present a "dynamic," "personalized" view of truth which is irreconcilable with the propositional, objectively historical approach to truth characteristic of plenary inspirationists. Emil Brunner, for example, asserts: "In the time of the apostles as in that of the Old Testament prophets, divine revelation always meant the whole of the divine activity for the salvation of the world. Divine revelation is not a book or a doctrine." [55] Frequently appealed to in support of this contention is Albrecht Oepke's article in Kittel's *Woerterbuch,* where one is told that in the Bible "revelation is not the communication of rational knowledge" but rather "Yahweh's offering of Himself in mutual fellowship." [56] Though James Barr's revolutionary book, *The Semantics of Biblical Language,* has decisively shown that Neo-Orthodox, "biblical-theology-movement" apriori, rather than linguistic objectivity, lies at the basis of such articles as Oepke's,[57] the general question remains as to whether the biblical view of revelation is anti-objective, anti-propositional. It is worthwhile noting that if the latter is the case, then the Bible, like many of its modern interpreters, will pass into the never-never land of analytical meaninglessness, for its content will be devoid of testability; like the Scriptures of the Eastern religions, its "truth" will be "known" only to those who read it through the glass of prior belief—and it will say nothing to all those who, not having had an (indefinable, unverifiable) experience in relation to it, are understandably wary of such "experiences"!

But in fact the Bible does not operate within an existential-dualistic frame of reference. Fundamental to the entire biblical revelation are the twin convictions that subjective truth is grounded in and verifiable through objective truth, and that the eternal has been made manifest in the temporal.

Consider such prominent Old Testament events as Gideon and the fleece (Judges 6) and Elijah on Mount Carmel (I Kings 18). Gideon, realizing how easy it is to deceive oneself in matters of subjective religious assurance, asks an objective sign from God by which he can know that the Lord will deliver Israel from her enemies. God willingly complies, not once but twice: first, dew falls on Gideon's fleece but not on the surrounding ground; second, dew falls on the ground but not on the fleece. The point? Gideon, like any spatio-temporally bound member of the human race, was incapable of knowing by subjective, existential immediacy that the voice within him was God's voice; yet he had to know, for the lives of others as well as his own safety depended upon his ability to make a true religious judgment. In this quandary, God provided Gideon with external evidence—in concrete, empirical terms—showing that it was indeed He who spoke within Gideon's heart.

Elijah was faced with a common religious problem— one which existential immediacy is totally unable to solve. This is the problem of conflicting religious claims. The "false prophets" said one thing to the people; Elijah said another. How were the people to know who was proclaiming God aright and who was the idolater? An objective test was the only way of ridding the situation of endless confusion and meaningless claims. So Elijah gave the false prophets the opportunity to demonstrate the "reality" of their God through his ability to perform an act of divine power on earth. The inability of the false prophets' truth-claim to hold up under such a test, when coupled with Yahweh's positive response to the identical test, provided the needed ground for belief in the true God.

Such examples could be multiplied in the Old Testament, but let us now turn to our Lord's own attitude toward religious verifiability. A close look at a frequently misunderstood event in His public ministry will be especially revealing. In all three Synoptic Gospels (Mt. 9; Mk. 2; Lk. 5) Jesus' healing of the palsied man is recorded in similar detail; here is the Marcan account:

> And again he entered into Capernaum after some days;
> and it was noised that he was in the house. And straightway
> many were gathered together, insomuch that there was no
> room to recieve them, no, not so much as about the door;
> and he preached the word unto them. And they come unto
> him, bringing one sick of the palsy, which was borne
> of four. And when they could not come nigh unto him for
> the press, they uncovered the roof where he was; and when
> they had broken it up, they let down the bed wherein the
> sick of the palsy lay. When Jesus saw their faith, he said
> unto the sick of the palsy, Son, thy sins be forgiven thee.
> But there were certain of the scribes sitting there, and
> reasoning in their hearts, Why doth this man thus speak
> blasphemies? who can forgive sins but God only? And
> immediately when Jesus perceived in his spirit that they
> so reasoned within themselves, he said unto them, Why
> reason ye these things in your hearts? Whether is it
> easier to say to the sick of the palsy, Thy sins be forgiven
> thee; or to say, Arise, and take up thy bed, and walk?
> But that ye may know that the Son of man hath power
> on earth to forgive sins, (he saith to the sick of the palsy,)
> I say unto thee, Arise, and take up thy bed, and go
> thy way into thine house. And immediately he arose, took
> up the bed, and went forth before them all; insomuch that
> they were all amazed, and glorified God, saying, We never
> saw it on this fashion.

It is generally assumed that the answer to Jesus' question,
"Is it easier to say, Thy sins be forgiven, or Take up
thy bed and walk?" is "Take up thy bed and walk."
Quite the opposite is the case. Perhaps it is easier to
restore a sick man to health than to forgive sin, but Jesus'
question has to do, not with acts but with *claims;* Jesus
asks, not "Which is easier?" but "Which is easier *to
say?*" Clearly it is easier to *claim* to be able to forgive sin than to be able to restore a palsied man to health
miraculously, for the former is a theological affirmation
which cannot *per se* be subjected to verification.

So what does our Lord do? Does He leave His forgiveness claim in the realm of the unverifiable, as have
numerous religious leaders through the ages? By no
means; he connects the theological claim with an empirical claim whose verifiability is not only possible but inevitable. The argument thus runs: "You do not believe that
I can forgive sins. Very well; I cannot show you that
directly. But if I show you that I can, by my Divine
power, remedy the empirical sickness that connects with

the sin problem, will you have any reason left for denying
my power to work in the theological sphere?" The empirical, objective healing of the palsied man was performed
that men might "know that the Son of man hath power
on earth to forgive sins"—a fact that, had our Lord not
coupled it with an objective test, could have been dismissed as meaningless and irrelevant by those who had
doubtless heard such claims many times before. In
precisely the same way does the New Testament present
Christ's resurrection as the objective ground for belief
in the theological significance of His death on the
Cross.[58]

The picture of the biblical conception of truth drawn
from the foregoing passages is in no way altered by Jesus'
affirmations, "I am the Truth" (Jn. 14:6), and "Everyone who is of the truth hears my voice" (Jn. 18:37), or
by any other "personalized" references to truth in the
Bible. Of course such statements are part of the scriptural
revelation; plenary inspirationists have never denied their
existence or importance. The question is not whether truth
is ever conceived of personally in the Bible, but whether
it is *only* conceived of personally there. We contend that
the biblical view of truth requires subjective (existential,
if you will) truth to be grounded in objective, empirical
facticity—for only then can existential truth be distinguished from existential error. Jesus' claim to be the
Truth hardly warrants the conclusion that the facticity
of His earthly acts, or the precise varacity of His words,
is unimportant. Quite the contrary: It is the truth of His
acts and words that drives us to commit our lives to
Him as the only final answer to man's quest for Truth.

The biblical conception of truth not only stands over
against analytically nonsensical existentialisms; it categorically opposes the equally meaningless notion of a
dualistic split between the "theological" and the "histori-
cal/empirical" or between "personal encounter" and "objective facticity." Here, indeed, we find ourselves at the
very heart and center of the Christian faith: the doctrine
of Incarnation. According to biblical teaching, the Old
Testament revelation typologically introduces, and the
New Testament writings express the fulfilment of, the
genuine Incarnation of God in human history. The Pro-

logue of John's Gospel summarizes this superlative teaching in the simple words: ὁ λόγος σὰρξ ἐγένετο. As the Ecumenical Creeds of the Church consistently testify, this
Incarnation was in every sense a real entrance of God
into the human scene; the gap between eternity and time
was fully bridged in Christ.

The soteriological necessity of this act has often been
stressed through Christian history,[59] but at the same
time the epistemological need for the Incarnation ought
never to be forgotten. Apart from empirical confrontation
with God in Christ, man's religious aspirations and conceptions would have forever remained in the realm of
unverifiable meaninglessness. This is why throughout the
New Testament the Apostles place such powerful stress
on having "seen with their eyes" and "touched with their
hands" the incarnate Word.[60] The biblical message
recognizes finite man's need to "try the spirits" representing diverse religious claims and ideologies; and the
only meaningful test is objective verifiability: "Every
spirit that confesseth that Jesus Christ is come in the
flesh is of God" (I Jn. 4:1-3).

In biblical religion it is impossible to conceive of theological truth divorced from historical, empirical truth;
this divorce would destroy the whole meaning of Incarnation. The theological truths of Scripture are thus inextricably united with earthly matters, and the truth of the
one demands the truth of the other. The Bible recognizes
as fully as does analytical philosophy that to speak of
"theological truth" or of "existential encounter with God"
apart from empirical veracity is to speak nonsense. When
Bishop Wand asserts that "there is no external guarantee
of inspiration," [61] he is asserting just such nonsense,
for without the "external guarantee" of empirical facticity, "inspiration" becomes no more than an emotive
plea—on the same level with the innumerable and conflicting immediacy claims to inspiration by religious
fanatics.

Even Beegle, in his recent attempt to demolish biblical
inerrancy, admits that "subjective truth cannot occur
without some minimal amount of objective truth";[62]
but here he gives his whole case away. For what amount
of objective truth is "minimal"? The Bible declares, as

does analytic philosophy, that only where objective truth is unqualifiedly present can one avoid meaninglessness on the subjective side. Thus the "minimum" is unrestricted objective truth, which, in the case of the Christian revelation, means nothing less than an inerrant Bible. For wherever the Scripture were to err objectively, there doubt would be warranted subjectively; and wherever the word of Scripture were to carry historically or scientifically erroneous ideas, there the reader would have every right to reject the theological affirmations, which, in the very nature of God's revelation, are inextricably entwined with empirical facts.[63]

And here, like it or not, we arrive at verbal inspiration, for, as contemporary linguistic analysis has so fully demonstrated, every genuine word carries genuine meaning and influences the context in which it is used. Therefore, each "jot and tittle" of Scripture has an impact, however slight, on the totality of the Bible; and this impact must be either for good or for ill. On the basis of the thoroughgoing incarnational theology of the Bible, we can affirm that the verbal impact is always veracious, not only theologically but also in all other aspects touched. For, in the final analysis, the biblical theology that centers on Christ the incarnate Word knows no distinction between "other aspects of life" and the religious: biblical truth is holistic, and its claim to theological validity is preserved from meaninglessness by its verifiability in the empirical domains that it touches.[64]

A Final Clarification and Caveat

It has been not infrequently argued by those who would move Lutheranism away from the inerrancy view of biblical inspiration that the Lutheran Church is fortunate in lacking explicit statements on verbal inspiration in its historic creeds. We are informed that it is to our advantage that, unlike the Calvinists, our creeds contain no assertions concerning "the entire perfection" and "infallible truth" of Scripture.[65] Therefore, the argument continues, we are free to embrace fully, without loss of intellectual integrity, the non-propositional, non-verbal view of inspiration which has become so popular in recent years.

The analytical discussions comprising the bulk of this

paper should have prepared us to see the fallacy in this superficially attractive line of reasoning. Let us see what the last of the Reformation Lutheran Confessions, the *Formula of Concord*, does say on the subject of biblical inspiration. The Formula's position in this matter is drawn from Luther:

> [Luther] diesen Unterscheid ausdrücklich gesetzt hat, dass alleine Gottes Wort die einige Richtschnur und Regel aller Lehre sein und bleiben solle, welchem keines Menschen Schriften gleich geachtet, sondern demselben alles unterworfen werden soll.
>
> Hoc discrimen (inter divina et humana scripta) perspicue posuit, solas videlicet sacras litteras pro unica regula et norma omnium dogmatum agnoscendas, iisque nullius omnino hominis scripta adaequanda, sed potius omnia subiicienda esse.
>
> Luther explicitly made this distinction between divine and human writings: God's Word alone is and should remain the only standard and norm of all teachings, and no human being's writings dare be put on a par with it, but everything must be subjected to it.[66]

Here, it is true, there is no reference to infallibility or inerrancy. Yet the Scriptures are declared to be the "only standard and rule," to which all other writings must be "subordinated." Clearly, the Bible is held to stand in judgment over all other books—in all fields—and no man is permitted to judge the Scripture in any particular. Such a view of biblical authority differs in no way from the verbal inspiration position set out in this paper.

And, indeed how could it, if Luther and the theologians of the Confessions understood the implications of scriptural inspiration? We have seen that the incarnational theology of the Bible demands the plenary truth of Scripture that the "historical-empirical" elements in the Bible must be regarded as no less veracious than the "theological" truths intimately bound up with them and epistemologically dependent upon them. Though the Lutheran fathers were not acquainted with the technical concept of analytic. meaninglessness, they understood the Bible too well to believe that it would retain its theological value if its truthfulness in other particulars were impugned. The writers of the Lutheran Confessions did not face the epistemological issue of biblical reliability that we face today, but they knew full well that to allow the

Scriptures to fall under *any* kind of negative criticism would tear the foundation out of all meaningful theology. That "the Word was made flesh" gripped them too powerfully to permit their losing the objective veracity of God's revelation.

Today the winds of philosophical change are veering away from existentialistic and dualistic world-views. The analytical tradition has delivered mortal body-blows to these metaphysical *Weltanschauungen*. And within the realm of analytical philosophy itself, every year that goes by sees greater stress placed upon "words," "language," and "propositions." [67] How unfortunate it would be if now, when the presuppositions of the anti-verbal inspirationists have been thoroughly undermined along with the aprioris of Existentialism and Dualism, and a new era of appreciation for the verbal proposition is on the horizon, Christians in the Reformation tradition should sell their biblical heritage for a mess of outdated philosophical pottage. In the Bible and in the Christ to whom it testifies God has given a πλήρωμα of meaningfulness. May we not lose it in chasing the phantoms of analytical nonsensicality.

Notes

[1] James Orr, *The Progress of Dogma* (4th ed.; London: Hodder & Stoughton [1901]), *passim*. The lectures comprising this book were originally delivered in 1897. Orr was Professor of Apologetics and Systematic Theology in the United Free Church College, Glasgow.

[2] In this connection it is instructive to note that a recurring theme in present-day "broad-church" Lutheran theological writing is that Bultmann should be regarded as a 20th-century Luther; as Luther directed men from ethical works-righteousness to the saving Christ, so it is argued, Bultmann points men from intellectualistic works-righteousness (i.e., relying on an inerrant Bible) to Christ. (See, for a typical statement of this view, Robert Scharlemann, "Shadow on the Tomb," *Dialog*, I [Spring, 1962], 22-29; and cf. Thomas C. Oden, "Bultmann As Lutheran Existentialist," *Dialog*, III [Summer, 1964,] 207-214.) This comparison has the single merit of emphasizing that, as justification was the key theological issue Luther faced, the Scripture problem is the theological

watershed of our time. Otherwise, the Luther-Bultmann parallel is completely wide of the mark. As I have written elsewhere: "Whereas Luther turned from moral guilt to confidence in the *objective* facts of Christ's death for his sin and resurrection for his justification, Bultmann turns from his intellectual doubts to *subjective* anthropological salvation—a direct about-face from the objective Gospel Luther proclaimed" (Montgomery, *The Shape of the Past* ["History in Christian Perspective," I; Ann Arbor, Michigan: Edwards Bros., 1963], p. 160).

 Roy A. Harrisville, "A Theology of Rediscovery," *Dialog*, II (Summer, 1963), 190.

 "Controversy on Inspiration," *Dialog*, II (Autumn, 1963), 273. The same editorial asserts that the inspiration controversy "is surely one of the emptiest"; if so, why devote a journal issue to an attempt to demolish the traditional position on inspiration?

 Of the Commission's *Report*, the *Dialog* editor writes: "The statement on biblical 'inerrancy' does not come off very well. Admittedly this is a sensitive question and an emotionally laden word in the Missouri Synod; and if public opinion is a determinant, one can understand why the only point raised against *A Brief Statement*—the official document of the Synod which describes the Scriptures as the infallible truth even in 'historical, geographical, and other secular matters'—is the question whether it 'does justice to the rich variety present in the content and mode of the utterances of the Scriptures.' But, synodical public opinion aside, the objection to that sentence in *A Brief Statement* surely is not that it is insufficient but that it is wrong; and the Report ought to say so" ("Right Key—Wrong Melody," *Dialog*, III [Summer, 1964], 165).

 Dewey M. Beegle, *The Inspiration of Scripture* (Philadelphia: Westminster Press, 1963), p. 187.

 Such a Bible could of course have a higher (quantative) degree of *literary* inspiration than the average book (cf. Shakespeare as compared with Mickey Spillane), but this is clearly not the type of "inspiration" with which any theologian (except the unreconstructed, pre-World War I liberal) is concerned.

 Warren A. Quanbeck, "The Bible," in *Theology in the Life of the Church*, ed. Robert W. Bertram (Philadelphia: Fortress Press, 1963), p. 23. This book is an outgrowth of the Conference of Lutheran Professors of Theology, and thus well reflects the general trends of Lutheran theological thought in America today.

 Robert Scharlemann, Letter to the Editor, *The Lutheran Scholar*, April, 1963.

¹⁰ John W. Haley, *An Examination of the Alleged Discrepancies of the Bible* (reprint ed.; Grand Rapids, Michigan: Baker Book House, 1958), p. 154.

¹¹ *Ibid.*, p. 153. Cf. also William F. Arndt, *Does the Bible Contradict Itself?* (5th ed.; St. Louis, Missouri: Concordia, 1955), pp. 51-53, 73-74; and Edward J. Young, *Thy Word Is Truth* (Grand Rapids, Michigan: Eerdmans, 1957), pp. 172-75.

¹² Andreas Althamer, *Conciliationes Locorum Scripturae, qui specie tenus inter se pugnare videntur, Centuriae duae* (Vitebergae:

Zacharias Lehman, 1582). This excellent work, of which I possess a personal copy, treats 160 "discrepancies" and went through at least sixteen editions (1st ed., 1527).

[13] A. Jaubert, *La Date de la Cène. Calendrier biblique et liturgie chrétienne* (Paris: Gabalda, 1957). I have treated this matter in some detail in my article, "The Fourth Gospel Yesterday and Today," (*Concordia Theological Monthly*, XXXIV [April, 1963], 206, 213) which is reprinted below in III. 5.

[14] For a semi-popular overview of this trend, see Werner Keller, *The Bible As History*, trans. William Neil (New York: William Morrow, 1956).

[15] On the invalidity of Hume's argument in light of the replacement of Newtonian by Einsteinian conceptions of scientific law, see Montgomery, *The Shape of the Past*, pp. 288-93; and C. S. Lewis, *Miracles* (New York: Macmillan, 1947), especially chap. xiii.

[16] I have discussed this matter in considerable detail in my lecture series, "Jesus Christ and History," delivered on January 29 and 30, 1963, at the University of British Columbia. These lectures have been reprinted in my book, *Where Is History Going?* (Grand Rapids, Michigan: Zondervan, 1969), and are also obtainable in pamphlet form (Address: *His* Reprints, 4605 Sherwood, Downers Grove, Illinois). See also in this connection, H. J. Rose, *Handbook of Greek Literature from Homer to the Age of Lucian* (London: Methuen, 1934), pp. 42-43; and A. H. McNeile and C. S. C. Williams, *Introduction to the Study of the New Testament* (2nd.; Oxford: Clarendon Press, 1955), pp. 52-58.

[17] If the Genesis 1-3 problem here comes to mind, the reader should consult such classic refutations of supposed "scientific error" in the biblical account as are found in two monographs of the American Scientific Affiliation: *Modern Science and Christian Faith* (2d ed., 1950) and *Evolution and Christian Thought Today* (2d ed., 1960).

[18] *Is the Bible Infallible? A Debate between John Wenham, Vice-Principal of Tyndale Hall, Bristol, and Rupert E. Davies, Tutor at Didsbury College, Bristol* (London: Epworth Press, 1959), p. 27.

[19] A. G. Hebert, *The Authority of the Old Testament* (London: Faber & Faber, 1947), pp. 306-307. Hebert's misrepresentations of biblical orthodoxy as "fundamentalism" have been decisively answered in J. I. Packer's *"Fundamentalism" and the Word of God* (Grand Rapids, Michigan: Eerdmans, 1958).

[20] Locke's statement is grounded in rationalism, not in empiricism, and as such offers no proper analogy to the biblical inerrancy position. Russell and Whitehead, in the *Principia Mathematica*, and Wittgenstein in the *Tractatus Logico-Philosophicus*, have shown that geometrical propositions are tautologous, i.e., that they have no necessary connection with "observable phenomena." Neither the biblical writers nor the plenary inspirationists have argued that biblical truth is mathematical/tautologous; rather, they have asserted that it is observationally reliable (as in the case of the historic revelation of Christ himself).

[21] Charles Joseph Costello, *St. Augustine's Doctrine on the Inspiration and Canonicity of Scripture* (Washington, D.C.: Catholic University of America, 1930), pp. 30-31. Costello's work constituted his thesis for

the doctorate in theology, and is fully grounded in the primary works of Augustine. It is noteworthy that Augustine, in the 5th century, effectively treated the Zacharias-Jeremiah "contradiction" which R. Scharlemann presented in 1963 as a decisive counter to biblical inerrancy! (see Costello, pp. 34-37, and cf. our text above at nn. 9-11).

[22] Quanbeck, op. cit., p. 25.

[23] Montgomery, "Karl Barth and Contemporary Theology of History," published in The Cresset, XXVII (November, 1963), 8-14, in the Bulletin of the Evangelical Theological Society, VI (May, 1963), 39-49, and now reprinted in Where Is History Going? (op. cit.). In this article I deal primarily with the baleful implications of the Geschichte-Historie dualism in christology and in theology of history.

[24] Martin H. Scharlemann, "The Bible As Record, Witness and Medium" (mimeographed essay), p. 11. The same approach is found in William Hordern's Case for a New Reformation Theology (Philadelphia: Westminster Press, 1959), where the amazingly circular statement appears: "Objectivity is possible only when there is a faith-commitment made to objectivity" (p. 44; cf. pp. 62-69).

[25] Cf. Jean Wahl, A Short History of Existentialism, trans. Forrest Williams and Stanley Maron (New York: Philosophical Library, 1949).

[26] Paul Tillich, "Existential Philosophy: Its Historical Meaning," in his Theology of Culture, ed. Robert C. Kimball (New York: Oxford University Press, 1959), p. 92.

[27] Ironically, to be sure, Existentialism has sought to destroy all metaphysical speculation, including Dualism. But since Existentialism itself has a metaphysic, it cannot successfully destroy metaphysics; and it often (as here) finds itself a strange bedfellow to other (uncongenial) metaphysical tendencies.

[28] For an introduction to these movements, see Victor Kraft, The Vienna Circle, trans. Arthur Pap (New York: Philosophical Library, 1953); G. J. Warnock, English Philosophy Since 1900 (London: Oxford University Press, 1958); and J. O. Urmson, Philosophical Analysis (New York: Oxford University Press, 1967).

[29] A. J. Ayer, Language, Truth and Logic (New York: Dover Publications, [1946]), p. 35. Since the publication of the first edition of his work (1936), Ayer has somewhat refined his statement of the "Verifiability Principle" (see his Introduction to the new edition, pp. 5-16); however, in substance, his original statement remains unaltered and its classic simplicity warrants its continued use.

[30] Attempts have been made, of course, to destroy the Verifiability Criterion. Few traditional, speculative philosophers have been happy with Feigl's remark that "Philosophy is the disease of which analysis should be the cure!" But the Verifiability Principle still stands as the best available road map through the forest of truth-claims. One of the most persistent attempts to refute the Criterion has been the effort to show that it is itself a meaningless assertion, being evidently neither an analytic nor a synthetic statement. However, this objection has been effectively met both by Ayer, who argues that the Criterion is actually a definition (op. cit., pp. 15-16) and by Hempel, who shows that it, "like the result of any other explication, represents a linguistic proposal

BIBLICAL AUTHORITY   353

which itself is neither true nor false" ("The Empiricist Criterion of
Meaning," published originally in the *Revue Internationale de Philosophie*, IV [1950], and reprinted, with newly appended remarks by the
author, in *Logical Positivism*, ed. A. J. Ayer [Glencoe, Illinois: Free
Press, 1959], pp. 108-129).

[31] The parable was told by Wittgenstein to Stout and is related
by Norman Malcolm in his *Ludwig Wittgenstein: A Memoir* (London:
Oxford University Press, 1962), p. 66.

[32] *Tractatus Logico-Philosophicus*, propositions 4.116 and 7.0 (cf.
Wittgenstein's "Vorwort"). For a discussion of these propositions in
light of the *Tractatus* as a whole, see Max Black's long awaited commentary, *A Companion to Wittgenstein's 'Tractatus'* (Ithaca, New York:
Cornell University Press, 1964), *passim*.

[33] This is a variation on Moritz Schlick's (now outdated!) propositional example: "There are mountains on the other side of the moon."

[34] Antony Flew, "Theology and Falsification," in *New Essays in
Philosophical Theology*, ed. Antony Flew and Alasdair MacIntyre (London, SCM Press, 1955), p. 96.

[35] This was shown in detail by Thomas H. Leith of York University,
Toronto, Canada, in a paper titled, "Some Logical Problems with the
Thesis of Apparent Age," delivered at the 19th Annual Convention of
the American Scientific Affiliation, August 27, 1964, and subsequently
published in the December, 1965, issue of the *Journal of the American
Scientific Affiliation* (cf. also the Letters to the Editor in the *JASA*
issue for June, 1966).

[36] Tillich, *Dynamics of Faith* (New York: Harper Torchbooks,
1958), p. 95.

[37] Cf. Jean-Paul Sartre, *Existentialism and Human Emotions* tr.
Bernard Frechtman and Hazel E. Barnes (New York: Philosophical
Library, 1957).

[38] Rudolf Carnap, "The Elimination of Metaphysics through Logical Analysis of Language," in *Logical Positivism*, ed. Ayer, pp. 69-73.
Carnap's paper originally appeared in German in Vol. II of *Erkenntnis*
(1932).

[39] Victor F. Lenzen, *Procedures of Empirical Science* ("International Encyclopedia of Unified Science," I/5; Chicago: University of
Chicago Press, 1938), p. 28. That the Heisenberg Indeterminacy Principle
does not in any sense break the subject-object distinction has been
shown by Lenzen and by many others.

[40] Sartre, *op. cit.*, p. 13.

[41] To avoid misunderstanding, I must anticipate myself by pointing
out here that my argument does *not* negate a "Christian existentialism"
(Christian subjectivity) *founded upon testable, objective considerations*
(specifically, upon an inerrant Scripture); indeed, I myself have made
much use of genuine Christian-existential categories (e.g., in my Strasbourg thesis for the degree of Docteur de l'Université, mention Théologie
Protestante, 1964). But it is this very idea of an objective basis for
existential subjectivity that the contemporary philosophical and theological existentialists decry; and this is the reason for my above-stated
counter to subjectivistic Existentialism. Apart from an objective foundation, all existentialism is analytically meaningless.

42 Cf. my *Chytraeus on Sacrifice* (St. Louis, Missouri: Concordia, 1962), p. 27.

43 Cf. the essays in Helmut Ristow and Karl Matthiae (eds.), *Der Historische Jesus und der kerygmatische Christus* (Berlin: Evangelische Verlagsanstalt, 1961).

44 C. B. Martin, "A Religious Way of Knowing," in *New Essays in Philosophical Theology*, ed. Flew and Macintyre, p. 83. See also my *Shape of the Past*, pp. 257-311.

45 This is the general position espoused in *Dialog*; see above, our text at notes 4 and 5.

46 M. Scharlemann, *op. cit.*, p. 14.

47 Tillich, *Dynamics of Faith*, p. 98.

48 Gordon H. Clark, *Karl Barth's Theological Method* (Philadelphia: Presbyterian and Reformed Publishing Co., 1963), p. 224.

49 M. Reu, *Luther and the Scriptures* (Columbus, Ohio: Wartburg Press, 1944), reprinted in *The Springfielder*, XXIV (August, 1960). Cf. my review of W. J. Kooiman's *Luther and the Bible*, in *Christianity Today*, VI (February 16, 1962), 498.

50 M. Scharlemann, *op. cit.*, p. 11.

51 Robert C. Schultz, "Scripture, Tradition and the Traditions: A Lutheran Perspective," *Dialog*, II (Autumn, 1963), 281.

52 When we do subject ourselves fully to the biblical testimony concerning Christ, we find, note well, that we must simultaneously accept the plenary inspiration and inerrancy of *all* of Scripture—for this was the belief of the biblical Christ Himself. This fact has been emphasized by numerous writers across the centuries; for a succinct marshalling of the evidence for it, see Pierre Marcel, "Our Lord's Use of Scripture," in *Revelation and the Bible*, ed. Carl F. H. Henry (Grand Rapids, Michigan: Baker Book House, 1958), pp. 119-34. Moreover, to employ kenotic arguments in an effort to lessen the binding force of Jesus' attitude toward Scripture is to board a vehicle whose logically inevitable destination is theological solipsism, since a Jesus who accommodates to the first-century thought world in one respect cannot be assumed to have stated any absolutes in other respects: thus all of Jesus' words lose binding force if His view of Scripture is not held to be normative.

53 Schultz, *loc. cit.*

54 On the Bible's view of itself, see B. B. Warfield's classic essays published under the title, *The Inspiration and Authority of the Bible* (Philadelphia: Presbyterian and Reformed Publishing Company, 1948). This volume is a new edition of Warfield's *Revelation and Inspiration*, published by Oxford University Press and now out-of-print.

55 Emil Brunner, *Revelation and Reason*, tr. Olive Wyon (Philadelphia: Westminster Press, 1946), p. 8.

56 *TWNT*, III, 575 (art. καλύπτω).

57 Barr takes Oepke as "a very bad example" of the absorption of philology by theological apriori in the *TWNT*. He shows that Oepke's ἀποκαλύπτω article "is assimilated to modern theological usage to a degree that the actual linguistic material will not bear" (*The Semantics of Biblical Language*[London: Oxford University Press, 1961], p. 230).

[58] See I Cor. 15, and cf. my University of British Columbia lectures (*op. cit.*).

[59] One thinks immediately of Anselm's *Cur Deus Homo?* and Aulén's *Christus Victor*. Cf. my *Chytraeus on Sacrifice (op. cit.)*.

[60] See, e.g., I Jn: 1:1-4, where existential "joy" (v. 4) is grounded in objective empirical contact with the incarnate Christ (vs. 1-3). Cf. also Jn. 20:24 ff.

[61] J. W. C. Wand, *The Authority of the Scriptures* (London: Mowbray, 1949), p. 61.

[62] Beegle, *op. cit.*, p. 191.

[63] The fallacy of "minimum" objective facticity has been implicitly recognized in Kaesemann's damning criticism of Bultmann's claim that Christian existential experience requires only the "thatness" of Jesus as a historical person—the mere fact that he existed. Says Käsemann (representing the "post-Bultmannian" reaction in contemporary European theology): Such minimal "thatness" will reduce the Christian gospel to a Gnostic redeemer myth and docetism.

[64] I am not arguing (note well) that empirical verifiability of the historical and scientific content of Scripture automatically produces subjective *commitment* to the truth of its religious claims. The Pharisees could (and doubtless many of them did) refuse to believe that Jesus was able to forgive sin even after he had healed the palsied man. However, only where objective verifiability is present can genuine faith be distinguished from blind faith. To engage in the existentialists' "leap of faith" is to topple headlong into the domain of analytic meaninglessness, where one man believes in "Christ" and another in a pantheon of six-headed monsters! Only biblical inerrancy preserves biblical faith from condemnation as nonsensically irrelevant.

[65] These phrases appear in the *Westminster Confession of Faith*, chap. i, sec. 5.

[66] *F. C.* (Sol. Dec.), Preface, para. 6.

[67] The analytical stage is now being occupied particularly by the "linguistic analysts," such as the "ordinary language philosophers" Ryle and Toulmin. Here also is to be classed the work of the later Wittgenstein (the posthumous *Philosophical Investigations*).

Inductive Inerrancy

In the months since the International Seminar on the Authority of Scripture that took place at Wenham, Massachusetts, during June of 1966, numerous articles and letters-to-editors have appeared dealing with biblical inerrancy. Having established a reputation for volubility at the seminar (Dr. Ockenga seemed ready to give me a prolixity prize at the final session), I find myself emotionally compelled to enter the post-mortem fray.

But what I have to say will be quite brief, since my concern is restricted to one key problem, which kept cropping up under various guises throughout the ten-day seminar: the question of induction vs. deduction in relation to the inerrancy of Scripture. I was amazed to find that a number of the seminar participants (generally exegetes) associated the historic Reformation, evangelical conviction that the Bible is factually errorless with a "deductive" process of reasoning from such passages as II Timothy 3:16, while preferring personally to leave the question of factual error open on the "inductive" ground that every problem passage of Scripture warrants interpretative consideration *sui generis*.

Such agruments have been making headway even without Dewey M. Beegle's *Inspiration of Scripture* (see *Christianity Today,* April 26, 1963). Thus Robert H. Mounce, in his June, 1966, *Eternity* article entitled "Clues to Understanding Biblical Accuracy," asks his readers the (to him) rhetorical question, "Are we to argue deductively that inspiration logically necessitates Cape Kennedy accuracy, or shall we adopt the inductive approach and ask Scripture to define its own terms?" In my judgment, even if we blast the "Cape Kennedy" straw man from this question, we are still left with a query as misleading as, "Have you stopped beating your wife?"

The great Wittgenstein, in a famous remark, claimed that the aim in philosophy is "to show the fly the way out of the fly bottle." Let's see if we can extricate the contemporary theological fly from the inductive-vs.-deductive fly bottle.

First and foremost, we must grant the priority of induction in setting out a doctrine of biblical inerrancy.

Why? Although all investigative operations involve the interplay of deduction and induction—together with a liberal dose of what Peirce called imaginative retroduction (see my paper, "The Theologian's Craft," reprinted in the present volume in III. 2)—only inductively justifiable results necessarily jibe with the phenomenal world. The only purely deductive procedures are logical or mathematical in nature, and they at best offer only a "scaffolding" for the world of fact, not an account of any particular facts. Independently of the Bible, no one has any right, on alleged "deductive" grounds, to pronounce on the nature of scriptural authority.

But (and a more important "but" cannot be imagined) to affirm the primacy of induction in the inerrancy issue in no way establishes the view that factual error can be compatible with a proper inspiration doctrine. "Induction" is not a monolithic, simplistic procedure in which one stares at one problematic fact at a time and then draws conclusions from these facts. Actually, one does not know how to treat particular factual problems until one has a *Gestalt* or pattern in which to fit them. This *Gestalt* is, of course, inductively derived from the material to be analyzed; but, since it provides the structure for understanding the particulars, its significance transcends that of the details. Unless it is properly induced, further induction will be fruitless.

Let us take some non-biblical literary examples. In understanding modern stream-of-consciousness writing (e.g., portions of James Joyce's *A Portrait of the Artist as a Young Man;* his *Ulysses;* parts of Faulkner's *The Sound and the Fury;* Salinger's *Catcher in the Rye*), the reader is hopelessly led astray by the indicia of the narrative until he discovers, through the express teaching of the novel, the actual age of the characters involved. Having learned this, he has an inductively derived *gestalt* for understanding the particular problems of the stream-of-consciousness narration; to reverse the procedure would be to lose all hope of meaningful interpretation.

The wild hilarity of Frederick C. Crew's *Pooh Perplex* (in which he "analyzes" *Winnie-the-Pooh* from the standpoint of "varying critical persuasions," such as the

Marxist and psychoanalytic literary schools) stems from an intentional overlooking of the *Gestalt* principle. Each interpreter hopelessly misconstrues *Pooh*, not because he doesn't employ genuine, inductively derived indicia from Milne's book, but because he never determines the *Gestalt:* the fact that *Winnie-the-Pooh* is a *children's book*, not a treatise on class war or the Oedipus complex.

To know how to treat biblical passages containing apparent errors or contradictions, we must determine what kind of book the Bible is. A doctrine of limited biblical authority derived from passages manifesting difficulties is as false an induction and as flagrant a denial of the analogy of Scripture as is a morally imperfect Christology derived from questionable acts on Jesus' part. In both cases, proper induction requires that we go to the express biblical teaching on the subject (Jesus' deity; Scripture's authority) and allow this to create the pattern for treating particular problems.

And how does one correctly determine the nature and extent of scriptural authority? Not by staring at genealogical difficulties or ancient king-lists as (to use Luther's figure) a cow stares at a new gate, but by going directly to the Bible's central character, Jesus Christ, who declared himself to be God incarnate by manifold proofs, and observing his approach to Scripture.

Christ's attitude toward the Old Testament was one of *total trust*: nowhere, in no particular, and on no subject did he place Scripture under criticism. Never did he distinguish truth "in faith and practice" from veracity in historical and secular matters, and he told the Evil Foe in no uncertain terms that man lives "by *every word* that proceedeth out of the mouth of God" (Matt. 4:4, quoting Deut. 8:3). To his apostles, under whose scrutiny the New Testament would be written, he promised his Holy Spirit, who "shall bring *all* things to your remembrance, whatsoever I have said unto you" (John 14:26, cf. II Pet. 3: 15, 16).

Inerrancy? Yes. Induction? Yes. The way out of the fly bottle? Approaching Scripture always and everywhere as did the Lord Christ.

The Relevance of Scripture Today*

Theology, no less than "secular" fields of endeavor, is subject to changing fashions in terminology. A semanticist could easily plot the course of 20th-century Protestant thought by analyzing the life cycle of in-group jargon such as "existential encounter" and "eschatological moment." Currently, no expression is quite as popular theologically as the word "relevance." On every hand—in book, magazine article, and sermon—we are told that the Christian faith and its Bible must be "made relevant to modern man."

The lengths to which contemporary churchmen are going in the quest for "relevance" seem endless; the March 10, 1967, issue of *Time* describes, under the appropriate rubric, "Secular Sermons," an Emory University chaplain who projected illustrations from *Playboy* onto the chancel wall as a backdrop for his Sunday sermon, and a Birmingham, Michigan, clergyman who passed out lumps of clay and cardboard to his congregations so that they could sculpt themselves.

Even within the Protestant theological establishment, the cult of relevance is beginning to call forth satire and parody—a sure sign that its coinage is in process of devaluation. Thus Robert McAfee Brown, in a chapter of his *Collect'd Writings of St. Hereticus* (1964), titled, "Making the Bible Relevant: Biblical Needs and How to Meet Them," offers a "relevant" retelling of the Easter story:

> But on the first day of the week, toward dawn, they arose and went to the garden in convertibles, ranch wagons, and Corvettes, wearing on their persons the spices they had prepared for the occasion. And behold, as the sun burst forth there was a great blast from four trumpets, drawn from the local high school marching band. And at the blast of the trumpets, an Easter bunny, wondrous large, stood before them. His appearance was like lightning, and his fur was white as snow. And he did carry a sign affixed to his hat bearing the words, "Courtesy of Jones's Department Store."

* An invitational presentation at the 7th General Assembly of the International Fellowship of Evangelical Students, held on August 9, 1967, in the Gemarker Kirche, Wuppertal-Barmen, Germany.

Brown notes, quite properly, that his contemporary "scripture lesson" is "sober and straightforward reporting of the various strata of twentieth-century religious insight." This is in point of fact the very difficulty in theologies of "relevance": they take modern man as normative and endeavor to reconstruct Christianity and the Bible in his cultural image. As I have written, modern theology has engaged in "an impossible attempt to make the Christian message fit the demands of the unregenerate man" (from "Renewal and Contemporary Theology," in *Why—in the World?*, ed. Harvey C. Warner [Waco, Texas: Word Books, 1965]; reprinted in the present volume as the last chapter; quoted in *Newsweek,* April 26, 1965).

It is the firm conviction of this writer that the Bible does not need to be "made relevant" to 20th-century man. Holy Scripture, as the utterance of the living God, is by its very nature the most relevant Word ever spoken. When Charles Finney was asked by a feverish young man how he could defend the Bible, the great evangelist replied: "How would you defend a lion? Let it out of its cage and it will defend itself!" Persuaded by the testimony of Scripture itself that God's word never returns void (Isa. 55:11) but is "quick, and powerful, and sharper than any twoedged sword" (Heb. 4:12), we shall endeavor to illustrate in the present essay that irrelevance exists not where a fully authoritative Scripture is proclaimed, but where it is denied: that in our age as in ages past the Bible meets the human situation in maximum relevance and power.

The Bible's Relevance in the Past

As background for any analysis of the Bible vis-à-vis contemporary life, one does well to note the testimonies to its relevance in former times. A common failing of men in every era is their naive belief that their own time constitutes a qualitatively different situation from all others, thereby rendering the biblical Word somehow irrelevant for them. In actuality, as Reinhold Niebuhr said in another connection, "the fabric of history is woven upon one loom" (*Christianity and Crisis,* May

4, 1942). Every period of history has had its special problems, but they are no different qualitatively from those of other eras, for man remains man. Throughout the centuries, the testimonies of those who have allowed the biblical message free rein in their lives show a remarkable similarity; they well illustrate that in spite of changing cultural conditions, man remains a sinner in desperate need of the Word of life. Consider a few typical examples.

In the 4th century Chrysostom voiced the common conviction of patristic Christianity as to the excellence of Holy Scripture:

> Yea, rather, the reading of the divine Scriptures is not a meadow only, but a paradise; for the flowers here have not a mere fragrance only, but fruit too, capable of nourishing the soul. Assuredly, then, we ought not hastily to pass by even those sentences of Scripture which are thought to be plain; for these also have proceeded from the grace of the Spirit; but this grace is never small nor mean, but great and admirable, and worthy the munificence of the giver; for pearls too, take their price, not from the size of the substance, but from the beauty of it. Even so is it with the reading of the divine Scriptures; for worldly instruction rolls forth its trifles in abundance, and deluges its hearers with a torrent of vain babblings, but dismisses them empty-handed, and without having gathered any profit, great or small.

Twelve centuries later the same reverence for the biblical Word infused the life and thought of the Reformers. Here are but a few of the remarks made by Luther concerning the Bible:

> No book, teaching, or word is able to comfort in troubles, fear, misery, death, yea, in the midst of devils and in hell, except this book, which teaches us God's Word and in which God Himself speaks with us as a man speaks with his friend (*W.A.* 48, 2).

> No book but Holy Scripture can comfort us. It alone has the title St. Paul gives it: "the book of comfort" [Rom. 15:4]. It can support the soul in all tribulations so that it does not give way to despair but keeps on hoping; for the soul apprehends the Word of God, in which it learns His gracious will, to which it firmly clings, and thus remains unshaken in life and death. But the man who does not know the will of God must doubt; for he does not know what his relation to God really is (*W.A.* 10I, 2, 75).

The Bible is the proper book for men. There the truth is distinguished from error far more clearly than anywhere else, and one finds something new in it every day. For twenty-eight years, since I became a doctor, I have now constantly read and preached the Bible; and yet I have not exhausted it but find something new in it every day (W.A. [Tischreden] 5, No. S193).

I beg and faithfully warn every pious Christian not to be offended by the simplicity of the language and the stories that will often meet him here. Let him not doubt that, however simple they may seem, they are the very words, works, judgments, and deeds of the exalted majesty, power, and wisdom of God. For this is the Writing that turns all the wise and prudent into fools and is an open book only to the small and foolish folk, as Christ says in Mt. 11:25. Therefore dismiss your own notions and feelings and think of this Writing as the most sublime, the most noble of holy things, as the richest of mines, which can never be entirely exhausted. Do this that you may find the wisdom of God which He here submits in a manner so foolish and simple in order to quench all pride. Here you will find the swaddling clothes and the manger in which Christ lies (W.A. [Deutsche Bibel] 5, 3).

Well after the onset of the modern secular era, 19th-century poet Heinrich Heine could still write of the Holy Scriptures:

What a Book! Vast and wide as the world, rooted in the abysses of Creation, and towering up behind the blue secrets of heaven. Sunrise and sunset, promise and fulfillment, birth and death, the whole drama of humanity, all in this Book!

And a few years after those lines were penned, the greatest saint of the century, Abraham Lincoln, addressed a letter to a Negro organization, in which, after discussing the issue of freedom ("it has always been a sentiment with me that all mankind should be free"), he spoke of the source of his religious and moral convictions:

In regard to this Great Book, I have but to say, it is the best gift God has given to man. All the good the Saviour gave to the world was communicated through this book. But for it we could not know right from wrong. All things most desirable for man's welfare, here and hereafter, are to be found portrayed in it.

Testimonies of this kind to the relevance of the scriptural Word through the ages could be multiplied virtually without limit. (Readers may wish to consult such collections as S. W. Bailey's *Homage of Eminent Persons to the Book* [1872] and D. W. Clark's *From a Cloud of Witnesses* [1897]). One could also set forth in detail the dynamic impact that Holy Writ has had upon man's life across the centuries; with David Mears (*The Deathless Book* [1888]), we could show that while other books have suffered from the temporal limitations of their human authors, the Bible, by virtue of its eternal Authorship, has acted as the most civilizing, radically transforming, and revolutionary piece of literature in every age and clime where it has penetrated.

At best such considerations would reduce the parochial arrogance of the modern man who assumes that the Scriptures have always been more or less irrelevant to basic human needs. But the marshalling of evidence for the Bible's impact on pre-20th century life would still leave the haunting question: Is the Bible relevant *today* —in the philosophical, religious, and cultural climate that will usher in century 21? Can a fully authoritative Scripture as witnessed to by historic evangelical Christianity, speak as cleaily to the needs of the present and the future as it evidently did to the needs of the past?

The Relevance of Scripture
in Today's Philosophical Climate

The great Anglican divine E. A. Litton emphasized the unanimity of all branches of the Christian Church in regard to the plenary inspiration of the Bible: "If there ever was a general consent of the Church Catholic on any question, it exists on this. East and West, from the earliest to the latest times, concurred in assigning to Scripture a pre-eminence which consisted in its being—as no other collection of writings is—the Word of God" (*Introduction to Dogmatic Theology*, ed. Philip E. Hughes [1960], p. 19). For classical Protestant theology, the Bible in its entirety is a message introduced by the eternal God into the human situation, and is therefore totally veracious both in its facts (its descriptive content) and in its values (its normative content). Moreover, having God as its Author, Scripture is a clear book whose teachings can be objectively determined through the study and comparison of one portion of the Bible with another. When the objective truths of God's Word—and particularly the factual reality of Christ's death for man's sin and resurrection for his justification—are brought to bear on human life, they have the power to transform existence totally: "If any man be in Christ," declares the Apostle, "he is a new creature: old things are passed away; behold, all things are become new" (II Cor. 5:17).

In a striking number of ways, this high view of biblical authority maintained by orthodox Protestantism can establish ideological links with the latest and most fruitful advances in contemporary philosophical thought. Orthodox Christians of the 19th and early 20th centuries had a hard row to hoe vis-à-vis the ideological climate of their day, for the 19th century was characterized by a philosophical idealism (Hegel and Bradley come immediately to mind) that confidently endeavored to set forth absolute truth apart from revelation, and, when these endeavors hopelessly failed, 20th-century existentialism (Heidegger, Sartre) gave up in principle the search for absolutes and substituted for objective truth and value a subjective relativism in which the individual determines the nature of his world through his own decisions. The 19th century tried to reach God through human reason, and the early 20th century, having failed in constructing this Tower of Babel and finding its language confused, gave up all hope of eternal truth and saw no other recourse than to make a philosophy of life out of the hopelessness of a confused existence. Both idealism and existentialism had been right and wrong simultaneously: idealism was right in believing that man desperately needed an absolute Word, but wrong in thinking that man could attain it by pulling himself to heaven by his own ideological bootstraps; existentialism was right in recognizing man's inability to arrive at absolute truth and value through his philosophical efforts, but wrong in giving up all hope of an eternal Word. The most recent developments in philosophical thinking point the way beyond this impasse and offer powerful testimony to the continuing relevance of the orthodox doctrine of biblical authority.

At the root of the new look in 20th-century philosophy

is Ludwig Wittgenstein (1889-1951), a strange, eccentric, passionate seeker after philosophical integrity who combined mathematical-logical genius with intense mysticism. Says Justus Hartnack—and he does not exaggerate —"Wittgenstein holds the key to modern philosophical activity." In his remarkable *Tractatus Logico-Philosophicus,* Wittgenstein effectively argued that "the sense of the world must lie outside the world" (6.41), that is, man never has sufficient perspective from within the world situation to build an eternal structure of truth and value. Absolute truth and eternal value, if they exist at all, must take their origin from outside the flux of the human situation.

This insight has revolutionized all branches of philosophy and has dealt a virtual deathblow to metaphysical idealism. Consider the realms of philosophy of history and ethics. The grandiose 19th- and early 20th-century attempts (Hegel, Spengler, *et al.)* to construct universally valid interpretations of history apart from revelation are now seen to be impossible in principle; the philosopher simply cannot gain the perspective outside the world needed to explain the human drama (cf. my article, "Where Is History Going?", *Religion in Life,* Spring, 1964; reprinted in my *Where Is History Going?* [Zondervan, 1969]). As Arthur C. Danto has shown, following in Wittgenstein's footsteps, the only "substantive philosophy of history" which is logically possible would be in reality *prophetic:* "It involves speaking in a prophetic vein, i.e. describing the present in the light of things which have not as yet happend ('Unto you a Saviour is born')" (*Analytical Philosophy of History* [Cambridge: Cambridge University Press, 1965], pp. 12-13).

Likewise in the realm of ethics. G. E. Moore, who considered Wittgenstein his best student and, with Bertrand Russell, examined him for his doctorate, labeled as the "naturalistic fallacy" any attempt to define "goodness' absolutely in the human sphere—particularly the attempt to create an absolute value system simply on the basis of what people do (*Principia Ethica,* chap. i). More recently, Kurt Baier, one of the foremost ethical thinkers to benefit from Wittgensteinian insights, has admitted that from within the human situation ethical values can never rise above the societal level: "Outside society, the very distinction between right and wrong vanishes" (*The Moral Point of View* [New York: Random House, 1965], p. 157). Human beings, in other words, are incapable of reaching absolute ethical norms by unaided reason; their ethic will always reflect their stance in society. As Wittgenstein put it in the *Tractatus:* "If there is any value that does have value, it must lie outside the whole sphere of what happens and is the case.... Ethics is transcendental" (6.41-6.421).

The plain consequence is that the only possible answer to modern man's quest for the ultimate meaning of history and for an absolute ethical standard would have to lie in a revelation from outside the world. If such a revelation does not exist, man will of logical (not merely practical) necessity remain forever bound to his cultural relativities, forever ignorant of life's meaning. But if such a revelation should exist, it would explode the world —turn it, as men said the early Christians did, upside down (Acts 17:6). Wittgenstein himself understood this very clearly, as one sees from the following passage in the only popular lecture he is known to have composed (the text remained unpublished until its appearance in the January, 1965, *Philosophical Review*):

> And now I must say that if I contemplate what Ethics really would have to be if there were such a science, this result seems to me quite obvious. It seems to me obvious that nothing we could ever think or say should be *the* thing. That we cannot write a scientific book, the subject matter of which could be intrinsically sublime and above all other subject matters. I can only describe my feeling by the metaphor, that, if a man could write a book on Ethics which really was a book on Ethics, this book would, with an explosion, destroy all the other books in the world.

It is the conviction of orthodox Christianity that in Holy Scripture just such a book exists: a Book "intrinsically sublime and above all other subject matters" because its Author is the transcendent Lord God, who is unconditioned by the human predicament that corrupts even our best attempts to find life's meaning, and who alone knows and is Absolute Truth.

But is the Bible the revelation Christians claim it is? Has it the power to explode the world of human speculation? Sad to say, neither Wittgenstein himself nor the analytical philosophy movement that stems from his work has seriously investigated the question (cf. Wittgenstein's *Lectures & Conversations on Aesthetics, Psychology and Religious Belief,* ed. Cyril Barrett [Oxford: Blackwell, 1966], pp. 57-59). In Wittgenstein's personal life, one sees only the profound and pathetic longings of one who recognized man's overwhelming need for a Word from God but did not think any avenue existed for its transmission; as his biographer Malcolm described it: "Often as we walked together he would stop and exclaim 'Oh, my God!', looking at me almost piteously, as if imploring a divine intervention in human events." But the analytical philosophy movement—Wittgenstein's continuing legacy—has provided the tools by which early 20th-century existential skepticism toward objective biblical truth can be effectively countered, and the fact of "divine intervention" through Scripture meaningfully proclaimed.

Characteristic of existential modes of thinking is Wilhelm Dilthey's historical relativism. Dilthey argued that the historian is never able to obtain a genuinely objective view of the past, for his own subjectivity inevitably enters into his investigations of earlier times. This viewpoint has been picked up by theological existentialists such as radical New Testament critic and demythologizer Rudolf Bultmann ("always in your present lies the meaning in history"), by post-Bultmannians such as Heinrich Ott ("the objective mode of knowledge is entirely inappropriate to historical reality because there are no such things as objectively verifiable facts"), and by death-of-God theologians such as Thomas J. J. Altizer (who, on the basis of his belief that objective knowledge of the past is impossible, freely creates a "hidden Christ" in terms of his own present experience).

The insights of Wittgenstein-inspired analytical philosophy have done much to show the fallacy in this kind of approach to historical reality and to the literary products of the past. Summarizing the results, J. W. N. Watkins notes that, over against the Dilthey tradition, analytical work by such philosophers as Ryle "dispels the old presumption . . . that to understand Ghengis Khan

the historian must be someone very like Ghengis Khan"
(*La Philosophie au milieu du vingtième siècle*, ed. R.
Klibansky [2nd ed.; Firenze, 1961-1962], III, 159). One can
most definitely arrive at an objective knowledge of a
Ghengis Khan—or of a Moses or of Jesus Christ! The most
recent and important collection of papers reflecting an
analytical approach to historiography is William H.
Dray's *Philosophical Analysis and History* (New York:
Harper, 1966); the essays by C. G. Hempel and J. A.
Passmore are especially devastating to the Dilthey-
existential variety of historical skepticism. Hempel's
closely reasoned paper on "Explanation in Science and
in History" demonstrates "the methodological unity of
all empirical science," i.e., the common ground between
scientific and historical investigations. Passmore, in his
essay on "The Objectivity of History," effectively argues
in the same vein that skepticism toward history will
necessarily involve one in skepticism both toward science
and toward one's present experience, resulting in total
solipsism; he concludes: "If we mean by 'science' the
attempt to find out what really happens, then history is
a science. It demands the same kind of dedication, the
same ruthlessness, the same passion for exactness, as
physics." Comparable realization in the literary field
that objectivity of interpretation is possible can be seen
in the work of the "neo-Aristotelians" such as Elder Ol-
son, who shows that existential blendings of literary
texts with their interpreters have produced "an endless
succession of free improvisations" instead of an objective understanding of the great literary products of the
past ("Hamlet and the Hermeneutics of Drama," *Modern
Philology*, February, 1964; cf. R. S. Crane, *Critics and
Criticism* [Chicago: University of Chicago Press, 1952]).
The biblical implications of this recovery of confidence
in historical and literary objectivity are no less than revolutionary: now the orthodox Christian claim that Scripture is objectively true historical revelation, capable of
yielding a clear message to all who without prejudice
study its literary content, must be taken with utmost
seriousness.

The analytical philosophy movement has provided
still another inestimable boon for evangelicals concerned

to maintain the classic view of biblical truth. Analytical philosophers have had much to say about "verifiability" and "meaningfulness"; they stress that truth-claims which are in principle unable to be confirmed or disconfirmed have no meaningful content. Philosopher Paul Edwards makes this point well in his critique of Tillich's theology (*Mind*, April, 1965):

> We normally regard as empty, as devoid of (cognitive) meaning or content a sentence which, while pretending to assert something, is on further examination found to be compatible with any state of affairs. If, for example, I say "Bomba is going to wear a red tie tonight" and if I do not withdraw my statement even if he shows up wearing a brown or a black or a grey tie, and if it further becomes clear that I will not consider my statement refuted even if Bomba wears no tie at all and in fact that I will consider it "true," no matter what happens anywhere, then it would be generally agreed that I have really said nothing at all.

Tillich and other contemporary theologians much influenced by existentialist modes of thought have been particularly prone to make religious statements that, being "compatible with any state of affairs" and totally without the possibility of confirmation or disconfirmation, are really meaningless. The attitudes toward Scripture taken by dialectic theologians such as Barth and by existential theologians such as Bultmann and his disciples precisely fit this category. For example, we are told that the Bible, though an erroneous book, is revelatory because "God encounters us there" (Barth) or because "self-understanding" occurs in contact with it (Bultmann) or because "the text interprets us" (Fuchs, Ebeling; cf. Merrill Abbey's *The Word Interprets Us* [1967]). These subjectivistic approaches to biblical inspiration are now revealed as hopelessly weak; they are in fact technically meaningless, for they are still maintained by the modern theologian regardless of the errors he purports to find in Scripture and regardless of the untestability of subjective experience.

The orthodox Christianity of the Reformers and of the evangelical divines has never fallen into this pit: orthodoxy has consistently affirmed that the dynamic effect of Scripture on man's personal life occurs because

Scripture is in fact objectively true. Personal truth is grounded in objective truth. Historic Christianity has always maintained a meaningful doctrine of inspiration which rests the case for the Bible's subjective validity on its *de facto* objective truthfulness. By a very precise and confirmable argument (the historical reliability of the New Testament documents *qua* documents; the demonstrable Deity of Christ in those records; Christ's stamp of approval on the Old Testament and his promise of identical, Spirit-led remembrance of His Word among the apostles under whose aegis the New Testament would be written), evangelical Christians offer to the world today the only meaningful revelation-claim for the truth of Holy Scripture.

Today, as never before, philosophical thought manifests a passion for objective, empirical truth, and the ordinary-language philosophers (whose work stems from Wittgenstein's *Philosophical Investigations*) are stressing the importance of verbal expression in conveying truth. Idealistic castles-in-air have been deflated and existential wanderings in the labyrinth of subjectivity have been discredited. Evangelicals of the second half of the 20th century have an unparalled opportunity to affirm the philosophical relevance of their high view of Scripture. The "divine intervention" for which Wittgenstein longed can with confidence be offered to modern man in the totally veracious, inscripturated Word of God.

The Relevance of Scripture for the Current Theological Situation

Protestant theology in the 1960's was characterized above all by the God-is-dead phenomenon. Though this movement, as represented particularly by Thomas J. J. Altizer and William Hamilton, had inherent instabilities which doubtless have shortened its ideological life, one must not underestimate its importance. As I have emphasized in my writings and debates on the movement, the death-of-God phenomenon reflects the increasing secularization of our time, which will certainly go on whether or not the theothanatologists retain their popularity; and, even more significantly, the God-is-dead movement demonstrates the consequences of the weak view of Holy

Scripture that has prevailed in Protestant theology since the advent of rationalistic biblical criticism. By noting the connections between God-is-dead thinking and destructive criticism of Holy Writ, we can see quite plainly how evangelical Christianity's belief in a totally authoritative Word has maximum relevance in a time of general theological collapse.

In a paper (see "The Death of God Becomes More Deadly" in I. 5 above) delivered at a program on radical theology sponsored by the University of Michigan's Office of Religious Affairs (October 28, 1966), William Hamilton unwittingly provided a laboratory example of how the demise of one's bibliology results in the demise of one's God. In answering the question, "Can you really maintain a loyalty to Jesus without a loyalty to God?" he said:

> Professor Altizer solves the problem more readily than I by his apocalyptic definition of Jesus, more Blakean than biblical, as the one who is born out of God's death. I am not yet ready to give up *sola scriptura* [!], and thus my answer must be more complex and tentative. . . . Early in the nineteenth century, we had to face, under the early impact of historical criticism, both that Jesus was firmly committed to demon-possession as the meaning of mental and physical illness, and that we were not so committed and needn't be. But obedience to Jesus was not destroyed. Later, at the time of Darwinian controversy, we had to face another instance of Jesus' full participation in the thought forms of his day—the three-story, primitive cosmology. But we do not go to the Bible for science, we were rightly told, and obedience to Jesus was not hurt. At the close of the century we had to face an even more disturbing fact—the fact brought before us by Weiss and Schweitzer that Jesus was completely committed to the apocalyptic views of the Judaism of his day. . . . If Jesus' demonology and cosmology and eschatology were taken as first-century views, appropriate then, not so now, needing reinterpretation and understanding but not literal assent, what is inherently different about Jesus' *theology*?

The significance of this argument for the current theological situation cannot be overestimated, for it explicitly maps the progressive demise of Christology through the consistent application of rationalistic biblical criticism. For over a century, orthodox Christians have vainly reminded their liberal confères of the Reformers' conviction that the "material principle" (the Gospel of

Christ) cannot possibly survive apart from "formal principle" (divinely inspired Scripture). "Fiddlesticks!" has been the reply: "*Of course* we can distinguish the true theological core of Scripture and the central message of Jesus from the biblical thought-forms of the ancient Near East." But in point of fact, as Hamilton well shows, the stripping of the cultural thought-forms from the "true" teaching of Scripture is like peeling an onion: when finished, you have no teaching at all, only tears (unless you happen to be a constitutional optimist like Hamilton, who finds mankind a satisfactory God-substitute).

Either Jesus' total teachings are taken as God's word (including His full trust in Scripture as divine revelation) or, as Luther well put it, "everyone makes a hole in it wherever it pleases him to poke his snout, and follows his own opinions, interpreting and twisting Scripture any way he pleases." The Bible has become just such a "wax nose" today, so that even a death-of-God theologian claims to follow *sola scriptura*. This is the inevitable outcome of rationalistic biblical criticism that refuses to distinguish between straightforward grammatical-historical explication of the biblical message and presuppositional judgment upon it. Has the time perhaps come for the Church to recognize that aprioristic biblical criticism has brought theology to the bier of Deity?

The path to solid ground is the doctrine of total biblical authority as taught by Christ Himself, at once the Lord of Scripture and its central figure. Dr. Kenneth Kantzer gives us weighty testimony in this regard from the critics themselves:

> H. J. Cadbury, Harvard professor and one of the more extreme New Testament critics of the last generation, once declared that he was far more sure as a mere historical fact that Jesus held to the common Jewish view of an infallible Bible than that Jesus believed in his own messiahship. Adolf Harnack, greatest church historian of modern times, insists that Christ was one with his apostles, the Jews, and the entire early church in complete commitment to the infallible authority of the Bible. John Knox, author of what is perhaps the most highly regarded recent life of Christ, states that there can be no question that this view of the Bible was taught by our Lord himself. The liberal critic, F. C. Grant, concludes that in the New Testament, "it is everywhere taken for granted that Scripture is trust-

worthy, infallible, and inerrant." Rudolph Bultmann, a radical anti-supernaturalist, but acknowledged by many to be the greatest New Testament scholar of modern times, asserts that Jesus accepted completely the common view of his day regarding the full inspiration and authority of Scripture.

If Christ did in fact "show Himself alive after His passion by many infallible proofs" (Acts 1:3), thereby validating His claims to Deity as He had predicted He would (Matt. 12:38-42; John 2:18-22), how can the Christian possibly rationalize a view of Scripture inconsistent with that of the Lord Christ? It will not do to argue in terms of modern "kenotic theory" that Jesus was limited or limited Himself to the thought forms of His day, for (as Hamilton has well demonstrated) such hypothetical limitations have no boundaries and are logically capable of reducing everything Jesus said to meaninglessness; moreover, as Eugene R. Fairweather concludes, after examining the whole kenotic question in detail: "It can hardly be claimed that Kenoticism is explicitly contained in the New Testament picture of Christ; rather, it depends on a complicated deduction, involving highly debatable presuppositions. . . . The Kenotic theory does not in fact vindicate the religious meaning of the Christian Gospel. On the contrary, in the severe words of Pius XII, it 'turns the integral mystery of the Incarnation and of redemption into bloodless and empty spectres' " (see Fairweather's appendix to F. W. Beare's *Philippians*).

Nor does one accomplish anything by endeavoring to maintain that Jesus stamped with approval only the "substance" or "message" of the Bible, not its "form" or "medium" (the former being absolute while the latter is culturally conditioned and therefore lacking in normative character). As contemporary communications specialist Marshall McLuhan has shown in his epochal works (*The Gutenberg Galaxy* and *Understanding Media: The Extensions of Man*), "the medium *is* the message": it is impossible to separate a message from its medium, since the medium makes an integral contribution to the very nature of the message. Orthodox Christianity has always recognized this in respect to Scripture: no "detail" of the Bible is unimportant; the literary form must itself be in-

spired in order for it not to detract from the message conveyed; every word of Scripture—every "jot and title"
of the text—has an impact, however slight, on the totality of the Bible, and this impact must, if Christ spoke
truly, be for good.

How pertinent and intensely practical this issue of
biblical authority is for the theology and personal Christian testimony of believers today was brought out recently by Donald R. Neiswender, one of my former students,
now a missionary in Japan. His "pilgrimage to faith in
the integrity of Scripture" is recorded in *Christianity
Today*, November 25, 1966; it warrants extended quotation here:

> More and more theologians of our day are saying that
> the Bible is both inspired and errant. Many of these theo-
> logians insist that the virgin birth, the physical resur-
> rection, and other supernatural elements in the life of
> Jesus are factual. They staunchly defend the deity of
> Christ, with all its implications for his personal author-
> ity. Yet they say that the proclamation of Christ needs no
> protective doctrine like biblical inerrancy. In this way they
> posit a strong dichotomy between the authority of the
> Bible and the Word made flesh.
>
> I have listened to them and thought and prayed about
> their views. But somehow I keep remembering the days
> when I, a young man just out of high school, first learned
> why Christ was crucified. I learned it from the Bible. I
> find there no hint that Christ was ever jealous of the at-
> tention men paid to Scripture. Rather, He made it plain
> that He accorded to Scripture the very highest authority,
> and He used the words of Scripture as the authoritative
> base of His own teaching.
>
> From personal experience I well understand the theo-
> logical attraction of an inspired yet errant Bible. Some
> years ago, while studying at a seminary in the Black
> Forest of Germany, I sat under two men who had taken
> their degrees under Karl Barth at the University of Basel.
> I had largely neglected Barth in my previous studies, and
> what a thrill it was to revel in the big, white volumes of
> *Die Kirchliche Dogmatik!* In what he said about Christ,
> how Barth nourished my soul! But though he often spoke
> highly of the Bible, Barth convinced me that there were
> errors, inaccuracies, and contradictions in the text. For
> the first time in my Christian life, I was faced with having
> to decide which verses of the Bible were authoritative for
> me and which were not.
>
> I clearly remember the morning when in my devotional

time I read the first chapter of Hebrews, where the writer addresses to Jesus the verse from Psalm 45, "Thy throne, O God, is for ever and ever . . ." The thought came to me: How do I know that we ought to call Jesus *God?* Wasn't Hebrews written by an unknown author? And don't many theologians doubt whether it should be in the Bible?

With deep shock I suddenly realized that, because I had come to limit the authority of the Bible, I no longer had any way to decide which verses were true. I had begun by believing that some records in the book of Kings contradict the books of Chronicles. I had gone on to wonder whether the Red Sea actually parted during the Exodus. I had doubted that Jonah could have lived for three days inside a fish. Now I was doubting whether or not Jesus was God.

For three days I struggled as the Christian Church struggled when it had to choose between the teachings of Arius and Athanasius. Like the Church, I chose to hold to faith in the full deity of Christ. And also like the Church, I made the decision because that is what the Bible teaches. Since that day the matter has been settled for me: To stick with the Bible is to stick with Christ. An inspired but errant Bible cannot teach me anything for certain, even about Christ. It cannot provide what I need more than life itself—assurance that my sins are forgiven.

Modern secularized theology most certainly needs—"more than life itself"—the assurance of the forgiveness of sins, and that assurance is available only through a totally trustworthy biblical revelation. The relevance of Holy Scripture in the current theological bewilderment could hardly be more evident: only the Word of God, which stands forever, can offer solid footing for theologians needing to recover not only a saving Christ but also His God and Father.

The Relevance of Scripture in a Disenchanted Era

The stir produced by the death-of-God movement is a genuine reflection of the loss of God by vast numbers of people in the 20th century. In Samuel Beckett's play, *En attendant Godot (Waiting for Godot)* the leading characters are typical of modern man, waiting in darkness and addressing himself to the unknown god who never appears. At one point Vladimir says:

We wait. We are bored. (He throws up his hand.) No, don't protest, we are bored to death, there's no denying it. Good. A diversion comes along and what do we do? We let it go to waste. Come, let's get to work! (He advances towards the heap, stops in his stride.) In an instant all will vanish and we'll be alone once more, in the midst of nothingness.

Elsewhere in the play, Estragon remarks:

Yes, now I remember, yesterday evening we spent blathering about nothing in particular. That's been going on now half a century.

How has such a cultural malaise come about in our time? Someone has sagely noted that in the 18th century the Bible died, in the 19th century God died, and in the 20th century mankind has died. This sequence is not accidental: the rationalistic criticism of Scripture during the 18th-century, deistic "Enlightenment" removed the most solid foundation for belief in God; and after Nietzsche and other 19th-century thinkers proclaimed His demise, it became impossible any longer to substantiate man's individual worth. No longer a creature of God, man could only regard himself as a clever, evolving animal, and the totalitarianisms of the 20th century are the inevitable result of stronger animals subjugating the weaker to their own ends. Without an eternal value system, available only in a veracious revelation from God, man is at the mercy of his fellows. Might makes right; in the words of Lord Acton's classic aphroism: "Power tends to corrupt; absolute power corrupts absolutely." Orwell's *1984* takes on nightmarish reality.

In the "secular theologians," however, an optimistic note is presently being sounded. We are informed that the "secular city" offers revelatory possibilities for acquiring a "new name" for God (see Harvey Cox's *The Secular City* and *The Secular City Debate*, ed. by Daniel Callahan); and one writer (Gibson Winter) goes so far as to speak of "the New Creation as Metropolis." A common axiom of the day, expressed by Cox and Altizer, is that "God is where the action is": in the dynamic social movements of our day, in the struggles for racial justice and human freedom. We are told that the "fully hidden Jesus" is now immanently to be experienced in such movements, and that "a whole new era in theology" is opening up through stress on the Spirit—"the God of the present" (so writes President James McCord of Princeton Seminary in *Time,* August 5, 1966).

But what is the actual situation? The urbanization of life is, as the greatest living phenomenologist of religion, Mircea Eliade, points out, desacralizing life by separating it from the cyclical, God-given patterns of nature. In the city we create our own environment and are therefore easily led not to God but to ourselves. We become convinced that we are "the masters of our fate and the captains of our soul," and we quickly reach the point where we endeavor to justify any "action" that we create. Much of the social action of our day is indeed God-honoring, for all races are "one in Christ Jesus" (Gal. 3:28) and "God is no respecter of persons" (Rom. 2:11, etc.); but apart from a revelatory, absolute ethic (as we saw earlier) supra-cultural standards of justice cannot be established. This means that the "secular theologian" without an authoritative Scripture can as easily find himself embroiled in the demonic, racistic, fascist activism of a Third Reich as in the contemporary freedom marches in behalf of minorities. Only a firm Word of God, coming from outside the flux of contemporary action, can serve as a roadmap to an honorable and just future. And as the Reformers properly observed, talk about "Christ" or the "Spirit" apart from an objective Word is a waste of breath; for without a stable criterion, each man can build a demonic Christ—an Anti-christ—in his own image, and deceive many. The spirits, most definitely including the spirits of the age, must be tested (I John 4:1); and the only touchstone remains the inscripturated Word.

The instability of current "action" philosophies and theologies is becoming evident as our contemporaries, à la Aldous Huxley and Timothy Leary, simultaneously seek answers in Eastern mysticism and reality-avoiding psychedelic drugs (see my article, "The Gospel According to LSD," *Christianity Today,* July 8, 1966; reprinted in the present volume in I. 4). Unconsciously, modern man recognizes that, whether in the metropolis or in the wilderness, whether in action or in silence, his heart—to recall Augustine's great truth—is restless till it rests in God. But to rest there, it must know who God is and what He has done for sinful man, and that can only be learned in the pages of Holy Writ.

Like the little lost creatures in Kenneth Grahame's *Wind in the Willows,* we long, each one of us, for "the piper at the Gates of Dawn." How desperately we need to hear the clear piping of eternity as century 21 approaches! Well did a great theologian over a hundred years ago (William Henry Green, *The Pentateuch* [1863]) point disenchanted modern man to that clear voice of God recorded in the most relevant Book of all:

> Who can tell us whether this awful and mysterious silence, in which the Infinite One has wrapped himself, portends mercy or wrath? Who can say to the troubled conscience, whether He, whose laws in nature are inflexible and remorseless, will pardon sin? Who can answer the anxious inquiry whether the dying live on or whether they cease to be? Is there a future state? And if so, what is the nature of that untried condition of being? If there be immortal happiness, how can I attain it? If there be an everlasting woe, how can it be escaped? Let the reader close his Bible and ask himself seriously what he knows upon these momentous questions apart from its teachings. What solid foundation has he to rest upon in regard to matters, which so absolutely transcend all earthly experience, and are so entirely out of the reach of our unassisted faculties? A man of facile faith may perhaps delude himself into the belief of what he wishes to believe. He may thus take upon trust God's unlimited mercy, his ready forgiveness of transgressors, and eternal happiness after death. But this is all a dream. He knows nothing, he can know nothing about it, except by direct revelation from heaven.
>
> The question, therefore, is one of life or death. We will not, we can not give up our faith in the Bible. To do so is to surrender ourselves to blank despair. It is to blot out the sun from the heavens and extinguish at once the very source of light and life and holiness. "All flesh is as grass, and all the glory of man as the flower of grass. The grass withereth and the flower thereof falleth away; but the WORD OF THE LORD endureth forever."

He who has ears to hear the piping, let him hear!

SUGGESTIONS FOR FURTHER READING

Henry, Carl F. H. (ed.). *Jesus of Nazareth: Saviour and Lord.* ("Contemporary Evangelical Thought.") Grand Rapids, Michigan: Eerdmans, 1966.

Lawrenz, Carl J. (ed.). *This Steadfast Word: A Series of Essays on the Holy Scriptures.* Milwaukee, Wisconsin: Northwestern Publishing House, 1965.

Montgomery, John Warwick. *Crisis in Lutheran Theology.* 2 vols. Grand Rapids, Michigan: Baker Book House, 1967.

Valen-Sendstad, Olav. *The Word That Can Never Die.* Translated by Madson and Strand. St. Louis, Missouri: Concordia Publishing House, 1966.

4.

Politics and Religion

God's Country?

Laugh-in's "flying fickle finger of fate" award was recently presented to state automobile license bureaus which sell names and addresses for direct-mail advertising. I have no idea whether this is the source of the vast quantities of junk mail I receive; perhaps such mail simply represents one of the occupational hazards of the ministry. The invitations to join Hefner's Bunny Clubs at a reduced rate I can stand (they are invariably well printed); what I have great difficulty in tolerating is the not inconsiderable quantity of politically rightist propaganda misled to me. Behind it seems to lie the tacit (and thoroughly fallacious) assumption that anyone who is "conservative" theologically must of course believe that the U.S. is "God's country" and must join the crusade to "bring America back to the Christian political philosophy of the Founding Fathers."

That this viewpoint is by no means limited to pamphleteers was evident when I received as a Christmas gift from an evangelical publisher Benjamin Weiss's book, *God in American History*, whose Preface sets the tone of the entire volume: "The purpose of this book is to present documentary evidence that the source of our nation's strength from its beginning has been faith in God. . . . Schools, colleges, charitable institutions, hospitals, orphanages, and other institutions are monumental proof of the Christian character of the United States of America."

Now there is an element of truth in these claims. As the dean of American church historians, William Warren Sweet, pointed out in his epochal work, *Religion in Colonial America*, the biblical orthodoxy of 17th century colonists cannot be disputed, nor can the religious motivations leading to Puritan and Pilgrim settlement in the new world. Such influence continued in the 18th century;

"between 1717 and the Revolutionary War some quarter of a million Ulstermen came to America" (J. G. Leyburn, *The Scotch-Irish: A Social History*), and these Ulster Scots were the products of a strict yet dynamic Presbyterian confessionalism. Moreover, the "natural rights" theory underlying the Declaration of Independence has its direct source not in the thought of French *philosophes* but in the work of Christian philosopher John Locke, and his ideas in this regard can be traced back to medieval Christian "natural law." Carl Becker nicely expressed it in the following terms: "The 18th century, having apparently ventured so far afield, is nevertheless to be found within hailing distance of the 13th; for its conception of natural law in the world of human relations was essentially identical, as Thomas Aquinas' conception had been, with right reason." Thus the efforts of Mrs. O'Hare and her ilk to rewrite American history in unqualifiedly atheistic terms are doomed to failure.

But what about the opposite viewpoint with which we began—the view that equates America with "God's country"? This stands no greater chance of success, and in fact turns out to be a kind of reverse mirror image of Mrs. O'Hare (just as extreme left and extreme right tend to display the same mentality across the political spectrum). The most influential Founding Fathers of the 18th century were not Christian in any biblical sense of the term: they were either outright Deists or mediating religious liberals.

Among the Deists were Jefferson, Paine, and Franklin. Jefferson had so little respect for the Scriptures that he created his own Bible—the so-called "Jefferson Bible" consisting of the ethical teachings of the New Testament (with the miraculous and divine aspects of Jesus' life carefully excised). Julian P. Boyd's account of *The Spirit of Christmas at Monticello* (1964) is a chilling barometer of the kind of religion maintained by one who endeavored, in his own words, "to shew by example the sufficiency of human reason." Paine's *Age of Reason* set forth the religion of Deism as a specific alternative and corrective to historic Christianity; the "Book of Nature" was now to replace the "Book of Scripture," and Paine devoted the entire second half of his work to a demonstration of alleged errors, contradictions, and immoralities in biblical religion.

As for Franklin, though his motion in behalf of morning prayer at the Constitutional Convention in 1789 has led some to speculate that he experienced Christian conversion before his death, there is no doubt that Deism and not Christian belief informed his political action during his career. George Whitefield found it necessary to confront Franklin with the claims of Christ throughout their long acquaintance; wrote Whitefield on one occasion: "As you have made a pretty considerable progress in the mysteries of electricity, I would now humbly recommend to your diligent unprejudiced pursuit and study the mystery of the new birth. . . . One hath solemnly declared that without it 'we cannot enter the kingdom of heaven.' You will excuse the freedom. I must have something of Christ in all my letters."

If outspoken Deists were few in number among the Founding Fathers, their influence was nonetheless considerable. Their philosophy of the natural goodness of man entered directly into the foundation documents of the nation. And the opponents of Deism among the Fathers of our country were not so much spokesmen of historic Christianity as advocates of religious liberalism who considered Deism too radical. The liberals themselves "generally held an Arian view of Jesus" (H. S. Smith, *American Christianity,* I [1960], 487), and therefore found Deistic anthropology quite hospitable. Representative of this viewpoint was Jonathan Mayhew, pastor of Boston's West Church, whose "Discourse" on the 100th anniversary of the execution of Charles I was called by John Adams "the opening gun of the Revolution."

In many ways the American frontier experience reinforced the anthropocentric self-confidence instilled by the Founding Fathers. F. J. Turner observed the "do-it-yourself" kind of religion which so easily developed in a frontier situation where self-reliance was the prime virtue. Americans have not generally been known for a sense of unworthiness or a willingness to accept aid from others—though such attitudes are fundamental to the

Christian gospel ("Except ye become as little children
....."; "I am not come to call the righteous but sinners
to repentance"). Bertrand Russell shrewdly points up an
American characteristic of which Americans themselves
are often oblivious: "If Job had been reincarnated as an
inhabitant of New York, and had been twitted, as the
original Job was, with the great size of Leviathan and
Behemoth, he would have been unimpressed, and would
have replied: 'Gee, they ain't half as big as a sky-
scraper'" (*The Impact of America on European Culture* [1951], pp. 9-10).

In reality, ours is no more "God's country" than is
any other part of this sin-impregnated globe. We are not
the Israelite theocracy repristinated, nor are we the
pinnacle of Christian civilization. What we have accomplished positively as a nation is due, not to ourselves, but
to God's grace. And for our Hiroshimas and My Lai mas-
sacres we stand under the wrath of the Almighty just
as others do for their Pearl Harbors and Buchenwalds.
Perhaps the judgment against us is even greater, "for
unto whomsoever much is given, of him shall be much
required." Let us therefore demythologize our American
religion, cease our presumptive removal of motes from
the eyes of other nations and ideologies, and return to
the Christ who stands in judgment (and—praise heaven
—in grace!) over the history of all peoples.

Demos and Christos

Most of us consider ourselves both Christians and—
regardless of our opinion of Pentagon bureaucracy—
democrats. But seldom do we try to relate the one to the
other. What connection, if any, exists between Christianity
and democracy? And what does the Christian message
have to say about our responsibility in a democratic society?

In Huysman's *fin-de-siècle* novel *Là Bas,* which por-
trays the disillusion and degradation of materialist European society on the eve of the twentieth century, one
of the characters says, "Conversations which do not treat
of religion or art are so base and vain"; yet not long
after, the opinion is expressed concerning the probable

victory of a democratic political candidate: "This certainly is the age of universal imbecility." Obviously no connection is seen here between religion—much less Christianity
—and democracy.

The great contemporary political philosopher Sidney
Hook takes much the same attitude. In his 1959 work
Political Power and Personal Freedom he asks: "Does
democracy as a way of life rest upon belief in supernatural religious truths in the sense that, if the latter are
denied, the former must necessarily be denied?" And
true to his pragmatic philosophy, he answers in the negative: "I shall argue that they constitute neither necessary
nor sufficient conditions."

Upon what grounds is a denial of relation between
Christianity and democracy usually based? Two arguments are common: First, democracy prededed Christianity (Greece is the cradle of the democratic state)
and was restored to Western civilizaticn through the consciously anti-Christian doctrine of the rights of man at
the time of the French Revolution; second, that Christianity, as represented by the Church, has historically
allied itself most frequently with hierarchical, non-demo-
cratic political philosophies.

But neither of these arguments is of much significance.
It is true that Athens had a democratic government—in
theory. Pericles is supposed to have orated: "Our government is called a democracy, because its administration
is in the hands, not of the few, but of the many"; but
he failed to add that political rights were in fact denied
to at least 90 per cent of the population, since neither
slaves, resident aliens, nor women were given a voice
in the public administration. Moreover, the greatest
Athenian philosopher, Plato, took a dim view of democracy—even in his later works, after he had been disil-
lusioned by his failure to turn the lazy boy-ruler of Syracuse into an ideal philosopher-king.

As for the eighteenth-century declarations of the rights
of man, stemming from the deistic philosophies of such
persons as Voltaire, Rousseau, and Paine, it has been well
shown that revolutionary movement was inflamed by
demands for *rights* rather than recognition of *duties*, and
therefore provided a very questionable basis for democracy. Indeed, the near-anarchy of the French revolu-

tionary governments led almost inevitably to the auto-
cratic Napoleonic era. Recent historical scholarship, as
a matter of fact, is much more inclined to see the roots
of modern representative democracy in the estates-
generals, parliaments, and cortes of medieval Christian
Europe than in the work of the anti-clericals of the Age
of Reason.

To determine the true attitude of Christianity to democracy, it is necessary to look not at the history of the Church
(which is, by definition, composed of sinful men who have
often erred) but at the Holy Scriptures, which provide
the only proper norm of the Church's teaching. On the
one hand, we find that Scripture presents no single govern-
mental form as obligatory (the theocracy of Israel, as
the Puritans failed to notice, was ideal only for Israel
as the vehicle of God's revelation preparatory to the advent of the Christ). Barth was quite right to tell the East
German pastors that they could "serve God in a Communist land"—and in fact had a divine responsibility to do
so (Romans 13).

But just as the Scripture, without explicitly condemning slavery, condemned it by the Gospel which sets
men free, so the New Testament message provides irre-
sistible impetus toward more democratic government,
i.e., toward government in the hands of the people. Jesus
said: "Let no man among you be called master; for ye
are all brethren"; the one man he called a fox was a
king. Bishop Berggrav quite rightly asserted that "the
cornerstone of democracy" was laid when Christ proclaimed that a man's soul is worth more than the whole
world.

In the central Christian doctrines of sin and grace, the
relation of Christianity to democracy becomes crystal
clear. Scripture asserts that "there is no difference, for
all have sinned and come short of the glory of God" (Rom.
3:22, 23); and because of this universal human predicament, the Gospel is declared that "God was in Christ,
reconciling the world unto himself" (II Cor. 5:19). If all
are sinners, then the best form of government is the one
that prevents any one sinner from gaining absolute control
over the rest; and if all are potential recipients of God's
saving grace, then the best government is the one that
permits each person to contribute the most to the well-

being of his fellows. Since a man is never perfect, he must always be checked by his fellows, or tyranny will loom on the horizon; and since no man can ever be more "saved" than another (for salvation is God's work for all men, not man's work for God), no one has the right to lord it over his neighbor in the political realm. In spite of its limitations, democracy has been found experientially to provide the greatest fulfillment of these ideals; it is unquestionably the best government for "sinners saved by grace." Thus it is not strange that democracy has flowered not in the East but in the West, where the Christian faith has served as the religious cement for civilization.

And what is the responsibility of the Christian in a democratic society? As Reinhold Niebuhr puts it:

> The preservation of a democratic civilization requires the wisdom of the serpent and the harmlessness of the dove. The children of light must be armed with the wisdom of the children of darkness but remain free from their malice. They must have this wisdom in order that they may beguile, deflect, harness and restrain self-interest, individual and collective, for the sake of the community.

This means that participation in the democratic processes is obligatory, not optional, for Christians. Unlike the sectarians, we must not run from government as an evil, but must realize that we have a holy responsibility to prevent evil and promote the good. This means a political vocation if we are called to it—and Luther wrote: "There is need in this office of abler people than are needed in the office of preaching, for in the preaching office Christ does the whole thing by His Spirit, but in the government of the world one must use reason" (WA, XXX, Pt. 2, 562)! It means also an intelligent concern for and awareness of political issues and problems—a vital, active citizenship. The popular judgment that "religion and politics should not be discussed in polite conversation" is as wrong in the one case as in the other; and Christ's warning that "because thou art lukewarm, and neither cold nor hot, I will spue thee out of my mouth" should be pondered both theologically and politically—both by the Christian Church and by the Western democracies.

5.

Wisdom, Love and Law

Wisdom as Gift

The Religious Meanings of Wisdom

The present study is not an examination of the so-called Wisdom Literature of the Old Testament, nor of the professional class of wise men active among the Hebrews in Old Testament times; rather, the subject for discussion here is the *concept* of wisdom (which appears chiefly in the Wisdom Literature but also in other Old Testament books), and the significance of this concept to the messianic belief set forth in the Judeo-Christian Scriptures. A clear understanding of the religious meanings of the wisdom concept is, therefore, fundamental to our investigation.

According to Girdlestone's standard work, *Synonyms of the Old Testament,* "The word wisdom . . . generally answers in the A. V. to the Hebrew *chakham.* This is an important word in Scripture, and is used to represent the discernment of good and evil, prudence in secular matters, skill in arts, experience in Divine things, and even dexterity in magic. . . . The general rendering of the LXX is σοφία, which is used in the same largeness of sense in the N.T." [1] The essence of the wisdom idea is well expressed in the following definition: "One is *wise* who is so discerning in his understanding of persons, conditions, or situations that he knows how to deal with them so as to correct what is wrong in them, how to get the best out of them considering their limitations or difficulties, or how to estimate them fairly and accurately: often also the term implies a wide range of experience or of knowledge or learning." [2] In brief, then, wisdom is distinguished from mere knowledge, or understanding, or even comprehension, in that it represents a greater degree of "discernment"—a greater depth of penetration of insight—than is signified by these other expressions.

But what does wisdom mean in the specifically reli-

Notes for this section, pages 400-403.

gious sphere? If we accept some such definition of religion as that of Professor William Adams Brown ("by religion is meant the life of man in his superhuman relations; that is, his relation to the power on which he feels himself dependent, the authority to which he deems himself responsible, and the unseen being with whom he is capable of communing"),[3] we shall need to relate the idea of wisdom, as presented above, to the god-idea, and more specifically to the God of Hebrew-Christian Revelation. This brings us necessarily to what Anders Nygren has termed *Motifforschung*, for the relation of wisdom to God involves two basic motifs. Wisdom is a relational concept; one can always ask, when wisdom is mentioned, what the object of the wisdom is ("wisdom about what?") and what the source of wisdom is ("wisdom from what?"). In the religious realm, the *source* of wisdom can be either God or man, and, depending upon which is emphasized, a given religious point of view will be theocentric or anthropocentric. This motif, as it relates to wisdom, can be called the "grace-works" motif. If wisdom is viewed as coming from God as a free gift, then we are operating in the realm of theocentric "grace." If, however, wisdom lies inherently in man, or can be achieved by him through some positive action on his part, then wisdom is being conceived of anthropocentrically, and a "works" emphasis is present.[4] When we consider the possible *objects* toward which religious wisdom can be directed, we arrive at the other basic motif with which we shall deal here: the "value-scale" motif.[5] On the most "earthly" level, religious wisdom can be concerned with the successful conduct of practical activities. On a higher level, it will center its attention on God's law. Moving higher yet, wisdom can be conceived of as a personal emanation from God, or as God himself incarnated. Finally, wisdom can mean a continuing, direct, personal experience with the God of the universe.

Since it is evident that both the "grace-works" and the "value-scale" motifs operate simultaneously in any religious concept of wisdom, and since it is also quite clear that religious wisdom concepts seldom manifest pure "grace" or pure "works," or lie entirely at one end of a value continuum, it seems useful at the outset of this study to combine these relationships in a schematic way. The following diagram attempts to do this—the ordinate representing the "value-scale" motif, and the abscissa representing the "grace-works" motif.

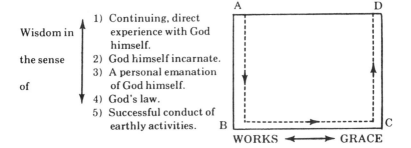

Wisdom in the sense of

1) Continuing, direct experience with God himself.
2) God himself incarnate.
3) A personal emanation of God himself.
4) God's law.
5) Successful conduct of earthly activities.

WORKS ⟵⟶ GRACE

The broken line ABCD introduces normative judgment into our discussion. Point D is the ideal, for it combines the maximum value with the conviction that wisdom has its source solely in God's grace. Point A is the most reprehensible, for it presumptuously attempts by works to reach the greatest value—continuing, direct fellowship with God. The fact that point C is more desirable than point B indicates that the worst exemplifaction of the grace-belief is better than the most innocuous attempt at a works concept of wisdom. Justification for these normative judgments need not be given here in detail, for two eminent philosopher-theologians have done so elsewhere. Rudolf Otto has shown that fundamental to all true religion is the *mysterium tremendum et fascinosum*— the qualitative distinction between God and the worshipper.[6] To the extent that this is lost sight of, religion disintegrates proportionately. Since the grace concept preserves this idea of the "wholly other," whereas a works point-of-view blurs the creator-creature distinction, it is evident that any point on the line CD in our diagram is religiously preferable to any point on line AB. Edward

John Carnell has rendered great service in showing axiologically that God himself is the highest value, because only God can solve the multifarious problems of human existence.[7] This being true, the ordering of values from C to D is self-evident; wisdom concerning God's law, for example, is preferable to practical wisdom in conducting earthly business, but is not to be compared with a personal revelation of, or a continuous experience with, God himself.

In this essay an attempt will be made to classify according to the above scheme the conceptions of wisdom set forth in the Judeo-Christian Scriptures, and to relate these conceptions to the Messianic belief present in these same sacred writings. We shall direct our attention first to the canonical[8] Old Testament—specifically the Psalms, Proverbs, Ecclesiastes, and Job, since these books contain the most significant material on the wisdom concept. Next, the Apocryphal books of Ecclesiasticus, Baruch, and Wisdom of Solomon will be analyzed for their views of religious wisdom. Thirdly, the Pauline and Johannine New Testament references to wisdom will be studied. Finally, we shall summarize the biblical view of wisdom, and compare it with the typical wisdom conception which developed outside the Hebrew-Christian stream of revelation.

The Wisdom Concept in the Canonical Old Testament
The Psalms

Although the concept of wisdom made an appearance in Israel long before the Exile, we shall touch on pre-exilic scriptural materials only incidentally—through the Book of Psalms, which certainly contains pre-exilic elements.[9] This emphasis on post-exilic biblical documents stems from our desire to concentrate on the most central and well-developed wisdom concepts of the Old Testament.[10]

The idea of wisdom in the sense of successful conduct of earthly activities is not entirely absent from the Psalter, but even when present it is clearly connected with a grace viewpoint. In Psalm 107:27 one reads of sailors in a storm: "They reel to and fro, and stagger like a drunken man, and are at their wit's end" (more literally: "their wisdom is swallowed up" [11]). Their lack of practical wisdom is in contrast to the Lord's ability, for the next verses speak of his power and grace: "Then they cry unto the Lord in their trouble, and he bringeth them out of their distresses. . . . Oh that men would praise the Lord for his goodness, and for his wonderful works to the children of men!" (vss. 28, 31). [12]

God's law is the focal point of wisdom in the Psalms. Psalm 37:30-31 illustrates this well: "The mouth of the righteous speaketh wisdom, and his tongue talketh of judgment. The law of his God is in his heart; none of his steps shall slide" (cf. the whole of Psalms 1 and 119). Psalm 110:10 demonstrates, however, that the coupling of wisdom with the law does not necessarily diminish a theocentric, grace emphasis (Nygren notwithstanding!): "The fear of the Lord is the beginning of wisdom: a good understanding have all they that do (translators supply: "his commandments"): his praise endureth for ever."

Indeed, the most obvious characteristic of the wisdom statements in the Psalter is their unequivocal stress upon God as the gracious source of all true wisdom. Consider the following verses: "O Lord, how manifold are thy works! in wisdom hast thou made them all: the earth is full of thy riches" (104:24; cf. 136:5). "So teach us to number our days, that we may apply our hearts unto wisdom" (90:12). "Behold, thou desirest truth in the inward parts: and in the hidden part thou shalt make me to know wisdom. Purge me with hyssop, and I shall be clean: wash me, and I shall be whiter than snow. . . . Create in me a clean heart, O God; and renew a right spirit within me. Cast me not away from thy presence; and take not thy holy spirit from me" (51:6-7, 10-11). [13]

The Proverbs

The book of Proverbs is composed of several collections of material, but since we are here engaged in conceptual analysis rather than in literary criticism, we shall concern ourselves only with the distinction between the first nine chapters and the material comprising the remainder of the book. Oesterley and most other reputable students of Proverbs hold that chapters 1-9 contain "the latest portion of the book." [14]

In Chapters 10 through 31 of Proverbs, the general view of wisdom presented is that of shrewd, practical skill in dealing with earthly activities. The grace emphasis is not absent (cf. 15:33: "The fear of the Lord is the instruction of wisdom; and before honour is humility"), but the constant stress on earthly accomplishment makes it easy to understand how these chapters have been fitted into a works-righteousness framework by many readers from Pharisaic times to the present.

Chapters 1—9 of Proverbs contain a personification of wisdom which virtually has the status of a divine emanation. Siegfried goes to an unnecessary extreme when he asserts that "wisdom is conceived of in Prov. 8:22 ff. as a separate Existence whom Yahweh formed as the first of His works prior to the creation of earthly things," [15] but there is no doubt that real hypostatizing (in the Nicene sense) occurs in the early chapters of Proverbs. Brown, Driver, and Briggs offer the following balanced description: "The divine wisdom is personified: she was begotten before all things to be the architect and counsellor of God in the creation (Prov. 8:22-31); she builds a palace and spreads a feast for those who will receive her instruction, 9:1 (cf. vss. 2-5); she teaches in public places, 1:20; 8:1, 5, 11, 12 (v. context); gives her pupils the divine spirit, 1:23; by her discipline simple become wise, rulers rule wisely, and those seeking her are richly rewarded, 8:14 (cf. vss. 1-21)." [16] This description makes evident why the passage "has been interpreted from early days in a christological sense." Indeed, "there can be no doubt that [chap. 8] v. 22 lies at the back of Col. 1:15-18 and Rev. 3:14." [17]

In these early chapters of Proverbs the exhortations to seek wisdom should not be allowed to obscure the grace emphasis present. It is significant that both near the beginning and close to the end of this section of the book the statement we have encountered before is repeated, "The fear of the Lord is the beginning of wisdom" (1:7; 9:10).

Ecclesiastes and Job

These two Old Testament books can logically be discussed together here, since they are both the product, not of practical wisdom teachers, but of "a group of dissidents who grappled with . . . more fundamental issues," [18] and because the wisdom concept presented in both writings is much the same. In general, Koheleth and Job are hardly concerned at all with the value-scale motif (the object of wisdom), but they are deeply concerned that wisdom be viewed from the standpoint of divine sovereignty and grace.

The Book of Ecclesiastes is now dated 275-250 B.C. by the most reputable authorities, and its integrity has been reaffirmed. Even the epilogue (12:9-14) is now believed to contain "valuable information about the author's life and work from a contemporary." [19] Koheleth is perceptive enough to realize that all wisdom attained "under the sun," that is, through human effort on earth, is, after all, but vanity (emptiness). He states this clearly in his opening chapter: "I communed with mine own heart, saying, Lo, I am come to great estate, and have gotten more wisdom than all they that have been before me in Jerusalem: yea, my heart had great experience of wisdom and knowledge. And I gave my heart to know wisdom, and to know madness and folly: I perceived that this also is vexation of spirit. For in much wisdom is much grief: and he that increaseth knowledge increaseth sorrow" (1:16-18). Anthropocentric wisdom indeed "excelleth folly" (2:13), but the wise man dies as the fool, so "this also is vanity" (2:15-16). "Wisdom is better than strength: nevertheless the poor man's wisdom is despised, and his words are not heard" (9:16). Moreoever, death destroys everything, including human wisdom (12:7-8). Koheleth offers no real solution to this problem (after all, no "solution" is possible for surd evil, *ex hypothesi!*), unless we consider his existential approach to be a solution. He makes crystal clear to his reader that man's only hope lies in his assenting to God's absolute sovereignty and otherness (3:11, 14; 5:2; 8:17; 11:5), and his living each day in the knowledge that "God will bring thee into judgment" for every decision and action (11:9; cf. 12:13-14).

The Book of Job sets forth a like view of wisdom, and in consummate literary style; indeed, the book is held by many to be "the greatest work of genius in the Old Testament, and one of the world's artistic masterpieces." [20] "Wide disagreement" still exists among scholars with regard to the critical analysis of the book; the date is usually placed at 400-200 B.C., and few defend absolutely the unity of its contents.[21] The wisdom chapter (28), the Elihu speeches (chapters 32-37), the second divine speech (contained in chapters 40 and 41), and certain other portions of the book are considered by many to be later additions or of secondary origin.[22] However, as Oscar Wilde put it, "When the work of art is finished it has, as it were, an independent life of its own, and may deliver a message far other than that which was put into its lips to say." [23] The central message of the book as a whole is given preliminary statement in chapter 28. In 28:27, "hypostatization of wisdom is as clear . . . as in Pr. 8," [24] but the basic message of the chapter lies in its answer to the question posed in verse 12: "Where shall wisdom be found?" "It is hid from the eyes of all living" (vs. 21); only "god understandeth the way thereof. . . . For he looketh to the ends of the earth, and seeth under the whole heaven. . . . And unto man he said, Behold, the fear of the Lord, that is wisdom" (vss. 23-24, 28). This God-oriented conception of wisdom is painted with vivid strokes as God answers suffering Job out of the whirlwind—thus providing a theocentric denouement for the drama. "After this tripartite presentation of argument—the proof of Job's inability to understand or fashion the mysterious arrangements of nature (38-39), the proof of the impossibility of his assuming or improving on the divine world-government (40:8-14), and the proof of his incompetence to cope with the most formidable of animals (40:14—41:26 ([34]), the hero has been sufficiently brought to his senses." He now fully realizes "the foolhardiness of his criticism of God," [25] and receives, purely out of grace, a restoration which is actually more than restoration, whether viewed from the material or from the spiritual standpoint (chapter 42, especially verses 5, 10, 12).

In general, then, we may say that in the four canonical Old Testament books which we have considered here (the four most directly concerned with the concept of wisdom), a strong grace emphasis exists, and the idea of wisdom is employed sometimes in the sense of successful conduct of earthly activities (a few Psalms and the later portions of Proverbs), sometimes with reference to God's law (the

Psalter as a whole), and sometimes with reference to a divine hypostasis (the early chapters of Proverbs, and Job 28). In terms of the diagram presented earlier, the Old Testament wisdom concept is represented by (3), (4), and (5) on the line CD. The significance of this for biblical messianism will be pointed out later; at this point we must hasten on into the realm of the Apocryphal writings.

The Wisdom Concept in the Old Testament Apocrypha

Ecclesiasticus and Baruch

The difference between canonical and Apocryphal Old Testament books is to some extent one of degree, as Luther recognized when he translated them and appended them to his German Bible of 1534, and called them useful and good to read.[26] Three of the Apocryphal books are concerned sufficiently with the concept of wisdom to warrant our attention here. The varying distances at which Apocryphal books lie in relation to the canonical writings can be seen readily by considering Ecclesiasticus and Baruch on the one hand, and the Wisdom of Solomon on the other.

Ecclesiasticus, or the Wisdom of Jesus the Son of Sirach, was composed in two volumes (Chapters 1-23 and 24-50 of the present book) by Sirach, a Jerusalem teacher and scribe. The date of writing was *circa* 180 B.C., and shortly after 132 B.C. Sirach's grandson translated it from Hebrew into Greek.[27] Prior to 1896, the only traces of the Hebrew extant were in Talmudic citations, but in the years 1896-1931 almost two-thirds of the Hebrew text came to light through medieval manuscript discoveries.[28] The best scholarly opinion believes that these Hebrew fragments substantially represent the original,[29] so the most accurate English translation of Ecclesiasticus probably remains that of Box and Oesterley, which, though made in 1913, takes into account practically all of the Hebrew fragments.[30] The first half of the book (volume one) provides the reader with numerous instructions for wise daily living, and the second part of Sirach's work is certainly not lacking in similar precepts. Volume two opens with a detailed personification of wisdom (Chapter 24)—a hypostasis more thoroughgoing than that presented in Job or Proverbs. This wisdom hypostasis is by no means divorced from the law, however; indeed, it "has found

its fullest expression in the Book of the law (24:23-29),
whose full stream is compared with that of the four rivers
of Paradise." [31] A grace framework of real strength
is provided by Sirach in his work: the book opens with
the lofty assertion, "All wisdom cometh from the Lord,
and is with Him for ever" (1:1), and the statement we
have encountered in canonical literature is repeated again
and again like a theme—"To fear the Lord is the beginning
of Wisdom" (1:14 *et passim*). It is not hard to understand why C. C. Torrey considers "this noble monument
of the Hebrew wisdom literature" to stand "at the head
of all the 'outside books'," and why it was given a traditional Latin name (Ecclesiasticus) designating it "as
the 'church book' *par excellence* in the extra-canonical
literature" and showing how highly it was esteemed in
Christian circles from the earliest times." [32]

Baruch is a composite work, originally written in
Hebrew, but now available only in a Greek version. We
are concerned here solely with the section 3:9—4:4 (180-
100 B.C.)[33] which consists of a poetic praise of wisdom.
As in Ecclesiasticus, wisdom is personified (though not
in such detail), and a specific connection is made with
God's law: "There is none that knoweth her [wisdom's]
way, nor any that comprehendeth her path. But he that
knoweth all things knoweth her. . . . This is our God, *and*
there shall none other be accounted of in comparison of
him. He hath found out all the way of knowledge, and
hath given it unto Jacob his servant, and to Israel that
is beloved of him. . . . This is the book of the commandments of God, and the law that endureth for ever" (3:31-
32, 35—4:1).[34] The theocentric, grace emphasis of the
Baruch wisdom poem is quite evident from this excerpt.

The Wisdom of Solomon

When we come to this famous Apocryphal book, "a
discourse attributed to Solomon, composed in Greek by
an Alexandrian Jew during the period 100-50 B.C.," [35]
we find ourselves in a strange and alien territory. Here
we meet a wisdom hypostatized in more specific terms
than was the case even in Ecclesiasticus—and in terms
unmistakably dictated by Platonic categories. "Wisdom
is more mobile than any motion; yea, she pervadeth
and penetrateth all things by reason of her pureness. For
she is a breath of the power of God, and a clear effluence

of the glory of the Almighty; therefore can nothing de-
filed find entrance into her. For she is an effulgence from
everlasting light and an unspotted mirror of the working
of God, and an image of his goodness. And she, though
but one, hath power to do all things; and remaining in
herself, reneweth all things" (7:24-27).[36]

The command ἀγαπήσατε is encountered as the very first
word of the book, but this is by no means the *agape* of
the New Testament revelation. The concept is rather that
of ἔρως , as the following typical passage shows: "She
[wisdom] goeth about, seeking them that are worthy of
her, and in their paths she appeareth unto them gracious-
ly, and in every purpose she meeteth them. For her true
beginning is desire of instruction; and the care for instruction is love *of her;* and love *of her* is observance of her
laws; and to give heed to *her* laws is the assurance of
incorruption; and incorruption bringeth near unto God;
so then desire of wisdom promoteth to a kingdom"
(6:16-20; cf. 9:15).[37] Nygren correctly notes that "again
and again during the early centuries of Christianity" the
book of Wisdom "came to serve as a bridge over which
Eros-theory was able to pass into Christianity." [38]

The Apocrypha which we have examined here contain
more sharply drawn personifications of wisdom than
appear in the canonical writings of the Old Testament.
In Ecclesiasticus and Baruch these hypostases are still
conceived of from the standpoint of grace, but in the
Wisdom of Solomon one sees a shift occur to a works
emphasis (line AB on the diagram presented *supra*). This
shift is a matter of no small significance, for it is a movement from a point of considerable theocentric value to
one of great anthropocentric presumption.

Wisdom and the Christ in the New Testament
The Pauline Teaching

"The Old Testament reached no final conclusion as
to how salvation was to be achieved. That God himself
would intervene dramatically and fulfil history, draw all
men to himself in the new Jerusalem, re-create human
nature with a new heart and a new spirit, send his Prince
of Peace to rule over the new community established by
an everlasting covenant—of this Israel was confident."
So states G. Ernest Wright near the close of his in-

fluential monograph, *The Old Testament Against Its Environment*.[39] The central message of Paul—and indeed of the entire New Testament—is that the fulfillment of this Old Testament hope occurred in Jesus of Nazareth. In the opening sentence of the Epistle to the Romans, for example, we read: "Paul, a servant of Jesus Christ [that is, Jesus the Anointed, the Messiah], called to be an apostle, separated unto the gospel of God, (which he had promised afore by his prophets in the holy scriptures) concerning his Son Jesus Christ our Lord, which was made of the seed of David according to the flesh; and declared to be the Son of God with power, according to the spirit of holiness, by the resurrection from the dead...." Paul's concern to proclaim Jesus as God's Messiah led him on occasions to make the astounding declaration that in Jesus one finds wisdom of God incarnated.[40] Let us direct our attention to these occasions.

Paul's First Letter to the Corinthians abounds with the words "wisdom" and "knowledge" and their antonyms. He is at pains to point out that Christ is the only adequate religious foundation (3:11), for he is "the power of God and the wisdom of God" (1:24, 30). The wisdom for which the Greeks seek (1:22) is found only in him. God's Spirit alone can bestow this Christ-wisdom upon a person (2:10-12), and the greatest evidence of such activity of the Spirit is *agape* love (12:4; 13). Why this preoccupation with wisdom in I Corinthians? The answer is suggested by two facts: the explicit mention of Greeks seeking wisdom, and the repeated references to an Apollos faction at Corinth (1:12 *et passim*). Acts 18:24—19:6 informs us that Apollos was an Alexandrian Jew who had preached Christ at Ephesus apparently without having heard of the Holy Spirit, and who, having subsequently received religious instruction from Aquila and Priscilla, proclaimed the gospel at Corinth also. It is not unlikely that Apollos' message at Corinth had been tinged with that blend of Hellenistic philosophy and Jewish mystical speculation which we have observed in the Wisdom of Solomon.[41] Whether Apollos was at the bottom of the problem or not, it is clear that some such wisdom notions were current among the believers at Corinth, and Paul wished to assert in his letter to them a grace view of wisdom which centered on Jesus the Christ and emphasized the work of the Holy Spirit.

At Colossae a somewhat similar situation existed. "The Colossian Christians were Gentiles, whom Jewish Christians were trying to seduce from pure Christianity. What they inculcated was not the plain Judaism which had been the chief trouble in Galatia a few years earlier. The danger now arose from a different quarter. Greek philosophical speculations were combining with a variety of oriental ideas to form a strange amalgam of mystical theosophy." [12] To the Colossians Paul wrote that Christ "is the image of the invisible God, the first born of every creature; for by him were all things created . . . and he is before all things, and by him all things consist . . . in whom are hid all the treasures of wisdom and knowledge" (1:15-17; 2:3; cf. 1:9, 28; 2:8, 23; 3:12; 4:5). [13]

The Johannine Teaching

In Ecclesiasticus wisdom says at one point, "They that eat shall still hunger, and they that drink me shall still thirst" (24:21). [14] John, like Paul, sets himself to show that in Jesus the Christ God himself (no mere emanation of God) has become incarnate (Jn. 1:1-5, 14), and for this reason Jesus can say to the Samaritan woman, "Whosoever drinketh of the water that I shall give him shall never thirst; but the water that I shall give him shall be in him a well of water springing up into everlasting life" (John 4:14). The Christ makes possible for the believer a continuing, direct experience with God himself, for upon his departure from this earth he sent "another [ἄλλον , another of the same kind] Comforter, that he may abide with you for ever; even the Spirit of truth" (John 14:16-17; cf. 14:26; 16:7-15).

This continuing fellowship between God and the believer is broken in this life only by sin, and "if we say that we have no sin, we deceive ourselves, and the truth is not in us" (I John 1:8). One day, however, Christ will come again, and God will "make all things new" (Rev. 21:5); in the holy city, new Jerusalem, "there shall be no more curse: but the throne of God and of the Lamb shall be in it; and his servants shall serve him: and they shall see his face; and his name shall be in their foreheads" (Rev. 22:3-4). [15] All this will be accomplished by the God who is *agape* love (I John 4:16), for "the law was given by Moses, but grace and truth came by Jesus Christ" (John 1:17).

Contrast and Conclusion

At the ruined city of Anuradhapura, eighty miles north of Kandy, India, the traveller finds the sacred Bo-tree, which has grown there for centuries and which is supposed to be derived from the original Bodhi-tree, beneath which Buddha attained perfect wisdom. To this day the tree is worshipped by throngs of pilgrims who come long distances to pray before it. According to Rhys-Davids, Buddha's Bo-tree is to the Buddhist what the cross is to Christians.[46] In a real sense this is symbolic of the opposition between the concept of wisdom presented in the Hebrew-Christian revelation, and that prevalent in non-Christian religions. The Bo-tree reaches up toward heaven, as did the tower of Babel; but on the cross, God reached down to give a wisdom not of this world to those who would receive it as a gift. Talmudic Judaism particularly demonstrates the contrast, for to the Talmudic writers, the time of Messiah's coming "was generally held to depend on the degree of progress men will have achieved in their development." [47] In Philo, as in the Eastern mystics, the heights of presumption are reached, for man climbs a self-made ladder of asceticism directly into the presence of God himself.[48]

The Christian Scriptures, on the other hand, assert unequivocally, "Say not in thine heart, Who shall ascend into heaven? (that is, to bring Christ down)" (Rom. 10:6). Wisdom begins in the Old Testament as practical guidance, becomes identified with God's law, is conceived as a divine hypostasis; in the New Testament, God's wisdom is declared to be incarnated in Jesus the Messiah, is available to believers through God's Holy Spirit, and will one day mean sin-free fellowship with the Creator in the New Jerusalem. At each stage, God initiates by his grace, and man acts as a recipient. Thus knowing that "when the fulness of the time was come God sent forth his Son," may we say with the seer of Patmos, "Even so, come, Lord Jesus."

Notes

[1] Robert Baker Girdlestone, *Synonyms of the Old Testament: Their Bearing on Christian Doctrine* (Grand Rapids: Eerdmans, 1951 [reprint of the 2d ed., 1897]), p. 74. Along with *chokhmah*, Girdlestone discusses briefly *bīn, sakhāl,* and *tūshiyyāh.* These synonyms may be profitably

studied in Brown, Driver, and Brigg's revision of Gesenius' *Lexicon of the Old Testament* (Oxford: Clarendon Press, 1952). On σοφία and its biblical synonyms, see Richard Chenevix Trench, *Synonyms of the New Testament* (London: Macmillan and Co., 1880), pp. 281-86; and Arndt and Gingrich's edition of Bauer's *Lexicon of the New Testament and Other Early Christian Literature* (Chicago: University of Chicago Press, 1957).

[2] *Webster's Dictionary of Synonyms* (Springfield, Mass.: G. and C. Merriam, 1951), p. 888.

[3] *Christian Theology in Outline*, p. 29; quoted in Robert Ernest Hume, *The World's Living Religions*. rev. ed. (New York: Scribner, 1955), p. 6.

[1] It will be noted that when we speak of a "grace-works" motif, we are combining Nygren's ἔρως. νόμος , and ἀγάπη motifs into a single, more general idea.Ἔρως and νόμος have in common the "works" emphasis and both are essentially anthropocentric. Ἀγάπη is God-centered and grace-centered. See Nygren's *Agape and Eros*, tr. by Watson (Philadelphia: Westminster Press, 1953).

[5] Cf. Chapter Three ("Religious Values") in Edgar Sheffield Brightman's *A Philosophy of Religion* (New York: Prentice-Hall, 1940), pp. 85-107.

[6] See Otto's classic, *The Idea of the Holy* (New York: Oxford University Press, 1926). Cf. also his *The Kingdom of God and the Son of Man*, rev. ed. (Boston: Starr King Press, 1957), pp. 41, 164-65. Otto's influence on Martin Buber and Karl Barth has been immense.

[7] *A Philosophy of the Christian Religion* (Grand Rapids: Eerdmans, 1952). Cf. Augustine's famous assertion *(Confessiones,* i. 1.): "Fecisti nos ad te et inquietum est cor nostrum, donec requiescat in te."

[8] The term "canonical" is used in the Protestant sense.

[9] H. H. Rowley writes of the Psalms: "To-day there is less effort to fix precise dates, but a general tendency towards earlier dating. It is commonly allowed that there may be a considerable pre-exilic element in the Psalter, and in some quarters there is a reluctance to find more than the slightest post-exilic element" (*The Growth of the Old Testament* [London: Hutchinson's University Library, 1950], p. 130). No attempt will be made here to date the individual psalms from which quotations are taken.

[10] The Exile was of profound relevance for Hebrew life and thought. All aspects of the people's experience were deepened, a transformation in which the wisdom movement shared to the full. Later wisdom, in so far as we can identify it, is markedly religious" (William A. Irwin, "The Wisdom Literature," *The Interpreter's Bible*, Vol. 1 [New York: Abingdon, 1952], p. 215).

[11] See E. C. Blackman, "Wise, Wisdom," in Alan Richardson's *A Theological Word Book of the Bible* (New York: Macmillan, 1950), p. 282.

[12] In Lutheran churches, the latter verse appears as part of the Gradual for the Second Sunday after the Epiphany.

[13] The apparent connection here between wisdom and the work of God's "holy spirit" is strongly suggestive of the New Testament, and serves to support E. Sellin's assertion that in the Psalter "a con-

sciousness of salvation is attained which already bears an almost New Testament character" (Quoted in Rowley, *op. cit.*, p. 136).

[14] W. O. E. Oesterley, *The Book of Proverbs* (New York: Dutton, 1929), p. xiii. Oesterley assigns Proverbs 1:1—9:18 to the third century B.C., but feels certain that some earlier material has found its way into the section. We shall here treat Chapters 1—9 as a unit, since our concern is with the admittedly late hypostatizing of wisdom which appears there. The remaining chapters of Proverbs are of an earlier date, but probably not pre-exilic (Pfeiffer denies that even 10:1—22:16, which is the oldest section, appeared before the Exile).

[15] "Wisdom," in Hastings' *Dictionary of the Bible*, Vol. IV (New York: Scribner, 1902), pp. 924-25. Siegfried's position that the early chapters of Proverbs are "un-Israelitish" and are due to the influence of Greek philosophy is less and less maintained today. A more reasonable parallel is with the wisdom literature of Egypt and Babylonia (Oesterley, *op. cit.*, pp. xxxiii-lv).

[16] *Op. cit.*, p. 315.

[17] Oesterley, *op. cit.*, p. 61.

[18] Robert Gordis, "Ecclesiastes, Book of," in Loetscher's *Twentieth Century Encyclopedia of Religious Knowledge; an Extension of the New Schaff-Herzog Encyclopedia of Religious Knowledge*, Vol. 1 (Grand Rapids: Baker Book House, 1955), p. 360.

[19] *Ibid.*, p. 361.

[20] Rowley, *op. cit.*, p. 143.

[21] Emil G. Kraeling, "Job, Book of," in Loetscher, *op. cit.*, Vol. I, p. 605.

[22] Rowley, *op. cit.*, pp. 143-45.

[23] From Wilde's *The Critic as Artist;* quoted in Kraeling, *The Book of the Ways of God* (New York: Scribner, 1939), p. 235.

[24] S. R. Driver and G. B. Gray, *A Critical and Exegetical Commentary on the Book of Job* (International Critical Commentary series), Vol. I (New York: Scribner, 1921), p. 243.

[25] Kraeling, *The Book of the Ways of God*, p. 161.

[26] Edgar J. Goodspeed, *The Story of the Apocrypha* (Chicago: University of Chicago Press, 1939), p. 135. I use the term "Apocrypha" in the Protestant sense (i.e., as equivalent to the Roman Catholic expression, "deuterocanonical writings"). This in part explains why I am not examining IV Maccabees at this point.

[27] Robert H. Pfeiffer, "Apocrypha: Old Testament," in Loetscher, *op. cit.*, Vol. I, p. 51.

[28] W. O. E. Oesterley, *An Introduction to the Books of the Apocrypha* (New York: Macmillan, 1935), pp. 244-48, 254-55.

[29] For example, Pfeiffer and Oesterley. Goodspeed believes that they are "probably retranslations" (*op. cit.*, p. 25).

[30] "The Book of Sirach," in R. H. Charles' *Apocrypha and Pseudepigrapha of the Old Testament*, Vol. I (Oxford: Clarendon Press, 1913), pp. 268 ff. This translation is employed where I quote Ecclesiasticus directly.

[31] Siegfried, *op. cit.*, p. 927.

[32] *The Apocryphal Literature: a Brief Introduction* (New Haven,

Conn.: Yale University Press, 1945), p. 93. Torrey, incidentally, like Goodspeed, questions the value of the Hebrew fragments of Ecclesiasticus.

[33] Pfeiffer, *loc. cit.*

[34] Charles, *op. cit.*, Vol. I, pp. 590-91.

[35] Pfeiffer, *loc. cit.* Weighty arguments have been adduced by some (for example, Eichhorn) to demonstrate composite authorship.

[36] Charles, *op. cit.*, Vol. I, p. 547.

[37] *Ibid.*, pp. 544-45. This chain-like form of argument (called "Sorites") was a favorite of the Stoics.

[38] *Op. cit.*, p. 228. Augustine's *caritas*, for example, is an amalgamation of pagan *eros* and Christian *agape*.

[39] London: SCM Press, 1950 (Studies in Biblical Theology, No. 2), p. 110.

[40] Cf. Luke 2:40; Mt. 13:54. Note the precedent established by the messianic prophecy in Isa. 11:1-3.

[41] E. C. Blackman states (*op. cit.*, p. 283) that "It is a fair assumption that St. Paul's thought was ... influenced by ... Wisdom 7.22-7 and Ecclus. 24.24-7; and by Rabbinic speculation which identified Wisdom and Law." This assertion is somewhat misleading, for Paul's grace emphasis is in striking contrast to the works point of view of the book of Wisdom and of most Rabbinic teaching. Robertson and Plummer (*A Critical and Exegetical Commentary on the First Epistle of St. Paul to the Corinthians* [International Critical Commentary series] , 2d ed. [Edinburgh: T. & T. Clark, 1914], p. 17) cautiously suggest that "St. Paul had possibly read" the Wisdom of Solomon. Of course, to read a book is not to agree with it. The same may be said with regard to the connection between the Prologue of the Gospel of John and contemporary Hellenistic thought (see the literature cited in Arndt and Gingrich, *op. cit.*, p. 480 [article," λόγος "]); in being "all things to all men," what was more natural than for the apostles to purify and then use current ideological conceptions in their preaching of the gospel of Christ?

[42] A. H. McNeile, *An Introduction to the Study of the New Testament*, 2d ed. rev. by C. S. C. Williams (Oxford: Clarendon Press, 1955), p. 159.

[43] See above, the text at note 17.

[44] Charles, *op. cit.*, Vol. I, p. 399. I follow the Greek and the old Latin versions in preference to the Syriac here.

[45] It will be noted that we are not concerned here with problems of Johannine authorship such as "the Apostle John" vs. "the Elder John."

[46] G. G. Atkins and C. S. Braden, *Procession of the Gods*, 3rd ed. (New York: Harper and Brothers, 1948), p. 155.

[47] Rabbi Ben Zion Bokser, *The Wisdom of the Talmud* (New York: Philosophical Library, 1951), p. 101.

[48] Eduard Zeller, *Outlines of the History of Greek Philosophy*, 13th ed., rev. by Wilhelm Nestle and trans. by L. R. Palmer (London: Routledge and Kegan Paul, 1931), pp. 262-63. Cf. the pseudepigraphical Book of IV Maccabees. Even the ancient Greeks in their deification of heroes did not reach such a level of effrontery.

Eros and Agape in Pico of Mirandola[1]

Introduction

Anders Nygren's remarkable work, *Agape and Eros*,[2] whose German edition appeared in Carl Stange's monographic series, "Studies of the Apologetics Seminar,"[3] and which opposes the interpretations both of Harnack[4] and of Scholz,[5] received from the outset high commendation as a classic theological production. In his review of the English translation of Part Two of *Agape and Eros* Sydney Cave wrote: "Dr. Nygren's fresh and suggestive study puts many an old problem in a new light and in particular shows how false were some of Harnack's brilliant generalizations on the history of early Christian thought and piety. . . . It is some years since we have read so suggestive and significant a book on the history of doctrine; or one that makes so clear the difference between Protestant and Roman Catholic theology and ethics."[6]

Although the main interpretative theme of the work has received criticism from some quarters,[7] Nygren could write in 1953, over 20 years after the publication of Part One of the original book: "In the discussion of the subject that has so far taken place, I have found no reason to abandon my original position at any point"[8]—and the vast majority of Protestant theologians seem to have agreed with this stand.

The author of *Agape and Eros* would be the first, however, to admit the limitations of the volume. The purpose of the work is very specific: to identify and investigate, by the sophisticated methodological technique of *Motivforsking* ("motif research"), the classical and Christian ideas of love as these have interacted in the patristic, medieval, and Reformation church. No attempt is made to provide an all-embracing historical study of the motifs; the historical data included serve chiefly as illustrations of the principle encounters between Eros and Agape. The survey character of Part Two of the work thus entails both an advantage and a disadvantage—the advantage of clarity and the disadvantage of overprecise categorization. A particular illustration of this latter difficulty will hold our attention in the present essay.

Nygren's section on "The Renewal of the Eros Motif in the Renascence" occupies three brief chapters in his total work. At the outset of the section he writes: "During the whole of the Middle Ages, Eros had been a living reality—but it was imprisoned in the Caritas-synthesis. . . . Toward the end of the Middle Ages, however, the situation is entirely altered. . . . The tension between the two motifs . . . has become so strong that the synthesis must disintegrate. The result of the disintegration may be expressed thus: the Renascence takes up the Eros motif, the Reformation the Agape motif. The most clear and interesting example of the concern of the Renascence for Eros is provided by Marsilio Ficino" (pp. 667, 669).

The succeeding discussion in Nygren's three Renaissance chapters consists entirely of an analysis of Ficino's teachings on love, and quite effectively demonstrates that Ficino presented a consistent, thoroughgoing Eros point of view. However, one is compelled to ask the question: Can we generalize from Ficino to the Renaissance as a whole? Granting that Ficino was "the life" of the Platonic Academy at Florence (to use Nygren's own expression), are we to assume from this that all important Renaissance figures maintained a static Eros conception of love? The mere fact that Nygren does not distinguish a "low" from a "high" Renaissance, or a "southern" from a "northern," gives us real cause for suspicion—particularly since the northern Renaissance seems to have had much more in common with the Reformation than with what Burckhardt termed "the civilization of the Renaissance in Italy." [9] But leaving these interesting considerations aside, we shall deal with a single figure of the High Italian Renaissance, a close friend of Ficino himself, and attempt to point out, through examining his conception of love, the dangers of assuming either that an historical epoch can be characterized by a single motif or synthesis or that a given philosopher-theologian must be associated with a single motif or harmonization of motifs.

We begin with a brief overview of the life of Giovanni Pico della Mirandola, designated the "Phoenix of the wits," [10] by Ficino and increasingly known in our own day through his "Oration on the Dignity of Man." [11]

Having provided the reader with biographical orientation, we shall discuss the concept of love in the thought of this remarkable Renaissance figure.

The Life of Pico of Mirandola

Our purpose in giving this sketch of Pico's brief life is not to reveal new facts about him (although the account will be based on original sources to a greater extent than is the case with most modern treatments).[12] It is rather our intention here to immerse the reader in the spirit of the times in which Pico lived and thus to provide an adequate background for understanding Pico's ethical point of view in general and his concept of love in particular.

J. M. Rigg's evaluation of Pico's personality makes an appropriate beginning for this account of his life.

> Giovanni Pico della Mirandola, "the Phoenix of the wits," is one of those writers whose personality will always count for a great deal more than their works. His extreme, almost feminine beauty, high rank, and chivalrous character, his immense energy and versatility, his insatiable thirst for knowledge, his passion for theorizing, his rare combination of intellectual hardihood with genuine devoutness of spirit, his extraordinary precocity, and his premature death make up a personality so engaging that his name at any rate, and the record of his brief life, must always excite the interest and enlist the sympathy of mankind, though none but those few in any generation who love to loiter curiously in the bypaths of literature and philosophy will ever care to follow his eager spirit through the labyrinths of recondite speculation which it once thridded with such high and generous hope.[13]

Giovanni Pico was born on Feb. 24, 1463, at Mirandola, a small territory not far from Ferrara, afterward absorbed into the duchy of Modena. Mirandola had become independent in the 14th century and had received the fief of Concordia from the emperor Sigismund in 1414.[14] Appropriately, Pico's birth was attended by an amazing prodigy. The story is well related by Ehrman, who retells it from G. F. Pico and More:

> Suddenly the stillness of the early morning was rudely shattered. The Prince and the priest, hurriedly crossing themselves, ran to a casement. A dazzling light in the shape of a fiery garland hovered about the chamber above.

Brighter and brighter it grew. It seemed almost as if in an effort to cast its portent far and wide, that this circlet of fire sought to blind its beholders. Then with no less remarkable speed than it had come, it disappeared in the heavens. Slowly the overseer of men and the guardian of the souls turned. In the light of the burning flambeau their faces. drained of all color, looked seared and grey. As they faced each other in questioning silence, the sound of women's voices raised in exclamations of joy was carried from the upper rooms of the castle. Of a sudden the noise ceased. The wail of a newborn babe floated through the quiet air. Both men fell to their knees and prayed. To the lord of Mirandola and Concordia another son had been born.[15]

In all probability Pico was very young when his father died, and the matter of his education devolved upon his mother. He was a remarkable child, and his powers of memory were particularly great. In More's *Life of Pico* we read:

Under ye rule and governaunce of his mother he was set to maysters & to lernynge: where with so ardent mynde he labored the studyes of humanite: yt within shorte whyle he was (and not without a cause) accompted amonge the chyef Oratours and Poetes of that tyme: in learnynge mervaylously swyfte and of so redy a wyt, that ye versis whiche he herde ones red he wolde agayne bothe forwarde and backwarde to the grete wonder of the herers rehearse. and over that wolde holde hit in sure remembraunce: whiche in other folkes wonte comenly to happen contrary. For they yt are swyfte in takyng be oftentymes slowe in remembrynge, and they yt with more labour and dyffyculte recyve hit more fast & surely holde hit.[16]

Pico's mother desired that he have a church career and sent him to Bologna at the age of 14 to acquire a knowledge of the pontifical letters (decretals). He disliked the dry, routine nature of the work and remained at Bologna for only two years. After this he spent seven years studying at Ferrara, Padua, Florence, and Perugia. During this time he started corresponding with Politian, formed a strong friendship with Ficino, and made the acquaintance of Savonarola. Of the latter contact Villari writes:

Meanwhile our hero, Savonarola, sat among the other monks, absorbed in his own thoughts, his cowl drawn over his head. His pale and haggard face, the fixed yet sparking glance of his deep-set eyes, the heavy lines seaming his forehead—his whole appearance, in short, indicated a profoundly thoughtful mind. Anyone comparing him with Pico, the one full of charm, courteous, sociable, and buoyant; the other full of gravity, lonely, severe, and almost harsh, might have judged the two characters to be thoroughly antagonistic and incapable of coming to an understanding. Yet from that day each felt drawn to the other, and their sympathy went on increasing.[17]

That Pico was involved in amours at this period seems evident from his correspondence.[18] He gave vent to his emotions in verses which he later destroyed.

In 1486 Pico wrote a commentary on Girolamo Benivieni's *canzone* on "Celestial Love." Since this work most fully sets forth Pico's early conception of the love idea, we shall examine it in detail in the next section of this paper. That same year Pico went to Rome and published his famous 900 "Conclusiones," or Theses, touching on all fields of knowledge—and intended to defend them against anyone who would dispute with him. He was willing even to pay the traveling expenses of scholars who did not live in Rome but who nevertheless desired to take part in the debate. His famous *De hominis dignitate* was written at this time. Concerning it Kristeller says:

> Pico's *Oration* was written as an introductory speech for this projected disputation, probably in 1486. Apparently it was not usual to furnish this kind of rhetorical introduction for a disputation. Yet introductory speeches at the beginning of the school year or at the opening of particular courses were an established custom of medieval schools and universities—a custom further developed by the Humanists of the Renaissance. Pico's disputation speech was obviously patterned after such examples of academic eloquence.[19]

This disputation never took place, however, because the ecclesiastical authorities accused Pico of heresy in 13 of his theses. He was ultimately cleared only through a special appeal to the Pope (Innocent VIII). The volume in which his theses were contained was suppressed.

Giovanni Francesco gives the impression that Pico's printing of the theses was motivated by a desire for glory and that his devotion to the religious was not very great at the time. The section concerned with the theses is titled in More's translation: "Of His Mynde and Vayngloryouse Dispicions of Rome," and in it More says, "Yet

was he not kendled in ye love of God." [20] The impression
that Pico was in a low spiritual state at the time is increased by the title of the next section of this work, which
reads: "Of the Chaunge of His Lyfe." [21] In order not
to receive a wrong impression here, one must note that
although Pico was undoubtedly motivated by a youthful
desire for fame in publishing his theses, he was beyond
reproach in respect to Roman orthodoxy. Concerning
Pico's theses even Paul Lejay (in the *Catholic Encyclopedia*) states unequivocally, "Innocent VIII was made to
believe that at least thirteen of these theses were heretical, though in reality they merely revealed the shallow-
ness of the learning of that epoch." [22] Greswell offers
decisive proof on this point:

> This undertaking of Picus, however extraordinary it may
> at present appear, was in some measure sanctioned by the
> custom of his own age, in which public disputations were
> not unusual or unprecedented. He had fortified himself
> with the express permission of Innocent VIII, who at this
> time occupied the chair of St. Peter. He studiously and
> avowedly professed all possible deference to the authority
> of the church, solemnly engaging to support his theses only
> "sub apostolicae sedis correctione." Nay more, when in
> his list of "Conclusiones," after a great number to be
> maintained "secundum opinionem aliorum," he intro-
> duces no fewer than five hundred "secundum opinionem
> propriam." Of these he says, "nihil assertive, vel pro-
> babiliter pono, nisi quatenus id vel verum vel probabile
> iudicat sacrosancta Romana ecclesia et caput eius bene
> meritum, Pontifex Innocentius Octavus; cuius iudicio qui
> mentis suae iudicium non summittit, mentem non ha-
> bet." [23]

It was chiefly the jealousy of the Roman divines which
resulted in Pico's condemnation, as he himself says in
his hastily composed *Apologia* (1489), which he dedicated
to Lorenzo de Medici.[24]

After his acquittal Pico journeyed to France, where
he was presented to Charles VIII.[25] Soon after, he was
ordered by the pope to return to Rome on account of renewed antagonism towards him, which had been incited
primarily by his *Apologia*. The pope permitted him to
take up residence in the vicinity of Florence, but it was
not until 1493 that he received complete exoneration (from
Pope Alexander VI).

About 1489 was published Pico's *Heptaplus*, "a rather rhapsodic treatment of the Biblical account of creation." [26] In March 1491 Pico completed his treatise *De Ente et Uno*, the theme of which he sets forth in his introductory address to Politian.

> Though you know me to have it in view (in a more extensive work, upon which I am at present employed) to shew the agreement of Plato and Aristotle; you earnestly solicit me briefly to commit to writing the principal arguments which I adduced to you in person, upon the beforementioned occasion, and when, if I am not mistaken, our friend Domenicus Benivenius was also present, who is endeared to us both, as well by his erudition as integrity. To Politian, whom I may term my almost inseparable associate, I can refuse nothing, especially of a literary nature. [27]

Pico remained in Florence until the summer of 1491, at which time he accompanied Politian to Venice. They returned to Florence in time to be present at the deathbed of Lorenzo (April 8, 1492). Then Pico went to Ferrara. From his correspondence we learn that here he almost blinded himself working with the Hebrew books of a Sicilian Jew who intended to leave the city in 20 days. [28]

Some years before his death Pico underwent a striking change in life. He burned the love poetry written in his youth and concentrated his whole attention on theological studies. From this final period of life comes the short devotional works which embody his mature conception of love and which we shall discuss below: "An Interpretation of Psalm Sixteen," "An Exposition of the Lord's Prayer," "Twelve Rules of Spiritual Battle," and "Twelve Properties of a Lover." For a very inadequate remuneration he transferred to his nephew, Giovanni Francesco, his share of the ancestral principalities of Mirandola and Concordia. He used the money for the support of his household and for charitable donations. He refused the highest ecclesiastical honors. More writes:

> When he sawe many men with grete labour & money desyre & bysely purchase ye offices & dygnites of ye chirche (whiche are now a dayes alas ye whyle communely bought & solde) him selfe refused to recyve them whan two knyges offred them; whan an other man offred hym grete worldely promocon yf he wolde go to ye kynges courte: he gave hym suche an answere, that he sholde well knowe that he neyther desyred worship ne worldly

ryches but rather set them at nought yt he might ye more
quyetly gyve hym selfe to study & ye servyce of God:
this wyse he persuaded yt to a phylosophre and hym yt
seketh for wysedome it was not prayse to gather rychesse
but to refuse them.[29]

He determined to devote his old age to the defense of the
faith; his intention was to produce a work *Adversus
hostes ecclesiae,* in which he would refute

I. The avowed and open enemies of Christianity; II.
Atheists and those who reject every religious system, upon their own mode of reasoning; III. The Jews, from the
books of the Old Testament and their own writers; IV.
The followers of Mahomet from the Koran; V. Idolators
and such as are addicted to any superstitious science,
amongst whom, he particularly directed the artillery of
his arguments against the partizans of judicial astrology;
VI. Those who, perverting the doctrine of Christianity, or
denying due obedience to the church, i.e., heretics, whom
he distinguished into no fewer than two hundred species,
intending to make them so many distinct subjects of his
animadversion; VII. Those Christians who "hold the truth
in unrighteousness" and discredit and contradict their profession by their practice.[30]

Only the section against astrologers was published (1495)
—the notes which Pico had written for other works were
in various types of shorthand that could not be deciphered
after his death. On the *Disputationes adversus astrolo-
giam divinatricem* Paul Lejay says, "Because of this
book and his controversy against astrology Pico marks
an era and a decisive progressive movement in ideas." [31]
Pico had even intended to take the crucifix in hand and
travel barefooted from city to city as a preacher of the
Gospel.

Pico died of a fever on Nov. 17, 1494, not yet 32 years
of age. His intimate friend Politian had passed away only
two months before. Pico died on the day Charles VIII of
France made his triumphant entrance into Florence. On
hearing of Pico's illness Charles sent with all possible
speed two of his own personal physicians and with his
own hand wrote the scholar a letter expressing his sympathy. Pico's remains were interred in the church of
San Marco, near those of Politian. His epitaph reads:[32]

Ioannes Iacet Hic Mirandula. Caetera Norunt et Tagus
et Ganges Forsan et Antipodes.

His death was mourned by the learned in all parts of Europe. Before his burial, although he had never taken orders, he was invested with the habit of the Fratri Predicanti (Dominicans) by the hands of their general, Savonarola, who had been Pico's confessor and who had almost persuaded him to become a member of his order.

The Concept of Love in Pico's Thought

Orientation

Little has been written on Pico's ethics in general or on his view of love in particular. Arthur Levy's doctoral dissertation at the Friedrich-Wilhelms-Universität, Berlin, in 1908, attempted to deal with the whole gamut of Pico's philosophical thought, and approximately one fourth of the work was devoted to his anthropology and ethics. But, unhappily, less than half of the total work was ever published, and the ethics section is known to us only by its table of contents.[33] From this table of contents it is evident, however, that Levy believed there is but a single unified concept of love in Pico—a concept involving the three aspects of *sinnliche Liebe, rationale Liebe,* and *intellektuelle Gottesliebe,* the latter making possible *die Erreichung der Glückseligkeit.*

Perhaps the importance of the love concept in Pico has been stressed most by Eugenio Garin, who makes it the subject of the final chapter of his standard work, *Giovanni Pico della Mirandola: Vita e dotrina.*[34] It is Garin's belief that the love idea acts as the harmonizing principle for the amazing religio-philosophical syncretism characteristic of Pico's thought.[35] In setting forth Pico's love concept, Garin cites the later devotional works *(Spiritualis pugnae arma; In orat. dom. expositio; In Psalmum XV [i.e., XVI] comm.)* in immediate conjunction with his early *Commento alla canzone d'amore.* Clearly Garin sees but a single love idea in Pico. He can say, in fact: "Pico is able to draw the work of his precocious maturity to a close by returning to the impetuous enthusiasm of his youth.[36]

The question before us is whether Pico really held a single, static conception of love or whether his thought on the subject underwent a change in the course of his religious development. From an a priori standpoint, it could be argued, on the one hand, that Pico's short scholarly life militates against the probability of such a change; on the other hand, one can reemphasize the biographical fact that Pico experienced a religious "conversion" several years prior to his early death. Pierre-Marie Cordier, though wishing to tone down the severity of this religious crisis, readily admits that Savonarola "exercised an undeniable influence on Pico from 1490 to his death" and that the short devotional works which Pico wrote in the last two years of his life "show the intense rhythm of his religious life in these final years."[37] Rigg asserts that "as his short life drew towards its close Pico's preoccupation with religion became more intense and exclusive." [38] However, such a question as we have posed cannot be answered a priori. It is obviously essential that we examine Pico's earlier and later writings themselves.

The Young Pico

It would undoubtedly be possible to induce the conception of love maintained by the young Pico if we were to analyze the anthropocentric anthropology in such writings as his *Oration on the Dignity of Man;* however, a much more direct approach is possible through his *Commento alla canzone d'amore,* which specifically sets forth his views on the subject. We shall therefore restrict ourselves in this section to a discussion of the *Comento.*

The occasion for the writing of the *Commento* was the production of Girolamo Benivieni's *Canzone d'amore secondo la mente e opinione de' Platonici.*

Benivieni ... was a Platonist, and having saturated himself with the Symposium and the Phaedrus, the fifth book of the third Ennead of Plotinus, and Ficino's commentaries, thought himself qualified to write a canzone on ideal love which should put Guinicelli and Cavalcanti to shame. The result was that he produced a canzone which has a certain undeniable elevation of style, but is so obscure that even with the help of Pico's detailed commentary it takes some hard study to elicit its meaning. The theme, however, is the purifying influence of love in raising the soul through various stages of refinement from the preoccupation with sensuous beauty to the contemplation of the ideal type of the beautiful, and thence to the knowledge of God, who, though, as Pico is careful to ex-

plain. He is not beautiful Himself, since beauty implies
an element of variety repugnant to His nature, is nevertheless the source of the beautiful no less than of the true
and the good.[39]

Pico's *Commento* on the poem is his "only important work
in the vernacular," [40] and breathes a thoroughgoing
Platonic atmosphere. Even Cordier, who avowedly wishes
to show that Pico is "the purest figure of Christian humanism," says of the content of the *Commento:* "Such
a teaching is far removed from Catholic thought." [41]
The *Commento* was not published until after Pico's death;
and Giovannie Francesco Pico insisted that it appear in
Latin rather than in Tuscan, in order not to "cast pearls
before swine." Benivieni himself wrote of it after Pico's
death:[42]

> When Pico and I reread that *Canzone* and the com-
> mentary on it, the spirit and fervor which had led me to
> compose it and him to interpret it had already given out,
> and there was born in our minds some shadow of doubt
> whether it was proper for one who professes the law of
> Christ and wishes to treat love, especially divine and
> celestial love, to deal with it in a Platonic and not in a
> Christian manner. Therefore we thought that it would be
> better to suspend publication of such a work, at least un-
> til we could by revision turn it from Platonic to Christian.

In reference to this statement of Benivieni's, Cordier
aptly remarks: "If we accept Benivieni, it was a concern
for orthodoxy, corresponding to an evolution in their
thought, which deterred them from publishing the *Canzone* and its *Commento*." [43]

The fact is that Benivieni's short poem and Pico's
lengthy commentary on it provide an illustration—as
clean-cut as Ficino's works[44]—of the Italian Renaissance tendency to destroy the medieval "caritas-synthesis" through the absorption of Agape into Eros. Pico's
Commento abounds with such assertions as the following, which present pure Eros in classic terms—as ac-
quisitive, egocentric love employed by man to carve out
a path to the Divine[45]:

> Venus then is Beauty, whereof Love is generated, prop-
> erly his Mother, because Beauty is the cause of Love,
> not as productive principle of this act, to Love, but as
> its object; the Soul being the efficient cause of it as of

all his acts; Beauty the material. . . . Celestial Love is an
Intellectual desire of Ideal Beauty.[46]

Now few would dipute such an interpretation of Pico's
Commento (we have already seen that Levy and Garin
would consider this interpretation as adequate for Pico's
entire philosophical-theological career). The question now
remains: Did the mature Pico view love in this same
way?

The Mature Pico

In the general introduction to this paper, we noted
that Nygren treats the Renaissance as a homogeneous
epoch, deals solely with Marsilio Ficino in analyzing it,
and arrives at the conclusion that, just as the Reformation represents the overthrow of the medieval "caritas-
synthesis" by a sole concentration upon Agape, so the
Renaissance displays the breakup of this synthesis by
absolute stress on Eros. To Nygren, then, the Renaissance and Agape are poles apart, and one should not find
in Renaissance thinkers evidences of a love which is
"spontaneous," "unmotivated," "indifferent to value,"
"creative of value," directed from God to man rather than
from man to God, and indeed the "initiator of fellowship
with God." [47] It is our contention that in his later devotional writings—those produced after his contact with
Savonarola had brought about a redirection of his religious life—Pico moves toward just such an Agape concept
of love.[48] Let us examine each of his mature devotional
productions in order to see at firsthand the view of love
presented in them.

We begin with his *Commentary on Psalm Sixteen*, the
only one of his psalm commentaries to appear in the collected editions of his *Opera omnia*. Apparently Pico's
intention had been to produce a comprehensive work on
the Psalms, but his comments on only six psalms have
come down to us (four in fragmentary form), and all but
the *Commentary on Psalm Sixteen* remained unpublished
until recent times.[49] The very fact that Psalm Sixteen
seems to have been the only psalm on which Pico produced a finished, publishable commentary is significant
in itself. This psalm is especially strong in its theocentric
emphasis—from its opening words, "Preserve me, O God,

for in Thee do I put my trust," through such assertions
as "O my soul, thou hast said unto the Lord, Thou art
my Lord: my goodness extendeth not to thee," and "I
have set the Lord always before me," to the closing
verse, "Thou wilt shew me the path of life." Pico's comments are thoroughly consistent with the God-oriented
character of the psalm and differ most markedly from
the youthful anthropocentrism of his *Oration on the Dignity of Man*. A short quotation from the *Commentary* will
provide sufficient evidence in this regard:

> Conserva me Domine. That is to saye, kepe me good
> Lorde: whiche worde kepe me: yf it be well consydered:
> taketh awaye all occasyon o pryde. For he that is able
> of hym self ony thynge to gete is able of him self that
> same thynge to kepe. He that asketh then of God to be
> kepte in the state of vertue signifyeth in that askynge
> that from the begynnynge he gote not that vertue by hym
> selfe. He then whiche remembreth yt he attayned his vir-
> tue: not by his owne power but by the power of God:
> may not be proude thereof but rather humbled before God
> after those wordes of th apostle. Quid habes quod non
> accepisti. What hast thou that thou hast not receyved.
> And yf thou hast receyved hit: why arte thou proude
> thereof as though thou haddest not receyved it. Two wordes
> then be there which we sholde ever have in our mouthe:
> ye one. Miserere mei Deus. Have mercy on me Lorde:
> whan we remembre our vyce: that other. Conserva me
> Deus. Kepe me good Lorde: whan we remembre our ver-
> tue.[50]

Pico's *Exposition of the Lord's Prayer* is given the most
prominent position in the 1572 edition of his collected
works, for it appears first in the folio volume.[51] However, strange to say, it has never been translated from
Latin into English. Pico begins with a short discussion of
the general problem of prayer, and then treats in turn
each of the petitions of the Lord's Prayer. He asserts as
axiomatic: "If . . . we ought to know how we should pray,
we must first learn what we should desire, for what we
desire above all, that we ask to receive in our prayers."
But then the question naturally arises as to how we are
to know what is desirable. Pico rejects carnal affec-
tions, knowledge, prophecies, miracles, and mystic experiences (and thereby rejects the previously sought
goals of his youth) and says: "But we shall ask

God *not* to give us such things; instead, we shall ask Him to give us His own pure love with perfect humility." Such God-bestowed love, he argues on the basis of Luke 11:27, 28, is better than having Christ in one's womb as Mary had. Then he adds the following statement, which does not greatly differ from Luther's remarks on Rom. 8:26, 27: "And because we do not know when the things of life are beneficial to us and when they are not, we should wholly abandon the matter to God's judgment" (thereupon he quotes Matt. 6:8). In discussing the opening ascription, "Our Father who art in heaven," he refers to his comments on Ps. 16:1 which we have quoted above. Of the first three petitions he writes: "These first three petitions concern the goodness of God, which we ought to desire far more than any personal good of our own—just as we ought to love Him above all things.... Therefore we should, in the first place, desire God's glory *per se,* and love His glory not merely to the extent that it is beneficial to us, but inasmuch as it is good in itself." His exposition of the last three petitions (dealing with human good) centers in "Give us this day our daily bread." Instead of giving an anthropocentric, moralistic commentary on this petition, Pico devotes a full three pages (out of the total of 11 comprising the entire treatise) to emphasizing the fact that our "bread" in the final analysis is Christ Himself. He uses John 6:51 as the basis of this argument and builds upon it a Christocentric understanding of the place of love in the Christian life: "Now we are united to God in this life through grace, which is the source (*radix*) of faith, hope, and love, and in the next life through seeing Him face to face and through experiencing the complete fruition of His goodness. All this is bestowed on us through Jesus Christ."[52] Pico's summary statement on the Lord's Prayer well reflects the atmosphere of the entire *Exposition:*

> All consideration of this Prayer is reduced to a consideration of Christ's Cross and our own death. Our own death shows us truly that we are pilgrims on earth, and the death of Christ made us sons of God; so that, thinking neither of an earthly father nor of an earthly fatherland, we may rightly say: "Our Father, who art in heaven." Our death keeps us from seeking our own glory, for we

shall soon be dust and ashes; and Christ's death makes us desire God's glory, for on our behalf He did not shrink from the disgrace of the Cross. Therefore we shall say: "Hallowed be Thy Name," as if we were saying: "Not to us, Lord, not to us, but to Thy Name give glory." Moreover, if we remember that all men swiftly perish through death, we shall want Christ to rule among them.

The *Twelves Rules of Spiritual Battle* and the *Twelve Properties of a Lover* are very brief in extent, but indicate the same movement from Eros to Agape in Pico which we have already observed. In the *Twelve Rules* we read:[53]

Also putte not thy truste in mannes helpe but in the onelye vertue of Christe Jesu whiche sayde: Truste well, for I have vaynquished the worlde. And in an other place He sayde: The prince of this worlde is caste oute thereof. Wherfore let us truste by his onelye vertue, to vaynquishe the worlde, and to subdue the divell. . . . Wherefore above al temptations manne or woman oughte to arme theym mooste stronglye agaynste the temptation of pryde, sens pryde is the rote of all myschyfe, agaynste the whiche the onelye remedye is to thynke alway that God humbled hym selfe for us unto the crosse.

The *Twelve Properties* read as follows:[54]

To love one alone and contempne all other for yt one.
To thynke hym unhappy that is not with his love.
To adourne hym selfe for the pleasure of his love.
To suffre all thyng, thoughe hit were death, to be with his love.
To desyre also to suffre shame harme for his love, and to thynke that hurte swete.
To be with his love ever as he may, yf not in dede yet in thought.
To love all thynge yt perteyneth unto his love.
To coveite the prayse of his love and not to suffre ony dysprayse.
To beleve of his love all thynges excellent, & to desyre that all folke sholde thynke the same.
To wepe often with his love: in presence for joye, in absence for sorrowe.
To languysshe ever and ever to burne in the desyre of his love.
To serve his love, nothyng thynkynge of ony rewarde or profyte.

These properties (which remind us somewhat of 1 Cor. 13) are explicitly applied to God in the following sentence: "He Himself is of all beings the best and most lovely and wisest . . . and has conferred on us the greatest favours, since He has both created us from nothing and redeemed us from hell by the blood of His Son." [55]

Conclusion

The preceding discussion has attempted to demonstrate that in Pico of Mirandola, one of the most striking personalities of the Italian Renaissance, a definite movement occurred from an Eros to a predominantly Agape conception of love. Our contention is not that Pico necessarily reached the point of pure Agape (no man, it seems safe to say, is able to achieve a complete about-face in life, since changes after all occur in the same person), but the quotations recorded above do indicate a definite alteration in general point of view.

What conclusions can be drawn from the above analysis? First of all, it appears that Pico should serve as a warning to practitioners of *Motivforsking*, for his spiritual progress demonstrates both that individuals change and should not be too quickly categorized and that epochs cannot be characterized without the investigation of many personalities related to them. Second, Pico comes to us as a troubled representative of those agonizing years on the eve of the Reformation and reminds us that Eros and Agape posed an existential issue for some (even in Renaissance Italy) who had no personal contact with the momentous events soon to transpire north of the Alps.

Notes

[1] At the outset of this study I wish to express appreciation to Dr. Gunnar Hillerdal of the University of Lund, Sweden, under whose supervision it was carried out.

[2] Published originally in Swedish at Stockholm (Part One, 1930; Part Two, 1936). German translation: *Eros and Agape. Gestalwandlungen der christlichen Liebe* (Gütersloh: C. Bertelsmann, 1930 [1. Teil], 1937 [2. Teil]). Part One was translated into English in abridged form by A. G. Hebert in 1932 and published by the SPCK in London. Philip S. Watson translated Part Two, which was issued in two separate volumes by SPCK in 1938-39. In 1953 Watson revised and completed Hebert's translation of Part One, and the work was finally published in a single English volume (London: SPCK; Philadelphia: Westminster Press,

1953). In this article all page references will apply to this latter edition of the English translation.

[3] The book was dedicated to Stange, who celebrated his 60th birthday on March 7, 1930. G. A. van den Bergh van Eysinga notes this and uses the apologetics connection as a point of departure for his excellent review of Part One of the work. See the "Boekbeoordeelingen" section of *Nieuw theologisch Tijdschrift* (Haarlem), XX (1931), 253-56.

[4] See the review of Part Two by Kurt Kesseler in *Theologische Literaturzeitung*, LXIV:6 (1939), 220-22.

[5] Heinrich Scholz's *Eros und Caritas: Die platonische Liebe und die Liebe im Sinne des Christentums* was published at Halle by Max Niemeyer in 1929. Cf. the composite review by W. Blossfeldt of Nygren's book, Scholz's work, and of L. Grünhut's *Eros and Agape* (Leipzig: L. Hirschfeld, 1931), in *Blätter fur deutsche Philosophie*, VI (1932/33), 413-17.

[6] *Congregational Quarterly*, XVII (1939), 101, 360.

[7] Note especially J. Burnaby, *Amor Dei* (London: Hodder & Stoughton, 1938); and M. C. D'Arcy, *The Mind and Heart of Love* (New York: Holt, 1947). Also see the review by Philip S. Watson in *Expository Times*, XLIX, 12 (1938), 537-40.

[8] *Agape and Eros*, p. vi. Hereafter page references to this work will be given in parentheses in the text.

[9] Cf. Albert Hyma, *The Christian Renaissance* (New York: Century Company, 1925).

[10] Other contemporary testimonies to Pico are given in Pearl Kibre, *The Library of Pico della Mirandola* (New York: Columbia University Press, 1936), pp. 3, 4.

[11] Conveniently available in English translation in Petrarca et al., *The Renaissance Philosophy of Man*, edd. Ernst Carrirer, Paul Oskar Kristeller, and John Herman Randall, Jr. (Chicago: University of Chicago Press, 1948), pp. 223-54. Kristeller asserts that in Pico "we have the picture of a many-sided if not 'universal' intellectual activity that corresponded to the best traditions and ideals of his time" (*ibid.*, p. 216).

[12] One of the chief sources upon which my biographical sketch of Pico is based is the little-known but scholarly thorough *Memoirs of Politianus, Picus, et al*, by W. Parr Greswell, 2d ed. (London: Cadell and Davies, 1805), which contains a book-length (200-page) account of Pico's life and works (pp. 153-367), based chiefly on Pico's letters and on some difficult-to-obtain original source materials. Greswell quotes these in the original languages (Latin, Greek, Italian) and occasionally gives translations as well. Pico's complete correspondence, it should be noted, is best consulted in the Basel (1572) edition of his works, *Opera omnia Ioannis Pici*, I, 340-410.

[13] *Giovanni Pico della Mirandola*, J. M. Rigg, ed. (London: David Nutt, 1890), p. v. Rigg here republishes Sir Thomas More's paraphrase translation of the primary source account of Pico's life by G. F. Pico.

[14] Paul Lejay, "Mirandola, Giovanni Pico della," *Catholic Encyclopedia*, X, 352.

[15] Sidney Hellman Ehrman, *Three Renaissance Silhouettes* (New York: Putnam, 1928), pp. 84, 85.

[16] Rigg, p. 8.

[17] Pasquale Villari, *Life and Times of Girolamo Savonarola*, trans.

Linda Villari (New York: Scribner and Welford, 1888), I, 77. This is the definitive biography of Savonarola.

[18] See Greswell, pp. 166-76, and Rigg.

[19] *The Renaissance Philosophy of Man*, p. 217. In a paper on "Renaissance Humanism," read before the 75th annual meeting of the American Historical Association on Dec. 28, 1960, Hanna H. Gray maintained that eloquence—the rhetorical emphasis—is one of the chief unifying characteristics of Renaissance Humanism.

[20] Rigg, p. 9.

[21] *Ibid.*, p. 12.

[22] Lejay, *loc. cit.*

[23] Greswell, pp. 230, 231.

[24] Pico, *Apologia*, in *Opera*, I, 114-25.

[25] Rigg, p. 86.

[26] Joseph Leon Blau, *The Christian Interpretation of the Cabala in the Renaissance* (New York: Columbia University Press, 1944), p. 28.

[27] Greswell, p. 304 (Greswell's translation).

[28] *Opera* I, 360. See also Blau, pp. 29, 30.

[29] Rigg, p. 19. Ivan Pusino, in his article, "Zur Quellenkritik für eine Biographie Picos," *Zeitschrift für Kirchengeschichte*, XLV (1927), 370-82, argues on the basis of some of Pico's surviving vernacular sonnets that his conversion was gradual, evolutionary, and "natural," not sudden, traumatic, and externally motivated; and that in stressing a sudden change of life G. F. Pico's biography was too much colored by its author's acceptance of Savonarola's religious approach. However this may be, the fact of a conversion cannot be doubted, as Pusino himself is quick to point out.

[30] Greswell, p. 331 (Greswell's translation).

[31] Lejay, *loc. cit.*

[32] Greswell, p. 355.

[33] Arthur Levy, *Die Philosophie Giovanni Picos della Mirandola: Ein Beitrag zur Philosophie der Frührenaissance (Einleitung, Kapitel I, Kapitel II, Abschnitt C)* (Berlin: Ebering, 1908), 49 p. The table of contents to the entire dissertation is given on pp. 3-6; ch. 4 dealt with Pico's anthropology and ethics. An examination of the *Jahresverzeichnis der deutschen Hochschulschriften* indicates that the dissertation was published only in this incomplete form.

[34] Pubblicazioni della R. Università degli Studi di Firenze. Facoltà di Lettere e Filosofia. Ser. III, Vol. 5 (Firenze: Felice Le Monnier, 1937).

[35] *Ibid.*, p. 209.

[36] *Ibid.*, p. 215.

[37] Pierre-Marie Cordier, *Jean Pic de la Mirandole* (Paris: Nouvelles Éditions Debresse, 1957), pp. 45, 47.

[38] Rigg, p. xxxvii.

[39] *Ibid.*, pp. xxiv-xxv. A detailed analysis of Pico's *Commento* is given in John Charles Nelson, *Renaissance Theory of Love* (New York: Columbia University Press, 1958), pp. 54-63.

[40] Edmund G. Gardner, ed. *A Platonic Discourse upon Love by Pico della Mirandola* (Boston: Merrymount Press, 1914), p. xx. Gardner has here republished a 1651 abridged English translation of Pico's *Commento* by Thomas Stanley. The original of the *Commento*, together

with Benivieni's poem, is best consulted in the critical edition of Pico's works by Eugenio Garin: Pico, *De hominis dignitate et al.*, Edizioni Nazionale dei Classici del Pensiero Italiano (Firenze: Vallecchi Editore, 1942), pp. 443-581.

[41] Cordier, p. 63.

[42] Quoted by Garin in Pico, *De hominis dignitate*, p. 13.

[43] Cordier, p. 64. Cordier notes (p. 112) the interesting fact that some copies of the Basel (1572) edition of Pico's *Opera omnia* have Reuchlin's *De arte cabalistica* substituted for Pico's *Commento*. Is this because some felt that the *Commento* did not reflect its author's final thinking on the problem of love, and was in fact inconsistent with his later writings? That the substitution occurred merely because of orthodox circumspection seems unlikely, since Reuchlin's work hardly served as a norm of orthodoxy at the time.

[44] See especially Ficino's *Commentarium in Convivium Platonis de amore*, in his *Platonis Opera omnia quae exstant, Marsilio Ficino interprete* (Lugduni, 1590), pp. 773, 774.

[45] See Nygren, pp. 175-81, 210.

[46] Gardner, pp. 29, 30.

[47] Nygren, pp. 175-81, 210.

[48] Nelson, though he attempts to present Pico's concept of love solely on the basis of the *Commento* (and thus of course finds Pico's love idea almost exclusively Platonic), vaguely suggests the true solution in his concluding statement: "Renaissance Neoplatonism tried to combine with the classical ideal of beauty the Christian ideal of religious and moral perfection. The difficulty of this fusion is shown by the fact that the preaching of a Savonarola could influence such men as Benivieni and Pico to forsake Platonistic philosophy for revivalist religion" (*op. cit.*, p. 63).

[49] Cordier, p. 75; Pico, *De hominis dignitate*, p. 93. The difficulty of dating the Psalm fragments has led us to concentrate attention on Psalm Sixteen. However, after working with all of this material, Garin states: "When we read in their entirety Pico's religious texts and Biblical commentaries, I believe that his detachment from external forms will appear in bold relief—those forms of Ficinian Platonism which beguiled him when he wrote his *Commento*" (quoted by Cordier, *loc. cit.*).

[50] Rigg, p. 48 (passage translated by Sir Thomas More).

[51] Pico, *Opera* I, leaves a1[r] a6[v]. My thanks to the Newberry Library, Chicago, which kindly permitted me to use this volume in its rare book collection.

[52] Cf. Ivan Pusino, "Ficinos and Picos religiös philosophische Anschauungen," *Zeitschrift für Kirchengeschichte*, XLIV (1925), 534 and 535.

[53] Here translated by Sir Thomas Elyot (author of the *Boke of the Governour)* and included in Rigg, pp. 91, 93.

[54] *Ibid.*, p. 67 (translated by More). It is noteworthy that Sir Thomas More translated three of Pico's four mature devotional works, together with G. F. Pico's biography of him, and several of Pico's letters. More apparently saw in Pico's life, and especially in his final labors, a powerful testimony to the transforming effects of the Christian message.

[55] *Ibid.*, p. 95 (translated by Rigg).

The Law's Third Use: Sanctification

In 1528—only a decade after the posting of the Ninety-five Theses—Erasmus asserted that "the Lutherans seek two things only—wealth and wives *(censum et uxorem)"* and that to them the Gospel meant "the right to live as they please" (letter of March 20, 1528, to W. Pirkheimer, a fellow humanist). From that day to this Protestants have been suspected of antinomianism, and their Gospel of "salvation by grace through faith, apart from the works of the Law" has again and again been understood as a spiritual insurance policy which removes the fear of hell and allows a man to "live as he pleases."

Sanctification Twice Desanctified

The claim that Protestantism is essentially antinomian seemed to have an especially strong basis in fact in the nineteenth century. Industrialization and urbanization brought about social evils which were overlooked and rationalized by many professing Protestants. Inevitably a reaction occurred, and in the social-gospel movement of the late nineteenth and early twentieth centuries one encounters a textbook illustration of what Hegel called the antithesis. In its fear that Protestantism had become ethically indifferent, the social-gospel movement of Washington Gladden and Walter Rauschenbusch identified the Christian message with social ethics. From an apparent justification without sanctification, the pendulum swung to a "sanctification" which swallowed up justification. In their eagerness to bring in the kingdom of God through social action and the amelioration of the ills of the industrial proletariat, the social gospelers generally lost track of the central insight of the Reformation: that the love of *Christ* must constrain the Christian, and that we can experience and manifest this love only if we have personally come into a saving relationship with the Christ who "first loved us" (I John 4:19) and gave himself on the cross for us (I Peter 2:24).

World War I burst the optimistic bubble of the social gospel; no longer did there seem to be much assurance that human beings had the capacity to establish a sanctified society on earth. But the reductionist biblical criti-

cism with which the social-gospel movement had allied
itself did not die as easily. So loud had been the voices
of modernism against a perspicuous, fully reliable Scripture that in the most influential Protestant circles it was
believed that a return to a propositional biblical ethic
could never take place. The result was (and is, for the
movement is by no means dead) an existential ethic.

The Protestant existentialists do not of course go to
the length of the atheist Jean-Paul Sartre, who says in
Existentialism and Human Emotions, "There are no
omens in the world." But when Sartre follows this assertion with the qualification that even if there were omens
(as the Christian believes), "I myself choose the meaning they have," he comes very close to the approach of
the contemporary Protestant existentialist. The latter,
unable to rely (he thinks) on a biblical revelation which
is objectively and eternally definitive in matters ethical,
must himself "choose the meaning" of Scripture for his
unique existential situation. In practice he agrees with
Simone de Beauvoir when she says that man "has no need
of any outside guarantee to be sure of his goals" (*The
Ethics of Ambiguity*). Right or wrong is never determined
absolutely in advance; the Bible is not a source of ethical
absolutes—it is rather the record of how believers of former times made ethical decisions in the crises of their experience. What distinguishes the Christian ethic from the
non-Christian, in this view? Only the motivation of love.
The Christian has experienced God's love, and so is in
a position to bring that love to bear upon the unique existential decisions he faces. This existential approach, at
root highly individualistic, has in recent years been given
a "group discussion" orientation by such writers as A.
T. Rasmussen, who, in his *Christian Social Ethics* (1956),
asserts that existential decision should take place in "the
higher community of God," where "Christian discussion"
serves as "the channel through which the Holy Spirit
moves in the dialectic or give-and-take of genuine spiritual intercourse to provide ethical guidance."

The contemporary existential ethic in Protestantism
is a second instance of desanctifying sanctification, for
it inevitably devolves into ethical relativism. Sartre,
when asked advice by a young man who, during World

War II, was torn between a desire to join the Free French Forces and a feeling that he should stay in France to take care of his mother, could only say, "You're free, choose, that is, invent." Likewise, the Protestant existentialist can never appeal to absolute law; he can only say, "You're free, choose to love." But what does this mean in concrete terms? Theoretically it can mean "anything goes"—an antinomianism indeed—for each existential decision is unique and without precedent. Thus the housemouther in *Tea and Sympathy* who committed adultery out of self-giving (*agape?*) love in order to prove to a student that he was not incapable of heterosexual relationships, cannot be condemned for her decision. As for Rasmussen's ethic of social existentialism, one can see that it merely compounds the problem on the group level. George Forell has well characterized this approach as "inspiration by bladder control," for the person who stays longest in the group discussion is frequently the one whose "responsible participation" determines the "contextual and concrete" ethic of the moment. The absence of an eternal ethical standard either in individualistic or in social existentialism totally incapacitates it for promoting Christian holiness.

Answer of Classical Protestantism

In the Protestantism of the Reformation, antinomianism is excluded on the basis of a clear-cut doctrine of the Law and a carefully worked-out relation between the Law and the Gospel. The Reformers assert, first of all, that no man is saved on the basis of Law. As the *Apology of the Augsburg Confession* puts it: *Lex semper accusat* ("The Law always indicts"). Whenever a man puts himself before the standard of the Law—whether God's eternally revealed Law in the Bible or the standard of Law written on his own heart—he finds that he is condemned. Only the atoning sacrifice of Christ, who perfectly fulfilled the demands of the Law, can save; thus, in the words of the Apostle, "by grace are ye saved through faith; and that not of yourselves: it is the gift of God: not of works, lest any man should boast" (Eph. 2:8, 9).

But God's Law as set forth in Scripture, remains

valid. Indeed, the Law has three functions (*usus*): the political (as a restraint for the wicked), the theological (as "a *paidagōgos* to bring us to Christ"—Gal. 3:24), and the didactic (as a guide for the regenerate, or, in Bonhoeffer's words, "as God's merciful help in the performance of the works which are commanded"). Few Protestants today dispute the first and second uses of the Law; but what about the third or didactic use? Do Christians, filled with the love of Christ and empowered by His Holy Spirit, need the Law to teach them? Are not the Christian existentialists right that love is enough? Indeed, is it not correct that Luther himself taught only the first two uses of the Law and not the *tertius usus legis?*

Whether or not the formulation of a didactic use of the Law first appeared in Melanchthon (Helmut Thielicke [*Theologische Ethik*] and others have eloquently argued for its existence in Luther's own teaching; cf. Edmund Schlink, *Theology of the Lutheran Confessions*), there is no doubt that it became an established doctrine both in Reformation Lutheranism and in Reformation Calvinism. One finds it clearly set out in the Lutheran *Formula of Concord* (Art. VI) and in Calvin's *Institutes* (II, vii, 12 ff.). It is true that for Luther the pedagogic use of the Law was primary, while for Calvin this third or didactic use was the principal one; yet both the Lutheran and the Reformed traditions maintain the three-fold conceptualization.

An Essential Doctrine

The Third Use is an essential Christian doctrine for two reasons. First, because love—even the love of Christ —though it serves as the most powerful impetus to ethical action, does not inform the Christian as to the proper *content* of that action. Nowhere has this been put as well as by the beloved writer of such hymns "I Heard the Voice of Jesus Say" and "I Lay My Sins on Jesus"; in his book, *God's Way of Holiness*, Horatius Bonar wrote:

> But will they tell us what is to regulate service, if not law? *Love*, they say. This is a pure fallacy. Love is not a *rule* but a *motive*. Love does not tell me *what* to do; it tells me *how* to do it. Love constrains me to do the will

of the beloved one; but to know what the will is, I must go
elsewhere. The law of our God is the *will* of the beloved
one, and were that expression of his will withdrawn, love
would be utterly in the dark; it would not know what to
do. It might say, I love my Master, and I love his service,
and I want to do his bidding, but I must know *the rules
of his house*, that I may know *how* to serve him. Love
without law to guide its impulses would be the parent of
will-worship and confusion, as surely as terror and self-
righteousness, unless upon the supposition of an inward
miraculous illumination, as an equivalent for law. Love
goes to the law to learn the divine *will*, and love delights
in the law, as the exponent of that will; and he who says
that a believing man has nothing more to do with law,
save to shun it as an old enemy, might as well say that
he has nothing to do with the will of God. For the divine
law and the divine will are substantially one, the former
the outward manifestation of the latter. And it is "the *will*
of our Father which is in heaven" that we are to do (Matt.
7:21); so proving by loving obedience what is that "good
and acceptable, and perfect *will of God*" (Rom. 12:2).
Yes, it is he that doeth "the *will* of God that abideth
forever" (I John 2:17); it is to "the *will of God*" that we
are to live (I Peter 4:2); "made perfect in every good
work *to do his will*" (Heb. 13:21); and "fruitfulness in
every good work," springs from being "filled with the
knowledge of *his will*" (Col. 1:9, 10).

Secondly, the doctrine of the Third Use is an essential
perservative for the entire doctrine of sanctification. The
Third Use claims that as a result of justification, it is
a nomological fact that "if any man be in Christ he is
a new creature: old things are passed away; behold, all
things are become new" (II Cor. 5:17). A man in Christ
has received a new spirit—the Spirit of the living God—
and therefore his relation to the Law is changed. True,
in this life he will always remain a sinner (I John 1:8),
and therefore the Law will always accuse him, but now
he sees the biblical Law in another light—as the manifestation of God's loving will. Now he can say with the
psalmist: "I delight in Thy Law" and "O how I love
Thy Law!" (Ps. 119; cf. Ps. 1 and 19). Only by taking
the Third Use of the Law—the "law of Christ" (Gal. 6:2)
—seriously do we take regeneration seriously; and only
when we come to love God's revealed Law has sanctification become a reality in our lives. Ludwig Ihmels made
a sound confession of faith when he wrote in *Die*

*Religionswissenschaft der Gegenwart in Selbstdarstel-
lungen*: "I am convinced as was Luther that the Gospel
can only be understood where the Law has done its work
in men. And I am equally convinced that just the humble
Christian, however much he desires to live in enlarging
measure in the spirit, would never wish to do without
the holy discipline of the *tertius usus legis*." The answer
to antinomianism, social-gospel legalism, and existential
relativism lies not only in the proper *distinction* between
Law and Gospel, as C. F. W. Walther so effectively
stressed, but also in the proper *harmony* of Law and
Gospel, as set forth in the classic doctrine of the Third
Use of the Law.

The Fourth Gospel Yesterday and Today:

An Analysis of Two Reformation and Two 20th-Century Commentaries on the Gospel According to St. John

Strange Bedfellows

In this paper a comparative study will be made of the
work of four Johannine interpreters who are widely
separated both in time and in theological approach:
Philipp Melanchthon (1497-1560), Luther's irenic asso-
ciate, rightly designated the "preceptor of Germany";[1]
Aegidius Hunnius (1550-1603), an uncompromising representative of early Lutheran confessional orthodoxy;[2]
Father Marie-Joseph Lagrange (1855-1938), one of the
greatest Roman Catholic Biblical scholars of the
twentieth century;[3] and Charles Kingsley Barrett, an
English Methodist, who since 1958 has served as professor of divinity at Durham University, and who is the
author of a highly reputed commentary on the Greek text
of the Fourth Gospel.[4] Such an essay content demands
immediate justification and on two counts: first, Why a
study of Johannine interpretations? and second, Why
the juxtaposition of these particular commentators, in
view of their obvious dissimilarities?

The first question is readily answered. For those in
the Lutheran tradition, the Fourth Gospel has always
held a preeminent place. It was Luther's favorite Bibli-

Notes for this section, pages 454-465.

cal book,[5] and whenever he referred to it he did so in
the most praiseworthy terms. The following remarks
are typical:

> John's Gospel and St. Paul's Epistles, especially that to
> the Romans, and Saint Peter's first Epistle are the true
> kernel and marrow of all the books. They should justly be
> the first books, and it would be advisable for every Chris-
> tian to read them first and most, and by daily reading
> make them as familiar as his daily bread. . . . John writes
> very little about the works of Christ but very much about
> His preaching, while the other Evangelists write much of
> His works and little of His preaching; therefore John's
> Gospel is the one, tender, true chief Gospel, far, far to be
> preferred to the other three and placed high above them.[6]

> Matthew, together with the other two Evangelists,
> Mark and Luke, does not point his Gospel so much at the
> sublime article of Christ as St. John and St. Paul do.
> They, therefore, speak and exhort much concerning good
> works, as indeed should be done in Christendom; both
> should be taught, yet in such a way that each continues
> in its nature and dignity. First and foremost, faith in
> Christ should be taught and then also works.[7]

The key position accorded to the Fourth Gospel in
Luther's thought provides ample reason to study significant commentaries on that Gospel. Added to this historical consideration one finds in present-day Biblical
scholarship a keen revival of interest in John's Gospel.
Thus Norman Sykes, in describing "some changes in
theological thought since 1900 in respect of the quest
of the historical Jesus," wrote in 1960:

> During the last half-century much attention has been paid
> to that [the Fourth] Gospel, and recent scholars are ready
> to allow to it a more important status in their recon-
> struction and interpretation of the ministry of Jesus. The
> opinion has gained ground that this Gospel embodies a
> tradition of our Lord's ministry which is independent of
> the Synoptic accounts, that its tradition retains distinct
> marks of a Palestinian origin, and that in some important
> respects, notably in its placing the Last Supper on the eve
> of the Passover, its testimony on historical episodes is
> of greater authenticity than the Synoptic tradition. From
> another standpoint also the application of the methods of
> Form-Criticism to the Synoptists has lessened the gulf
> between them and the author of the Fourth Gospel, since
> the latter is recognized as presenting the ministry and
> teaching of Jesus in the *Sitz im Leben* of a later and

different generation of Gentile Christians from those of
the Synoptics. More attention will therefore have to be paid
to the distinctive features and witness of the Fourth Gospel in the contemporary quest of the historical Jesus.[8]

Both in terms of Lutheran tradition and of contemporary
scholarly interest there is every reason to add to the
literature on the history of Johannine exegesis.

But why a combined treatment of such diverse interpreters as Melanchthon, Hunnius, Lagrange, and
Barrett? The choice of each of them could, of course,
be defended on the basis of individual merit and historical significance, and the absence of English translations of the commentaries written by three of the four
theologians would in itself provide sufficient ground for
a careful analysis of these works; but such justification
would still leave the question of combined treatment
unanswered. The four commentaries have been chosen
for unified study because they represent two different
epochs of interpretation and two different mind sets,
and thereby provide an opportunity to cast doubt upon
two commonly held generalizations with regard to the
history of exegesis.

One of these generalizations is that the unbiased exegete
of catholic tastes is preferable to the opinionated exegete
bound by Biblicistic and confessional presuppositions.[9]
The other generalization (not entirely unconnected with
the first) is that, other things being equal, a Biblical
commentator of the modern period (i.e., the post-Astruc
period) is preferable to the exegete who lived prior to
the advent of documentary criticism.[10] A corollary of
this second generalization is the judgment that 17th-
century Protestant orthodoxy contributed virtually nothing in a positive way to the history of Biblical exegesis.[11]
Much light can be shed on each of these generalizations
by a combined study of the above-mentioned Johannine
interpreters, for both generalizations lead us to expect
certain things—good and bad—of the four commentaries,
and these expectations can be tested through inductive
examination of the commentaries themselves.

It has already been noted that the four commentators
to be discussed represent two widely different time
periods; but of equal significance is the fact that they

represent different personality types as well. Melanchthon has been characterized by his most recent American biographer as "the quiet reformer," [12] and such a characterization seems eminently just. Melanchthon said of himself: "Ego sum tranquilla avis," and "Non sum φιλόνεικος." [13] Undoubtedly Neve went too far when he referred to Melanchthon as "the feminine principle of the Reformation," [14] for, as the recent Melanchthon revival has emphasized, he was "in no sense a weakling." [15] However, unlike Luther, Melanchthon was much concerned with mediation and the reconciliation of opposites; indeed, his tolerance and catholicity may be a factor in the present repristination of interest in him.[16]

Of a far different cast of mind was Aegidius Hunnius, the orthodox Lutheran controversialist. What Luther supposedly said of Melanchthon, Hunnius could also have said: "Philip can sting you too, but he does it with needles and pins. . . . I stab you with boar's spears." [17] Hunnius' personality is manifest both in his life and in his writings.[18] His career was largely spent in energetic opposition to Crypto-Calvinists, Flacians, and Romanists. In 1576, at age 26, he obtained a professorship at the University of Marburg and received his doctorate in theology from Tübingen; forthwith he entered upon a vigorous campaign of anti-Calvinist polemic. So successful was he that in 1592 he was invited into Saxony to reform the electorate.

In his position as chief professor of divinity at Wittenberg, minister of the castle church, and member of the Consistory, he so successfully cleared the country of Calvinists that he was invited to Silesia to perform a similar function there. At the end of his life he opposed the Jesuits Gretser and Tanner at the Regensburg colloquy (1601). In Hutter's funeral oration for him such statements as the following are typical:

> In what strong as well as frequent contests he was forced
> to engage in Hesse, as well at Kassel as at Marburg, one
> moment against secret enemies, and another against open
> ones, who are called Sacramentarians by the Lutherans;
> what mighty combats he sustained, on account of that
> most holy article of the Christian faith, concerning the
> person of Christ and His adorable majesty sitting at the

right hand of God—these things, I say, are known to God, who sees and judges all things, nor are they unknown to many pious and judicious men.[19]

The controversial nature of most of his publications is evident from such representative titles as:[20] *Examen et refutatio assertionum jesuiticarum Laur. Arturi Fauntei . . . de ordinatione ac vocatione ministrorum in Ecclesiis reformatis* (Francoforti ad Moenum: J. Spies, 1591); *Calvinus judaïzans* (Witebergae: M. Welac, 1595);[21] *De indulgentiis et iubilaeo Romani pontificis tractatus, scriptus et oppositus duobus libris R. Bellarmini Jesuitae* (Francofurti: J. Saurius, 1599); *Antipareus, hoc est Invicta refutatio venenati scripti a D. Davide Pareo* (2 vols.; Witebergae: C. Berger, 1603);[22] *Articuli Christianae religionis de lege et Evangelio . . . forma quaestionum ac responsionum pertractati, confutatis etiam pontificiorum, antinomorum, calvinianorum aliorumque novatorum erroribus* (Wittebergae: J. J. Porsius, 1606).

Hunnius' two most important and influential doctrinal writings were concerned with the central dogmas of the majesty and omnipresence of Christ as man (*Libelli IV de persona Christi, ejusque ad dextram Dei sedentis divina Majestate* [Wittebergae: B. Raab, 1612]), and the absolute authority of the Bible (*Tractatus de sacrosancta majestate, autoritate, fide ac certitudine Sacrae Scripturae* [Francofurti ad Moenum: J. Spies, 1590]). His exegetical labors included not only the commentary on the Fourth Gospel, but also works on Matthew, the Pauline epistles, and I John; and he wrote Biblical dramas (e.g., *Josephus, comoedia sacra*) as well.

To a certain extent the two modern Johannine interpreters to be discussed here parallel the two Reformation commentators. In Father Lagrange one sees an exegete firmly wedded to a powerful confessional tradition. Granted, Lagrange was no controversialist,[23] yet, like Hunnius, he was more frequently motivated by faithful adherence to a doctrinal tradition than by a Melanchthonian desire to reconcile opposites. W. F. Howard wrote of Lagrange and his John commentary:

When a fruitful and very absorbing ministry in South America prevented Père Calmes from bringing out the new edition of his excellent commentary, the duty of writing a new work devolved upon Père M.-J. Lagrange, whose unusual equipment on the linguistic side gives to all his discussions of grammar, especially on questions where a Semitic background is in dispute, an unsurpassed authority. It is unfortunate that the Biblical Commission of May 29, 1907, has prevented a really unbiased discussion of the critical points at issue, for the great learning and sound judgment of this scholar, who lives in Palestine, would carry weight beyond that of any ecclesiastical committee. But the second sentence in the Introduction reads: "It is no longer a question of knowing if it had as author the Beloved Disciple, John, son of Zebedee. This point is fixed by ecclesiastical tradition." [24]

It seems that Lagrange, no less than Hunnius, would be subject to modern criticism for representing what Burton and Goodspeed term the "dogmatic method, which assumes that the results of the interpretation of a certain body of literature must conform to the dogmas of an accepted body of doctrine or system of thought." [25] Moreover, like Hunnius, Lagrange held a very high view of the inspiration of Scripture, for he accepted without question the Roman position on inspiration and Biblical studies expressed not long after his death in the papal encyclical *Divino afflante Spiritu* (1943): What task can be more sublime than to study, interpret, expound to the faithful, and defend against unbelievers the very word of God given to men under the inspiration of the Holy Ghost?" [26]

In C. K. Barrett one finds a modern counterpart to the irenic Melanchthon. It is true that Melanchthon took a far more conservative view of the inspiration and authority of the Bible than Barrett is able to maintain,[27] yet in their basic concern to present all sides of an issue they have much in common. Many critics of Barett's commentary on John have pointed out the *media via* character of his approach. G. D. Kilpatrick writes: "Mr. Barrett's commentary belongs to the same kind as that of Dr. Vincent Taylor [on Mark]. It is a work of reference rather than a vehicle for a particular view or thesis about the Gospel." [28] E. Kenneth Lee notes Barrett's "mediating position" in such matters as John's sacramental teaching.[29] W. H. Cadman of Mansfield College, Oxford, states that "by the time they are through with it readers of this Commentary who are not new to the serious study of St. John will be reflecting that the author has taken a middle-of-the-road course with the problems which have to be faced in connexion with the Gospel." [30] The distinguished Roman Catholic theologian William Grossouw of the University of Nijmegen, author of *Revelation and Redemption, a Sketch of the Theology of St John*,[31] argues: "Of the three authors under discussion [Dodd, Barrett, Bultmann] Barrett is the one who expresses himself in the most cautious terms about the question of the background of St. John, his whole work for that matter being distinguished by a great carefulness. For all its laudability this wariness does not unoften refrain the author from taking sides." [32] In his reticence to "take sides," Barrett shows himself to be a kindred spirit with the Quiet Reformer.

On the ground of contemporary *ad hominem* argumentation, it would seem that the more "tolerant" commentators, Barrett and Melanchthon, would be preferable to the more "opinionated" commentators, Lagrange and Hunnius. Moreover, on the present-day assumption that, other considerations being equal, modernity is a positive virtue, Barrett would be preferred to Melanchthon, and Lagrange to Hunnius. And in light of the severe criticism directed today against the theologians and Biblical commentators of the 17th century, Hunnius would be certain to receive last place in an evaluative arrangement of these four Johannine interpreters. How well do these *ad hominem* evaluations stand up when the four commentators are studied inductively in the light of the Gospel they purport to interpret? That is the question to which we shall address ourselves. But in order to make the required comparison, it is necessary first to set forth briefly our conception of John's Gospel.

The Thrust of the Fourth Gospel

Rudolf Bultmann, one of the greatest contemporary interpreters of the Fourth Gospel, has raised the vital question, "Is exegesis without presuppositions possible?" [33] His answer is that although exegesis must not presuppose its results, it always presupposes the method of historical-critical research and requires an existential "life-relation" between the Biblical subject matter and the exegete himself. Thus there is a necessary "circularity" involved in all Biblical exegesis,[34] and no exegesis can be definitive in an absolute sense.

With certain elements of Bultmann's approach we readily agree: he is correct when he asserts, following Kant, that presuppositionless intellectual endeavor is impossible; and he is likewise correct that no exegesis can be absolutely definitive, for all exegesis involves the communication of a text to the historical situation of the exegete. However, when Bultmann argues that not only historical method[35] but also existential "life-relation" must be presupposed in exegesis, he blurs the aim of objectivity which is essential to all proper literary and historical study. Following Dilthey[36] as well as the general stream of philosophical existentialism, Bultmann attempts to "cut under the subject-object distinction";[37] he claims that "for historical understanding, the schema of subject and object that has validity for natural science is invalid."[38] But in fact the subject-object distinction is of crucial importance in history as well as in natural science, and only by aiming to discover the objective concern of the text (rather than blending it with the subjective concern of the exegete) can successful exegesis take place.

For us then, in analyzing John's Gospel there is only one valid question—not a multiplicity of existentially determined questions—to be put to the text, namely: What is the intended message of the book? Unless this question is objectively posed, exegesis will inevitably presuppose its results, regardless of Bultmann's strictures to the contrary. The "circularity" of exegesis must be broken by the subject-object distinction, or criteria for distinguishing sound from unsound interpretation will forever be rendered impossible.[39]

A second methodological issue requiring clarification at the outset is the question of literary unity. Here we argue on the basis of Aristotle's dictum that the benefit of the doubt should be given to the work being studied, not arrogated by the interpreter to himself.[10] In practice this means that we regard as unproven all theories of textual displacement—e.g., the recent theory of MacGregor and Morton[41]—which cannot be supported by objective manuscript evidence.[42] This is not to say that such theories *cannot* be true; we say only that subjective literary speculation and the "scissors and paste" method must not be allowed to substitute. for patient exegesis of the text as determined by the objective canons of lower criticism.[43]

The Johannine authorship problem must be faced by anyone who intends to interpret the Fourth Gospel. In applying the above stated Aristotelian principle of literary criticism to such passages as 19:35 ("he that saw it bare record, and his record is true: and he knoweth that he saith true") we must agree with William Temple when he asserts in his *Readings in St. John's Gospel:* "I regard as self-condemned any theory about the origin of the Gospel which fails to find a very close connection between it and John the son of Zebedee. The combination of internal and external evidence is overwhelming on this point." How strong this evidence actually is may be seen in a detailed article by Hugo Odeberg which takes into account 20th-century papyrus discoveries.[44]

The important issue is not whether the apostle John was the actual amanuensis of the Gospel that bears his name, but whether the Gospel represents the first-century apostolic witness; we find the affirmative arguments of Odeberg and Temple compelling in this regard. It follows, moreover, that if the Fourth Gospel is a product of the apostolic witness, and if the Synoptic Gospels were written even earlier—within a half-century of the death of our Lord, according to the best evidence—then the exegete should expect to find harmony rather than disharmony between John on the one hand and Matthew, Mark, and Luke on the other. So, for example, when faced with an issue such as the date of the Last Supper, where the Synoptics and John appear to disagree, sympathetic attention should be given to a reconciliation of the kind offered by Jaubert, who, by successfully demonstrating that two calendars (the official lunar and a Jubilees-Qumran) were employed at the time, provides a harmonization which does not do violence to any of the records.[45]

Assuming, then, the literary unity of the Fourth Gospel

and its source in the apostolic witness, what is its intended message? Obviously a direct statement of purpose within the book itself would carry maximum weight, and we are provided with such an assertion in 20:31: "ταῦτα δὲ γέγραπται ἵνα πιστεύητε ὅτι Ἰησοῦς ἐστιν ὁ χριστὸς ὁ υἱὸς τοῦ Θεοῦ, καὶ ἵνα πιστεύοντες ζωὴν ἔχητε ἐν τῷ ὀνόματι αὐτοῦ."

Here the writer stresses two elements: *belief* and the *object of belief*. He wishes to bring his readers to belief (and thus life), and he has in mind a specific content of belief, namely that Jesus is "the Messiah, viz., the Son of God." We can term these two foci of John's interest the "evangelical-apologetic" and the "testificatory."

The former—John's aim to bring readers to belief— is evident in the prologue, where the author employs the λόγος concept familiar to Greeks, to Hellenistic Judaism, and even to Rabbinic Judaism, in an effort to show that all their hopes are fulfilled in the historic Jesus.[46] Concern for an apologetic evangel is also seen in John's use of σημεῖα[47] and dialogues[18] to induce belief. E. C. Colwell is thus quite correct when he titles his interpretation, *John Defends the Gospel.*[49] But the Fourth Gospel is not simply a "Gospel of belief" in the traditional sense of a book which centers attention on the subjective production of faith. More important by far to John than the believer (or unbeliever) is the "ontology of belief," that is to say, the object—and source—of belief, Jesus the Messiah. This is evidenced especially by the prominence in the Gospel of the idea of "witness."[50]

A word count reveals that the verb μαρτυρέω appears in only one verse in Matthew, in only two verses in Luke, and not at all in Mark, but in 33 verses in John; likewise, the noun μαρτυρία is found not at all in Mathew, in only three verses in Mark, and in just one verse in Luke, but in 14 verses in John.[51]

The writer of the Fourth Gospel introduces believers and unbelievers alike into the narrative in order to point to Jesus—and on occasion summarily dismisses them (e.g., Nicodemus) after they have served this function. The witness of unbelievers to Christ is often unconscious by way of double meanings, but it is no less real because of that; especially clear examples of such Johannine irony are provided by Caiaphas (11:49-52) and Pilate (19:19-22).[52] Thus the thrust of the Fourth Gospel is in the most real sense Christocentric; Luther recognized this when in 1537 he commented as follows on John 14:5, 6:

> The evangelist St. John is wont to write and to emphasize that all our doctrine and faith should center in Christ and should cling to this one Person alone, and that we, brushing aside all science and wisdom, should simply know nothing but the crucified Christ, as St. Paul says in 1 Cor. 1 and 2.[53]

It is imperative to see, moreover, that the Christ on whom the Fourth Gospel centers attention is conceived *historically*, not just existentially. The Christ is viewed not primarily as a means to existential self-understanding (as Bultmann leads us to believe in his *Kommentar* and in his *Theology of the New Testament*[54]), but as the Divine in human flesh, whose historical reality provides the only proper focus for existential commitment.

The historicity of the Christ of John is seen particularly in the key verse of the prologue, 1:14 (ὁ λόγος σὰρξ ἐγένετο); in the historical detail of the Passion account (Dodd, in approaching the Johannine Passion narrative, writes: "It is as though the evangelist, having sufficiently set forth the meaning of the death and resurrection of Christ, turned to the reader and said, 'And now I will tell you what actually happened, and you will see that the facts themselves bear out my interpretation' "[55]); and in the exceedingly great stress placed upon the facticity of Christ's resurrection—both through the preparatory miracle of the raising of Lazarus and through the "doubting Thomas" incident that climaxes the Gospel.[56] As Dr. Wright well says, John's Gospel "was a Gospel *of God*—he knew that there was no 'Gospel' at all unless it was God's own Gospel: but it was a Gospel of God *incarnate in a real man*."[57]

The Commentators Compared

The preceding inductive analysis of the message and

approach of the Fourth Gospel will now be employed as a standard of comparison for the four Johannine commentators under discussion. In each case an attempt will be made to see how successfully the given commentator deals with such central hermeneutic issues as the purpose of the Fourth Gospel (with special reference to 20:31 and the prologue), the general function of the σημεῖα, the interpretation of a key discourse (the Nicodemus incident in chap. 3),[58] recognition of unconscious testimony to Christ and of the ironic use of double meanings (11:49-52; 19:19-22), the significance of the Lazarus story (11:1-44), and the treatment of alleged contradictions between the Johannine and Synoptic Passion chronologies.

Melanchthon

For Melanchthon the theme of the Fourth Gospel is the declaration of grace in Jesus Christ over against the old dispensation of Law as represented by Moses. The reformer introduces his commentary with a lengthy section entitled "Legis et Evangelii differentia,"[59] which forms the backdrop for his entire presentation. In his detailed discussion of the Johannine prologue he places particular stress on 1:17 ("The Law was given by Moses, but grace and truth came by Jesus Christ"),[60] and the incarnation is viewed from the standpoint of the Law-Gospel distinction. Interestingly enough, Melanchthon makes no comment at all on 20:31.[61]

The Johannine "signs" are generally regarded as symbolic of the Gospel-vs.-Law issue. Thus the miracle at Cana (2:1-11) is interpreted allegorically (the six waterpots = the Law; wine = the Gospel; the governor of the feast = the apostles and preachers, who dispense the Word);[62] and the feeding of the 5,000 (chap. 6) provides an opportunity to distinguish between the manna of the Israelites (i.e., justification by the Law), and the Bread of life (i.e., righteousness provided through Christ's Gospel).[63] The Nicodemus dialogue, typical of the other Johannine dialogues, is regarded from the same standpoint as the signs: Nicodemus represents "the wisdom and righteousness of the flesh" which seeks to be justified before God through the "external works of the Law,"

while Christ preaches justification through the Gospel
of regeneration.[61] In discussing the raising of Lazarus,
Melanchthon cautions against allegorical interpretation,[65] but then characteristically sees in Christ's ad-
monitions to believe in Him as the Resurrection and the
Life an opposition to reliance upon "good works,"
"human works." [66]

In spite of his preoccupation with the Law-Gospel
distinction, however, Melanchthon does not entirely lose
sight of the testificatory emphasis of the Fourth Gospel.
It is true that he does not catch the unconscious testimony and ironic double meaning in the superscription
incident (19:19-22),[67] but he does see such a witness
in Caiaphas' statement that "it is expedient for us that
one man should die for the people" (11:49-52); indeed,
Melanchthon parallels this testimony with that of Ba-
laam's ass and with God's use of Pharaoh in the Old
Testament.[68]

Melanchthon does not of course deny the historicity
of the picture of Christ presented in the Fourth Gospel,
but his main concern is with doctrine rather than history, and thus it is not strange that he nowhere deals
with the problem of reconciling the chronology of the
Passion narratives—in spite of his willingness to include
bits of factual *antiquaria* throughout the commentary.[69]
His commentary becomes especially brief and sketchy
when he reaches the Passion narrative, and this contrasts markedly with the detail at the beginning of the
work—particularly in his section on the prologue, which,
of course, provides much material for doctrinal exegesis.[70]

In summary, then, one finds Melanchthon's commentary to be *dogmacentric*—to suffer from an unfortunate
tendency to force John's Gospel into the straitjacket of
a single doctrinal motif—the proper distinction between
Law and Gospel—which, though a sound doctrine *per
se*, and possibly even a minor theme of the fourth evangelist, is unquestionably not the central concern of the
Gospel writer.[71]

Hunnius

It is a striking experience to pass from the some-

what flat, static, abbreviated, and doctrinally oriented
commentary of Melanchthon to the work of Aegidius
Hunnius, whom Johann Gerhard called "der trefflichste
unter allen neueren Theologen." Hunnius quite obviously
reacted to the Gospel of John as J. B. Phillips did to the
Pauline epistles: "Again and again the writer felt rather
like an electrician rewiring an ancient house without
being able to 'turn the mains off.' " [72]—and this same
dynamic reaction is conveyed to the reader of Hunnius'
commentary. This characterization of Hunnius' work
might seem exaggerated in the light of his use of a *loci
communes* method of approach,[73] but in actuality his
presentation gains in systematic effectiveness through
the controlled use of this methodology. As I have pointed
out elsewhere, it is manifestly unfair to condemn 17th-
century writers for their concern with "system"; every
writer employs some kind of system, and problems
arise only when a given form is allowed to twist and
pervert content.[74]

In his prefatory section dealing with the *argumentum*
of the whole Gospel, Hunnius begins with the title of the
book: "the Gospel according to John," and underscores
the two elements in it: the Gospel ("the joyous and
salutary news of our Savior, the eternal Λόγος and Son
of God, manifested in the flesh") and the eyewitness
character of the testimony to it, which assures both its
"historicity" and the "indubitable veracity of its doctrine." John 20:31 is then quoted, and Hunnius comments:
"This Gospel sets forth the One who is the beginning
and end of all our salvation, viz., Christ—in the knowledge
of whom eternal felicity has its focal point, as Christ
Himself said, 'This is life eternal, that they might know
Thee the only true God, and Jesus Christ whom Thou
hast sent.' " [75] Thus a thoroughgoing *Christocentric*
tone is set for the entire commentary to follow.

Mention was made earlier of Hunnius' important
treatise, *De persona Christi*; indeed, he was "the most
able representative of the Swabian theology of Brenz and
consequently of the doctrine concerning the majesty
and omnipresence of Christ as man." [76] Not un-
naturally, then, one finds a powerful treatment of the
Incarnation in his comments on the Johannine prologue.

The victorious majesty of the incarnate Word stands forth in spite of the blind ignorance of the world and rejection by His own people.

Hunnius regards the σημεῖα in the Fourth Gospel not as allegorical symbols of doctrinal truth, but as pointers to the Christ. At the conclusion of his discussion of the raising of Lazarus (which, incidentally, Hunnius recognizes as the crucial event that polarizes opposition to Christ and brings about the plan to kill Him),[77] Hunnius states the "purpose, fruit, and result of Christ's miracles, that by them men may be convicted in their own consciences with regard to faith toward Jesus. Thus the evangelist John testifies in chapter 20 that he has described these signs (among which the resurrection of Lazarus hardly receives last place) in order that we might believe that Jesus is the Messiah, the Son of God, and that believing we might have life in His name."[78] Indeed, "all the miracles of Christ declare His divinity, inasmuch as He performed them by the power of divinity alone."[79]

Hunnius' interpretation of the Nicodemus dialog is remarkable for its Christocentric emphasis. The verse upon which Hunnius concentrates most is 3:13 ("No man hath ascended up to heaven but He that came down from heaven, even the Son of man which is in heaven"), and he inserts two essays at this point to expand his treatment ("De descensu Filii hominis de coelo"; "De ascensione Filii hominis in coelum").[80] In this way the stress is placed not on Nicodemus (as representing the law, or as a potential believer, etc.), but on the Christ whose descent from and ascent to heaven provide the only basis for the birth "from above" (ἄνωθεν) which Nicodemus so desperately needs.

That Hunnius is well aware of the basic testificatory character of the fourth evangelist's message is also evidenced in his recognition of the ironic, *Doppeldeutigkeit*[81] character of the unconscious, unbelieving witness portrayed in it. Thus with reference to Pilate and the superscription (19:19-22), Hunnius says: "This title, composed by Pilate to dishonor Jesus, was so regulated by the overruling God that it redounded to the highest and everlasting glory of Christ."[82] On Caiaphas' proposal to kill Jesus (11:49-52), Hunnius writes: "The words of Caiaphas have a double meaning [*duplicem sensum*]. One sense is that of Caiaphas himself, namely that Jesus be put to death for the peace and quiet of the Jewish nation. . . . But the other sense is that which the Holy Spirit intended, namely that Christ alone should die to save the people of the whole world, lest the entire human race perish in eternal death." [83]

Hunnius' concern with the historicity of the Johannine account is shown by his efforts to solve the apparent discrepancy between the Synoptic and Johannine chronologies of the Passion week. In commenting on 13:1, he asserts that Jesus and His disciples ate the Last Supper as a Passover meal,[84] and he reconciles this with 18:28 and 19:31 by stating that the (main) Passover meal (with the lamb) did not take place until after Jesus' crucifixion,[85] and that the Jews wished to remove the body from the cross "because of the coming high Sabbath, on which they customarily began the Passover celebration." [86] In other words, Hunnius regards the crucifixion as occurring on Friday, 14 Nisan, and the official Passover as beginning that evening with the onset of the Sabbath (15 Nisan); at the same time he holds that in some genuine sense the Last Supper was a Passover meal.

This harmonization accords beautifully with Jaubert's recent researches,[87] and it may even be possible that Hunnius also was thinking in terms of two calendars, since (as we shall see forthwith) he employs analogous reasoning in the "third hour-sixth hour" problem (19:14). Be that as it may, Hunnius' attempt certainly demonstrates a praiseworthy concern for the historicity of the key events in our Lord's earthly ministry; for him (unlike Melanchthon) the historical element in the Fourth Gospel could not be subordinated to the doctrinal.

Hunnius attempts to resolve the apparent contradiction between John 19:14 ("about the sixth hour" Jesus is sentenced to be crucified) and Mark 15:25 (He goes to the cross at "the third hour") by arguing that the Jews divided the day both into twelve hours and into four quarters (the latter consisting of the period from dawn to the third hour; the period from the third to the sixth hour; the period from the sixth to the ninth hour;

and the period from the ninth hour to sunset)—as is indicated by the parable of the laborers in the vineyard, Matt. 20:1-16. Since the whole period from the third to the sixth hour was customarily called the third hour, Mark, in speaking of the third hour as the time of the crucifixion, is referring to the quarter of the day between the third and sixth hours. And John informs us precisely that the third hour had almost passed, for he tells us that Jesus was crucified about the sixth hour, i.e., about noon.[88]

This is the same type of harmonization that one finds in the master exegete of the Reformation, John Calvin;[89] and an analogous method, involving two schemes of time reckoning, has been persuasively argued by the modern Johannine expert Westcott.[90] Here again, one may not agree with the specifics of Hunnius' answer, but respect should be accorded him for perceiving that the historical details of Messiah's earthly life are not un-important as compared with His "theology"; indeed, as Hunnius well recognized, at the heart of the Johannine theology is the affirmation that the Word became *flesh*.

Lagrange

In many respects Lagrange appears as a Hunnius *redivivus*. It is true that in the last section of the intro-duction to his commentary he lays great stress on the concept of unity and on the verse so popular today in ecumenical discussion, "that they may be one" (17:22), and he makes the inevitable Romanist connection with the need for a united Christendom under a single papal shepherd.[91] But in practice he tacitly admits that unity is not the fourth evangelist's central theme, for he makes no attempt to relate each event in the Gospel to it.[92] Moreover, he flatly states that "we do not have to con-jecture about the author's purpose; it is written at the end of the book (20:30-31)." [93] His comments on these verses evidence his sensitivity to the testificatory and evangelical aims of the Fourth Gospel and to their focus on the Christ Himself:

> The author's purpose was not to recount all the signs Jesus did; the σημεῖα are not miracles which simply as-tonish or console or lift a burden, but which at the same

time point out something; they have been performed before all the people and the Christ has publicly
set forth their lesson. If John then says here that the signs
have been done before the disciples, the point is that they
alone have understood that lesson and are charged with
transmitting it to others. . . . The evangelist made a selection, stressing what was most appropriate for engen-
dering and nourishing faith. The present πιστεύητε (N, B,
O) is much better suited than the aorist πιστεύσητε to
indicate progress rather than genesis of faith. John addresses those who already believe, but who need to believe
to a greater extent, as has so often been indicated even
by the aorist directed to those who were already disciples
(cf. 1:50; 2:11, 22; 4:50, 53; 13:19; 14:29). The object of
faith is the belief that Jesus is the Christ, that is to say,
the Messiah promised by the Scriptures, and that He is
at the same time the Son of God, in the particular sense
always affirmed by the evangelist, i.e., truly God, as
Thomas has just confessed.[94]

One might object to Lagrange's preoccupation with
those who are already disciples (cf. his unity theme mentioned above), but he does not fail to see the wider
audience of unbelievers and the need for reaching them
with the Christian message, viz., the message about
Christ.

It will be noted that Lagrange has interpreted the
σημεῖα *Christocentrically*;[95] the same is true of his treatment of the prologue and of such a typical dialogue as
the Nicodemus incident. In the contrast between Nicodemus' salutation, "Rabbi, we know that thou art a
teacher come from God" (3:2), and Jesus' rebuke, "Art
thou the teacher of Israel and knowest not these things?"
(3:10), Lagrange sees "incontestablement une pointe
d'ironie,"[96] for Jesus shows Himself to be the only One
who can reveal heavenly things.[97] Moreover, with
reference to 3:13, John was "not able to forget the first
page of his Gospel. The Son of man is thus the Word
incarnate, in the reality of His human nature, which does
not prevent Him from still being in heaven as the
Word."[98]

As for the prologue itself, Lagrange sees it as "a most
solemn preface which sketches in a few words the person
of Jesus Christ and the nature of His mission."[99] The
prologue has a "conclusion historique," expressed in 1:

16-18. The material relating to John the Baptist must not be viewed as the work of a redactor, as Loisy claims; and Bultmann's conjecture that the entire prologue, except for verses 6-8 and 15 (17), were borrowed from a baptismal text in praise of the Baptist need not be regarded seriously. Actually the Baptist's testimony is integral to the prologue, for "the splendor of the light [i.e., from the Word] produces its effect on John, who reflects back its rays.... If one considers the prologue as a poem, the two references to John can figure as antistrophes which allow the thought to reecho."

In the light of the strong testificatory character of Lagrange's general treatment, it is disappointing to find him weak in the recognition of unconscious testimony to Christ in the Fourth Gospel. He fails entirely to grasp the high irony of Pilate's superscription, and instead devotes himself to somewhat irrelevant obiter dicta (e.g., "Palestine still today has three official languages, English, Arabic, and Hebrew"!).[100] He sees the double meaning in Caiaphas' words in 11:49-52, but the powerful witness to Christ is obscured by Lagrange's painstaking discussion of such questionable arguments as whether Caiaphas needed a special anointing of the Spirit to say what he did, and whether Urim and Thummim were involved![101]

Here one encounters examples illustrating the chief failing of the commentary: a tendency to lose thematic perspective through preoccupation with antiquarian and philological details. As has been previously noted, Lagrange's detailed mastery of Semitics greatly enhances the value of his commentary; but it is well to see that its strength is not totally unrelated to its weakness.

Lagrange was particularly concerned with the facticity of the Johannine narrative. He had no patience with the critical-psychological method of Goguel, which claimed to prove the purely human character of the religion of Jesus but actually presupposed it.[102] Loisy's modernist-allegorical interpretation of the Fourth Gospel comes under heavy criticism throughout Lagrange's commentary.[103] Renan's criticism of the Johannine discourses, and his famous assertion that "because the

Gospels relate miracles they are legends" come under heavy fire in Lagrange's book dealing with Renan's *Life of Jesus.*[104] Lagrange's position on the historicity of the Fourth Gospel has been well summarized by Vénard:

> P. Lagrange does not dispute the symbolical character John gives to his accounts, but he insists on their probability. "Solidly fixed on the ground," anchored in a geographical, historical, well-determined chronological framework which can be checked, they are anything but transpositions of an idea under the guise of history. . . . The theologian, then, meaning by this the author of the fourth gospel, has not swallowed up the witness, either in the discourses he records, or in the facts which he relates.[105]

It should not be surprising, consequently, that Lagrange defends the historicity of the Lazarus episode and the possibility of harmonizing the Passion chronologies. He argues the facticity of the raising of Lazarus on the ground that the story is not purely "theological"—for along with the picture of the divine Christ appear the most touching human details (e.g., "Jesus wept," 11:35)[106] —and on the ground that the story has a position of "bold relief" in the structure of the Fourth Gospel.[107] He recognizes that to John the Lazarus event provided the backdrop for Christ's own resurrection, for he suggests that the Synoptic writers, in their regard for catechumens, may have omitted the raising of Lazarus for fear that attention would be distracted from the "great and decisive" miracle of Christ's resurrection.[108]

The Passion chronology problems are handled by Lagrange much as Hunnius deals with them. He considers the Fourth Gospel to provide a more precise chronology than the Synoptics, but this does not mean that the Synoptics are in error: John "wished to correct the inexact affirmations which would erroneously have been able to be derived from their text."[109] Thus Lagrange maintains the validity of the 14 Nisan crucifixion and 15 Nisan Passover, but holds that in some genuine sense the Last Supper must have been a Passover meal; "it does not seem to us impossible," he writes, "that a given group celebrated the Passover on the eve of the official day."[110] Considering the fact that Lagrange did not have the benefit of Jaubert's researches, this tentative solution must be regarded with admiration.

In the matter of the "third hour" vs. the "sixth hour" (Mark 15:25 and John 19:14), Lagrange holds that "John wished to designate the time more precisely. He attached a great importance to that moment because it marks the end of Judaism, which condemned itself in condemning Jesus. In this entire passage the pursuit of historical accuracy is too patent for us to settle on a symbolic explanation, e.g., noon as the midpoint of history." [111]

As for Mark, Lagrange writes in his commentary on that book: "He seems to have conceived a time-scheme which skips in three-hour intervals: morning (15:1), the third hour, the sixth hour (15:33), and the ninth hour (15: 34). Consequently, there is good reason to take these numbers as approximate and to think that John is nearer to reality. Mark, who makes things move rapidly, could thus speak of the third hour as the time of the crucifixion." [112] Again the parallel with Hunnius' harmonization is very close.

Barrett

It has been pointed out earlier that Barrett's commentary is noted for its "cautious," "careful," "mediating," "middle-of-the-road" approach, and that it is regarded as a valuable reference work because of this characteristic. Here we shall look at the other side of the same coin—the disadvantages which result from Barrett's "wariness." A. Viard suggests the problem when he asks, "Perhaps Barrett is at times too prudent, too reasonable?" [113] C. Kenneth Sansbury touches the nerve of this issue with the following witty remark: "Sometimes even a Cambridge man may find Mr. Barrett's Cambridge caution a little excessive—there is *something* to be said for the Oxford willingness to take a plunge, if only because it provides another Oxford man with an occasion for writing another book to point out how wrong the plunge was!" [114] In a work of reference the "unwillingness to take a plunge" may have real value, but in a commentary attempting to catch the spirit of a Biblical book which, from its opening sentence to its concluding event, takes the greatest plunge of all—by asserting that the divine Word actually became flesh—mediating caution (we might call it *medenaganocentrism!*) [115] can do more harm than good.

Barrett's discussion of the purpose of the Fourth Gospel provides a concrete illustration of the weakness of his approach. He begins by quoting 20:31, but then, instead of proceeding directly to its testificatory and evangelical-apologetic foci, centering on the Christ, he offers the following equivocating statement which (perhaps in line with his Methodist orientation) suggests that man's faith rather than the source and object of faith is the major concern of the fourth evangelist. "It is not always observed that this verse, important as it is, raises more questions than it answers, and provides no more than a starting point for a discussion of the purpose of the gospel; for merely to say that John was written in the interests of faith is to say nothing at all, beyond that it is a Christian book, which is hardly in dispute." [116] Barrett then goes on to make the amazing assertions: "It would be a mistake to press too far the question of the purpose of the gospel. . . . It is easy, when we read the gospel, to believe that John, though doubtless aware of the necessity of strengthening Christians and converting the heathen, wrote primarily to satisfy himself. His gospel must be written: it was no concern of his whether it was also read." [117]

In spite of the utility of the material Barrett thereupon supplies with reference to the Johannine problems of eschatology, gnosticism, and authority, it would seem that the quoted statements tell us far more about the commentator himself than about the author of 20:31—a verse which the evangelist certainly regarded as the unequivocal climax rather than a vague "starting point" in his Gospel.

The same lack of decisive Christocentricity is manifested in Barrett's treatment of the prologue, the σημεῖα, and the exemplary Nicodemus dialogue. Instead of seeing the prologue as a witness to God's incarnational victory over the ignorance and unbelief of sinful man, Barrett misses the ironic paradox of apparent, penultimate defeat and ultimate, actual victory which is so characteristic of the Biblical "tragic vision";[118] he describes the

Johannine account of incarnation as "a coming which
was an almost unmitigated failure. Even those who were
most privileged did not believe when they saw the light;
though John is careful to note and allow for the few who
heard, believed, and received, and so constituted the
Church, whose spokesman he was." [119]

In discussing the Johannine σημεῖα, Barrett correctly
notes that "the miracles of this gospel are a function of
its Christology" [120] and that even though the death
and resurrection are not so designated in the Gospel,
they are "the supreme σημεῖον" and in them alone "sign
and its meaning coincide." [121] But he appreciably
weakens the Johannine thrust by making the signs relative to faith rather than objective testimonies to the
Messiahship and divine Sonship of Jesus: "to those who
do believe, the miracles are signs which feed their faith;
to those who do not, signs may be multiplied indefinitely
without producing faith (12:37)." [122]

But the doubting Thomas incident at the climax of the
Gospel belies this interpretation, for Thomas is compelled by the objective "supreme σημεῖον" of the risen
Christ; and even 12:37, taken in context, explains unbelief not in terms of a supposedly ambiguous character
of the σημεῖα, but as a result of the blinding and harden-
ing action of the sovereign God (12:38-41, concluding with
the Christocentric verse: "These things said Isaias, when
he saw His glory, and spake of Him").

At the outset of his analysis of the Nicodemus incident, Barrett recognizes that as the discourse proceeds
Nicodemus "is quickly forgotten"; one expects that this
insight will lead to a focusing of attention on Christ Himself, who is the source of the "new birth/birth from above."
But such a personalistic Christocentrism does not appear;
rather, says Barrett, "we are made to hear not a conversation between two persons but the dialogue of Church
and Synagogue." [123] It is noteworthy also that Barrett
completely misses the irony in the contrast between
διδάσκαλος (3:2) and ὁ διδάσκαλος (3:10) [124]—a contrast
which especially heightens the distinction between Nicodemus (who should have known the highest spiritual
truths but did not) and Jesus, who could reveal the true
nature of spiritual life because He alone "came down

from heaven." This unawareness of irony, however, does not extend throughout the commentary; Barrett clearly brings out the ironically unconscious testimony of Caiaphas (11:49-52) and of Pilate (19:19-22).[125] But unhappily he seems to view such irony as no more than a "consummate dramatic touch of the evangelist's";[126] that much it is, of course but the central function of the evangelist's ironic technique is to affirm God's victory in Christ, to which all men must testify, whether they consciously believe in Him or not.

In the matter of the facticity of the Fourth Gospel one finds Barrett at his weakest. It would seem from his assertions on the Johannine conception of authority that Barrett would stanchly maintain the specific accuracy of the apostolic testimony in the Gospel:

> [John] 21:24 ... emphasizes the importance of the testimony of a veracious eyewitness, and adds "we know that his witness is true"—the Church sets its seal upon the veracity of its spokesman. The Church itself is thus the heir of the apostles and of their authority. It is clear that if this statement were left unqualified a door would be left open to a worse anarchy than that of gnosticism; but it is not left unqualified. The Church is the Church—the authoritative, apostolic Church—so far as it rests upon the word of the apostles (17:20).[127]

But in evaluating the ostensive "word of the apostles," Barrett in fact manifests "skepticism and minimism ... in the question of the historical authority (not general, but particular) of the Fourth Gospel."[128] Thus Barrett suggests that the Lazarus story may be a "miracle" which developed out of a parable, or a narrative which John drew "from tradition, where of course it may already have been modified."[129]

J. N. Sanders, in his review of Barrett's commentary, very properly questions the consistency and validity of such an approach:

> It is a nice question how far one can go in maintaining both that John asserted the primacy of history and that one cannot place any reliance on his historical details. In the Commentary, as each incident comes up for consideration, Dr. Barrett gives the impression of such hesitancy in affirming anything to be historical that his brave words about John's concern for history in the Introduction

452   THE SUICIDE OF CHRISTIAN THEOLOGY

ring a little hollow. . . . A general impression of inconclu-
siveness remains.[130]

Predictably, Barrett gives possible explanations for the
"third hour" (Mark 15:25)—"sixth hour" (John 19:14)
crucifixion problem, but does not commit himself
to a solution.[131] With reference to the date of the
Passover in the Synoptics and in John, he flatly asserts:
"Here again is a real contradiction; it is impossible to
reconcile the dates (for example by the hypothesis that
in the time of Jesus two different modes of reckoning
the Passover dates were in use); one must be preferred
to the other."[132] Granted, Barrett's work was published prior to Jaubert's, and so he did not have the benefit of the latter's research, but it is noteworthy that
Barrett absolutely closes the door to harmonization,
rather than giving the benefit of doubt to the evangelists,
as Hunnius and Lagrange do.

Barrett prefers the "Marcan chronology," and says
of John: "On his dating Jesus died on the cross at the
moment when the Passover lambs were being slaughtered
in the temple. This may not be good history; but it does
seem to be Johannine theology."[133] To this assertion,
which shows better than any other how little Barrett
understands the central message of John, that ὁ λόγος σὰρξ
ἐγένετο (1:14), D. M. Stanley properly retorts: "It is an
essential consequence of the truth of the Incarnation that
Christianity is *de natura sua* an historical religion. There
can be no 'good theology' which may at the same time
be dubbed 'bad history.' "[134]

"Dogmatism" vs. "Impartiality" in Biblical Interpretation

The foregoing study of two Reformation and two
20th-century commentaries on the Fourth Gospel has
brought us to a surprising conclusion. The high value
placed today on impartiality and modernity suggested
that the four commentators to be analyzed could be
ranged axiologically thus:

1. Barrett—impartial, modern
2. Melanchthon—impartial, premodern
3. Lagrange—dogmatic, modern
4. Hunnius—dogmatic, pre-modern

But in fact our detailed investigation of the commentaries leads to a reversal of value judgment and to a
reversal of axiological order:

1. Hunnius—Christocentric
2. Lagrange—Christocentric (qualified)
3. Melanchthon—dogmacentric
4. Barrett—medenganocentric[135]

Such a result offers three exegetical warnings: First,
one should be wary of all attempts to prejudge a commentator on the basis of *ad hominem,* a priori reasoning. Second, a commentator's historical epoch should
not be held against him and employed as a criterion of
prejudgment. Third, a commentator's theological temper-
ament likewise is no proper basis for a priori negative
evaluation of his work.

But how can we explain the peculiar results of the
present investigation? How could Barrett and Melanchthon, two mediating commentators, achieve less satisfactory exegetical insights than the "opinionated" theologians Hunnius and Lagrange? And how could the orthodox controversialist Hunnius possibly find the heart of
the Fourth Gospel? I suggest that the "impartiality" of
Barrett and Melanchthon is a singularly inappropriate
cast of mind for interpreting such Biblical books as John's
Gospel, for there one finds absolute and unqualified commitment to a God who, beyond question, revealed Himself in Jesus Christ. Thus a Barrett, who remains warily
cautious, misses the essential teaching of the book; and
a Melanchthon, whose *media via* approach is felt even
by him to be experientially unsatisfying,[136] tends toward an exegetical instability which can result in hyper-
preoccupation with a single doctrine. Moreover, Barrett
(and to some extent Lagrange) suffer from the ill effects (as well as benefit from the unquestionable values)
of modernity; W. H. Cooper has perspicaciously observed
that "items of literary and historical criticism . . . fas-
cinate and often sidetrack the modern investigator" and
prevent him from getting to the heart of Biblical teaching.[137]

In the case of Hunnius it seems possible to argue that
his radical commitment to the Scriptural Christ gave him
the theological stabilization necessary to create a classic

commentary on John. Like Chesterton's fictional detective
Father Brown, his unshakable confidence in "heavenly
things" kept him from aberrational judgments in "earthly things." [138] For Hunnius the Johannine proclamation of the Incarnation—the historical facticity of the Word
—was not to be questioned but to be testified to; and in
taking this position, he aligned himself completely with
the fourth evangelist himself. [139] If Menoud was correct when he wrote in 1958, "the works of the last ten
years have not solved the enigma which is the Fourth
Gospel," [140] perhaps the failure lies in not standing
where Hunnius stood. The opening sentence of his commentary leaves no doubt concerning his starting point,
and suggests the root strength of his approach: "Author
Evangelicae huius historiae est Spiritus Sanctus." [141]

Notes

[1] Philipp Melanchthon, *Annotationes in Evangelium Ioannis*, in
Corpus Reformatorum, XIV (1847), 1043-1220. Luther himself was responsible for the publication of this commentary, which originated in
the lectures Melanchthon delivered at Wittenberg in the winter of 1523.
Luther was so pleased with the lectures that he sent them to the
printer Nikolaus Gerbel with an accompanying letter which is repro-
duced in *CR*, XIV, 1043-1046. In this paper we shall concentrate on this
Johannine commentary rather than on the *Enarratio in Evangelium
Ioannis* (*CR*, XV [1848], 1-440), which, though a more detailed work,
may well represent the combined labors of Melanchthon and Kaspar
Cruciger rather than the work of Melanchthon alone.

[2] Aegidius Hunnius, *Commentarius in Evangelium de Iesu Christo,
secundum Ioannem, perspicuis annotationibus illustratus* (Francoforti
ad Moenum: Iohannes Spies, 1585), [18], 443 leaves. In the preparation
of this paper I have been privileged to use the copy of Hunnius' *Commentarius* which once belonged to the great New Testament textual
critic C. R. Gregory and which is now in the possession of the University of Chicago Library's Department of Special Collections.

[3] Marie-Joseph Lagrange, *Évangile selon Saint Jean*, 8th ed., reprint of the 5th ed. of 1936 (Paris: Librairie Lecoffre, J. Gabalda et
Cie, Éditeurs, 1948), cxcix, 559 pp. The growth of a strong Biblical
movement in present-day European Roman Catholicism is regarded as
stemming in large part from Fr. Lagrange's influence; Jean Levie, in
his indispensable treatment of contemporary Roman Catholic Biblical
exegesis, writes of Lagrange: "Since the foundation of the Biblical
School in Jerusalem, through his own work, through the *Études bibliques*,
(studies of abiding value, coming one after another since 1902, forty

WISDOM, LOVE AND LAW 455

of them by 1958; Paris, Gabalda), through the *Revue biblique,* which
was from the start, and now in its sixty-eighth year still remains, the
supreme Catholic review devoted to the Bible, he had been the principal master and the greatest benefactor of Catholic exegesis" (*The Bible,
Word of God in Words of Men,* trans. S. H. Treman [New York: Kenedy,
1962], p. 128, *et passim*). M. Zerwick (*Verbum Domini* [Rome],
XXXIV [1956], 49, 50) points out the interesting fact that Lagrange's
work is the one Roman Catholic commentary specifically cited by C.
K. Barrett in his work on the Fourth Gospel.

⁴ Charles Kingsley Barrett, *The Gospel According to St. John: An
Introduction, with Commentary and Notes on the Greek Text* (London:
S.P.C.K., 1960 [c. 1958]), xii, 531 pp. Vincent Taylor's high praise of
Barrett's commentary is worth quoting: "It may be said at once that
Mr. Barrett's work is a very notable achievement. Among British
commentaries on John it is without a parallel, and it is worthy to stand
side by side with the great works of M.-J. Lagrange (1948) and R.
Bultmann (1950)" (*Expository Times,* LXVII [1955-1956], 7). Barrett's
work, incidentally, is the first English commentary on the Greek text
of John to appear since J. H. Bernard's contribution to the International Critical Commentary series in 1928. Raymond T. Stamm writes
of Barrett's work: "The pressing need for an up-to-date critical and
theological commentary in English on the Greek text of the Gospel of
John has now been met" (*Journal of Biblical Literature,* LXXV [1956],
349).

⁵ Cf. Roland H. Bainton, *The Reformation of the Sixteenth Century*
(Boston: Beacon Press, 1952), p. 45.

⁶ Preface to the New Testament (1522); *D. Martin Luthers Werke:
Kritische Gesamtausgabe* (Weimar: Hermann Böhlaus Nachfolger,
1883—), *Deutsche Bibel,* VI, 10; freely translated. Hereafter this ed.
of Luther's works will be referred to as *WA.*

⁷ *WA,* XXXII, 352, 353 (exposition of Matt. 5:16 in 1532).

⁸ Norman Sykes, *Sixty Years Since: Some Changes in Theological
Thought Since 1900 in Respect of the Quest of the Historical Jesus,*
Montefiore Memorial Lectures, No. 3 (Southampton: University of Southampton, 1960), p. 16. We shall have more to say later on the question
of Gentile vs. Jewish *Sitz im Leben* for the Fourth Gospel, and on the
problem of the chronology of the Last Supper in John and in the Synoptics; it should not be assumed that we necessarily agree with the views
presented by Sykes.

⁹ The older works on Biblical hermeneutics invariably discuss the
characteristics of the ideal interpreter, and among these one generally
finds such phrases as "a sound, well-balanced mind," "imagination
needed, but must be controlled," "sober judgment," "correctness and
delicacy of taste" (Milton S. Terry, *Biblical Hermeneutics,* [2d ed.,
reprint; Grand Rapids, Michigan: Zondervan, n.d.] pp. 151 ff.). Cf.
the 1950 selection policy for religious books at the Enoch Pratt Free
Library: "The Library ... attempts to provide authoritative and objective presentations, avoiding inflammatory, extreme, or unfair statements and highly emotional treatments" (*Book Selection Policies and
Procedures, Pt. I: Policies* [Baltimore: Enoch Pratt Free Library,

1950 (mimeographed)] pp. 55, 56); for the fallacies in this evaluative criterion of religious literature, see my article, "A Normative Approach to the Acquisition Problem in the Theological Seminary Library," *American Theological Library Association Proceedings*, XVI (1962), 65-95.

[10] See, e.g., Harry Emerson Fosdick's *The Modern Use of the Bible* (New York: Macmillan, 1924), esp. pp. 10, 11. This widely held conviction is briefly treated in my editorial Introduction to *Chytraeus on Sacrifice: A Reformation Treatise in Biblical Theology* (St. Louis, Missouri: Concordia, 1962), pp. 26, 28, 29.

[11] Samuel Terrien writes: "Although the Protestant Reformation spurred in every land an unprecedented interest in the Bible, the dogmatic intolerance of the post-Reformation period was not favorable to the development of Biblical studies" ("History of the Interpretation of the Bible: III. Modern Period," *The Interpreter's Bible*, I [New York, Nashville: Abingdon Press, 1952], 127). Frederick W. Danker also dispenses with these exegetes in one paragraph with the comment: "The 17th-century commentaries are notable chiefly for their prolixity and for their curioso-like display of what Spurgeon called 'intellectual crockery.' ... Time which one may be inclined to spend on the works of these men who wrote *currente calamo* will be more wisely invested in the study of the patristic commentators who supplied much of their bulk. A gust of fresh air enters with Matthew Henry...." (*Multi purpose Tools for Bible Study*[St. Louis, Missouri: Concordia, 1960], p. 257).

[12] Clyde L. Manschreck, *Melanchthon, the Quiet Reformer* (New York: Abingdon, 1958).

[13] *CR*, VI, 474 (epistle to Butzer, Aug. 28, 1544); 880 (epistle to Carlowitz, April 28, 1548).

[14] J. L. Neve, *A History of Christian Thought*, I (Philadelphia: Muhlenberg Press, 1943), 256.

[15] Wilhelm Pauck, "Luther and Melanchthon," in Vilmos Vajta (ed.), *Luther and Melanchthon in the History and Theology of the Reformation* (Philadelphia: Muhlenberg Press, 1961), p. 27.

[16] Cf. Walter G. Tillmanns, *The World and Men About Luther* (Minneapolis, Minnesota: Augsburg, 1959), p. 106.

[17] *WA (Tischreden)*, I, No. 348 (1532).

[18] For biographical data on Hunnius see, as the basic primary source, Melchior Adam's sketch, based on Hutter's funeral oration for Hunnius: *Vitae Germanorum theologorum* (Haidelbergae: J. Rosa, 1620), pp. 723-31. Cf. also Pierre Bayle, *A General Dictionary, Historical and Critical*, trans. J. P. Bernard et al., VI (London: G. Strahan et al., 1738), 318-22; Friedrich Wilhelm Strieder, *Grundlage zu einer hessichen Gelerhten und Schriftsteller Geschichte* (Cassel: Cramer, 1780-82), VI, 243 ff.; IX, 391; *Philipp's des Grossmüthigen hessiche Kirchenreformationsordnung*, ed. Karl August Credner (Giessen, 1852), *passim*; Alexander Schweizer, *Die protestantischen Centraldogmen* (Zürich, 1854-56), I, 529 ff., 568 ff.; and Gustav Frank, *Geschichte der protestantischen Theologie*, I (Leipzig: Breitkopf & Härtel, 1862), 248, 249, 257, 265, 275, 280, 343. The most accessible biographical article in

English on Hunnius is that by Johannes Kunze in *The New Schaff-Herzog Encyclopedia of Religious Knowledge*, V. 409, 410.

[19] Adam, p. 727.

[20] Copies of these works are held either by the British Museum or by the Bibliothèque Nationale (Paris), and citations have been obtained from the printed catalogs of their departments of printed books. A complete edition of Hunnius' Latin works was prepared by his son-in-law H. Garth(ius), and published in five volumes folio at Wittenberg, 1607-09; it is titled, *Tomus primus [—quintus] Operum Latinorum*.

[21] Of this work Bayle says: "Calvin was there accused of so many heretical crimes, that he might have been afraid of being treated like Servetus, had he lain at Hunnius's mercy" (VI, 321).

[22] David Pareus (1548-1622) was one of the most distinguished Calvinist theologians of the early 17th century; on him, see my *Seventeenth-Century View of European Libraries: Lomeier's "De bibliothecis,"* Chapter X (Berkeley, California: University of California Press, 1962), pp. 27, 28, 100, 101, 161.

[23] For a full bibliography with detailed subject index of M.-J. Lagrange's prolific exegetical writings, see F.-M. Braun, *L'oeuvre du Père Lagrange: Étude et bibliographie* (Fribourg en Suisse: L'Imprimerie St.-Paul, 1943). Cf. also *Mémorial Lagrange* (Paris: Librairie Lecoffre; J. Gabalda et Cie, Editeurs, 1940), pp. 1-11.

[24] Wilbert Francis Howard, *The Fourth Gospel in Recent Criticism and Interpretation*, ed. C. K. Barrett (4th ed.; London: Epworth Press, 1955), p. 88.

[25] Ernest DeWitt Burton and Edgar Johnson Goodspeed, "The Study of the New Testament," in *A Guide to the Study of the Christian Religion*, ed. G. B. Smith (Chicago: University of Chicago Press, 1916), p. 176.

[26] Quoted in James D. Wood, *The Interpretation of the Bible: A Historical Introduction* (London: Gerald Duckworth, 1958), p. 169.

[27] See, for example, Melanchthon's "The Church and the Authority of the Word" (1539), in *Melanchthon: Selected Writings*, trans. Charles Leander Hill (Minneapolis, Minnesota: Augsburg, 1962), pp. 130-86. It is noteworthy, however, that Melanchthon never stressed the doctrine of Scriptural authority as much as Hunnius did in his *Tractatus de sacrosancta majestate, autoritate, fide ac certitudine Sacrae Scripturae*.

[28] *Theology* [London], LIX (1956), 369.

[29] *Scottish Journal of Theology*, VIII (1955), 429, 430.

[30] *Hibbert Journal*, LIV (1955-1956), 294.

[31] Trans. and ed. Martin W. Schoenberg (Westminster, Md.: Newman Press, 1955).

[32] "Three Books on the Fourth Gospel," *Novum Testamentum*, I (1956), 41.

[33] "Ist voraussetzungslose Exegese möglich?" *Theologische Zeitschrift*, XIII (1957), 409-17; published in English trans. in *Existence and Faith: Shorter Writings of Rudolf Bultmann*, ed. Schubert M. Ogden (New York: Meridian Living Age Books, 1960), pp. 289-96.

[34] Bultmann's circularity principle is well set forth and persuasively defended in Armin Henry Limper's thesis, "Hermeneutics and

Eschatology: Rudolf Bultmann's Interpretation of John, Chapters 13-17," unpubl. Ph.D. diss. (Chicago, 1960).

[35] We readily agree that the canons of historical method must be presupposed in historical investigation, but such presuppositions are properly heuristic and do not limit freedom of inquiry. However, when Bultmann asserts that historical method requires us to "understand the whole historical process as a closed unity" and that "this closedness means that the continuum of historical happenings cannot be rent by the interference of supernatural, transcendent powers and that therefore there is no 'Miracle' in this sense of the word" (*Existence and Faith*, p. 292), he confuses historical method (empirical method applied to history) with historicism (rationalistic scientism operative in the historical realm).

[36] Bultmann's dependence on Dilthey in this respect is evident from Bultmann's essay, "The Problem of Hermeneutics," which appeared originally in the *Zeitschrift für Theologie und Kirche*, XLVII (1950), 47-69; published in English trans. in Bultmann's *Essays, Philosophical and Theological*, trans. J. C. G. Greig (London: SCM Press, 1955), pp. 234-61.

[37] Tillich so describes this basic characteristic of existentialism in his "Existential Philosophy: Its Historical Meaning," first published in the *Journal of the History of Ideas*, V (January 1944), and republished in Tillich's *Theology of Culture*, ed. Robert C. Kimball (New York: Oxford University Press, 1959), p. 92.

[38] Bultmann, *Existence and Faith*, p. 294.

[39] I have argued this point with reference to philosophy of history and have criticized Bultmann's approach in detail in my book, *The Shape of the Past: An Introduction to Philosophical Historiography*, ("History in Christian Perspective," I; Grand Rapids, Michigan: Edwards Brothers, 1962), esp. pp. 120-22.

[40] Aristotle, *De arte poetica*, 1460b, 1461b. Cf. my article, "Some Comments on Paul's Use of Genesis in His Epistle to the Romans," *Bulletin of the Evangelical Theological Society*, IV (April, 1961), 4-11.

[41] G. H. C. MacGregor and A. Q. Morton, *The Structure of the Fourth Gospel* (Edinburgh: Oliver and Boyd, 1961).

[42] The adulterous woman pericope (7:53—8:11) must be rejected on textual grounds; for a summary of the manuscript evidence see Nestle's text.

[43] "I conceive it to be the duty of an interpreter at least to see what can be done with the document as it has come down to us before attempting to improve upon it" (C. H. Dodd, *The Interpretation of the Fourth Gospel* [Cambridge: Cambridge University Press, 1953], p. 290).

[44] Hugo Odeberg, "The Authorship of Saint John's Gospel," *Concordia Theological Monthly*, XXII (April, 1951), 246.

[45] A. Jaubert, *La date de la Cène. Calendrier biblique et liturgie chrétienne* (Paris: Gabalda, 1957). Cf. F. F. Bruce's excellent review of this work in the *Journal of Semitic Studies*, III (1958), 219-21.

[46] See Dodd, pp. 263-85, and my article, "Wisdom as Gift: The Wisdom Concept in Relation to Biblical Messianism," *Interpretation*, XVI (January, 1962), 43-57 (reprinted *supra* in the present section).

In his *Authority of the Bible* (rev. ed.; London: Nisbet, 1955), pp. 200, 201, Dodd presents the following balanced judgment: "Some critics, approaching it (the Fourth Gospel) from the side of Judaism, have pronounced it the most Jewish of the Gospels, while others, approaching it from the other side, see in it a thoroughly Hellenistic book. Nowhere more evidently than here does early Christianity take its place as the natural leader in new ways of thought, uniting in itself the main tendencies of the time, yet exercising authority over them by virtue of the creative impulse proceeding from its Founder." In spite of recent tendencies to understand the Fourth Gospel in thoroughgoing Jewish terms (Cf. Howard, pp. 158, 159), it is important to note that a "Greek" (i.e., non-Jewish) audience is not entirely removed from the purview of the author (note especially 12:20 ff.: "And there were certain Greeks among them that came up to worship at the feast . . . and they said, Sir, we would see Jesus"). As to the frequently debated question whether the Fourth Gospel was written for "believers" or "unbelievers" (cf. the debate on the reading πιστεύητε vs. πιστεύσητε in 20:31—both of which have excellent manuscript support), two considerations render the argument superfluous: (1) "Believing" in the Fourth Gospel is consistently presented as a continuous, moment-by-moment experience, and therefore witness can be meaningfully directed to believers as well as to unbelievers (cf. the theological aphorism, "No Christian is more than one day old"); (2) As we shall see, the major focus of attention in John's Gospel is on the source and object of belief, not on the one believing or the one about to believe; John is concerned not with the psychology of belief but with its ontology.

[47] Note, for example, John's apologetic use of the supreme σημεῖον, the Resurrection: "Then answered the Jews and said unto Him, What sign [σημεῖον] showest Thou unto us, seeing that Thou doest these things? Jesus answered and said unto them, Destroy this temple, and in three days I will raise it up. Then said the Jews, Forty and six years was this temple in building, and wilt Thou rear it up in three days? But He spake of the temple of His body. When therefore He was risen from the dead, His disciples remembered that He had said this unto them; and they believed the Scripture, and the word which Jesus had said" (2:18-22). Cf. also J. H. Bernard's discussion of the "signs," in his *Critical and Exegetical Commentary on the Gospel According to St. John*, ed. A. H. McNeile ("International Critical Commentary;" Edinburgh: T. & T. Clark, 1928), I, clxxvi, clxxvii.

[48] A particularly clear example is the dialog with Nicodemus in chap. 3, where Jesus' object is to bring Nicodemus to a "new birth/ birth from above" (ἄνωθεν). Vv. 14 ff. (probably representing John's comments on the incident) connect this transcendent birth with a believing relationship to Christ (πιστεύειν εἰς αὐτόν), who will be "lifted up" on the cross for man's salvation.

[49] Chicago: Willett, Clark, 1936.

[50] See Bernard, I, xc—xciii.

[51] These word counts are derived from Moulton and Geden's *Concordance to the Greek Testament* (3d ed.; Edinburgh: T. & T. Clark, 1926), pp. 616, 617.

[52] I am indebted for these latter two points to Dr. David Granskou of the Department of Theological Cooperation, National Lutheran Council.

[53] *WA*, XIV, 489.

[54] Thus Bultmann existentializes the Johannine concept of "true light" by defining it as "the state of having one's existence illumined, as illumination in and by which a man understands himself, achieves a self-understanding which opens up his 'way' to him, guides all his conduct, and gives him clarity and assurance" (*Theology of the New Testament*, trans. Kendrick Grobel [London: SCM Press, 1955], II, 18). In actuality the fourth evangelist, at the very outset of his Gospel, defines the "true light" as the "Word made flesh" (1:9-14).

[55] Dodd, *Interpretation of the Fourth Gospel*, pp. 431, 432.

[56] "Thomas stops short at the glorious scars, and the book, as originally planned, ends with his adoration and the challenge to all readers to believe. The reader is bound to be left gazing with Thomas" (Barnabas Lindars, "The Fourth Gospel, an Act of Contemplation," *Studies in the Fourth Gospel*, ed. F. L. Cross [London: Mowbray, 1957], p. 35). On the historical significance of this Thomas incident, see my *Shape of the Past*, pp. 173-75. Bultmann greatly weakens the factual thrust of the Johannine resurrection accounts when he warns against "taking the Easter-stories for more than they are able to be: signs and pictures of the Easter faith—or, perhaps still better, confessions of faith in it" (*Theology of the New Testament*, II, 57).

[57] C. J. Wright, in Major, Manson, and Wright's *Mission and Message of Jesus* (New York: Dutton, 1938), p. 675; Wright's italics. Dodd makes the same point when he thus describes the Johannine theology: "The knowledge of God which is life eternal is mediated by an historical transaction. Only through the 'departure' and 'return' of Christ, that is, through His actual death on the cross and His actual resurrection, is the life He brings liberated for the life of the world" (*Interpretation of the Fourth Gospel*, p. 423).

It will be noted that in the foregoing analysis of the basic message of John's Gospel we have not dealt with any of the "special" hermeneutic theories such as the allegorical (Loisy), the mystical (Von Hügel), the sacramental-liturgical (Cullmann), etc. This is not to say that we totally reject these emphases, but we believe that where applicable they must be regarded as subordinate and contributory to the central purpose of the Gospel as set forth in the direct and literal statements of its author. With regard to the "realized" vs. "futurist" eschatology issue, we reject Bultmann's argument that the Fourth Gospel is absolutely nonfuturist; his claim that 5:28, 29, 6:54, and 12:48 are later additions to the book has no textual basis and actually represents the operation of exegetical presuppositionalism.

[58] Excellent precedent for the use of the Nicodemus dialogue in comparative exegesis has been provided by Barrett himself who, in his revision of Howard's *Fourth Gospel in Recent Criticism* (pp. 243 ff.), examines the treatment of the Nicodemus episode given by Hoskyns, Bultmann, and Dodd.

[59] *CR*, XIV, 1047-1049.

[60] *Ibid.*, cols. 1065, 1066.

[61] *Ibid.*, cols. 1216, 1217.

[62] *Ibid.*, col. 1078.

[63] *Ibid.*, cols. 1099-1103.

[64] *Ibid.*, cols. 1079, 1080.

[65] "In historia resuscitati Lazari non quaeremus allegoriam, ut Lazari morte repraesentetur animae mors, et hoc genus alia. Sed factum ipsum consyderandum est" (*ibid.*, col. 1138). Unhappily, Melanchthon does not restrain himself from employing allegorical method elsewhere in the commentary, and here he does not see the *factum ipsum* of Lazarus' resurrection as a pointer to the *factum ipsum* of Christ's own resurrection.

[66] *Ibid.*, col. 1139.

[67] *Ibid.*, cols. 1213-1215.

[68] *Ibid.*, cols. 1144, 1145.

[69] For example: "*Altera die vidit, etc.* [1:29] Altera die, i.e. alio die, quia graecismus est, ne urgeat esse sequenti die" (*ibid.*, col. 1071).

[70] Of the 169 columns of the commentary, 28 are spent on John 1. This is three and a half times the emphasis one would expect if equal stress were placed on each chapter of the Fourth Gospel. In contrast, only four columns are devoted to John 18 and only two columns each to chaps. 19 and 20; in the case of chap. 18 this is half what one would expect, and in the case of chaps. 19 and 20, it is but one fourth of the expected emphasis.

[71] It was undoubtedly Luther's legitimate preoccupation with the Law-Gospel issue that caused him to look with such favor on Melanchthon's commentary. It has also been suggested that Luther appreciated Melanchthon's support of his position on free will over against Erasmus (*ibid.*, cols. 1043, 1044). Luther himself saw the doctrine of justification in John's Gospel (*WA*, XXXIII, 82—sermon on John 6:37-39 [1531]), but he clearly recognized that the focus of the Gospel was not on doctrine but on the source and object of doctrine, Christ Himself.

[72] J. B. Phillips, *Letters to Young Churches* (London: Bles, 1947), p. xi.

[73] After presenting the general *argumentum* of a chapter, he divides the chapter into two or three major subject units or paragraphs; then he makes general explanatory comments on each unit; finally, he derives specific *loci* from the units. The approach is not greatly dissimilar to that employed in the *Interpreter's Bible*, where historical-philological comments form the background for theological-devotional insights.

[74] In my *Chytraeus on Sacrifice, loc. cit.* It can be argued, in fact, that the concern for system in the 17th century was the epoch's greatest strength and most permanent contribution; see my "Libraries of France at the Ascendancy of Mazarin: Louis Jacob's *Traicté des plus belles bibliothèques,*" unpubl. Ph. D. diss. (Chicago, 1962), Editorial Introduction.

[75] "Proponit enim eum, qui omnis salutis nostrae principium & finis est, Christum scilicet, in cuius cognitione cardo aeternae foelicitatis vertitur, dicente ipso Christo: Haec est vita aeterna, ut cognos-

cant te solum verum Deum, & quem misisti Iesum Christum [17:3]"
(Hunnius, *Commentarius* . . . , fol. 3v).

[76] J. Kunze, "Hunnius, Nicolaus," *New Schaff-Herzog Encyclopedia*, V, 409.

[77] Hunnius, *Commentarius* . . . , fol. 277r.

[78] *Ibid.*, fols. 291v, 292r.

[79] *Ibid.*, fol. 291v; the Latin reads: "Itaque omnia miracula Christi divinitatem eius astruunt, siquidem ex solius divinitatis potentia haec miracula fecit." (On the meaning of *astruo* here, see Baxter and Johnson's *Medieval Latin Word-List* [London: Oxford University Press, 1934], p. 34; and Alexander Souter's *Glossary of Later Latin* [Oxford: Clarendon Press, 1957], p. 8.)

[80] Hunnius, *Commentarius* . . . , fols. 63r to 67r.

[81] To be distinguished sharply from *Zweideutigkeit* (ambiguity), as Oscar Cullmann correctly points out.

[82] "Hic titulus in ignominiam Iesu à Pilato scriptus à Deo gubernante sic temperabatur, aut [sic: ut] ad summam ac sempiternam Christi gloriam vergeret" (*ibid.*, fol. 408r).

[83] *Ibid.*, fol. 293v. Hunnius makes this point very strongly; see the entire discussion, fols. 293v, 294r.

[84] *Ibid.*, fols. 320v, 321r. Hunnius writes: "Ante festum, id est, sub [= just before] eam ipsam vesperam, qua & Pascha comedit cum discipulis, & abrogatis veteris Testamenti sacris typicis, Sacrementum novi Testamenti Coenam Domini instituit." On resolving the problem involved in the phrase "before the feast of the Passover," cf. R. V. G. Tasker, *The Gospel According to St. John* (London: Tyndale Press, 1960), pp. 153, 154.

[85] *Ibid.*, fols. 395v, 396r.

[86] *Ibid.*, fol. 414r. Strack and Billerbeck note that "if this Sabbath was 15 Nisan, as the Fourth Gospel supposes, then it could be called 'high' since it was simultaneously the first festival day of the Passover" (*Kommentar zum Neuen Testament aus Talmud und Midrasch*, II [München, 1924], 581).

[87] Jaubert (*op. cit.*) effectively argues that the Last Supper was eaten as a Passover meal (but without the lamb) on Tuesday evening, in accord with the Jubilees-Qumran calendar; that the arrest took place that evening; that on Wednesday, 12 Nisan, Jesus was brought before the Sanhedrin; that on Thursday morning the Sanhedrin, following the Mishnaic rules, promulgated their verdict, and took Jesus to Pilate, who referred Him to Herod Antipas (Thursday afternoon); that on Friday, 14 Nisan, Jesus was returned to Pilate and summarily crucified; and that on Friday afternoon the Passover lambs were sacrificed in the Temple, thus ushering in the official Passover meal that evening (15 Nisan, the Sabbath) for those who followed the lunar calendar.

[88] Hunnius, *Commentarius* . . . , fol. 404v.

[89] Calvin writes: "This [the alleged contradiction] may be easily explained. It is plain enough from other passages that the day was at that time divided into four parts, as the night also contained four watches; in consequence of which, the Evangelists sometimes allot not more than four hours to each day, and extend each hour to three, and,

at the same time, reckon the space of an hour, which was drawing to a close, as belonging to the next part. According to this calculation, John relates that Christ was condemned *about the sixth hour,* because the time of the day was drawing towards *the sixth hour,* or towards the second part of the day. Hence we infer that Christ was crucified at or about *the sixth hour;* for, as the Evangelist afterwards mentions (v. 20), *the place was near to the city. The darkness* began between the sixth and ninth hour, and lasted till the ninth hour, at which time Christ died" (*Commentary on the Gospel According to John,* trans. William Pringle, [reprint ed.; Grand Rapids, Michigan: Eerdmans, 1956], II, 224).

[90] B. F. Westcott (*The Gospel According to St. John; the Greek Text with Introduction and Notes* [reprint ed.; Grand Rapids, Michigan: Eerdmans, 1954]) reasons on the basis of the *Martyrdom of Polycarp* that our present-day midnight-to-noon, noon-to-midnight hour-reckoning system was in use in Asia Minor when the Fourth Gospel was written, and that John is therefore saying that Pilate sentenced Jesus at about 6 a.m. Consistency is thus established with Mark, who, following the Jewish system, states that the crucifixion itself began at 9 a.m. ("the third hour").

[91] Lagrange, *Évangile selon Saint Jean,* pp. clxxxiv, clxxxv.

[92] In point of fact it is difficult to find the unity concept presented explicitly in the Fourth Gospel except in the high-priestly prayer, John 17.

[93] Lagrange, *Évangile selon Saint Jean,* p. lxx.

[94] *Ibid.,* p. 519.

[95] Cf. *ibid.,* p. 60 (discussion of the miracle at Cana): "In John the σημεῖον is used in its proper sense of sign; it is a miracle supernaturally pointing in a special way to the person of Jesus (c'est un miracle contenant une indication surnaturelle spécialement sur la personne de Jésus)."

[96] *Ibid.,* p. 78. Hunnius is also aware of the relation between 3:2 and 3:10—see his *Commentarius . . . ,* fol. 62r. Unhappily, neither interpreter brings out the full ironic force of the anarthrous διδάσκαλος in 3:2 vs. the articular ὁ διδάσκαλος in 3:10; the AV, it will be noted, completely misses the point by translating the same word "teacher" in 3:2 and "master" in 3:10, and by using the *indefinite* article in the second instance.

[97] Lagrange, *Évangile selon Saint Jean,* p. 80.

[98] *Ibid.,* p. 81.

[99] *Ibid.,* p. 1. Lagrange's frequent emphasis on "la personne de Jésus-Christ" reminds one of the personalistic concern of a number of *avant-garde* contemporary Roman Catholic scholars, particularly in Europe; see my *Chytraeus on Sacrifice,* pp. 120, 121, note 281.

[100] Lagrange, *Évangile selon Saint Jean,* p. 490.

[101] *Ibid.,* pp. 315, 316.

[102] See Lagrange's review of Goguel's *Life of Jesus,* in *Revue biblique,* XLI (1932), 598-614.

[103] Cf. Lagrange, *Monsieur Loisy et le modernisme* (Paris: Éditions du Cerf, 1932).

[104] See Lagrange, *Christ and Renan: A Commentary on Ernest Renan's "The Life of Jesus,"* trans. Maisie Ward (New York: Benziger, 1928), p. 54.

[105] Vénard, in *Père Lagrange and the Scriptures,* trans. Richard T. Murphy (Milwaukee, Wisconsin: Bruce Publishing Co., 1946), pp. 80, 81.

[106] Lagrange, *Évangile selon Saint Jean,* p. 312.

[107] *Ibid.,* p. 294.

[108] *Ibid.,* pp. 310, 311.

[109] "Il a . . . voulu corriger les affirmations inexactes qu'on aurait pu tirer à torte de leur texte" (*ibid.,* p. cxxvii).

[110] *Ibid.,* p. 471; cf. also pp. 319, 350, 469 f., 497 f., 504.

[111] *Ibid.,* p. 487.

[112] Lagrange, *Évangile selon Saint Marc* (4th ed.; Paris: Gabalda, 1947), p. 429.

[113] *Revue des sciences philosophiques et théologiques,* XL (1956), 146.

[114] *Church Quarterly Review,* CLVII (1956), 18.

[115] Coined from μηδὲν ἄγαν ("nothing too much"), the Greek expression for the Golden Mean.

[116] Barrett, *The Gospel According to Saint John,* p. 114.

[117] *Ibid.,* pp. 114, 115.

[118] Cf. Edmond LaB. Cherbonnier, "Biblical Faith and the Idea of Tragedy," in *The Tragic Vision and the Christian Faith,* ed. Nathan Scott (New York: Association Press, 1957), pp. 23-55.

[119] Barrett, *The Gospel According to Saint John,* p. 125.

[120] *Ibid.,* p. 62.

[121] *Ibid.,* p. 65.

[122] *Ibid.,* p. 64. Cf. Bultmann's assertion that the Johannine miracles "are ambiguous signs whose meaning can only be found in faith" (*Theology of the New Testament,* II, 60).

[123] Barrett, p. 169.

[124] *Ibid.,* pp. 171, 176.

[125] *Ibid.,* pp. 337, 457.

[126] *Ibid.,* p. 457; see also p. 454.

[127] *Ibid.,* p. 119.

[128] M. Zerwick, *Verbum Domini* [Rome], XXXIV (1956), 50.

[129] Barrett, p. 323.

[130] *New Testament Studies,* III (1956-1957), 75. Sanders illustrates his point with reference to Barrett's treatment of the Cana miracle (*The Gospel According to St. John,* p. 157), the Samaritan woman incident (*ibid.,* p. 191), and Jesus' trial before the high priest (*ibid.,* p. 438).

[131] *Ibid.,* p. 454.

[132] *Ibid.,* p. 39.

[133] *Ibid.,* p. 41.

[134] *Theological Studies,* XVII (1956), 250.

[135] It should be emphasized that we are not depreciating the value of Barrett's commentary *as a reference work* (in this respect it is of paramount significance); we are saying, however, that it is less successful at penetrating to the heart of John's message than even Melanch-

thon's commentary with its preoccupation with Gospel and Law.

[136] Cf. the revealing *pecca fortiter* advice which Luther found it necessary to give to Melanchthon.

[137] W. H. Cooper, "Martin Chemnitz on Justification; with Special Reference to His Use of the Old Testament," part II, *Northwestern Seminary Bulletin*, XXXV (January, 1960), 8.

[138] Anthony Boucher writes of Father Brown: "It is not so much the crime as the *appearance* of the crime that is fantastic; and it is the credulity of modern man, 'emancipated' from religion and failing to comprehend the science which has 'replaced' it, which turns the commonplace into the fantastically miraculous. (See, for example, 'The Hammer of God,' in which Father Brown, who can discount the supernatural because he knows it exists, meets a 'miracle' and finds a simple and most literally down-to-earth explanation.)" (Anthony Boucher, Introduction to G. K. Chesterton's *Ten Adventures of Father Brown*, Chapel Books [New York: Dell Publishing Co., 1961], p. 11).

[139] Maurice F. Wiles makes a point worth pondering when he says: "There are some books of the Bible whose interpretation has been so completely revolutionised by modern critical methods that the exegesis of earlier centuries is unlikely to add much of value to our understanding of them. There is probably no book of which this is less true than the Fourth Gospel. It is of such a nature that it seems to reveal its secrets not so much to the skillful probings of the analyst as to a certain intuitive sympathy of understanding. We need not, therefore, despair of finding amongst such early interpreters significant examples of a true insight into the meaning of the Gospel" (*The Spiritual Gospel: The Interpretation of the Fourth Gospel in the Early Church* [Cambridge: Cambridge University Press, 1960], p. 1).

[140] Philippe H. Menoud, "Les études johanniques de Bultmann à Barrett," in *L'évangile de Jean: Études et problèmes*, Recherches bibliques, No. 3 (Louvain: Desclée de Brouwer, 1958), p. 30.

[141] Hunnius, *Commentarius . . .* , fol. 1r. For a faithful and sympathetic treatment of the doctrine of inspiration held by Hunnius and other major orthodox Lutheran theologians of the time, see Robert Preus, *The Inspiration of Scripture . . .* (Edinburgh: Oliver and Boyd, 1957).

6.

Can We Recover the Christian Devotional Life?

The Issue

A Great Gulf

In Christ's parable of Dives and Lazarus, we are told that between paradise and hell "there is a great gulf fixed: so that they which would pass from hence to you cannot; neither can they pass to us, that would come from thence." An analogous gulf seems to separate Christians of the present day from the great saints and devotional writers in the church's past. Such approaches to life as are advocated or described in the following quotations could hardly be more foreign to the actual life-pattern of the average American Christian—whether layman or cleric:

> Flee the company of worldly-living people as much as thou mayest: for the treating of worldly matters abateth greatly the fervour of spirit: though it be done with a good intent, we be anon deceived with vanity of the world, and in manner are made as thrall unto it, if we take not good head . . . . Therefore it is necessary that we watch and pray, that the time pass not away from us in idleness. If it be lawful and expedient to speak, speak then of God and of such things as are to the edifying of thy soul or of thy neighbour's.[1]

> I looked then, and saw a man named Evangelist coming to him, who asked, "Wherefore dost thou cry?"
> He answered, "Sir, I perceive by the book in my hand, that I am condemned to die, and after that to come to judgment; and I find that I am not willing to do the first, nor able to do the second." Then said Evangelist, "Why not willing to die, since this life is attended with so many evils?" The man answered, "Because I fear that this burden that is upon my back will sink me lower than the grave, and I shall fall into Tophet. And, sir, if I be not fit to go to prison, I am not fit to go to judgment, and from thence to execution; and the thoughts of these things make me cry."

Notes for this section, pages 474-475.

Then said Evangelist, "If this be thy condition, why standest thou still?"

He answered, "Because I know not whither to go." Then he gave him a parchment roll, and there was written within, "Flee from the wrath to come."

The man, therefore, read it, and looking upon Evangelist very carefully, said, "Whither must I fly?" Then said Evangelist (pointing with his finger over a very wide field), "Do you see yonder wicket gate?" The man said, "No." Then said the other, "Do you see yonder shining light?" He said, "I think I do." Then said Evangelist, "Keep that light in your eye, and go up directly thereto: so shalt thou see the gate; at which, when thou knockest, it shall be told thee what thou shalt do." So I saw in my dream that the man began to run. Now, he had not run far from his own door, when his wife and children perceiving it, began to cry after him to return; but the man put his fingers in his ears, and ran on, crying, "Life! Life! eternal life!" So he looked not behind him, but fled toward the middle of the plain.[2]

I found in myself a spirit of love, and warmth, and power, to address the poor Indians. God helped me to plead with them to "turn from all the vanities of the heathen to the living God." I am persuaded the Lord touched their consciences for I never saw such attention raised in them before. And when I came away from them, I spent the whole time, while I was riding to my lodgings three miles distant, in prayer and praise to God.

After I rode more than two miles, it came into my mind to dedicate myself to God again; which I did with great solemnity and unspeakable satisfaction. Especially gave up myself to Him renewedly in the work of the ministry. And this I did by divine grace, I hope, without any exception or reserve; not in the least shrinking back from any difficulties that might attend this great and blessed work. I seemed to be most free, cheerful and full in this dedication of myself. My whole soul cried: "Lord, to Thee I dedicate myself! Oh, accept of me and let me be Thine forever. Lord, I desire nothing else: I desire nothing more. Oh, come, come, Lord, accept a poor worm. 'Whom have I in heaven but Thee? and there is none upon earth, that I desire besides Thee.' "[3]

The reading of the Word and meditation on the promises have been increasingly precious to me of late. At first I allowed my desire to acquire the language (Chinese) speedily to have undue prominence and a deadening effect on my soul. But now, in the grace that passes all understanding, the Lord has again caused His face to shine upon me . . . .

> I have been puzzling my brains again about a house,
> etc., but to no effect. So I have made it a matter of prayer,
> and have given it entirely into the Lord's hands, and now
> I feel quite a peace about it. He will provide and be my
> guide in this and every other perplexing step.[4]

The Winds of Modernity

It is natural to ask why such passages as these breathe an atmosphere almost totally different from that in church life today. Several contributing factors can be cited, all of which must be taken into account for a full explanation. First of all, one must note what Andrew Dickson White termed "the warfare of science with theology," which, since the middle of the nineteenth century, has resulted in the growth of a mechanistic, reductionist attitude on the part of both scientist and non-scientist. Scientific method presupposes a closed universe, governed by invariable law; in such a universe religious devotion and prayer for specifics, in particular, seems archaic and meaningless. "Among the professional and scientific classes it has been the inability of traditional religion to justify it-self in the light of modern science . . . that has led to the rapid growth of a tolerant indifference, a skepti-cal agnosticism, or a dogmatic atheism." [5] Secondly, and more important, we have the secular "success-philosophy" which has turned generations of Americans (church members included) from seeking God to seeking personal achievement and recognition by society. "The major influence affecting religious beliefs and attitudes has been the growth of our manifold secular faiths and interests . . . . Though men repeat the old phrases their real concern has turned elsewhere." [6] In the secularistic activism of modern life, few find time or motivation for devotional exercises. Thirdly, observation of the churches themselves reveals that organized religion has shifted its goals to accord more fully with the modern temper. "The main stress of religious energy has been turned away from the supernatural to the social, from transcending the human to the serving of human needs . . . . It is not that the churches practice a conscious hypocrisy about Chris-tian teachings but rather that religious doctrines have been turned into counters in a game men play to bring their consciences to terms with their universe. It is less a question of what the pastors say than the fact that they are no longer listened to; having lost the capacity for belief, they have lost also the power to instill belief." [7] But this is not the only contribution that the church has made to widening the gap between the ideal and the real in Christian devotional life.

Modern Theology Widens the Gulf

In their writings, not a few twentieth-century theologians have (in many cases unwittingly encouraged the trend away from Christian devotional exercises. I refer not merely to publications by religious liberals who would justify an anthropocentric religion,[8] nor solely to works by those who would interpret prayer largely in terms of introspection or meditation[9]—influential as such writings have been. What concerns me to a far greater extent is the doctrinal emphasis characteristic of some of the foremost theologians within the Reformation framework of belief.

For several decades, Karl Barth and the so-called "neo-orthodox" school of Christian thought excessively stressed the sovereignty and transcendence of God.[10] The work of Rudolph Otto[11] and the Kierkegaard revival [12] contributed to and reinforced this shift in the gravitational center of theology. Nygren's *Agape and Eros*[13] sharply distinguished God's unmotivated, selfless, unconditioned love from all varieties of human desire. Now obviously no Christian who subjects his theology to the testimony of Revelation would deny the great contribution which this transcendence movement has made; in an era of watered-down, man-centered, social-gospel liberalism Barth's *Commentary on Romans* came as a clarion-call to a re-emphasis on justification by grace alone. However, the neo-orthodox and Lundensian movements do not seem productive of a positive attitude in the devotional realm. Specifically, one notes that Nygren's *agape*-emphasis is interpreted ethically to mean that man cannot in the ultimate sense love God, for if he could a form of synergism would have crept into Christian doctrine. In his *Basic Christian Ethics* Ramsey writes:

> One has to go in heavily for analogy, or even commute back and forth from one meaning to another, ever to

suppose that "love," *or any other single term* can adequately convey the meaning of a Christian's response
to God and also his love for neighbor. The words "faith,"
"obedience," "humility," and—to indicate greater intimacy and warmth—the words "gratitude" and "thank-
fulness" and—to keep the distance between God and man
—the expression "to glorify" are preferable, singly or
as a cluster, for describing how Christians think of themselves standing in relation to God. . . . Strictly speaking,
the Christian church is not a community of prayer, but
a community of memory . . . . Strictly speaking, Christians
are not lovers of God; they are *theodidacti,* "taught of
God." [14]

When such radical stress is placed upon the "otherness of God," and when one observes the frightening extent to which Christian devotional writers have sometimes
slipped into eros-synergism,[15] it does not seem strange
that the present-day Christian pastor and priest find it
easy, amid their hectic and activistic responsibilities, to
rationalize a very loose attitude toward the "quest for
holiness." And the clergyman's personal reticence in this
regard has as a logical consequent a *laissez faire* approach
to the devotional lives of his parishioners—out of whose
homes come a good number of the church members of
the next generation. If one assumes that this situation is
not the ideal one, can a Revelation-based theology present
a more balanced approach? To this question we now address ourselves.

The Solution

The Life of Faith As a Scriptural Paradox

Not all great exhibitions of Christian devotion are to
be found in the distant past. The following is a 1951 diary
entry by James Elliot, who in January, 1956, was killed
while attempting to bring the Christian message to the
Auca Indians in Ecuador.

I walked out to the hill just now. It is exalting, deli-
cious. To stand embraced by the shadows of a friendly
tree with the wind tugging at your coat tail and the
heavens hailing your heart—to gaze and glory and give
oneself again to God, what more could a man ask? Oh the
fullness, pleasure, sheer excitement of knowing God on
earth. I care not if I never raise my voice again for
Him, if only I may love Him, please Him. Perhaps in

> mercy He shall give me a host of children that I may
> lead them through the vast star fields to explore His
> delicacies whose finger ends set them to burning. But if
> not, if only I may see Him, smell His garments and smile
> into my Lover's eyes—ah then, not stars nor children shall
> matter, only Himself.[16]

How have such modern saints of God reconciled a life of
personal devotion with the principle of *sola gratia?* The
basic answer is, I believe, that they have given proper
weight to the two other cardinal watchwords of Reformation theology: *sola scriptura* and *sola fide.*

One finds upon a careful examination of Holy Scripture that faith is the absolute requisite in the Christian
life, for it is the open hand which admits a radical need
for salvation from sin, and accepts God's offer of pardon
on His terms. "Without faith," says Divine Revelation,
"it is impossible to please Him" (Heb. 11:6). Of faith,
hope, and love, love is indeed the greatest (I Cor. 13:13),
for God Himself is love (I John 4:8), and His plan of salvation was motivated by love (John 3:16); but faith and
faith alone appropriates God's love personally (John 5:24;
Rom. 10:9). Now a thorough study of the faith-concept in
the Bible leads inevitably to the conclusion that Christian
faith is essentially paradoxical: on the one hand, faith is
a free, unmerited gift of God, and not in any sense the
product of human effort (Eph. 2:8-9); yet, on the other
hand, men must be encouraged, and indeed commanded,
to believe the Gospel of Christ (Acts 16:30-31). This paradox is stated with particular acuteness in passages such
as the following:

> As many as received Him, to them gave He power to
> become the sons of God, even to them that believe on His
> name: which were born, not of blood, nor of the will of
> the flesh, nor of the will of man, but of God. (John 1:12-13)

> Work out your own salvation with fear and trembling.
> For it is God which worketh in you both to will and to do
> of His good pleasure. (Phil. 2:12-13)

It follows from the nature of the faith-paradox that
preaching the necessity of faith to unbelievers is neither
meaningless nor synergistic. Meaninglessness exists only
if the Gospel is *not* preached; and synergism is manifest
only if the believer attributes his existing faith to the
"will of man" rather than to God.

THE SUICIDE OF CHRISTIAN THEOLOGY

One cannot stress too strongly that the sharp edge of this Scriptural paradox must not be blunted by verbalizing. Kierkegaard asserted quite correctly in his *Journals* that "the paradox is not a concession but a category, an ontological definition which expresses the relation between an existing cognitive spirit and eternal truth" [17]; as such, a true Biblical paradox must be asserted in its fullness by sinful men who cannot hope to unravel it by logic or semantics. In speaking of one's own faith, then, the Christian unabashedly attributes all glory to God; and in preaching the message of salvation, he calls for actual, personal commitment. He does not, in the first instance, assert that God gave him faith because he "did not resist the Spirit" (for even such non-resistance is God's work); in the latter instance, he does not preach merely that sinners should "place themselves where God can reach them," but with the Apostle Paul decisively cries, "Believe on the Lord Jesus, and thou shalt be saved." Such a paradox, like that of the Trinity or the Incarnation, is certainly foolishness to the unbeliever, but it is at the same time truly meaningful to the Christian; for the latter does not view it as a metaphysical contradiction, but (in the words of Aulén) as a "mystery of faith" [18] which points to the qualitative distinction between a holy Creator and a sinful creature.

Devotional Implications of the Faith-Paradox

Great Christians of all ages have acknowledged the faith-paradox, and in acknowledging it have found a solid basis for the devotional life. For this paradox applies not only to the beginning of the spiritual life (the new birth), but also to the continuing life of faith. The aphorism that "no Christian is more than one day old" is profoundly true. Faith is not a once-for-all act in the Christian experience; rather, it is a daily relationship between the individual and the living God. And since the Christian, though justified by grace, is never free of sin here on earth (I John 1:8), both sides of the faith-paradox apply to him constantly. Because he is *justus* (to use Luther's formula), he thanks God for giving him sanctifying faith; but since he is also *peccator,* he is bound to strive, as Paul did, to "keep under my body, and bring it into subjection: lest that by any means, when I have preached to others, I myself should be a castaway" (I Cor. 9:27). Adolf Köberle makes this point with telling effect when he writes of prayer, discipline, and service:

> The justification of prayerlessness has never been derived from the article of justification. It was the age of the Illumination that first brought about that weakening of fervor and of discipline in prayer which our race has not yet succeeded in overcoming. . . . Properly under stood the use of such discipline can never endanger the nature of the Gospel but, on the contrary, will only demonstrate and strengthen it. . . . That the suppression of our self-love requires unrelenting self-discipline certainly deprives us of every basis for self-satisfaction, every idea of meritorious action, and sternly directs the one who is fasting to seek the forgiveness of sins. . . . The admonition of Scripture to the disciples and the congregations to crucify the flesh with the affections and lusts thereof, to mortify our members, to strive to enter in through the strait gate, to fight a good fight, to strive to attain the goal—all these admonitions after all only testify how easily the believer may still be lost and what full measure of grace is needed if any one is to be saved.[19]

It follows, therefore, that the devotional life is not a synergistic compromising of the Christian message, but is an essential element in the ongoing life of faith. To deny this is to misunderstand the very nature of belief as it is set forth in Revelation. Unquestionably, a Scylla of synergism can exist where devotional exercises are practiced and love for God is experienced; but one hardly solves the problem by destroying one's spiritual life on the Charybdis of antinomianism.

The Warning

"You could not step twice in the same rivers; for other and yet other waters are ever flowing on," the pre-Socratic philosopher Heraclitus is supposed to have said.[20] Scientific ideologies, cultural values—and even theological schools of thought—have a habit of flowing on with frightening speed. All too soon, one can find that the *Weltanschauung* to which he has given himself has become passé, and another has replaced it. It seems worthwhile, in light of this, to point out that the Word of our God is unique in that it alone "stands forever" (Isa. 40:8), and that its first and great commandment is still to "love the Lord thy God with all thy heart, and with all thy soul, and with all thy mind, and with all thy strength" (Mark 12:30). If the paradoxes of Holy Writ are rendered ineffective through submerging one of their aspects in the other, the result will always be heresy and weakness. God grant then, where the faith-paradox is concerned, that we may pray not only "God be merciful to me a sinner," but also "Lord, increase our faith."

Notes

[1] Thomas à Kempis, *The Imitation of Christ*, i. 10; trans. Richard Whitford (New York: Pocket Books' Cardinal Edition, 1953), pp. 17-18.

[2] John Bunyan, *The Pilgrim's Progress*, i. 1 (Philadelphia: Universal Book and Bible House, 1933), pp. 8-10.

[3] Jonathan Edwards, ed., *The Life and Diary of David Brainerd*, vi, July 1, 1744; newly ed. by Philip E. Howard, Jr. (Chicago: Moody Press' Wycliffe Series of Christian Classics, 1949), p. 169.

[4] Dr. and Mrs. Howard Taylor, *Hudson Taylor's Spiritual Secret* (Philadelphia: China Inland Mission, 1950), pp. 38-39 (extracts from Hudson Taylor's letters of 1854).

[5] John Herman Randall, Jr., *The Making of the Modern Mind* (rev. ed.; Boston: Houghton Mifflin, 1940), p. 535.

[6] *Ibid.*, p. 538.

[7] Max Lerner, *America As a Civilization*, (New York: Simon and Schuster, 1957), pp. 708, 711. The Rev. Mackeral is a fictional example of the suburban modernist clergyman; he receives a salary raise when he makes the stirring sermonic point that "It is the final proof of God's omnipotence that he need not exist in order to save us" (Peter DeVries, *The Mackerel Plaza* [Boston, Little, Brown, 1958], p. 8). Needless to say, such religious soil is not particularly conducive to the growth of Christian spirituality.

[8] E.g., Curtis W. Reese, *The Meaning of Humanism* (Boston: Beacon Press, 1945).

[9] E.g., William Adams Brown, *The Life of Prayer in a World of Science* (New York: Scribner, 1927), especially pp. 13-15 ("The Fourfold Function of Prayer").

[10] Cf. Walter Leibrecht, ed., *Religion and Culture: Essays in Honor of Paul Tillich* (New York: Harper, 1959), pp. 6, 10.

[11] Note especially Otto's *Idea of the Holy* (1923; rev. ed., 1929).

[12] Cf. Jaroslav Pelikan, *Fools for Christ* (Philadelphia: Muhlenberg, 1955), chap. i (pp. 1-27).

[13] Anders Nygren, *Agape and Eros*, trans. Philip S. Watson (Philadelphia: Westminster, 1953); see especially Pt. I.

[14] Paul Ramsey, *Basic Christian Ethics* (New York: Scribner, 1950), pp. 129, 132; Cf. Nygren, *op. cit.*, pp. 212-14, 219.

[15] Examples of synergistic error in Christian devotional classics may be found in such works as Francis de Sales' *Introduction to a Devout Life*, ed. Thomas S. Kepler (Cleveland: World Publishing Company, 1954). A precedent for all such *eros*-related devotional literature was Augustine's *De quantitate animae*, a work much influenced by neo-Platonic philosophy; here Augustine "distinguishes seven aspects of the Soul, or rather seven steps, *gradus*, by which it climbs to its perfection" (Edward Kennard Rand, *Founders of the Middle Ages* [New York: Dover Publications, 1957], p. 260).

[16] "Excerpts from Jim Elliot's Diary," *His*, XVI (April, 1956), 9.

[17] Quoted by Stanley Romaine Hoppe in his article "Paradox," *A Handbook of Christian Theology*, ed. Marvin Halverson and Arthur Cohen (New York: Meridian Living Age Books, 1958), p. 262.

[18] Gustaf Aulén, *The Faith of the Christian Church*, tr. from the 4th Swedish edition by Wahlstrom and Arden (Philadelphia: Muhlenberg, 1948), especially pp. 47, 101-103.

[19] Adolf Köberle, *The Quest for Holiness*, tr. from the 3d German edition by John C. Mattes (Minneapolis: Augsburg, 1938), pp. 174, 184-85.

[20] Milton C. Nahm, ed., *Selections from Early Greek Philosophy* (3d ed.; New York: Appleton-Century-Crofts, 1947), p. 91.

100 Select Devotional Books

The following list provides pastor and layman with a bibliography of the best available books additional to the Bible for deepening the spiritual life. Not all these works are in the strict genre of devotional literature, and some were certainly not written with a devotional intent. But it is safe to say that all are capable of performing radical spiritual surgery on sensitive Christian hearts.

Several criteria have been employed in the selection of titles:

1. Excluded on principle are works of general religiosity (for example, books by K. Gibran), works of general mysticism (Jakob Boehme, Madame Guyon), works doctrinally objectionable (Fulton Sheen's *Life of Christ*), works of a social-gospel cast (Sheldon's *In His Steps*), works reflecting simply the peace-of-mind or positive-thinking mood (Peale, Blanton), and works of sweetness-and-light (Grace Livingston Hill).

2. Only titles in print as of 1961 are included. Thus the reader should not expect such classics as Adolph Saphir's *The Lord's Prayer,* David McIntyre's *Prayer Life of Our Lord,* or Isaac Watts' *The World to Come;* it is hoped that publishing houses engaged in reprinting services will bring back these and other great devotional writings of the past.

3. Only works written in English or available in English translation are included. Many writings of Continental divines of the late sixteenth to early eighteenth century are therefore outside the scope of this list (English translations are badly needed of such works as Johann Gerhard's *Homiliae XXXVI seu meditationes breves diebus dominicis atque festis accomodatae).*

4. No more than one entry is given for a single author. The list could have been extended almost indefinitely under such names as Oswald Chambers; it is assumed that readers will make such extensions for themselves.

My thanks to the Knox College Library, Toronto (Dr. Neil Smith, librarian); to the Moody Bible Institute Library, Chicago (Dr. Elgin S. Moyer, librarian) for access to a vast number of devotional writings from which this list has been in part prepared; also to the editorial staff of *Christianity Today* and to Dr. William H. Wrighton, formerly professor of literature at the University of Georgia, for several helpful suggestions.

Alleine, Joseph. *An Alarm to Unconverted Sinners.* Sovereign Grace Publishers.

Allen, Charles L. *All Things Are Possible through Prayer.* Revell.

Andrewes, Lancelot. *Private Devotions.* World.

Arndt, Johann. *Devotions and Prayers* (selected and translated by John Joseph Stoudt). Baker.

Arthur, William. *Tongue of Fire.* Light and Life.

Athanasius. *The Incarnation of the Word of God.* Macmillan.

Auden, W. H. *Collected Poetry.* Random House. (Note especially "The Age of Anxiety").

Baxter, J. Sidlow. *Going Deeper.* Zondervan.

Baxter, Richard. *The Saint's Everlasting Rest.* Sovereign Grace Publishers.

Bonar, Horatius. *God's Way of Holiness.* Moody Press.

Bonhoeffer, Dietrich. *Life Together.* Harper.

Boston, Thomas. *Human Nature in Its Fourfold State.* Sovereign Grace Publishers.

Bounds, E. M. *Preacher and Prayer*. Zondervan.

Brainerd, David. *Life and Diary* (edited by Jonathan Edwards). Moody Press (condensed; unabridged edition out-of-print).

Browne, Thomas. *Religio Medici*. Henry Regnery Co. (Gateway edition).

Browning, Robert. *Poetry and Prose* (edited by Humphrey S. Milford). Oxford University Press.

Bunyan, John. *The Pilgrim's Progress*. John C. Winston (This edition especially recommended because it identifies Scriptural quotations and allusions, and reproduces the Frederick Barnard illustrations; cf. C. S. Lewis' *The Pilgrim's Regress*).

Calvin, John. *Thine Is My Heart* (compiled by John H. Kromminga). Zondervan.

Chambers, Oswald. *My Utmost for His Highest*. Dodd, Mead.

Chytraeus, David. *On Sacrifice* (translated and edited by John Warwick Montgomery). Concordia.

Clarke, Samuel. *Precious Bible Promises*. Grosset & Dunlap.

Doberstein, John W. *Minister's Prayer Book*. Muhlenberg Press.

Doerffler, Alfred, *et al. The Devotional Bible*. 2 vols. Concordia.

Donne, John. *Sermons*. Meridian (The great, critical edition of Donne's sermons is published by the University of California Press).

Drummond, Henry. *The Changed Life*. Revell.

Durbanville, Henry. *Three Deadly Foes*. B. McCall Barbour, 28 George IV Bridge, Edinburgh 1, Scotland.

Edman, V. Raymond. *Storms and Starlight*. Van Kampen Press.

Edwards, Jonathan. *The History of Redemption*. Kregel. (Note also the modern, critical edition of Edwards' works, now published by Yale University Press).

Eliot, T. S. *Complete Poems and Plays, 1909-1950*. Harcourt.

Elliot, Elisabeth. *Through Gates of Splendor*. Harper.

Fletcher, Lionel B. *Life Quest and Conquest*. Marshall, Morgan & Scott, London, England.

Fuller, Thomas. *The Holy State and the Profane State*. 2 vols. Columbia University Press.

Gockel, Herman W. *What Jesus Means to Me*. Concordia.

Gordon, A. J. *The Ministry of the Spirit*. Zondervan.

Gordon, S. D. *Quiet Talks on Prayer*. Grosset & Dunlap.

Goudge, E. *Reward of Faith*. Coward.

Graham, Billy. *The Secret of Happiness*. Doubleday.

Grubb, Norman. *The Law of Faith*. Christian Literature Crusade.

Guinness, Howard W. *Sacrifice*. Inter-Varsity Press.

Guthrie, Malcolm. *Learning to Live*. Marshall, Morgan & Scott, London, England.

Guthrie, William. *The Christian's Great Interest.* Kregel.
Haakonson, R. P. *Family Altar Readings.* Moody Press.
Hallesby, O. *Under His Wings.* Augsburg Publishing House.
Henry, Matthew. *Quest for Communion with God.* Eerdmans.
Hoffmann, Oswald C. J. *Life Crucified.* Eerdmans.
Hopkins, Evan H. *The Law of Liberty in the Spiritual Life.* Sunday School Times.
Ironside, Henry A. *Continual Burnt Offering.* Loizeaux.
Krummacher, F. W. *The Suffering Saviour.* Moody Press.
Kuyper, Abraham. *The Death and Resurrection of Christ.* Zondervan.
Law, William. *A Serious Call to a Devout and Holy Life.* Dutton (Everyman's Library).
Lawrence, Brother. *The Practice of the Presence of God.* Revell.
Lewis C. S. *The Narnia Chronicles.* 7 vols. Bles, London, England; and Bodley Head, London, England (cf. John Warwick Montgomery's article, "The Chronicles of Narnia," in *Religious Education,* Sept.-Oct., 1959).
Luther, Martin. *Day by Day We Magnify Thee.* Muhlenberg Press (note also the 55-vol. edition of Luther's most important works which is issued by Concordia Publishing House and Muhlenberg Press).
M'Cheyne, Robert Murray. *Memoirs.* (edited by Andrew Bonar). 2 vols. Moody Press.
Macdonald, George. *An Anthology.* (edited by C. S. Lewis). Macmillan.
Marshall, Peter. *Prayer.* McGraw-Hill.
Maxwell, L. E. *Crowded to Christ.* Eerdmans.
Meyer, F. B. *Our Daily Walk.* Zondervan.
Milton, John. *Paradise Lost* (edited by Northrop Frye). Rinehart (cf. C. S. Lewis' magnificent *Preface to Paradise Lost*).
Morgan, G. Campbell. *The Life of the Christian.* Revell.
Morris, Leon. *The Lord from Heaven.* Eerdmans.
Moule, H. C. G. *Charles Simeon.* Inter-Varsity Press.
Murray, Andrew. *God's Best Secrets.* Zondervan.
Nelson, Marion H., M.D. *Why Christians Crack Up.* Moody Press.
Oswald Chambers: His Life and Work (second edition). Christian Literature Crusade.
Owen, John. *Temptation and Sin.* Zondervan.
Oxenham, John. *Bees in Amber.* Revell.
Pascal, Blaise. *The Pensées.* Dutton (Everyman's Library).
Paton, Alan. *Cry, the Beloved Country.* Scribner's.
Paxson, Ruth. *Life on the Highest Plane.* Moody Press.
Pelikan, Jaroslav. *The Shape of Death: Life, Death, and Immortality in the Early Fathers.* Abingdon.
Pollock, J. C. *The Cambridge Seven: A Call to Christian*

Service. Inter-Varsity Press.

Rainsford, Marcus. *Our Lord Prays for His Own.* Moody Press (condensed).

Redpath, Alan. *Victorious Christian Living.* Revell.

Rutherford, Samuel. *Selected Letters.* Allenson.

Ryle, J. C. *Holiness.* Kregel.

Sanders, J. Oswald. *Christ Incomparable.* Christian Literature Crusade.

Sauer, Erich. *In the Arena of Faith.* Eerdmans.

Simpson, A. B. *The Self Life and the Christ Life.* Christian Publications.

Smeaton, George. *The Doctrine of the Atonement As Taught by Christ Himself.* Zondervan.

Spurgeon, Charles H. *Morning and Evening.* Zondervan (unabridged edition).

Stalker, James M. *The Trial and Death of Jesus Christ.* Zondervan.

Taylor, Dr. and Mrs. Howard. *Hudson Taylor.* 2 vols. Lutterworth Press.

Taylor, J. Hudson. *Union and Communion.* Moody Press.

Taylor, Jeremy. *The Rule and Exercises of Holy Living.* World.

Taylor, Mrs. Howard. *Bordon of Yale.* Moody Press.

Theologia Germanica. World.

Thomas, W. H. Griffith. *Grace and Power.* Eerdmans.

Thomas à Kempis, supposed author. *The Imitation of Christ.* Pocket Books (especially attractive edition because of the illustrations by Valenti Angelo).

Thompson, Francis. *The Hound of Heaven.* Morehouse.

Thomson, James G. S. S. *The Praying Christ.* Eerdmans.

Tolkien, J. R. R. *The Lord of the Rings.* 3 vols. Houghton and Ballantine Books (Includes: *The Fellowship of the Ring, The Two Towers, The Return of the King*).

Torrey, R. A. *The Power of Prayer.* Zondervan.

Tozer, A. W. *The Divine Conquest.* Christian Publications.

Walther, Carl F. W. *The Proper Distinction between Law and Gospel.* Concordia.

Wesley, John. *Devotions and Prayers* (compiled by Donald E. Demaray). Baker.

Whyte, Alexander. *Lord Teach Us To Pray.* Harper.

Williams, Charles. *The Descent of the Dove.* Meridian. (Readers should also be reminded of his more difficult works— the supernatural novels, such as *All Hallow's Eve,* and the poetical masterpieces, such as *The Region of the Summer Stars*).

Woolman, John. *Journal.* World.

Zwemer, Samuel. *The Glory of the Cross.* Zondervan.

Choice Books on the Holy Spirit

To write of the Holy Spirit is to write of God, as the ecumenical creeds affirm; to write of his works is to write of the action of God through all of human history (he "convicts the world of sin, righteousness, and judgment") and throughout the history of the Church (he is the Paraclete in every Christian heart). Thus the compilation of a bibliography of books on the Holy Spirit is a task requiring great delimitation.

The present bibliography is limited in these respects:

1. It includes only works written in English or available in English translation. Thus such important books as Werner Krusche's *Das Wirken des Heiligen Geistes nach Calvin* (Göttingen: Vandenhoeck & Ruprecht, 1957) are omitted.

2. It includes only separately published books on the person or mission of the Holy Spirit. Works of general dogmatics (e.g., Calvin's *Institutes*, Barth's *Church Dogmatics*), though containing sections on the Holy Spirit, are therefore excluded; and so are books which are devoted to other subjects but which touch on pneumatology (e.g., William Anderson's *Regeneration* [London: Hodder & Stoughton, 1875]; and Robert Preus's *Inspiration of Scripture: A Study of the Theology of the Seventeenth Century Lutheran Dogmaticians* [Edinburgh: Oliver & Boyd, 1957], which has a valuable chapter (pp. 50-75) on the relation between the work of the Holy Spirit and the doctrine of biblical inspiration).

3. It includes only works not previously listed in my bibliography of "100 Select Devotional Books" (*supra*). Readers must consult that list for such works as William Arthur's *Tongue of Fire*, A. J. Gordon's *Ministry of the Spirit*, Ruth Paxson's *Life on the Highest Plane*, and Charles Williams' *Descent of the Dove*.

4. It excludes for doctrinal reasons works orientated toward what Professor E. A. Burtt of Cornell has called "Constructive [i.e., subjective] Religious Empiricism" (e.g., H. Wheeler Robinson's *Christian Experience of the Holy Spirit*); works of unreconstructed liberalism (e.g., T. Rees's *The Holy Spirit in Thought and Experience*; E. F. Scott's two books on the Holy Spirit; *The Spirit*, B. H. Streeter, ed.; H. P. Van Dusen's *Spirit, Son and*

Father); and anti-Reformation, non-evangelical treatments such as L. Dewar's *The Holy Spirit and Modern Thought.*

Astute readers will note that, in contrast to my book list of devotional works, almost 50 per cent of the present bibliography consists of out-of-print titles (specifically, 27 of the 60 items are in this class). Every effort was made to concentrate on in-print titles, but it is an unhappy fact of mid-twentieth century life that many currently available books on the Holy Spirit are not worth bibliographical listing, and many of the truly classic books on pneumatology have been neglected since their original publication. It is hoped that a publisher with a flair for photolithographic reprinting will bring out a "Library of Classical and Devotional Pneumatology" to fill the gap.

Readers interested in purchasing in-print titles (those in print as of 1963 are identified by an asterisk) will find the addresses of United States publishers in *Books in Print* or in the *Cumulative Book Index,* and the addresses of British publishers in the *Reference Catalogue of Current Literature.* In some instances British prices are considerably lower than American, and the Christian bibliophile can benefit economically from an international orientation.

Athanasius, *Letters concerning the Holy Spirit,* trans. C. R. B. Shapland (London: Epworth, 1951). By the great fourth-century defender of the divinity of the Holy Spirit against Arianism. His letters deserve to be read today as a historical counteractant to the essentially Arian views of Unitarianism, religious liberalism, and the Jehovah's Witnesses.

* Barclay, William, *The Promise of the Spirit* (Westminster, 1960; London: Epworth). Barclay, author of *A New Testament Wordbook* and *More New Testament Words* and editor of the *Daily Study Bible* commentary series, as usual combines expert Greek scholarship with penetrating devotional insight.

* Barrett, C. K., *The Holy Spirit and the Gospel Tradition* (Seabury, 1947; and S.P.C.K.). Deals primarily with the Synoptic Gospels. Author holds inadequate doctrine of biblical authority, but his book is still of great value. Cf. his "The Holy Spirit in the Fourth Gospel," *Journal of Theological Studies,* 1950, pp. 1-15, and R. Hoeferkamp's article under the same title in *Concordia Theological Monthly,* September, 1962.

Barth, Karl, *The Holy Ghost and the Christian Life,* tr. by R. B. Hoyle (London: F. Muller, 1938). Study of the Holy Spirit as Creator, Reconciler, and Redeemer. Cf. Barth's sermon collection, *Come Holy Spirit* (Edinburgh: T. & T. Clark, 1934); and G. W. Bromiley, "The Spirit of Christ," *Essays in Christology for Karl Barth*, ed. T. H. L. Parker (London: Lutterworth, 1956).

* Bickersteth, Edward H., *The Holy Spirit, His Person and Work* (Kregel, 1959). This nineteenth-century Anglican divine evidenced his spiritual depth in writing such hymns as "Stand, Soldier of the Cross."

Biederwolf, William Edward, *A Help to the Study of the Holy Spirit*, 4th ed. (Revell, 1904). In the Introduction Dr. William G. Moorehead rightly praises this work for its "complete subjection to the authority of Scripture" and for its excellent bibliography.

* Boer, Harry R., *Pentecost and Missions* (Eerdmans, 1961). A doctoral study "concerned with the significance of Pentecost for missions." Author is a theologian-missionary of the Christian Reformed Church to Nigeria.

Burton, Edward, *Testimonies of the Ante-Nicene Fathers to the Doctrine of the Trinity and of the Divinity of the Holy Ghost* (Oxford, 1831). Still the standard work.

Candlish, J. S., *The Work of the Holy Spirit* (Edinburgh: T. & T. Clark, n.d.). A brief, lucid work, published originally in the series "Handbooks for Bible Classes and Private Students," ed. by Marcus Dods and Alexander Whyte. Candlish was professor of systematic theology, Free Church College, Glasgow.

* Chafer, Lewis Sperry, *He That Is Spiritual* (Findlay, Ohio: Dunham, 1918). By the former president and professor of systematic theology at Dallas Seminary. Practical yet profound analysis of Holy Spirit-created spirituality.

* Come, Arnold B., *Human Spirit and Holy Spirit* (Westminster, 1959). Strongly Kierkegaardian in outlook. Its anthropocentric starting-point and its lack of clear revelational criterion of authority are great weaknesses, but it offers stimulating insights via depth psychology and process philosophy.

*Cumming, James Elder, *"Through the Eternal Spirit"*: A Bible Study on the Holy Ghost (Minneapolis, Minn.: Bethany Fellowship, Inc.; originally published 1891). Correctly regarded by Wilbur Smith as a "standard work"; scholarly, comprehensive, beautifully organized, thoroughly scriptural and devotional.

* Davies, J. B., *The Spirit, the Church and the Sacraments* (London: Faith). An exceedingly attractive presentation from the standpoint of contemporary evangelical Anglicanism; shows acquaintance with the best literature, ancient and modern, English and non-English, on the subject.

* Dillistone, F. W., *The Holy Spirit in the Life of Today* (Westminster, 1947). Short, well-written book "for the average man." Author is chancellor of Liverpool Cathedral, England; previously he served as professor of systematic theology at Wycliffe College, Toronto, and at the Episcopal Theological School, Cambridge, Massachusetts.

Dixon, A. C., ed., *The Holy Spirit in Life and Service* (Revell, 1895). Consists of 19 addresses delivered before the Conference on the Ministry of the Holy Spirit held in New York in 1894; authors include, *inter alia*, W. J. Erdman, A. J. Gordon, and A. T. Pierson. The papers relate the work of the Holy Spirit to a wide range of church activities.

* Downer, Arthur Cleveland, *The Mission and Ministration of the Holy Spirit* (Edinburgh: T. & T. Clark, 1909,). "A book that deserves the widest circle of readers"—Wilbur Smith. Comprehensive, well organized. Comparable to Kuyper, though shorter, and orientated more to biblical than to dogmatic theology. Author was Anglican.

Faber, George Stanley, *A Practical Treatise on the Ordinary Operations of the Holy Spirit*, last edition, with a biographical notice (New York: Protestant Episcopal Society for the Promotion of Evangelical Knowledge, 1857). By the nineteenth-century bishop, apologist, and student of biblical prophecy.

* Hamilton, Neill Q., *The Holy Spirit and Eschatology in Paul* (Naperville, Ill.: Allenson, 1957; London: Oliver & Boyd). In the series *Scottish Journal of Theology Occasional Papers* (No. 6). Contains useful bibliography.

Hare, Julius Charles, *The Mission of the Comforter*, ed. by E. H. Plumptre (London: Macmillan, 1886). Sermons preached at Cambridge University in 1840.· Archdeacon Hare added numerous valuable scholarly notes.

* Hendry, George S., *The Holy Spirit in Christian Theology* (Westminster, 1956). Regarded by T. N. Tice of Princeton as "at this point the one indispensable treatise on the subject by an English-speaking theologian." Excellent on the problem of the Holy Spirit in current theological thought, but marred by a neo-orthodox view of Scripture.

* Henry, Antonin M., *The Holy Spirit*, tr. by Lundberg and Bell (Hawthorn, 1960). In the "Twentieth Century Encyclopedia of Catholicism" series. An exceedingly valuable work demonstrating once again that Protestants cannot afford to ignore contemporary Roman Catholic theological writing.

* Köberle, Adolf, *The Quest for Holiness; a Biblical, Historical and Systematic Investigation*, trans. J. C. Mattes (Augsburg, 1930). Contemporary Lutheranism's greatest contribution to the study of sanctification; the book combines scholarly thoroughness with devotional depth.

* Kuyper, Abraham, *The Work of the Holy Spirit*, trans. Henri De Vries, Introduction by B. B. Warfield (Eerdmans, 1900). An unsurpassed classic. Undoubtedly the most comprehensive work in print on the subject. In the tradition of Reformation-Calvinist systematic theology.

Macgregor, G. H. C., ed., *"The Things of the Spirit": The Teaching of the Word of God about the Spirit of God* (London: Marshall, 1898). A valuable classification of the biblical passages on the Holy Spirit by a close friend of G. Campbell Morgan. Cf. Wilbur Smith's classification in his *A Treasury of Books for Bible Study* * (Wilde).

McIntyre, David M., *The Spirit in the Word* (London: Morgan

484   THE SUICIDE OF CHRISTIAN THEOLOGY

& Scott, 1908). An excellent treatment of the work of the Holy Spirit in the inspiration of the Bible. Cf. L. Gaussen's *Theopneustia.*

* Morgan, G. Campbell, *The Spirit of God* (Revell, 1900). One of the finest books written by this great preacher and Bible expositor.

Moule, H. C. G., *Veni Creator: Thoughts on the Person and Work of the Holy Spirit of Promise* (London: Hodder & Stoughton, 1890). A superlative book by the prolific doctrinal and devotional writer well known for his contributions to the *Cambridge Bible for School and Colleges,* for his Christian poetry, and for his biography of Charles Simeon.

* Murray, Andrew, *The Spirit of Christ* (Zondervan). Meditations of extraordinary depth by the nineteenth-century Dutch Reformed pastor.

* Nuttall, Geoffrey F., *The Holy Spirit in Puritan Faith and Experience,* 2nd ed. (Oxford: B. Blackwell, 1947). A valuable historical study, particularly with regard to Quakerism, though marred by its author's enthusiastic proclivities. The book originated as an Oxford University D.D. thesis.

* Ockenga, Harold John, *The Spirit of the Living God* (Revell, 1947). High-quality sermons by the former pastor of Park Street Church, Boston, and past-president of Fuller Theological Seminary. Cf. his *Power Through Pentecost** (Eerdmans, 1959).

* Owen, John, *The Holy Spirit, His Gifts and Powers* (Kregel, 1954). Regarded by Kuyper in 1888 as "still unsurpassed"; the same must be said today. Owen, a Presbyterian Nonconformist of the seventeenth century, was one of the most learned and prolific theological writers of all time.

* Pache, René, *The Person and Work of the Holy Spirit,* trans. J. D. Emerson (Moody, 1954). A carefully outlined, lucid exposition of biblical teaching on the Holy Spirit by the president of Emmaus Institute, Lausanne, Switzerland. Particularly helpful for sermon construction and in Bible study preparation.

Parker, Joseph, *The Paraclete: An Essay on the Personality and Ministry of the Holy Ghost, with Some Reference to Current Discussions* (Scribner, 1886). The first edition of this fine work appeared anonymously.

Phelps, Austin, *The Work of the Holy Spirit; or, The New Birth* (Boston: D. Lothrop, 1882). By the brilliant Congregationalist homiletician who served as professor of sacred rhetoric (1848-79) and president (1869-79) of Andover Seminary.

Pierson, Arthur T., *The Acts of the Holy Spirit, Being an Examination of the Active Mission and Ministry of the Spirit of God, the Divine Paraclete, As Set Forth in the Acts of the Apostles* (Revell, 1895). By the nineteenth-century authority on missions and voluminous Christian writer who edited the *Missionary Review of the World.*

* Prenter, Regin, *Spiritus Creator,* tr. by J. M. Jensen (Muhlenberg, 1953). The first comprehensive study in the twentieth

century of Luther's concept of the Holy Spirit.

* Ramm, Bernard, *The Witness of the Spirit; an Essay on the Contemporary Relevance of the Internal Witness of the Holy Spirit* (Eerdmans, 1959). A trenchant systematic-historical analysis, with a final chapter criticizing Romanism, liberalism, and fundamentalism; by the neo-evangelical apologist and professor of systematic theology at California Baptist Seminary.

Redford, R. A., *Vox Dei: The Doctrine of the Spirit As It Is Set Forth in the Scriptures of the Old and New Testaments* (London: J. Nisbet, 1889). By the nineteenth-century biblical apologist and contributor to *The Pulpit Commentary*.

* Sanders, J. Oswald, *The Holy Spirit of Promise; the Mission and Ministry of the Comforter* (Fort Washington, Pa.: Christian Literature Crusade, 1959). For the general reader; a short but penetrating overview of the central problems of pneumatology by the director of the China Inland Mission.

* Shoemaker, Samuel M., *With the Holy Spirit and with Fire* (Harper, 1960). Typically warm and practical book from the prolific pen of this much-loved Episcopalian rector.

* Simpson, A. B., *The Holy Spirit, or, Power from On High*, 2 vols. (Harrisburg, Pa.: Christian Publications, 1924). Subtitle: "An unfolding of the doctrine of the Holy Spirit in the Old and New Testaments." Originally presented as sermons in the Gospel Tabernacle, New York City, by the founder of the Christian and Missionary Alliance.

* Smeaton, George, *The Doctrine of the Holy Spirit* (Christian Literature Crusade). A classic, worthy to be placed with Downer, Kuyper, and W. H. Griffith Thomas. Includes a historical survey of the doctrine of the Holy Spirit from New Testament times through the nineteenth century.

* Snaith, Norman H., et al., *The Doctrine of the Holy Spirit* (London: Epworth, 1937). Contents: "The Spirit of God in Jewish Thought," by Snaith; "The Spirit in the New Testament," by Vincent Taylor; "The Holy Spirit in the Church," by Howard Watkin-Jones; and "The Holy Spirit and the Trinity," by Harold Roberts. Exceedingly valuable, though not always manifesting a high view of biblical inspiration.

* Starkey, Lycurgus M., Jr., *The Work of the Holy Spirit: A Study in Wesleyan Theology* (Abingdon, 1962). A historical study of Wesley's concept of the Holy Spirit.

Swete, Henry Barclay, *The Holy Spirit in the New Testament* (London: Macmillan, 1909). To be used in conjunction with Swete's other three standard works on the early history of doctrine: *The Holy Spirit in the Ancient Church* (London: Macmillan, 1912), covering the patristic age; *On the Early History of the Doctrine of the Holy Spirit with Especial Reference to the Controversies of the Fourth Century* (Cambridge: Deighton, Bell, 1873); and *On the History of the Doctrine of the Procession of the Holy Spirit, from the Apostolic Age to the Death of Charlemagne* (Cambridge: Deighton, Bell, 1876).

* Thomas, W. H. Griffith, *The Holy Spirit of God*, 3rd ed. (Eerdmans, 1955). A masterly work by the conservative Anglican theologian who served as professor of Old Testament literature and exegesis in Wycliffe College, Toronto. The book, which first appeared in 1913, studies the doctrine biblically, historically, systematically, and practically; its comprehensiveness ranks it with Downer, Kuyper, and Smeaton.

Tophel, Gustave, *The Work of the Holy Spirit in Man*, trans. T. J. Després (Edinburgh: T. & T. Clark, 1882). Five discourses of great devotional power.

* Torrey, R. A., *The Holy Spirit: Who He Is and What He Does* (Revell, 1927). In the perceptive and lucid style characteristic of this great pastor, evangelist, and onetime (1889-1908) superintendent of the Moody Bible Institute.

* Unger, Merrill F., *The Baptizing Work of the Holy Spirit* (Wheaton, Ill.: Scripture Press, 1953). Provocative study of a difficult aspect of pneumatology by the eminent Old Testament scholar and professor at Dallas Seminary.

Walker, James Barr, *The Doctrine of the Holy Spirit, or Philosophy of the Divine Operation in the Redemption of Man*, 6th ed. (Cincinnati: Jennings and Pye, 1901). A continuation of the author's *Philosophy of the Plan of Salvation*, which deservedly attained great popularity in the nineteenth century.

* Walvoord, John F., *The Holy Spirit*, 3rd ed. (Findlay, Ohio: Dunham, 1958). By the president and professor of systematic theology at Dallas Seminary. Contains a valuable appendix on "The Holy Spirit in Contemporary Theology."

Watkin-Jones, Howard, *The Holy Spirit in the Medieval Church* (London: Epworth, 1922). A continuation of the work of Swete. It deals with the history of the doctrine from the post-patristic age to the Counter-Reformation, and is itself continued by Watkin-Jones' *Holy Spirit from Arminius to Wesley* (London: Epworth, 1929), which covers the seventeenth and eighteenth centuries.

Weidner, Revere Franklin, *Pneumatology, or, The Doctrine of the Work of the Holy Spirit* (Wartburg, 1915). Systematic treatment from the standpoint of conservative Lutheranism. Author was professor of dogmatics and president of Chicago Lutheran Seminary (1891-1915).

* Winslow, Octavius, *An Experimental and Practical View of the Work of the Holy Spirit* (London: Banner of Truth Trust). First published in 1843. Powerfully evangelical and deeply devotional, as were all of this prolific writer's works, some 100 of which are listed by the British Museum's Department of Printed Books.

Winstanley, Edward William, *Spirit in the New Testament* (Cambridge: University, 1908). Subtitle: "An enquiry into the use of the word *pneuma* in all passages, and a survey of the evidence concerning the Holy Spirit."

* Wislöff, Fredrik, *I Believe in the Holy Spirit*, trans. Ingvald

Daehlin (Augsburg, 1949). By a European Lutheran pastor who represents a contemporary blend of classical orthodoxy with the evangelical pietism characteristic of the Norwegian Inner Mission movement. His book cannot be too highly recommended for its faithfulness to Scripture and its genuine experiential impact.

7.

The Descent and Ascent of God

Remythologizing Christmas

Christmas is not the most pleasant time to go to church. Not only unbelievers suffering from the compulsions of a churchgoing childhood but even fervent believers often have to steel themselves when the clergyman rises to deliver his Christmas sermon. There is always the grim possibility that the focus will be upon those wretched persons in the congregation who have not been seen since the previous Easter; such sermons agonize the unbeliever without helping him and fail to edify the faithful (since Law is confused with Gospel and good advice is substituted for the central Christian message of Good News). But even if the Christmas churchgoer is fortunate enough to miss a law preachment, he will seldom avoid the twin agonies of sermonic rationalism and homiletic iconoclasm.

At the liberal side of the ecclesiastical spectrum, the person who has the temerity to enter a Christmas service has every chance of hearing an urbane plea to make his religion "relevant to the twentieth century" by chucking the supernatural baggage of the Christmas story. Influenced both by the Bultmannian efforts at "demythologizing" the New Testament message (penetrating beneath the miraculous accretions to its "genuine" existential center—the quest for "self-authentication") and by the current vogue of "secular Christianity" (redefining the faith in terms of modern humanistic values), the liberal clergyman derides or pities the childish parishioner who must still hitch his religious wagon to the burnt-out Christmas star. Such legends were meaningful to our prescientific forebears, one is told, but to hold on to them now is to remain hopelessly wedded to an irrecoverable past. Magi and shepherds, annunciations and virgin births —surely we must locate the kernel of truth that is imbedded in these mythological shucks.

So loudly do such sentiments resound on the clear, crisp air each December that Anglo-Catholic philosophical theologian E. L. Mascall has immortalized them in two poems entitled, "Christmas with the Demythologizers" (*Pi in the High* [1959], pp. 49-51). Here are sample stanzes:

> *Hark, the herald angels sing:*
> *"Bultmann is the latest thing!"*
> *(Or they would if he had not*
> *Demythologized the lot.)*
> *Joyful, all ye nations, rise,*
> *Glad to existentialize!*
> *Peace on earth and mercy mild,*
> *God and Science reconciled.*
>
> *Lo, the ancient myths disperse.*
> *Hence, three-storied universe!*
> *Let three-decker pulpits stay:*
> *Bultmann has a lot to say,*
> *Since Kerygma still survives*
> *When the myths have lost their lives.*
> *Hark, the herald angels sing:*
> *"Bultmann shot us on the wing!"*

But the agonies of the Christmas sermon are not entirely avoided even if our hapless seasonal churchgoer stumbles into an evangelical setting. There, though rationalistic shreddings of the New Testament account of the Incarnation are rigorously excluded, often an iconoclasm is promoted that leaves the congregation only slightly less unsettled. The preacher inveighs against all the unbiblical trappings that have accumulated around the Saviour's cradle (better, swaddling clothes): the carols that do not express precise scriptural teaching; the emphasis on material gift-giving; the pagan Christmas tree; the gluttonous centrality of the Christmas dinner and the anthropocentric family reunions; the stress on our own children instead of on the Christ-child; and the evil genius of the whole occasion: Santa Claus. Depending upon the closeness of his confessional and temperamental alignment with Cromwellian times, the evangelical pastor may even give the impression that Christmas should be radically de-emphasized—or done away with altogether. After all, the holiday is nowhere commanded or even recommended in Scripture; and look at the appalling ways in which non-Christian Western society has secularized it since the eighteenth century!

Versus a Rationalistic Christmas

These two forms of sermonizing, the modernistic and the evangelical, though poles apart theologically, are bedfellows in their antipathy to "myth." Where specifically has the follower of Bultmann gone off the track?

The Bultmannian demythologizer is convinced that the gospel accounts, particularly the infancy narratives at the beginning of Matthew and Luke, are the end products of an oral tradition that was shaped and freely altered by the early Church in light of its own needs and the mythological view of the world current at that time. By the techniques of "form criticism," as practiced by the Dibelius-Bultmann school, one can reach behind the New Testament documents as they have come down to us and find the existential heart of the Christmas message.

But what assures the advocate of such "demythologizing" that he is arriving at bedrock reality when he reaches the level of existential experience? Is there any reason to assume that Heideggerian existential categories are less "mythical" than the simple New Testament accounts? As some nasty but profound critics of Bultmann such as Fritz Büri have pointed out, he may well be accomplishing nothing more than substituion of a modern philosophical myth for the original Christian conviction. The same could even be the case when the Bultmannian replaces the ancient "supernatural" conception of the universe by a modern cosmology. Contemporary cosmologies have not exactly excelled in durability; the twentieth century, with its high obselescence in cosmic explanations, has done no little myth-making on its own.

Moreover, if the purportedly historical accounts of gospel events such as the Virgin Birth are not to be taken as factually true—if they require "demythologization"—why is the "core" message to be accepted at all? "History" and "theology" are painfully intertwined in the infancy accounts: "There went out a decree from Caesar Augustus, that all the world should be taxed. (And this taxing was first made when Cyrenius was governor of Syria.) . . . And suddenly there was with the angel a multitude of the heavenly host praising God, and saying, Glory to God in the highest, and on earth peace to men of good

will." If the early Church could not get its historical facts
straight, why do we think it succeeded so well when making high theological judgments? Here again Professor
Mascall has the poetical word for the occasion (this time
to the tune of "Good King Wenceslas"):

> Sir, my thoughts begin to stray
> And my faith grows bleaker.
> Since I threw my myths away
> My kerygma's weaker.

What is retained in the demythologizing process is, of
course, a naive faith in the methodology of the demythologizer. One is reminded of the encounter between Alice
and (William Ellery) Channing-mouse in R. C. Evarts's
clever parody, *Alice's Adventures in Cambridge*, published by the Harvard Lampoon in 1913; after the mouse
has demythologized General Washington, the American
revolutionary army, Paul Revere, and the Queen, he is
forced to say to those who appeal to historical facts, *"Your
memory is simply a legend"*—and when Alice finally asks
the Black Knight, "Doesn't he believe in anything?," the
inevitable reply comes: "Nothing but himself."

The form-critical method of the demythologizer, however, is anything but believable, as its loss of ground in
non-theological areas well exemplifies. In Greco-Roman
and comparative Near Eastern studies, less and less reliance is being placed on such techniques as every year
passes (cf. *Composition and Corroboration in Classical
and Biblical Studies* [1966] by Edwin Yamauchi), for these
methods are intensely subjectivistic. In the case of the
New Testament material, the unscholarly character of
this methodology appears especially in its gratuitous use
of rationalistic presuppositions against the miraculous
(how do the Bultmannians *know* that "the nexus of natural
causes is never broken"?), and in its failure to recognize
that the interval of time between the recording of the
events of Jesus' life and the events themselves was too
brief to allow for communal redaction by the Church—
especially in a hostile environment in which so many
competing faiths were interested in destroying Christianity's particularistic claims. In the study of English ballads, John Drinkwater (*English Poetry*) has rejected
redaction-theory because of inadequate time for exten-

sive alteration of the original ballads; yet the infancy narratives of our Lord never passed through such a long period of oral tradition as did the ballads, and the gospel narratives were in circulation when Mary and the other principals were still alive and when the opponents of the faith would have blasted accounts of Jesus' divine origin had they not been factual.

This Christmas, should one have the misfortune to wander into a demythologization service, the recommended Rx is serious contemplation of a typical assertion by one who knew both Mary and Jesus intimately: "We have not followed cunningly devised fables [Greek, *mythoi*]. when we made known unto you the power and coming of our Lord Jesus Christ, but were eyewitnesses of his majesty" (II Pet. 1:16).

Versus an Iconoclastic Christmas

"Quite right! Well done!" declares our evangelical iconoclast from his Christmas pulpit: "The very factuality of the Christmas story requires us to strip away from this season all that *is* mythical—all the extrabiblical accretions, both ancient and modern, that have become associated with the birth of the Christ." Certainly the iconoclast is right to demand that we maintain a clear distinction between the truly historical facts of the Incarnation and the non-historical, traditionalistic additions (for example, the impossible view evidently held by all crèche-makers that the wise men arrived at the same time as the shepherds). The iconoclasts perform a valuable service by emphasizing the distinction between retaining the old oaken bucket of solidly factual theology and scraping off the traditional moss that clings to it.

Yet the iconoclast misses a profound point as to the nature of the Christmas story—a point that applies with equal force to the entire Christian story. The genuine historicity of the Gospel does not prevent it from being at the same time genuinely mythical—in the special sense of a story that cuts to the heart of man's subjective need. The greatest contemporary creator of literary myth, J. R. R. Tolkien, author of the three-volume masterpiece *The Lord of the Rings*, has argued this case in a manner that bears repeating ("On Fairy-Stories," *The Tolkien*

Reader [Ballantine Books, 1966], pp. 71-73):

> The Gospels contain a fairy-story, or a story of a larger
> kind which embraces all the essence of fairy-stories. They
> contain many marvels—peculiarly artistic, beautiful, and
> moving: "mythical" in their perfect, self-contained signi-
> ficance; and among the marvels is the greatest and most
> complete conceivable eucatastrophe. But this story has
> entered History and the primary world. . . . The Birth of
> Christ is the eucatastrophe [decisive event of maximum
> value] of Man's history. The Resurrection is the eucatas-
> trophe of the story of the Incarnation. This story begins and
> ends in joy. It has pre-eminently the "inner consistency
> of reality." There is no tale every told that men would
> rather find was true, and none which so many skeptical
> men have accepted as true on its own merits. . . . To reject
> it leads either to sadness or to wrath.
>
> It is not difficult to imagine the peculiar excitement
> and joy that one would feel, if any specially beautiful
> fairy-story were found to be "primarily" true, its narra-
> tive to be history, without thereby necessarily losing the
> mythical or allegorical significance that it had possessed.
> . . . The Christian joy, the *Gloria,* is of the same kind; but
> it is pre-eminently (infinitely, if our capacity were not
> finite) high and joyous. But this story is supreme; and it
> is true. Art has been verified. God is the Lord, of Angels,
> and of men—and of elves. Legend and History have
> met and fused.
>
> But in God's kingdom the presence of the greatest does
> not depress the small. Redeemed Man is still man. Story,
> fantasy, still go on, and should go on. The Evangelium
> has not abrogated legends; it has hallowed them, especial-
> ly the "happy ending."

What Tolkien says here is most assuredly true: the
myths and legends and tales of the world that give symbolic expression to man's fundamental needs (Carl Gustav
Jung called them "the archetypes of the collective unconscious") serve as pointers to the reality of the Christian
message in which they are historically fulfilled. A tale
as common as Sleeping Beauty is fully comprehended only
in this light: the princess, subjected to a deathlike trance
by evil power that cannot be thwarted despite all the good
intentions and concerted efforts of her family, represents
the plight of the human race; the prince, who comes by
prophecy, enters the castle of death from the outside,
and conquers the evil spell by the kiss of love, is the
Redeemer of mankind; and the marriage and happy

ending express the eschatological future of the redeemed and the marriage supper of the Lamb. God becomes the Lord of angels, and of men—and of elves.

Seen in this light, as the fulfillment of the deepest longings men have brought to expression in their myths, the Christmas story is not to be set over against the traditional lore of the Christmas season. Indeed, that lore, when properly understood, will reinforce and heighten the truth of the Incarnation itself. The traditional carols will be listened to more closely, and even the most "secular" will yield the eternal message:

> *God rest you merry, gentlemen, let nothing you dismay,*
> *For Jesus Christ our Saviour was born upon this day,*
> *To save us all from Satan's power when we were gone*
>   *astray,*
> *O tidings of comfort and joy, comfort and joy.*

The Christmas tree will inevitably and properly suggest the One who grew to manhood to "bear our sins in his body on the tree, that we might die to sin and live to righteousness." Family reunions will point to the truth that where two or three are gathered together, there Christ is in the midst, as well as to the family of the Redeemed, the clouds of witnesses, and the Church Triumphant that we shall ourselves join by God's grace before many more Christmases have passed. The dinners and the parties will speak of the Christ who hallowed feasts when he walked this earth and who constitutes "living Bread come down from heaven." The centrality of children at this blessed season should remind us that childlike faith before the mysteries of the Incarnation is a requisite for participation in his kingdom. And even (or especially?) the archetypal and ubiquitous Santa Claus, who comes from a numinous land of snow-white purity to give gifts to those who have nothing of their own, proclaims to all who have ears to hear the message of the entrance of God into our sinful world to "give gifts to men."

The Way of Affirmation

Christmas thus calls for total appropriation and reconsecration. It calls not for demythologizing but for remythologizing. It calls for what Christian littérateur

Charles Williams termed "the Affirmative Way":

> The Negative Way of the mystics is fulfilled and cor-
> rected by the Affirmative Way. . . . To its adherents,
> the heavens indeed disclose the glory of God, and the
> firmament shows clearly that it is his handiwork. They
> witness that he discloses himself in all things. Human love
> manifests divine love; particular beauties exhibit ulti-
> mate beauty [Shideler, *The Theology of Romantic Love*
> (1962), p. 25].

All the glories of the Holy Season, and all its tales—
from Van Dyke's *The Other Wise Man* to Seabury Quinn's
retelling of the Christ-oriented legend of Santa Claus—can
in this way be reaffirmed. The Christian, solidly grounded
in the eucatastrophe of man's history, the birth of Christ,
finds that the Evangelium has indeed hallowed every
genuine manifestation of Christmas joy. The believer can
affirm them all; to each he can say with thanksgiving:
"This also is Thou."

And as he remythologizes the season, another transformation occurs: in contact with the Christ who hallows
all things, he is himself hallowed and becomes a living
symbol by which others are pointed to the Incarnate
Saviour. Like the Santa Claus of the legend (Quinn, *Roads*
[1948], p. 110), he receives the wondrous commission:

> His is the work his Master chose for him that night
> two thousand years ago; his the long, long road that has
> no turning so long as men keep festival upon the anni-
> versary of the Saviour's birth.

Ascension Perspective*

My remarks this morning—shortly before Christendom
again celebrates the Festival of the Ascension—will attempt to contrast what may be termed an "Ascension
perspective" with a perspective of a far different, but
more familiar, kind. As a firm reference point for our
meditation, I shall read Psalm 121:

> I will lift up mine eyes unto the hills, from whence cometh
> my help. My help cometh from the Lord, which made
> heaven and earth. He will not suffer thy foot to be moved:
> he that keepeth thee will not slumber. Behold, he that

---

* Originally delivered as a sermon in the Joseph Bond Chapel of the
University of Chicago.

keepeth Israel shall neither slumber nor sleep. The Lord is thy keeper: the Lord is thy shade upon thy right hand. The sun shall not smite thee by day, nor the moon by night. The Lord shall preserve thee from all evil: he shall preserve thy soul. The Lord shall preserve thy going out and thy coming in from this time forth, and even for evermore.

Currently a number of good and not-so-good psychiatric jokes and cartoons have been making the rounds. Among those which I can tell here in the Chapel without fear of looking for a new position next year is the short story of the two psychiatrists passing on the street. Psychiatrist A: "Good morning, doctor." Psychiatrist B (mumbling to himself after psychiatrist A has gone by): "I wonder what he meant by that." Also we have the *New Yorker* cartoon of the busy psychoanalyst with a double-decker couch. Now the former editor of the British humor magazine *Punch* wrote in the April, 1958, *Esquire*:

Humor, I have come to feel, is an expression in terms of the grotesque of the enormous disparity between human aspiration and human performance. Thus, for instance, sex is funny because the impulses associated with it demonstrate dramatically and unmistakaby how ludicrously what men do mocks what they hope or try to do. In the same way, death is funny. Any comedian knows that he has only to mention a hearse or a corpse to bring down the house. Why? Because the fact that men die translates into farce all the pretensions and vain glory whereby, while they are alive, they seek to magnify and glorify themselves. In the same way, self-importance is funny because everyone really knows in his heart that, whatever else is conceivable, it is quite outside the bounds of possibility that one mortal man should be inherently more important than another.

Following this line of approach, we might well say that psychiatric humor strikes us as particularly funny today because we sense the disparity between what psychoanalytic psychiatry has claimed to be able to do, and what it actually has done. Not too many years ago, depth analysis was declared by many—analyst and layman alike —to be the only sufficiently penetrating way to fulfill the Greek injunction *gnothe seauton*—"know thyself." The frustrating experiences of such distinguished men as Harvard psychology professor Edwin Boring, who underwent analysis; plus the cost and length of analytic sessions; plus the not-too-rare suicide of a prominent psychoanalyist (one occurred at the University of California while I was a graduate student there)—all these and many other facts have tended to make the public question the panacea for human ills here offered. Psychoanalytic performance has not reached the level of psychoanalytic aspiration.

However, the psychological perspective is much with us. My wife and friends tell me that I suffer from frequent attacks of Dibdin's disease, more commonly known as "bibliomania," and this is certainly true—but it has its advantages. While puttering about in bookstores, I recently encountered the paperback history of philosophy series published by the New American Library. The 18th-century volume is of course entitled "The Age of Enlightenment"; the 19th-century is "The Age of Ideology"; and the 20th-century—our time—is significantly represented as "The Age of Analysis." I believe that I am safe in saying that the perspective of our era is in many respects a *subjective* one—involving inner probing of our thoughts, motives, experiences. In discussing the current marriage problem from the standpoint of Christian ethics, Emil Brunner writes in his *Divine Imperative*—pp. 343, 345—"Two theories are at our disposal, one is objective ... in tendency, and the other individualistic and subjective; they represent the ancient and modern points of view respectively. . . . It is . . . subjective individualism, more than anything else, which has caused the present crisis in marriage." Let us take a rapid look at the subjective perspective of our time—with special reference to life on a university campus—and then see if the Christian message offers a more satisfactory life-viewpoint.

First (because of its inherent interest for most of us), I mention the area of personal (especially marital) relationships. Brunner claims, as we have just seen, that subjectivism is the basic problem in marriage today. He asserts that most modern marriages are built on the sand of emotional attachment. The Greeks had a word for this— *eros*. Love someone to satisfy your own emotional needs— and if the person no longer accomplishes this purpose, find a new partner who will. This hyper-emotional stress is a disease today. Women are treated in advertising as if they were commodities; soupy popular music has not ceased to declare that "we kiss and the angels sing." Of course, this creates a real problem when the girl (or boy) of your choice begins to wear a bit from the effects of time, as even a few movie stars are prone to do. Hair pieces and superstructure of one sort and another represent the pitiful attempts of many to remain in the emotional rat-race.

Secondly, consider the area of education and career. Few would deny that in the last several decades American education has in many quarters undergone a shift from objective, propositional learning to subjective adjustment. Instead of stressing "dry, academic" disciplines such as history, languages, and the sciences, educators of the progressive stamp have concerned themselves with courses in everything from beauty care to flycasting—all in the interests of personal adjustment. The result has been, as one of *Life*'s editorials soundly (but ungrammatically) put it, "U.S. high school students are plain ignorant of things grammar school students would have known a generation ago." And one of the tragic results is that many students arrive at college with no real understanding of what academic *work* involves—and make every effort while they are in the institution not to find out. Vocationally, the person educated in the current subjectivistic, individualistic system seldom views the choice of career from any other standpoint than personal satisfaction—which is generally identified with salary. Why be a scientist, for example, when with far less work you can become a business executive who hires and fires scientists and makes double or triple what they do?

Finally, let us look at the religious sphere. Here subjectivism has particularly reigned in the 20th century. The liberal theologies which have stemmed from the scholarly Ritschl and the popular Fosdick are firmly rooted in a subjective perspective. What is true in religion? Why, obviously, that which satisfies the religious needs of people. Let's not be dogmatic; if Roscrucianism makes a man happy and adjusted, fine. Wasn't Jesus primarily interested in creating integrated personalities? The neo-orthodox movement which appeared in reaction to religious modernism has unfortunately not escaped the latter's subjectivity. The Bible is still viewed chiefly as a product of human religiosity—not primarily as the work of men objectively inspired by God's Holy Spirit. The Bible merely interprets events from a religious viewpoint—and is therefore hardly the objective norm of faith and practice. A "living Christ" has been set over against the Christ of Scripture—and "living Christ" is frequently created in the image of the theologian who describes him—or at a minimum reflects the latter's religious presuppositions. The general result of all this religious subjectivity has been a Christianity of adjustment rather than of saving, transforming power. And if all else fails, we are told, one can buoy up his spirits with Christianized positive thinking.

What has the Biblical revelation to say to all of this? Scripture would have us change our perspective radically. It would have us stop looking within ourselves—like Buddha staring at his navel, or Aristotle's prime mover contemplating himself because there is nothing greater to think about—and "lift up our eyes unto the hills, from whence cometh our help," for "our help cometh from the Lord, which made heaven and earth." With Luther, we are to shift our perspective from subjective wallowing in our sins and our psyche to an objective concentration on the Lord who saves by grace through faith—on His glory and the world which He has made and the other people whom He has placed upon it. We are to deal with other persons as objects of our love—not as means of our own satisfaction. We are to learn as much as we can of God's world, and seek to serve our fellowmen and God Himself with the knowledge we have attained—not waste in self-indulgence the precious time He has given us.

And, most important of all, we are to come to terms with the Lord Himself—the God of the Scriptures—who is, in the last analysis, wholly other than ourselves (as the author of *The Humanity of God* would be the first to admit!). God tells us that we (all of us) have sinned and come short of His glory, and therefore that we cannot have communion with Him on the basis of our human attainments. He tells us, moreover, that He came to earth in the historical person of Jesus Christ to die for us—to cancel out our sins on the Cross. Objectively and finally, Christ dealt with our sin and our *Angst* as His life's blood was poured out. But this fact, true as it is, will do us no good if we insist upon preferring our own problems to the acceptance of His great solution for them.

This Biblical approach I call the "Ascension perspective"—for if the Ascension says anything to us, it says that when God became man and worked out our salvation in our midst, this was a unique event, a *kairos*-time, and we make a great mistake if we attempt to find Him by delving into human consciousness in general or into the depths of our own souls in particular. In our time especially—a period strangely like the subjectivistic, emotionalistic era which Huizinga describes in *The Waning of the Middle Ages*—we must see the absolute necessity of looking away from ourselves to the One who said, "If I be lifted up, I will draw all men unto Me." Only then will we understand the full impact of Wesley's joy when he sings:

> The Saviour, Jesus, reigns,
> The God of truth and love;
> When He had purged our stains,
> He took His seat above:
>> Lift up your heart, lift up your voice;
>> Rejoice, again I say, rejoice. AMEN.

8.

The Reformation and World Evangelism

Some Christians are moved to tears by romanesque basilicas; three stanzas of a Toplady hymn rouse others to emotional heights. As for me, the Reformation era turns me on. Luther before the Emperor or Knox before the Queen sends my blood tingling. I would rather catch pneumonia in Wittenberg than dysentery in Joppa any day. Therefore I am especially sensitive to criticism of the Reformers or of the seventeenth-century Protestant systematicians who followed close on their heels.

Particularly excruciating is criticism of the Reformation that has some basis in fact. That Luther "left the monastery to marry a nun" is an allegation over which little sleep should be lost. But what about the following claim, made by the great Protestant missiologist Gustav Warneck of Halle: "The comprehension of a continuous missionary duty of the Church was limited among the Reformers and their successors by a narrow-minded dogmatism combined with a lack of historical sense. They knew of the great missions of the past, but according to their ideas the apostles had already gone forth to the whole world and they and their disciples had essentially accomplished the missionary task. Christianity, therefore, had already proved its universal vocation as a world religion" (*The New Schaff-Herzog Encyclopedia of Religious Knowledge,* VII, 404).

Though painful to admit, this allegation has truth in it. Warneck is in part correct when he goes on to point out that Luther "never thought of sending a mission to the heathen of his time," that Calvin "regarded the apostolate as a *munus extraordinarium,* while a special effort of man, that is to say, the establishment of a mission for the heathen, was not necessary," and that "even Zwingli and Butzer do not recognize continuous mission work as a duty of the Church." When Count Truchsess inquired of the Wittenberg theological faculty as to the scope of the Great Commission, the faculty issued an

official document declaring that the command to go into
all the world was only a *"personale privilegium"* of the
apostles, and had already been fulfilled; were this not
so, the faculty reasoned, the duty of becoming a missionary evangelist would fall to every Christian—an absurd conclusion! World evangelism would violate the
creative orders (*Schöpfungsordnungen*) by which God
gives each man a stable place in society, sets rulers
over their subjects and requires a definite and limited
call for ministerial service. In his *Abriss einer Geschichte der protestanischen Missionen* (Berlin, 1905, p.
65), Warneck states the sobering fact that the Moravian
Herrnhutters established more missionary posts in two
decades than did all of Reformation Protestantism in two
centuries.

But it is possible to miss the forest for the trees in
dwelling on such considerations. The historical and cultural situation in the Europe of the sixteenth and seventeenth centuries is a necessary explanatory backdrop to
the facts just adduced. The religious wars of the Reformation era, culminating in the unbelievably brutal Thirty
Years' War that devastated Germany and cast a pall over
the whole seventeenth century, attenuated the perspective
of Protestants and left them with little energy for world
evangelism (cf. C. V. Wedgwood's *The Thirty Years' War*
and Sir George Clark's *War and Society in the Seventeenth
Century*). The uncritically accepted ideological framework of the "great chain of being" (see Arthur Lovejoy's
superlative treatment of the theme) led to a basic conservatism in social outlook and to a natural predilection for
the state church. And the Protestant states, unlike the
Catholic ones, were not much engaged in overseas expansion; thus they did not benefit from the alliances between crown and church that led to the early introduction
of the Catholic faith into America, Africa, and Asia.

Admittedly, the main thrust of the Protestant Reformation was intensive, not extensive. Lutheranism was an
outlaw faith prior to the Religious Peace of Augsburg
(1555), and Calvinism remained in this unenviable position
in the Empire until the Peace of Westphalia, concluding
the Thirty Years' War (1648). Protestants had to fight
for their very existence and for the basic truth of the

Gospel, that salvation is indeed by grace alone and not by the deeds of the law. Rome had formulated her theology over many centuries; the Protestants were compelled to perform the herculean task of systematizing and competently defending newly recovered biblical truth in a matter of decades. Calvin's *Institutes* and Chemnitz's *Examination of the Council of Trent* demonstrate how well they succeeded, but this expenditure of energy left little for other tasks, even important ones.

One can legitimately argue that had the Reformers not set Protestantism on so firm a doctrinal footing, the great missionary activities of late seventeenth-century Pietism, the eighteenth-century evangelical awakenings, and what Latourette has called "the great century" of Christian expansion (the nineteenth century) would have been impossible. Like members of the Church, who have their individual gifts and should not depreciate others or say "I have no need of thee" (I Cor. 12), so the eras of church history are part of one body and do not perform identical functions; at the last trump we shall find (as Charles Williams put it) how much the ages have "coinhered" and been dependent upon one another.

Indeed, the anti-evangelistic criticism of the Reformation seems particularly unfortunate when we recall that the Reformers were above all concerned to recover and proclaim the "evangel"! Werner Elert (*The Structure of Lutheranism*) has rightly taken Warneck to task for missing this point: "How could Luther, who expounded the Psalms, the Prophets, and Paul, have overlooked or doubted the universal purpose of the mission of Christ and of His Gospel? From Col. 1:23 and Mark 16:15 he concludes that the Gospel is not to be kept in a corner but should fill the whole globe." Elert cites such orthodox dogmaticians of the time as Jakob Herrbrand: "We are intent, so far as is humanly possible, on winning for the Lord Christ many for eternal life, and we do not want to neglect any opportunity of which we are aware." Examples of the practical outworking of this zeal included the Jews at home, the Turks in the Balkans, and the Laplanders in Scandinavia.

Though each evangelistic activity may seem small in comparison with Catholic work, in qualitative terms the picture is far different; the recovery of the Gospel among the Protestants eliminated in principle such *ex opere operato* methods as Xavier's aspersion (Christianizing tribes by mass application of baptismal water). The Reformers' stress on lay Bible reading and the priesthood of all believers inevitably led to a sense of personal responsibility for those who had not heard of Christ, and the Wittenberg faculty's provincialism evaporated as better demographic information replaced the faulty data that had convinced Philipp Nicolai, Johann Gerhard, and others that the apostles had virtually evangelized the globe.

George Forell, in his fine work, *Faith Active in Love,* has shown how fully the Reformation dynamic impels believers to social action. Precisely the same motive—Christ's gracious love—constrains heirs of the Reformation (as the Student Volunteer Movement put it) to "evangelize the world in this generation." For, in the last analysis, who *will* evangelize our generation if we do not?

9.

95 Theses for the 450th Anniversary of the Reformation

"Out of love and zeal for the elucidation of truth, the following theses will be debated . . . in the name of our Lord Jesus Christ," wrote an obscure monk at the head of a series of propositions four and a half centuries ago this week. Those theses were posted not simply on a Castle Church door (which the ravages of time have long since claimed) but on the conscience of Christendom. Both the formal theology and the practical church activity of Luther's day were leading men away from, rather than to, Christ's salvation, for the Church had embraced the greatest error of all: the belief that man can earn his own way to Life. On the Eve of All Saints, 1967, "love and zeal for the elucidation of truth" demand that this same fundamental error—today appearing in a different but no less deadly form—be revealed for what it is. (Readers of these theses may enjoy comparing them, number by number, with the orignals, some of which have been freely used here in various degrees of modification. Concordia Publishing House publishes an English translation of the theses in attractive booklet form with introduction by E. G. Schwiebert.)

1. Our Lord and Master Jesus Christ, in saying: "Repent ye," etc., intended that the whole life of believers should be penitence.

2. In the sixteenth century, indulgences diverted men from a life of repentance; in the mid-twentieth century, "secular religion" achieves the same purpose.

3. Then the world was kept from the Gospel by hyper-religiosity on the part of churchmen; now, by their hyper-irreligiosity.

4. Which is another way of saying that false religion and irreligion amount to the same thing.

5. The lamentable condition Bonhoeffer called "cheap grace" can result either from selling grace cheaply (as

THE SUICIDE OF CHRISTIAN THEOLOGY

then) or from cheapening the very idea of grace (as now.)

6. Grace is cheapened and man becomes his own pseudo-saviour when God is considered dead—either metaphorically or literally—for as God diminishes, man assumes his place.

7. Yet true religion begins with the Baptist's affirmation: "He must increase, but I must decrease."

8. A world without a name for God is a world without a name for salvation; all hope in such a world is man-made hope and therefore chimerical.

9. Secular towers of Babel, built over the alleged coffin of Deity, invariably produce confusion of tongues.

10 A "secular Christ" is a contradiction in terms, for he plainly said: "My kingdom is not of this world."

11. The way is narrow and the gate strait leading to that Kingdom; to enter it, one must give up all hope of saving oneself and rely fully upon the Christ.

12. To rely on Christ is to take him at his word.

13. To question his teachings at any point is to stand in judgment upon one's Judge and Advocate.

14. To translate the Christ of the New Testament into a secular "man for others" is to re-do God in our image instead of permitting him to re-do us in his image.

15. If the Christ in whom one believes is unable to say, "He who has seen me has seen the Father," he is no Christ at all.

16. A "fully kenotic Christ" is by definition un-knowable.

17. If nonetheless believed in, a "fully hidden Christ" will necessarily turn out to be the mirror-image of his worshiper or of the times in which the worshiper lives.

18. Salvation through such a Christ is self-salvation, which is in reality damnation.

19. If we are on the threshold of a "new age of the Spirit," we had better be sure which "spirit" he is before we worship him; the spirit of the age is generally "the god of this world."

20. "Test the spirits," says Scripture, intending that God's Word judge the spirit of the age.

21. But when Scripture itself is judged, what ultimate judgment remains?

22. Human judgment of Scripture assumes that we

know more than God and must in the last analysis save ourselves.

23. Indeed, all "secular theology" is grounded in an optimistic view of man's abilities.

24. How quickly has theology in our century come the full circle from modernistic optimism to secularistic optimism!

25. How very fast sinners forget the piles of eyeglasses and teeth and the bodies of naked children at Dachau.

26. How readily sinners forget that apart from the living God of Scripture and his Son's death in our behalf, we turn our secular existence into a seething cauldron of hell and hatred.

27. They preach human doctrine who say that the soul achieves bliss as soon as the divine truths of biblical Christianity are reduced to "secular cash-value."

28. What is achieved is "sinful cash-value," nothing less, nothing more.

29. One wallows in secularity, without hope of a solution for its self-centered condition.

30. In the words of Tillich, one destroys proper theological correlation by turning revelational answers into existential questions.

31. Unless a clear and unimpeachable Word from outside the human situation is available to man, his existential predicament will remain overwhelming and secular optimism will stand revealed as naive folly.

32. Those who believe that they are made sure of their own salvation by "finding God where the social action is" will be eternally damned along with their teachers.

33. We must especially beware of those who say that such social and political action is that inestimable gift of God by which men are reconciled.

34. The "horizontal" reconciliation of man with man depends squarely upon the "vertical" reconciliation of God and man at the Cross, even as the Second Table of the Decalogue follows and rests on the First.

35. They preach no Christian doctrine who teach that contrition and faith in Christ are not necessary for doing God's will in society.

36. Every Christian who feels true compunction over his sins has plenary remission of pain and guilt, even with-

out involvement in social and political causes.

37. Involvement in politics and society will follow as a fruit of faith, for "we love because he first loved us."

38. But when the Christ-relationship is not seen as the ground of Christian social action, Law is confused with Gospel, and neither faith nor properly motivated social action remains.

39. It is a most difficult thing, even for the most learned theologians, to exalt before the people the great riches of political action and, at the same time, the necessity of true contrition.

40. True contrition seeks and loves chastisement for its sins, while stress on changing society makes it seem relatively unimportant.

41. It is well to remember that the Great Commission had to do with the proclamation of the Gospel, not the reformation of the Roman Empire.

42. The Empire was much transformed through the Gospel, but where this occurred it happened because believers "sought first the Kingdom of God and his righteousness."

43. Christians should be taught that he who proclaims to a man an eternal word of grace does better than he who participates in a sit-in.

44. For by a preachment of God's Word, which never returns void, the believer grows in sanctification, while by sit-ins he does not become better but only less subject to adverse social conditions.

45. Christians should be taught that he who substitutes political lobbying for the proclamation of divine grace is not obtaining God's favor but calls down upon himself God's wrath.

46. Christians should be taught that he who does not perform charitable acts to his immediate neighbor accomplishes little in attempting to improve the lot of those at a distance.

47. Christians should be taught that while they are free to engage in social and political action, they are not commanded to do so for their soul's salvation.

48. Scripture nowhere sets forth a normative political or social system; Christians are to proclaim the eternal riches of Christ under political systems of the "right" and of the "left."

49. Christians should be taught that political and social philosophies are useful if they do not put their trust in them, but most hurtful if through them they lose the fear of God.

50. Adherence neither to the "American way of life" —conservative or liberal—nor to socialism nor to Communism will save or damn a man; adherence to Christ, and Christ alone, saves, and rejection of him, and him alone, damns.

51. To demand that all Christians accept a given political or social philosophy as a test of "consistent Christianity" is to elevate man's word to the level of God's word.

52. Vain is the hope of salvation through secular activity, even if a divinity-school dean—nay, the President of the World Council of Churches himself—were to pledge his own soul for it.

53. They are enemies of Christ and of the Church who, in order that a secular salvation may be preached, condemn the Word of God to utter silence in their churches.

54. Wrong is done to the Word of God when in a sermon as much time is spent on secular topics as on God's Word, or even more.

55. If secular participation by Christians is celebrated with single bells, single processions, and single ceremonies, the Gospel should be preached with a hundred bells, a hundred processions, and a hundred ceremonies.

56. A theology derived from the sinful human situation will be humanistic and sinful, likewise an ethic stemming from man's situation instead of from God's revelation.

57. A "contextual" or "situation" ethic foolishly assumes that proper norms will automatically arise from descriptive action; this is a precise example of what G. E. Moore called the "naturalistic fallacy."

58. If human "contexts" and "situations" are self-centered, will not the ethic found there have the same qualities? Can water rise above its source?

59. The importing of *agape*-love into a situation as a norm is of little help apart from God's revealed law, for *agape* is a motive, not a guide for specific action; it will be interpreted in whatever direction the sinful interpreter wishes.

60. How ironical that churchmen today combine "absolute" social and political programs with relativistic situational ethics! Is this not the predictable imbalance of Paul's "natural man"?

61. Only the eternal Word of God can show the relative to be truly relative (e.g., political systems) and the absolute to be truly absolute (e.g., God's moral law).

62. The true treasure of the Church is still the holy Gospel of the glory and grace of God.

63. This treasure, however, is understandably—today as yesterday—most hateful because it causes the first to be the last.

64. But the treasure of salvation through secularity is understandably the most acceptable because it causes the last to be the first.

65. Hence the treasures of the Gospel are nets wherewith churchmen of old have fished to save men from a sinful society.

66. The treasures of secularity are nets wherewith churchmen now fish for acceptance by a sinful society.

67. Those activities which the preachers loudly proclaim to be the greatest graces are seen to be truly such as appeal most to unregenerate standards.

68. They are in reality in no degree to be compared with the grace of God and the piety of the Cross.

69. Christians ought to receive with all reverence exhortations to racial justice, open housing, and equality before the law, for these are demonstrably the will of the God of scriptural revelation.

70. But they are still more bound to open their eyes and ears lest churchmen preach their own fancies in place of the biblical Word.

71. He who speaks against legitimate and proper social action, let him be anathema and accursed.

72. But he, on the other hand, who is seriously concerned about the wantonness and licenses of speech of the preachers of social action, let him be blessed.

73. We should justly thunder against those who by rationalization impede the advance of social justice.

74. And, much more, we should thunder against those who, under the cloak of social programs, depreciate the proclamation of divine grace and the gospel message.

75. To think that secular involvement has such power that it can absolve a man even if he denies the atoning death and bodily resurrection of God's Son, is madness.

76. We affirm, on the contrary, that all of man's good works cannot take away even the least of venial sins as regards its guilt.

77. The saying that Jesus was "the most"—the ideal man and "the place to be"—but not, as he claimed, the very incarnate God, is blasphemy.

78. We affirm that the true grace the Lord Christ has to grant is not a program but himself: his death for our sins and his resurrection for our justification.

79. To say that any earthly goal is of equal rank with the Cross of Christ is blasphemy.

80. Those bishops, curates, and theologians who allow such ideas to have currency among the people will have to render an account for this.

81. The preaching of "secular Christianity" today makes it no easy thing, even for learned men, to protect the reverence due to the visible church against the calumnies of unbelievers and the criticisms of the laity.

82. For instance: Why do the secular theologians always claim credit for jumping on social bandwagons that have been put into motion outside the Church?

83. Again: Why bother with all the theological jargon if Christianity really reduces to humanism?

84. Again: Why not study sociology or politics or psychiatry instead of attempting to be a sloppy representative of these fields with irrelevant theological training?

85. Again: If the Church's beliefs are derived from the fallible human situation like everyone else's, why does the Church presume to judge others or declare grace to them?

86. Again: If God is *ipso facto* "where the action is," was he motivating the action of the Third Reich, as National Socialist theologians said he was?

87. Again: If the theologian judges the Bible and its Christ, who judges the theologian?

88. Again: When Christ demanded fidelity to the "once for all" character of his saving work, how is it that the contemporary Church is satisfied only when it continually proclaims "some new thing"?

89. And how does it happen that faithful preaching of the eternal Word of grace is despised, while the most bizarre theological and ecclesiastical innovations are lauded to the skies as a true mark of "relevance"?

90. Repressing these scruples and arguments is to expose the Church to the ridicule of her enemies and to make Christian men unhappy.

91. If, then, churchmen would subordinate themselves to God's Word, and seek first to bring their wills into accord with Christ's will, and make his Gospel their Gospel, all other things would be added, and the troubles of today's Church would be resolved with ease; nay, they would not exist.

92. Away, then, with all those prophets who say to the people of Christ, "Peace, peace!" though there is no peace.

93. Blessed be all those prophets who say to the people of Christ, "The cross, the cross," and there is no cross.

94. Christians should be exhorted to strive to follow Christ, their Head, through pain, death, and hell;

95. And thus to enter heaven through the tribulations of his cross rather than in the pseudo-security of optimistic secularity.

10.

Renewal and Contemporary Theology

No single word is more frequently on the lips of the contemporary theologian than "renewal." From the *aggiornamento* of the progressives at the Second Vatican Council to the recent three-volume study, *The Renewal of the Church,* by theologians of the Disciples of Christ, all eyes seem to turn toward new beginnings in ecclesiastical life. Not too many years ago it was only the professional evangelists who made a special point of "revival in our time"; now the mainstream of theology has taken up the cry. What has brought about this remarkable theological concern for renewal, and what forms is it now taking?

A little over a decade ago, Cyril Garbett, archbishop of York, wrote a book which serves as a roadmap to the appalling problems faced by the Christian church in the mid-twentieth century. This book, entitled *In An Age of Revolution,* describes the radical changes in modern life which have more and more separated contemporary man from the Christian message. Consider a representative sampling from Garbett's table of contents:

Seventy Years of Change: Revolution, not evolution. Technics—machinery; the airplane; weapons of destruction. Political changes. Social and economic upheaval. Loss of confidence in man. The danger of catastrophe.

Religion in the Twilight: Widespread disturbance on matters of faith in Christian and non-Christian lands. An age of faith replaced by an age of questioning and atheism. Darwinism; the discoveries of the vastness of the universe; comparative religion; psychology. Two wars dislocated religious work. Falling away from the church.

Moral Chaos: The rejection of traditional ethical standards. Group and provincial loyalties substituted for universal loyalty. Changed values seen in the relationships between nations, revival of cruelty, and in sexual conduct. Promiscuity for the unmarried, easy divorce for the married. Crime's increase.

Substitutes for Christianity: Humanism. King Mammon: uncontrolled capitalism; social injustice. King Demos: the dangers of democracy—secularism, overconfidence, soullessness under numerical pressure. The God-State: totalitarianism demands the obedience due to God alone. Marxian Communism: its attack on Christianity.

The mere reading of such a catalog of non-Christian pressures (and it is but a partial catalog at that!) leaves the sensitive churchman with a sense of profound frustration. Depth study of any one of the areas here referred to reveals even greater problems for Christianity than appear on the surface: The two world wars and continuing international tension, for example, have so revealed man's inhumanity to man and his hypocrisy in asserting ethical ideals that vast numbers of people have turned from the church to existentialistic philosophies which relativize the world and preach in effect, "Eat, drink and be merry: for tomorrow you die."

Clearly Christianity is not making the impact that it should on our fearfully changing, increasingly secularistic age. The need—indeed, the necessity—for Christian renewal thus presses upon contemporary theology from all quarters. No theologian, whatever his orientation, has been able to ignore the gauntlet thrown down by such writers as Gerhard Szczesny (*The Future of Unbelief*) who maintains that "as long as public opinion in the West insists that the world can be saved only by accepting Christian postulates as true, the period of unbelief will be greatly prolonged and ever new generations will be driven to cynicism, superficiality and stupidity." To the theologian of our day it is axiomatic that only a renewed Christianity can meet the challenge of this gravity.

The question is, of course, what form or forms shall renewal take? Many theological panaceas have been suggested by both Roman Catholics and by Protestants. Leaving aside the more fanciful contributions to church renewal (such as the substitution of non-verbal art forms, e.g., the modern dance, for verbal proclamation of Christian truth!) one can see five main thrusts in contemporary renewal efforts. These occur in the realms of *worship, church organization, secular involvement, doctrine* and *ethics.*

Worship and organization

All branches of Christendom are at present experiencing a revived interest in forms of *worship*. The argument runs somewhat as follows: church worship is not meaningful to contemporary man; therefore it must be made significant for him. In Roman Catholicism, as Ernest Koenker pointed out in his important work, *The Liturgical Renaissance in the Roman Catholic Church* (1954), herculean efforts are being made to render centuries-old worship forms more relevant to mid-twentieth century man. The most dramatic result of this trend is the recent and widely-publicized permission—subject to the approval of local bishops—for the use of the vernacular in large portions of the Mass. Protestants likewise have been reevaluating their forms of worship—and this has by no means been restricted to the "liturgical denominations" (Episcopalians and Lutherans). Books such as *An Outline of Christian Worship* by Presbyterian William Maxwell can be paralleled in virtually all theological traditions: they make a conscious effort to enrich worship through greater use of historic forms. The conviction exists that in many Protestant services only the religious experience of the pastor or of the local "pillars of the church" has really been reflected in corporate worship; by the introduction of more historic usages, a fuller gamut of meaningful Christian experience can be made available to today's churchgoer, thereby more fully meeting his personal spiritual needs. At the same time it should be stressed there are Protestants who wish to move in the other direction entirely; away from historical worship to unabashed contemporaneity. For them, worship must be stripped of its "pious" overtones and fully reflect the modern communications revolution; thus group discussion may be preferable to preaching, mutual self-criticism a desirable substitute for testimonies and silent meditation a worthwhile equivalent for the old-time prayer meeting.

Organizationally, theological renewal centers on ecu-

516 THE SUICIDE OF CHRISTIAN THEOLOGY

menicity. Here also both Roman Catholics and Protestants appear to be moving in the same general direction. The so-called Ecumenical Council has given every evidence of concern for the "separated brethren" outside the Roman fold. In the last decade Roman Catholic theologians have published book after book relating their own ecumenical concerns to those of Protestantism (e.g., George Tavard's *Two Centuries of Ecumenism*). As for Protestants themselves, there is no doubt that ecumenicity has played a larger part in their thinking on all levels in the twentieth century than has any other single problem. Church histories now, as a matter of course, conclude with a chapter on ecumenicity (see Winthrop Hudson's representative *Story of the Christian Church*). One need not read *The Ecumenical Review* to discover that for many of Protestantism's theologians the renewal of the church demands above all the organizational unity of Christendom. Only thus, it is argued, can Christianity possibly present a united front against the overwhelmingly powerful forces of unbelief in our time. Separated and divided, we will surely be conquered; united, we can oppose with suitable vigor and untarnished image the inroads of secularism. Ours is an age of "larger units": the history of business and government in the twentieth century has demonstrated to all that victory goes to the well-organized, and that the small unit cannot effectively resist organized power. Thus the church cannot expect to appeal to twentieth-century man or to rout the forces that would destroy him unless she herself unify her tragically divided forces.

Secular involvement

Ours is not only an age of "larger units"; it is an epoch of secular concerns. Therefore, if the church is to have any real impact on modern man she must meet him where he is—in the midst of his *secular involvements*. Here we have one of the most characteristic emphases in contemporary "renewal" theology: theology must focus on man's secular needs. At this point the prophet is Dietrich Bonhoeffer, who was martyred by the Nazis in 1945. Of his position Martin Marty writes:

Bonhoeffer's rejection of any sort of cosmic nostalgia,

of most romantic yearnings for the past, ... of false dreams for the future; his willingness to accept what God gave in the present has caused others in a generation without ground beneath its feet to identify with him. It has also led him and his students to pursue an analysis of history which has gathered many followers, drawn much attention, and in the eyes of some become the totality of what he represents. I refer to the understanding of a "world come of age," the maturation of secularity revealed in the last letters in *Prisoner of God*. Bonhoeffer, it is well known, foresaw the end of the religious phase in Western man's development and wanted to provide a theological base for the Christian displaced both spatially "from the ground of Western Civilization" and temporally from Christendom's unfolding.

"Religion," for Bonhoeffer, is an evil; and by "religion" he means, as Marty points out, "devotion to a particular metaphysic, stance or piety." Bonhoeffer was convinced that in a day when traditional Christian religiosity is no longer meaningful to the modern man, the church categories and Christian experience" *(The Place of Bonhoeffer)*. In practice, this means maximum stress on the problems the non-Christian faces in his secularized milieu; and it means that the solutions offered by the church must be rigorously purged of those traditional theological overtones which will alienate a "world come of age." For Bonhoeffer himself, one must hasten to add, this "secular Christianity" did not mean a return to the naïveté of liberalism's social gospel; he was far too thoroughly existentialized by war for that. But in the minds of many of his American followers, his teachings have been boiled down to the conviction that the church is truest to her mission when she engages in projects of maximum "secularity," such as NCC voter registration drives in the South ("the Delta Ministry"). The Jesus of this secular-focused church renewal becomes, quite naturally, more of an existentially involved representative man than a supernaturalistically conceived Saviour; to use Bonhoeffer's phrase, He is "the man existing for others."

Doctrine and ethics

As the preceding remarks have made patent, contemporary renewal emphases cannot exist without theological reconstruction, both in doctrine and in ethics. *Doctrinally,* Roman Catholicism has its "new shape," reflected in the dynamic-personal (rather than static Aristotelian) theological interpretations of Karl Rahner, and the Reformation stress on justification by grace (rather than by divine-cum-human cooperation) in the revolutionary writings of Hans Küng (cf. C. Davis, *Liturgy and Doctrine).* Protestantism is—predictably— far more radical in its renewal thinking. Here the thought of Rudolf Bultmann still sets the tone, though many of his particular emphases have been rejected by his "post-Bultmannian" disciples. To Bultmann, and to the moderns who follow him, it is self-evident that:

> The cosmology of the New Testament is essentially mythical in character. The world is viewed as a three-storied structure, with the earth in the centre, the heaven above, and the underworld beneath. . . . Supernatural forces intervene in the course of nature and in all that men think and will and do. Miracles are by no means rare. . . .
>
> This then is the mythical view of the world which the New Testament presupposes when it presents the event of redemption which is the subject of its preaching. It proclaims in the language of mythology that the last time has now come. "In the fulness of time" God sent forth his Son, a pre-existent divine Being, who appears on earth as a man. He dies the death of a sinner on the cross and makes atonement for the sins of men. His resurrection marks the beginning of the cosmic catastrophe. . . .
>
> Can Christian preaching expect modern man to accept the mythical view of the world as true? To do so would be both senseless and impossible. It would be senseless, because there is nothing specifically Christian in the mythical view of the world as such. It is simply the cosmology of a pre-scientific age. Again, it would be impossible, because no man can adopt a view of the world by his own volition—it is already determined for him by his place in history.

This argument, quoted from Bultmann's famous essay, "New Testament and Mythology," is the charter for "demythologizing"—for removing from the Christian proclamation those "pre-scientific" elements which offend contemporary secular man. Though there is disagreement on details, such advocates of renewal as Schubert Ogden, Carl Michalson and Reginald Fuller are convinced that modern man will never listen to the church as long as it persists in preaching a gospel studded with a virgin birth, miraculous healings and resurrections.

But when doctrine has been demythologized, what remains? Advocates of renewal point to the vital need for a Christian existential *ethic* in a disintegrating age. Quite consistently, Bishop Robinson's *Honest to God* follows its demythologizing program with a chapter on "The New Morality," and the Bishop's latest book, *Christian Morals Today,* expands his basic contention that agape-love is the whole of the Christian faith and thus that absolute moral codes must be discarded in favor of the flexible ethic of "acting responsibly in love." Such a "dynamic" approach to moral problems, it is contended, will make sense in a secular world where the old morality simply cannot obtain a hearing. Modern man is in dire need of ethical guidance; he cannot accept the straitlaced standards of the traditional church; therefore, he must be given a renewal ethic which will be meaningful to him in his existential situation and will restore his respect for a church in process of renewal.

The Canker in Renewal Theology

Now what must be said in evaluating the present-day "renewal theology"? On the positive side, several important considerations should be underscored. First, the motive behind efforts toward church renewal is highly commendable: Christianity has (K. S. Latourette notwithstanding!) been falling behind in its impact on large segments of the Western world during the twentieth century. How often, with our heads in the sand, we Christians have avoided the challenges of the day and permitted secular philosophies and programs to make headway at our expense! How often we evangelicals have been satisfied to preach against the vintage sins of "card-playing," "theatre-going," et al., and neglected entirely the great issues of our own day (the immorality of segregation, atomic aggression, etc.) which are crying for prophetic analysis! The church in all her branches *should* repent in sackcloth and ashes for her lack of renewal in an age demanding theological vitality.

Second, many of the particular emphases in renewal

theology are deserving of praise and support. The desire to enrich what is all too frequently a cold, bare, un-aesthetic Protestant worship through the reintroduction of great worship patterns of the past could well be re-garded with great appreciation. Ecumenical efforts, where they do not do violence to biblical freedom, are worthy of the strongest support for surely a Protestant-ism often divided over no more significant issues than pipe smoking is an abomination both before the Lord and before the non-Christian world. Renewal theology is also making an important point when it stresses the need for Christianity to become relevant to the secular needs of the day; as I pointed out in a review of Marty's *Second Chance for American Protestants* which cor-rectly argues that the days of an "established" Protes-tantism in America are over: "In a pluralistic post-Christendom, believers had better wake up to the abso-lute necessity of serving as lights of the world by living and preaching the gospel, not by expecting any form of generalized social or official establishment to do it for them" (*Christianity Today,* August 30, 1963; reprinted in the present volume in II. B. 2).

Nonetheless, after granting all the positive insights of renewal theology, one is left with a sense of horror at the overall impact of the movement. Liturgical revival can (and frequently has) led to a substitution of form for the content of the Christian message; ecumenicity has confused transcendent oneness in Christ and quali-tative spirituality with organizational unity and sheer big-ness; Bonhoeffer's "nonreligious interpretation of bibli-cal categories and Christian experience" leads almost inevitably (though Bonhoeffer himself would not have wished it) to a de-Christianized religiosity fitting well with the paganization of the gospel in Bultmann and the ruination of Christian ethics in Robinson (cf. Montgomery, "The Law's Third Use: Sanctification," *Christianity To-day,* April 26, 1963; reprinted in my *Crisis in Lutheran Theology* [Baker, 1967]), and *supra* in III. 5).

Whence comes this canker in renewal theology? It comes, I suggest, from *an impossible attempt to make the Christian message fit the demands of the unregener-ate man.* Paul Tillich, in presenting his famous "principle of correlation," rightly points out that theology tends to err in one of two directions: either it tries to diagnose the sins of the non-Christian without regarding his real existential situation or it tries to find the remedy for his ills within the framework of the disease itself. Both approaches are devastating for they destroy either the world or the church; true theology has to apply the pure revelational message of the gospel to the genuine existential need of the non-Christian. Renewal theology is committing the second error: it is so preoccupied with sinful man's need in our times that it is allowing the gospel to be swallowed up in the sinful situation itself. To "demythologize" the gospel in order to make it relevant" to the unbeliever is actually to give the unbeliever a sinfully corrupted gospel which is no gospel at all (Gal. 1:8-9); to present modern man with an agapeistic, situational ethic is to offer him no Christian ethic at all for he will simply bend it in his own situationally sinful direction.

Ironically, one of the major reasons why the Christian church needs renewal in our time is that Protestant theology in the twentieth century has so consistently sold its birthright for a mess of culturally sinful pottage (cf. J. V. Langmead Casserley's *The Retreat from Christianity in the Modern World*). Modernism, Neo-Orthodoxy and Bultmannianism have all made higher-critical accommodations to secularism which have emasculated Christian theology, rendering it impotent to cope with contemporary unbelief. Renewal will come—if it does come—only when we take a cue from such Roman Catholic renovators as Hans Küng, who are trying to restore fundamental biblical emphases to present-day theology rather than attempting to rewrite theology in the image of fallen man.

In a word, theological renewal necessitates radical reorientation of our perspective: instead of trying to re-create God in our image, we had better let Him recreate us in His image. Philip Watson has emphasized that the Reformation of the sixteenth century was a theocentric revolution in theology—a revolution that put God and His grace, instead of man and his works, at stage center. This is precisely what we need for theological reformation in our time and such radical theocentrism demands that we take God at His Word as inerrantly revealed in Holy Scripture, and accept the Christ proclaimed there, who was indeed Bonhoeffer's "servant," but a servant who came to give His life a ransom for the sins of the world (Mark 10:44-45). If any man be in *that* Christ, he is indeed a new creature: "old things are passed away; behold, all things are become new" (II Cor. 5:17).

Index of Names

This index includes the names of all individual persons —ancient and modern, real and fictitious—discussed or cited in the book.